THE
EQUINE
DICTIONARY

HORSEWORDS: THE EQUINE DICTIONARY

Maria Ann Belknap

Trafalgar Square Publishing

First published in the United States of America in 1997 by
Trafalgar Square Publishing, North Pomfret, Vermont 05053

Printed by Dah Hua Printing Press Co. Ltd., Hong Kong

© J.A. Allen & Co. Ltd., London, England, 1997

Library of Congress Catalog Card number 97-60992

ISBN 1-57076-101-9

Typeset by Textype Typesetters, Cambridge, England

Disclaimer of Liability
The author and publisher shall have neither liability nor responsibility to any person or
entity with respect to any loss or damage caused or alleged to be caused directly or indirectly
by the information contained in this book. While the book is as accurate as the author can
make it, there may be errors, omissions and inaccuracies.

DEDICATION

'with all beings and all things
we shall be relatives.'

Sioux Indian precept

TO THE READER

If you find an error or omission, please write and tell us; this will help us make the next edition even more comprehensive.

ACKNOWLEDGMENTS

A book of this magnitude is born from the efforts of countless individuals from around the world, most of whom remain nameless though not forgotten. Those who left the most indelible mark on me and this work are noted below.

First and foremost, my thanks to Lee and Corry for realizing that real nurturing is about facilitating, sharing, and giving, rather than control.

Also, to Walter de la Brosse for getting me started. . . a voice now quiet.

To Michelle for picking up the slack for so many months thus enabling me to focus.

To Kevin for cheering me along the homestretch.

And finally to Caroline, for giving my voice an audience and preparing the ground for my footprint.

Maria Belknap is an avid horsewoman. She currently rides and writes in Southern California, USA.

A

AAAI The acronym for the American Albino Association, Inc. (q.v.).

Aachen One of the world's chief show jumping (q.v.), eventing (q.v.), and dressage (q.v.) centers located in Germany; the home of Germany's International Horse Show held annually in July.

AAEP The acronym for the American Association of Equine Practitioners (q.v.).

AAHC The acronym for the American Albino Horse Club, Inc. (q.v.).

AAOBPPH The acronym for the American Association of Owners and Breeders of Peruvian Paso Horses (q.v.).

abandoned race A racing term; any race or race meeting (q.v.) which was not held and will not be rescheduled for a later date; may be due to adverse weather conditions which make the track unsafe for either the horses or jockeys.

abasia A trembling or quivering of the legs or an inability to walk due to a defect in coordination.

Abats le Sultan An aggressive mounted game popular in Russia in which mounted participants, wearing feather-covered fencing masks and padded shirts, chase after and attempt to cut the feathers off their opponents' masks using swords or sharp daggers; the participant with the most feathers remaining on his mask at the end of the competition is considered the winner.

abaxial Situated out of or directed away from the axis.

Abbot buggy A horse-drawn Australian buggy designed by the Abbot-Downing Company of Concord, New Hampshire, USA, popular during the second half of the 19th century for both town and country use; hung on semi-elliptical side springs with a fairly short wheelbase and had pedal brakes and a half hood usually kept in a raised position.

abdomen Also known as the belly; the portion of the horse's body between the chest and pelvis.

abdominal Of or pertaining to the abdomen.

abdominal cavity The hollow portion of the body between the chest and pelvis which contains most digestive, reproductive, and excretory organs, i.e., liver, kidney, and bladder.

abduction To draw away from the median plane of the body.

Aberdeen plait To braid (q.v.) the top portion of the mane of a draft horse with colored yarn.

abort To expel the fetus or embryo from the uterus before it is viable.

abortifacient Any substance that causes abortion.

abortion *see* EQUINE ABORTION

abortion storm Simultaneous abortion in mares stabled or pastured together; may be triggered by viruses such as rhinopneumonitis (q.v.).

above the bit Also known as over the bit; said of a horse who evades bit contact by bringing his nose in front of the vertical, thus carrying his head too high and hollowing his back.

abrasion A superficial wound (q.v.); an injury caused by a scraping or rubbing away of the top layer of hair and minimal loss of skin by friction; usually characterized by an oozing serum (q.v.), some slow ooze of blood, and a lack of damage to the subsurface.

abrupt transition A change from one gait (q.v.) to another, e.g., walk to trot, trot to canter etc. or an alteration of the stride within a gait performed too suddenly; often caused by the rider who gives his aids too suddenly and/or without sufficient preparation.

abscess Also known as pus pocket; a collection of pussy matter in the tissue of a body organ or part, with pain, heat, and swelling.

absolute dry matter The percentage of feed less the water content subtracted from 100 percent; used in feed analysis.

absolute ensurer Slang; a whip (q.v.).

absorbent A substance such as surgical gauze, applied to a wound to stanch or arrest the flow of blood.

acari *see* MITES

acariasis *see* MANGE

accept the bit Said of a horse who holds the bit confidently in his mouth and responds to the contact and influence of the rider's hands on the reins without resistance or hesitation.

acceptance time The time by which a horse must be entered, registered, or nominated to participate in an event.

accessory carpal bone One of eight carpal bones comprising the knee; a disc-shaped bone located behind and to the outside of the other seven carpal bones and which forms a sharp ridge at the back of the knee.

Acchetta pony A pony breed from Sardinia.

accommodation A short-distance, horse-drawn, public-service stage coach first constructed in the United States about 1827; seated 12 inside with one additional seat outside adjacent to the driver; entered through side doors.

account Also known as account for or account for the fox; a hunting term; said of the hounds when they drive a fox into a hole or kill it in the open.

account for *see* ACCOUNT

account for the fox *see* ACCOUNT

accouterments *see* ACCOUTREMENTS

accoutrements Also spelled accouterments; the tack including the saddle, bridle, and bit, worn by the horse.

accumulator bet *see* PARLAY BET

ace The acronym for acetylpromazine (q.v.).

acepromazine Also known by the acronym ACE; the trade name for acetylpromazine (q.v.), a commonly used tranquilizer for horses.

acetabulum Also known as the hip joint; a depression in the pelvis created by the ilium and ischium bones which forms the pelvic component of the hip joint and receives the head of the femur.

acetylcholine A chemical found on the nerve endings which allows the transmission of impulses from one nerve fiber to the next or to a muscle fiber.

acetylpromazine Also known as ACE; one of a group of antihistamines (q.v.), including chlorpromazine and promethazine, administered orally, intramuscularly, or intravenously, to tranquilize and sedate a horse; over stimulation may result in the horse overcoming the calming effects of the drug; decreases blood pressure and may help to reduce the muscle spasm and pain associated with conditions such as azoturia (q.v.); intra-arterial injection results in convulsion and death.

acey-ducey A racing term; a riding style in which the right stirrup leather is shorter than the left, or inside, leg which enables a jockey to maintain balance more easily on the turns; popularized by Hall of Fame jockey Eddie Arcaro.

ACHA The acronym for the American Cutting Horse Association (q.v.).

Achean An ancient pony breed indigenous to Greece, now extinct.

Achenbach, Benno von (1861–1936) A horseman who developed the modern international sport of driving.

Achilles tendon *see* HAMSTRING

acid (1) A category of joint-lubricating substances including sodium hyaluronate or hyaluronate sodium; a component of normal synovial fluid that, when injected directly into an inflamed joint or into the bloodstream, improves the quality and production of synovial fluid in the horse's joints. (2) A compound containing hydrogen as an essential constituent and which possesses a sour taste; changes blue vegetable colors to red, neutralizes alkalis, and combines with bases to form salts.

acid brand (1) Also known as acid mark; an identifying symbol, character, letter, or series of numbers, or any combination thereof, burned into the flesh of the horse using an acid such as hydrochloric acid (q.v.); difficult to distinguish from a hot brand (q.v.). (2) To apply a registration mark to the horse using acid.

acid detergent fiber The residue in plant material remaining after complete acid digestion of same.

acid mark *see* ACID BRAND

acidosis An accumulation in the body due to a disruption of the normal acid-base balance.

acme sporting cart A light, Australian horse-drawn gig (q.v.) popular in the late 19th century, having a three-ring suspension system, fully upholstered driving seat, arm rests, and mud guards above both wheels.

acquired defect An imperfection, function, or condition of the horse resulting from disease or accident following birth.

acquired leukoderma The whitening of previously pigmented hair or skin due to skin trauma.

acquired marks Any permanent mark appearing on the coat or skin of the horse, e.g., saddle marks, bridle marks, collar marks, girth marks, and other harness marks, permanent bandage marks, firing and branding marks, surgical scars, and tattoo marks in which the pigment of the hair or skin is altered; may be used for identification purposes.

acridine dyes A group of coloring agents including acriflavine, aminocrine, and proflavine having microbe-inhibiting properties; used in wound powders, solutions, or emulsions for skin and wound disinfection.

across the board A racing term; a combination pari-mutuel (q.v.) bet in which the bettor (q.v.) collects if the selected horse finishes the horse race in first, second, or third place.

ACTH The acronym for adrenocorticotropic hormone (q.v.).

actin The structural protein of the muscles; important for muscle contraction and relaxation.

acting hand see ACTIVE HAND no. 1.

acting master A hunting term; one appointed temporarily to organize a hunt for one or more days, pending the appointment of a permanent Master.

actinobacillus equuli A species of bacteria responsible for foal abortion (q.v.) or death shortly after birth.

action (1) The manner and degree of movement of the horse's feet and legs. (2) A racing term; wagering activity on a horse, e.g., the horse took a lot of action.

active hand Also known as ACTING HAND. (1) The rider's hand on the side to which the horse is turned when neck reining (q.v.). (2) To move the hands or fingers to work the reins and activate the bit; the opposite of a quiet hand (q.v.).

active immunization An acquired immunity due to the presence of antibodies formed in response to an antigen (q.v.).

active member Said of an individual whose membership dues with an organization are paid for the current calendar year.

acupressure To control pain, illness, and/or injury through pressure applied to trigger points along body meridians (q.v.).

acupuncture Also known as traditional acupuncture; Chinese medicine practiced for more than 3,500 years; based on the Chinese medicine of Chi – the flow of energy comprising positive (Yang) and negative (Yin) components that travel on meridians (q.v.) throughout the body; imbalances or blockages along these meridians cause stiffness, pain, swelling, and/or sickness; to re-establish harmony between the Yin and Yang (electrical fields), acupuncture points (q.v.) are stimulated with the insertion and twirling of one or more fine needles (traditional), electrical current (electro-acupuncture [q.v.]), laser beam (laserpuncture [q.v.]), burning herb moxa (moxibustion [q.v.]), the injection of fluids such as water, oil, and vitamin-B solution (aquapuncture [q.v.]), injection of air (pnemopuncture [q.v.]), gold implants, blood-letting (hemo-acupuncture) and metal staples; used to control pain, treat internal malfunctions, anesthetize, and reduce stress.

acupuncture points Small areas, 1 inch (12–25mm) in diameter located in the skin that have increased electrical conductivity; most are motor points located near the spots where the nerves enter the muscles, while the others are situated, for the most part, on other neurological pathways; lie along 12 meridians, paired in two groups of six (there are also two unpaired meridians and a band of independent trigger points not connected to any particular channel); external points are linked by the meridians to limbs, joints, sense organs, superficial tissues, and to the internal visceral organs.

acute Having a short and relatively severe course.

acute arthritis Severe, rapidly developing inflammation of a joint; may eventually dissipate or develop into chronic arthritis (q.v.).

acute equine respiratory syndrome A condition caused by the lethal virus, equine *Morbillivirus* (q.v.) of the family *Paramyxoviridae* first isolated in Australia in 1994; symptoms include shallow breathing and respiratory distress, lethargy, nervous disorders, staggers, and head butting; afflicted horses ultimately die of cardiac arrest.

acute laminitis A clinical type of laminitis (q.v.); inflammation of the laminae (q.v.) having a rapid onset and a brief duration; characterized by the horse's marked resistance to exercise and reluctance to stand; may result in founder (q.v.) or lead to chronic laminitis (q.v.) if left untreated.

acute mastitis Rapid onset of inflammation of the mammary gland due to bacteria-related infection; occurs occasionally in lactating mares brought on by the presence of streptococci (q.v.) or staphylococci (q.v.) organisms; symptoms may include painful swelling of the affected gland and adjacent tissue, fever, depression, stiffness at the walk, or standing with the hind legs apart; if left untreated the affected gland may abscess.

acute metritis Rapid onset of inflammation of the muscular and endometrial layers of the uterus (q.v.) caused by the introduction of contaminants following abnormal parturition (q.v.); often accompanied by retention of the fetal membrane, fetid discharge, fever, depression, anorexia, laminitis, and if left untreated, sterility.

acute poison Any fast-acting agent or toxin that chemically destroys life or health within a short period of time following consumption.

acute rhabdomyolysis *see* EXERCISE RELATED MYOPATHY

ADA *see* ADENOSINE DEAMINASE

Adayevsky A Russian horse breed similar to, but lighter than, the Kazakh (q.v.).

added-money (1) A racing term; money added to the winner's purse in addition to nomination, entry, eligibility, and starting fees paid by the owners and breeders. (2) The purse put up by the event organizing committee added to the contestants' fees to make up the total prize money.

added weight A racing term; said of a horse who carries more weight than the conditions of the race require, usually because the jockey (q.v.) exceeds the stated weight limit.

Addison's disease A degenerative condition caused by deficiency in the secretion of adrenocortical hormones; seen occasionally in horses, especially race horses in training.

adduction To draw towards the median plane of the body.

adductor muscles The group of muscles responsible for drawing the thigh inward.

Adeav One of two types of Kazkh (q.v.), an ancient pony breed originating in Kazakhstan; thought to have descended from the Asiatic wild horse (q.v.); the appearance has been refined by significant infusions of Don (q.v.), Akhal-Teké (q.v.), Iqmud (q.v.), and Karabair blood; stands 12.1 to 13.1 hands, may have a bay, gray, palomino or chestnut coat, and has a small, light head and compact body; is less resistant to harsh conditions than the Dzhabe (q.v.), although frugal, hardy, and possessed of great stamina; used for riding.

adenoma A benign tumor originating in and affecting the glands.

adenosine deaminase Also known by the

acronym ADA; one of the enzymes active in the chemistry of energy transfer.

Adequan A brand name for polysulfate glycosaminoglycan (q.v.) injected to treat some arthritic conditions.

adhesion An abnormal firm fibrous attachment between two structures as in scar tissue.

adhesive tape Also known as tape (q.v.); a cloth, paper, or synthetic strip with a sticky substance on one side and having various uses, as holding a bandage in place.

adipose Also known as fat; of or relating to body fat (q.v.).

adipose tissue Body tissue which can readily store and release fat as energy to the horse when normal energy sources such as glucose and the volatile fatty acids found in the blood stream are depleted.

a distance A racing term; a separation of more than 20 lengths between the horses in a race at the finish.

adjusted monitor system A cutting horse (q.v.) term; a system by which scores may be adjusted during National Cutting Horse Association (q.v.) major events held in the United States; in case of a discrepancy on a major penalty (q.v.), the judge monitor reviews the incident on video tape to determine if the query is valid, in which case, he will ask the judges to review the run again on video tape to assess if they want to alter their scores.

adjusted score A cutting horse term (q.v.); a competitor's score reviewed and changed under the rules of the adjusted monitor system (q.v.) used by the National Cutting Horse Association (q.v.); is posted on the scoreboard after it has been reviewed.

ad lib *see* AD LIBITUM

ad libitum Also known by the acronym ad lib; Latin; to give a horse, whether stabled or at pasture (q.v.), free access to feed.

ADMS The acronym for The American Donkey & Mule Society (q.v.).

adopticon A float or show wagon drawn by a minimum of six horses first used in North America during the late 19th century for advertising purposes, street parades, and to carry a small payload.

adrenaline Also known as epinephrine; a hormone secreted by the medulla of the adrenal gland (q.v.); acts primarily as a stimulant.

adrenal cortex The outer cell layer of the adrenal gland (q.v.); produces hormones including those responsible for the utilization of glycogen by the muscles, provides part of the body's shock protection mechanism, and controls electrolyte balance in the body.

adrenal gland One of two ductless, flat glands located on the front of the kidneys responsible for the secretion of hormones into the bloodstream.

adrenal medulla The internal portion of the adrenal gland which produces, stores, and releases hormones including epinephrine (q.v.) and noradrenaline into the body.

adrenocorticotropic hormone Also known by the acronym ACTH; a hormone secreted by the pituitary gland responsible for controlling the secretion of hormones from the adrenal glands (q.v.); contributes to the control of energy use and prevention of shock through the secretion of corticosteroids; production increases during times of stress.

ADS (1) The acronym for American Driving Society (q.v.). (2) The acronym for the Australian Driving Society (q.v.).

ADT The acronym for the American Discovery Trail (q.v.).

adult The age at which a horse stops growing; may be four, five, six, or seven years depending on the geographic region and in some cases the breed.

adventitial marks Also known as adventitious marks; white coat hairs resulting from destruction of the pigment cells of the underlying skin due to trauma as in acquired leukoderma (q.v.), bridle marks, collar marks, girth marks, harness marks, surgical marks, tattoo marks, etc.; must be recorded on all identification charts and breed registrations.

adventitious marks *see* ADVENTITIAL MARKS

AEI The acronym for Average-Earnings Index (q.v.).

a-equi-1 A strain of the equine influenza (q.v.) virus.

a-equi-2 A strain of the equine influenza (q.v.) virus.

aerobe A micro-organism whose existence requires the presence of air or free oxygen to thrive and live.

aerobic Requiring air or free oxygen to live and thrive.

aerobic bacteria Bacteria which require air or free oxygen to live and thrive.

aerobic exercise Any activity level that utilizes the horse's capacity to supply oxygen to the cells.

aerobic respiration The breakdown of energy producing nutrients, principally glycogen, in the presence of oxygen, which are dissolved in the blood and carried throughout the body from the lungs.

aerophagia *see* WIND SUCKING

AFA The acronym for the American Farriers Association (q.v.).

AFCL The acronym for the Worshipful Company of Farriers (q.v.).

afebrile Without fever (q.v.).

afferent Leading or conducting inward, as certain nerves and veins.

affiliated show Any horse show run in accordance with the rules of a larger organization and the results of which are recognized by that organization.

African Ass Also known by the scientific term *Equus africanus*; all but extinct today; had a large black or brown patch at the base of the ears as well as at the tip and legs the same color as the body; the progenitor of the domestic donkey (q.v.).

African horse sickness An insect-borne, highly fatal, viral infection of horses caused by reovirus, a virus of the family *Reoviridae*, *genus orbivirus*; characterized by high fever, labored breathing, patchy sweating, and a dry cough; donkeys are more resistant than horses; controlled by an annual vaccine; gnats are the principal vectors; occurs between insect seasons and recovered animals do not appear to be carriers; a major epidemic disease throughout Africa, Pakistan, Spain, most Middle Eastern countries, and India.

afterbirth *see* PLACENTA

afterwale The body of the harness collar (q.v.) fitted behind the hames (q.v.); consists of padding made from stout woolen cloth with straw and leather side pieces.

against the clock *see* JUMP OFF

agalactia An absence of milk in the mare's udder after foaling.

age *see* AGE OF A HORSE

aged *see* AGED HORSE

aged horse Also known as aged or past the mark of the mouth; in Thoroughbreds (q.v.), a horse seven years or older while in most other breeds any horse 16 to 20 years of age.

age of a horse Also known as age; the time a horse has lived; may be determined by registration papers, breeder's certificate, the eruption and wear of the teeth, or the feel of the ribs, jaw, or tail; for show and registration purposes, is computed from the first of January, regardless of the actual date on which the horse was foaled; the horse's age on January 1 shall be maintained throughout the year; one horse year is said to be equivalent to five to seven human years.

agent (1) Any substance, compound, or drug capable of producing a physical, chemical, or biological effect. (2) Also known as authorized agent; any person, other than the owner of the horse, authorized to act or conduct business on behalf of the owner; such authorization is usually given in writing.

agglutination Said of the red blood cells; to collect or clump into groups.

agglutination antibodies Antibodies that cause red blood cells to collect or clump together abnormally.

agglutination test A stall-side diagnostic

test (q.v.) performed to detect endotoxemia (q.v.).

aging (1) The process of determining the age of a horse by evaluating the eruption and wear patterns of the teeth. (2) The process of growing older.

agistment Also known as gisted, stint, horse gait, gaited out, gait, or at gait; generally the prepaid use of pasture for grazing purposes, as on a weekly or monthly basis.

ah Also known as ahve or arve; a voice command used when driving agricultural horses to indicate a turn to the left.

AHC The acronym for the American Horse Council (q.v.).

AHSA The acronym for the American Horse Shows Associations (q.v.).

ahve *see* AH

AI *see* ARTIFICIAL INSEMINATION

aids Any natural or artificial touches employed by the rider to address reflexes and communicate instruction to his horse; include natural aids (q.v.), artificial aids (q.v.), driving aids (q.v.), diagonal aids (q.v.), rein aids (q.v.), weight aids (q.v.), upper aids (q.v.), voice aids (q.v.), and lower aids (q.v.).

Aimé Felix Tschiffely *see* TSCHIFFELY, AIME FELIX

Aintree A 4-mile, 856-yard (7,220 m) long race course located near Liverpool in Lancashire, England, where the first Grand National Steeplechase (q.v.), then known as The Grand Liverpool Steeplechase, was held in 1839.

Aintree breast girth Also known as a racing girth, Aintree girth, Newmarket girth, Newmarket breast girth, or racing breastplate; a breastplate (q.v.) made of canvas webbing used to prevent a racing saddle from slipping backwards.

Aintree girth *see* AINTREE BREAST GIRTH

air The correct bearing of a horse in its movements (q.v.) and gaits (q.v.) or paces (q.v.).

air above the ground *see* AIRS ABOVE THE GROUND

air dried feed Any feed such as hay allowed to dry naturally as in the sunlight and air.

airer saddle A wooden stand on which a saddle is placed to air out or dry.

aires relevés A French term; airs above the ground (q.v.).

airing Also known as workout; a racing term; said of a horse who runs a race as if he were only out for exercise.

airs (1) Formalized posture or movement of the horse; include low airs (q.v.) and high airs or airs above the ground (q.v.). (2) *see* AIRS ABOVE THE GROUND.

airs above the ground Also known as high airs, airs, air above the ground, schools above the ground, movements off the ground, aires relevés, and historically as bounds; any of the various High School (q.v.) movements performed either with the forelegs or with the fore and hind legs while the horse is above the ground; of seven types in the classical equitation of 17th-century Europe, while at the Spanish School today they have been distilled into three: levade (q.v.), courbette (q.v.), and capriole (q.v.); others include the pesade (q.v.), croupade (q.v.), ballotade (q.v.), and un pas un saut (q.v.); derived from movements performed by medieval war-horses to discourage the close proximity of foot soldiers intent on unhorsing the knight.

AIT The acronym for Area International Trial (q.v.).

Akaster Turk *see* ALCOCK ARABIAN

Akhal Teké A warmblood indigenous to the former Soviet Union, descending more than 3,000 years ago from the Turkmene (q.v.); bred around the oases of the Turkmenistan desert, north of Iran; possesses outstanding endurance, resistance to heat, and speed; stands 14.2 to 15.2 hands, is wiry with a long head and neck set on a long body and legs, has a low-set tail, and silky, sparse, and short mane and tail hair; has a flowing movement with little swing to the body; the predominant coat color is dun with its striking gold bloom (q.v.), although black, gray, and silver do occur; can be obstinate and bad-tempered; used for long-distance riding, racing, jumping, and dressage; the first Russian breed to have its own stud book.

a la brida A late 15th-century riding style popular around the Iberian Peninsula; the rider rode a saddle with a high pommel (q.v.) and cantle with his legs very straight and feet pushed forward; a severe curb with a high port and cheekpieces up to 16 1/2 inches (37 cm) long was commonly used.

à la flèche A circus act in which the rider drives a horse in the lead on long reins (q.v.).

a la gineta A late 15th-century riding style practiced by the Gineta, a Moorish tribe which populated the Iberian Peninsula; similar to a la brida (q.v.), but a ring bit was used instead of the severe curb.

Alazan Refers to point (q.v.) color; a Spanish term; red or dark flaxen points; sometimes used in combination with other color distinctions such as sorrel (q.v.) and chestnut (q.v.) to provide greater specificity, e.g., chestnut alazan.

Albany cutter *see* CUTTER

albarda *see* APAREGO PACK

albata *see* GERMAN SILVER

ALBC The acronym for American Livestock Breeds Conservancy (q.v.).

albinism The state or condition of being albino (q.v.).

albino A color type; a horse having a white coat due to lack of pigmentation, pink skin, and pale translucent eyes.

Albino *see* AMERICAN WHITE AND AMERICAN CREAM

Al Borak The mythological winged horse of the Prophet The Prophet Mohammed; supposedly white in color with a human head, and possessed of incredible speed.

Alcock Arabian Also known as Pelham Arabian, Ancaster Arabian, or Akaster Turk; a gray Arabian stallion from which all gray Thoroughbreds (q.v.) are descended in direct male line; stood at service 1720 to 1725.

alcohol block To inject alcohol into the nerves of the tail of Appaloosa (q.v.), Quarter Horse (q.v.), Paint (q.v.), stock-type Pinto (q.v.), and other breed show horses to deaden or numb the nerves to achieve a quiet tail carriage; formerly achieved by nerving (q.v.); as it is now an illegal procedure for show purposes, show horses are tested for neurological response using an electrical prod.

Alderney milk float A horse-drawn English dairyman's float popular during the 1900s; hung on sideways-positioned, semi-elliptical springs, had a cranked axle, low-slung body work, mud flaps above the wheels, curved top or name board, and a seat positioned crosswise in the center of the body work.

Alexandra car A horse-drawn vehicle; an American version of the dogcart phaeton (q.v.); had back-to-back seating and cut under forewheels.

Alexandra dogcart An English single- or two-wheeled horse-drawn dogcart (q.v.) used in the late 19th century; constructed with straight rather than curved lines, a high dashboard, and high, broad mud guards; sat slightly lower to the ground than the ordinary dogcart; originally designed for Queen Alexandra; thought to be more suitable for women.

alfalfa (1) Also known as Lucerne; a perennial legume plant of the medic family; thought to be the first cultivated forage for horses, being carried into Greece by the Persians during Xerxes' invasion in 490 BC to feed the war horses; has an average life of four to 16 years, is an excellent source of protein, carotene, and nitrogen, and grows in temperate and subtropical regions; will produce up to three times as much hay per acre as many of the grass hays (q.v.) and many cuttings may be made on the same field in one year; contains a fiber content of approximately 30 percent and a digestible protein content ranging from around 7.7 to 12.3 percent depending on the bloom of the alfalfa; the protein found in alfalfa contains all ten essential amino acids; may be fed green or as hay. (2) Also known as alfalfa hay; cut and dried alfalfa; generally pressed into 50–100 lb (23–45 kg) bales strung with wire or rope; may be stored for many months without sacrificing quality.

alfalfa cubes *see* CUBES

alfalfa hay *see* ALFALFA no. 2

alfalfa leaf meal *see* ALFALFA MEAL

alfalfa meal Also known as alfalfa leaf meal; finely ground and heat dried alfalfa (q.v.); generally of uniform quality and composition; an excellent source of protein, minerals, and vitamins; can be made into alfalfa pellets (q.v.) immediately after drying.

alfalfa pellets A compressed feed pellet, usually cylindrically shaped, made from dehydrated alfalfa hay or dehydrated alfalfa leaf meal (q.v.); may be fed as roughage or as part of a concentrated ration; generally have a higher protein and carotene content than alfalfa (q.v.), are less dusty and are not as subject to mold, aging, and weathering.

alga The singular of algae (q.v.).

algae One of many plants of the subdivision of thallophytes found for the most part in both salt and fresh water, including pond scums, kelps, and some seaweeds.

alight *see* DISMOUNT

aliment That which nourishes; food.

alimentary Relating to food.

alimentary canal Also known as alimentary tract or alimentary system; the embryonic canal from the mouth to the anus through which food passes; evolves into the gastrointestinal tract (q.v.), esophagus, lips, etc.

alimentary system *see* ALIMENTARY CANAL

alimentary tract *see* ALIMENTARY CANAL

alkaloid A class of nitrogenized compounds found in living plants and containing their active principles, such as morphine, quinine, caffeine, etc.

a la jineta A 15th-century Spanish term; a balanced seat riding style in which the rider's ankles hang vertically below the hips; encourages loin coiling in the horse, ensuring rider comfort and mobility.

all-age race A racing term; a horse race for two-year horses and older.

allantonic fluid The watery substance filling the space between the alanto-amnion and the chorio-allantois membranes surrounding the fetus in the uterus; lubricates the birth canal during birth and expulsion from the vagina precedes appearance of the foal.

All England Jumping Course A continental-style jumping course with permanent obstacles built by Douglas Bunn in the fields of his home, Hickstead Place (q.v.), in 1960 for British horses and riders; evolved into Hickstead (q.v.) one of the greatest show jumping centers in the world.

allergen Any substance that induces an allergic reaction.

allergy Excess sensitivity producing a bodily reaction to certain substances such as food, drugs, pollen, heat, or cold which are harmless to other animals or humans.

Alley Bodger A small, low-sided, horse-drawn wagon frequently run on iron wheels; drawn by one horse and used for general purposes in the hop fields of Kent, England.

Alliance Phaeton A horse-drawn sporting version of the Park Phaeton (q.v.) popular during the 1850s and 1860s.

alligator (1) A cutting term; a cow who is difficult to control. (2) *see* CLINCHER

all on A hunting term; said by the whippers-in (q.v.) to let the huntsman (q.v.) know that all hounds are up with the pack and accounted for.

all out Said of a horse who gives maximum effort and exertion when asked by the rider.

allowance race A racing term; a non-claiming event in which published conditions drafted by the racing secretary (q.v.) stipulate jockey weight allowances according to their previous purse earnings and/or number and type of victories; a horse is allowed to carry less weight if he has won fewer times than the other competitors, or if he has earned less money; generally considered a higher class race than claiming races (q.v.), but of a lower class than stakes races (q.v.).

allowances A racing term; reductions in weight carried by competing horses due to race conditions: because an apprentice jockey (q.v.) is riding, or to female horses competing against males and three-year olds competing against older horses.

all-purpose saddle Also known as general purpose saddle; an English saddle having a slightly deeper seat than a close contact saddle (q.v.), round cantle (q.v.), and slightly forward and padded flap; used for jumping, trail riding, and eventing.

all-round cow horse A western term; any horse capable of performing the duties required of it by a cowboy (q.v.).

all-rounder A polo term; a player sufficiently confident and knowledgeable of the game of polo (q.v.) to be able to read and interpret the game at every moment of play.

allures The gait (q.v.) or pace (q.v.) of the horse; of two types: natural allures (q.v.) and artificial allures (q.v.).

alopecia Local or general loss of hair, fur, or wool in the absence of other visible skin disease; may be congenital (q.v.) or associated with inflammatory skin disorders such as mange (q.v.) or ringworm (q.v.).

alpung The Austrian practice of raising young Haflinger (q.v.) stock on Alpine pastures where the thin air develops their hearts and lungs.

also eligible A racing term; a horse officially entered in a race who will not compete unless other horses are scratched creating vacancies in the field (q.v.).

also-ran A racing term; any horse who does not complete a race in the top three finishers.

Altai A horse breed indigenous to Russia used for riding.

Alter *see* CASTRATE

Alter A Spanish-bred warmblood with similar lineage to the Andalusian (q.v.) used for riding and jumping.

Alter-Real A horse breed indigenous to Portugal; descended from Andalusian (q.v.) mares imported from the Jerez region of Spain to Portugal by the House of Braganza in 1847 where they were bred and maintained at a stud farm at Villa de Portel in Portugal's Alentejo province; the stud was later moved to Alter, from which the breed name derived; the purpose of the stud was to develop a Haute Ecole (q.v.) horse; blood lines were seriously conta-

minated during the Napoleonic invasion at which time Thoroughbred (q.v.), Hanoverian (q.v.), Arab (q.v.), and Norman (q.v.) blood was introduced; government intervention enabled the consistent reintroduction of Andalusian blood in the 20th century which re-established the breed to its former type; is compact, standing 15.1 to 16.1 hands, and has a bay, brown, chestnut, and sometimes gray coat; is intelligent, quick to learn, and athletic; the action (q.v.) is elevated, but lacks extension; a good riding horse, particularly well suited to the Haute Ecole.

alum A class of double sulfates containing aluminum and such metals as potassium, ammonium, and iron; common or potash alum is used in medicine as an astringent and styptic.

alveolar emphysema *see* CHRONIC OBSTRUCTIVE PULMONARY DISEASE

Amalgamated Society of Farriers and Blacksmiths An organization founded in 1805 in Great Britain to regulate the wages and employee/employer relations for farriers and blacksmiths; one of the oldest trade unions in existence.

amarinda A Spanish term; horses trained to stay with a bell mare (q.v.).

amateur *see* AMATEUR RIDER

amateur huntsman A hunting term; a gentleman, usually a master (q.v.) who chooses to hunt his own hounds.

amateur-owner A competitive division restricted to non-professional adult riders who ride horses owned by themselves or their families in hunter/jumper competitions.

amateur rider (1) Also known as amateur or gentleman rider; one who rides a horse solely for pleasure and not for monetary award or financial gain; excludes stable hands, grooms, hunt servants, etc. (2) A rider who lacks the polish or talent of a professional.

amateur whipper-in *see* HONORARY WHIPPER-IN

amble A four-beat lateral gait derived from the pace (q.v.) and performed in four-time without suspension: (i) left hind, (ii) left fore, (iii) right hind, and (iv) right fore; the sequence is the same as the walk (q.v.), although the rhythm and execution make it closer to the pace; is smooth, comfortable, easy to ride, and can be collected; most horses that perform the gait have a natural affinity for it.

Americaine *see* AMERICAN BUGGY

American Albino *see* AMERICAN WHITE HORSE

American Albino Association, Inc. Also known by the acronym AAAI; an organization founded in the United States which superseded the American Albino Horse Club, Inc. (q.v.) in 1970; in the interest of allaying public fear about the word "albino," began registering pure white horses, ponies, and miniature horses as "American White" and also accepted cream colored horses in a new division as American Cream (q.v.); superseded by the International American Albino Association, Inc. (q.v.).

American Albino Horse Club, Inc. Also known by the acronym AAHC; an organization founded in the United States in 1936, and incorporated in 1937 to promote and preserve the breeding records of the American Albino (q.v.), known as the American White Horse (q.v.) since 1970; reincorporated in 1970 under the American Albino Association, Inc. (q.v.) and reincorporated again in 1985 as the International American Albino Association, Inc. (q.v.).

American Association of Equine Practitioners Also known by the acronym AAEP; an organization founded in 1954 in the United States to oversee and regulate the activities of equine veterinarians in the United States.

American Association of Owners and Breeders of Peruvian Paso Horses Also known by the acronym AAOBPPH; an organization founded in the United States in 1962 and incorporated as a non-profit corporation in 1967 to register pure-bred Peruvian Pasos (q.v.), promote the breed, and educate the public; the only registry recognized by the Association Nacional de Criadores and Propietarios de Caballos Peruanos de Paso, the registry in Peru.

American Bashkir Also known as American Bashkir Curly; a centuries-old pony breed originating in Bashkiria, around the southern foothills of the Urals in the former Soviet Union; reputed to have run wild in the United States in the early 1800s at which time it was quite popular with the American Indian for riding, packing and light draft; stands 13.1 to 14, hands; has a distinctive thick, curly winter coat and thick mane, tail, and forelock that enable it to survive in sub-zero temperatures; is kept outdoors where it can withstand winter temperatures of -22–40°F (-30–40°C); the coat is usually bay, chestnut or palomino; has a short and long neck, low withers, elongated and sometimes hollow back, a wide and deep chest, short and strong legs, and a small foot for its size; the breed standard quotes a bone measurement of 8 inches (20 cm) below the knee and a girth measurement for stallions of 71 inches (180 cm); is docile, strong, quiet, and hardy; during a seven- to eight-month lactation period a mare can yield as much as 350 gallons (1,590 liters) of milk; the long winter coat hair is spun into cloth; due to the exceptionally hard hoof, is generally left unshod.

American Bashkir Curly *see* AMERICAN BASHKIR

American break A horse-drawn passenger vehicle used in the Western United States for swift, long-distance travel; had a short wheel base, seating for six, slatted under-boot, ample luggage space, and was hung front and rear on sideways-elliptical springs, drawn by four or more horses.

American buggy Also known as buggy, Americaine in Western Europe, or spelled buggie; any of the family of medium-sized, light and fast, two- and four-wheeled, horse-drawn driving wagons popular in the United States from the 1830s to the 1920s; a phaeton (q.v.) with equirotal or near equirotal wheels; similar in outward appearance to a Model T Ford; modern versions are still used by the Amish sect; drawn by a single horse.

American cab A two-wheeled horse-drawn cab first used in New York, United States around 1832; had a driver roofseat with angled footboard, two interior seats for a total of four passengers, and rear entry; mounted on cranked axles with sideways elliptical or semi-elliptical springs.

American cabriolet A four-wheeled, horse-drawn, low-slung carriage popular in North America during the second half of the 19th century; drawn by a pair of horses in pole gear (q.v.), hung on full sideways elliptical springs, front and rear, and protected at the rear by a half hood.

American Cream *see* AMERICAN CREAM HORSE

American Cream Horse Also known as an American Cream and incorrectly as an Albino or American Albino; an American color breed with diverse bloodlines; descended from a white foundation stallion of Morgan (q.v.) and Arab (q.v.) blood known as Old King (1906) put to Arab, Morgan, and Thoroughbred (q.v.) mares beginning in 1917; due to public demand for a registration for horses whose coats were cream-colored instead of pure white, the American Albino Association (q.v.) opened a separate stud book for creams in 1970; the result of a dilute gene, a cream bred to a cream will produce a cream 100 percent of the time; have pale cream hair varying in shades from almost white to a rich cream or any other shade that does not qualify as Palomino (q.v.), pink to pinkish-orange (pumpkin) skin pigmentation, and a mane and tail which may vary from white to russet in color; any eye color is acceptable with blue, hazel, and amber occurring most often; gray or black skin is not acceptable; is different than the American White (q.v.).

American Cutting Horse Association Also referred to as ACHA.

American Discovery Trail Also known by the acronym ADT; the first nonmotorized, coast-to-coast thoroughfare in the United States traversing 6,000 miles (9,656 km) of urban as well as rural areas from Point Reyes National Seashore in California to Henelopen State Park in Delaware; developed in the late 20th century.

American Donkey & Mule Society, The Also known as ADMS; an organization founded in the United States in 1968 to maintain the registry for all types of asses (q.v.) and ass hybrids such as mules (q.v.).

American Farriers Association Also known by the acronym AFA; an association of farriers (q.v.) practicing in the United States organized in 1971; provides certification tests for its members since 1979, the levels of which include Certified Farrier and Certified Journeyman Farrier.

American Foxhound Club A non-profit organization founded in the United States in 1912 originally founded to promote the Virginia strain of American Foxhounds (q.v.), now promotes all pack hounds in North America, is the primary financial supporter of hound shows, and publishes materials and books on foxhunting (q.v.).

American Horse An all-purpose, generic riding horse developed in the Eastern United States in the early 1700s by crossing Narragansett Pacers (q.v.) mares with Thoroughbred (q.v.) stallions; larger and prettier than the Narragansett, but possessed of the same easy gaits and stamina; recognized as a breed in 1776; a precursor to the American Saddlebred (q.v.).

American Horse Council Also known by the acronym AHC; an organization founed in 1969 in Washington, DC, USA to promote and protect the horse industry by communicating with Congress, federal agencies, media, public, and the horse industry itself on behalf of all horse-related interests.

American Horse Shows Association Also known by the acronym AHSA; an organization founded in the United States in 1917 to represent the United States in international equestrian affairs and to govern equestrian sport competition in the United States.

American Horse Shows Association Hunter Seat Equitation Medal A year-long horsemanship competition for junior riders culminating at the Pennsylvania National Horse Show in Harrisburg, Pennsylvania, USA each October; riders must qualify for the finals by winning a specified number of AHSA (q.v.) Medal classes throughout the year.

American Livestock Breeders Conservancy Also known by the acronym ALBC; a nonprofit membership organization chartered to preserve heritage breeds of cattle, horses (Spanish Mustang [q.v.], Gotland [q.v.], etc.), goats, asses, sheep, swine, and poultry from extinction; also acts in the United States as a clearing house for information on livestock and genetic diversity.

American mail coach, the *see* CONCORD COACH

American Novice Horse Association

Also known by the acronym ANHA; an organization founded in Texas, USA in 1990, to organize rodeo (q.v.) competitions for inexperienced horses such as barrel racing (q.v.), pole bending, and breakaway and calf roping events; classes have career-earning limits to encourage parity of competition.

American Paint Horse Association Also known by the acronym APHA; an organization founded in the United States in 1962, following the merger of the American Paint Stock Horse and American Paint Quarter Horse Associations; dedicated to the continuance, registration, performance, and record keeping of Stock-Type Paint Horses (q.v.); started the Pinto Horse Stud Book in 1963; registers foals born of registered American Paint Horses (q.v.), Quarter Horses (q.v.), or Thoroughbreds (q.v.) registered with the Jockey Club or Jockey Club-recognized organizations having a white spot on the body at least 2 inches (50 mm) long, with unpigmented skin beneath it; solid-colored horses will not be registered.

American Pelham bit A single-piece or mullen mouth bit, with a slightly curved mouthpiece and cheeks (q.v.) angled backwards at the bottom; equipped to handle four reins – two snaffle and two curb.

American Quarter Horse Association Also known by the acronym AQHA; an organization founded in the United States in 1940 to establish breed specifications and maintain a registry for the Quarter-type horse; merged with the American Quarter Racing and National Quarter Horse Associations in 1949; the world's largest breed organization.

American Quarter Racing Association Also known by the acronym AQRA; an organization founded in the early 1940s in the United States to establish breed specifications and registry for the Quarter-type horse; merged into the American Quarter Horse Association (q.v.) in 1949.

American Saddlebred Also known as the Kentucky Saddlebred, Kentucky Saddler, Saddlebred, American Saddle Horse, or Saddle Horse; a horse breed indigenous to the United States where it was developed in Kentucky by putting a Thoroughbred (q.v.) foundation sire to American Horse (q.v.), Canadian Pacer (q.v.), and Narragansett Pacer (q.v.) mares; identified as a distinct breed in the early

1800s; more than 60 percent of the horses in the first three breed registry volumes trace to the foundation sire Gaines' Denmark and today the two prominent bloodlines remain: Denmark and Chief; Morgan (q.v.) blood was introduced in the 1850s; may be three- or five-gaited depending on the training; has a high-set tail achieved by nicking (q.v.), a high head set, long and arched neck, and a sloped shoulder; the gait is free and natural and has high action; stands 15 to 16 hands with an average weight of 1,000–1,200 (454–544 kg); all coat colors are acceptable, with the most prominent being chestnut, bay, black, and brown; gray, palomino, roan, and pinto colors also occur; used for saddle, show, and harness; shown in three types of classes: light harness (q.v.), three-gaited saddler (q.v.), and the five-gaited saddler (q.v.).

American Saddlebred Horse Association Also known by the acronym ASHA; an organization founded in 1891 in Louisville, Kentucky, USA to maintain the breed registry for the American Saddlebred (q.v.); was the first public association and breed registry established for an American horse breed.

American Saddle Horse see AMERICAN SADDLEBRED

American Saddlehorse see AMERICAN SADDLEBRED

American Standardbred see STANDARDBRED

American Stage Coach see STAGE COACH

American Stud Book, The The American-held registry for all Thoroughbred (q.v.) horses foaled in the United States, Puerto Rico, and Canada and of all Thoroughbreds imported into those countries from jurisdictions having a registry recognized by The Jockey Club (q.v.) and the International Stud Book Committee.

American Team Penning Championships Also known by the acronym ATPC; one of three national events established in the United States after 1980 which is devoted solely to the sport of team penning (q.v.).

American Triple Crown see TRIPLE CROWN

American Trotter see STANDARDBRED

American Vaulting Association Also known by the acronym AVA; an organization established in California, USA in 1968 to promote vaulting in the United States through training of judges, creation of rules, and publishing of a bi-monthly magazine.

American White *see* AMERICAN WHITE HORSE

American White Horse Also known as Albino, American Albino, American White, and incorrectly as an American Cream; an American color breed with diverse bloodlines; descended from a white, stock-horse type of Morgan (q.v.) and Arab (q.v.) blood, known as Old King, put to Arab, Morgan, and Thoroughbred (q.v.) mares from 1917 on; physical characteristics vary considerably and may resemble the Quarter Horse (q.v.), Morgan, Thoroughbred, or Arab; has snow white coat hair, pink skin, and dark brown eyes, with black, blue and hazel also occurring; mottled skin, spotted hair or spotted skin are unacceptable, but a few, small spots on the skin of the extremities is permitted; a dominant color; white bred to color will result in white offspring 50 percent of the time, and white bred to white will produce white approximately 75 percent; since 1970, two studbooks have been maintained: the American White Horse and the American Cream Horse (q.v.); due to the diversity of the bloodlines, must stand a minimum of 13.1 hands; the only pure white, non-albino horse breed in the world; the name derived from the Latin albus meaning white.

America's 500-year-old new breed *see* PASO FINO

amino acid An organic compound containing the amino group NH_2 (nitrogen) and at least one carbon group which form the basic constituents of proteins (q.v.); essential amino acid (q.v.) content determines the quality of the protein.

amino acid supplement A feed additive containing one or more of the essential amino acids (q.v.) fed to a horse to correct a deficiency.

Amish buggy A horse-drawn American buggy (q.v.) used by the Amish religious community in the United States from the 18th century through modern day; originally had a basic tray shape with a high-backed driving seat, wide enough for two passengers, leather-covered dashboard, folding hood, and brass-mounted candle lamps; now, box-shaped and enclosed on three sides with leather screens; always painted black and drawn by a single horse.

ammonia A compound of nitrogen and hydrogen; may be applied to sprains or injuries as a liniment or inhaled, when in vapor form, to stimulate respiration and the respiratory system when these are depressed.

ammoniac An exudation of an umbeliferous plant with a fetid smell used as an antispasmodic and expectorant and in plasters (q.v.).

amnion *see* AMNIONIC SAC

amnionic sac Also known as amnion or water bag; the innermost membrane surrounding the fetus (q.v.).

Ampeton A light, horse-drawn open carriage of the landau (q.v.) type first used in London, England during the 1850s.

ampoule Also spelled ampule; a hermetically sealed glass vial or container used to hold solutions for laboratory tests or injection into the horse.

ampule *see* AMPOULE

amulet Anything worn or carried upon the person or animal, intended to act as a charm or preservative against evil, accident, or mischief, such as disease and witchcraft; originally used on camels in the desert; when used on horses, known as horse brasses (q.v.).

anabolic steroids A group of substances including tenbolone, testosterone, and nadrolone used to accelerate the recovery of weight lost due to debility or undernutrition, increase muscular development and tone, speed up tissue regeneration to help resolve bone and tissue injuries, assist in the recovery from infectious diseases, and to increase the efficiency of protein utilization; may produce male-like behavior in some mares and fillies; sudden withdrawal after prolonged administration may result in a marked loss of condition in the treated horse.

anaemia *see* ANEMIA

anaerobic exercise A period of strenuous exercise demanding muscle function without adequate oxygen.

anaesthetic *see* ANESTHETIC

anal atresia A congenital condition of foals born without an anal opening; a true lethal (q.v.) resulting in death.

analeptic A restorative; any substance which gives strength and/or stimulates the central nervous system.

analgesic A substance that relieves or removes pain.

anaphylactic shock Also known as anaphylaxis; a shock (q.v.) condition characterized by acute, violent and often fatal systemic allergic reaction triggered by the introduction of an antigen (q.v.) to a horse who has already been exposed to and acquired sensitivity to that antigen (q.v.); may result from the injection of vaccines or drugs, exposure to food or airborne allergens, or insect bites; symptoms occur within seconds after the allergen enters the circulation and include constriction of bronchial airways and the pulmonary vascular bed which results in severe respiratory distress and death within minutes if untreated.

anaphylaxis *see* ANAPHYLACTIC SHOCK

anatomy The structure of the horse body and the relation of its parts.

Ancaster Arabian *see* ALCOCK ARABIAN

anchor pull A metal tip attached to the lower half of the hames (q.v.) fitted with an eye through which the hame clip or hame tug ring passes; the most common method of securing the traces, shoulder-pieces, or hame tugs on modern horse-drawn driving vehicles.

Ancient English Pacer Also known generically as palfrey or pad; the primary horse breed used throughout the British Isles from 500 to 1500 AD; specific types were known by the location of their origin such as the Irish Hobby Horse and the Scottish Galloway (q.v.) transported by the Vikings to Iceland where they remain today as the Icelandic (q.v.); the foundation stock for the American Saddlebred (q.v.).

Andalucian *see* ANDALUSIAN

Andalusian Also spelled Andalucian and

known as the Spanish Horse; a breed originating in Spain around the 8th century AD thought to have either descended from Barb (q.v.) and Arab (q.v.) stock crossed with native breeds or descended from the Iberian Horse (q.v.); influenced the development of most European breeds (i.e., Friesian (q.v.), Holstein (q.v.), Lippizzaner (q.v.), and Oldenburg (q.v.)) and, thanks to Columbus, most American breeds (Quarter Horse [q.v.] and Criollo [q.v.]) as well; strictly and systematically bred since 1571 with the founding of the Royal Stables in Cordoba where it is still bred and now also in Jerez and Seville; is short-coupled and powerfully built, stands 15.1 to 15.3 hands, has a gray, black, bay, chestnut, or roan coat with bay and shades of gray occurring most commonly a straight or sometimes convex profile, small, inward-facing ears, curved neck, rounded quarters, low-set tail, a thick, long, and wavy mane and tail, an airy action, a high-stepping, impulsive trot, and a rocking canter; is a good jumper and particularly well suited to dressage and the movements of Haute Ecole (q.v.); less than 20,000 world wide.

anemia Also spelled anaemia; a deficiency in red blood cell count and/or blood hemoglobin content; commonly caused by excessive bleeding, infection, worms, dietary deficiency, and the presence of toxins in the body; symptoms include pale mucous membranes of the eyelids and a weak pulse; types include hemorrhagic anemia (q.v.), hemolytic anemia (q.v.), and nutritional anemia (q.v.).

anesthesia An artificially induced state of insensibility, especially to the sense of pain.

anesthetic Also spelled anaesthetic; of or belonging to anesthesia; having the power to deprive of feeling or sensation; any substance that has the power to deprive of feeling or sensation; may be injected or inhaled to achieve different levels of desensitization: local anesthetic (q.v.), regional anesthetic, and general anesthetic (q.v.).

anestrus A period of sexual inactivity in the mare during which there is an absence of observable heat (q.v.) or acceptance to the stallion.

aneurine hydrochloride Synthetic thiamin (q.v.) or vitamin B_1.

Anglo-Arab A horse breed resulting from

crossing Thoroughbred (q.v.) stallions with Arab (q.v.) mares or vice versa; originated in Britain, but is also bred elsewhere, particularly France, where it has been selectively bred for more than 150 years; in some countries, the mix may be no less than 50 percent Thoroughbred and 50 percent Arab, while in others the percentage is not stipulated; the breed registry is maintained by the Arab Horse Society in each country; has the soundness, endurance, and stamina of the Arab and the scope and speed of the Thoroughbred, but without its excitable temperament.

Anglo-Argentine A breed developed in South America by crossing the Thoroughbred (q.v.) with the Criollo (q.v.).

Anglo-Norman *see* NORMAN

Anglo-Persian A breed developed in Iran by crossing the Arab (q.v.) with Persian; an all purpose riding mount.

Angular Landau *see* SHELBURNE LANDAU

ANHA The acronym for American Novice Horse Association (q.v.).

anhydrosis The failure of the body's sweating mechanisms; commonly occurs when both the temperature and humidity are high; symptoms include inability to sweat, increased respiratory rate, elevated body temperature, and decreased exercise tolerance; may be reversed if the horse is moved to a more temperate climate.

aniseed Also spelled anise seed; the seed of the anise, an annual umbelliferous plant, Pimpinella anisum, which has a licorice-like taste and aromatic smell; used in drag hunts (q.v.) as a line for the hounds to follow in the absence of live fox.

anise seed *see* ANISEED

ankle (1) *see* FETLOCK JOINT. (2) A leg marking (q.v.); any white mark extending from the coronary band (q.v.) to just above the fetlock (q.v.).

ankle boot Also known as Kersey protection boots or sesamoid boots; a light-duty brushing boot (q.v.) used to protect the fetlock joint (q.v.) including the associated ligaments and tendons above the joint; made of Kersey (q.v.), leather, or felt and held in place with buckle straps or velcro.

ankle cutter A racing term; a horse who cuts his fetlock (q.v.) with the opposite foot while running.

ankylosing arthritis Arthritis (q.v.) characterized by severe degeneration and ulceration of the articular cartilages in conjunction with erosion and flattening of the underlying bone; degeneration results in new bone growth which fills the joint space; may be the end result of osteoarthritis (q.v.), infectious arthritis (q.v.), or severe injury such as a fracture (q.v.) or puncture wound.

ankylosis The fusion of bones in part or all of a joint due to disease, injury, or surgical procedure; results in loss of movement.

annular Shaped like a ring.

anodynes Medicines or drugs used to relieve or soothe pain, particularly as associated with colic (q.v.).

Anoplocephala manga A species of tapeworm (q.v.) varying in length from 8 to 25 cm and found in the small intestine and stomach; in light infestations, no signs of disease are present, while in heavy infestations, digestive disturbances, and anemia (q.v.) may occur.

Anoplocephala perforliata A species of tapeworm (q.v.) varying in length from 8 – 25 cm; found in the cecum, and in some cases, the small intestine; ulceration of the mucosa occurs quite commonly in the area of attachment; in light infestations, no signs of disease are present; in heavy infestations, digestive disturbances, unthriftiness, and anemia (q.v.) may occur.

ante-post betting A racing term; a betting option in which wagering on a race, for an agreed upon price, occurs on any day prior to the race.

anterior Toward the front of the body.

anterior enteritis An acute inflammation of the small intestine resulting in signs of abdominal distress such as colic (q.v.) and diarrhea (q.v.).

anthelmintic Also known as antiparasitic; any drug or compound administered to the horse by injection, drenching, or oral paste to destroy internal parasites.

anthrax An acute, infectious disease caused by *Bacillus anthracis*; symptoms include elevated temperature, abnormal swelling in the throat and neck, great pain, and sudden death; rare in horses.

anti A prefix; against, as in antibacterial (q.v.).

antiarrhythmic agent Any drug used to regulate cardiac arrhythmia (q.v.).

antibacterial A group of substances topically applied to destroy or inhibit the growth of bacteria and other disease-causing organisms.

antibiotic A group of substances used to destroy or inhibit the growth of bacteria and other disease-causing organisms; may be administered orally, topically, or by injection depending on the drug used and the nature of the infection; includes penicillin and mycin drugs.

antibody Any of various substances existing in the blood or developed in immunization which counteract toxins or bacterial poisons in the system.

antibody test A laboratory test performed by technicians to measure the titer, or blood concentration, of immune activity against a known virus; in a diagnostic setting, two tests are taken several weeks apart to compare titers which rise with recent infection; a shortcoming of this test is that by the time antibody production is measurable, the disease has often run its course.

anti-cast roller Also known as arch-roller; a girth or surcingle fit around the girth of a stabled horse to prevent him from rolling over (q.v.) and/or casting (q.v.); a 3 to 4 inch wide girth made of leather or webbing with pads attached to the underside that fit on either side of the withers (q.v.) to prevent rubbing or pressure; bridged by an arched metal bar which sits approximately 3 inches (7.5 cm) above the withers.

anticipate Said of a horse who thinks he is aware of what is about to happen, as in what the rider or trainer will request of him, and acts accordingly, e.g., the horse may try, or succeed in trying, to make a transition before

receiving the rider's aid.

anti-cribbing device Also known as cribbiting device; a collar fitted around the upper neck of the horse to apply pressure to the horse's gullet to prevent cribbing (q.v.) and wind sucking (q.v.).

antifebrile Having the quality of abating fever (q.v.).

antifungal Any substance having the quality of inhibiting, controlling, or destroying a fungal infection.

antigen The molecules, primarily proteins, comprising a portion of an organism invading the body; once the body identifies an antigen, it produces antibodies (q.v.) that only attach to that antigen.

antihistamine A class of drugs used to neutralize histamine (q.v.) production resulting from conditions including sweet itch (q.v.), laminitis (q.v.) azoturia (q.v.) and allergic skin and respiratory diseases.

anti-inflammatory Any agent, drug, or compound that reduces inflammation including redness, heat, pain, and swelling.

antimere One of two or more corresponding parts on opposite sides of the horse.

antiparasitic *see* ANTHHELMINTIC

antiphlogistic Any agent, drug, or compound which counteracts inflammation and/or fever.

antipost bet A racing term; a wager placed on a horse(s) before the opening price is known.

antipyretic A remedy effective in reducing fever.

anti-rearing bit *see* CHIFNEY BIT

antiseptic (1) Devoid of germs. (2) An agent that inhibits the growth of micro-organisms such as germs.

antiserum A serum inclusive of antibodies acquired from the blood of an animal and used for injection into other animals to provide immunity against a certain disease.

antisweat sheet A cloth covering for the body of the horse made of a breathable, cellular cotton mesh or linen that enables the horse to cool down slowly following exercise.

antitoxin (1) A substance formed in a body, capable of counteracting a specific toxin. (2) The antibody formed in immunization with a given toxin; used to treat certain infectious diseases or produce immunity against them.

antivenin (1) Also spelled incorrectly as antivenom; an antitoxin (q.v.) produced in the blood by repeated injections of venom, as of snakes. (2) The antitoxic serum obtained from blood treated with repeated injections of venom, as of snakes.

antivenom *see* ANTIVENIN

antler A branched, bony, seasonal protection grown by the male of such species as the deer preparatory to the mating season; begins to grow from the crown in April, the bone is fully developed by July or August, and the antler is generally shed by late fall or early winter; has a blood supply unlike a horn; when growing, is covered by dermis and epidermis known as velvet (q.v.).

Antoine de Pluvinel *see* DE PLUVINEL, ANTOINE

anvil (1) A heavy iron block with a flat surface upon which a horseshoe (q.v.) is formed. (2) In human anatomy, the middle bone of the ear; the incus.

anvil shooting (1) Also known as anvil blowing; a recreational farrier practice; to place and ignite an explosive charge between two anvils (q.v.) stacked one on top of the other to launch the top anvil into the air. (2) Also known as anvil blowing; a farrier practice; to hammer a white-hot piece of iron against a wet anvil thus producing a pistol-like sound.

aparego pack Also known as albarda or asparego; a pack saddle of Spanish origin, constructed without a tree and consisting of long stems of straw sewn into two, square-shaped cloth cases joined by padded straps which pass over the back of the horse; straw-stuffed cases are placed on top of the square cases and a saddle cloth, secured by surcingles, covers the entire saddle; pack loads are distributed into two bundles and attached to the saddle; no weight is placed on the spine of the horse.

APHA The acronym for the American Paint Horse Association (q.v.).

ApHC The acronym for the Appaloosa Horse Club, Inc. (q.v.).

Appaloosa Also known as spotted horse or historically as Palouse Pony or Palousy; an American-bred warmblood descended from Spanish stock – some of which carried the hereditary spotting gene – introduced by the conquistadors in the 16th century and crossed with native and Quarter Horse (q.v.) -type mares; breed characteristics were initially fixed by the Nez Percé Indians; was nearly eradicated in 1876 as United States troops seized tribal lands and was revived by the Appaloosa Horse Club (q.v.) in 1938 at which time it was officially recognized as a breed; six symmetrical coat patterns are recognized: frost (q.v.), leopard (q.v.), varnish roan (q.v.), white blanket (q.v.), spotted blanket (q.v.), and snowflake (q.v.); a white sclera encircling the eye and at least one striped hoof on a solid-colored leg, mottled nose, lip, and genital skin are breed requirements; the mane and tail are characteristically sparse, the result of selective breeding to prevent entanglement in brush and undergrowth; originally short-coupled and of the stock type, but recent infusions of Thoroughbred (q.v.) blood have added height and more elegant lines to the breed; in Europe, and to some extent, the United States, crossed with warmbloods; possess good stamina, speed, and agility; the name derives from a corruption of the word Palouse, a river area located in northeastern Oregon where the Nez Percé Indians selectively bred this horse throughout the 18th and 19th centuries; the highly-valued horses of this area were soon known as Palouse ponies, which led to the singular a Palouse Pony, and ultimately Appaloosa.

Appaloosa Horse Club, Inc. Also known by the acronym ApHC; an organization founded in Moscow, Idaho, USA in 1938 to preserve, improve, promote, and enhance the Appaloosa (q.v.); the third largest breed registry in the world; original registration requirements included a classic blanket (q.v.) or leopard coat pattern (q.v.), mottled (q.v.) skin, white sclera (q.v.), and at least one striped hoof with a solid-colored leg.

appeal To address another person or authority for a decision regarding a score, time, penalty, disqualification, suspension, and the like received in a competition or from an association.

appendageal system An outgrowth of the epidermis (q.v.), with which it is contiguous; consists of hair follicles and sebaceous and aprocrine glands.

appointment card Also known as card or fixture card; a hunting term; an invitation sent out to interested hunters by the hunt Secretary to inform them of the date, time, and place of meets occurring in the subsequent month.

appointments Saddlery and harness worn by a horse at work or show.

apprentice One bound, often by a legal document, to learn a profession, as in an apprentice jockey (q.v.), apprentice trainer, etc.

apprentice allowance A racing term; a reduction in the weight carried by an apprentice jockey (q.v.) when competing against jockeys; the amount of the allowance as well as the conditions relating to such varies from area to area; usually 5 pounds (2.25 kg) until the jockey has five wins, 7 pounds (3 kg) until the 35th win, or 5 pounds (2.25 kg) for one calendar year from the 35th win; a 3 pounds (1.35 kg) allowance is occasionally granted to a jockey under contract to a specific stable or owner for two years from his first win; is not granted apprentice jockeys when competing in stakes races (q.v.).

apprentice jockey Also known as apprentice, jockey apprentice, bug, or bug boy; a racing term; a rider, usually young, serving an indentured apprenticeship to a jockey (q.v.); so called because of the "bug" or asterisk appearing next to the jockey's name in the official racing program; the asterisk is used to denote that the weight carried includes the apprentice allowance (q.v.).

apprentice, the Slang; a severe whip formerly used by drivers of heavy coaches.

approach The act of drawing near to an object or point, as in a horse to a jump.

appui Also spelled appuy; a historical French dressage term; the feeling of contact between the horse and rider achieved through the reins as the horse accepts the bit on the bars of his mouth; is ideally firm, yet light.

APPUY *see* APPUI

appuyer A French dressage term; two track (q.v.).

appuyer en renvers A French dressage term; haunches out (q.v.).

appuyer en travers A French dressage term; haunches in (q.v.).

appuyer épaule en dedans A French dressage term; shoulder in (q.v.).

appuyer épaule en dehors A French dressage term; shoulder out (q.v.).

apricot dun Refers to coat color; the lightest shade of red dun (q.v.); the body hair is light red tending to a yellow shade with a pale red, brown, or flaxen mane and tail.

apron (1) Also know as shoeing chaps; a leather or canvas leg covering worn by a farrier (q.v.) to protect thigh while shoeing a horse; worn just above the hips and held in place by means of a belt. (2) A heavy skirt worn by a side-saddler (q.v.) to cover her legs, boots, and the side saddle horns when mounted. (3) A cloth, rubber, or leather covering used by drivers of horse-drawn vehicles to keep them warm, dry, and clean. (4) A racing term; the paved area located between the grandstand and the racing surface.

apron face A face marking (q.v.); a wide, white blaze extending from the forehead to the muzzle and wrapping around and including both upper and lower lips.

AQHA The acronym for the American Quarter Horse Association (q.v.) and the Australian Quarter Horse Association.

AQRA The acronym for the American Quarter Racing Association (q.v.).

aquapuncture A type of acupuncture (q.v.); stimulation of precise body points along body meridians (q.v.) by injection of fluid such as water, oil, vitamin-B, or herbal and homeopathic solutions into trigger points; the solution continues to stimulate the points for an additional 10 to 15 minutes after removal of the needles; used to control pain, treat physical issues, anesthetize, and/or reduce stress.

Arab Also known as Arabian horse and Arabian; one of the oldest and purest horse breeds dating back more than 3,000 years, when it originated in Saudi Arabia; popular tradition states that it descended from the five mares of the Prophet Mohammed; of three main types: Assil (q.v.), purebred Arab (q.v.), and the Arab breed (q.v.); used for riding and light draft; has excellent endurance and speed, a straight or distinctively dished profile, small ears, fine bone structure, and stands 14 to 15 hands; has only 17 thoracic vertebrae instead of 18 and five lumbar vertebrae instead of six; may have a gray, bay, chestnut, black or, more rarely, roan coat.

Araba A Turkish horse-drawn wagon popular in the 18th and 19th centuries having a canopy top and crosswise seating; drawn by a pair of horses or oxen, driven by harem women, and guided by dismounted servants.

Arab breed One of three basic types of Arabian horse; includes the blood of horses with uncertain origins, or whose pedigree reflects the influence of the Berber, Persian, Syrian, Egyptian Arab, and other related breeds.

arabesque A vaulting position in which the vaulter (q.v.) stands on the back of a moving horse on one leg with the other leg, usually straight, stretched out behind.

Arab Horse Society An organization founded in 1918 in England to promote the breeding and encourage the re-introduction of Arab (q.v.) blood into English light-horse breeds; maintains registries for Arabs, Anglo-Arabs (q.v.), and part-bred Arabs (q.v.).

Arabian *see* ARAB

Arabian horse *see* ARAB

Arabian Race A part-bred Arab (q.v.) bred at the Bablona stud, located in Hungary after 1816; the progeny of purebred Arab stallions crossed with mares of oriental appearance who carried strains of Spanish, Hungarian, and Thoroughbred (q.v.) blood; the foundation of the Shagya Arabian (q.v.).

arc A barrel racing term; the bend achieved by the horse when turning around a barrel, which correctly extends from his nose, through the poll, shoulder, and into the loin.

Arcera An ancient Roman four-wheeled, horse-drawn, covered carriage used by the sick or infirm; alleged to be the oldest Roman vehicle on record; drawn by either horses or oxen; superseded by the litter (q.v.).

arched back *see* ROUNDED BACK

arch pelham A bit having a single-piece mouthpiece which curves characteristically in the center to accommodate the tongue; has cheeks and is used with two sets of reins, a curb chain, and sometimes a lip strap.

arch roller *see* ANTI-CAST ROLLER

Ardennais Also known as "the cart horse of the north" or French Ardennais; a heavy-draft breed from the Ardennes region of France from which the name derived; originated approximately 2,000 years ago at which time it was smaller and less massive; in the early 19th century crossed with Arab (q.v.), Thoroughbred (q.v.), Percheron (q.v.), and Boulonnais to increase size and draft capability; is gentle, docile, and calm yet energetic, is tough, has a compact, yet large frame, stands 15 to 16 hands, and weighs 1,540–2,200 pounds (699 – 998 kg); may have a bay, roan, red roan, gray, palomino, or chestnut coat although brown and light chestnut coats are tolerated and black excluded; has a heavy head, a straight or snub profile, small ears, large eyes, a short neck and back, heavily muscled quarters and shoulders, short, feathered legs with a broad hoof, and an enormous bone structure; the stud book was established in 1929; used for heavy draft, farm work, and raised for human consumption.

Ardennais du Nord *see* TRAIT DU NORD

Ardennes *see* BELGIAN ARDENNES

Area International Trial Also known by the acronym AIT; a show jumping competition put on by the British Show Jumping Association.

arena The specific area of any work-out, competition, or contest – physical, mental, or figurative; Latin meaning sand as used in an arena; from ancient Rome where the ground of the amphitheaters, upon which gladiators fought or wild animals were turned on human victims, was covered with sand to soak up spilled blood.

arena director A rodeo term; one responsible for conducting rodeos (q.v.) according to PRCA (q.v.) rules.

arena footing The surface material used in an arena (q.v.); may consist of grass, sand, wood products, rubber, leather, stone, or some combination thereof.

arena polo Also known as indoor polo; a polo game (q.v.) played in an enclosed arena approximately 300 by 150 ft (91 by 46 m) in size and having goal posts set at either end, 10 ft (3 m) apart; considerably smaller than a polo field (q.v.); the game follows the same basic rules and principles of field polo, although the strategies are different, and teams consist of only three members.

Argentine Criollo *see* CRIOLLO

Argentine polo pony Also referred to as Argentine pony; a polo pony (q.v.) developed in Argentina by putting imported Thoroughbred (q.v.) stallions to native Criollo (q.v.) mares; is tough, distinctly Thoroughbred in appearance, but shorter strided and possessing better bone, stronger joints and sturdier hooves; stands about 15.1 hands.

Argentine pony *see* ARGENTINE POLO PONY

Argentine snaffle A snaffle bit (q.v.) having a broken snaffle mouthpiece and hinged shanks; used with a curb chain.

arginine An essential amino acid (q.v.), vital in the composition of proteins.

Ariègeois *see* MERENS

Arkwright bit Also known as Lowther bit or Lowther riding bit; a curb bit (q.v.) in which the curb rein hangs directly from the cheekpiece without a neck.

armchair ride A racing term; an easily won victory which did not require the jockey (q.v.) to urge the horse forward.

aromatherapy The use of essential oils (q.v.) to treat and heal emotional and physical ailments through the sense of smell.

arrhythmia Also known as cardiac arrhythmia or heartbeat irregularity; a fairly common disturbance of the heart rate and rhythm; may be treated with antiarrhythmic agents and may disappear or be less pronounced following exercise.

arterial bleeding The loss of blood from an artery (q.v.); bleeding is profuse, brisk, and bright red; pulsations may be visible and tissues surrounding the wound may swell rapidly.

arterial fibrillation A gross irregularity of heart rhythm with a variation in heart sound intensity and pulse due to rapid and ineffective contractions of the chambers of the heart; may occur in the absence of underlying cardiac disease or in conjunction with other cardiac disease such as mitral insufficiency; occurs most commonly in draft and other large horses; may be definitively diagnosed by the electrocardiogram (q.v.).

arteritis *see* EQUINE VIRAL ARTERITIS

artery One of a system of cylindrical vessels or tubes which convey the blood from the heart to all parts of the body, to be brought back to the heart by the veins.

arthritis Generally, inflammation of a joint (q.v.); specifically a complicated condition that may involve the bones, articular cartilages, joint capsule, and associated ligaments of a joint(s); includes serous arthritis (q.v.), osteoarthritis (q.v.), infectious arthritis (q.v.), and ankylosing arthritis (q.v.).

Arthrobotrys oligospora A species of predatory fungus found in many parts of the world used to control small strongyle (q.v.) populations by trapping and penetrating them, then absorbing their contents; research is underway to develop an oral product containing the fungal predator which, when administered to livestock, will be excreted in the feces (q.v.) along with the eggs or larvae, enabling them to attack the parasites before they can migrate onto surrounding soil or grass where they would be ingested during grazing; considered an effective alternative to chemical anthelmentics (q.v.).

arthroscope A narrow tube containing a fiber optic instrument connected to a video camera which is inserted into a joint via a small incision to enable viewing inside a joint or through which to conduct microscopic surgery.

arthroscopic surgery Also known as arthroscopy; micro-surgery, generally in or around a joint, performed using an arthroscope (q.v.); less invasive than conventional surgery techniques, resulting in a more swift recovery.

arthroscopy *see* ARTHROSCOPIC SURGERY

articular cartilage Also known as joint cartilage or commonly as gristle; one of six types of cartilage (q.v.) found in the body structure of the horse; is firmly attached to and covers the ends of the bones where they meet in a joint (q.v.), protects the underlying bone, and transmits forces to the underlying subchondral bone; has limited powers of regeneration, and damage to it cannot be completely repaired

articular fracture A break in a bone which extends into a joint.

articular windgall *See* ARTICULAR WINDPUFF

articular windpuff Also known as ARTICULAR WINDGALL; a soft, painless, fluid-filled swelling which develops between the cannon bone and the suspensory ligament (q.v.) due to excessive accumulation of synovial fluid; often occurs in conjunction with a tendonous windpuff (q.v.); may be caused by intense training followed by a period of rest, excessive exercise on hard surfaces, and the cumulative effects of imbalances produced by poor conformation or improperly trimmed hooves.

articulating ring bone A ring bone (q.v.) condition where the bony growth has attached to the joints between the long and short pastern or the short pastern and the pedal bone; lameness usually results and there is no effective cure.

articulation (1) Limb joints; where two or more bones meet forming a joint. (2) The act or manner of moving a body part.

artificial aids Any means by which the rider communicates instruction to the horse including the use of spurs (q.v.), whips (q.v.), martingales (q.v.), and/or other gadgets.

artificial airs *see* ARTIFICIAL ALLURES

artificial allures Also known as artificial airs; any trained gait or pace of the horse, other than the walk, trot, and canter, i.e., the high and low airs (q.v.).

artificial breeding To generate progeny

(q.v.) by means other than natural cover (q.v.); includes artificial insemination (q.v.) or embryo transfer (q.v.); not approved by some breed associations such as The Jockey Club (q.v.).

artificial coloring Any change of color to the coat, mane, tail, or forelock that does not result from natural processes, e.g., dying.

artificial drag A hunting term; a man-laid trail of scent used in a drag hunt (q.v.); left by dragging, on foot or horseback an object soaked in any of a number of types of strong-smelling liquid similar to the scent of a fox, but not from the fox, e.g., a scent produced from aniseed (q.v.).

artificial insemination Also known as capsule or by the acronym AI; an unnatural method of impregnating the mare for the purpose of producing offspring; semen collected from the stallion, using nonsurgical methods, is generally frozen and transported to the mare where it is deposited in the body of the uterus during the mare's oestrus (q.v.) using a plastic insemination pipette; utilized when the stallion (q.v.) serves mares in widely spread locations, to protect a valuable stallion from injury during breeding, to increase the number of mares a given stallion can service, and to impregnate mares whose anatomical conformation precludes natural cover (q.v.); banned by some breed associations such as the Tennessee Walking Horse Breeder & Exhibitors Association, Jockey Club (q.v.), United States Trotting Association, and the American Saddle Horse Association

artificial scent A hunting term; a manufactured scent similar to that of a fox or other prey laid in a drag hunt; may be produced from aniseed (q.v.), fox feces, solid litter from tame fox's kennel, or fox or mink secretions.

artificial vagina A device used to collect semen from stallions for artificial insemination (q.v.) or laboratory purposes; generally a rubber sheath, surrounded by warm water, encased in a metal cylinder into which the horse's penis is inserted and in which the semen is collected.

artzel A face marking; any form of white marking on the forehead of the horse.

arve *see* AH

arytenoid cartilage Triangular-shaped cartilage (q.v.) located in the upper part of the entrance to the larynx (q.v.), the opening and closing of which it controls.

ascarid *see* LARGE ROUNDWORM

ascorbic acid *see* VITAMIN C

Ascot Landau A horse-drawn English vehicle of the landau (q.v.) type used for the British Royal Family's traditional drive down the course at Royal Ascot.

aseptic Free from germs that cause disease.

ASH The acronym for Australian Stock Horse (q.v.).

ASHA *see* AMERICAN SADDLEBRED HORSE ASSOCIATION

as hounds ran A hunting term; the distance covered by the hounds in a run (q.v.), measuring each turn from field to field, as opposed to the distance measured in a straight line from start to finish.

Asian Wild Horse *see* ASIATIC WILD HORSE

Asiatic wild ass A wild ass (q.v.) of the genus Equus; of two subspecies: *Equus hemionus* and *Equus kiang*; has a rust-colored coat with a light dorsal stripe; travels in herds throughout Iran, Afghanistan, and northern India; has no domestic descendants.

Asiatic Wild Horse Also known as Asian Wild Horse, Mongolian Wild Horse or by the scientific name *Equus przewalski* "Poliakov"; an ancient pony breed first discovered in 1881 by Colonel Poliakov in the Daqin Shan Mountains bordering the Gobi desert in Mongolia; although now extinct in the wild, a few animals remain in captivity; efforts are underway to re-establish the breed in the wild; historically used as mounts for the Huns and Chinese; stands 12 to 14 hands, has a palomino or yellow dun coat with dark legs, mane, and tail, mealy markings on the muzzle and zebra markings (q.v.); has a large, heavy head, broad forehead, long ears, small, almond-shaped eyes, short, bristly mane and tail, long back and short legs; is strong and hardy.

asil Also spelled asl; an Arabic word; a purebred Arab (q.v.) as out of an Arab mare served by a purebred Arab stallion.

Asinus isabellinus The scientific name for the Isabella quagga (q.v.).

ask the question Also known as question; to push a horse to its physical limits as in a race or gallop.

asl *see* ASIL

asparego *see* APAREGO PACK

asphyxia Interrupted breathing causing a lack of oxygen or excess of carbon dioxide in the body.

ass Also known as burro (particularly west of the Mississippi River, USA), donkey (particularly east of the Mississippi in the United States), jack stock, or by the Scientific term *Equus asinus* from which the current name derives; a quadruped of the horse family historically used as a beast of burden; descended from the African wild ass and includes the African wild ass, domestic donkey (q.v.), and onagers (q.v.); of four size classifications: miniature donkey (up to 36 inches [91 cm]), standard donkey (36–48 inches [91–122 cm]), large standard donkey (48–56 inches [122–142 cm]), and mammoth jack stock (54 inches [137 cm]. and up for jennets and 56 inches [142 cm] and taller for jacks); used for breeding mules (q.v.), driving, packing, show, sheep protection, post-weaning foal companionship, and halter breaking young calves and horses; an easy keeper and long lived, often living 30 to 40 years.

Assateague Also known as an Assateague pony; a pony originating on the island of Assateague off the Atlantic coast of the United States; adjacent to the Chincoteague Islands on which originated the Chincoteague pony (q.v.), to which it is identical.

Assateague pony *see* ASSATEAGUE

assil Also known as Kocklani, Kohuail, Koklani, Koheil, Khamsa or Kansat; one of three basic types of Arabian (q.v.) horse; said to be the true Bedouin Arab; classified into three sub breeds: the Kuhailan, the Siglavy, and the Muniqi.

Associate Farriers Company of London Also known by the acronym AFCI; a recognition of advanced farrier skill awarded by the

Worshipful Company of Farriers (q.v.), London, England; superseded by the Associate of the Worshipful Company of Farriers (q.v.).

Associate of the Worshipful Company of Farriers Also known by the acronym AWCF; a certification of advanced farrier skill awarded by the Worshipful Company of Farriers (q.v.), London England; recipients must have obtained and held for a minimum period of two years, a Diploma of the Worshipful Company of Farriers (q.v.) and have passed written, oral, and practical examinations.

asterisk A figure resembling a star, thus *, used in printing and writing such as in breeding publications, to denote an imported horse when placed in front of a horse's name, or when placed in front of a jockey's name, or beside the weight a horse is to carry, denotes an apprentice jockey (q.v.).

asternum A structure or piece of tissue in the region of, but not attached to, the sternum (q.v.).

as the hounds ran *see* AS HOUNDS RAN

Astley, Philip The father of the modern circus (q.v.); in 1769, 1,500 years after the last known Roman circus, he left the British Army and began to give trick riding exhibitions in London, England; his program included clowns, rope artists, acrobatics, High School (q.v.) acts, trick riding, and ballet on horseback; having determined it was easier to maintain balance on a horse if it was cantering in a circle rather than in "en linge" (q.v.), he seated his audience in the round; the circus ring became standardized at 42 ft (13 m) in diameter, a size large enough to allow a horse to go fast, yet small enough to keep him under control.

astride Said of the rider; seated with one leg on each side of the horse.

astringent Any liquid substance used to constrict or tighten the tissues.

Asturcon *see* GALICIAN

Asturian *see* GALICIAN

ataxia Also known as wobbles, wobbler disease, or wobbler syndrome; a group of diseases of the spinal column and spinal cord characterized by various defects of coordina-

tion and movement; may be caused by pressure on the spinal cord exerted by a malformed or injured spine, destructive protozoal infection, or other degenerative or infective processes; the common term describes the wandering or staggering gait of affected horses.

at bay A hunting term; the position of the hounds (q.v.) when kept off the quarry (q.v.).

ATCP The acronym for the American Team Penning Championships (q.v.).

at fault A hunting term; said of hounds (q.v.) who have lost the fox's scent.

at gait *see* GAIT no. 2

atlas The first vertebra of the vertebral column which unites the neck with the bones at the back of the head in the cervical region and enables the head to move up and down.

at pasture *see* PASTURE no. 2

Atropa belladonna *see* DEADLY NIGHTSHADE

atrophy The wasting away of the body, an organ, or body part, as caused by inadequate nutrition, injury, or inactivity; generally used to describe muscles.

at stud *see* STAND AT STUD

at the end of the halter Said of a horse sold with no guarantee other than title.

at walk *see* WALK no. 2

auction A public sale of property such as horses, tack, and/or real estate to the highest bidder; payment is generally required at the "fall of the hammer" or declaration of sale delivered by the auctioneer (q.v.) unless other arrangements have been made.

auctioneer One whose business it is to sell things by auction (q.v.).

Australian bow wagon A horse-drawn farm wagon originally used in Victoria, Australia in the 1870s; drawn by a single heavy horse in shafts or by a tandem pair; had low, single plank sides, a short wheelbase, curved sideboards protecting both the front and rear wheels, and an unsprung axle.

Australian loose ring cheek snaffle
Also known as Fulmer snaffle; a bit consisting of a single jointed mouthpiece with long cheeks (q.v.) on either side and loose rings attached to the long cheeks; may be used with or without bit keepers (q.v.) to alter pressure.

Australian pony A pony breed native to Australia which descended from Welsh Mountain ponies (q.v.) and Welsh ponies (q.v.) brought to Australia in 1803; by 1920 established as a fixed type; stands 12 to 14 hands, generally has a gray coat although any color is permitted by the breed society except piebald (q.v.) and skewbald (q.v.), has a light head, arched neck, full mane, high withers, short and straight back, a full girth, and short legs with good bone; is strong and well-balanced; used for riding; the stud book, maintained by the Australian Pony Stud Book Society (q.v.), was established in 1929.

Australian Pony Stud Book Society An organization established in Australia in 1929 to oversee breeding and registration of, and maintain the Stud Book for, the Australian pony (q.v.).

Australian road wagon A horse-drawn driving wagon, similar to the phaeton (q.v.), used on the rougher roads of the Australian outback; had a large umbrella basket and rearward boot (q.v.), narrow perch, pedal brake that operated on the rear wheels, and was hung on crosswise elliptical springs front and back.

Australian simplex safety iron A safety stirrup designed to ensure the escape of the foot in the event of a fall; has a forward curve on the outer side of the iron that allows the rider to readily kick free of a stirrup should trouble arise.

Australian spring dray A horse-drawn, two-wheeled heavy cart historically used in Australian cities to recover dead and/or injured horses; could be tipped in a rearward direction, had an ample, slatted ramp on which to load the horse or carcass, plank or panel sides, a low cross bench in the front from which the dray was driven and was hung on sideways semi-elliptical springs.

Australian Stock Horse Also known by the acronym ASH; originally horses of Waler (q.v.) origin; a warmblood descending from Arab (q.v.), Thoroughbred (q.v.), and Anglo-Arab (q.v.) stock put to native Australian mares; since the beginning of the 20th century outside contributions have been limited to Anglo-Arab blood; stands 14.2 to 16 hands, may have a coat of any solid color, has well-muscled legs, solid hooves, strong joints, good endurance, and ability to carry weight; appearance varies greatly; used in competitive sports including polo, on cattle stations, and as a cavalry mount; the Australian Stock Horse Society (q.v.) maintains the stud book which was established in 1971.

Australian Stock Horse Society An organization founded in New South Wales, Australia in the 1960s to promote and standardize breed characteristics of the Australian Stock Horse (q.v.), formerly known as Walers (q.v.), and maintain the stud book.

Australian Veterinary Association Also known by the acronym AVA; the professional body representing veterinarians in Australia.

Australian Waler *see* WALER

Authorisation Spécial A pink card issued by the National Equestrian Federation (q.v.) to a rider which permits him to participate in international dressage, show jumping, or combined training events.

authorized agent *see* AGENT no. 2

automatic timer Also known as electronic eye; an electronic apparatus used to record the times of equine competitions such as show jumping and rodeo; two timers are used, one placed at the start and the other at the course finish; the horse breaks an electronic beam as it passes the starting and finishing points, which triggers and stops the timer.

autonomic nervous system That part of the nervous system which innervates the blood vessels, heart, viscera, smooth muscles, and glands, regulates involuntary actions.

autopsy *see* POST-MORTEM EXAMINATION

Auto-top buggy A horse-drawn, tray-bodied American buggy (q.v.) with a folding top similar to that of the Model T Ford, popular in the United States during the 1900s.

Autumn Double A racing term; an event consisting of two races, the Cesarwitch Stakes and the Cambridgeshire Stakes, held annually each autumn in Newmarket, England.

auxiliary reins Any rein (q.v.) used in conjunction with the normal reins, as when training or schooling a horse; include side reins (q.v.), draw reins (q.v.), etc.

auxiliary starting gate A racing term; a second starting gate (q.v.) placed along side of the primary gate when the number of entrants exceeds the capacity of the primary starting gate.

Auxois A horse breed indigenous to 6th-century France at which time it descended from the old Burgundian horse; received infusions of Percheron (q.v.) and Boulonnais (q.v.) blood in the 19th century and, more recently, Ardennais (q.v.) and the Trait du Nord (q.v.); is quiet, good natured, willing, very strong, and possessed of great endurance; stands 15.1 to 16 hands and weighs 1,650–2,425 pounds (748–1,100 kg); may have a bay or roan coat, although chestnut and red roan do occur; the head is light and the legs slender in proportion to the heavy body; the breed is strictly controlled according to type and coat color; the Stud Book has been maintained since 1913 by the Syndicat du Cheval de Trait Ardennais de l'Auxois; used for heavy draft and farm work; branded on the left neck with the letters TX.

AVA (1) The acronym for the American Vaulting Association (q.v.). (2) The acronym for the Australian Veterinary Association.

Avelignese An ancient coldblood pony originating in Avelengo, Italy, from which the name derived; traces to the Middle Ages, sharing heritage with the Haflinger (q.v.) through the foundation sire Folie out of a native mare and sired by the Arab stallion El Bedavi XXII; bred in the mountain areas of northern, central, and southern Italy; generally has a chestnut or golden coat with a flaxen mane and tail; a blaze is common and white on the legs is minimal; has a light head with a slightly concave profile, broad forehead, muscular neck, short back and legs, muscular croup, hard hoof, and stands to 14 hands; is frugal, hardy, docile, quiet, trustworthy, and resistant to fatigue; bear a brand featuring the edelweiss with the letters HI in the center (Haflinger Italy) while the Haflinger has the same brand centered with an H (Haflinger); used for medium-heavy draft, riding, packing, and farm work.

average The mean sum of a score; timed competitions such as calf roping (q.v.) and barrel racing (q.v.) with more than one round will pay prize money for each individual round and for the best 'average' time or score; the competitor with the best overall average is considered the contest winner and will generally receive additional money.

Average-Earnings Index Also known as AEI; a racing term; a breeding statistic that compares racing earnings of a stallion or mare's foals to those of all other foals racing at that time; 1.00 is considered average.

Avondale *see* GOVERNESS CAR

avulsion The pulling or tearing away of a part of a structure.

avulsion of the hoof wall at the heel Also known as heel crack or heel avulsion; a disruption in the horny wall at the heel; may begin as a small separation at the heel and gradually progress until the hoof wall at the quarter becomes separated from the underlying dermal laminae (q.v.); most commonly the result of trauma; lameness ranges from mild to severe.

AWCF The acronym for Associate of the Worshipful Company of Farriers (q.v.).

axle-tree maker Also known as fireman; one responsible for forging and shaping the iron used in the making of axle trees for horse-drawn vehicles.

axial Situated in, around, or along the axis of the body.

axis (1) An imaginary line through the center of the body of the horse around which all or part of the body is symmetrically arranged. (2) The second bone in the backbone or vertebral column of the horse which allows for rotation of the head; connects to the atlas (q.v.).

away from you A hunting term; said by a member of the field to indicate there is a ditch on the far side of a fence.

Aylesbury wagon A box-type, horse-drawn English farm or road wagon with high spindle sides and a relatively short wheelbase; drawn by a single horse.

Ayrshire harvest cart A low-sided cart used in the western Lowlands of Scotland; had an unsprung or dead axle and semi-permanent end ladders.

azotemia An excess of nitrogen containing compounds in the blood.

azoturia A severe form of exercise related myopathy (q.v.) occurring shortly after the horse has begun work; muscle stiffness and muscle spasms of the loin and hind limbs, profuse sweating, tachycardia, hyperventilation, and an anxious facial expression are common; a reluctance to move, recumbence, and red-brown to black-colored urine depending on the amount of myoglobin content may also occur.

azulejo Refers to coat color; a coat consisting of blue and white combinations; the Spanish name for the South American Blue-bird.

Azteca A relatively new breed developed in Mexico by crossing Andalusian (q.v.) stallions with Quarter Horse (q.v.) mares or vice versa, or by crossing Andalusian stallions with improved Criollo (q.v.) mares; must have a minimum of 3/8 and a maximum of 5/8 Spanish or Quarter Horse blood, while blood from horses not registered as Criollo (q.v.) may not exceed 1/4; breed selection began in 1972; a hardy, fast, and agile horse used for leisure riding, competitive sports, light draft, and farm work; females must stand at least 14.3 hands and males 15 hands; all solid coat colors are acceptable.

B

babble A hunting term; the speaking of a hound other then when on the line of a fox (q.v.).

babbler A hunting term; a hound who barks for reasons other than being on the line of a fox (q.v.) when on the hunt, e.g., from excitement, when unsure of the scent, or when trailing the lead hound by a good distance.

Babieca The Andalusian (q.v.) mount of Spain's national hero Ruy Diaz, El Cid; died in the 11th century at the age of 40 and was buried at the monastery of San Pedro de Cardena where a monument stands in his honor.

babesiosis *see* EQUINE PIROPLASMOSIS

Babolina The Hungarian state stud, famous for its Arab (q.v.) breeding program.

baby A racing term; a two-year old horse.

baby race A racing term; a 2, 3, or 4-furlong (402, 604, or 805 m) race for two-year olds, held early in the year.

babysitter (1) A made, gentle horse used by a trainer to give lessons to novice riders. (2) A cow or horse who is easy to control.

baby teeth *see* DECIDUOUS TEETH

back (1) *see* REIN-BACK. (2) A racing term; to place a bet on a horse. (3) That portion of the horse's body between the withers (q.v.) and the loins (q.v.). (4) *see* NUMBER FOUR POSITION

back at the knee *see* BACKWARD DEVIATION OF THE CARPAL JOINTS

back band The leather strap that passes over the back of the horse to which the tugs are buckled in harness tack.

back blood A hereditary trait found in a family of horses which may influence the conformation of succeeding generations.

backbone *see* VERTEBRAL COLUMN

back breeding To breed a horse factoring in conformation traits common to the line.

back cinch *see* FLANK CINCH

Back Door Cab A horse-drawn vehicle of the wagonette-brougham (q.v.) type popular in the late 19th century; entered from the rear, hung on sideways-elliptical springs front and rear, and used for both public and private transportation purposes.

Backdoor omnibus *see* BOULNOIS CAB

backed *see* BACKHANDER

back 'em off A cutting term; said of the rider; to back (q.v.) the horse away from the cow because he is either stepping into the cow, or is ahead of it.

backer (1) A racing term; one who places a bet on a horse. (2) One who rides a horse for the first time.

back fence A cutting term; the designated area of the fence located directly behind the herd; in competition, the horse is penalized three points each time the cow being worked stops or turns within 3 feet (91 cm) of this fence.

backgammon board *see* GAMMON BOARD

backhand cut A polo term; any stroke of the ball hit backwards at an angle away from the horse.

back hander Also known as backed, backhand shot and back shot; a polo stroke in which the player hits the ball in the direction opposite to that traveled by the horse; may be a backhand cut (q.v.), tail shot (q.v.), or cut away shot (q.v.).

backhand shot *see* BACKHANDER

backing (1) An English term; to mount a horse for the first time after breaking (q.v.) and sit upon back. (2) A harness term; to make a horse put its weight into the shafts (q.v.).

backing up *see* REIN-BACK

back jockey The top skirt (q.v.) of a western saddle.

back line (1) A polo term; a line drawn perpendicular to each side of the goal area on either end of a polo field (q.v.) which marks the longitudinal terminus of the playing field; a ball passing beyond this line is considered out of play. (2) *see* TOP LINE

back not round Said of a horse who hollows or flattens his back, instead of dropping his haunches and swinging well under his body with his hind legs.

back of the knee *see* BACKWARD DEVIATION OF THE CARPAL JOINTS

backover saddle fall A maneuver performed by trick riders or stunt people working in the movie industry; to kick out of the stirrups and roll backwards off the croup (q.v.) of a running or galloping horse.

back pad A non-rigid protective pad used to protect the back of the horse and to provide secure footing for the vaulter (q.v.) when standing on the horse's back; may not extend more than 28 inches (71 cm) from the back edge of the vaulting roller (q.v.), nor exceed 36 inches (91 cm) width or 4/5 inches (2 cm) in thickness, except directly under the roller where any thickness is allowed.

back racking The removal of feces (q.v.) from the horse's rectum by hand.

back shot *see* BACKHANDER

backside *see* BACKSTRETCH

back strap (1) A single or double leather strap that holds the crupper dock (q.v.) in position around the dock (q.v.) of the horse's tail; passed through a dee on the back of the pad in a harness crupper and to the saddle on a saddle crupper to which it may be buckled or stitched; prevents the saddle or harness pad from shifting onto the horse's withers (q.v.). (2) The strip of leather that runs from the top of the counter (q.v.) down the back seam of a riding boot to protect the stitching from wear and to create a more finished look.

backstretch (1) Also known as backside; a racing term; the straight part of the track on the far side (q.v.) between the turns. (2) Also known as backside; a racing term; that area of the track consisting of the stable area, dormitories, track kitchen, chapel, and recreation area for stable employees.

back up (1) A racing term; said of a horse who slows down noticeably when being raced. (2) *see* COLD BACK. (3) *see* REIN BACK

backward deviation of the carpal joints Also known as palmar deviation of the carpal joints, calf knees, sheep knees, back at the knee, back of the knee, and incorrectly, as tied in below the knee; a conformation defect in which the horse's forelegs bend slightly back at the knees giving a concave or cupped appearance; the opposite of buck knee (q.v.).

backwards shoe Also known as reverse shoe, open toe egg bar, or Napoleon shoe; a conventional horseshoe attached to the hoof in reverse position; the heels of the shoe support the toe of the hoof while the toe of the shoe supports the heels of the hoof; generally requires extra nail holes.

bacteria Any of the disease-producing microscopic organisms of the class *Schizomycetes*, having round, spiral, or rod-shaped bodies, which occur in soil, water, organic matter, and animal tissues.

bactericidal Any substance used to destroy the growth of bacteria (q.v.) and other disease-causing agents.

bacteriostatic Any substance used to prevent the multiplication of some bacteria (q.v.) and other disease-causing agents, but not destroy them.

bacterin A suspension of killed or attenuated bacteria (q.v.) injected into a living body to stimulate development of immunity to the same kind of bacteria.

bacterium A singular bacteria (q.v.).

bad actor A horse who is difficult and uncomfortable to ride.

bad cow *see* ALLIGATOR

bad doer A horse who lacks appetite, usually because of illness, pain, fatigue, nervousness, and/or loneliness.

Badge of Honor An award presented by the FEI (q.v.) to riders competing in Prix des Nations (q.v.) events.

badge horse *see* BADGER

badger Also known as badge horse; a racing term; an inexpensive horse used by the owner to qualify him for track privileges.

badger-pied Refers to hound coat color; having a fawn- or cream-colored head, legs, body, and stern with the ears and back shading into black with lighter tips to the ears.

bad hands Said of a rider whose hands are heavy, rough, and insensitive on the rein and therefore on the mouth of the horse through the bit; the opposite of good hands (q.v.).

badikins A swingle tree (q.v.) when used with a farm horse.

Badminton (1) Also known as Badminton House; the location of the first three-day event horse trials held in Great Britain; first sponsored by the then Duke of Beaufort in 1949, it has been held annually since as the Badminton Horse Trials (q.v.). (2) The home of the Duke of Beaufort's Foxhounds, a line of foxhunting hounds dating to 1720.

Badminton Horse Trials Also known as Badminton Three Day Horse Trials; a three-day horse trial (q.v.) event held annually since 1949 in the village of Badminton, England from which the name is derived.

Badminton House *see* BADMINTON

Badminton Three Day Horse Trials *see* BADMINTON HORSE TRIALS

bad traveler A horse who does not travel nor haul well, being anxious.

bag fox Also known as bagman or dropped fox; a hunting term; a fox caught and held in captivity until needed for the hunt (q.v.), at which time it is turned loose at a specified location in advance of the oncoming hounds (q.v.); prohibited by some foxhunting associations.

Baggage Cart A two-wheeled, horse-drawn vehicle used to transport military stores; usually hooded with low, wickerwork sides and solid or disc-type wheels; sometimes drawn by a pair of horses in double shafts or pole gear (q.v.), but more commonly drawn by a single horse; used from the late Middle Ages through the mid-17th century.

Baggage Wagon A larger, four-wheeled version of the Baggage Cart (q.v.) drawn by two or more horses in pole gear (q.v.).

bagging A breaking (q.v.) technique similar to sacking out (q.v.), in which the horse is restrained on either side by sidelines attached to the halter on one end and affixed to two sturdy posts or walls on the other; a bag is waved about his head and body to encourage him to kick, which when he does so, throws himself to the ground.

bagman *see* BAG FOX

Bagman's Gig A two-wheeled horse-drawn vehicle of the gig (q.v.) type; seated two, was drawn by a single horse, and equipped with a large luggage boot (q.v.).

bag of marbles Said of a horse who has multiple bone fractures (q.v.) in a small area.

Bahama grass *see* BERMUDA GRASS

Baiga Any Russian horse race 9 to 18 miles (15-30 km) long when held cross country and open to unlimited numbers of riders or 9 to 12 miles (15-20 km) long when conducted on a racetrack, in which case there is a limit of 20 riders.

balance (1) Said of the horse when his weight and the weight of the rider are distributed equally over the foot of each leg; a balanced horse will move freely and correctly. (2) Said of the horse's foot, when viewed from the front or rear, if the medial axis of the leg, pastern, and foot are in a straight line, and when viewed from the side if the medial axis of the pastern coincides with the axis of the foot which is parallel to the hoof wall at the toe.

balanced seat The position of the mounted rider; the rider is relaxed in the seat of the saddle and does not interfere with the movements or equilibrium of the horse.

balance not maintained Said of the horse when his weight, and that of the rider, are not equally distributed over the foot of each leg resulting in poorly executed movements or gaits.

balance rein A training tool utilized to teach bridleless riding to a horse using such methods as TTEAM (q.v.); a round, 1/2 inch (25 mm) rope or strap placed around the base of the horse's neck which, in conjunction with a bridle, acts much like a rein; an upward motion of the rein can encourage the horse to shift his weight off his forehand and move into self-carriage thus enabling him to achieve roundness and lengthening of the neck.

balancing strap A leather strap attached to the center of the off-side cantle of the sidesaddle (q.v.) which runs on top of the girth; used as a stabilizing hand hold for the sidesaddler (q.v.).

bald Without hair.

bald face Also known as a white face; a face marking (q.v.) consisting of a wide, white blaze covering most of the face including the forehead, the area around the eyes, the nostrils, and most of the upper lip, or a portion thereof, often extending into the cheeks.

balding gag bit A bit (q.v.) consisting of a jointed mouthpiece (q.v.) with large, loose-ring cheek gags used with a single rein; prevents the effect of the gag until considerable pressure is applied; commonly used on polo ponies.

balding gag bridle A headstall used in conjunction with a balding gag bit (q.v.).

balding girth A leather girth (q.v.) consisting of a single piece of leather split into three sections below the buckle attachment, which are plaited under the belly; reduces the width of the girth in the area of the forearm and the potential of chaffing or galling the horse; the center section is generally reinforced by additional leather.

baldy A white-faced cow.

bale (1) To form into a bundle or bale, as in hay (q.v.). (2) Compressed hay formed into a square-shaped bundle and bound with wire or twine. (3) A partition suspended horizontally from the ceiling at trace height to separate horses tied parallel to each other in an enclosed area, thus creating open, individual stalls; usually a thick piece of wood about 7 ft (213 cm) long by 1 ft 6 inches (46 cm) wide.

Balearic An ancient pony breed found on the island of Majorca off the coast of Spain; may have a bay or brown coat, is generally Roman nosed, and has a fine head; used for draft and driving.

balk Also spelled baulk and known as jib; a vice; the refusal of a horse to pass or jump a certain point or object, ultimately stopping and refusing to move forward; may back away from the object.

balking Said of a horse who balks (q.v.).

balky horse A horse who stops and refuses to move.

Bali A pony breed originating on the island of Bali, Indonesia, believed to have descended from the Ancient Asiatic pony; has an upright mane and is generally bay with a black mane and tail, eel stripes on the legs, a black dorsal stripe, and dark points; is strong, frugal, quite docile and very quiet, has low withers and a short, straight back, and stands 12 to 13 hands; used for riding and packing.

balios *see* XANTHUS

ball *see* MEDICINE BALL

ball a horse Also known as balling; to administer medicine to a horse which is encapsulated in gelatin using a balling gun (q.v.), balling iron, or by hand.

ball and bucket race A mounted event in which competitors make repeated trips from one end of an arena to the other carrying one ball at a time and placing that ball in a bucket; the winner is the one who moves all the balls in the shortest amount of time.

ball and socket joint A joint (q.v.); the point of junction of two moveable bones in which the end of one bone rests in a socket or cup of another, as in the hip joint.

balling (1) Said of snow when it forms into a compact ice-like lump in the space within a horseshoe (q.v.) in horses ridden in the snow; may be prevented by applying grease to soles of the hoof or use of a balling pad. (q.v.) (2) *see* BALL A HORSE

balling gun An out-dated tubular device made of wood, leather, steel, or brass used to administer a ball (q.v.) to a horse.

balling pad A rubber pad fitted between the horseshoe (q.v.) and hoof to prevent snow from packing into the area.

balloon bit A hack curb bit (q.v.) with a

fancy cheek (q.v.) in the shape of a balloon.

ballotade An air above the ground (q.v) in which the horse half rears, then jumps forward, drawing his hind legs up below his quarters (all four feet are at the same height), before landing on all four feet; the horse shows his heels as though he is about to kick, but does not throw them out.

balloted out Said of a horse nominated to compete in a race or other event in which the number of contestants exceeds a safe limit, or whose nomination or entry is rejected or withdrawn by the organizing committee.

Baluchi A pony breed indigenous to India.

Bampton Fair A fair held in Devon, England annually each October, since 1258; noted for the sale of Exmoor Ponies (q.v.) which occurs there.

banamine The trade name for a non-steroidal, anti-inflammatory (q.v.) drug known as flunixin meglumine used to control inflammation and pain associated with colic (q.v.) and muscle injury.

Banbury bit *see* BANBURY CURB and BANBURY POLO PELHAM

Banbury curb Also known as Banbury bit; a bit with cheeks (q.v.) independently revolve around the hour-glass-shaped mouthpiece; the shape of the bit prevents the horse from taking hold of it with his teeth, while the independently moving cheeks discourage one-sidedness (q.v.).

Banbury polo pelham Also known as Banbury bit; a pelham bit (q.v.) having a straight mouthpiece with an hour-glass shaped center; the mouthpiece slots into the cheeks, which allows the cheeks to move independently of each other.

band *see* HERD

bandage (1) A leg wrapping used to provide support or protection against injury to the horse's lower leg; types include standing bandage (q.v.), exercise bandage (q.v.), stable bandage (q.v.), and stocking bandage (q.v.). (2) A strip of cloth or gauze used in dressing and binding wounds, restraining hemorrhages, etc.; includes pressure bandage (q.v.) and spider-web bandage (q.v.). (3) To dress a wound; to apply a bandage to.

bandage bow Also known as compression bow; a bowed tendon (q.v.); enlarged, swollen, and/or torn or broken tendon fibers and/or tendon sheaths caused by too tight or uneven wrapping of the front or back legs, which results in a loss of circulation to the tissue and swelling, reduced nutrition to and removal of waste products from the tissue, and reduced viability of the tendon (ability to contract and expand); soft tissue fibers are pushed towards the cannon bone and tear; has the appearance of a bowstring drawn back from the wood of the bow.

bandana Also spelled bandanna; a large, colorfully printed kerchief popularized by the cowboys of the American west.

bandanna *see* BANDANA

bandy A native horse-drawn cart used in India; had a small platform rigged between two disc wheels supported by an unsprung or dead axle and sometimes hooded by a canopy of rough matting; drawn either by a pair of large ponies or a yoke (q.v.) of small oxen.

bandy legs *see* LATERAL DEVIATION OF THE CARPAL JOINTS

bandy-legged (1) Also known as bow-legged; said of a horse displaying lateral deviation of the carpal joints (q.v.). (2) Said of a rider having legs set wide apart at the knees and close at the ankles; results in greater comfort when riding a horse; the term may have been coined in the 17th century by a comparison of the legs to a curved stick called a "bandy" used in the game of hockey.

banged *see* BANG TAIL

bangtail (1) Slang; a race horse (q.v.). (2) *see* BANG TAIL

bang tail Also known as square tail, banged or bangtail; said of the horse's tail when tied short or cut off square below the points of the hocks; in Australia, a tail which has been squarely cut below the last bone of the tail.

bang up Also known as banging up; to tie up the tail of draft or harness horses so the tail hair does not catch in the harness (q.v.) and reins (q.v.).

banging up *see* BANG UP

bank A jumping obstacle consisting of a constructed mound of dirt with a platform or flat top, a slope on the take-off side, and a steep downside; usually covered with grass.

bank and ditch A jumping obstacle consisting of a constructed mound of dirt with a platform or flat top and a ditch located at the base of the mound on the take off side; usually covered with grass.

banker A horse who jumps on and off a bank (q.v.) rather than over it.

bant A racing term; to reduce a jockey's weight.

bar (1) Also known as bars of the mouth; the portion of the lower jaw of a horse between the incisors (q.v.) and molars, on which the bit mouthpiece lies. (2) Also known as bars of the saddle; a metal projection located under the saddle flap and built into the sweat flap, to which the stirrup leathers (q.v.) are attached; opens towards the rear of the saddle. (3) Also known as bar of the hoof; the continuation of the wall of the hoof which turns inward at the heel and runs parallel to the frog; an important portion of the weight-bearing surface of the foot. (4) *see* SWINGLE TREE

Barb Formerly known as Barbary Horse; an ancient oriental breed originating along the Barbary coast region of North Africa which is now Morocco, Algeria, Tunisia, and Libya; introduced into Europe in the 7th century where it had considerable influence on other breeds such as the Andalusian (q.v.); nearly died out as a purebred in the mid-19th century; is currently raised as a purebred among the nomadic populations of North Africa, while elsewhere the breed has been crossed with the English Thoroughbred (q.v.) or Arab (q.v.) as in the Libyan Barb or Libyan; is athletic and unusually resistant to changes in climate, fatigue, and disease; develops late and does not reach maturity until its 6th year; the coat may be brown, black, bay, black chestnut, or gray; stands 14 to 15 hands and has a long head, sloping quarters, and rather low-set tail; is extremely fast over short distances and possesses great stamina over longer ones; is an easy keeper; used for riding.

Barbary horse *see* BARB

barbed wire Also known as wire and formerly as Devil's Rope; thin strands of wire twisted together, having sharp-pointed barbs projecting at even and short intervals, stranded between fence posts to contain livestock; until 1868 all fencing wire used in the United States was smooth, without barbs of any kind.

barbed wire boom The period between 1868 and 1888 during which more than 700 barbed wire (q.v.) designs were patented in the United States.

bar bit A driving bit with a straight or slightly curved solid mouthpiece.

Barco-de-tierra The Spanish equivalent of an American landship (q.v.); a rough-made horse-drawn earth-boat or wagon used by the Spanish settlers on the South American Pampas; had wickerwork sides, high wheels with numerous spokes, and was drawn by pairs or larger teams of horses or oxen.

bardella A heavy stock saddle (q.v.) with hooded stirrups, used by the Italian buttero (q.v.).

Bardi horse *see* BARDIGIANO

Bardigiano Also known as Bardi horse; an ancient mountain pony originating in the northern Appenine region of Bardi, Italy; is almost identical to the Haflinger (q.v.) and resembles the Dale (q.v.) and Mèrens; stands 13.1 to 14.1 hands (males under 13.2 hands cannot be registered); the coat may be bay, brown, or black, while chestnut and light bay are not allowed by the breed registry; limited white markings on the legs and a small star are allowed; has a small head, broad forehead, full fetlock, small ears, a substantive neck with a good arch, wide withers, medium back, short loins, deep girth, wide chest, and well-formed legs with clean joints; is strong, hardy, docile, and quick moving; used for riding, light draft, and farm work

bardot A French term; a hinny (q.v.).

bards Any of various pieces of defensive armor historically worn by the horse to protect the breast and flanks from wounds in combat and, occasionally, for ornamental purposes.

bareback *see* BAREBACK RIDING

bareback riding Also known as bareback

or Indian style; to ride a horse without the aid of a saddle or blanket.

barefoot Also known as unshod or smooth; said of a horse without horseshoes (q.v.).

Bareme A French term; any of three tables of rules established by the Fédération Equestre Internationale (q.v.) by which show jumping competitions are judged; Table A covers jumping only, and Table C, speed.

Barenger, James (1780–1831) A noted British equestrian artist.

bark A hunting term; the cry of a hound or fox.

barker Also known as dummy foal, wanderer, convulsive foal, or barker foal; a foal afflicted with neonatal maladjustment syndrome.

Barker Brougham A small, four-wheeled, horse-drawn carriage of the brougham (q.v.) type drawn by a single horse in shafts; seated two forward-facing passengers, was lowslung, fully paneled with an upholstered and fully enclosed body, and had elegant and generous curves.

barker foal *see* BARKER

Barker Quarter Landau A horse-drawn vehicle of the landau (q.v.) type used in the mid-19th century; had a dropped center or well for the passengers' feet and curved rather than square corners.

barge (1) An American horse-drawn vehicle used to transport large numbers of passengers and luggage; had a long, covered body with open sides, curtains, and inward-facing bench seats, was entered from the rear, and drawn by four horses driven from a low, front seat. (2) A roomy, usually flat-bottomed boat used chiefly for the transport of goods on inland waterways; usually propelled by towing as by a horse.

barge horse Any horse used to pull a barge along a canal as was common in England and North America until the late 19th century; horses were either ridden or led along towpaths located parallel to the waterways, or walked freely if fitted with a nosebag to prevent browsing en route.

barley Also known as barley grain; a grain from the cereal plant of the same name and of the species Hordeum; the most widely grown grain crop in the world today and the fourth most commonly grown crop in the United States; comparable to oats with a protein content of 12 percent and a fiber content ranging from 5 to 6 percent; high in niacin, low in fiber, and considered a heavy feed; easier to overfeed than oats or corn and may upset the digestive system; more easily digested and its nutrient better utilized if fed in a crushed, crimped, rolled, or ground form.

barley grain *see* BARLEY

barley hay Cut and dried grass hay (q.v.) made from barley (q.v.) grain grass; contains approximately 5 percent digestible protein and 27 percent fiber.

Barlow, Francis (1626–1704) A noted sporting artist.

bar mouth A generic term; any straightmouth snaffle bit (q.v.).

barn (1) A covered building in which hay and grain are stored and domestic animals housed. (2) *see* TRAINING BARN.

barn crazy Said of a horse who resents being retained in an enclosed area such as a barn, preferring movement and open space as provided by a pasture, paddock, or an in-andout stall.

barn sour Also known as herd-bound behavior; the reluctance of a horse to leave a group of horses (the herd), a particular equine buddy, or a physical location that represents security (the barn or the pasture which represents the herd's focal point – food, water, and social interaction) because of the anxiety produced by separation; a primal safety instinct.

bar of the hoof *see* BAR no. 2

baroque movement The manner in which a horse moves as characterized by high, round, and elastic strides with much suspension; so called because it was characteristic of the manège horses of the 17th century; today such movement is typical of Andalusians (q.v.) and Lipizzans (q.v.).

Barouche An ancient four-wheeled horsedrawn vehicle of the coach family; had full undergear and lower panels, but no upper panels, a half-hood which covered the rear seat only, and a box seat for the driver raised well above the body work; passengers normally faced in the direction of travel, although some vehicles had folding seats on which others might be seated vis-à-vis (q.v.); generally a town vehicle used for summer driving drawn by a pair of horses in pole gear (q.v.); derived from the Latin birotus meaning two-wheeled.

Barouche Landau Also known as Landau Barouche; A horse-drawn vehicle of the barouche (q.v.) type; popular particularly in England from the 18th through the early 19th century on; had a higher than average box seat (q.v.), a rumble seat for two grooms, and was driven to a four-in-hand team generally by amateurs.

Barouche Sociable A horse-drawn vehicle of the barouche (q.v.) type having a double hood or two half hoods protecting both the front and rear of the vehicle.

barrage *see* JUMP OFF

Barraud, Henry (1811–1874) A British equestrian artist of French descent; collaborated with his brother William Barraud (q.v.) to create portraiture of Hunts, huntsmen, and well-known Masters of the Hounds including the famous work of John Warde (q.v.) on his horse Blue Ruin.

Barraud, William (1810-1850) A British equestrian artist of French descent; collaborated with his brother Henry Barraud (q.v.) to create portraiture pictures of Hunts, huntsmen, and well-known Masters of the Hounds including the famous work of John Warde (q.v.) on his horse Blue Ruin.

barrel (1) The part of the horse's body between the forearms (q.v.) and loins (q.v.). (2) An empty metal or wooden 44 gallons (200 liter) vessel, approximately cylindrical, used as a turning point in a barrel race (q.v.). (3) *see* VAULTING BARREL

barrel horse Any horse used as a mount by a barrel racer (q.v.) to compete in a barrel race (q.v.); generally exhibits great speed, power, and agility; Quarter Horses (q.v.) or Quarter Horse crosses are commonly used.

barrel race A timed western riding competition in which the rider must circle three barrels set in a clover-leaf pattern; the distance between the barrels may vary; the winner is the rider who successfully rides around all three barrels and crosses the finish line without toppling a barrel, in the fastest time.

barrel racer One who barrel races (q.v.).

barrel turn A cutting horse term; an undesirable turn of the horse executed on the forehand rather than the haunches; undesirable for a cutting horse.

barren Also known as barren mare or, in Scotland, eild; said of a mare who is sterile (q.v.), infertile (q.v.), or not in foal.

barren mare *see* BARREN

barrier Also known as tape; a string, elastic band, or electronic beam that serves as a temporary barricade across the start- or finish-line of a race or other competition as in timed rodeo events.

barrier draw A racing term; the position a horse assumes in the starting gate (q.v.) at the start of a race.

bar pressure Pressure on the indenture gap in the lower jaw as applied by the bit.

bars The plural of bar (q.v.).

bar shoe Any horseshoe (q.v.) that is not interrupted by an opening between the heels; the most frequently used of all therapeutic horseshoes; used to apply pressure to, or relieve pressure from, one part of the foot; are fitted so that 1/16 to 1/8 inches of daylight can be seen between the heels of the shoe and the heels of the hoof wall when the bar is resting on the frog; so called because an extra length of steel, a bar, attaches the heels of the shoe; of several types including the curved bar shoe (q.v.), heart bar shoe (q.v.), mushroom bar shoe (q.v.), egg bar shoe (q.v.), tongue bar shoe (q.v.), jumped-in bar shoe (q.v.), and whip-across bar shoe (q.v.).

bars of the mouth *see* BAR no. 1

bars of the saddle *see* BAR no. 2

barstock Also known as stock; the metal from which hand- or ready-made horseshoes are forged.

Barthais Also known as Barthais Pony; a French-bred pony indigenous to the plains of Challosse near the Adour River; a taller and heavier version of the Landais (q.v.) from which it was originally considered a separate breed.

Barthais Pony *see* BARTHAIS

basal Relating to, or being essential for, the maintenance of the fundamental vital activities of an organism.

basal cell Any one of the innermost cells of the deeper epidermis of the skin.

basal crack A sand crack (q.v.) beginning at the ground surface of the hoof which splits towards the coronet (q.v.).

basal metabolic rate The rate at which heat is given off by a horse at complete rest.

bascule The shape or line of a horse when jumping.

baseball Also known as wheeling; a racing term; a daily-double play in which the bettor (q.v.) couples a horse in one race with all horses in another other.

base color Refers to coat color; the dominant color of the horse as determined from the body, neck and head area.

base narrow Refers to conformation; said of the horse when the distance between the center lines of the hooves at their placement on the ground is less than the distance between the center lines of the limbs at their origin in the chest as viewed from the front, or the center lines of the limbs in the thigh region when viewed from behind; may be accompanied by toe-in (q.v.) or toe-out (q.v.) conformation.

base wide Refers to conformation; said of the horse when the distance between the center lines of the hooves on the ground is greater than the distance between the center line of the limbs at their origin in the chest when viewed from the front.

Bashkir Also known as Bashkir Curly or Bashkirsky; a centuries-old pony breed originating in Bashkiria, around the southern foothills of the Urals in the former Soviet Union; of two distinct types: the Mountain Bashkir (q.v.) and the Steppe Bashkir (q.v.); stands 13.1 to 14 hands, has a distinctive thick, usually bay, chestnut, or palomino coat which becomes curly in the winter and a thick mane, tail, and forelock; is kept outdoors where it can withstand winter temperatures of minus 22–minus 40°F (minus 30–minus 40°C) and locate food under heavy snow; the coat is usually bay, chestnut or palomino; has a short and long neck, low withers, elongated and sometimes hollow back, a wide and deep chest, short and strong legs, and a small foot for its size; the breed standard quotes a bone measurement of 8 inches (20 cm) below the knee and a girth measurement for stallions of 71 inches (180 cm); is docile, strong, quiet, and hardy; used for packing, light draft, riding, and to provide meat, milk and clothing (the long winter coat hair being spun into cloth); in a seven- to eight-month lactation period a mare can yield as much as 350 gallons (1,590 liters) of milk; due to the exceptionally hard hoof, it is generally left unshod; when bred in the United States, known as the American Bashkir Curly (q.v.).

Bashkir Curly *see* BASHKIR

Bashkirsky *see* BASHKIR

basic seat A compulsory exercise performed in vaulting (q.v.) competitions in which the vaulter (q.v.) sits in the deepest part of the horse's back with both arms stretched outwards from the sides of his body with the finger tips held at eye level and the shoulders, hips, and heels on the same vertical line.

Basil Nightingale *see* NIGHTINGALE, BASIL

Basket Phaeton Also known as Lady's Basket Phaeton, beach carriage or, in America, wagon; a horse-drawn vehicle of the phaeton (q.v.) type designed during the 1860s for park driving in fashionable districts; had an optional rumble seat and basketwork sides of a curved or rounded profile; British versions had sideways-elliptical springs, while the American type had crosswise elliptical springs.

Basque Also known as Basque pony, Basque Pottok, Pottok (meaning small horse in Basque), and spelled Pottock; a semi-wild pony breed indigenous to the mountainous Basque regions of Spain and Southwest France; thought to have descended from the prehistoric horse of the Solutrè; improved by crosses to Welsh Section B (q.v.) stallions and

Arabs (q.v.); the coat is generally brown or black, although bay, chestnut, piebald, and skewbald do occur; has a well-proportioned head, but long ears, an over-hanging upper lip covered with whiskers, a short neck, long back, full, but shaggy mane and tail and small hooves; the hind legs are commonly cow-hocked (q.v.); of three types the Standard (q.v.), Piebald (q.v.), and Double (q.v.) standing 11 to 14.2 hands; less refined than the Landais (q.v.); is very hardy and tough; used for riding, light draft, farming, and jumping.

Basque pony *see* BASQUE

Basque Pottok *see* BASQUE

Basse Ecole Exercises by which students learn to mount a horse; the basse in 19th century riding schools was an incline.

Basseri A horse breed indigenous to Iran; contributed to the development of the Plateau Persian (q.v.).

bastard strangles A condition occurring when the swollen glands typical of strangles (q.v.) burst, releasing the bacteria which caused the infection into the blood stream, infecting other organs in the body such as the spleen, kidneys, lungs, liver, and brain, in which case, death may result.

Basterna A Roman horse litter (q.v.) with poles attached to a horse in front and a horse behind, as in the form of a sedan chair.

bastos *see* SADDLE SKIRT

Basuto Also known as Basuto Pony; a pony breed originating in Basutoland (now Lesotho) South Africa; derived from the Cape Horse (q.v.) crossed with native stock and, after 1822, English Thoroughbred (q.v.), Persian, and Arab (q.v.) blood; a hardy and courageous breed with tremendous endurance capable of covering 60–80 miles (97–129 km) per day carrying more than 200 lbs (91 kg); used extensively as a troop mount in the Boer War and is now used for polo and flat racing as well as general riding; may have a bay, brown, gray, or chestnut coat, stands 14 to 14.1 hands, is thickset, having a long, muscular neck, prominent withers, long back, low-set tail, and slender, strong legs; is reliable, hard-working and tolerant.

Basuto Pony *see* BASUTO

bat (1) Also known as cosh; a whip (q.v.) generally less than 24 inches (61 cm) in length and having a flattened end. (2) A racing term; slang; to strike a horse with a whip to encourage increased speed or to gain attention.

Batak Also known as Batak pony or Deli pony; a pony breed originating on the island of Sumatra, Indonesia; descended from Arab (q.v.) stallions put to selected native mares; stands 12 to 13 hands and may have a coat of any color although brown is most common; is gentle, lively, and frugal; used for riding; has a light head, arched, well-shaped neck, short back, and sturdy legs.

Batak pony *see* BATAK

bathing machine A box-like horse-drawn dressing room mounted on large, straight or dished wheels drawn by a single horse attached to the vehicle by chain trees; ridden rather than driven into the sea water; when the axletrees were level with the water, the horse was unhitched and steps let down from the front of the vehicle into the water for the bathers to descend; to remove the machine from the water, the unhitched horse was harnessed to the rear of the vehicle and the front steps retracted; the sides of the bodywork were often striped in primary colors; the prototype was first used in Weymouth, England, by George III when seabathing became popular for both fashion and health.

battery Also known as machine or joint; a racing term; an illegal electrical device used by a jockey to encourage the horse to run faster.

Battlesden car *see* BATTLESDEN CART

Battlesden cart A small, two-wheeled, horse-drawn pleasure vehicle, popular in England during the second half of the 19th century; pulled by a large pony or cob; similar in design to a single- or two-wheeled dogcart (q.v.), but with a much lower body and hung on elliptical springs with shafts interior to the body and splashboards which formed a semicircle over the wheels.

batwing chaps Also known as batwings; a type of chaps (q.v.); a full-length leather covering of the legs held together and onto the body by means of a belted waistband; wraps around the leg, closing on the outside of the leg by means of buckles or zippers; are wide and flared at the bottom to cover the foot and stirrup; worn by western enthusiasts, specifically cutters (q.v.) to camouflage the action of the leg and spur in cutting horse (q.v.) competitions.

batwings *see* BATWING CHAPS

baulk *see* BALK

bay (1) Refers to coat color; any shade of red with black points ranging from almost yellow to yellow mixed with black; may be confused with brown; variations include red bay (q.v.), mahogany bay (q.v.), blood bay (q.v.), and sand bay (q.v.). (2) A hunting term; the noise made by a hound (q.v.) when on the scent.

bay brown Refers to coat color; a variation of bay (q.v.); a brown coat with a bay muzzle (q.v.), black limbs (q.v.), mane, and tail.

bay roan Also known as red roan; refers to coat color; a variation of roan (q.v.); any shade of red coat mixed with white hairs and dark to black points with no white hairs.

bayo *see* DUN

bayo cayote Refers to coat color; a dun (q.v.) colored horse with a black dorsal stripe (q.v.).

Beach Carriage *see* BASKET PHAETON

Beach Phaeton An American four-wheeled, horse-drawn vehicle of the phaeton (q.v.) type; generally used for summer excursions at seaside resorts; easy to enter due to the low open sides; hung on sideways-elliptical springs front and rear and drawn by a pair of cobs or large ponies in pole gear (q.v.).

Beach Wagon A horse-drawn American pleasure wagon used for holiday excursions, especially around the coastal regions of New England; from 1860 through the early 1900s had a simple tray-like construction, double rows of forward-facing seats, a canopy top, open sides, and was hung on sideways-elliptical springs; drawn by a single horse.

beagle One of a breed of small hounds having a smooth coat, short legs, and drooping ears, used to hunt hares and other small game on foot; provide early hunting experience to many Masters (q.v.).

beagling A hunting term; to hunt hare on foot using beagles (q.v.) to flush and follow the prey; beagles are followed by the huntsman (q.v.) assisted by numerous whippers-in (q.v.) and followed by the field (q.v.).

beak Also known as horn or bick; the round, tapered, and relatively pointed end of a farrier's anvil (q.v.).

beaked shoe *see* EXTENDED-TOE SHOE

beam A hunting term; the distance between the main antlers of a stag.

bean (1) A mass of smegma (q.v.) collected in the cavity in the head of the penis, surrounding the end of the urethra; sometimes obstructs or prevents passage of urine by pressing on or stopping up the urethra. (2) Any of several kinds of smooth, edible, kidney-shaped seeds of any leguminous plant of a genus *Phaseolus* including the kidney bean, string bean, lima bean, etc.; sometimes fed to horses at hard work in combination with corn to reduce the heat value of the feed. (3) *see* CUP no. 1

beaning Also known as wedging; to temporarily disguise unsoundness in a horse using any number of methods, such as wedging a stone in the shoe of the sound foot to cause a temporary pain, so that, being tender in both front feet, the horse appears to go sound.

bean-shooter A horse who throws its front feet vigorously forward at the trot, with little or no flexion, effectively "landing" before the feet touch the ground; an undesirable trait.

bear foot *see* CLUB FOOT

bear in Also known as bearing in or lug in; a racing term; said of a horse who runs with his body turned to the inside rail rather than straight, often deviating from a straight course; may be due to weariness, infirmity, inexperience, or overuse of the whip or reins by the jockey.

bearing The general balance (q.v.) and carriage of the horse.

bearing in *see* BEAR IN

bearing out *see* BEAR OUT

bearing rein (1) Sometimes known as check

rein; a rein (q.v.) attached to either side of the bit, which runs through loops on the bridle located just below the ears and through a bearing rein post (q.v.) fixed to the top of the harness backband to the driver's hands; used to maintain high head carriage of the carriage horse. (2) *see* INDIRECT REIN

bearing rein drop *see* GAG RUNNER

bearing rein post A circular hook inserted perpendicular to the harness backband through which the bearing rein (q.v.) passes to the driver's hands.

bearing strap Also known as trace bearer, trace carrier, quarter strap, or hip strap; a narrow piece of leather which passes over the loins and through a slot in the back strap of the crupper (q.v.); on each side of the bearing strap there is a loop through which the traces (q.v.) are passed to keep them level; always used on a tandem leader where long traces are employed and sometimes on team and pair harnesses; also used to support the breeching (q.v.) used on cart horses.

bearing surface (1) The points in the mouth of the horse upon which the bit acts through applied pressure. (2) The ground-side surface of the hoof upon which the horse's weight is borne.

bear out Also known as bearing out or lug out; a racing term; a horse who runs with its body turned away from the inside rail, especially on the turns and which often deviates from a straight course; may be due to weariness, infirmity, inexperience, or overuse of the whip or reins by the rider.

Bear Step Katouche A special award presented to specific class winners at the National Appaloosa Show each year in the United States; hand-crafted from solid silver and turquoise by Shatka Bear Step and donated by him to the Appaloosa Horse Club (q.v.).

bear-skin cape Historically, a cape worn by coachmen (q.v.) of elite town carriages during cold weather; made out of bear hide with the hair still attached.

beast Any four-footed animal as distinguished from birds, fishes, insects, and man; used by some to refer to a horse.

beat (1) To flog a horse with a whip. (2) A

racing term; an unfortunate defeat, as when a horse is passed in the last stride of a race. (3) Exhausted; tired.

Beaufort Phaeton Also known as Hunting Phaeton; a horse-drawn vehicle; a large version of the Mail Phaeton (q.v.) accommodating six instead of four passengers and having an extra middle seat; used mainly in hunting country to transport viewers to hunt meets and to exercise coach and carriage horses; designed by the Duke of Beaufort for which it was named.

Beberbeck A horse breed descended from Arab (q.v.) and Thoroughbred (q.v.) stallions put to local mares bred at the Beberbeck Stud near Kassel, Germany, from the 1700s through 1930 at which time the Stud was closed; still bred today, but in greatly reduced numbers; resembles a heavy Thoroughbred; stands about 16 hands, generally has a bay or chestnut coat, and is used for riding and light draft.

bed *see* BEDDING

bedding Also known as litter and bed; the material placed on the floor of a stall, stable, or trailer as a bed for horses; used to provide cushion against a hard floor and lessen leg problems, insulate against the cold, absorb urine, and make removal of feces (q.v.) easier; different materials are used depending on availability and cost factors, including straw (q.v.), rice hulls, wood shavings (q.v.), sawdust (q.v.), shredded paper (q.v.), bracken, and sand.

bed down To put bedding (q.v.) in a stall (q.v.), stable (q.v.), or loose box (q.v.) for a horse.

Bedford Cart A two-wheeled, horse-drawn English farm cart with fixed sideboards above high wheels and an unsprung or dead axle popular in the 19th century with farmers or dealers for carrying goods; passengers sat dos-à-dos (q.v.) with two facing forward and two backward; the rear passengers placed their feet against a tailboard let down on chains to form a foot rest; had a square-shaped body hung on two semi-elliptical springs with shafts interior to the bodywork; made in various sizes and capacities; drawn by a single horse.

Bedford cord A very hard wearing fabric used as a cushion and valance cover on horse-drawn vehicles such as dogcarts (q.v.) and gigs (q.v.) and for driving aprons and breeches (q.v.).

Bedouin Arab *see* ASSIL

beef A racing term; a protest filed by one jockey, usually about another.

beefy hocks Said of the horse's hocks (q.v.) when thick and meaty.

Beetewk A heavy-draft breed originating on the banks of Beetewk river in the former Soviet Union; bred by Peter the Great who put Dutch stallions to local mares, and the progeny to Orlov Trotting (q.v.) stallions; is docile, obedient, and has high spirits, good action, great strength behind, and is capable of pulling up to 3 tons (3 tonnes).

beet pulp *see* SUGAR-BEET PULP

BEF The acronym for the British Equestrian Federation (q.v.).

behind the bit Also known as behind the bridle, overbent, or below the bit; an over responsiveness to the bit in which the horse evades rein contact by refusing to take hold of the bit in his mouth and draws his chin into his chest; the nose of the horse will be at an angle greater than 90 degrees to the ground rather than perpendicular to it.

behind the bridle *see* BEHIND THE BIT

behind the movement Said of a rider whose body is behind the imaginary vertical drawn perpendicular to the back of the horse; may result in too much weight placed on the loins of the horse thus impeding the action of the hind legs and movement of the horse's back.

behind the vertical Said of the position of the horse's head when he carries his muzzle (q.v.) behind, e.g., towards the chest, an imaginary line drawn perpendicular to the ground; the opposite side of the vertical line from in front of the vertical (q.v.).

belch To expel gas from the stomach suddenly through the mouth; uncommon in horses and a sign of a more serious condition.

Belgian Ardennais *see* BELGIAN ARDENNES

Belgian Ardennes Also known as an Ardennes or Belgian Ardennais; a coldblood once considered an offshoot of the Belgian Brabant (q.v.), but now classified as a division of the French Ardennais (q.v.) with which it shares the same features; originally from the Ardennes plateau in France from which the name derived; thought to have descended from the heavy draft horses used by Julius Caesar put to Arab (q.v.) in the 18th century; breed characteristics were firmly established in the 19th century; is hardy and frugal having tremendous endurance, stands about 15.3 hands, is compact and heavily built with a wide, deep chest, a big, broad head, short, heavily feathered, massive legs, and a well-crested neck; predominant coat colors are bay, roan, and chestnut; has a gentle temperament; used for heavy draft and agricultural work and is particularly well suited to work in hilly country; the stud book is maintained by the Societé Royale pour le Cheval de Trait Ardennais.

Belgian Brabant *see* BRABANT

Belgian Draft *see* BRABANT

Belgian Draft horse *see* BRABANT

Belgian Heavy Draft *see* BRABANT

Belgian road cart A light, two-wheeled, horse-drawn driving and exercise cart popular in Belgium during the 1900s; hung on a three-spring system with pivoting shackles; noted for its low bodywork and wide gauge track which made it safe for road work with inexperienced horses.

bell (1) A signal sounded to initiate a performance, to identify when a competitor goes off course (q.v.), when the starter opens the starting gate at a race track, or to mark the close of betting at a racetrack. (2) A hollow metallic device that when struck gives forth a ringing sound; attached to the harness for decoration, coaches for safety, etc.

Bellas Formas A Paso Fino (q.v.) show class in which horses are judged 60 percent on conformation, 30 percent on quality and naturalness of gait, and 10 percent on appearance, grooming, and manners; the horse is generally shown with two handlers using Bellas Formas lines (q.v.); Spanish meaning "beautiful lines".

Bellas Formas lines Two long lines approximately 20–30 feet (6–9 m) in length, attached to either side of a halter by which handlers show the Paso Fino (q.v.) horse in Bellas Formas (q.v.) classes; the handlers stand to either side and to the rear of the horse.

bell boots *see* OVERREACH BOOTS

Bellerophon The Prince of Corinth in Greek mythology who tamed the winged horse, Pegasus (q.v.) and rode him to destroy the dragon-like monster, the Chimera; success encouraged him to attempt to fly Pegasus to Olympia to live with the gods; Zeus, angered by his mortal ambition, sent a gadfly to bite Pegasus, which spooked the horse and unseated Bellerophon who fell to the earth crippled and blinded.

belling The sound a stag (q.v.) makes during mating season.

bell-mare Also known in South America as madrina; originally, in America, any mare with a specially toned bell strapped around her neck, used to lead a mule train (it is generally accepted that a mule train will pull harder and faster if led by a mare); in the rest of the world and in America today, any mare with a bell around her neck who other horses will follow when in pasture or range, hobbled or free.

belly band (1) A wide double leather strap that passes under the belly of the horse just to the rear of the fore flank to keep the harness tugs (q.v.) in place and to prevent the collar (q.v.) from choking the horse. (2) *see* GIRTH no. 1

belly clip To shave or cut the body hair of the horse from under the belly upwards between the forelegs, and up along the lower line of the neck to the jaw.

belly strap A leather strap with a buckle on each end attached to a dee (q.v.) on the lower side of each harness trace (q.v.) between the pad and the trace carrier and passed through a loop on the rear of the girth; used to prevent the traces from slipping over the back of the horse if he turns towards the shaft horse (q.v.).

Belmont Stakes One of three classic races for three-year-old horses comprising the American Triple Crown (q.v.) instituted in the United States between 1865 and 1875; a 1-1/2 mile (2.4 km) race first run in 1867 at Jerome Park; moved to Belmont Park located in New York in 1905 where it has been run annually every June since; named for August Belmont, the leading owner and breeder of race horses in the 1860s.

below the bit *see* BEHIND THE BIT

Belvoir tan Refers to foxhound coat color; dark rich mahogany and black coloring with no white unless in the form of a collar; descended from a black and tan hound named Senator which is currently mounted and on display at Belvoir Castle, Great Britain.

bench A hunting term; a slatted, wooden bench raised approximately 1 ft (30 cm) off the ground upon which kenneled hounds sleep; in the winter they are bedded with straw.

bench knees *see* LATERAL DEVIATION OF THE METACARPAL BONES

bend (1) A racing term; any turn in the race track. (2) The flexion of the horse from nose to tail; may be to the left or right; is more of a rider sensation than a physical actuality.

bending line A jumping term; an imaginary curved line from one obstacle to another where such obstacles are not placed in a straight line; a rider follows this line when jumping.

bending race Also known as a pole race; a mounted competition in which competitors weave, one at a time, in and out of a number of vertically placed poles set in a straight line; the winner is the competitor who completes the course in the fastest time without knocking down any poles.

bending tackle A type of tack used to alter the carriage (q.v.), e.g., raise the head, of the horse by encouraging flexion of the neck and jaw; the best known version is the Gooch Set.

Benjamin Also known as upper Benjamin; a coaching term; an overcoat worn by coachmen made of boxcloth (q.v.).

benign Any illness or medical condition which is neither malignant (q.v.) nor likely to re-occur; has a good chance of responding to treatment.

Benna A crude horse-drawn farm cart used in Ancient Rome having a wooden plank floor and rope sides woven with straw or grass;

drawn by either a pair of oxen or horses.

Bennett, James Gordon Considered the father of American polo (q.v.); introduced the game in the United States in 1876 by assembling players, knowledge, equipment, and Texas horses to play in the first loosely structured matches; the first game was played indoors at Dickle's Riding Academy located in New York.

Bentinck bit A curb bit (q.v.) with a gate-port mouth.

bent-panel cart A light, horse-drawn, two-wheeled dogcart (q.v.) with outwardly curved sides, a shallow foot well, and false side slats or louvers; favored by lady drivers on account of the protection from mud and splashes it provided; drawn by a small horse or large pony in curved shafts.

Berkley bit A pelham bit (q.v.) with auxiliary rings attached to the top ring on the cheeks; usually mullen mouthed; similar to the rugby pelham.

Beradi The progeny (q.v.) of a Persian Arab (q.v.) mare and a non-Arab stallion.

Berlin (1) Also known as a Berlin coach and spelled Berline; a horse-drawn coach or chariot developed in the mid-17th century and so named because its first public appearance was made in the streets of Berlin, Germany; had a Berlin suspension (q.v.) and two parallel braces in a longitudinal plan outside the main bodywork; on some models, the braces could be tightened, raised, or lowered by means of an attached windlass; not popular in Britain or the United States until the mid-18th century; usually drawn by a pair of horses in pole gear. (2) *see* BERLIN SUSPENSION.

Berlin coach *see* BERLIN

Berlin suspension Also known as Berline suspension; the undergear on which a Berlin was supported.

Berline *see* BERLIN

Berline suspension *see* BERLIN SUSPENSION no. 2

Berlingot *see* VIS-À-VIS

Berlin Rockaway A light, horse-drawn pas-

senger vehicle popular in North America having full-sized panels and glazed upper quarters; not a true Berlin (q.v.) as it was hung on leaf springs rather than braces.

Bermuda grass Also known as Bahama grass, devil grass, scutch grass, or couch grass; a trailing and stoloniferous grass, Cynodon dactylon, native to southern Europe and grown in other warm climates, particularly India, the Southern United States, and the Caribbean islands, for pasture, lawns, etc.

Bermuda hay Cut and dried hay (q.v.) made from Bermuda grass (q.v.); common to the southern and coastal regions of the United States; may be cut four to five times per year from the same stem of grass; similar in nutritional content to early bloom Timothy (q.v.) and has a protein content higher than that of cereal grass hays such as oat or barley.

bestride To ride astride, as on a horse.

bet (1) Also known as wager, play, or box; a betting term; a sum of money laid, staked, or pledged on the result of any uncertain event such as a horse race. (2) A betting term; also known as lay, wager, or betting; to pledge a sum of money on the outcome of an uncertain event, e.g., a horse race; includes post betting (q.v.) and ante-post betting (q.v.).

beta-carotene A derivative of vitamin A.

bet declared off A racing term; any wager announced as no longer valid or canceled by the race stewards (q.v.); as due to the scratch of an entry or part of an entry at the gate.

better (1) Having good qualities in a greater degree than another. (2) To make better; to improve. (3) A state of improvement. (4) *see* BETTOR

betting The act of placing a bet (q.v.).

betting board A betting term; a board upon which bookmakers (q.v.) display the odds of any horse competing in a given race.

betting book Also known as book; a betting term; a ledger maintained by a bookmaker (q.v.) in which all bets made and paid are logged.

betting favorite A betting term; the horse, as in one competing in a race, upon which most bets (q.v.) are placed.

betting ring (1) The area at a racetrack where authorized bookmakers (q.v.) conduct their business. (2) An organized, yet illegal group of bookmakers (q.v.).

betting shop A betting term; a licensed, off-track bookmaker's (q.v.) office which takes bets (q.v.) on events such as horse races.

betting ticket *see* TICKET no. 2

bettor Also known as a punter or player and spelled better; one who places a wager or bet (q.v.).

between hand and leg *see* ON THE AIDS

between the flags The area between the red and white flags (q.v.) on a jumping obstacle or course through which a mounted rider must pass when in competition.

BEVA The acronym for British Equine Veterinary Association (q.v.).

Beverly Car A square-sided version of the governess cart (q.v.), finished with clear varnish over natural wood rather than painted in solid colors.

Beyer number A racing term; a handicapping tool in which a numerical value is assigned to each race run by a horse based on his final time and the track condition; enables one to objectively compare different horses running on different racetracks; popularized by Andrew Beyer from which the name derives.

BDS The acronym for the British Driving Society (q.v.).

Bhotia *see* BHUTIA

BHS The acronym for the British Horse Society (q.v.).

BHSAI The acronym for British Horse Society Assistant Instructor (q.v.).

BHSI The acronym for British Horse Society Instructor (q.v.).

Bhutia Also spelled Bhotia; a pony breed originating in the Himalayan mountains of northern India; is similar in genetic makeup to

the native Tibetan and Spiti (q.v.) pony breeds; stands 13 to 13.1 hands, has a gray coat, short neck, shaggy mane, straight shoulder, short, strong legs, is frugal, and has good endurance; used for riding and packing; divided into three subgroups: the Tattu (q.v.), Chyanta (q.v.), and the Tanghan (q.v.).

Bian Also known as a Bianconi car or Biancononi car; a horse-drawn, four-wheeled, public passenger vehicle of the Irish jaunting car (q.v.) type introduced in the early 19th century; used primarily for long-distance journeys in Southern Ireland in districts not served by stage coaches prior to the advent of railways; passengers sat dos-à-dos down the sides of the vehicle, facing outwards; had knee flaps to protect the passengers' lower legs and was drawn by a either a unicorn (q.v.) or pair (q.v.).

Bianconi Car *see* BIAN

Biancononi Car *see* BIAN

bib A stout piece of leather strapped to the throat latch of the halter (q.v.) which prevents a horse from reaching and biting at its blanket (q.v.).

bib martingale Also known as web martingale; a running martingale (q.v.) in which the area between the split auxiliary reins is covered or filled with baghide or similar material; used on excitable and young horses to prevent them from entangling their legs and other equipment in the martingale.

bick *see* BEAK

bid A price offered to purchase a horse, tack, or real estate at an auction (q.v.).

bidder One who offers a bid at an auction (q.v.).

Bidet Breton Also known as Bidet d'Allure; one of four types of Breton (q.v.) defined according to size, the others being the Postier Breton (q.v.), Corlay (q.v.), and Heavy Draught Breton (q.v.); a horse breed originated in Brittany, France more than 4,000 years ago; highly prized as a military mount during the Middle Ages because of its alluring gait; stood about 14 hands.

Bidet d'Allure *see* BIDET BRETON

bienséance A 17th-century French term; to

have mores and manners; to adhere to the Classical Rules, as the rules proposed by Aristotle, which included the banning of violence at such events as mounted duels, on stage.

big apple An American racing term; any major racing circuit.

bighead *see* OSTEODYSTROPHIA FIBROSA

bighead disease *see* OSTEODYSTROPHIA FIBROSA

big hitch Four, six, eight, or more horses connected to a vehicle for the purpose of pulling it.

big knee *see* CARPITIS

big leg *see* STOCK UP

Bigourdan A horse breed descended from the Iberian Horse improved with Arab (q.v.) and Thoroughbred (q.v.) blood; basically, a tall Tarbenian (q.v.).

big race A racing term; the primary race of any race day.

Big Red Either of two chestnut-colored, Thoroughbred (q.v.) racing champions: Man O'War (q.v.) or Secretariat (q.v.).

bight of the reins That portion of the reins (q.v.) passing between the rider's thumb and finger and out on top of the hand to the bit (q.v.).

big Q A racing term; a betting option in which the bettor (q.v.) selects two quinellas (q.v.) in two nominated races.

bike American slang; a harness racing sulky (q.v.).

bilateral Pertaining to or affecting both sides.

Bilgoraj Konik A breed of Konik (q.v.) believed to be a direct descendant of the wild horse.

biliary fever *see* EQUINE PIROPLAMOSIS

Bill Daly A racing term; a famous American 19th-century racehorse trainer who promoted the racing style of taking the lead as soon as possible out of the gate, setting the pace, and remaining in the lead to the finish (q.v.); such jockeys are said to be "on the Bill Daly" (q.v.).

billet Also known as bridle stud billet; the metal clip, hook, or buckle by which the reins attach to the headstall (q.v.) of the bridle (q.v.).

billets (1) Fox manure. (2) *see* STUD FASTENING

binder A hunting term; the top horizontal branch of a cut and laid fence (q.v.) or jump, e.g., a small sapling woven between the stakes or a rail placed on top of a wire fence; used to make the jump safer for the horse.

biological control A method of suppressing and/or controlling fly (q.v.) populations in and around the stable using natural enemies of targeted flies, bolstered with commercially raised reinforcements delivered at the right time.

biopsy (1) The process of removing tissue from living patients for diagnostic examination. (2) A sample obtained by biopsy.

biotin Also known as vitamin H; an intestinally synthesized, B-complex vitamin necessary for proper skin, hair, and hoof-wall health.

biothane Plastic-covered nylon from which some tack such as bridles and martingales (q.v.) is made; popular with eventers and those who compete in ride & tie (q.v.) competitions.

birdcatcher spots Refers to coat color; random, small white spots scattered over any base color; named after the Thoroughbred (q.v.) stallion, Birdcatcher, who had them; unrelated to any other pattern and the genetics that cause them are unknown; usually frowned upon in breeds that favor dark, solid colors.

birdsville disease A frequently fatal disease of horses occurring in central and northern Australia caused by the ingestion of the poisonous plant *Indigophera enneaphylla*; early signs include incoordination, drowsiness, and some lack of control of the hind limbs including dragging; affected horses are prone to stand rather than move about; recovery is rare.

bird-eyed An antiquated term; a horse who shys at imaginary objects.

Birotum A small, horse-drawn gig or chariot used in Ancient Rome, particularly during the period 313 to 337 AD; used for both public hire and private use, drawn by a single horse, and generally had a rearward luggage rack.

birth bag *see* AMNIONIC SAC

bishop (1) Any old, horse-drawn vehicle refurbished to appear new and up-to-date. (2) *see* BISHOPING

bishoping Also known as bishop or tampering; the dishonest practice of artificially altering the teeth of older horses to represent them as young horses; where black marks on the incisors have disappeared with age, they are reproduced by drilling and staining or burning holes in the tooth surface; easily detected by evaluating tooth table shape and evaluation of enamel rings.

bit A device normally made of metal or rubber attached to the bridle, and placed into the horse's mouth to control head position, pace, and direction; manipulated by the rider through the reins; consists of the cheekpieces (q.v.) and the mouthpiece (q.v.).

bit burr Also known as burr; a round piece of leather, plastic, or rubber 2 to 3 inches (5-7-1/2 cm) in diameter faced with bristles on one side, slit from one outside edge to the center, and fitted around the bit mouthpiece just inside the cheekpiece (q.v.); the bristled side lies against the corner of the horse's mouth which it irritates; prevents the horse from leaning to, and assists in turning from, the side; generally used on only one side of the bit.

bitch (1) *see* BITCH HOUND. (2) *see* BITCH FOX.

bitch fox Also known as bitch; a female fox.

bitch hound Also known as a bitch; a female hound (q.v.).

bitch pack A hunting term; a pack of hounds composed entirely of bitch hounds (q.v.).

bit cover A tubular piece of rubber fit over the bit mouthpiece; used to enlarge the bit.

bite To cut, break, penetrate, or seize with the teeth; a vice.

bit guard Also known as bit shield, cheek leather, cheek guard, or in England, as lozenge; a round piece of leather or rubber 2 to 3 inches diameter, slit from the outside edge to the center, where there is a hole large enough to fit the bit mouthpiece; prevents the bit from catching on the horse's lips.

biting louse Also known as *Damalinia equi*; a lice (q.v.); an external, biting and sucking parasite which feasts on the dander and hair of the horse; less than 1/10 inch in length and visible to the naked eye as a small or light-gray object; may be detected by inspecting the mane, root of the tail, inside the thighs, or on the underside of the saddle blanket following exercise; are not transmitted to people.

bit keys *see* KEYS

bitless bridle Any bridle without a bit where control is achieved through pressure on the nose and the curb groove instead of the mouth; the hackamore (q.v.) is the most common.

bit roller *see* ROLLER

bit shield *see* BIT GUARD

bitted *see* BITTED UP

bitted up Also known as bitted; said of a horse when the bridle and bit are in position on his head and in his mouth.

bitting rig Tack used to artificially achieve a head set in the horse; consists of a surcingle, backstrap, crupper (q.v.), overcheck (q.v.), side reins (q.v.), bridle (q.v.), or any combination thereof.

black Refers to coat color; coat hair and points must be black with no obvious hairs of other colors including brown on the muzzle or flanks; may have white markings on the face and/or legs; may fade to a rusty color in the sun; rare in most breeds except the Percheron (q.v.), Fell pony (q.v.), North American Spanish horse, and Friesian (q.v.); variations include jet black (q.v.) and smoky black (q.v.).

Black and tan American slang; a four-wheeled, black and tan-colored, horse-drawn cab of the growler (q.v.) type used in the United States from the 1880s on for cheap service; considered disreputable in more fashionable areas.

Black Beauty Perhaps the best known fictitious story about the life of a horse, published in 1877 and written by Mrs. Anna Sewell.

Black Bess The high quality mare, perhaps fictitious, owned by British highwayman, and common thief, Dick Turpin (1706–1739); Turpin is said to have ridden Black Bess in his famous ride from London to York as recounted in Harrison Ainsworth's novel *Rookwood.*

Black Brigade Black horses, usually Flemish (q.v.) stallions, used in the late 19th century to pull hearses; also sterilized black stallions used in London, England to transport coal.

black brown Refers to coat color; a black body with the muzzle, and sometimes the flanks, a brown or tan.

black bullfinch A type of jumping obstacle; an excessively thick, live hedge which is jumped over, not through.

black cell tumor *see* MELANOMA

black fly Any of several small, black-bodied flies of the genus *Simulium*; a swarming daytime feeder that delivers painful bites, feeding on blood from relatively hairless body areas such as inside the ears, the genitals, and along the belly line and chest; bites may result in severe allergic reactions such as itching wheels (q.v.) and small hemorrhages.

black-letter work *see* BULLET WORK

Black Maria A four-wheeled, box-like police or prison van drawn by two horses in pole gear (q.v.) and driven from a high seat at roof level; entered from the rear, had a slatted clerestroy for ventilation, generally no windows, and was hung on sideways elliptical springs front and rear; used in Britain and North America from the 1830s through the 1920s; named for Queen Victoria whose nickname was Maria.

black marks Refers to coat color; small areas of black hairs among white or other colored coat appearing anywhere on the body.

Black Mass The quadrille of the Cadre Noir (q.v.) in which French traditional classical equitation is preserved.

Black Masters Funeral service owners who,

prior to the advent of the automobile, used sterilized black stallions known as the Black Brigade (q.v.) to draw funeral carriages.

black points Refers to coat color; the tail, ear rims, mane, tail, and lower legs of the horse when black.

black saddler A saddle maker specializing in cart and carriage harnesses.

blacksmith Also referred to incorrectly as farrier; one who forges all types of items out of hot metal.

blackthorn A thorny European shrub, the wood of which is used to make whips owing to its elastic quality.

black tobiano *see* PIEBALD

black type A racing term; a type of print often used in sale catalogues to distinguish racehorses who have won or been placed in at least one stakes race (q.v.).

black water *see* EXERCISE RELATED MYOPATHY

bladder A distendible sac with muscular and membranous walls which serves as a receptacle for the urine secreted by the kidneys.

Blagden Also known as Chubbarie and spelled Blagdon; a breed of spotted horse previously bred at the Royal Stud in Britain; now thought to be extinct.

Blagdon *see* BLAGDEN

Blair bridle *see* MECHANICAL HACKAMORE

blank (1) Also known as drawn blank; a hunting term; said of a fox den or hiding place which does not contain a fox. (2) *see* BLANK DAY

blank day Also known as blank; a hunting term; any day in which the hounds (q.v.) fail to find a fox.

blanket (1) Refers to a coat color pattern; a symmetrical pattern of white on the haunches of a non-white horse; common to many breeds of horses, but most notably the Appaloosa (q.v.) and the Pony of the Americas (q.v.); may vary in size from a pattern covering the croup and hips of the horse, to one which covers most of the body; of three types: solid with sharply defined edges, roan whose edges blend into the colored coat, and flecked where the edges blend into the body color with flecks of white hairs. (2) *see* HORSE BLANKET. (3) *see* SADDLE BLANKET. (4) To put a horse blanket (q.v.) on a horse.

blanket clip To shave or cut the body hair of the horse from the neck and belly; useful for horses pastured during the day and stabled at night.

blanketed Said of a horse wearing a horse blanket (q.v.).

blanket finish A racing term; an extremely close race finish in which the horses are so closely grouped they could be, figuratively, covered with one blanket.

blanket riding To ride a horse without the aid of a saddle, using instead a saddle blanket (q.v.) held in position with a surcingle (q.v.); now replaced by a bareback pad (q.v.).

blaze A face marking (q.v.) consisting of a band of white which covers most of the forehead between the eyes, the entire width of the nasal bone, and the area between, but not including, the nostrils.

Blazers, the Also known as Galway Blazers; a famous fox-hound pack from County Galway, Eire founded in the early 19th century.

blazing scent *see* BURNING SCENT

bleed (1) To draw blood from a horse using a syringe. (2) To lose blood.

bleeder (1) A horse who bleeds from the nostrils, as during a workout or race; a condition resulting from rupture of the capillaries surrounding the alveoli in the lungs known as exercise-induced pulmonary hemorrhage (q.v.); 75 percent of racehorses may have blood in their upper airways after racing. (2) Any horse from which blood is drawn under controlled conditions for use in the production of serums and vaccines.

blemish A minor conformation fault, mark, or scar which is not inherited and is considered unattractive, but does not affect the horse's soundness or performance in any way; includes, but is not limited to, capped hock

(q.v.), corneal scars (q.v.), dermal inclusion cysts (q.v.), and rope burns (q.v.).

blind (1) Also known as blind of an eye; devoid of the sense of sight; may be inherited in which case it is a delayed lethal (q.v.) condition, due to injury, or deficiency in the diet where it is known as moon blindness (q.v.); a blind horse will rely more heavily on sound as a sense and will be very hesitant in its gait; horses blind in one eye only may be prevented from competing in certain events for safety reasons; horses blind in both eyes may still be useful when driven in harness. (2) *see* BLINKERS. (3) *see* BLIND COUNTRY

blind boil A painful suppurating inflammatory sore forming a central core, caused by microbic infection which does not break or erupt the skin's surface.

blind bucker A horse who bucks without discrimination or any sense of direction; will often collide with objects in his path.

blind country Also known as blind; a hunting term; said of the country when the summer's growth of weeds and brush obscures the obstacles and terrain ahead making it difficult for riders to gage the jumps and footing.

blinder A horse who performs beyond expectations.

blinders *see* BLINKERS

blindness The condition of being blind (q.v.).

blind obstacle Any obstacle (q.v.) to be jumped by the horse for which the landing side is not visible at take off.

blind of an eye *see* BLIND no. 1

blinds *see* BLINKERS.

blind spavin Arthritis (q.v.) of the lower joints of the hock where the bone has degenerated without visible bone growth; the horse will go lame without showing outward signs of spavin (q.v.).

blind splint An inflammatory process of the interosseous ligament in the leg; difficult to detect because swelling occurs on the inner side of the splint, between the small metacarpal bone and suspensory ligament.

blind switch A racing term; said of a jockey who finds his mount pocketed (q.v.) behind other horses and who must decide whether to hope for an opening or to drop back and go around the pack.

blinkers Also known as blinders, blinds, or winkers; racing and harness equipment consisting of leather-covered metal plates attached to the cheek-pieces of the bridle or hood; used to restrict the horse's vision to the sides and rear in either or both eyes; in harness or driving available in round, hatchet, dee, or square shapes which are often decorated with a metal ornamentation; racing blinkers (q.v.) consist of a hood which fits over the head with the ears protruding and leather cups shielding the eyes.

blister (1) A collection of watery matter or serum which causes the skin to rise and separate from the lower tissues. (2) Also known as a vesicant or resciant; a liquid or paste counterirritant (q.v.) applied to the skin of the leg to cause blistering and inflammation; used to increase blood supply and flow, and therefore to promote healing. (3) Also known as blistering; to apply a counterirritant to the skin to cause blistering and inflammation, to treat chronic or subacute inflammation of joints, tendons, and bones by encouraging blood flow to the area to hasten the healing process.

blister beetle A small poisonous insect often present in alfalfa (q.v.) or lucerne hay (q.v.) grown in low-humidity areas of the United States during late August and early September; contains a chemical toxin, cantharidin, an irritant that will blister the skin, or if ingested by the horse in the hay, the lining of the digestive tract; signs of poisoning appear six to eight hours after ingestion of the insects and include colic (q.v.), loss of appetite, sweating, fever (q.v.), frequent attempts to urinate, and/or dehydration; if left untreated, may result in shock and/or death; no antidote exists, although aggressive treatment including administration of fluids, diuretics, and painkillers, as well as calcium (q.v.) and magnesium (q.v.) supplements, improves prognosis.

blistering *see* BLISTER no. 3

bloat *see* COLIC

block *see* NERVE BLOCK

blocked heels (1) Said of the heels of the

horse when a nerve block (q.v.) has been performed to the area. (2) Also known as corks; the heels of a horseshoe when folded down against the ground surface of the shoe to create a heel calk or to raise the heels of the shoe.

blocks Large, square heel calks on manufactured racehorse shoes.

blond sorrel ruano Refers to coat color; a variation of sorrel (q.v.); a light sandy-red coat with pale areas around the eyes and on the muzzle, flanks, and the inside of the legs, with pale lower legs; a common color of the American Belgian Draft Horse (q.v.).

blood (1) The fluid that circulates in the arteries and veins of the horse and conveys oxygen, hormones, and food to the tissues and organs and returns waste products to the liver and kidneys where it is excreted; assists in the control of body temperature; is red in color and consists of 60 percent pale yellow plasma and 40 percent red and white blood cells; red blood cells transport oxygen and white blood cells act as a defense mechanism against infection; accounts for approximately $\frac{1}{18}$ of the horse's total body weight. (2) *see* BLOODED no. 1

blood bay Refers to coat color; a dark shade of bay (q.v.) in which the coat is a dark purplish red with little or no black hairs mixed in.

blood blister *see* HEMATOMA

blood cell A basic, structural unit of the blood.

blood count A determination of the number and proportion of red and white cells in a specific volume of blood.

blooded (1) Also known as blood; a hunting term; said of a young hound given its first taste of blood from the kill. (2) A hunting term; said of a hunter who, having never before been present when a fox was killed, has the blood of the kill applied by the Master of the Hunt (q.v.) to the forehead or cheeks; a ceremony dating to the days of the Druids. (3) Of good blood or breed, as Thoroughbred (q.v.) horses.

blood heat The normal temperature, about 98 to 100°F (36–37.7°C), of horse blood.

blood horse A pedigree horse.

blood horse *see* THOROUGHBRED

blood hound One of a breed of medium to large, powerful dogs with a very acute sense of smell, used for tracking game.

bloodhounding A version of fox hunting originating in Britain in 1993 in which hunted prey, a group of seven men and women, a quarry, is given a 20-minute head start over approximately 24 bloodhounds and the same number of horses, ridden by members of the local Bloodhound Society; the hounds and horses track the quarry until it is captured at which time the hunt horn is blown; following a spot of sherry and biscuits for all, including the dogs, the hunt resumes, with the same chase repeated three to four times to total approximately a 10 to 12 mile (16–19 km) run.

blood-letting The act of letting blood or bleeding a horse, as by opening a vein, as a remedial measure.

blood line The lineage of a horse; the pedigree.

blood marks Refers to coat color; patches of red colored hairs growing into a gray coat; can become progressively larger, ultimately resulting in a uniformly red coat; an extremely rare occurrence.

blood plasma The clear almost colorless fluid of the blood when separated from blood corpuscles by centrifuge.

blood poisoning *see* SEPTICEMIA

blood pressure The pressure exerted by the blood against the inner walls of the blood vessels, varying in different parts of the body, with exertion, excitement, strength of the heart, age, or health.

blood spavin Displacement of the main vein of the hind leg appearing on the inside of the upper part of the hock above a bog spavin (q.v.); the resulting soft lump can be emptied by manipulation, but frequently refills; is rarely treated.

blood sport Any pastime, as foxhunting (q.v.), in which killing is involved.

bloodstock The stock or blood lines used to perpetuate a breed.

blood-stock Thoroughbreds (q.v.), particularly race and stud horses.

blood stock sale A sale or auction of Thoroughbred (q.v.) horses, particularly those used, or whose bloodlines are used, in racing.

blood-stock agent One who represents or advises a buyer or seller of Thoroughbreds (q.v.) at a public auction or private sale, generally on a commission basis.

blood test Analysis of a blood sample to obtain information on blood cells present, enzyme activity, and electrolyte balance; includes packed cell volume (PCV), total plasma protein (TPP), glucose concentrations, and hormone and enzyme assays.

blood tit *see* BLOOD WEED

blood-typing A method of examining blood factors unique to each horse, much like fingerprinting, to determine the true identity and parentage of a horse; required of all newborn foals before they can be registered, raced, or used for breeding purposes; is 96 percent accurate; now being replaced by DNA testing (q.v.) which is 99 to 100 percent accurate.

blood 'un *see* THOROUGHBRED

blood urea nitrogen Also known by the acronym BUN; the urea nitrogen level in the blood; an indicator of the kidney's ability to excrete urea from the body.

blood weed Also known as blood tit; an antiquated term; a lightly built Thoroughbred (q.v.) lacking substance and/or bone.

blood worm *see* LARGE STRONGYLES

bloom The shine or luster on the horse's coat as achieved by grooming or from added dietary fat in the form of oil.

blow (1) Also known as blow wind and blowing; said of the horse; to exhale with heavy, loud, and accelerated breathing following strenuous exercise in an effort to return to normal respiration. (2) Said of the horse who exhales air forcefully from the nostrils; a sign of suspicion, unfamiliarity, etc.

blow a stirrup Said of the rider when his foot falls out of the stirrup.

blow away Also known as blowing away; a hunting term; to send the hounds after the fox with a signal from the hunting horn (q.v.).

blower An antiquated racing term; telephone service between a bookmaker (q.v.) and his connection at the racetrack.

blow fly A species of fly that breeds in animal flesh.

blow him Also known as cook him; said of a rider or trainer who overtrains a young horse causing it to tire, sour, or burn out emotionally from stress.

blow his nose A racing term; to give a horse a short gallop prior to a race to clear his nose in prepare for a horse race.

blow home Also known as blow hounds home; a hunting term; a series of long, connected notes blown on the hunting horn (q.v.) indicating the hunt (q.v.) is over.

blow hounds home *see* BLOW HOME

blowing *see* BLOW no. 1

blowing away *see* BLOW AWAY

blowing out (1) A hunting term; said of the huntsman who calls the hounds out of an empty covert or one in which they lost the fox. (2) A racing term; the act or process of running a blow out (q.v.).

blowing the anvil *see* ANVIL SHOOTING

blow off a cow, to A cutting term; said of a horse who makes a bigger move than necessary to stay with the cow or when tricked by the cow, overanticipates its movements, and moves in the opposite direction.

blow out A racing term; a brief workout, usually three furlongs (q.v.) or a half mile in length occurring one or two days prior to a race; designed to sharpen or maintain the condition of the horse.

blow up (1) A dressage term; said of a horse who breaks from the gait or pace, misbehaves, or panics. (2) Said of a horse who bucks (q.v.). 3) Said of a horse who inhales and holds its breath whilst the girth is being tightened.

blow wind *see* BLOW no. 1

blue dun *see* GRULLO

blue eye *see* WALL EYE

blue grass One of several, fine-leafed grasses of the Poa genus of temperate and arctic forage grasses, as bluestem grass, more especially the grass of Kentucky, United States, which due to the limestone soil and water, is rich in phosphates and lime, two minerals which contribute to the building of strong bones.

blue grass country An area located in Kentucky, USA, where the grass is so rich in phosphates and lime, which produce strong bones, that it is ideal for breeding horses.

blue nose *see* PHOTOSENSITIZATION

blue riband *see* BLUE RIBBON

blue ribbon Also known as blue riband; a piece of blue ribbon signifying the highest award, as for first prize or place.

blue roan (1) Refers to coat color; any roan (q.v.) horse with a bluish color. (2) Refers to coat color; a mixture of red, black, and white coat hairs.

bluestem Also known as bluestem grass; any of the various tufted grasses, genus Andropogon, grown in the United States for hay and forage.

bluestem grass *see* BLUESTEM

bluestem grass hay Cut and dried hay made from bluestem grass (q.v.) common to the central United States; is highly palatable and contains a digestible protein content of approximately 3 percent and a fiber content of approximately 34 percent which is slightly higher than Timothy (q.v.) and Bermuda grass (q.v.) hays.

blue stone *see* COPPER SULFATE

blue vitriol *see* COPPER SULFATE

bluff A head covering or wrap having covered leather eye sockets put over the head of a bad-tempered or excitable horse to keep it quiet and calm.

Boadicea (d. AD 62) A British queen thought to have maintained the first racing stud (q.v.).

board *see* TOTALIZATOR BOARD

board fence Also known as plank jump; a jumping obstacle consisting of long, narrow, flat, and often painted board supported by the standards (q.v.).

boards A polo term; also known as side boards or polo boards; 9 x 11 inch (23 x 28 cm) wooden boards which define the side lines (q.v.) of the polo field (q.v.) in England, the United States, and Argentina; use is optional and today chalk is more commonly used.

boat race *see* FIXED RACE

bobbery pack A hunting term; a mixed pack of hounds (q.v.) or dogs used for hunting; the practice and term are believed to have originated in India.

bobble A racing term; said of a horse who takes a bad step out of the starting gate; generally due to the track surface giving way under foot; may cause the horse to duck its head, stumble, or nearly fall to its knees.

bobbing Said of the head of horse which rises and falls with each stride when the horse is lame or evading the bit.

bobby back *see* SWAY BACK

bobby backed *see* SWAY BACKED

bob tail *see* DOCKED TAIL

bob-tailed (1) Said of a horse with a short or docked (q.v.) tail. (2) A hunting term; said of a fox with little or no tail.

bocado (1) A Spanish term; a mouthpiece (q.v.). (2) A bit popular in South America, consisting of a strip of leather passed under the tongue and tied under the chin.

body (1) Also known as torso; the main part of the horse as distinguished from the head and limbs. (2) *see* INTERIEUR

body brush A grooming tool consisting of tightly packed, soft, natural or synthetic bristles or hair set in an attached handle of wood or plastic, used to remove dust, dirt, and sweat from the horse's coat.

body break *see* SHOOTING BREAK

body clip *see* FULL CLIP

body horse The middle horse of a lead team pulling a horse-drawn vehicle.

body roller *see* ROLLER no. 1

bodyside A driving term; the part of the collar (q.v.) which lies against the shoulders of the horse.

body team A driving term; the pair of horses positioned between the wheelers (q.v.) and the swing team (q.v.) in an eight-horse hitch.

body wash *see* BRACE no. 1

bogey (1) A jumper, hunter, and eventing term; a problem fence. (2) Muddy ground.

bog rider A cowboy (q.v.) whose responsibility it is to rescue cattle mired in the mud.

bog spavin Also known as tarsal hydrarthrosis; a soft liquid- or tissue filled swelling in the synovial bursa or sheath surrounding the hock joint; generally occurs on the inside and upper front of the hock joint; rarely interferes with the usefulness of the horse and may not cause lameness, although it does create an unsightly blemish; may be caused by poor conformation, overwork, and strain; may appear and disappear spontaneously in weanlings or yearlings given too much work before the bones fully mature, and has a tendency to recur; rest is essential.

boil A painful suppurating inflammatory sore forming a central core, caused by microbic infection; may break or erupt the skin.

boil over (1) Said of a horse; to start bucking (q.v.). (2) A racing term; said of a horse who has won a horse race by a decisive margin when not expected to do so.

Bokara Also known as Bokara pony and spelled Bokhara; a pony descended from the Persian horse (q.v.) from Turkestan.

Bokara pony *see* BOKARA

Bokhara *see* BOKARA

bold eye The eye of the horse when large,

expressive, and prominent.

bold-face type A racing term; a darker type style used to highlight a horse's name in a sales catalogue; when in bold letters, the horse has won at least one stakes race (q.v.), while bold and lowercase letters, denote a second or third placing in at least one stakes race.

bold front Said of the horse whose well-muscled neck is set squarely onto the forequarters resulting in a proud head carriage.

bolet *see* BOLUS

bollard *see* ROLLER BOLT

bolster The timber framing running parallel to the axles, front and rear, on a horse-drawn vehicle which connected the body of the vehicle to the axles by means of leather thoroughbraces (q.v.) or similar fittings.

Bolster Wagon A primitive, horse-drawn, four-wheeled buggy developed in the United States in 1814; lacked rearward springs, but had side bar suspension and crosswise bolsters (q.v.) to support an overhanging load.

bolt (1) *see* BOLTING. (2) To break out of control or try to run away as in a horse; may be a vice or caused by momentary fright. (3) *see* BOLT A FOX

bolt a fox Also known as bolt; a hunting term; said of the hounds to remove or force a fox out of a drain, hole, or other protection.

bolter (1) A horse who eats too fast. (2) A horse who breaks out of control or runs away, refusing to respond to the control of the bit, to turn, to slow down, or to stop; may be due to bad teeth, a poorly fitting bit, a hard mouth (q.v.), fear, etc.

bolting (1) Also known as bolting food or bolt; a vice; said of a horse who eats its food too quickly; may be due to boredom, bad teeth, insufficient feed, or lack of roughage and may result in digestive problems including colic (q.v.) and choking (q.v.); may be prevented by placing large stones in the manger, feeding smaller amounts more frequently throughout the day, and increasing roughage. (2) Said of a horse who bolts (q.v.).

bolting food *see* BOLTING no. 1

bolus Also known as bolet; any mass of food swallowed by the horse.

bomb calorimeter *see* GROSS ENERGY

bomb proof A British and Australian term; a safe, reliable, and quiet horse, as used by a green rider.

Bonaventia An American term; a Jenny Lind (q.v.).

bone (1) The measurement describing the circumference around the cannon bone halfway between the knee and fetlock joint; used to define conformation of a horse or hound, e.g., to have good bone; the ability of the bone to carry weight. (2) The hard, porous material which forms the skeleton of the horse and from which all soft tissues are suspended or joined; contains most of the minerals in the horse's body, specifically calcium (q.v.) and phosphorus (q.v.); strength is directly related to collagen composition, not mineral mass; classified into five categories depending on shape: compact, flat, long, roofing, and irregular. (3) *see* BONING

bone chip A loose bone fragment resulting from injury to a bone that does not result in fracture (q.v.).

bone in the ground A hunting term; the state of the ground during or immediately following a frost in which the ground is hard under a soft surface.

bone meal Crushed or finely ground bones fed as a calcium-phosphorus feed supplement.

bone shaker Antiquated slang; any cheap, hired, horse-drawn carriage.

bone spavin An ossification, or new bone growth as the result of chronic irritation, such as arthritis; may result in the fusing of the small bones of the hock; appears as a bony enlargement on the inside and front of the hind legs below the hock joint at the point where the hock tapers into the cannon bone; may be caused by concussion, over exertion, injury, faulty hock conformation, and mineral imbalance; all breeds are affected but it is most prevalent in Standardbreds (q.v.) and Quarter Horses (q.v.); the affected horse may drag the toe, display shortened forward flight of the hoof, and decreased hock action.

boning Also known as bone; an antiquated practice of polishing black riding boots made of Bordeaux leather using a bone, preferably a shank bone of a deer, in conjunction with paste or liquid blackening; the shank is rubbed over the surface of a cleaned and polished boot prior to rubbing with a chamois.

bonnet (1) A face marking (q.v.); a white head with pigmented ears and a pigmented area around the eyes. (2) Also known as Chaunter; an antiquated term; one who boasts about the merits of a horse to assist the owner in selling it; does not admit that he knows the owner of the horse; now replaced by shill (q.v.).

bon veneur A French hunting term; a good huntsman (q.v.) or Hunt Master (q.v.).

bony growth *see* EXOSTOSIS

book (1) A racing term; a jockey's schedule of riding assignments. (2) Also known as betting book; a racing term; a bookmaker's (q.v.) tally of bets placed, the amounts of each bet (q.v.) and the odds necessary to assure profit. (3) The group of mares bred to a stallion in one given year; if he is bred to the maximum number of mares allowed by his manager (about 40 for race horses), he is said to have a full book (q.v.). 4) *see* THE BOOK

bookie Slang; a bookmaker (q.v.).

bookmaker Also known as bookie; a professional betting man/woman who accepts wagers, cash or credit, placed by others on horses competing in a race or performance.

booster An additional dose of a vaccine given to a horse to either enhance or continue protection against a particular disease.

boot (1) A protective and/or supportive covering for the legs or feet of the horse made of leather, plastic, rubber, or other synthetic materials. (2) *see* RIDING BOOT. (3) To clip the long hair of the fetlock and lower leg. (4) A receptacle on a coach or carriage used to contain luggage; differentiated as front boot (q.v.) and rear boot (q.v.). (5) A racing term; said of a jockey who kicks his horse, as when coming in on the home stretch. (6) *see* HALF STOCKING

boots and saddles A racing term; a bugle call sounded when jockeys (q.v.) mount and enter the racetrack (q.v.) for the post parade; formerly a bugle call to cavalrymen; from the French cavalry command "bout selle" meaning to put saddle, which became "boot and saddle" in England and "boots and saddles" in the United States.

boot home a winner A racing term; to ride a winning horse in a race.

boot hook A J-shaped metal hook with wooden, bone, plastic, or ivory handle attached perpendicular to the long, straight side of the hook; used to pull on riding boots.

boot jack A contrivance, usually made of wood, used to assist in removing a boot from the foot of the rider; of many shapes and sizes; in one design, the rider stands on the rear portion of the wood with one foot, wedges the heel of the boot into the "V", and pulls up on his leg; the boot remains in the jack.

boot tred The step attached to the front boot (q.v.) of a horse-drawn coach, used by travelers to get into the box (q.v.).

boot tree A wooden or plastic form put into the leg, and in some cases foot, of a tall boot, to preserve its shape when not being worn.

borer Said of a horse who constantly pulls on the bit by thrusting his head forward and downward.

boring Said of a horse in action when he pulls on the bit by thrusting his head forward and downward.

bosal A semi-oval, braided, rawhide, leather, or rope noseband which terminates in a heel knot (q.v.) tied under the jaw; used with a bosal hackamore (q.v.); rests at a 45 degree angle between the bridge of the nose and the chin of the horse; control is achieved by pressure applied to the bridge of the nose by the bosal and the tender area behind and under the jaw by the heel knot when the reins are raised by the rider; available in various sizes and diameters.

Bosnian An ancient pony breed descended from the Tarpan (q.v.) and originating in Bosnia-Herzegovina; stands 12.1 to 14 hands and may have a bay, brown, black, gray, chestnut, or palomino coat; has refined features overall, yet a rather heavy head and short neck, deep and wide chest, and short, muscled legs; is docile, steady, and hardy; used for riding, packing, light farm work and light draft; breeding stallions are government controlled, while mares are in private ownership; resembles the Hucul (q.v.).

bosomy Said of a horse with an over-wide chest (q.v.).

boss Also known as rosette; a disc, often emblazoned with the owner's monogram, crest, or engraving, attached to the sides of the browband (q.v.) of a harness bridle; depending on the type of team, may be attached to the left, right, or both sides of the bridle (q.v.); designed in many different styles and materials; rosettes with outward protruding terrets, through which the leader's reins pass, were often used with a tandem (q.v.) shaft horse or the wheelers (q.v.) of a unicorn or four-in-hand team (q.v.).

botfly *see* HORSE BOTFLY

bot larvae *see* HORSE BOT

bot *see* HORSE BOT

both legs out of the same hole A horse with a very narrow chest whose forelegs are set too close together.

both sides of the road Also known as two sweats; a phrase used into the early 20th century; to work a coach team twice in the same day.

bots The plural of bot (q.v.).

bottom (1) A racing term; the foundation of a race track. (2) A racing term; equine stamina, strength, and resolution. (3) A racing term; a horse assigned an outside post position and listed last in the race program. (4) An English hunting term; a fence with a big deep, and jumpable ditch. (5) An English hunting term; an unjumpable ditch or brook running at the bottom of a deep gully or ravine.

bottom bar The lowest slot or ring into which a rein (q.v.) can be buckled or secured on a curb bit (q.v.).

botulism Also known as forage poisoning or shaker foal syndrome; an intoxication, not an infection, resulting from the ingestion of the toxin Clostridium botulinum, a spore-forming anaerobic (q.v.) bacterium found in food; reproduces in decaying plant or animal matter and persists in most farm soils, animal intestines, and feces; the bacteria live for years in a benign spore form, waiting for warmer, wetter conditions and a protein source to feed on; toxins bind to nerve endings rendering them useless and paralysis ensues; as little as one milligram can kill a horse with 98 percent of the cases fatal; of the five known types: types B and C are most common in horses; type B progresses slowly and is easily diagnosed while type C does not impair eating until just prior to death and is often confused with tying up (q.v.), equine encephalomyelitis (q.v.), or plant poisoning; is particularly destructive of foals; symptoms in foals include impaired nursing, inability to swallow, decreased eyelid and tail tone, dilated pupils, and progressive muscular weakness and tremors leading to collapse and an inability to rise; symptoms in adults include motor weakness to total paralysis of the entire voluntary and much of the involuntary musculature, muscle tremors over the flanks after exertion, drool, a weak and unsteady gait, falling and an inability to rise, and ultimately death from respiratory paralysis; an antitoxin is available.

bought sight unseen To purchase a horse on the basis of verbal or written description rather than visual evaluation.

Boulnois Cab Also known as backdoor omnibus, duobus, minibus, or slice of an omnibus; a four-wheeled, closed, horse-drawn carriage with a small, elongated body resembling a small Omnibus (q.v.); developed by Mr. Boulnois in 1830; seated two passengers vis-à-vis (q.v.); driven from a seat on the front of the roof and drawn by a single horse, hung on sideways elliptical springs front and rear and entered by a step and door from the rear; used privately and for hire; because it was easy for passengers to slip from the cab undetected upon arriving at the destination, thus leaving the fare unpaid, the life of this cab was short.

Boulonnais A coldblood breed originating in Northern France; descended from the ancient north European heavy horse crossed with eastern horses sometime in the first century AD; Arab (q.v.) blood was introduced during the time of the Crusades and in the 14th century the breed was crossed with Andalusian (q.v.) and Mecklenburg (q.v.); in the 17th century, it was named Boulonnais at which time two types emerged: (1) the smaller Mareyeur (q.v.) and (2) the larger horse standing 15.3 to 16.2 hands which is still bred and used for draft; has a distinctive head with a straight profile and particularly large eye, a thick, but graceful neck, prominent withers, silky skin with visible veining, a compact body, broad and straight back, short, strong limbs with wide joints, thick cannons and a lack of feathering, and a characteristic double-muscling of the croup; the mane and tail are full and the tail is set high; the predominant coat color is gray, usually dappled, although chestnut and bay occur occasionally; has straight, relatively long, swift, and energetic action; the Stud Book dates to 1886.

Boulster Wagon A four-wheeled, horse-drawn vehicle; a large version of the bolster wagon (q.v.) frequently used in public service; had two or three rows of crosswise seating, a hard standing top, open sides, roller blinds, side curtains, and a driving apron across the forward seating; drawn by one or two horses harnessed in pole gear (q.v.); the bodywork was raised on bolsters (q.v.), but all seats were sprung individually.

bounce fence A jumping obstacle consisting of two parallel fences without a stride between them; the horse touches down between the two elements and takes off without taking a stride.

boundary rider An Australian term; a ranch worker whose responsibility it is to ride the perimeter of the property or range fence line on large cattle and sheep stations to look for and repair holes in the fence.

bounder *see* OXFORD CART

bounds *see* AIRS ABOVE THE GROUND

Bourbannais *see* CHAROLLAIS

bowed Said of a horse who has had, or is currently suffering from, a bowed tendon (q.v.).

bowed tendon Also known as tendosynovitis; any true physiological damage to the tendon or tendon sheath, specifically tearing or breaking of one or more of the tendonous fibers; usually occurs in the superficial flexor tendon of the front leg, although bows of the hind legs do occur; may be precipitated by fatigue, deep going, uneven terrain, improper shoeing, obesity, excessively tight fitting running bandages or boots, work on slippery surfaces, long, weak pasterns, sudden changes in stress loads, low heel angles, and long toes; symptoms may include diffuse swelling over the tendon area, heat, and pain; lameness may or may not be present; hemorrhage and inflammation cause swelling and development of adhesions between the tendon and tendon sheath; a chronic bow is characterized by a firm, prominent swelling; of three classifications depending on the location: high bow (q.v.), low bow (q.v.), and middle bow (q.v.); as much as one year's rest may be required for a bowed tendon to heal completely.

bow hocks A conformation defect in which the hock joints are turned to the outside.

bowing A barrel racing term; said of a horse who when rounding a barrel, strides out too quickly before in position for the next barrel; results in a wide, gradual turn which leaves the horse out of position for the next turn and a slower time.

bow legs *see* LATERAL DEVIATION OF THE CARPAL JOINTS

bow legged *see* BANDY LEGGED

bowline knot One of the few knots tied in a rope in which the loop does not get smaller when pulled.

bowling *see* THROW-IN

box (1) Also referred to as the box; an eventing term; an enclosed collecting area where competitors and their mounts spend the 10-minute compulsory halt before beginning Phase D of the Speed and Endurance test (q.v.) and where the second compulsory veterinary inspection occurs. (2) A competitive calf roping term; the area along the side of the chute where the horse and rider wait until the start of a calf-roping run. (3) Also known as coachman's seat; the seat from which the coachman drives a horse-drawn vehicle. (4) An English term; a stall (q.v.). (5) An English term; a horse trailer (q.v.). (6) *see* BET. (7) *see* BOX SEAT

boxcloth A fabric historically used for gaiters and outdoor wear, especially that used in coach driving.

boxed A horseshoe (q.v.) in which the outer edge of the hoof-facing side is rounded or beveled.

boxed in A racing term; said of a horse trapped behind or to the side of other horses in the field (q.v.).

boxed trifecta A racing term; a betting option in which the bettor (q.v.) selects first, second, and third place horses which may finish in the exact or any order.

box foot *see* CLUB FOOT

boxing (1) A racing term; a technique in which the bettor (q.v.) selects three key horses in a trifecta (q.v.) and bets them in all possible combinations; an expensive option, that may yield high monetary rewards. (2) An outdated English term; to transport a horse in a trailer, van, truck, or rail car.

box loop Also known as full safe or pipe loop; a large, box-shaped leather keeper used on harness to hold the point of straps on the bridle cheek-pieces, hame and shaft tugs, crupper, and breeching; much wider than standard keepers (q.v.).

box seat Also known as box; a cushioned passenger's seat in a horse-drawn vehicle located adjacent to the coachman's seat (q.v.); a seat of honor.

box spur A spur (q.v.), consisting of a long, straight shank terminating in a thin, square.

box stall *see* STALL no. 1

box wagon Also known as show wagon or Hackney (q.v.) show wagon; a light, four-wheeled, pneumatic-tired, wagon used for showing Hackney horses and ponies; has a shallow, box-shaped body hung on a perch undercarriage with two transverse-elliptical springs and a single, stick-backed driving seat; the shafts curve downwards towards the front axle.

boxy foot *see* CLUB FOOT

boxy hooves *see* CLUB FOOT

boy Racing slang; a jockey (q.v.).

boy's horse, not a Said of a horse having a strong mouth which requires a strong and experienced rider.

Brabancon *see* BRABANT

Brabant Also known as Brabancon, Belgian Brabant, Belgian Draft, Belgian Draft horse, Belgian Heavy Draft, race de trait Belge, or Flanders horse; an ancient horse breed descended from the Ardennais (q.v.) and the product of centuries of selective breeding; principally bred in Brabant, Belgium from which the name derived; by 1890 there were three main groupings based on bloodlines rather than conformation: Orange I, Bayard, and Jean I; a massive horse standing 16 to 17 hands and weighing up to 2,200 pounds (998 kg); has a thick back, short and extremely strong limbs with feathering (q.v.), huge and powerful quarters, a short, thick neck, and a small head in comparison to the body size; coat colors vary from line to line with bays, duns, and grays occurring, but red-roans with black points, sorrels and chestnuts predominating; is docile and obedient, strong, willing, matures early, long lived and has a slow but vigorous action; the stud book dates back to 1885; used for slow heavy pulling and farm work; instrumental in the development of the Shire (q.v.), Great Horse (q.v.), Clydesdale (q.v.), Suffolk Punch (q.v.), Irish Draft (q.v.), and American Belgian.

brace (1) Also known as body wash; any solution, liniment, or lotion containing menthol, worm wood, aromatics, alcohol, or other counterirritant applied to the horse's body and/or legs to create mild topical stimulation and increase circulation. (2) A hunting term; two foxes; one fox equals half a brace, e.g., five foxes equals two and a half braces. (3) A pair or couple of geldings (q.v.). (4) A sewn leather strip from which the bodies of some horse-drawn vehicles were hung on the chassis; used to check excessive motion in the vehicle body. (5) Also known as the brace; a polo term; the stance from which a polo player takes a stroke (q.v.) on the ball. (6) To make rigid, as in the rider's back when communicating direction to the horse.

brace bandages *see* EXERCISE BANDAGE

brace, the *see* BRACE no. 5

brachygnathism *see* OVER-SHOT JAW

bradoon *see* BRIDOON

bradoon hanger *see* GAG RUNNER

brain fever *see* ENCEPHALOMYELITIS

brain staggers *see* ENCEPHALOMYELITIS

brake (1) A 19th-century, open, heavy, four-wheeled, horse-drawn passenger vehicle with an elevated driving seat used for sporting and general purposes; drawn by a pair of horses in pole gear (q.v.) or a team; had a longitudinal seat which could be removed when luggage was carried; types include the shooting brake (q.v.), skeleton brake (q.v.), and wagonette brake (q.v.); the name derived from its original purpose which was to train and break young horses to drive, although it was also used for exercising. (2) A mechanical device which decelerates or stops the motion of a wheel or vehicle by means of friction.

brake lever A long-handled metal bar used to apply the brakes on a horse-drawn vehicle through either forward or reverse pressure applied to the lever.

bran Also known as broad bran; the outer coating of wheat, rye, or other grain kernel which is separated from the flour in milling; contains less digestible energy, but more protein, fiber, and phosphorus than whole grain; highly laxative when fed as a mash (q.v.); may inhibit calcium absorption.

branch (1) An offshoot or subdivision of blood vessels, nerves, air tubes, lymphatics and so on. (2) The surface of a horseshoe from toe to heel on each side of the foot. (3) Also spelled branche; *see* CHEEK no. 1. (4) An arm-like part diverging from the main stem, as in a stag's antler.

branche *see* BRANCH no. 3

brand (1) Any mark of a simple, easy, recognizable pattern on the hide or tissue of a horse made by burning with a hot iron or acid, freezing using cryogenics, or tattooing to designate ownership; designs and/or numbers must be registered and issued to the owner, and may only be placed on the body on an area of the animal designated by the registration. (2) Also known as punch; the process of applying a brand (q.v.) to a horse.

brander (1) One who marks with a brand (q.v.). (2) *see* BRANDING IRON

branding iron Also known as brander; an iron rod with a simple, easy, recognizable pattern at one end used to apply a brand (q.v.) to the hide of a horse.

bran disease *see* OSTEODYSTROPHIA FIBROSA

bran mash A mixture of bran (q.v.), usually wheat, and boiling or hot water mixed to a wet, but not sloppy consistency; used as a laxative, poultice, and, when mixed with sweeteners, to administer medications such as bute (q.v.) to a horse; salt may be added to make it more palatable.

bray (1) The characteristic cry of the donkey (q.v.). (2) A loud or discordant noise resembling a donkey's bray.

braze To join metal surfaces using brass, bronze, or copper as a filler material, as in farriery.

break (1) To train a young horse to obey commands and accept direction and control. (2) *see* FRACTURE. (3) Also known as break stride; said of the horse; to change the gait at the command of the rider, as in "to break into a gallop". (4) To turn and run, as in the cow is going to break for the gate; to run away. (5) A racing term; to leave the gate at the start of a race.

breakage A racing term; the difference between true mutuel odds and the lesser, rounded amounts (to the nearest $0.10) given to the winning bettor(s); the difference is usually divided between the track and the state.

break covert A hunting term; said of a fox who leaves or escapes his hiding place.

breakdown (1) Said of a horse; to lose soundness or ability to perform due to an incapacitating illness or injury representing a physical disorder. (2) To lacerate the suspensory ligament or fracture a sesamoid bone, so that the back of the fetlock drops to the ground.

break-in cart *see* BREAKING CART

breaking *see* BREAK no. 1

breaking bit Also known as mouthing bit; a straight bar bit to which keys (q.v.) are attached in the center, used on a horse who has not previously had a bit in his mouth; the keys distract the horse from the bit and give it something to play with using his tongue.

Breaking Cart Also known as break-in cart, single shaft cart, or single break; a low, two-wheeled, training or exercise vehicle used to break single horses to draft; usually built to trainer specifications; had an elevated driving seat, an open, skeletal body, long shafts equipped with tug attachments to prevent breeching, and sometimes a rear drop extension to protect the driver in the event the horse fell over backward; a smaller version of the Skeleton Break (q.v.).

breaking cavesson *see* LUNGEING CAVESSON

breaking head collar *see* LUNGEING CAVESSON

breaking out Also known as break out; said of a horse who begins to sweat again after having been cooled out following exercise; may also occur due to illness, lack of fitness, excitement, stress and/or electrolyte imbalance.

breaking tackle A generic term; any tack used when breaking (q.v.) a horse such as lungeing cavesson (q.v.), side reins (q.v.), driving and lungeing reins (q.v.), bridle (q.v.), and crupper (q.v.).

break in the air A racing term; said of a horse who leaps into the air at the start of a race rather than moving forward.

break maiden Also known as earning a diploma; a racing term; said of a horse or rider who wins the first race of his career.

break out *see* BREAKING OUT

breakover Said of the foot; the act of the hoof rolling forward, lifting from the ground heel first to the toe.

breakover point The functional toe over which the hoof naturally rolls at each lift off; determined by the conformation of the coffin bone and the leg joints above it.

break stride *see* BREAK no. 3

break the barrier A rodeo term; said of a horse and rider who ride through the barrier (q.v.) before it is released; results in a 10-second penalty.

break to harness To train a horse to drive.

break up A hunting term; said of the hounds (q.v.) when they eat the carcass of the hunted fox.

break water A generic term; the expulsion of allantoic fluid during the first stages of the process of giving birth.

breast Also known as brisket; that part of the horse's body below and in front of the insertion of the neck into the shoulder; the lowest portion of the breast.

breast bone Also known as sternum; the bone in the center of the chest to which the lower ends of the ribs are attached.

breast collar Also known as Dutch collar when used for driving; a wide leather strap fitted around the front of the shoulders just below the juncture of the neck, held in place by a narrow wither strap; easily adjusted to fit various horses of similar size, but with different shaped necks; used in conjunction with driving, western, and some English saddles to prevent the saddle from slipping backwards.

breast girth *see* BREASTPLATE

breast high A hunting term; said of the quarry's scent (q.v.) when it rises from the ground to the level of the hounds' noses so they are able to hunt at full speed.

breast piece *see* BREASTPLATE

breast plate *see* BREASTPLATE

breastplate Also known as breast piece or breast strap, incorrectly as breast girth and spelled incorrectly breast plate; a wide leather strap that encircles the horse's chest and attaches on both sides of the saddle to the dees, directly to the girth on either side, or to the girth between the forelegs; depending on the type, may be used in conjuction with a neck strap; used to prevent the saddle from slipping backward when dictated by conformation or terrain and for ornamental and show purposes.

breast strap *see* BREAST PLATE

breather A slowing of pace or speed to allow a horse to rest, conserve, or renew his strength for a short spell during exercise such as a race.

breathing bridoon A narrow, straight snaffle (q.v.) having a number of holes drilled through the mouthpiece (q.v.); thought to be effective with windsuckers (q.v.).

bred (1) The past tense of breed (q.v.). (2) Said of a horse from a specific geographic area, as in Kentucky-bred.

bred horse *see* THOROUGHBRED

breech birth Also known as breech delivery; birth of a foal in which the foal's hindquarters (q.v.), instead of the front legs and nose, are presented first in the birth canal.

breech delivery *see* BREECH BIRTH

breeches Also spelled britches; previously, trousers reaching to or just below the knees and often tapered to fit closely; now, any snugly fitting riding pant made of natural and/or synthetic fabric that closes tightly at the ankle; generally worn with a top or knee-high boot (q.v.).

breeching Also known as britchin when used on farm horses; a broad leather band fitted around the haunches of the horse and attached either to the driving harness and shafts or directly to the saddle; supports the weight of brakeless, two-wheeled horse-drawn vehicles when pulling up or descending a hill, backing, and to prevent riding and pack saddles from slipping forward.

breeching body A driving term; that part of the breeching (q.v.) which rests against the body of the horse.

breed (1) The progeny or race from a particular stock or line of horses that, as a result of selective breeding, have certain distinguishable characteristics which are passed on through successive generations; generally resulting from known parents, the pedigree of which can be traced back a minimum of three generations; pedigrees are recorded in a stud book. (2) *see* COVER

breed class Any horse show class held for a specific horse breed.

breeder (1) One responsible for the selection of a sire (q.v.) to which a dam (q.v.) is mated; one who breeds horses. (2) One who owns a stud or stud farm where mares are bred. (3) The owner of a dam at the time of service unless the dam was under lease at the time of breeding. (4) *see* BROOD MARE

Breeders' Cup American Thoroughbred racing's year-end championship; consists of seven races – the Breeders' Cup Sprint (q.v.), Breeders' Cup Juvenile Fillies (q.v.), Breeders' Cup Distaff (q.v.), Breeders' Cup Mile (q.v.), Breeders' Cup Juvenile (q.v.), Breeders' Cup Turf (q.v.), and the Breeders' Cup Classic (q.v.) conducted on one day at a different racetrack each year; purses and awards total $10 million; the $250,000 Breeders' Cup Steeplechase (q.v.) was formerly (dropped in 1994) part of the Breeders' Cup, but was not conducted on the same day or necessarily the same track

Breeders' Cup Classic A 1-1/4 mile (2 km) race for three-year old horses and older first run in 1984; one of seven Thoroughbred year-end championship races run on one day in the United States; currently pays $3 million.

Breeders' Cup Day The single day per year on which the seven Breeders' Cup (q.v.) races are conducted in the United States.

Breeders' Cup Distaff A 1-1/8 mile (1.8 km) race for three-year olds and older, mares and fillies, first run in 1984; one of seven Thoroughbred year-end championship races run on one day in the United States.

Breeders' Cup Juvenile A 1-1/16 mile (1.6 km) race for two-year old horses first run in 1984; one of seven Thoroughbred year-end championship races run on one day in the United States.

Breeders' Cup Juvenile Fillies A 1-1/16 mile (1.6 km) race for two-year old fillies first run in 1984; one of seven Thoroughbred year-end championship races run in one day in the United States.

Breeders' Cup Mile A 1 mile (1.6 km) turf race for three-year old horses and older first run in 1984; one of seven Thoroughbred year-end championship races run on one day in the United States.

Breeders' Cup Sprint A six furlong race for three-year old horses and older first run in 1984; one of seven Thoroughbred year-end championship races run on one day in the United States.

Breeders' Cup Steeplechase A 2-5/8

mile (4.2 km) jump-race event for three-year old and older Thoroughbred horses in the United States; conducted over a turf course; a year-end Breeders' Cup (q.v.) event first run in 1986 and dropped, due to financial deficits, from the annual slate of racing events in 1994; was not conducted on Breeders' Cup Day (q.v.) or necessarily on the same track.

Breeders' Cup Turf A 1-1/2 mile (2.4 km) turf race for three-year old horses and older first run in 1984; one of seven Thoroughbred year-end championship races run in one day in the United States.

breeding (1) The quality of the bloodline achieved through careful and controlled selection of the dam (q.v.) and sire (q.v.). (2) The act of reproducing the species.

breeding boots Also known as covering boots; a padded felt boot, heavily reinforced with leather, strapped onto the hind feet of mares during natural cover (q.v.) to protect the stallion from damaging kicks.

breeding certificate Written verification signed by the stallion owner listing the name of the breeding stallion, the mare bred, the dates the breeding or breedings took place, or the period the mare was exposed to the stallion, in the case of pasture breeding.

breeding contract A binding agreement between the owners of the stallion and mare stating the amount of the payment due for breeding services and the contractual obligations of each party.

breeding fund A state fund established in the United States on a state-by-state basis to provide cash bonuses to horses bred within the state in which a fund is established.

breeding hobbles Also known as serving hobbles or mating hobbles; straps that encircle the hocks of the mare which prevent her from kicking the stallion during natural cover (q.v.); in another version, a rope is connected to a collar around the mare's neck, passed between her forelegs and attached to the hind pasterns.

breeding season The period during which males and females of a species demonstrate receptivity to mating.

breeding soundness evaluation of the mare An examination of a mare's breeding potential based on her history and a reproductive examination including estrus detection, visual examination of the perineum, rectal examination, examination by vaginal speculum, endometrial culture, endometrial biopsy, and cytology.

breeding soundness evaluation of the stallion An examination of the stallion's breeding potential based on his history and a reproductive examination including an evaluation of the sexual organs and semen collection.

breed type Also known as type; the ideal or standard of perfection for any breed (q.v.) as detailed in the appropriate stud book or in registration papers.

breeze (1) Also known as breezing; a racing term; to exercise the horse at a controlled and relaxed speed. (2) A racing term; a rider hired to exercise or breeze race horses.

breeze in A racing term; said of a horse who easily wins a race.

breezing *see* BREEZE no. 1

Breton A coldblood breed originating in Brittany, France more than 4,000 years ago; descended from native Brittany stock crossed with Norfolk Roadster, its descendant the Norfolk Trotter (q.v.), Ardennais (q.v.), Percheron (q.v.), and Boulonnais (q.v.); of three distinct morphological types: the Fast Heavy Draft Breton (q.v.), the Postier-Breton (q.v.), and the Corlay (q.v.); the coat is generally chestnut, but bay, gray, roan, and red roan also occur, black is not a breed color; has a well-proportioned head with a heavy jaw, broad forehead, short ears, flared nostrils, a short, broad, muscular and arched neck, short and straight back, broad loins, sloping croup and short and powerful legs with heavy joints; the tail is commonly docked; stands 15 to 16 hands and weighs 1,540 to 1,980 pounds (699–899 kgs); registered foals are branded on the left side of the neck with a cross surmounting a splayed, upturned V; has been used to improve other heavy draft breeds as well as heavy draft and farm work; is energetic, lively, and has great endurance.

Brett A horse-drawn vehicle; a transatlantic version of the European britzka (q.v.); had a shallow body hung on two elliptical springs in front and two elliptic and two cee springs behind, one forward-facing and one rear-facing passenger seat, and a folding hood which covered the forward seat; seated four passengers; drawn by two or more horses in pole gear (q.v.).

brewers dried grains Also known as brewers grains and erroneously as distillers grains; the dried extracted residue of barley malt, alone or in mixture with other cereal grains or grain products; high in protein and fiber and containing a digestible energy content equal to or higher than that of oats; may contain pulverized, dried, or spent hops; generally fed dry although may be fed wet if obtained fresh from the breweries and fed immediately.

brewers grains *see* BREWERS DRIED GRAINS

brewer's horse Heavy, shire-type horses used by the breweries to pull brewer's vans prior to the 1900s; usually stood between 17 and 18 hands.

brewers yeast A yeast, Saccharomyces, suitable for use as a ferment in the making of malt liquors; filtered from beer following the fermentation process; a good source of B-complex vitamins.

Breyerfest The largest show in the world for Breyer horses (q.v.) held every July in Lexington, Kentucky, USA; a four-day event for enthusiasts sponsored by Breyer Molding Company; includes performance horse, breed, and costume classes for models in original finish and remade as well as lectures by experts and hundreds of vendors selling everything for the enthusiast from tack to costuming and the limited edition Breyerfest model.

Breyer Horse Model horses made of plastic or porcelain noted for their realistic appearance; often modeled after live horses; manufactured since 1954 by Breyer Molding Company, are sold as toys, collected by hobbyists and shown at model horse shows, the largest being Breyerfest (q.v.).

brick wall A solid jumping obstacle consisting of faux brick blocks; a wall (q.v.).

bridesmaid A horse/rider combination placed second in a competition.

bridge jumper A racing term; a bettor (q.v.) who specializes in placing large show bets (q.v.) on odds-on favorite, short-priced horses

to show.

bridging the reins A method of holding the reins (q.v.); the right rein is run through the rider's right hand to the left and the left rein run through the left hand to the right; the reins overlap or "bridge" between the rider's hands with the rider holding both right and left reins in each hand.

bridle (1) Tack usually made of leather, or synthetic materials, placed on the horse's head and fitted over the ears to control the horse with or without a bit; consists of the headstall (q.v.), bit (q.v.), and reins (q.v.). (2) To put a bridle on.

bridle cheekpiece *see* CHEEKPIECE no. 2

bridled Said of a horse fitted with a bridle (q.v.).

bridle gate Also known as hunting gate and hand gate; a hunting term; any small gate, the height of a fence, wide enough to accommodate the passage of a horse and rider.

bridle hand A 16th and 17th-century term; the left hand; the reins were held in the left hand, to free the right to hold a weapon.

bridle head *see* HEADSTALL

bridle hook A fixture suspended at shoulder height from the ceiling or a cross bar, used to hold bridles prior to cleaning; consists of four or more J-shaped hooks sharing a common center stem.

bridle lame *see* UNEVEN

bridleless cutting A cutting term; to demonstrate the cow sense (q.v.) of a horse by cutting a cow(s) without the use of a bridle; weight, leg, and spur aids may be used.

bridle path (1) Also known as bridle trail; a path or road used only for riding horseback. (2) The area near the poll (q.v.) and just behind the ears on the crest of the neck across which the crown piece of the bridle passes; the mane is commonly clipped in this area.

bridles well *see* GOES WELL INTO THE BRIDLE

bridle wise Said of a horse trained to obey the aids of the bridle and bit.

bridle teeth *see* CANINE TEETH

bridle trail *see* BRIDLE PATH

bridling A predominantly English term used in the 18th through the 20th centuries; to render the head and neck light and flexible by teaching the horse to bend his neck at the poll and to relax his lower jaw; the lightness of the head and neck reacts on the shoulders and through them on the entire forehand.

bridoon Also spelt bradoon and formerly known as a flying trench; a light, jointed, usually narrow gaged, snaffle bit used in conjunction with a curb bit (q.v.) in a double bridle (q.v.); controlled by reins other than those attached to the curb; may be plain, twisted, egg-butt, or have a ring in the center.

bridoon rein The rein attached to the bridoon bit.

bright (1) Quick-witted or intelligent. (2) A cutting horse term; alert, as in "the horse is bright on the cow."

brindle Refers to hound coat color; tawny with streaked or spotted darker markings.

brisket *see* BREAST

Briskie *see* BRITZKA

britchin *see* BREECHING

Britchka *see* BRITZKA

British Driving Society, The Also known by the acronym BDS; an association founded in Great Britain 1957 to perpetuate interest in, and encourage and assist those involved with, driving horses and ponies; associated with the British Horse Society (q.v.).

British Equestrian Federation Also known by the acronym BEF; an organization established in 1972 which represents both the British Horse Society (q.v.) and the British Show Jumping Association (q.v.) in policy issues pertaining to the FEI (q.v.).

British Equine Veterinary Association Also known by the acronym BEVA; the governing body representing most veterinarians licensed in Great Britain.

British Field Sports Society An organi-

zation founded in 1930 in Great Britain to encourage interest in all equine field sports.

British Horse Society, The Also known by the acronym BHS; an organization founded in Great Britain in 1947 by an amalgamation of the National Horse Association of Great Britain and The Institute of the Horse and Pony Club, Ltd.; headquartered in London, England, is responsible for the organization and promotion of all horse-related activities in Great Britain as well as the regulation of riding instructor standards.

British Horse Society Assistant Instructor Also known by the acronym BHSAI; an assistant riding instructor (q.v.) certified by the British Horse Society (q.v.).

British Horse Society Instructor Also known by the acronym BHSI; a riding instructor (q.v.) certified by the British Horse Society (q.v.).

British Percheron Horse Society, The An organization founded in Great Britain in 1919 to establish and maintain the purity of the Percheron (q.v.) in Great Britain.

British Racehorse, The An illustrated journal devoted to the bloodstock (q.v.) industry in Great Britain and Ireland; established in 1949 by a resolution of The Thoroughbred Breeders' Association (q.v.).

British Riding Club, The An organization founded in Great Britain in 1936 to improve training of the riding horse.

British Show Hack and Cob Association An organization founded in 1938 in Great Britain to further interest in riding hacks and cobs (q.v.).

British Show Jumping Association An organization founded in 1923 in Great Britain to regulate all show jumping activites conducted there.

British Show Pony Society An organization founded in Great Britain in 1949 to regulate showing of children's riding ponies.

British Spotted Horse A type rather than a breed; a British-bred horse of mixed lineage who carries the spotting gene common in such breeds as the Appaloosa (q.v.) and Knabstup (q.v.); bred for coat pattern rather than conformation.

British Spotted Horse Society An organization founded in Great Britain in 1947 to promote the interests of the riding-type British Spotted Horse (q.v.).

British Thoroughbred *see* THOROUGHBRED

Britschka *see* BRITZKA

brittle feet *see* BRITTLE HOOVES

brittle hooves Also known as brittle feet; abnormally dry hooves which are prone to breaking due to a dry condition of the horn; associated with dry air and lack of moisture in the soil.

Britzka Also known as britchka, britzska, britzschka, britschka or briskie; originally an open, four-wheeled, horse-drawn traveling wagon popular in Poland and Eastern Europe; developed into a traveling carriage in Austria in 1818; later versions had a rearward platform with a rumble seat large enough to accommodate three carriage servants and a straight rather than a curved bottom line; the interior could be converted to a sleeping compartment for one or two persons lying at full length; generally hung on cee-springs; drawn by four or six horses and driven by a coachman (q.v.), although it was later postillion controlled (q.v.).

Britzschka *see* BRITZKA

Britzska *see* BRITZKA

broad bran *see* BRAN

brockamore *see* MECHANICAL HACKAMORE

brocket Also known as knobbler or knobbler; a two-year-old male deer.

broke Tamed and trained, as in a horse.

broken amble *see* RACK

broken canter *see* DISUNITED CANTER

broken crest A heavy neck which breaks over and falls to one side.

broken down Said of a horse in less than perfect physical condition due to injury, trauma, or overuse.

broken kneed Said of a horse having knees scarred by injury.

broken knees The knees of the horse when scared, indicating he has fallen or had some type of injury.

broken wind *see* CHRONIC OBSTRUCTIVE PULMONARY DISEASE

brokk One of five gaits of the Icelandic Horse (q.v.); a trot (q.v.) used when traversing rough country.

bromegrass hay Cut and dried grass hay generally made from the smooth variety of bromegrass; hardy and grown in the Central Plains of the United States; frequently mixed with legumes (q.v.) for improved palatability, yield, and quality; contains a digestible protein content ranging from approximately 6.2 percent to 1.8 percent and a crude fiber content ranging from 34.2 to 38.5 percent.

bronc *see* BRONCO

bronc buster Also known as buster, bronco buster, bronc twister, bronc peeler, or bronc snapper; one who breaks or trains broncos (q.v.).

bronc busting The handling and breaking of broncs (q.v.) so they may be ridden.

bronc chaps Chaps (q.v.), generally brightly colored, loosely fitted and secured only to mid thigh so that the lower leg portion may move freely; makes the spurring of the rider look wilder and the bucking of the horse harder than it is.

bronchioles Small, tubular air passages in the lungs.

bronchitis A respiratory condition characterized by inflammation of the bronchial tubes and forced expiration.

broncho *see* BRONCO

bronchoconstriction A narrowing of the smaller airways of the lungs triggered by the release of histamines (q.v.).

bronchodilator Any substance that, when inhaled, causes the air passages of the lungs to widen.

bronchospasm Abnormal involuntary contraction of the muscles surrounding the bronchioles (q.v.).

bronco Also known as bronc and spelled broncho and bronk; an unbroken or imperfectly broken wild horse; Spanish for rough and rude.

bronco buster *see* BRONC BUSTER

bronc peeler *see* BRONC BUSTER

bronc rider One who rides wild, unbroken horses usually in a rodeo event.

bronc riding Also known as buck jumping; a rodeo event in which a competitor rides a bareback bronco fitted with a wide leather band strapped circumferentially around his body just behind the shoulder to which a leather hand hold protrudes and onto which the rider secures his grip.

bronc saddle A saddle used in breaking horses.

bronc snapper *see* BRONC BUSTER

bronc twister *see* BRONC BUSTER

bronk *see* BRONCO

broodmare A mare who has previously foaled and is expected to continue to have foals; kept primarily for breeding purposes.

broodmare sire *see* DAM SIRE

broomtail (1) *see* SWITCH TAIL. (2) Also known as broomstock; any small horse, such as some mustangs (q.v.), not considered worth the effort to break (q.v.).

Brotherhood of Working Farriers Association Also known by the acronym BWFA; an organization of farriers founded in the United States in 1989.

brothers Also known as full brothers or own brothers; a relationship of male horses by the same sire (q.v.) and out of the same dam (q.v.).

brothers in blood Said of male horses by the same sire out of full sisters, or by full brothers out of the same dam.

Brougham Also known as a fly, fly-by-night, and from the mid-19th century on, as a small station cab; a small, four-wheeled, horse-drawn town carriage first built around 1839; inspired if not actually designed by Lord Brougham, a statesman of the early 19th century, for whom it was named; seated two forward-facing passengers, was low-slung, fully paneled and had an upholstered and fully enclosed body fitted with windows; popular well into the 1920s; of two main types: Peter's Brougham (q.v.) and Barker Brougham (q.v.).

browband Also known, in driving terms, as front; that part of the bridle that lies flat across the forehead below the ears and above the eyes of the horse, attaches to the headstall (q.v.) by the cheekpieces (q.v.) and passes through loops on either side of the browband on both sides; prevents the headstall (q.v.) from slipping backwards on the neck.

brown Refers to coat color; having the color of coffee or chocolate, a combination of red, black, and yellow without red tones and having black points; variations include dark brown (q.v.), medium brown, light brown (q.v.), and seal brown (q.v.).

brown saddler A saddle maker specializing in saddles, bridles, etc., as opposed to a black saddler (q.v.).

Bruce Lowe System *see* BRUCE LOWE FIGURE SYSTEM

Bruce Lowe Figure System Also known as the Bruce Lowe System or Lowe Figure System; a method of identifying racing Thoroughbred (q.v.) families; each family is identified by number according to the female ancestor from which it descended; all Thoroughbred progeny were traced back to 43 foundation mares (q.v.) and were allotted numbers according to the number of times their descendants won classic (q.v.) races; developed by Australian Bruce Lowe in the early 20th century.

bruise (1) To injure by a blow or pressure without laceration. (2) A discoloration due to bruising.

bruised sole A contusion of the foot, without laceration, resulting from stones, irregular ground, or other trauma such as poor shoeing which can predispose a horse to bruising; may or may not be associated with lameness.

Brumby A wild horse indigenous to Australia descended from domestic horses turned loose on the ranges during the mid-19th century following the gold rush; is hardy and unrefined, stands approximately 15 hands, and has a rather heavy head, short back, sturdy legs, and a coat of any color; in the 1960s, due to organized culling of the wild herds, was brought close to extinction; the name derived from the aboriginal word baroomby meaning wild.

Brumby runner An Australian bush horseman who chases, captures, and tames Brumbies (q.v.).

brush (1) To run a horse at top speed over a short distance. (2) A hunting term; the tail of a fox. (3) A hand-held instrument consisting of natural or synthetic bristles or hair set in an attached handle of wood, plastic, or leather used for removing dirt or dust, polishing or smoothing, or applying cream, paint, or conditioner. (4) A hunter jumper term; said of a horse when jumping who lightly touches a rail or plank, but does not drop it. (5) A racing term; said of two horses that slightly touch or collide while running. (6) A harness racing term; the brief peak(s) of speed reached by a horse in a race or training mile.

brush box An artificial jumping obstacle consisting of brushwood or other suitable hedging material grown in a planter box.

brush boots *see* BRUSHING BOOTS

brush fence A jumping obstacle (q.v.), either natural or artificial, consisting of brush wood or some other suitable hedging material.

brushing Said of a horse in motion in which one limb lightly strikes another as in forging (q.v.) or interfering (q.v.).

brushing boots Also known as brush boots or splint boots; a protective covering of the front legs of the horse made of felt, leather, or synthetic materials used to protect the fetlock joint and cannon bone against brushing (q.v.) or knocks from the shoe or hoof of another leg when the horse is in action.

brushing ring boot *see* FETLOCK RING BOOT

bubble A cutting term; the imaginary area or space surrounding a cow or herd of cattle in which they feel secure; size is determined by how far a cutter can penetrate the herd before it reacts to his presence; the fresher the cattle the larger the bubble; the direction and speed of a cow's movements can be influenced by the position of the cutter's horse near the edge of the bubble.

Bucephalus The horse of Alexander the Great; could not be broken or ridden by anyone but Alexander; died in 326 BC and was buried by the Jhelum River, India.

buck (1) Action of the horse when in good spirit or when intending to unseat his rider; a series of acrobatic jumps in which the horse springs with a quick leap, dropping its head and arching its back and simultaneously kicking with its hind legs and landing on stiffened forelegs; may be considered a vice. (2) The lower part of the body of a horse-drawn vehicle. (3) Also known as stag in parts of Europe and Great Britain; the male of the deer, antelope, rabbit, or the hare. (4) *see* BUCKED

buckaroo Also known as vaquero and spelled buckeroo; a cowboy; a bronco (q.v.) buster; a herder of cattle.

buckboard A four-wheeled, open-passenger, horse-drawn vehicle popular in the United States from 1826 through the 1900s in which a long flexible board or frame was fastened to the axle without the use of springs; had one or two rows of crosswise seating, was drawn by a single horse or pair, and was generally driven by a coachman from a box (q.v.).

bucked Also known as buck; said of a horse suffering from bucked shins (q.v.), "the young thoroughbred bucked."

bucked knees *see* FORWARD DEVIATION OF THE CARPAL JOINTS

bucked shins Also known as shinbuck or sore shins; a temporary, usually bilateral, unsoundness involving the horse's forelimbs resulting from skeletal immaturity and concussion; associated with the stretching or tearing of the overlying periosteum (q.v.) of the large metacarpal (cannon bone) or, less frequently, the small metatarsal bone and characterized by a warm, painful swelling over the front of the bones, initial lameness, and a shortened stride; bone abnormality is not common although saucer fractures (q.v.) are sometimes seen; confined almost chiefly to young Thoroughbreds (q.v.) in training or racing, although it is possible for older horses to buck (q.v.); occurs more commonly in the United States than other countries, probably due to different training and racing conditions.

buckeroo *see* BUCKAROO

bucket (1) A cylindrical container for scooping up or holding liquids or solids. (2) To ride hard, as a horse.

buck eye An antiquated term; a prominent eye.

buckhound A hound used by hunters to pursue deer.

bucking Said of a horse who performs more than one buck (q.v.) in a row, usually until either the rider is unseated or the horse tires; may be considered a vice.

buck itself out Said of a horse who has stopped bucking due to exhaustion or because it cannot unseat the rider.

buckjumping (1) The act of a bucking (q.v.) horse whereby he arches his back, lowers his head, and jumps into the air off of all four legs at once; repeated with great rapidity. (2) *see* BRONC RIDING

buck-kneed Said of a horse displaying forward deviation of the carpal joints (q.v.).

buckle (1) A clasp consisting of a rectangular or curved rim with a tongue and catch; used to fasten together two loose ends. (2) To fasten or join together with a buckle.

buckle guard Also known as buckle safe; any piece of shaped leather incorporated into the tack between a buckle and the horse to prevent the buckle from rubbing on the horse's hide.

buckle safe *see* BUCKLE GUARD

buck line A line attached to the draw chain used in multiple draft hitches (q.v.) to keep a horse from getting ahead of his mate.

buckskin Refers to coat color; a type of dun (q.v.) having a grayish-brown yellow coat, black points, and a head of a similar, but darker color than the body; wither and dorsal stripes (q.v.) and stripes over the knees and hocks may occur; variations include zebra dun (q.v.), dusty buckskin (q.v.), smutty buckskin (q.v.), and silver buckskin (q.v.).

budget A leather storage box attached to the fore-carriage of a horse-drawn vehicle when used for out-of-town travel.

Budenny *see* BUDYONNY

Budonny *SEE* BUDYONNY

Budyonny Also known as Budonny, Budenny, or Budyonovsky; a Russian warmblood developed at a military stud in Rostov in the 1930s by Marshal Budyonny who intended to create a military mount by putting Thoroughbred (q.v.) stallions to Don (q.v.) mares with the best of the resulting progeny interbred; an officially recognized breed since 1948; has excellent conformation, a strong, close-coupled body which is deep through the girth, strong and has generously boned legs, an elegant head, long neck, and stands 15.1 to 16 hands; 80 percent of the breed have a chestnut coat with a rich golden sheen, although bays and grays also occur; is calm, sensible, and has great stamina; rigorously tested over long distances and on the track; excels at steeplechasing and, due to its jumping ability, performs well as an all-round sport and riding horse.

Budyonovsky BUDYONNY

buffer *see* CLINCH CUTTER

bug *see* APPRENTICE JOCKEY

bug boy *see* APPRENTICE JOCKEY

buggie *see* BUGGY AND AMERICAN BUGGY

buggy (1) Also spelled buggie and known as a hooded gig; a light, English-type, horse-drawn vehicle of the gig (q.v.) type having curved shafts and a folding head (q.v.); drawn by a single horse; popularized in the early 19th century. (2) *see* AMERICAN BUGGY. (3) *see* HOODED GIG

bulbs *see* HEEL BULBS

bull (1) *see* STALLION. (2) *see* GRUNTER

bulla A large blister (q.v.).

bull dog (1) Refers to conformation type; a small horse having huge, muscled quarters, a short back and an over-muscled front end between the shoulders; used to describe conformation in such breeds as Quarter Horses (q.v.) and Pintos (q.v.). (2) Harness racing slang; a stayer (q.v.). 3) *see* BULL DOG QUARTER HORSE

bull-dog bite *see* UNDER-SHOT JAW

bulldogger *See* STEER WRESTLER

bulldogging *see* STEER WRESTLING.

bulldogging A horse used for steer wrestling (q.v.).

bull dog Quarter Horse Also known as bull dog; a Quarter Horse (q.v.) conformation type; a small horse having huge, muscled quarters, a short back, and an over-muscled front end between the shoulders which is more massive than a standard Quarter Horse.

bullfinch A jumping obstacle; a thick, overgrown live hedge which, due to the height, must be jumped through, not over; the hedge may be placed on top of a small bank with a ditch on either the take off or landing side; of two types: black bullfinch (q.v.) and hairy bullfinch (q.v.).

bullet work Also known as black-letter work; a racing term; the best workout time clocked by a horse for a particular distance on a given day at a track; from the printer's "bullet" that precedes the time of the workout in the daily listings.

bull neck Said of the horse's neck when short, thick and difficult to flex.

bull nose foot *see* DUBBED

bull pen (1) Also known as a round pen; an enclosed area at least 30 feet (9 m) in diameter, with high, solid walls more than 8 feet (2.6 m) tall, in which a horse can be worked or trained. (2) An auction ring. (3) Also known as a bull ring; an American racing term; a small racetrack usually less than 1 mile (1.6 km) in length with sharp turns.

bull riding A standard rodeo event, in which the contestant rides a bull equipped only with a rope wrapped around its body behind the shoulder and over the withers (q.v.); the rider may hold onto this rope with only one hand, the other hand held up in "high salute" until the ride is completed.

bullring *see* BULL PEN no. 3

bump A polo term; a movement in which one player rides into, or bumps, another to spoil his shot on the ball; the angle of the collision should not exceed 45 degrees, although the faster the horse of the player performing the bump is traveling, the smaller this angle should be.

bumper (1) A racing term; an amateur rider. (2) A racing term; a race for amateur riders.

bump the bit A cutting term; said of the rider; to inadvertently pull back with one or both reins just enough to make the horse feel and react to the bit; may be caused by holding the reins unevenly or too tightly.

burner A small piece of rawhide or leather laced onto the honda of a lariat (q.v.) which prevents the honda from wearing out.

Burford saddle Previously known as a Morocco saddle; a military saddle used in the first half of the 17th century.

Burghley An area in England near Stamford in Lincolnshire which is the home of the Burghley Horse Trials (q.v.).

Burghley Horse Trials The principal autumn three-day event held annually in Burghley, Britain since 1961.

burning scent Also known as screaming scent, red hot scent, or blazing scent; a hunting term; said of the scent of the quarry (q.v.) when so strong that the hounds are able to pursue the line without hesitation.

burr *see* BIT BURR

burro A Spanish term; an ass (q.v.).

bursa A sac or sac-like cavity containing synovial fluid (q.v.) situated over bony prominences or between tendons, which acts as a pad or cushion.

bursatii *see* CUTANEOUS HABRONEMIASIS

bursitis Inflammation of a bursa (q.v.) characterized by rapid swelling due to an accumulation of synovial fluid, local heat, and pain; may be location specific as in capped hocks (q.v.), capped elbow (q.v.), shoe-boil, or navicular bursitis.

burst A hunting term; said of the hounds (q.v.); a fast, quick run on a fox.

bury A jumping term; said of a rider who rides his horse too close to the fence to jump it from the proper distance.

bush track A racing term; in the United States, an unofficial race meeting.

Butazolidin A brand name for phenylbutazone (q.v.).

Butazone A brand name for phenylbutazone (q.v.).

butcher boots Black hunt boots (q.v.) without tops.

bute *see* PHENYLBUTAZONE

butteri Mounted cattlemen from the Maremma regions of Tuscany and Latium, Italy, who commonly used the Maremmana (q.v.) for light draft and as an all purpose riding horse.

butteris An ancient farrier tool used for trimming hooves; a long, sharp chisel pushed by means of the farrier's shoulder; although still used in some parts of the world, it has not been in use in the United States since the 1930s.

butterfly bars *see* JUMPED-IN BARS

buttermilk horse *see* PALOMINO

buttermilk roan *see* SABINO

buttress foot *see* PYRAMIDAL DISEASE

buxton bit A heavy harness curb (q.v.) bit having curved cheeks with two slots for the reins, one halfway down the cheek and one at the bottom; the lower ends of the cheeks are connected by a narrow bar to prevent the lead reins from becoming caught under the bit; mouthpiece size varies considerably.

buy-back Also known as charge-back; a racing term; said of a horse put through public auction who did not reach his reserve (q.v.) set by the consignor and so was retained.

Buzkashi Also known as dragging the goat; a rudimentary form of mounted rugby, the object being to pick up a stuffed goat skin from the ground without dismounting, tuck it under the knee, gallop around a far goal post and return to the circle; the skin of a freshly killed goat is stuffed with sand, sewn up, and left to soak in water overnight, and may weigh as much as 66 to 88 pounds (30–40 kg); may be played by several teams consisting of 25 or more players; each participant carries a whip with a short wooden handle with which they may strike an opponent, but not his mount; the size of the playing field is not limited in size and obstacles such as hills and rocks are looked upon with favor; two single goal posts are positioned approximately 1/2 mile (800 m) apart about which are drawn circles of about 50 yards (46 m) in diameter; the game is started by an umpire who throws the goat (now, often a goat-skin ball is used) into the middle of the pack; umpires decide which team wins; a contraction of buz meaning goat, and kashidan meaning to pull; its origins are uncertain, although it is still played in central Asia.

buzzer A battery-powered vibrator or other electric-shock device used to frighten a horse into running faster or jumping; is illegal on the track or in the show ring, but is often used as a training device.

BVMS The acronym for Bachelor of Veterinary Medicine & Surgery.

BVSc The acronym for Bachelor of Veterinary Science.

BWFA The acronym for Brotherhood of Working Farriers Association.

by Also known as sired by; a foal is said to be "by" its sire and "out" of its dam.

bye day A hunting term; an extra hunt meeting held by a Hunt (q.v.) during the Christmas holiday or to make up for hunt days lost due to bad weather.

Byerley Turk An Arab (q.v.) stallion, one of the three founding sires of the English Thoroughbred (q.v.), who was captured from the Turks at the siege of Budapest and brought back to England by Captain Byerley for which it was named; was never raced; all Thoroughbreds (q.v.) in the world today trace their ancestry in direct male line to this horse, the Godolphin

Arab (q.v.), or Darley Arabian (q.v.).

by the rack A betting term; said of a bettor, to purchase every possible daily-double (q.v.) or other combination ticket.

C

CAA The acronym for the Carriage Association of America (q.v.).

cab A horse-drawn, two-wheeled coach brought to London, England from Italy, via Paris, during the early 19th century; frequently used for public hire; the first rival of the Hackney coaches; from the 1820s on, developed in many two- and four-wheeled versions; by the 1860s, the primary types included the four-wheeled Growler (q.v.), driven from a box seat, and the two-wheeled Hansom (q.v.) driven from a rearward skeleton seat situated at roof level; later types were fitted with taximeters, for recording distances and fares, from which the name taxi derives; Derived from cabriolet, meaning two-wheeled coach.

caballero A Spanish term; a cowboy (q.v.).

caballo A Spanish term; a horse (q.v.).

Caballo Chileno *see* CHILENO

Caballo Peruano de Paso *see* PERUVIAN PASO

cabbage Any of various cultivated varieties of the cruciferous plant, *Brassica oleracea*, especially one of the varieties with a short stem and leaves formed into a compact, edible head; in a wider sense includes such plants as the cauliflower, Brussels sprouts, kale, etc.; suitable as horse feed.

cable link Also known as cable-link snaffle; a snaffle bit (q.v.) in which the mouthpiece consists of a rough-link chain.

cable-link snaffle *see* CABLE LINK

Cabriole *see* CABRIOLET

Cabriolet Also known as cabriole; a two-wheeled, open, boxless, horse-drawn carriage with a shell-shaped body mounted high above road level, with flexible shafts, a folding hood, and either whip or cee-spring suspension originating in the 1700s; in 19th-century England, it was used by the wealthy class; usually drawn by a powerful coach horse of a hunter type, and driven by the owner with a short youth or mature short man, standing on a rearward platform; from the French version of the Italian capriolo meaning kid or young goat as related to the skipping or swaying movements of the vehicle.

Cachar Polo Club A polo club found in Cachar, India in 1859; considered the oldest polo club in existence.

cactus cloth A coarsely woven cloth used to rub out sweat marks from the horse's coat and to stimulate blood flow.

cad (1) English slang; a conductor of London's early horse buses; noted for their rough demeanor. (2) A 19th-century term; a man who worked in the stables which supplied post-horses (q.v.); looked after the horses, washed the Post Chaises (q.v.), called the post-boys (q.v.) at night when a chaise was needed for hire, lit the lamps, and occasionally rode the post chaise.

cade An English term; a bottle-raised foal.

cadence The quality of the horse's pace demonstrating rhythm and impulsion; elastic steps.

cadenettes Curls that form in the long ear hair of the Poitou ass (q.v.).

Cadre Noir A select group of horsemen of the French Cavalry School at Saumur (q.v.) who practice High School (q.v.) riding in accordance with the French tradition of classical equitation (q.v.); became the instructor's corps for the school at Saumur; the name means black frame which was derived from the distinctive uniform these horsemen wear: a black three-pointed hat, black high-neck tunic, and white or black breeches.

CAF I The acronym for Certified Apprentice Farrier, Level One (q.v.).

CAF II The acronym for Certified Apprentice Farrier, Level Two (q.v.).

Café-au-Lait *see* PALOMINO

cala One of nine scored events in a charreada (q.v.); an individual reining competition for charros (q.v.).

Calabrese A warmblood indigenous to the district of Calabria, Italy; originally of Arab (q.v.) derivation, it was later crossed with Andalusian (q.v.) and presently Thoroughbred (q.v.) blood; Oriental blood is periodically reintroduced to perpetuate breed characteristics; stands 16 to 16.2 hands, has a brown, black, bay, chestnut, or gray coat, a well-formed, although slightly convex head, prominent withers, slanted croup, short loins, and is short-coupled; used for riding.

calash *see* CALECHE

calcification The deposition of calcium salts in degenerating muscle tissue.

calcium A soft, metallic, white chemical element which, in conjunction with phosphorus (q.v.), comprises 75 percent of the minerals in the horse's body and approximately 90 percent of the minerals in the skeleton; is required for bone mineralization including bone formation, growth, maintenance, and repair; required for normal muscular activity, blood clotting, release of hormones, and enzyme activation; the dietary requirement is much greater during early growth of the foal than for maintenance of the mature horse, is appreciably higher in the final stages of pregnancy and during lactation, and is up to 50 percent higher for aged horses than for the maintenance of younger horses; work does not increase calcium requirements as a proportion of the diet; an improper calcium-phosphorus ratio (q.v.) may result in serious diseases or physical problems such as osteomalacia, osteoporosis, osteofibrosis, crooked or enlarged joints or weakening of the bones, shifting lameness, especially connected with the hocks, and rickets; first added routinely to commercial horse feeds manufactured in the United States in the mid 1930s; excess levels can interfere with absorption of trace minerals such as zinc (q.v.), while excessive zinc, iron (q.v.), and/or manganese (q.v.) can disrupt calcium and phosphorus absorption.

calcium blood level The amount of the mineral calcium (q.v.) carried in the blood.

calcium carbonate A colorless, crystal or gray powder occurring naturally in chalk, calcite, limestone, and marble; used as an antacid and protectant in the treatment of diarrhea.

calcium-phosphorus ratio The amount of calcium (q.v.) compared to phosphorus (q.v.) in the horse's diet; the average optimal ratio in the feed is 1.1 up to 1.5 to 1; if the ratio is higher than 1.5 to 1, phosphorus is either added to the feed or pastures.

calculator A racing term; a clerk responsible for computing pari-mutuel (q.v.) odds.

calcutta A gambling option utlized for some western and/or English performance events; each exhibitor is given a number which is auctioned off to the highest bidding spectator; the bet pays places 1-6 and in some cases 10th with the amount of the payoff contingent on the type of event and/or if there is any added money (q.v.).

Calèche Also spelled Calash and in Germany, kalesch; (1) A two-wheeled, vehicle of the chaise or gig type drawn by a single horse; generally hooded, driven from a narrow seat above the dashboard, and hung on side and cee-springs. (2) A horse-drawn vehicle; a development of the four-wheeled barouche (q.v.) or German wagon, but with extra seating and improved suspension; one of the first vehicles to be equipped with springs.

Calesa A two-wheeled, horse-drawn passenger cart or heavy gig used in the Philippines from the mid-1800s through the 1940s; hung on semi-elliptical springs, drawn by a single horse, and driven by a coachman seated on the rear of the vehicle.

calesh The folding top on a horse-drawn carriage (q.v.).

Calesso A two-wheeled, horse-drawn, hooded gig, popular in Italy from the late 1700s through the early 1900s; drawn by one horse in shafts and a second horse harnessed along side, but outside the shaft.

calf (1) A stag (q.v.), hind (q.v.), or cow in its first year. (2) *see* GASKIN

calf horse Any horse from which a rider ropes a calf.

calf-knees *see* BACKWARD DEVIATION OF THE CARPAL JOINTS

calf-roping: (1) A standard rodeo event in which a mounted rider lassoes a calf using a lariat (q.v.), dismounts quickly, and ties the calf by three legs with a piggin string (q.v.). (2) Said of a cowboy (q.v.) or ranch hand who ropes a cow using a lariat (q.v.).

calico paint *see* SABINO

Caligula *see* INCITATUS

calk Also known as caulk, calkin, caulkin, cawk, sticker, cork, or mud sticker; a cleat or grip formed on the heels and sometimes the toes of horse shoes to increase traction, alter movement, or adjust stance; used as early as the 10th century, now largely replaced by studs (q.v.).

calkin *see* CALK

calking An injury such as a nick, cut, or bruise to the coronary band (q.v.) caused by the horseshoe; most common in horses whose shoes have calks (q.v.) or in rough-shod (q.v.) horses.

calking boot *see* STABLE BOOT

call (1) A racing term; the stage of a race at which the running positions are recorded, e.g., quarter-mile call. (2) A racing term; to describe a race to the audience.

calling A polo term; said of the team captain (q.v.) or any team member who calls out instructions to the player in control of the ball, e.g., turn back, back-hander (q.v.), mine, etc.

calling the odds *see* CALL OVER

call of the card *see* CALL OVER

call over Also known as call of the card and calling the odds; a racing term; to name the horses in a race and give the latest betting odds on each.

calorie The amount of heat required to raise the temperature of one gram of water one degree centigrade; now used by the National Research Council as a method of describing food energy values.

Calorie Also known as kilocalorie; the equivalent of one thousand calories (q.v.).

Camargue Also known as Camargue pony, Camargue horse, or white horse of the sea; a breed indigenous to the salt-marsh delta of the Rhône, in the Camargue area of Southern France; thought to have descended from the prehistoric horse of Solutré the origins of

which date to around 20,000 BC; in the 19th century received infusions of Arab (q.v.), Thoroughbred (q.v.), Anglo-Arab (q.v.), and Postier-Breton (q.v.) blood, but this did not result in modifications to type; lives in the wild and is used by the Gardiens (q.v.); risked extinction in the mid 20th century; has had its own breed registry since 1967; develops slowly and is not full-grown until it is five to seven years old, stands 13.1 to 14.2 hands, rarely exceeding 15 hands, and usually has a white or light gray coat, although bay and brown occur very rarely; foals are born black, dark gray or brown, but their coat lightens with age; has a large head, with pronounced jaws, short, broad ears, a short neck which is thick at the base, straight back, and long loins; noted for its depth of girth; the mane is full and shaggy; is firey, independent, and courageous; the action is peculiar to the breed, having an active, high-stepping, and long-strided walk, a jarring and rarely used trot, and a free gallop and canter; branded on the left hind hip; used for riding and packing.

Camargue pony *see* CAMARGUE

Camargue horse *see* CAMARGUE

Cambridge mouth A bit in which the mouthpiece (q.v.) is slightly ported and roughed on only one side.

camera patrol A racing term; equipment used to film a race while in progress.

campagne school Elementary dressage (q.v.).

camp drafting An Australian rodeo contest in which a rider separates a bull from the herd and drives it at a gallop around a course marked with straight poles.

camped in front A conformation defect in which the entire forelimb, from the body to the ground, is too far forward when viewed from the side; may also be present in such conditions as laminitis (q.v.) and bilateral navicular disease (q.v.).

camped behind A conformation defect in which the entire hind limb is placed too far backward when viewed from the side; a perpendicular line dropped from the hip joint would hit at the toe instead of halfway between the toe and heel; often associated with upright pasterns behind.

camphor A whitish, translucent, volatile, and aromatic crystalline substance obtained chiefly from the tree *Cinnamomum camphora*, the camphor tree; used as an irritant, stimulant, and a pain reliever when applied to areas of inflammation, sprains, etc.; is a mild blister (q.v.) and a rubefacient (q.v.).

Campolino One of three types of Criollo (q.v.) found in Brazil, the other two being the Criollo of Rio Grande do Sul (q.v.) and the Mangalarga (q.v.); descended from Andalusian stock brought to South America by the conquistadors in the 16th century; similar to the Mangalarga but with a heavier frame and more bone; stands 14.3 to 15.4 hands and is used for riding and light farm work.

camp wagon *see* CHUCK WAGON

Canadian bars *see* WHIP-ACROSS BARS

Canadian Cutting Horse The Canadian equivalent of the American Quarter Horse (q.v.) from which it descended and closely resembles in both physical appearance and temperament; a warmblood standing between 15.2 and 16.1 hands; is intelligent, fast, and agile; any coat color is acceptable.

Canadian Mounted Police, The Royal Also known as The Mounties or Mounties; the famous mounted police force of Canada; founded in 1873.

Canadian Pacer An easy gaited horse breed indigenous to Canada during the period 1800 to 1840; believed to have been Narragansett Pacers (q.v.), some perhaps having crosses to French stock; Tom Hal, Copperbottom, and Davy Crockett were three of the original 17 foundation sires of the American Saddlebred (q.v.).

Caned Whiskey A light, one-horse chaise popular in the late 18th and early 19th centuries; hung on shallow, sideways platform springs, was seldom headed, frequently lacked a dashboard, seated either one or two passengers, and had canework covered bodywork; so named because it could whisk over the ground at great speed.

canine (1) The singular of canines. (2) Of or like a dog; pertaining to or characteristic of dogs.

canines *see* CANINE TEETH

canine teeth Also known as canines, bridle teeth, or tush; small pointed teeth (q.v.) located one on each side, top and bottom, in the interdental space between the third incisor and second premolar of the horse's mouth; four appear in the male horse at age five or those horses cut (q.v.) after puberty, with two to four appearing in five-year-old males who were cut before the onset of puberty; two small vestigial lower canines may appear on mares.

canker A chronic softening of the horn-producing tissues of the foot, involving the frog and the sole in one or all four feet, although most commonly the hind feet; primarily a disease of heavy draft horses, although it is found in light horses as well; is frequently well advanced before detection; the frog may appear to be intact, but has a ragged, oiled appearance; the horn tissue of the frog loosens easily, revealing the swollen, foul-smelling corium; the disease may extend to the sole and to the hoof wall which is what differentiates it from thrush (q.v.); treatment must be radical and intensive.

cannon (1) *see* CHEEK no. 1. (2) *see* CANNON BONE

cannon bone Also known as cannon, shin, large metacarpal bone, or large metacarpal; the principal bone of the foreleg located between the knee and the pastern joint; the only bone in the body of the horse which has attained its full length at birth and will not grow during the life of the horse; the circumference just below the knee is often used as a measurement of bone (q.v.); the corresponding bone in the hind leg is known as the shank (q.v.).

canola meal A meal bi-product derived from varieties of rapeseed (q.v.) containing less than three milligrams of glucosinotate per gram of seed.

canteen A small vessel or flask, as of tin, used by soldiers and others for carrying water and other liquids for drinking; from the Spanish cantina (q.v.).

canter A rocking, three-beat pace or gait in which the horse's hooves strike the ground in the following order: near hind, near fore and off hind together, off fore or off hind, off fore, and near hind together, near fore; there is a moment of suspension when all four legs are in the air before the sequence begins again; of a number of types including broken canter (q.v.), collected canter (q.v.), cross canter (q.v.), counter canter (q.v.), disunited canter (q.v.), extended canter (q.v.), false canter (q.v.), flat canter (q.v.), medium canter (q.v.), and working canter (q.v.).

canter, change of the leg *see* FLYING CHANGE

canter left Said of a horse working at the canter (q.v.) when he leads with his left leg or near foreleg (q.v.).

canter right Said of a horse working at the canter (q.v.) when he leads with his right or off side foreleg (q.v.).

cantina (1) A Spanish term popularized in the American southwest from which the term canteen (q.v.) derived; a pouch or bag hung on a saddle used to carry water. (2) An establishment where alcohol is sold; a saloon.

cantle The protuberant afterpart or rear bow of the saddle located behind and perpendicular to the seat.

cantle-boarding A rodeo term; said of a bronc rider (q.v.) who spurs his horse so far back that his spurs (q.v.) strike the cantle (q.v.) of the saddle.

Canute's Forest Law A law proclaimed in England in 1016 to protect and improve New Forest Pony (q.v.) stock.

cap (1) Also known as cap fee or capping fee; a hunting term; the fee payable by a visitor, who is not a member of a Hunt (q.v.), to participate in a day of hunting; historically visitors paid in silver dropped into the hunt cap (q.v.) of the hunt Secretary (q.v.). (2) A driving term; that part of the harness which extends upwards in front of the top hame strap (q.v.). (3) *see* HUNT CAP

caparison (1) Ornamental covering for a horse. (2) Decorative trappings and harness.

cap case A large trunk attached to the rear body of a horse-drawn traveling coach.

cap curb *see* JODHPUR CURB

cape (1) A driving term; a waterproof garment worn over the coachman's coat which covered the top of the apron and box cushion. (2) A driving term; the flap of leather attached to the top of the harness collar (q.v.) which covers the seam; in dress harness, is adorned with a crest, while in working harness, it bears the number of the horse.

Cape cart Also known as Cape wagon; a large, two-wheeled, horse-drawn country cart used in South Africa; seated three passengers and a driver; hung on thoroughbraces and protected by a falling hood; driven to a pair of swift horses in a type of curricle gear with a center pole; developed by Dutch settlers in Cape Province during the early 19th century and later exported to New Zealand and Australia; the rear part could be converted to a sleeping compartment; frequently used for military transport during the Boer War.

Cape Horse A horse breed originating in South Africa which descended from Barb (q.v.) and Arab (q.v.) horses imported by the Dutch East India Company in 1653; Thoroughbred (q.v.) and English Roadster blood was later added; its numbers have declined greatly in recent years; served as foundation stock for the Basuto Pony (q.v.).

Capel A thick-set farm horse used in medieval times.

capel Also known as capulet; a swelling on the point of the hock (q.v.) or point of the elbow (q.v.).

Cape Wagon *see* CAPE CART

cap fee *see* CAP no. 1

capillaries More than one capillary (q.v.).

capillary One of the minute blood vessels between the termination of the arteries and the beginnings of the veins; from the Latin capillus meaning hair.

capillary refill time Also known by the acronym CRT; the amount of time required for blood profusion to return to a gum area following application of pressure; normal refill time is one to two seconds; a slower time may indicate low blood pressure, shock, or dehydration.

capped elbow Also known as shoe boil; a fluid-filled inflammation of the bursa over the elbow joint; may result from lying on poorly bedded hard floors, kicks, falls, the stirrup iron hitting the elbow, or horse shoes projecting beyond the heel; considered a blemish which may or may not interfere with performance.

capped hock A fluid-filled inflammation of the bursa over the point of the hock; may result from lying on poorly bedded hard floors, kicks, falls, horse shoes projecting beyond the hoof heel, leaning against the tailgate of the trailer, or hitting the stable wall; considered a blemish (q.v.).

capped knee *see* CARPITIS

capping fee *see* CAP no. 1

Caprilli, Federico (1868-1907) A turn of the century Italian cavalry officer considered to be the father of the forward seat (q.v.) jumping technique which he introduced in 1907; published the Principi di Equitazione di Campagna in 1907.

capriole A classical air above the ground (q.v.); the highest and most complete leap of the high airs (q.v.) in which the horse half rears with his hocks drawn under his body, then jumps forward and high into the air; at the height of the horizontal jump, the horse kicks out strongly with his hind legs, the soles of his feet turned upwards; when the movement is completed, the horse lands, collected, on four legs; originated in medieval times, where, by using such leaps and kicks of the horse, the rider in combat could rid himself of his adversaries.

capsular ligament The outer covering of a joint capsule in the ball and socket, shoulder, and hip joints.

capture myopathy *see* TYING UP

capulet *see* CAPEL

car (1) A four-wheeled, horse-drawn vehicle first used in the territory of Gaul, in the ancient Roman province of Gallia; the term derived from the Latin carrus meaning, four-wheeled vehicle. (2) A generic term; any superior two-wheeled, horse-drawn vehicle such as a governess car (q.v.); used in Britain in the early 19th century.

caravan (1) A horse-drawn house-on-wheels used by Gypsies, showmen, and other nomadic people from the mid-19th century through the 1930s; developed from a tent fixed to a cart which was used for business during the day and for sleeping at night; of many different types. (2) A medieval passenger wagon popular in the 13th and 14th centuries; unsprung, drawn by three horses in tandem (q.v.), controlled by a postillion (q.v.) on the shaft horse.

carbohydrates A chemical compound consisting of hydrogen, oxygen, and water; the major source of energy and heat in the horse's diet; include starches, sugars, and fiber; most are consumed in the form of green plants which constitute a major class of animal food.

card (1) *see* RACE CARD. (2) *see* FIXTURE CARD. (3) *see* TICKET no. 2

cardiac Pertaining to the heart.

cardiac arrhythmia *see* ARRHYTHMIA

cardiac muscle An involuntary, striated muscle (q.v.) that controls the rhythmic contraction of the heart.

cardiac shock Circulatory collapse characterized by a progressive diminishing circulating blood volume relative to the capacity of the vascular system, leading to acute failure of blood perfusion to the vital organs; caused by damage to the heart pump.

cardiovascular Pertaining to the heart and blood vessels.

care dog *see* CUR DOG

career (1) A historic battle term; the demarcation of the line a rider must take when making a charge or a tilt against an opponent; from the French carrière. (2) A dressage term; the line to take in the manège. (3) *see* TRACK

Caretta (1) A horse-drawn country cart popular in Sicily and southern Italy from about 476 AD through the mid-20th century; drawn by a single horse or pony in straight shafts (q.v.); had a richly carved body and framework with side panels painted with scenes from legends, biblical stories, and so on. (2) An early four-wheeled, horse-drawn coach or carriage used in Italy for ceremonial purposes; frequently lined with scented leather and expensive fabric; records pertaining to the use of this vehicle date to 1273.

car fit Said of a horse who experiences severe fright while being shipped, e.g., in a truck, trailer, van, train, or plane.

caries Also known as tooth decay; a bacterial infection of the tooth (q.v.) recognizable by strong, foul-smelling breath; is rarely a problem in horses unless resulting from trauma.

Cariole A two-wheeled, horse-drawn gig with a narrow body and unsprung or dead axle; used in the country districts of Norway throughout the 19th century; driven from a low rearward platform that was also used as a luggage grid; drawn by a single horse or large pony harnessed between exceptionally long shafts; seated one passenger.

carnation A flower; any of the numerous varieties of the clover-pink *Dianthus caryophillus* having fragrant flowers of many colors; yellow carnations are worn in the lapels of British Driving Society (q.v.) members at their meets.

Caroche An open, dead axle, horse-drawn carriage generally used for ceremonial purposes in France during the late 15th and early 16th centuries; drawn by six or more horses, was box shaped, had luxurious internal appointments, and ran on equirotal wheels.

carousel Also spelled carrousel; an orchestrated ride to music performed by a group of riders who execute figures on horseback; designed to resemble formal dances of the era such as the quadrille (q.v.) or the lancers; usually performed in fancy attire; first presented in 1828 at the French Cavalry School at Saumur (q.v.), where it is still officially performed by the Cadre Noir (q.v.); also presented at the Spanish Riding School in Vienna (q.v.).

carpal joint *see* CARPUS

Carpentum (1) Either a two- or four-wheeled, horse-drawn passenger vehicle used in Ancient Rome from the first century AD; a luxury vehicle, hung on side braces of toughened leather; entered from the rear; drawn by a pair of horses harnessed in curricle gear; named after Camenta, a worthy matron and mother of Evander, one of the founders of Rome. (2) A low-slung, elegant, and headed carriage with a fixed or standing top designed about 1840.

carpitis Also known as popped knee, sore knee, big knee, capped knee, or swing leg;

acute or chronic inflammation of the joint capsules and associated structures of the knee (q.v.) resulting from torn knee ligaments or fractures of any of eight carpal bones; common to horses in hard training, especially when unfit or immature Thoroughbreds (q.v.).

carpus Also known as knee, carpal joint, or radio carpal joint; the gliding joint (q.v.) in the front leg of the horse that connects the foreleg (q.v.) to the lower leg (q.v.), and consists of eight carpal bones held together by ligaments (q.v.).

carpus varus *see* LATERAL DEVIATION OF THE CARPAL JOINTS

carpus vulgus *see* MEDIAL DEVIATION OF THE CARPAL JOINTS

Carrera de sortijas A mounted gaucho game popular in Argentina; a form of tilting (q.v.) at the ring; two gauchos, starting side by side simultaneously, gallop towards two rings no bigger than finger rings suspended parallel so high that the riders must stand in their stirrups and stretch out their arms to reach the rings; riders use small pieces of wood about pencil size to pick up the rings; the rider who successfully picks up the ring and crosses the finish line first is the winner.

carrette (1) A four-wheeled horse-drawn bus or short stage coach used in many Australian towns and cities between 1895 and 1920; driven from a raised seat at the fore-end protected by an extended roof canopy; had longitudinal, inward-facing seating and was drawn by two horses in pole gear (q.v.). (2) A low-slung horse-drawn omnibus hung on sideways-elliptical springs and having cranked axles; drawn by two horses in pole gear; mainly used in Chicago, USA between the early 1890s and 1900s.

carriage (1) Also known as carriage parts, chassis, under-carriage, or gear; the supporting underworks of a horse-drawn vehicle consisting of the wheels, springs, axles, forecarriage sections, fifth wheel, perch, splinter bar, and futchells. (2) An open or semi-open, horse-drawn passenger vehicle of superior quality; generally run on four wheels, but some two-wheeled types such as the curricle (q.v.) and cabriolet (q.v.) existed; from the Latin carrus meaning car and the old French carier meaning wagon or cart. (3) The manner in which a horse carries itself with or without a rider;

evaluated in terms of attitude, manner, and style when standing or moving; requirements differ according to breed and use specifications.

Carriage Association of America Also known by the acronym CAA; an association of carriage drivers formed in 1961 in the United States to promote the sport/art of carriage driving in the United States and abroad.

carriage horse Any relatively light, elegant horse suitable for pulling a private or Hackney carriage (q.v.).

carriage hood Also known as a head, hood, or top; the fabric top of a carriage whether in a raised or lowered position.

carriage parts *see* CARRIAGE no. 1

carries the scent *see* CARRY THE SCENT

Carrinho The Portuguese equivalent of the carretta (q.v.).

Carromata A two-wheeled pony cart with a standing or fixed top used in the Philippines during the mid-19th century; drawn by a single pony.

carrot A biennial plant, *Dacus carota*, of the parsley family, with fern-like leaves and a long, orange-red root fed as a supplement; high in beta carotene which is converted into vitamin A (q.v.) in the digestive tract.

carrousel *see* CAROUSEL

carry (1) A hunting term; said of the ground when it holds the scent of the fox picked up from contact with the pads of the foot. (2) Said of a tent pegger (q.v.) when he successfully places the tip of his lance through the eye of the tent peg in the mounted sport of tent pegging (q.v.).

carry a good head Also known as carry a wide head; a hunting term; said of the hounds, when running a fox, who spread out, fan like, to catch every turn and twist in the line of the fox (q.v.).

carry a line Also known as work a line; a hunting term; to follow the line of the fox (q.v.).

carry a wide head *see* CARRY A GOOD HEAD

carry both ends *see* WEAR ITSELF WELL

carry scent *see* CARRY THE SCENT

carry the ball A polo term; said of a player who retains possession and control of the polo ball while moving down the field towards the goal (q.v.).

carry the bar A driving term; a horse whose bar (q.v.) is an inch or two in front of its partner's.

carry the horn A hunting term; to hunt (q.v.) hounds.

carry the line *see* CARRY THE SCENT

carry the scent Also known as carries the scent, carry scent, or carry the line; a hunting term; said of a hound (q.v.) when he actually follows the line of a fox (q.v.) when the pack is running.

carry the target A racing term; said of a horse who runs in last position the entire race.

cart (1) A generic term; any two-wheeled, horse-drawn vehicle designed for speed and flexibility over rough terrain. (2) A country or sporting vehicle drawn by a cob or pony; less expensive and ornate than coaches (q.v.) or carriages (q.v.), and generally owner driven; many named for the territory in which they were used, e.g., the Essex cart, while others were named for the purpose for which they were constructed, e.g., the governess cart (q.v.), or for the builder, e.g., Morgan Cart. (3) Said of a rider whose mount has run away with him.

cart horse Generally a heavy, cold-blooded (q.v.) draft horse.

cart horse of the north, the *see* ARDENNAIS

Carthusian A horse breed indigenous to Spain originating at studs founded by Carthusian monks in Seville and other parts of Andalusia, who from 1476, devoted themselves to the selective breeding of Andalusian horses; considered a type of Andalusian (q.v.); has good conformation, elegant action and is strong and athletic; stands approximately 15.2 hands and the coat is usually gray, although chestnut and black also occur; most descended from the stallion Esclavo; used for riding and light draft.

cartilage Also known as soft bone; tissue composing most of the skeleton in embryos and young vertebrates, then converted, for the most part, into bone in mature higher vertebrates; is insensitive, has no blood supply, and is dependent upon synovial fluid for nutrition; in the mature horse, cartilage is soft and pliable and absorbs shock to the skeleton; bone may convert back to cartilage due to mineral imbalance as in big head disease (q.v.), this however, is reversible; of three types: elastic cartilage (q.v.), hyaline cartilage (q.v.), and fibro cartilage (q.v.).

carting *see* CARTY

carting bred Said of a medium to heavy boned horse of mixed breeding whose body type is well suited to light draft.

carty Also known as carting; a horse of mixed breeding, but generally containing some cold blood (q.v.).

Caslick's operation Commonly referred to as suturing; the process of stitching a section of the mare's vulva lips together to prevent air and contaminants from entering her reproductive track when not being bred.

Caspian An ancient pony breed originating in what is now Iran around 3000 BC; thought to be a progenitor of the Arab (q.v.); believed extinct in the 10th century, but in 1965 a number of specimens were found in the Elburz Mountains and on the shores of the Caspian Sea; stands 9.2 to 11.2 hands although breed requirements specify the height between 10.2 and 12 hands; the coat may be chestnut, bay, or gray with white head and leg markings the exception; has a small head, short ears, large eyes, flared nostrils, a slightly arched neck with a full mane and tail, short back, and sturdy, well-built legs; is strong, quiet, and docile, has good endurance, and is a natural jumper; used for riding.

cast (1) Said of a horse when he becomes lodged on the ground between a vertical surface and his withers (q.v.); occurs when a horse falls, rolls, or lies down in too small a space or too close to a fence, wall, or manger and is unable to get up without assistance; the more strenuously he struggles to right himself, the more prone he is to injury. (2) Said of a horse; to throw a horseshoe. (3) A plaster bandage used to set broken bones or torn ligaments. (4) A hunting term; any effort made by the hounds, whether on their own initiative or at the direction of the huntsman (q.v.), to recover the scent of the fox at a check (q.v.). (5) An inferior or unsuitable horse. (6) Also known as casting a horse; to throw a horse onto the ground using ropes or hobbles (q.v.) or other means to break, clip, shoe, administer medical treatments, etc. (7) *see* CAST THE HOUNDS

cast horse (1) Also known as a principal horse; any horse used by a principal actor when shooting a movie; a horse who has a primary role in a film as opposed to a horse used in the background. (2) Said of a horse who is cast (q.v.).

cast coat *see* SHED OUT

cast the hounds Also known as cast; a hunting term; said of the huntsman (q.v.) who, when the hounds (q.v.) following the line of a fox (q.v.) have lost the scent, moves the pack in the direction in which he thinks a fox has moved in an attempt to recover the lost line.

casting a horse *see* CAST no. 6

castor *see* CHESTNUT

castrate Also known as cut, mark, geld, alter, or emasculate; to remove the testicles of a male horse to render him sterile, more docile, and to facilitate control in the presence of mares; may be performed at any age, although generally not prior to one year of age; may be performed at any time of the year, although it is most commonly carried out in the spring or autumn because of the absence of flies; commonly performed using an emasculator.

castration Also known as gelding; the act of removing the testicles from a male horse.

cataract Optification of the lens of the eye as due to genetics, illness such as diabetes, or trauma such as ultraviolet radiation; may lead to impaired vision or blindness.

cataplasm (1) To anoint or to spread as a plaster. (2) A treatment or plaster used to reduce inflammation and pain; mud or clay is one of the basic ingredients; when applied to the entire circumference of the leg provides the support normally associated with bandages or wrapping.

catch To find a mare in season (q.v.) when she is turned out to pasture (q.v.).

catch-as-catch-can A calf-roping term; said of a roper (q.v.) allowed to rope a calf in any fashion he chooses so long as he turns the rope loose when throwing the loop, and so long as the rope holds the calf until the roper reaches it.

catch colt An antiquated term; an orphaned colt (q.v.).

catch-driver A harness racing term; a driver not directly employed by a stable who is hired for his skill; receives a flat fee plus a percentage of winnings (generally 5 percent) for each race.

catch hold Said of a horse who suddenly takes hold of the bit and begins to pull.

catchhold A hunting term; said of a huntsman (q.v.) when he moves the hound pack to a point where he thinks the fox (q.v.) has moved or where it was last seen.

catching a double thong Also known as catching a whip or folding a whip; a driving term; to double up a long thong (q.v.) onto the whip when the extra length is not necessary; when doubled, the thong length would preferably be about 2 feet 6 inches (2 m), the rest of the thong being wound around the stick and the handle; long driving whips are customarily used when driving a tandem (q.v.), unicorn (q.v.), or team (q.v.).

catching a whip *see* CATCHING A DOUBLE THONG

catch pigeons A racing term; sprinting racehorses.

catch rope A roping term; the lariat holding a roped animal.

catch up *see* ROUND UP

catch weight A racing term; the optional weight carried by a horse competing in a race when the conditions of a race do not specify a weight.

catechu An astringent used to soothe intestinal inflammation associated with enteritis (q.v.) or diarrhea (q.v.); usually combined with chalk (q.v.) and kaolin and administered by stomach tube.

caterpillar *see* LARVA

cat foot A hunting term; said of a hound having a round foot with short toes and high, well-developed knuckles; characteristic of English hounds.

cat hairs The long, untidy hairs which grow in a horse's coat following a second clipping; appear early in the new year.

cat-hammed Said of a horse having weak hocks (q.v.) and long, relatively thin thighs and legs.

cathartic *see* PURGATIVE

catol A two-wheeled, horse-drawn Norwegian dogcart (q.v.); seats two passengers sitting one behind the other.

cattle (1) Domesticated four-legged bovine animals, including cows, bulls, and steers. (2) *see* HORSES

cattle blocking A mounted South American rodeo game held in a round arena surrounded by a wooden partition; the guacho, riding a horse trained to maneuver a steer in position up against the wooden partition, uses the horse's chest, legs, etc. to block the steer against the partition; points are awarded according to which part of the horse's body is used to block the steer.

Cattle Men's Carnivals *see* RODEO

cattle settler A cutting term; a mounted rider who quiets a herd of cattle (q.v.) so that when another rider penetrates the herd they do not scatter; achieved by riding back and forth in front of the cattle, allowing them to become familiar with the horse.

caudal Situated near or directed toward the hind quarters or tail of the horse.

caught one Also known as one healed; a roping term; said of the roper, to lasso (q.v.) only one of two hind feet of a steer (q.v.) when roping.

caulkins *see* CALK

caulks *see* CALK

caustic A group of substances including copper sulfate (q.v.), phenol, antimony trichloride, and silver nitrate, used to destroy excess granulation tissue and minor superficial tumors in the horse; cause cell death and precipitation of protein (q.v.) to form a scab.

cavaletti Also spelled cavalletti in correct Italian; a series of small wooden jumps, generally 4 inches x 10 ft (3 m) long, used in the basic training of a riding horse; invented by Federico Caprilli (q.v.) for his system natural; used to encourage the horse to lengthen its stride, improve its balance, and loosen and strengthen its muscles; although the plural of cavalletto, corruption of the language has led English-speaking equestrians to use cavalletti for both singular and plural forms; from the Italian meaning little horses.

cavalletti *see* CAVALETTI

cavelletto An Italian term; the singular form of cavaletti (q.v.).

cavallo An Italian term; a horse (q.v.).

cavalry Mounted soldiers collectively; that part of a military force whose troops serve on horseback (q.v.).

cavalry hold A method of holding the reins (q.v.) when mounted; the rider holds all four reins of a double bridle (q.v.) in either the right or left hand, thus freeing the other hand to carry a weapon.

cavalryman Also known as a horseman; a soldier who serves on horseback.

cavalry remount Any horse used for service in an army unit.

cavalry twill A type of fabric used for cavalry uniforms after 1914; was first made in khaki in western England for regiments serving in the First World War.

cavesson *see* NOSEBAND

cavesson noseband From the French cavecon meaning to curb or restrict; *see* CAVESSON.

cee-spring A driving term; a metal, c-shaped spring used in vehicle suspension first introduced in 1790 as an improvement to the whip-spring.

Celle Stud A breeding facility located near Hanover, Germany, where it is believed to have existed for more than two centuries.

CEM The acronym for contagious equine metritis (q.v.).

centaurs (1) Ancient mythical Greek people dwelling in the mountains of Thessalay who were imagined as men with the bodies of horses and half bestial natures; according to fable, they were the offspring of the god Ixion and a cloud. (2) A race of people who hunted wild cattle (q.v.) and lived almost continuously on horseback.

center line (1) An imaginary line dividing a defined area into two equal halves. (2) A dressage term; an imaginary line down the middle of the long side of the dressage ring used as a grid in the performance of many dressage moves.

center of gravity An imaginary point or axis around which the mass of a body or limb is balanced.

central incisors Also known as centrals or first incisors; four of the 12 incisor teeth (q.v.) in the horse consisting of the two front middle teeth, upper and lower; present at birth as milk teeth (q.v.) and later replaced by permanent teeth (q.v.).

centrals *see* CENTRAL INCISORS

cereal grass hay Also known as seeds hay; a cut and dried grass hay (q.v.) made from common cereal grain grasses such as oat, barley, wheat, and rye with oat hay (q.v.) being the most commonly fed; contains a lower calcium content than other hays; important to monitor the calcium-phosphorus ratio (q.v.) of the horse when feeding without supplements; generally cut when green to ensure palatability; varieties include barley hay (q.v.), Timothy (q.v.), Bermuda (q.v.), bluestem grass (q.v.), bromegrass (q.v.), wheat grass hay (q.v.), Sudan grass hay (q.v.), and prairie hay (q.v.).

cerebellar hypoplasia A genetically based disease in which a foal is born with an inadequately formed brain motor control center; the foal will be stiff-legged and uncoordinated.

certificate of registration A legal document attesting to the horse's age, pedigree, breeder, owner, and physical description; generally issued by the appropriate breed and/or performance associations.

certificate of veterinary inspection Also known by the acronym CVI; a certificate prepared by a veterinarian that certifies a horse is free of communicable diseases and is vaccinated against specific diseases; required when a horse is transported across state or country lines; in the United States (Arkansas, Delaware, Florida, Georgia, Ohio, and Rhode Island) and Canada, temperature readings are also required.

Certified Apprentice Farrier, Level One Also known by the acronym CAF I; a certification awarded to student and novice farriers by the Brotherhood of Working Farriers Association (q.v.) on the basis of a practical examination.

Certified Apprentice Farrier, Level Two Also known by the acronym CAF II; a certification awarded to graduates and professional farriers just starting practice by the Brotherhood of Working Farriers Association (q.v.) on the basis of written and practical examinations.

Certified Farrier Also known by the acronym CF; a certification of knowledge and skill awarded to farriers practicing in the United States by the American Farriers' Association (q.v.) on the basis of written and practical examinations.

Certified Journeyman Farrier Also known by the acronym CJF; a certification awarded to a farrier by the American Farriers' Association on the basis of written and practical examinations.

Certified Journeyman Farrier, Level One Also known by the acronym CJF I; a certification awarded to farriers with more than one year of practical experience by the Brotherhood of Working Farriers Association (q.v.) on the basis of written and practical examinations.

Certified Journeyman Farrier, Level Two Also known by the acronym CJF II; a certification awarded to farriers with more than three years of practical experience by the Brotherhood of Working Farriers Association

on the basis of written and practical examinations.

Certified Master Farrier Also known by the acronym CMF; the highest level of achievement and certification awarded to a farrier by the Brotherhood of Working Farriers Association (q.v.).

certified pedigree option Also known as CPO; a registration option offered by the Appaloosa Horse Club (ApHC) (q.v.) since 1982 for non-characteristic horses, that is those not showing typical Appaloosa characteristics, e.g., a blanket (q.v.); must have at least one ApHC-registered parent; can be used in Appaloosa (q.v.) breeding programs when mated with colored horses (q.v.) and can compete in ApHC-sanctioned events.

cervix The narrow or neck portion of an organ; generally the outer end of the uterus.

CF The acronym for Certified Farrier (q.v.).

chafe Said of the skin when rubbed to the point of irritation, but not to gall (q.v.).

chaff (1) Also known as chop; any mixture of hay (q.v.), such as meadow hay, green-cut oat hay, or straw, cut into small lengths and used as a feedstuff; often blended with molasses to increase nutritive value and palatability. (2) Also known as cravings; the residue from corn after removal of the kernel from the cob.

chain horse Also known as chain team; a driving term; the center or swing pair in a team of six horses; so called because the center pair are frequently separated by a chain instead of a pole.

chain-mouth snaffle A bit (q.v.) consisting of a flat, or cable-link chain mouth attached to two cheek rings (q.v.).

chain shanks *see* CROSS TIES

chain team *see* CHAIN HORSE

Chair-back Gig A horse-drawn vehicle of the gig (q.v.) type popular during the late 18th century; had a rounded cabriolet-type body fitted with a chair or stick-back seat; originally hung on leather braces swung on cee- or shallow whip springs, with semi-elliptical springs used in later models.

chair seat Said of the English rider when he sits too far back in the saddle, with the stirrups too short, and thus the thigh too horizontal.

Chaise Also referred to in 19th-century North America as shay; a horse-drawn vehicle widely used in Western Europe and the North American Colonies in the late 18th and early 19th centuries; drawn by a single horse or cob in curved shafts; generally mounted on thoroughbraces, cee-springs, a combination of both, or balanced on resilient shafts without further suspension; seated at least one passenger alongside of the driver; the driver's seat was protected by a falling hood.

chalk *see* CHALK HORSE

chalk board A racing term; a board or slate upon which the betting odds of horses competing in a given race are identified by bookmakers (q.v.).

chalk horse Also known as chalk; a racing term; the betting favorite or most heavily played horse in a race; from the days when bookmakers identified the odds of each horse in chalk written on chalk boards.

chalk jockey An obsolete racing term; a rider who has not ridden in a sufficient number of races to warrant placing his name on the number-board (q.v.).

chalk player A racing term; one who prefers to place bets (q.v.) on favored horses.

challenge (1) A racing term; said of a horse vying for the lead. (2) *see* CHALLENGE A LINE

challenge a fox *see* CHALLENGE A LINE

challenge a line Also known as challenge a fox or challenge; a hunting term; said of a hound who speaks to the line of a fox (q.v.) before the rest of the pack, or when a hound speaks to support another hound who opens on a fox (q.v.).

Challon, Henry Bernard (1770-1849) Appointed painter of animals to Kings George IV and William IV; some of his racehorse portraits and hunting scenes were engraved in mezzotint.

chambon Also known as a chambon martingale; an advanced piece of schooling and/or training equipment designed to lower the head

and upper neck while simultaneously raising the base of the neck to obtain a rounded top line (q.v.) and improved engagement of the hocks under the body; consists of a martingale (q.v.) attached to the girth (q.v.) between the legs, the branches of which (usually of cord) pass through rings on either side of a poll pad and attach to the bit (q.v.) rings; the action is on the poll (q.v.).

chambon martingale *see* CHAMBON

chambrière A 16th and 17th-century term; a lunge whip (q.v.) used to school a horse in the pillars (q.v.) and to punish if necessary.

chamfrain *see* CHAMFRON

chamfron Also known as chamfrain and spelled chanfron; (1) A headstall (q.v.) used in medieval armor. (2) To fasten a rein or bridle on a horse. (3) Medieval armor used to protect the head of the horse when in battle.

champ Said of a horse who chews or plays with the bit while it is in his mouth.

Championnat Hippique International Also known by the acronym CHI; *see* ROYAL INTERNATIONAL HORSE SHOW.

Championnat Hippique International Officiel Also known by the acronym CHIO; *see* ROYAL INTERNATIONAL HORSE SHOW (CHIO).

Championnat Hippique National Also known by the acronym CHN; a nationally authorized horse show.

chanfron *see* CHAMFRON

changar Polo (q.v.) played in Persia more than 2,500 years ago; from the Persian word meaning mallet.

change An antiquated coaching term; a location along a route traveled by horse-drawn public transportation vehicles where tired or spent team horses could be swapped out for rest horses (q.v.).

change hands A 16th and 17th-century French term; the action (q.v.) of the horse's legs when changing leads (q.v.).

change in the air *see* FLYING CHANGE

change lead *see* CHANGE OF LEAD

change of hand *see* CHANGE OF REIN

change of lead Also known as change lead or lead change; a change of the horse's leading leg (q.v.) performed at a gallop or canter.

change of leg *see* FLYING CHANGE

change of leg in the air *see* FLYING CHANGE

change of leg through the trot *see* SIMPLE CHANGE

change of ponies A polo term; to exchange a horse used in one chukker (q.v.) for a fresh horse; required after each chukker or at any point during a chukker if a horse is injured; an interval of three minutes is permitted to change horses, while if a change is due to injury, the clock is stopped.

change of rein Also known as change of hand; said of the rider; to change direction of travel from left to right or vice versa when riding.

change rhythm To alter the steps of the horse within a pace by breaking the length of the stride for one or more steps.

channel Also known as saddle channel or saddle chamber; the open portion of the saddle between the two panels and beneath the seat which runs from the pommel (q.v.) to the cantle (q.v.) parallel to the vertebral column of the horse's back.

chaparajos *see* CHAPS

chaparreras *see* CHAPS

chape The white tip of the fox's tail.

chaperos *see* CHAPS

Chapman Horse *see* CLEVELAND BAY

chappararos *see* CHAPS

chaps Also called chaperos, chappararos, chaparajos, or chaparreras, and spelled shaps; leather leggings which cover the rider's leg from the ankle to the hip or from midcalf to the hip; originally used to protect the legs of cowboys from heat, cold, and thorny native vegetation; in addition to the historical uses, now used to obtain better grip in the saddle, to prevent chafing of the rider's leg, ornamentation, and as usual show attire in the western riding circuit in the United States or in rodeos (q.v.); from the Spanish chaparreras.

Charabanc Also known as charabanc break; a four-wheeled, horse-drawn passenger vehicle of French origins introduced in the 1830s; had two or more rows of crosswise seating for passengers seated either vis-à-vis (q.v.) or facing each other; driven to either a two- or four-in-hand team by a coachman from a high box; usually open, but sometimes fitted with a canopy head or a cover mounted on standards; frequently used as a mobile grandstand at race meetings and other sporting events; some were fitted with front and rear slatted under boots (q.v.) to carry sporting dogs.

Charablanc Break *see* CHARABLANC

charbon *see* ANTHRAX

charge-back *see* BUY-BACK

charger A cavalry (q.v.) mount, generally used by an officer.

chariot From the French *char* meaning wheeled vehicle or the Latin *carrus* for car or wagon; (1) A two-wheeled, horse-drawn hunting or war vehicle thought to have originated in China or the Middle East around 2000 BC; drawn either by a single horse or several horses abreast, in which case the center horse was positioned between shafts while the outer horses were only connected by traces (q.v.); was high in the front, had sturdy wheels, a low center of gravity, and was entered from the rear; used for racing, some types of military training, and ceremonial purposes. (2) A four-wheeled coupé or cut-down coach which usually seated two forward-facing passengers; popular from the late 17th through the late 19th centuries; eventually replaced by the Brougham (q.v.); drawn by two horses in pole gear (q.v.); originally hung on cee-springs, but later on sideways-elliptical springs, had an underperch, high box seat with an elaborate hammercloth, and a dummy board on which the servants or footmen rode.

chariot racing The national sport of ancient Greece in which two-wheeled, horse-drawn, open-backed vehicles were raced on a straight or oval course; a popular spectator sport for more than 1,500 years which became an Olympic sport in 408 BC.

Charley *see* FOX

Charlie *see* FOX

Charlier shoe Also known as periplantar shoeing; a type of horseshoe (q.v.) now obsolete; the shoe is placed in a groove cut into the hoof wall, thus allowing the frog, in theory, to be in constant contact with the ground; invented by a Frenchman of the same name.

Charolais *see* CHAROLLAIS

Charollais Also spelled Charolais and Charrolais and known as a Charollais Half-Bred; a coldblood descended from Thoroughbreds (q.v.) crossed with Anglo-Normans (q.v.); stands 15 to 16.2 hands, may be of any solid color, and is renowned for its soundness; together with two similar breeds, the Bourbannais (q.v.) and the Nivernais, are collectively known as Demi-Sang Charollais.

Charollais Half-Bred *see* CHAROLLAIS

charreada Also known as a charro rodeo; a Mexican style rodeo (q.v.) consisting of nine scored events including the cala (q.v.), coleaderos (q.v.), jinete de novillos (q.v.), terna en el ruedo (q.v.), paso de la muerte (q.v.), piales en el lienzo (q.v.), and the mangana (q.v.) in which special attention is paid to specific customs of costumes and mannerisms; dates back to post-revolutionary Mexico in the early 20th century when it was a fiesta conducted to pay homage to the traditions of Mexican horsemanship including skilled riding and roping; some events are now outlawed in parts of the United States.

charro A Mexican cowboy (q.v.).

Charrolais *see* CHAROLLAIS

charro rodeo *see* CHARREADA

chart *see* RESULT CHART

chase (1) *see* STEEPLECHASE. (2) A hunting term; the pursuit of foxes or coyotes by a pack of hounds.

Chatelaine A small pony-drawn gig (q.v.) frequently driven by ladies in the southern states of North America during the mid-19th century.

chatter Also known as shower, shower the ground, shower down on one, chatter the ground, or dancing; a cutting term; said of the horse who, in anticipation of the movement of the cow, patters his front feet in small, vertical steps.

chatter the ground *see* CHATTER

chaugan An ancient Persian mounted game resembling lawn tennis developed around 525 BC from which polo (q.v.) derived.

chaunter *see* BONNET no. 2

cheap John American slang; a horseshoer who attempts to build his/her clientele by charging rates for his services below those customarily charged in the area.

check (1) A hunting term; said of the hounds when they lose the scent of the fox and stop pursuit; the field (q.v.) will wait while the hounds search for the line or are cast (q.v.) by the huntsman (q.v.). (2) *see* CHECK REIN. (3) A quick take and give of the outside rein by the rider to slow the forward impulsion (q.v.) of the horse.

checkerboard team *see* CROSS TEAM

check rein Also known as check, over draw bearing rein, overcheck, and spelled checkrein; a rein commonly used on trotting and pacing harness horses; runs from each side of the bit, comes together on the bridge of the nose, and passes between the eyes, over the poll, to the backband of the harness or to the saddle; maintains the horse's head and neck in an upward-extended position while racing.

checkrein *see* CHECK REIN

cheek (1) Also known as a cheekpiece, branch, cannon, sidepiece, or on western bits, shank; the vertical portion of the bit outside of the mouth; generally attached at right angles to the mouthpiece and connects to the reins; prevents the bit from slipping through the horse's mouth; of two types: full-cheek (q.v.) and half-cheek (q.v.). (2) *see* CHEEKPIECE. (3) Either side of the face of the horse below the eye and above the lower jaw bone.

cheek guard *see* BIT GUARD

cheek leather *see* BIT GUARD

cheekpiece (1) *see* CHEEK no. 1. (2) Also

known as bridle cheekpiece; that portion of the bridle which lies flat against the cheek (q.v.) of the horse, attaches to the bit on the lower end and buckles to the crownpiece (q.v.) on the upper; is adjustable to obtain the correct position of the bit in the mouth.

cheek teeth *see* MOLARS

cheer A hunting term; the call of the huntsman (q.v.) to encourage the hounds.

Chef d'Equipe The manager of a national equestrian team responsible for making all arrangements for team competition abroad.

chef-de-race A racing term; a list of superior Thoroughbred (q.v.) sires used in the Dosage (q.v.) formula.

cherry bay *see* BAY

cherry rollers *see* ROLLERS no. 2

Cheshire martingale A standing martingale (q.v.) consisting of an auxiliary, adjustable strap attached on one end to the girth which passes between the forelegs, splits into two branches and attaches on the other to the bridoon rings of a double bridle (q.v.); the split ends have chains and spring hooks attacked; may be fitted with a neck strap (q.v.) to keep it in place.

chesnut *see* CHESTNUT no. 2

chest Also known as thorax or thoracic cavity; the cavity of the body of the horse formed by the spine, ribs, and breast bone between the shoulders and below the windpipe which contains the lungs and heart.

Chester A city located in England; considered the earliest home of modern English horse racing where it commenced in 1540.

chestnut (1) Also known as night eyes or castors; horny growths or calluses located on the inside of the horse's leg, above the knees on the forelegs and below the hocks on the hind; differently patterned from horse to horse, as finger prints, and may be used to identify a horse through a process known as chestnut imprinting (q.v.). (2) Also spelled chesnut; refers to coat color; a medium red coat color with points of the same color; determining the difference between sorrel (q.v.) and chestnut depends largely on the breed under considera-

tion; the differences between sorrel (q.v.), chestnut, and liver chestnut are very subtle with some horses changing color during their lifetimes; in Thoroughbred (q.v.), Arab (q.v.), Morgan, (q.v.) and Suffolk (q.v.) breeds, all reds are designated as chestnut; draft horses may be classified as either chestnut or sorrel depending upon the depth of the red; color variations include chocolate chestnut (q.v.), liver chestnut (q.v.), chestnut tostado (q.v.), chestnut alazán (q.v.), and chestnut ruano (q.v.).

chestnut alazán Refers to coat color; of the chestnut (q.v.) color group; a medium red coat color with red or dark flaxen points.

chestnut imprinting The process of identifying a horse on the basis of the pattern of his chestnuts (q.v.); similar to finger prints in that each pattern is unique.

chestnut ruano Refers to coat color; of the chestnut (q.v.) color group; a medium red coat color with light flaxen points.

chestnut tostado Refers to coat color; of the color group chestnut (q.v.); a medium red coat color with brown points.

Cheval de Selle Français The general heading under which half bred horses bred in France are grouped.

Cheval du Poitou *see* POITEVIN

chew wood *see* WOOD CHEWING

CHI The acronym for Championnat Hippique International (q.v.).

chicken coop A hunting term; a two-sided panel (q.v.) with a peaked roof placed over the top wire of a wire fence to make it safe for horses to jump; so called because it resembles a chicken hutch roof; the most popular type of panel.

Chien de Gascoigne *see* GASCOIGNE, CHIEN DE

Chileno Also known as Caballo Chileno; a Criollo (q.v.) horse bred in Chile; similar in appearance and temperament to the Argentine Criollo from which it descends, but is more sturdy and disease resistant.

Chifney bit Also known as anti-rearing bit;

a circular bit developed in the late 1700s by Samuel Chifney for whom it is named; may have a reversed half circle mouth in which case it is used to prevent rearing.

chime A hunting term; said of the hounds when they give tongue (q.v.) in unison when on the scent of the quarry.

China eye *see* WALL EYE

Chincoteague Also known as Chincoteague pony; a pony breed indigenous to the Chincoteague Islands located off of the eastern coast of Virginia and Maryland, USA; believed to have descended from Moorish ponies sometime in the 1600s; improved by the introduction of Shetland (q.v.) blood; all coat colors are found although piebald (q.v.) and skewbald (q.v.) occur most often; breed appearance and conformation have degenerated over the years; stands about 12 hands, has a long head and neck, slightly pronounced withers, straight back, and solid legs; is rebellious, stubborn, hardy and resistant to harsh weather conditions; used for light draft and riding; wild herds spend most of the year on the uninhabited island of Assateague; every last Thursday and Friday of July a group of the ponies are swum across the channel to the island of Chincoteague where they are sold in a public auction; those ponies not swum across the channel remain known as the Assateague (q.v.).

Chincoteague pony *see* CHINCOTEAGUE

Chinese A pony breed indigenous to China which descended from the Asiatic wild horse (q.v.); similar to other breeds found throughout the Far East and is therefore more of a type than a true breed; breeding has never been controlled; frequently yellow dun (q.v.) although other colors do occur; primitive markings (q.v.), specifically zebra markings (q.v.) on the legs and the eel stripe (q.v.) are common; stands 12 to 13 hands, has a small head, with a straight profile, shaggy forelock, mane, and tail, slanty eyes and small ears, short neck, and straight back; is quite hardy, strong, sure-footed, and quite rebellious; is fast over short distances and used for riding, packing, and some farm work.

chin groove *see* CURB GROOVE

chinked back *see* JINKED BACK

CHIO The acronym for Championnat Hippique International Officiel (q.v.).

chip Said of a horse who adds a stride when jumping an obstacle which may or may not be needed; a stutter step.

chiropractic A system of healing based on the theory that disease results from a lack of normal nerve function and employing treatment by scientific manipulation, specifically adjustment of body structures (spinal column) and utilizing physical therapy when necessary.

chloral hydrate A infrequently used drug, now largely replaced by modern sedatives and analgesics, used as a general anesthetic and administered intravenously (q.v.).

chlorhexidrine An antiseptic agent found in powders, creams, and pre-operative skin preparations.

chloride A compound of chlorine, an electrolyte responsible, in conjunction with sodium, for maintaining osmotic pressure (q.v.), acid-balance metabolism, and kidney function.

chlorine A gaseous element used in such applications as bleech, disinfectant, and in water purification.

chlorpromazine *see* ACETYLPROMAZINE

CHN The acronym for Championnat Hippique National (q.v.).

chocolate chestnut Refers to coat color; a variation of chestnut (q.v.); the coat color is uniformly dark- to medium-brown chocolate with brown points.

choke To stop or restrict the breath of, by a partially or completely blocked esophagus (q.v.) as caused by rapid inhalation of improperly chewed food or consumption of non-food items such as wood, fabric, etc.; symptoms include repeated gulping efforts to swallow, oozing alarming amounts of saliva mixed with food from the nose, distress, straining for breath, arching the neck, and trying to cough; veterinary treatment may be necessary to dislodge the impaction; less dangerous than choking (q.v.).

choked down *see* CHOKING UP

choking Said of a horse with an obstruction in his windpipe; usually arises from inflammatory disease, allergic reaction, trauma, such as a kick to the throat, or a lodged foreign object; signs include an audible snoring sound as the horse strains to get air into his lungs and frantic behavior; a modified Heimlich maneuver, a swift powerful kick just behind the ribs, may dislodge an object, this method will not work in cases of disease, allergy, or trauma; in most cases, an immediate tracheotomy must be performed to allow air to enter below the obstruction; extremely rare; a desperate situation that often ends in death; more dangerous than choke (q.v.).

choking down see CHOKING UP

choking up Also known as choked down, choking down, soft palate disease, or tongue swallowing; thought to be related to a disruption in the anatomical relationship between the larynx and the soft palate (the larynx fits into a small hole in the soft palate, forming an airtight, food-tight seal); when the seal between the larynx and soft palate is broken, as in a racing horse, the normally nasally, breathing horse breathes through its mouth causing air to pass above and below the soft palate, producing a gurgling noise and severe airway obstruction; the situation corrects itself when the horse swallows and the soft palate and larynx return to their normal positions; occurs most commonly in race horses, but also seen in eventers and hunters; may be prevented by the use of a drop noseband (q.v.), tying the tongue forward with a tongue strap, and use of a milder bit; in horses where no primary cause can be identified, surgery is usually advocated.

Chola The sturdiest of three types of Criollo (q.v.) or Salterno horses bred in Peru, the other two being the Costeño (q.v.) and the Morochuco (q.v.); descended from Spanish stock brought to South America by the conquistadors in the 16th century.

choline An intestinally synthesized B-complex vitamin important in the metabolism of fat and for maintaining cell structure; deficiency is unreported in horses.

chrondroprotective Any animal-derived protein identical to the cartilage and joint-fluid components found in the connective tissue, particularly the fascia, throughout the horse's body, used to reduce athletic pain mechanically and physiologically by encouraging more normal joint function; may be injected or ingested; the proteins migrate to the joints via the bloodstream, unless injected directly into the joint where they reduce inflammation and destructive enzymes; in most cases they stop and/or heal existing cartilage damage; from chondro, relating to the cartilage (q.v.).

chondroitin sulfates Also known by the acronym CS; a popular nutraceutical (q.v.) used to reduce or relieve joint problems; extracted from bovine trachea, animal cartilage, and the Australian Perna canalculus mussel.

chop (1) see CHAFF. (2) A mixture of corn or roots with bran. (3) A hunting term; said of the hounds when they kill a fox before it has been hunted or had a chance to run. (4) The exchange of two horses between two parties, usually accompanied by a payment on one side.

chop bedding Chopped straw, waste hay, fodder, or corn cobs when used to bed a stall.

chopped fox A hunting term; a fox killed in his covert (q.v.) before having the opportunity to make a run (q.v.).

chopping (1) An old driving/coaching term; to hit a horse with the whip (q.v.) on the thigh rather than between the collar (q.v.) and the pad. (2) A driving term; to signal a team to turn by pulling either set of reins to the desired side.

chorioptic mange Also known as leg mange, itchy heel, itchy leg, foot mange, or ear mange; mange (q.v.); a skin disease caused by a species of mite Chorioptes equii, characterized by skin lesions found primarily on the lower part of the hind legs, although in severe cases they may spread to the flanks, shoulders, and neck; characterized by severe itching, scales, crusts, thickening of the skin, and in neglected cases, a moist condition in the fetlock region; symptoms subside in the summer, but reappear with cold weather; an affected horse will stamp his feet and rub his lower legs in an attempt to relieve the pain.

chromogen A molecule capable of changing color when adjusted by the appropriate enzyme.

chronic Long lasting or recurring frequently over a long period of time.

chronic arthritis A slowly developing, low-grade inflammation of the joint usually resulting in some degree of permanent damage.

chronic laminitis A persistent and long-term inflammation of the laminae (q.v.) characterized by changes in the shape of the foot; the hoof will grow rapidly, especially at the heel, resulting in long, dished feet with many laminitic rings (q.v.) which are close at the toe and divergent at the heel; as the condition progresses, the sole becomes thickened and either flattened or convex, and the pedal bone (q.v.) begins to rotate, and is forced downward to press on the horny sole; in severe cases the pedal bone may penetrate the sole just in front of the point of the frog and the hoof may sluff.

chronic obstructive pulmonary disease Also known as obstructive pulmonary disease, heaves, broken wind, alveolar emphysema, equine asthma or by the acronym COPD; a chronic allergic airway disease due to developing hypersensitivity to allergens such as organic dust, pollen, and fungal spores found in moldy or dusty hay and stables with poor ventilation; allergens cause constriction of the muscles in the walls of the small airways, swelling of the airway lining, and excess mucus production, all of which contribute to narrowing of the airways and require increased effort to breathe, especially exhale; the horse attempts to compensate for restricted air flow by coughing to clear the mucus from its breathing passages; symptoms include coughing, wheezing, reduced exercise capacity, labored breathing, and a slight increase in respiratory rate and expiratory effort; the most common cause of chronic coughing in horses; seen most frequently in confined horses aged five or older; is not curable but is manageable by placing the horse in a minimal-dust environment.

chronic poison Any toxin, e.g., plant, for which the degree of physiologic damage is a function of quantity consumed; poisoning may result over a period of days or weeks and may be fatal.

Chubbarie *see* BLAGDEN

chuck wagon Also known as a camp wagon, round-up wagon, or food wagon; a four-wheeled horse-drawn vehicle pulled by two or more horses in pole gear (q.v.) used as a mobile kitchen on farms and ranches in the Western states of North America; usually dead axle, but having a fully sprung driving seat and a covered canvas top stretched over hoops attached to the frame.

chukka *see* CHUKKER

chukker Also called period and spelled chukka in Britain; one of six periods in a polo game (q.v.) consisting of seven minutes of regular play with up to 30 seconds of overtime; if during the 30-second overtime period the ball goes out of play for any reason, e.g., a foul, the chukker will be ended by the umpire; play is stopped at the end of each period to allow players to change their mounts which are usually only played for two periods, with at least one chukker of rest in between those played; from the Hindi language meaning a circle.

chute (1) A racing term; an extension of either the homestretch (q.v.) or the backstretch (q.v.) of a race track; gives competing horses the opportunity to run a long straight stretch from the starting gate to the first turn or the last turn prior to the finish, rather than starting or ending on a turn; 6, 6-1/2, and 7 furlong races are started there. (2) A rodeo term; a stall in which rodeo horses and bulls are saddled, bridled, and mounted and from which they are released and/or ridden into the arena.

Chyanta A subgroup of the Bhotia (q.v.) pony breed which originated in the Himalayan mountains of northern India; stands about 12.2 hands, has a gray coat, short neck, shaggy mane, straight shoulder, and short, strong legs; is frugal and has good endurance; used mainly for riding.

CI The acronym for comparable index (q.v.).

CID The acronym for combined immunodeficiency (q.v.).

cimarron A South American term; a wild horse.

cinch (1) *see* GIRTH. (2) Also known as cinch up; to fasten or tighten the girth (q.v.) of a western saddle. (3) *see* BACK CINCH

cinch bound Also known as girth shy, cinchy, or girthy; said of a horse who objects to tightening of the cinch (q.v.) or girth (q.v.) by inhaling and/or holding his breath, crow hopping (q.v.), or bucking.

cinch up *see* CINCH no. 2

cinchy *see* CINCH BOUND

circle curb hook *see* MELTON

circuit A geographical grouping of tracks or horse shows which are coordinated to run in sequence within a given season.

circus A grand scale entertainment, generally performed in round rings in one or more large tents since 1769; performance rings are surrounded by tiers of seats for spectators; features acts performed by both humans and animals; unlike the Roman circus (q.v.), the spectacle does not end fatally for man or beast; Philip Astley is considered the father of the modern circus.

Cisium A two-wheeled, horse-drawn Roman gig driven by fashionable men at high speeds; had high, light, and flat wheels for speed, slatted sides for lightness, and decoration; drawn by a single horse or less frequently by two or three abreast; derived from the Latin cito meaning quick or speedy.

cisplatin A heavy-metal derivative of platinum used in chemotherapy (q.v.).

citrus pulp The peel and residue of citrus fruit resulting from juice production; contains an acid detergent fiber almost as high as that found in hay (q.v.) which is more efficiently digested than hay fiber, a digestible energy content equivalent to that of oats (q.v.), and a crude protein content of about 7 percent which is not efficiently digested.

CJF The acronym for Certified Journeyman Farrier (q.v.).

CJF I The acronym for Certified Journeyman Farrier, Level One (q.v.).

CJF II The acronym for Certified Journeyman Farrier, Level Two (q.v.).

CL *see* CORPUS LUTEUM

claim (1) A racing term; the money paid by a licensed buyer of a horse to the owner of that horse when claiming (q.v.) him following a claiming race (q.v.). (2) *see* CLAIMING

claimer Also known as claiming horse; a racing term; a horse who runs in a claiming race (q.v.).

claiming Also known as to halter; a racing term; the process by which a licensed person may buy a horse entered in a designated race for a predetermined price; the new owner assumes title to the claimed horse (q.v.) once it leaves the starting gate (q.v.), although the original owner is entitled to any purse won.

claiming box A racing term; a small storage box in which claims (q.v.) are placed before the start of a claiming race (q.v.).

claiming horse *see* CLAIMER

claiming race A racing term; an event in which all entered horses are eligible for purchase at a set price by any owner of another starter (q.v.) in the same race, his agent, or those who have received a claim certificate from the stewards; claims must be made before the race; are generally of a lower class than allowance races (q.v.); the lower the claiming price, the lower the class of the horse.

Clarence A horse-drawn farm coach first used in England in the 1840s; hung on either cee or elliptical springs without an underperch, seated four passengers inside vis-à-vis (q.v.), was drawn by a single horse, and coachman driven from a low box; use declined in the 1880s, with many being converted to cabs; an enlarged version of the brougham (q.v.); named for the Duke of Clarence.

Clarence cab Also known as a growler; a horse-drawn vehicle popular in the late 1800s which seated four passengers inside vis-à-vis (q.v.), was hung on either cee or elliptical springs without an underperch, drawn by a single horse, and coachman driven from a low box; an enlarged version of the brougham (q.v.).

Clarence surrey A more formal version of the Clarence (q.v.), outfitted with a hammer cloth box and a rear platform for footmen.

class A racing term; a horse possessing a combination of pedigree, stamina, speed, conformation, endurance, and heart.

Classic Any of five primary English flat races for nominated three-year-old horses; the Derby, the Oaks (fillies only), the St. Leger (entire colts and fillies only), the 1,000

Guineas (fillies only), and the 2,000 Guineas; in the United States, the equivalents are the Kentucky Derby (q.v.), the Preakness Stakes (q.v.), the Belmont Stakes (q.v.), and the Coaching Club American Oaks.

classic Also known as classic distance; a racing term; a specific distance; the American classic distance is 1-1/4 miles (2 km), while the European classic distance is 1-1/2 miles (2.4 km).

classical airs A dressage term; any of the movements of the High School (q.v.) or Haute Ecole (q.v.) consisting of movements on the ground (q.v.) and airs above the ground (q.v.).

classical equitation A riding style developed in the baroque riding halls of Europe during the Renaissance based on the works of Xenophon (c.430-355 BC).

classic distance *see* CLASSIC no. 2

classic fino One of three distinct forward speeds of the lateral, four-beat paso fino (q.v.) gait of which it is the most collected form; is extremely slow, with exceedingly rapid footfall, and short steps and extension; performed on a fino board (q.v.).

claybank Also known as claybank dun; refers to coat color; a variety of dun (q.v.), most commonly, a yellow dun (q.v.), in which the coat hairs are mixed with red and the points red.

claybank dun *see* CLAYBANK

clay bed A bed of thick, wet clay in which horses affected with laminitis were historically stood for treatment.

clean (1) Without defect, blemishes or unsoundness. (2) *see* CLEAR ROUND. (3) Free from dirt or filth.

clean bred An animal of any breeding whose pedigree contains only pure blood (q.v.).

clean ground A hunting term; ground which has not been stained or soiled by the scent of a fox other than the one being hunted or other activity.

clean leg (1) Said of the leg of the horse which has little or no feathering (q.v.) around the fetlock (q.v.). (2) Said of a horse's leg when free of blemishes or signs of prior injury.

clean round *see* CLEAR ROUND

clear Also known as clean or jump clean; a jumping term; to jump an obstacle without touching or dropping a rail.

clear round Also known as clean round or clean; a show jumping or cross country term; said of a horse/rider who completes an event or round without incurring jumping or time faults; when more than one horse per competition has a clear round, a jump-off (q.v.) results.

cleat *see* TOE GRAB

cleft (1) Also known as crosscrack; an interruption of the continuity of the hoof wall occurring at right angles to the direction of the horn tubes; may result from injury to the coronet (q.v.). (2) Partially split, divided half way, having deep fissures, as in a lip or hoof.

cleft lip Also known as harelip and formally as chelloschisis; disruption of the continuity of the lip due to a disturbance of the process making up the jaws and face during embryonic development; cleft of the lower lip is rare and usually occurs at midline; cleft of the upper lip is usually associated with cleft palate (q.v.) and may be complete or partial.

cleft palate Also known as absence of the turbinate bone; disruption of the continuity of the roof of the mouth due to incomplete fusion of the embryonic processes of the upper jaw; previously thought to be solely hereditary, but recent evidence indicates that ingestion of toxic agents, use of steroids, and some viral infections during pregnancy are also causes; may involve the palate alone, or may extend from the lip, through the alveolar bones of the upper jaw; evidenced by milk dripping from the nostrils of the foal when nursing, or respiratory infection; in some cases may be surgically treated, otherwise euthanasia is recommended; considered a partial lethal (q.v.).

clench *see* CLINCH

clench block *see* CLINCH BLOCK

clench cutter *see* CLINCH CUTTER

clencher *see* CLINCHER

clerk of the course A racing term; a mounted (unmounted in the United Kingdom), licensed race official responsible to the race stewards (q.v.) for general race arrangements including conduct of the horses to the starting gate, return of the horses to the saddling enclosure following the race, and the control and safety of riderless horses.

clerk of the scales A racing term; one responsible for weighing the jockeys and their tack prior to, and following, a race.

Cleveland Bay Also known as Chapman Horse and previously as Yorkshire Packhorse; a horse breed originating in the Middle Ages in the Cleveland district of Yorkshire, England where it was used by traveling merchants known as "chapmen," as a packhorse, hence the nickname; during the 18th century infused with Thoroughbred (q.v.) and Arab (q.v.) blood at which time it became a prized coach horse; the coat may be brown or bay with a small star and a few white or gray hairs around the coronet or heels with no other white markings accepted; stands 16 to 16.2 hands and is docile, strong, and clean-legged; used for eventing, combined training, hunting, and driving.

Cleveland Bay Horse Society of Great Britain An organization founded in Great Britain in 1884 to promote interest in the Cleveland Bay (q.v.).

click (1) *see* FORGE no. 1. (2) *see* CLUCK

clicketing A hunting term; said of a female fox when in season (q.v.).

clicking *see* FORGE no. 1

client (1) One who turns to another for professional services such as training, hauling, grooming, etc. (2) A racing term; one who purchases betting information from a tipster.

climb Also known as climbing; a racing term; a fault in a horse's stride in which the horse exhibits unusually high foreleg motion which results in an inefficient stride; often occurs when the horse is tired or flustered.

climbing *see* CLIMB

clinch (1) Also spelled clench; the visible point of the nail left projecting from the wall of the hoof which the farrier (q.v.) bends over

and hammers in and downward into the hoof wall to secure the horseshoe to the foot. (2) To nip off the portion of the horseshoe nail (q.v.) which protrudes from the hoof wall, leaving sufficient length to turn down using a clencher (q.v.) to form a clinch (q.v.).

clinch block Also spelled clench block; a farrier's tool; a small rectangular or square-shaped piece of metal which the farrier (q.v.) holds against the wall of the hoof below the point of the protruding horseshoe nail; after the nail has been driven into the hoof wall, the clench block is held against the base of the point of the nail, while the head of the nail is struck.

clinch cutter Also known as a buffer and spelled clench cutter; a farrier's tool consisting of two metal heads, a blade and a point, connected by a span of metal; the blade is approximately 1 inch (25 mm) wide and is used to cut or raise the clinches while the point is used to push nails and broken stubs out of the hoof.

clincher Also spelled clencher and known as a clinching tong or alligator; a farrier's tool; a large, pritchel-tipped tool used by a farrier (q.v.) to pull the protruding tip of the horseshoe nail down against the hoof wall.

clinching tong *see* CLINCHER

clinker (1) A top-class horse. (2) A 16.1, bay hunter (q.v.) Thoroughbred (q.v.) gelding owned by Captain Ross and ridden by Dick Christian in the famous 1829 horse race staged in Britain against Squire Osbaldenstone's horse Clasher.

clip (1) To shave or cut the body hair of the horse, as in winter growth before it has shed or to trim whiskers, bridle path (q.v.), etc.; clip patterns include blanket clip (q.v.), full clip (q.v.), hunter clip (q.v.), body clip (q.v.), and trace clip (q.v.). (2) A thin, V-shaped or round, extension of the horseshoe used to hold the shoe onto the hoof in situations where the nails alone are insufficient; the metal of the shoe is pulled up in a triangle shape along the outside of the hoof wall and pressed into the hoof; of two types: toe clips (q.v.) and quarter clips (q.v.). (3) Said of the horse; to strike and cut the leg or foot with the opposing or rear foot or horseshoe attached thereon.

clipped oats The edible grain of oat (q.v.)

grass which has been processed to remove the pointed ends of the hulls, a process that lowers fiber content and increases weight.

clipped out right *see* FULL CLIP

clipper One who removes body, mane, tail, and face hair from the horse using devices such as clippers (q.v.).

clippers A battery- or electrically operated mechanical device used to cut body, mane, tail, and face hair from the horse; available with interchangeable blades.

clocker A racing term; one who times workouts and races, generally for betting information.

clop To produce a sharp, hollow sound, as if by a horse's hooves.

close (1) A racing term; the final odds on a horse as in 2 to 1. (2) A racing term; said of a horse who is gaining ground on the leader.

closer A racing term; said of a horse who runs best in the later part of the race, coming off the pace (q.v.).

close basket *see* RALLI CAR

close contact saddle Also known historically as a forward seat saddle, hunt seat saddle, hunting saddle, or Italian saddle; an English saddle with a relatively flat seat, square cantle (q.v.), rounded and padded flap, and small knee rolls used for jumping.

close-coupled *see* SHORT-COUPLED

closed carriage Any horse-drawn vehicle with a falling hood and permanently or semi-permanently raised sides.

closed fracture Said of a broken bone which is not exposed through the skin.

closed top A driving term; a falling hood on a horse-drawn vehicle.

close fast A racing term; said of a horse who gains on the leader (q.v.).

close nail *see* NAIL BIND

clothes *see* HORSE BLANKET

clover hay A legume hay (q.v.) made from cut and dried clover of the subgroup trifolium; generally grown and dried in mixtures with other legumes such as alfalfa (q.v.) or grasses such as Timothy (q.v.), as clover is low growing and tends to mat when dried; red, white, crimson, alsike, and ladino varieties are most commonly fed to horses; contains approximately the same digestible protein content and total nutrients as found in alfalfa hay.

club foot Also known as box foot, boxy foot, donkey foot, donkey hooves, or bear foot; the horse's hoof when abnormally upright, having a foot axis of more than 60 degrees, in which the heels are closed instead of open; prevents the frog from contacting the ground and functioning as an anti-concussive and non-slip device; is unilateral (q.v.), due to injury and when bilateral (q.v.), it may be an inherited condition or due to nutritional deficiency.

clubhouse turn A racing term; the turn of the race track to the right of the grandstand, generally beginning on the homestretch (q.v.); so called because the clubhouse is usually to the right of the general stands.

club the reins A driving term; said of the driver who takes all of the reins into one hand.

cluck Also known as click; a sound made by the rider or driver with the tongue usually as a signal to the horse to increase speed.

Clydesdale A popular heavy-draft breed which originated at the beginning of the 18th century in Scotland's Clyde valley from which the name derived; descended from hardy native breeds put to Flemish and Friesian (q.v.) stallions; stands 16 to 17 hands and weighs approximately 1,540–2,000 pounds (699 – 907 kg); generally has a brown, bay, or black coat, with chestnut and roan occurring less frequently; white markings on the face and legs are quite common as is prominent feathering (q.v.) on all four legs which often extends over the wall of the hoof; the hind legs are frequently cow-hocked (q.v.); is calm, sociable, strong and hardy; the stud book was established in 1878; historically used for hauling coal, farm work, and carriage while the modern horse is used for heavy draft, farm, and some carriage work.

Clydesdale Horse Society of Great Britain and Ireland An organization established in England in 1877 to maintain and perpetuate the quality and purity of the Clydesdale (q.v.).

coach Any enclosed, four-wheeled, horse-drawn passenger vehicle, used either in private or public service; usually drawn by a team (q.v.), but sometimes by a pair and driven by a coachman or postillion (q.v.); introduced during the late Middle Ages in the town of Krocs (pronounced croach) Hungary, from which the corruption of the name survived; used in continuous service in a variety of types through the 1920s including the stage coach (q.v.), concord coach (q.v.), drag coach (q.v.), mail coach (q.v.), state coach (q.v.), and park coach (q.v.).

coach-dog *see* DALMATIAN

coach horn Also known as yard of tin, three feet of tin, horn, or coaching horn; a straight funnel-ended horn, commonly made of brass or copper used by coachmen and/or coach guards to clear the road and announce the approach of a horse-drawn vehicle by means of a series of short notes or snatches of tunes; in pre-railway days were seldom more than 36 inches (91 cm) in length, while modern ones measure 52 inches (132 cm) or more.

coach horse Any middle- to heavy-weight horse such as a Hackney (q.v.), Friesian (q.v.), Cleveland Bay (q.v.) or Percheron (q.v.), used to draw a coach (q.v.).

Coaching Club An organization established in 1870 in England to organize and conduct coaching events; the constituency was comprised of owners of private four-in-hand coaches (q.v.) which met regularly through 1939 for organized drives, usually starting from the Magazine in Hyde Park, London.

coaching crop Also known as a coaching whip, driving whip, or tandem whip; a wood, fiberglass, bone, plastic, metal, or leather rod attached to a thong of leather or cord used as an aid by coachmen to drive harness and coach horses.

coaching horn *see* COACH HORN

coaching marathon A long-distance race for four-horse coaches first organized by the Royal International Horse Show (q.v.) in 1909 in England; coaches depart from a specified location at staggered intervals, the drive

ending in the show ring within a specific amount of time without a change of coachman; points are awarded for turnout (q.v.) and condition of the horses on arrival in the show ring, not for speed.

coaching whip *see* COACHING CROP

coachman Also known as dragsman; a man employed to drive one or more horses pulling a coach (q.v.) or carriage.

coachman's elbow The salute given by a coachman (q.v.), who, rather than raising his hat, raises the whip hand to face level, with the whip held aslant to the body thus raising the elbow, a position from which the name derived.

coachman's seat *see* BOX no. 3

coarse Said of a horse lacking refinement and quality.

coarseness around the jowl Said of a horse who has an accumulation of flesh at the jowl which restricts the flexion of the head.

coarse punched A nail hole in a horseshoe located towards the inner edge of the horseshoe web (q.v.).

coat (1) The hair (q.v.) covering the body of the horse. (2) A warm outer garment covering at least the upper part of the human body.

coating *see* COVERT CLOTH

coat patterns Refers to coat color; the patterns of white hair found in the coat; of three types: individual white hairs, asymmetric patches of white, and symmetric patches of white; horses are described first by the appropriate color designation followed by the pattern of white present, e.g., black patterned leopard; such patterns include, but are not limited to, tobiano (q.v.), overo (q.v.), sabino (q.v.), splashed white (q.v.), piebald (q.v.), skewbald (q.v.), rabicano (q.v.), frosty (q.v.), blanket (q.v.), leopard spotting (q.v.), varnish marks (q.v.), snowflake (q.v.), and mottled (q.v.).

cob Originally known as rouncy and spelled runcy; a type not a breed; a small, heavy-boned, short-coupled, and muscular horse or pony usually standing under 15.3 hands, having great depth of girth, and a short neck, legs, and cannon bones; most are a combination of two or more breeds; is capable of carrying up to 200 pounds (91 kg); originally used as a hack for heavy riders.

cobalamin *see* VITAMIN B$_{12}$

cobalt A mineral component of vitamin B$_{12}$ (q.v.) required for the synthesis thereof; the dietary requirements for a mature horse are extremely low and are usually met by a normal diet.

cobby Said of a close-coupled (q.v.) and stoutly built horse as a cob (q.v.).

cockade A brooch or fastening for three-cornered hats introduced into England and Germany in the second half of the 18th century; now an oval- or fan-shaped rosette (q.v.) used as a badge of office; fastened to the side of a liveried servant's top hat when in formal dress.

cocked ankles An American term; bent forward or cocked fetlocks (q.v.), a condition usually found in the hind feet and commonly attributable to improper hoof trimming; results in short toes, long heels, and in some cases, lameness.

cock eye Also spelled cockeye; an oval-shaped metal eye attached to the end of lead trace (q.v.); the means by which the trace is secured to the lead bar hook in harness tack.

cockeye *see* COCK EYE

cock fence A jumping obstacle; a natural hedge or thorn fence trimmed to a low level.

cockhorse A driving term; an extra horse, usually of a flashy color, used in the lead of a team (q.v.) to assist in pulling a heavily loaded stage uphill; always ridden by a cockhorse boy (q.v.).

cockhorse boy Generally, a young, light-weight boy trained to ride a cockhorse (q.v.).

Cocking cart Also known as a suicide gig; a two-wheeled, horse-drawn English vehicle popular in the late 18th century for travel to sport events such as cock fights from which the name derived; mounted on high wheels and had a slatted underboot for carrying fighting cocks or dogs; seated two in the front and had a high rearward seat for a groom; gener-

ally drawn by a tandem (q.v.); a later version, popular in the 1890s and 1900s for pleasure driving, could be drawn by three horses abreast.

cocktail (1) The common name for a half breed English hunter (q.v.). (2) A racing term; a horse of racing quality, but not a Thoroughbred (q.v.). (3) Slang; a horse with a docked tail (q.v.).

Cock Tail An antiquated term; a horse with one or no parents registered in the General Stud book (q.v.).

cock throttled *see* SWAN NECK

cocoa shells The thin covering of the cocoa bean; contain approximately 15 percent protein, 17 percent fiber, 10 percent ash and 0.5 to 2.0 percent theobromine, which when used in small amounts may increase cardiac output, urine excretion, appetite and may function as a smooth muscle relaxant; high intake may cause a loss of appetite, diarrhea, and death.

codeine A white, crystalline, slightly bitter alkaloid obtained from opium used as an analgesic, constipant, sedative, and hypnotic; administered orally or mixed with honey or molasses into a paste to be applied to the tongue.

co-favorite A racing term; two or more horses equally favored to win a race who are generally given the same odds.

coffee-housing A hunting term; said of mounted riders who chat with each other rather than attending to the activity of the hunt (q.v.).

coffin cab A two-wheeled, horse-drawn, coffin-shaped vehicle of the Hackney (q.v.) type used in London, England prior to the hansom cab (q.v.); carried two passengers and was drawn by a single horse.

coffin bone *see* THIRD PASTERN

coffin head Said of a horse with a coarse, ugly face, and a jaw lacking prominence.

Coggins test A blood test conducted to detect the presence of antibodies for the equine infectious anemia (q.v.) virus.

cold A racing term; said of a horse unfit to

win a horse race due to his physical condition or jockey intervention.

cold back Also known as back up; said of a horse showing initial resistance to fitting the saddle and tightening the girth; a condition generally alleviated by fitting the saddle loosely and walking the horse for some time before mounting.

cold blood A generic term; any heavy-boned, even-tempered Northern European horse breed descended from the northern forest type horse, e.g., the tundra and steppe horses; not actually coldblooded, but originally from the colder climates; does not have any Arab blood; includes such breeds as the Shire (q.v.), Suffolk (q.v.), Percheron (q.v.), Clydesdale (q.v.) and the Punch (q.v.).

cold-blooded Said of a cold blood (q.v.) horse.

cold brand *see* FREEZE BRAND

cold fit *see* COLD SHOE no. 2

cold-jawed Said of a horse having a tough mouth, one resistant to the effects of the bit.

cold hose To run a stream of cold water on or over an injury to reduce inflammation.

cold line *see* STALE LINE

cold scent *see* STALE LINE

cold shoe (1) *see* READY-MADE SHOE. (2) Also known as cold fit or cold shoeing; to shoe a horse with ready-made (q.v.) shoes shaped to fit the hoof cold, on the anvil, without the benefit of the forge (q.v.); a much faster shoeing process than hot shoeing (q.v.).

cold shoer Any farrier who shoes horses without the benefit of a forge (q.v.) to shape the horseshoe (q.v.) to the hoof.

cold shoeing *see* COLD SHOE no. 2

cold trailing A cutting horse term; said of a horse in a working position who lags well behind the movement of the cow.

coleaderos One of nine scored events in a charreada (q.v.) in which a charro (q.v.) tails a wild bull.

colic Also known as gripes, stomach staggers, spasms of the gastrointestinal tract, or incorrectly as bloat and enteric fever; abdominal pain of any origin; caused by digestive disorders which may result from improper chewing, systemic disease, circulatory disturbances, digestive system infection, neuromuscular disturbances, twisting of the intestine, fatty tumors, gastric dilation caused by grain overload, toxicity, bots, water deprivation, nutritional factors such as feed high in fiber or poor in quality, sudden changes in feed, and feed too high in energy; associated pain is caused either by obstruction of the ingesta (q.v.), resulting in increased gas production that stretches the intestines, or by spasms in the alimentary canal; symptoms include lack of appetite, pawing, kicking at the abdomen, getting up and down, rolling, restlessness, flank watching and/or biting, elevated skin temperature, sweating (due to pain), increased and/or thready pulse, abnormal mucosa color, gut sounds, feces or the lack thereof, and body postures such as dog-sitting or a sawhorse stance; Arabs (q.v.) are 2.5 times more likely to colic than Thoroughbreds (q.v.); types include torsion colic (q.v.), sand colic (q.v.), impaction colic (q.v.), intussception colic (q.v.), and false colic (q.v.).

colic in foals A digestive tract disorder of foals characterized by acute abdominal pain; most commonly caused by intussusception (q.v.) which only responds to immediate surgery; colic (q.v.) occurring within the first 48 hours of life is caused chiefly by impaction of the large intestine due to meconium retention; may also be caused by a ruptured bladder or *atresia coli*.

colitis-X A sporadic disease which on occasion may affect several horses within a group; all ages other than foals are affected, but it occurs most commonly in two-to five-year-olds; the cause is unknown, although it may be associated with endotoxic shock; many affected horses have a history of stress or upper respiratory infection one to three weeks prior to onset; symptoms include copious, watery, mucoid, and occasionally blood-stained diarrhea, depression, mild abdominal discomfort, rapid onset of hypovolemic shock, and elevated heart rate as the disease progresses; death may occur within three hours of onset, or in less acute cases, within 24 to 48 hours.

collagen granuloma A condition in which

rotten collagen fibers in the skin's structure are buried between layers of healthy tissue, forming hard bumps; are slow growing and commonly appear on the back and sides of the horse where they may be rubbed raw by tack and/or blankets; may be surgically cored to allow expulsion of the dead fibers.

collar (1) *see* HARNESS COLLAR. (2) *see* COLLAR OF A WHIP

collar buttons Refers to coat color; a few concentrated spots of black hair on the neck just below where it joins the body; common to donkeys.

collar of a whip Also known as collar; the narrow, metal band which separates the leather, bone, or synthetic handpiece from the shaft of a whip (q.v.).

collar work A driving term; any work uphill, pulling heavy loads, or that which requires the horse to strain against the collar (q.v.).

collect (1) To shorten the pace of the horse using light hand contact on the reins and steady pressure from the rider's legs to make the horse flex its neck, relax its jaw, elevate the back, and bring its hocks well under its body; impulsion created by the hind legs is contained by the rider's hands. (2) Said of a bettor (q.v.); to win a wager on a horse, event, etc.

collected Said of a horse moved forward from behind and ridden into the bit with its neck flexed, jaw relaxed, hocks well under the body, back up, and his weight over the haunches.

collected canter A pace in which the horse is ridden at the canter (q.v.) into the bit with his neck flexed and arched, jaw relaxed, hindquarters engaged and active, forehand light, and shoulders supple and free; the stride is shorter than at other canters but lighter and more mobile.

collected trot A pace in which the horse is ridden at the trot (q.v.) into the bit with his neck flexed and arched, jaw relaxed, hocks well under the body with energetic impulsion, and the weight over the haunches; the horse is moved forward from behind; the steps are shorter, but lighter and more mobile than at other trots.

collected walk A pace in which the horse is ridden at the walk (q.v.) into the bit with his neck flexed, jaw relaxed, hocks well under the body with good action, and the weight over the haunches; the horse is moved forward from behind; the pace is vigorous with each step placed in regular sequence; the stride is shortened and shows greater activity than at the medium walk (q.v.).

collection Also known as self carriage and engaging the hindquarters; a learned weight-bearing posture of the horse; the increased and energetic engagement of the hind legs, elevation of the back, and lightening the forehand resulting in improved balance; the degree of desired collection varies greatly from sport to sport.

collier *see* PIT PONY

Collier's horse *see* KNOCKER

colon impaction Also known as constipation; difficult, painful, or infrequent passage of feces resulting from inactivity, debility, senility, obstruction due to a foreign body, or poor feeding.

Colorado Ranger A type of horse evolved from the Appaloosa (q.v.) to which it is similarly colored; found in the Colorado region of the United States.

color breed To develop desired coat colors by means of selective breeding.

colored (1) Also known as colored horse; said of an Appaloosa (q.v.) showing any coat color combination approved by the Appaloosa Horse Club (q.v.). (2) Also known as colored horse; any horse showing more than one coat color.

colored horse *see* COLORED

colors (1) Also known as silks, racing silks, or racing colors; a racing term; a silk or nylon, uniquely patterned jockey jacket and cap as selected by the owner of the mount and worn by the jockey (q.v.) during a race, a practice introduced in Newmarket, England in 1767; the distinctive patterns and colors are registered annually with The Jockey Club (q.v.) and with the appropriate state racing authority by the owner; at some smaller tracks, colors designate post positions (q.v.), e.g., yellow for post position one, blue for two, etc.; known as silks because they were originally made of that material. (2) A hunting term; distinctively colored hunt coat collars (q.v.) worn by the hunt staff and such members of the field as have been invited to wear them by the Hunt Master (q.v.).

colostrum Also known as first milk; the thick, extra-rich milk secreted by the mare's mammary glands upon birth of a foal; contains globulins and proteins that provide the foal with temporary, two to three months' immunity, against infectious disease until such time as the foal's system begins producing sufficient antibodies.

colt A young, uncastrated, horse less than three years of age or, in Thoroughbreds (q.v.), less than four years.

colt bit *see* TATTERSALL BIT

colt foal The male sex of a foal (q.v.).

comb (1) A toothed instrument of bone, rubber, plastic, or metal used for arranging, cleansing, or adjusting the hair, as the mane. (2) To dress, as the hair, with or as with a comb.

combination (1) *see* COMBINATION FENCE. (2) Also known as combination bet; racing term; any across-the-board (q.v.) bet for which a single mutuel ticket is issued.

combination bet *see* COMBINATION no. 2

combination horse A horse used for both riding and driving.

combination fence Also known as combination or combination obstacle; any obstacle (q.v.) consisting of two or more separate jumps or elements of any type which are numbered and judged as one which usually have a single or double non-jumping stride between each portion; the maximum distance between any two of the fences may not exceed 39 feet 4 inches (11.98 m), as measured from the inside element of the two fences at ground level.

combination obstacle *see* COMBINATION FENCE

combined   immunodeficiency Also known by the acronym CID; a genetically based fatal disease resulting in a failure of the immune system.

combined driving trial A driving competition consisting of four phases: Competition A, section one, presentation, Competition A (q.v.), section two dressage test, Competition B (q.v.), the marathon phase, and Competition C (q.v.), the obstacle course; the competitor with the lowest overall score is the winner.

combined test An eventing (q.v.) term; a special combined training event conducted in one day which consists of dressage and show jumping phases.

combined training Also known as eventing; a generic term; a three-phase competition consisting of dressage, jumping, and endurance phases, the latter including steeplechase, roads and tracks, and cross country; conducted over a period of one, two, or three days and performed by the same rider/horse team; in three-day (q.v.) and two-day events (q.v.), the endurance competition is made up of Phase A, short roads and tracks, followed by Phase B, steeplechase, followed by Phase C, long roads and tracks, followed by Phase D, cross-country; in horse trials (q.v.), the endurance competition is made up of only the cross-country component; originated as a military sport known as military trials or horse trials (q.v.) which was a test of the stamina and versatility of the military mounts; a rigorous sport for the all-round rider and mount; on the international level conducted over a three-day period.

combined training competition *see* COMBINED TRAINING

combined   training   event *see* HORSE TRIALS

come back to A racing term; said of a horse who slows down after taking the lead in the start of a horse race allowing the other horses in the field to close the gap.

comes again *see* SECOND WIND

come in front of the vertical Said of the horse who moves his head forward from a position perpendicular to the ground, thus raising his nose and hollowing his back.

come to a halt To slow up a horse gradually, from any pace or gait, through a step or two at the walk, to a controlled and collected standstill.

coming Said of a horse approaching one year of age, as in "the bay was coming three years of age."

command Gogue One of two types of de Gogue (q.v.); an advanced piece of schooling equipment consisting of an arrangement of straps, fastened on one end to the girth or chest ring, which split and run through rings on either side of a poll pad, down through the bit rings on the same side, and attach to a rein, other than the snaffle rein, on the other; assist the action of the bit by restricting the position of the horse's head and neck through action on the poll (q.v.); may be controlled by the rider.

commingle A racing term; to combine the mutuel pools from off-track sites with the host track.

comminuted fracture A break in a bone consisting of more than two fragments.

commission bet Any wager in which a percentage of the resulting winnings is paid to the party who placed the bet on behalf of the first.

commit A cutting horse term; said of a horse/rider team who demonstrates its intention to work a specific cow by looking at and stepping towards it.

committed A cutting term; said of a horse in competition when he has visibly cut a cow from the herd and is obligated to work it.

common Said of a horse of coarse appearance; generally the progeny of cold-blood, non-pedigree, or generic stock.

common alum Also known as potash alum; a type of alum (q.v.) used in medicine as an astringent and styptic.

common bay *see* BAY

common blood Non pedigree or purebred, as in the breeding of a horse.

common bone Said of bone of inferior quality, one which lacks density, is coarse-grained, and has a large central core.

common-bred Said of a horse bred from mixed, non-pedigree or generic stock.

common riding *see* HAYWICK COMMON RIDING

common salt *see* SODIUM CHLORIDE

Commons, Open Spaces and Footpaths Preservation Society An organization founded in England in 1865 to create, protect, and maintain public footpaths, bridlepaths, and other highways.

Comparable Index Also known by the acronym CI; an Average-Earnings Index (AEI) (q.v.) for stallions; establishes statistics for all the progeny of mares to whom a stallion was bred when the mares were bred to other stallions, e.g., a stallion with an AEI of 2.00 might have a CI of 1.00 which means that those same mares produced foals who earned a 1.00 AEI when bred to other stallions; a stallion can improve the mare or the converse.

competition An athletic contest between riders, horses, and/or horse and rider combinations.

Competition A Section One A driving term; usually the first phase of the four-phase combined driving trial (q.v.); a total of 50 marks can be gained based on presentation, consisting of 10 potential points each for: the driver and grooms or social passengers acting as grooms, the horse or horses, the vehicle, the harness, and the overall impression; a score of 10 is deemed excellent and one very bad.

Competition A Section Two A driving term; usually the second phase of the four-phase combined driving trial (q.v.); a dressage test in which the driver maneuvers a horse-drawn vehicle around markers (q.v.) to demonstrate that the horse(s) is obedient, calm, supple, and has correct paces; full use of the arena and smooth transitions are important in achieving a good score; 11 movements are required.

Competition B Also known as the marathon phase; a driving term; usually the third of four phases of a combined driving trial (q.v.) the objective of which is to test the fitness and stamina of the horse or horses and to test the judgment of pace and horse mastership of the competitors; usually occurs on one or two days following Competitions A Sections One and Two; consists of sections A – E, with section E involving the negotiation of obstacles.

Competition C Also known as the obstacle course; a driving term; the final phase of a four-phase combined driving trial (q.v.) the objective of which is to test the fitness, obedience, and suppleness of the horse following Competition B; drivers navigate a course consisting of up to 20 obstacles such as cones, on top of which rubber balls are balanced, laid out in a smooth pattern in a dressage arena; faults are incurred when either cones or balls are toppled; competitors with the lowest score going into this phase go first.

complete fracture A break in the bone which extends through both bone surfaces.

complete test *see* THREE-DAY EVENT

complementary lameness Lameness in a previously sound limb due to pain in another limb; pain will cause uneven distribution of weight on another limb(s).

compound fracture Also known as an open fracture; a break in a bone in which the broken bone penetrates the skin and exposes the bone; the risk of infection is very high.

compression bow *see* BANDAGE BOW

compulsory exercises A vaulting term; a group of movements in a vaulting competition consisting of the vault on, simple dismount, basic seat, flare (q.v.), stand (q.v.), mill (q.v.), scissors (q.v.), and flank (q.v.); are the basis of all freestyle compositions.

compulsory halt The 10-minute break between the speed and endurance test phases in a three-day event (q.v.).

computerized tomography Also known as CT scanning; a diagnostic technique in which a large scanning instrument revolves around a body part in a 180-degree arc, while a pencil-thin electromagnetic beam records images in slices of the structure; the resulting images are used to pinpoint abscesses, tumors, cysts, etc. that escape detection by traditional X-rays.

concave face *see* DISH FACE

conchal sinus *see* DENTIGEROUS CYST

concord *see* CONCORD COACH

Concord coach Also known as American mail coach and, in the 1820s, as the Concord; the most popular horse-drawn coach or stage used in North America with versions later used in Australia, New Zealand, and South Africa; was oval shaped, hung on leather thoroughbraces, and had double benches for passengers seated vis-à-vis; mail and valuables were carried in a fore-boot while ordinary luggage was strapped to the roof or contained within the rear boot, the latter having a sloping top; drawn by teams of from four to eight horses, depending on the terrain and vehicle size; driven from a box seat which the driver generally shared with a guard; on some 16 seaters, there was a separate guard's seat in the rear, perched on a skeleton framework; developed by Downing and Company of Concord, New Hampshire, USA, for which the vehicle was named.

Concours Complete *see* THREE-DAY EVENT

Concours Complete d'Equitation *see* THREE-DAY EVENT

Concours Voltige d'Amitie Also known by the acronym CVA; an international vaulting (q.v.) event open to competitors from the host country and up to four foreign nations.

Concours Voltige Frontière Also know by the acronym CVF; an international vaulting (q.v.) event open to competitors from the host country and up to four foreign nations.

condition The state of health and fitness of the horse.

Condition Book A racing term; a publication produced by the track racing secretary which identifies the purses, terms of eligibility, and weight formulas for each race to be run over a period of about two weeks at a specific track; used by horsemen to determine in what race to enter a horse based on eligibility.

conditioner (1) *see* TRAINER. (2) A racing term; a workout or race used to encourage fitness in the horse. (3) A liquid or cream applied to the mane and tail of the horse to moisturize and prevent tangling.

condition race Also known as terms race; a racing term; any race other than a handicap race (q.v.) for which specific entry conditions exist, e.g., for horses that have not won a race of $1,000.

conditions A racing term; the specifics of a race such as purse size, eligibility for entry, and weight formulas or concessions.

condition scoring A method of rating the relative thinness or fatness of a horse on a scale of one to nine developed at Texas A&M University, USA; provides a framework for visual weight assessment; not an objective method of calculation.

condylar fracture A break in the distal (q.v.), knobby end of a long bone such as the cannon bone, which serves to form an articulation with another bone.

Conestoga Wagon A large, horse-drawn, covered farm and freight wagon popular in the United States during the 1750s; had a canvas top supported by between 8 and 13 sloping tilts, a floor and bodywork of wooden planking curved slightly downwards to the fore-carriage, front boards and tail gates inclined outwards at both the front and rear, with a significant amount of overhang beyond the axletrees, and a driving seat pulled out from the front of the wagon on the near side; drawn by teams of six or more horses or oxen depending on the weight of the load pulled; much larger than the Prairie Schooner (q.v.).

confidential An antiquated British term; a horse suitable for a novice or elderly rider.

confinement *see* PARTURITION

conformation The shape or body structure of a horse, with particular attention paid to proportion.

congenital (1) Acquired during the development of the fetus in the uterus and not through heredity. (2) Exisiting at or dating from birth.

congenital abnormality *see* CONGENITAL TRAIT

congenital defect *see* CONGENITAL TRAIT

congenital deformity *see* CONGENITAL TRAIT

congenital mark Any mark on the coat of the horse inclusive of the limbs, body and head, present from birth, but not as a result of heredity; may be used for identification purposes.

congenital trait Also known as congenital abnormality, congenital deformity, or congenital defect; any structural or functional defect acquired during the development of the fetus in the uterus; may or may not have clearly established causes, although environmental, nutritional, or genetic factors may contribute; not necessarily hereditary.

congestive heart failure Also known by the acronym CHF; cessation of the horse's heart function; occurs when a horse's heart muscle is so severely damaged or overworked it loses its strength and can no longer pump blood efficiently; symptoms include flared nostrils, a swollen chest and belly, weak or erratic pulse, and an increased heart rate while at rest; the blood pools around the heart and in the lung area, eventually leaking through the tissues, collecting under the skin, causing the horse's underline to appear swollen; diagnostics include X-rays (q.v.), echocardiography (q.v.), and electrocardiography (q.v.); although rare, may strike horses of any age.

connections A racing term; the owner, trainer, and others involved with custodianship of a horse.

Connemara Also known as Connemara pony or, generically, as a native pony; the only breed of horse indigenous to Ireland; an ancient pony breed which benefited from crosses with Barbs (q.v.) and Spanish Horses (q.v.), infusions of Arab (q.v.) blood, and more recently the English Thoroughbred (q.v.); is hardy, docile, intelligent, sound, and generally raised in the wild; stands 13 to 14.2 hands, has a small head with a straight profile, a long, well-formed neck, high withers (q.v.), full mane and tail, sturdy and well-muscled legs often measuring 7-8 inches (18-20 cm) at the cannon, and a slightly sloping croup; coat colors include gray, dun, black, bay, brown, and occasionally roan or chestnut; piebalds and skewbalds are not accepted by the breed society; historically used for farming and packing, but now used for riding and jumping; the Stud book was established in 1924.

Connemara Breeder's Society *see* CONNEMARA PONY BREEDER'S SOCIETY, THE

Connemara Pony *see* CONNEMARA

Connemara Pony Breeder's Society, the Also known as the Connemara Breeder's Society; an organization founded in Eire in

1923 to encourage the breeding of the Connemara (q.v.), to develop and maintain them as a pure breed, and to maintain the Stud Book.

Connemara Pony Society, The English
see ENGLISH CONNEMARA SOCIETY

Conquistadors The 16th-century Spanish conquerors of Mexico credited with the reintroduction of horses to the western hemisphere following their disappearance millions of years before.

consignor One who offers a horse for sale through an auction.

consolation double A racing term; a payoff to holders of daily double (q.v.) tickets which pair a scratched horse from the second race with a winning horse from the first.

constipation *see* COLON IMPACTION

Con Sullivan *see* SULLIVAN, CON

contact The connection between the rider's hands and the horse's mouth achieved through the reins.

contagious equine metritis Also known by the acronym CEM; a highly contagious bacterial venereal disease; resides in infected stallions in the prepuce and on the surface of the penis and is transmitted during coitus; mares develop a profuse, sticky discharge two to six days following service; the conception rate is low, but after the infection subsides, fertility is regained in ensuing estrual periods; may be passed to foals at birth, which retain the infection until they reach breeding age.

continental   martingale A   martingale (q.v.); an auxiliary rein or strap used to assist the action of the bit by restricting the position of the horse's head and neck; consists of an arrangement of straps, fastened to the girth at one end which pass through the bridle on either side of the poll (q.v.), and down to the bit rings on the other; encourages a low head set through applied pressure on the poll and bridge of the nose.

contract rider A racing term; a jockey (q.v.) obligated by contract to provide his services first to the contract holder/owner of the mount (q.v.) before riding for another.

contracted feet *see* CONTRACTED HEELS

contracted heels Also known as contracted feet; a narrowing of the heels (q.v.) and frog (q.v.) of the hoof due to a lack of frog pressure; more common in the fore than the hind feet of light horses; may be caused by improper shoeing or trimming of the feet; symptoms include a shortened stride and heat around the quarters (q.v.) and heels; a narrow foot is not necessarily a contracted one.

contusion A blunt injury that does not break the skin, but which damages the deep tissues and/or bone; characterized by swelling, heat, and tenderness.

convulsive foal *see* BARKER

cooked Said of a young horse overtrained to the point of souring; as due to stress and other associated emotional strain.

cook him *see* BLOW HIM

cool down *see* COOL OUT

cooler (1) A horse blanket made of wool, acrylic, cotton, or other fabrics draped over the neck and back of a horse while it cools down after a workout, race, show, etc.; allows the horse to lower its body temperature slowly. (2) A racing term; a horse restrained by the rider to prevent it from running well.

cool out Also known as cooling out or cool down; to restore a horse, overheated by exercise, to its normal body temperature following a workout, as by walking it quietly.

cooling out *see* COOL OUT

coon foot Said of the hoof of the horse when the pastern slopes more than the dorsal surface of the hoof.

coon-footed Said of a horse having a foot in which the pastern slopes more than the dorsal surface of the hoof wall, the axis being broken at the coronary band (q.v.); may occur in either the fore or hind feet.

Copaicut Also spelled Copicutt; a four-wheeled, horse-drawn passenger wagon or phaeton (q.v.) widely used in North American colonies during the late 18th century; outfitted with two parallel, forward-facing cross seats, the rear seat was hung on thoroughbraces rather than springs; the rear portion of the vehicle slanted outwards; drawn by a single

horse.

COPD The acronym for chronic obstructive pulmonary disease (q.v.).

cope A hunting term; a cheer of the whippers-in (q.v.) meaning to ride forward as in "cope-forward."

coper Also known as horse-coper or horsecouper; one who deals in horses using shrewd or underhanded methods to influence the sale or purchase.

copicutt *see* COPAICUT

Coppa Delle Nazione *see* PRIX DES NATIONS

copper A reddish-brown, malleable, ductile, metallic element that is required in trace amounts in the diet of the horse for bone, cartilage, and elastin formation, utilization of iron, and formation of the pigments of the hair; dietary requirements are estimated at between 5-8 ppm; deficiency is rare and excess copper can be toxic.

copper sulfate Also known as blue stone or blue vitriole; a compound occurring in large, transparent, deep-blue triclinic crystals used as an astringent (q.v.) and caustic (q.v.) agent in the reduction of granulation tissue (q.v.) when applied either as a paste or dry crystal or as an anti-fungal treatment for ringworm (q.v.).

coprophagy To eat manure; a vice in mature horses and in foals considered a normal stage of development.

cording The cruel, and now illegal, practice of tying a stiff cord around the horse's tongue and attaching the ends to either side of the bit cheekpieces so that a slight jerk on the reins cuts the tongue with the cord; it was believed that the sudden pain would cause the horse to step higher.

cording up *see* TYING UP

cordobán Cordovan (q.v.) leather.

cordovan (1) Made of cordovan leather. (2) A soft, fine-grained, colored leather manufactured of split horse hides, pig skin, and goat hides. (3) Of or belonging to Córdoba, Spain. (4) Also known as shell cordovan; leather tanned from the inner layer of horse hide from the haunches and distinguished by its non-porosity, density, and long wearing qualities. (5) A variable color averaging a dark grayish red that is darker and slightly more yellow than average rose brown.

Corinthians A British term popular in the 1800s; aristocratic, wealthy amateur sportsmen, who liked to drive well-horsed coaches, curricles (q.v.) and highflyer phaetons (q.v.).

corium Also known as cutis or true skin; the sensitive vascular layer of the skin beneath the epidermis (q.v.)

cork (1) *see* BLOCKED HEEL no. 2. (2) *see* CALK

Corlay A coldblood originating in Brittany, France more than 4,000 years ago; the smallest of three distinct morphological types of Breton (q.v.) descended from native Brittany mares crossed with Norfolk Roadsters (q.v.); used for riding and light, fast draft work; is now quite rare if not extinct.

corn (1) A low fiber (2 to 2-1/2 percent), high carbohydrate, low-protein (about 10 percent digestible protein which is deficient in several amino acids, notably lysine), high starch (65 to 75 percent), high fat (4 percent) and high energy grain second only to oats (q.v.) as a feed for horses; may range in color from white to yellow; contains a higher level of vitamin A than other feed grains and is a good source of vitamin E, thiamin, niacin, and riboflavin; may be fed whole, cracked, or on the ear. (2) A specific type of bruising occurring in the sole of the foot at the angle between the hoof wall and the bar; most common in the forefeet on the inner quarter and is usually associated with poor shoeing. (3) Refers to coat color pattern; small dark spots appearing in the coat which are unrelated to scarring; the number of dark spots generally increases with age; provides further detail to the roan (q.v.) classification by identifying the color of the spots, e.g., a blue roan with corn spots would be known as a blue corn; the term originated in the American West as the color pattern resembles the arrangement of dark kernels on an Indian ear of corn.

corneal scar A mark appearing on the cornea of the eye after a wound has healed; when fresh, surrounded by a bluish, misty cloud; tends to dissipate over a period of months or years and may turn brown with age.

corner incisors Also known as corners or third incisors; four of the 12 incisor teeth (q.v.) of the horse located on either side of the laterals (q.v.) top and bottom; appear about 10 months after birth.

corner man A cutting term; a mounted rider responsible for keeping a herd of cattle to be worked by a cutter (q.v.) in the center of the pen and flowing around the cutter when he is selecting a cow, and to prevent a selected cow from returning to the herd.

corners *see* CORNER INCISORS

Cornet's Chase The principal event of the Haywick Common Riding held annually the first full week of June in Scotland; the event re-enacts the capture of a standard from the men of Haywick in 1514; the Cornet, a bachelor and the standard-bearer, is chased at a gallop by the townsmen up the steep slope of Vertish Hill.

Corinthian whip A driving whip fashionable in England between 1811 and 1820.

coronary (1) Related to the vascular system of the heart. (2) Related to the coronet (q.v.).

coronary band Also known as coronet or coronet band; the part of the leg at the distal (q.v.) end of the pastern where the hair stops and hoof growth begins between the perioplic ring (q.v.) and the sensitive laminae (q.v.); consists of fibro-fatty tissue covered by a vascular fleshy covering from which the hoof wall emanates; lies in the coronary groove located on the upper border of the hoof wall; similar to the quick in the human nail.

coronary crack A sand crack (q.v.) emanating from the coronary band (q.v.) and traveling downward.

coronary contraction of the foot Also known as local contraction of the foot; a narrowing of the heels at the horn immediately below the coronary cushion; an arbitrary subdivision of contracted heels (q.v.).

Coronation Coach *see* STATE COACH

coronet (1) *see* CORONARY BAND. (2) A leg marking (q.v.); a white mark on the leg of the horse consisting of a narrow band of white extending from the coronary band (q.v.) upward approximately one inch; extends cir-cumferentially around the foot and includes the heel.

coronet band *see* CORONARY BAND

corpora nigra An irregular, awning-like projection of the eye's iris, located over the upper edge of the pupil; shields the retina from excessive light.

corpus luteum Also known as yellow body and by the acronym CL; a mass of endocrine cells formed in the ruptured ovarian follicle after departure of the unfertilized egg; secretes progesterone, the hormone that maintains pregnancy.

corral (1) A round enclosure used to turn out, break, or hold horses and other animals. (2) To confine in, as in a corral; to seize or capture.

corrected score Any score awarded in a competition (q.v.) that is changed by the officials due to objection or a calculation or posting error.

corrective shoe (1) Any horseshoe (q.v.) that compensates for a defect in the stance or gait of a horse. (2) *see* THERAPEUTIC SHOE

corrective shoeing To put horseshoes on a horse to change its balance or way of traveling as to modify gait and conformation faults.

corrida de toros A classic Spanish bullfight performed by the bullfighter and picador (q.v.).

corse dei Berberi The famous Berber horse race conducted in Rome in 1400 of which Pope Paul II was the patron.

cortex *see* DIAPHYSIS

corticosteroids Analogs of the hormone cortisol primarily produced by the adrenal glands (q.v.) which function as anti-inflammatory hormones and influence metabolism, healing, allergic reactions, kidney function, and the body's electrolyte balance; the anti-inflammatory effects cannot be realized without side effects that influence tissue healing, hormonal balance, and so on; may be used intravenously (q.v.), intramuscularly (q.v.), intra-articularly (q.v.), locally, or topically (q.v.); may be natural or synthetically produced for injection.

cortisol Also known as hydrocortisone; a hormone produced in the adrenal gland (q.v.) which affects the metabolism of fat and water, muscle tone, nerve stimulation, and inflammation.

cortisone A colorless crystalline steriod hormone produced in the adrenal cortex prepared from the adrenal glands of certain domesticated animals or made synthetically; acts chiefly on carbohydrate metabolism, and used to treat inflammation; administered either orally or intramuscularly.

corvina A horse-drawn Gallic war chariot with scythe-hubbed wheels first used in Britain and Gaul during the time of the Roman conquests; entered from the rear rather than the front and drawn by a pair of fast horses harnessed with side traces and a neck yoke.

cosh *see* BAT

costal arch The arch of the chest cavity formed by the last nine ribs and the costal cartilage (q.v.) that connects them.

costal cartilage Cartilage (q.v.) that joins the ribs to the sternum to create the costal arch (q.v.); remains as cartilage for the life of the horse.

Costeño One of three types of Criollo (q.v.) or Salterno (q.v.) horses bred in Peru, the other two being the Morochuco (q.v.) and the Chola (q.v.); descended from Spanish stock brought to South America by the conquistadors in the 16th century; has a distinctive high-stepping gait known as the paso lano (q.v.).

cottage windows Windows used in horse-drawn stage coaches when divided into four small panes.

cotton eye Said of the eye of the horse when a lot of white shows around the iris.

cottonseed meal Also called cottonseed oil meal; a high protein, high energy concentrate produced from the residue of the cotton seed after oil extraction; total protein varies from 30 to 40 percent and the fat from 2 to 6 percent in an inverse relationship to the protein; higher in fiber, but lower in lysine than soybean meal; supplementation should not exceed 15 to 16 percent of the total ration due to the presence of gossypol, a chemical substance which may be toxic.

cottonseed oil meal *see* COTTONSEED MEAL

cough Expulsion of air from the lungs marked by sudden loud noise; may result from inflammation or irritation to the lower or upper airways including the pharynx, larynx, or trachea.

couldn't beat a fat man A racing term; a slow horse.

counter (1) The rear strip which covers the seam on the leg of a riding boot. (2) *see* HEEL no. 2. (3) A hunting term; said of a hound when he runs the line of a fox (q.v.) in the opposite direction to that the fox is traveling.

counter canter Also known as galop faux, false canter, or counter lead; an elementary dressage movement performed on a single track, where the horse leads with his outside leg (q.v.) on a circle or bend instead of the inside leg (q.v.) or natural lead; used as a suppling, balancing, strengthening, and straightening exercise.

counter half-pass A dressage movement in which the half-pass (q.v.) is performed in a zigzag formation through X (q.v.); the horse, on changing direction, must change flexion evenly throughout the entire length of his body.

counterirritant An agent that when applied produces a localized irritation to counteract irritation or relieve pain or inflammation elsewhere.

counter lead *see* COUNTER CANTER

country (1) A hunting term; the area over which a pack of hounds may hunt as authorized by the governing associations. (2) A rural district as opposed to cities or towns.

coup *see* COUP STICK

coupe *see* COUPE no. 1

coupé (1) Also spelled coupe; a closed, four-wheeled, horse-drawn town carriage with a truncated body designed for greater compactness and improved appearance; seated four, was drawn by a single horse or pair, and driven by a coachman from a box located in front of the box window; hung on elliptical springs under the coachman's seat in which the wheels turned; from the French word for cut.

(2) A class of accommodation offered on diligence (q.v.) vehicles during 19th and 20th-century Europe; the seats were enclosed with windows; and located behind the wheelers (q.v.), accommodated three forward-facing passengers and had limited leg space due to the proximity to the horses.

couple (1) A hunting term; two hounds; the number of hounds in a pack is counted in couples and couples and a half, e.g., four and half couples equals nine hounds; one hound is known as one hound rather than one half a couple. (2) To fasten, link, or join together in a pair or pairs as in hounds by means of leather collars connected by a short chain, or one horse to another by means of a harness.

coupled (1) Also known as coupled entry or entry; a racing term; said of two or more horses belonging to the same owner or trained by the same person who run as an entry (q.v.) and comprise a single betting unit; a bet on one horse of an entry is a bet on both; in the program the horses would be listed, regardless of post position, as 1, 1A, and so on. (2) A hunting term; said of two hounds joined together by means of leather collars connected by a short chain.

coupled entry *see* COUPLED

couples (1) A hunting term; hound collars joined by a metal distance link; this link is generally carried on the dee-ring (q.v.) of the whipper-in's saddle. (2) A driving term; the two buckle or snap-hook ends of a lead rein.

coupling (1) The length and muscle development of the loin area of the horse between the last rib and the point of the hip which connects the hindquarters to the front end. (2) A driving term; an adjustment of the coupling reins (q.v.) on the draft reins (q.v.).

coupling buckle The buckle on the coupling rein (q.v.) which joins it to the draft rein (q.v.) in pair and team harnesses.

coupling rein The shorter piece of a pair rein buckled to the bit on one end and to the draft rein (q.v.) on the other; used in pair and tandem team driving.

coupling up A driving term; to fasten the coupling reins (q.v.) to the draft reins (q.v.) in pair and team driving.

coup stick A light pole between 5 and 6 feet (1.5–1.8 m) in length to which the feathers or scalps taken by an American Indian were attached; believed that the more coups on a stick, the greater the warrior; historically attached to the lodge pole of the teepee, or carried by the mounted warriors as proof of bravery; replicas of the coup sticks are often carried in Appaloosa (q.v.) Indian Costume classes in horse shows; from the American Indian coup (pronounced coo) meaning a trophy of the scalp or feathers.

courbette Also known as curvet; a classical air above the ground (q.v.) in which the horse rears to an angle of 45 degrees, 30 degrees in a more advanced courbette, and when reaching a height of over 8 ft (2.4 m), leaps forward several times on his hind legs while maintaining bent forelegs; usually performed on a straight line, but in the past, also executed bearing right and left.

course (1) *see* TRACK. (2) A show-jumping or cross-country circuit consisting of a number of obstacles which the horse and rider must jump in a particular order or within a specified amount of time. (3) A hunting term; said of hounds who hunt by sight rather than scent.

course builder One responsible for building show-jumping or cross-country courses.

course designer One responsible for designing show-jumping or cross-country courses constructed by the course builder (q.v.).

course de brague A mounted military exercise or sport performed in 16th and 17th-century Europe in which a lance was used to hook a ring and carry it off.

court An antiquated hunting term; the paved yard attached to a hound kennel.

Cossack hang strap *see* VAULTING ROLLER

cover (1) Also known as breed, serve, or cover a mare; said of a stallion when he breeds a mare. (2) The width of the horseshoe. (3) A hunting term; any natural area that provides protection for animals from disturbances such as the elements.

cover a mare *see* COVER

covered Said of a mare bred by a stallion.

covered school An enclosed building used for riding and or schooling horses measuring minimally 65 x 22 yards (59 x 20 m).

covered up A harness racing term; said of a harness horse competing in a race who has other horses in front of him.

Covered wagon *see* PRAIRIE SCHOONER

covering boots *see* BREEDING BOOTS

covert Also known as a draw; a hunting term; a thicket or small wooded or bushy area less than 100 acres (40 hectares) in size in which foxes (q.v.) may hide or lay.

covert coat A light-weight, shower-proof, thigh-length top coat historically made of fine light-weight, Venetian twill and worn by men who hacked to the covert (q.v.) side.

covert cloth Also known as coating or covert coating; a top quality twilled cloth made with a whip-cord weave of ply yarns of cotton, wool, or worsted used for raincoats, overcoats, and covert coats; warp threads of worsted twist resulted in a flecked appearance to the fabric.

covert coating *see* COVERT CLOTH

covert hack A smooth-riding horse capable of negotiating small jumps, used to ride to a hunt meeting (q.v.), but not used in the hunt.

cow (1) The female of the bovine species. (2) Generically, a male or female bovine.

cowboy (1) Also known as cow poke, cow hand, or cow puncher; an American term; one who looks after cattle on a ranch and who, historically, performed this work on horseback. (2) A man who possesses the skill of a cowboy as those associated with the rodeo.

cowboy polo A game played by two teams of five mounted players; the purpose being for the players to move a small white ball down the field and through goal posts located at either end of the arena using a long mallet carried in the right hand; the game features longer mallets and is played at a much slower pace than high-goal polo (q.v.) where the goals can be no more than 250 yards (229 m) apart and the width of the field cannot exceed 200 yards (183 m); consists of six, 7-1/2 minute chukkas or periods.

cowboy shoe (1) A short-heeled horseshoe available in the same sizes as hot shoes (q.v.), developed for use when a forge is not practical; both front and hind shoes have the same web width and weight where formerly, the front shoes would be wider and heavier; nail holes are roughly punched, require opening with a pritchel (q.v.), and are spaced far apart and close to the outside edge; heels are square-cut and unfinished; secure nailing requires dubbing (q.v.); used by the military, ranchers, packers, and outfitters; a difficult shoe to fit and frequently results in a poor shoeing. (2) To shoe a horse without fitting the shoe to the foot; the shape of the shoe is only opened or closed at the heel; once the shoe is nailed on, the foot is trimmed to fit the shoe and rasped down to match its shape.

cowboy shoeing *see* COWBOY SHOE no. 2

cowboy shod Also known as rough shod; said of a horse who has had horseshoes put on without consideration for hoof shape; the hoof is shaped to fit the shoe.

cowgirl (1) A woman who looks after cattle on a ranch and does this work on horseback. (2) A woman who possesses the skill of a cowgirl as those associated with the rodeo (q.v.).

cow hand *see* COWBOY

cowhide The hide or skin of a cow, may or may not be made into leather; 95 percent of all saddlery is made from cowhide.

cow-hocked Said of a horse whose limbs are base-narrow (q.v.) to the hock and base-wide from the hock to the feet.

cow hocks *see* MEDIAL DEVIATION OF THE HOCK JOINTS

cow horn A hunting term; an American hunting horn (q.v.) used exclusively when hunting with American foxhounds.

cow horse Also known as a cow pony or range horse; a horse ridden by a cowboy when working cattle; commonly Quarter Horses (q.v.) or Quarter Horse crosses less than 16 hands tall.

cowing A cutting horse term; said of a horse when focused on a cow.

cow kick A type of kick in which the horse strikes forward and to the outside with one of his hind legs; enables a horse to strike a rider or handler standing beside him.

cowlick A hair pattern on the head of the horse; a tuft of hair which grows in a wayward direction and turns upward as if licked by a cow; may be used for identification purposes.

cow man A western United States term; an owner of cattle; a rancher; a cowboy (q.v.).

cow poke Western American slang; a cowboy (q.v.).

cow pony *see* COW HORSE

cow puncher Historically, one whose responsibility it was to punch or brand (q.v.) cattle.

cow sense *see* COW SMART

cow-side leg A cutting term; the rider's leg parallel to the cow being worked.

cow smart Also known as cowy, cow sense, good cow sense, or to have a lot of cow; a cutting term; said of a horse possessed of the innate ability, desire, and mental aptitude to read and anticipate the movements of a cow.

cow with a lot of feel A cutting term; said of a cow who works and turns well against a horse.

cowy *see* COW SMART

coyote dun Refers to coat color; a yellow coat with black hairs mixed in, black points, and primitive marks (q.v.); the equivalent of the dark buckskin (q.v.).

CPO The acronym for certified pedigree option (q.v.).

crab (1) A driving term; the hook and crosshead at the end of the pole on to which the main and lead bars are connected in a team harness; may be made of stainless or polished steel. (2) To give unfavorable criticism of a horse as to reduce his value. (3) An unfavorable feature of a horse such as a blemish, fault, or unsoundness.

crabber One who gives an unfavorable criticism of a horse.

crab bit A bit with prongs extending upwards towards the horse's nose, the purpose of which is to tip the horse's head up and help prevent him from pulling hard on the rein.

crack *see* SAND CRACK

cracked heels *see* SCRATCHES

cracked hoof A vertical split in the hoof wall; may extend from the coronary band (q.v.) down or from the base of the hoof upwards; may result from injury, concussion, improper shoeing, or environmental or stabling conditions and can be remedied with corrective shoeing (q.v.); identified on the basis of location on the hoof, e.g., quarter crack (q.v.) and toe crack (q.v.).

cracking the nostrils *see* HIGH BLOWING

cradle A light frame made of wood or aluminium dowels fastened at intervals by leather straps to form a wide "necklace" which is fitted around the horse's neck from the throat to the shoulder; used to prevent the horse from biting or licking wounds, blankets, etc.

cramped action Said of a horse who does not move freely.

cranial Of or pertaining to the skull or cranium.

crash skull *see* RACING HELMET

cravings *see* CHAFF no. 2

crawler An antiquated driving or coaching term; a cab driver who loitered to pick up fares rather than returning to a cabstand as was customary; considered a nuisance by other cabbies and a finable offense by the police.

creamy dun *see* GOLDEN DUN

crease A groove cut into the ground-side surface of a horseshoe which fills with dirt to create mild traction; permits the easy removal of the horseshoe nails (q.v.).

creasing Also known incorrectly as fullering; the act or process of cutting a crease (q.v.) into the ground-side surface of a horseshoe.

creep feeder A manger (q.v.) that allows a

foal, but prevents his dam, from feeding; available in many designs.

creeping splint One of four types of splints (q.v.); slowly multiply end-to-end, like a string of pearls, from the top to the mid-point of the splint bone, filling the splint groove; may result from inadequate rest following an interosseous splint (q.v.).

cremello Refers to coat color; a nearly white, cream-colored coat and points with blue eyes.

crescent brasses One of four primary historic patterns of horse brasses (q.v.); the pattern of the crescent moon, one of the images of the pagan gods struck into brass or other metal and placed on the harness or other tack of the horse to ward off the Evil Eye; worshippers of water used a crescent pointing down, since water always descends.

crest The uppermost part of the horse's neck (q.v.).

crested whorl A hair pattern; a whorl (q.v.); a change in direction of the flow of the hair in which two opposing sweeps of hair meet from diametrically opposite directions along a line and rise up to form a crest.

crew hole *see* DART HOLE

crib (1) *see* CRIB BITING. (2) *see* MANGER

cribber (1) Also known as crib-biter; a horse who cribs (q.v.). (2) *see* WIND SUCKER

cribbing *see* WIND SUCKING

crib-biter *see* CRIBBER

crib-biting Also known as wood-chewing; said of a horse who chews wood surfaces such as a manger, stable, door, etc.; a vice; may be due to a mineral or vitamin deficiency or boredom.

crib-biting device *see* ANTI-CRIBBING DEVICE

cricket A small roller (q.v.) in the port of a curb bit (q.v.) commonly used in western bits.

cricket bit Any ported western bit in which a roller is inserted into the port.

cricoid cartilage One of six types of cartilage (q.v.) found in the body structure of the horse; forms rings.

crinet Medieval armor used to protect the neck and throat of the horse.

Criollo Also known as Argentine Criollo; a horse breed indigenous to Argentina which descended from Spanish stock (Arab, Barb, and Andalusian) brought to South America in the 16th century by the Conquistadors; is sturdy, compact, and very muscular, with a short, broad head, straight profile, wide-set eyes, short legs with plenty of bone, strong joints, and hard feet; is willing, tough, agile, and possesses great endurance; all coat colors are acceptable; stands 14 to 15 hands; historically the mount of the gauchos and when crossed with the Thoroughbred (q.v.) became the base for the Argentine polo pony (q.v.); the stud book was established in 1918; other South American countries breed their own versions of the breed, all of which have the same origins as the Argentine Criollo, but which possess different names and slightly different characteristics according to their environment; these include the Chileno (q.v.), Guajira (q.v.), Llanero (q.v.), Salterno (q.v.), Mangalarga (q.v.), Campolino (q.v.), and Criollo of Rio Grande do Sul (q.v.).

Criollo of Rio Grande do Sul One of three types of Criollo (q.v.) horses bred in Brazil, the other two being the Mangalarga (q.v.) and the Campolino (q.v.); of the same origins as the Criollo, but possessing slightly different characteristics attributable to local environmental conditions; descended from Spanish stock brought to South America by the conquistadors in the 16th century; has a Barb-like appearance.

Crioulo A Brazilian-bred Criollo (q.v.) cross; obtained by crossing Altér Reals (q.v.) with Brazilian Criollos: Mangalarga (q.v.), the Criollo of Rio Grande do Sul (q.v.), and the Campolino Criollos (q.v.); has a high-set tail, long neck, is frugal and tough, and used for riding and herding.

crockery eye *see* WALL EYE

crooked halt A dressage term; said of a horse who stopped with his quarters (q.v.) to one side or the other of his forehand so that he is not straight.

crop (1) A short, stiff, straight-stock whip with a loop at one end; commonly used by jockeys, hunters, and jumpers. (2) A group of foals sired during a single stallion's season at stud. (3) A group of horses born within the same year.

crop-eared A horse whose ears or tips thereof have either been cut or frozen off.

crop out Also known as a crop-out Quarter Horse; any foal produced by two registered Quarter Horses (q.v.) who has more white on it than the American Quarter Horse Association color rule allows; cannot qualify for registry with the American Quarter Horse Association (q.v.), but will qualify for the American Paint Horse Association registry; crop-out Thoroughbreds (q.v.) also occur, but the Jockey Club does not have a registry color requirement.

cropper A racing term; a spill of the horse and rider; usually occurring in jump-type races.

cross *see* THE CROSS

cross-breeding Also known as outcrossing or outcross; the mating of two registered purebred horses of two different breeds.

crossbred Said of a horse produced by a sire (q.v.) and dam (q.v.) of different breeds.

cross canter *see* DISUNITED CANTER

crosscrack *see* CLEFT

cross firing Said of a horse in motion when the diagonal fore and hind feet contact on the inside i.e. the inside of the hind foot hitting the inside quarter of the diagonal forefoot (q.v.); common in pacers.

cross hook A polo term; said of a defensive player who reaches over his opponent's mount with his mallet (q.v.) in an attempt to hook (q.v.); a foul.

crossing Also known as crossing the line; a polo term; a principal infringement in the game of polo occurring when a defensive player crosses the imaginary projectory of the ball in front of the oncoming offensive player in control of it.

crossing feet *see* ROPE WALKING

cross noseband *see* GRACKLE NOSEBAND

crossing the line *see* CROSSING

crossing traces *see* CROSS TRACES

cross matched *see* CROSS TEAM

cross noseband *see* GRACKLE NOSEBAND

cross team Also known as checkerboard team or cross matched; a driving term; a team of four horses of two different colors; the horses of similar colors are usually positioned diagonal to each other, i.e., the near leader and the off wheeler are of the same color.

cross the stirrups Said of a mounted rider; to take the right stirrup (the leather and iron), cross it over the withers of the horse, and lay it on the left shoulder and vice versa with the left stirrup; improves the rider's seat and is a test in some hunt seat equitation classes in the United States.

cross tie To secure the head of a horse by means of two straps both attached at one end to the side of the horse's halter and to a stable object on the other.

cross ties Also known as pillar reins, rack chains, or headcollar chain shanks; 2 to 3 feet (61-91 cm) long leather, chain, elastic, or other straps fitted with hooks or clips at one end and attached to walls, posts, or other secure objects on the other between which the horse is tied as when grooming or tacking up.

cross traces Also known as crossing traces; a driving term; the practice of hooking the inside traces (q.v.) of one of the lead horses to the inside hook of his partner's bar to better distribute the draft from an unequally matched team.

crotch seat *see* LIGHT SEAT

croup (1) Also known as rump, crupper, or crupper line; the upper line of a horse's quarters, from the root of the tail to the loins. (2) An acute obstruction of the voice box.

croupade A High School (q.v.) air above the ground (q.v.) in which the horse rears from a standstill and performs a single vertical jump with the fore and hind legs drawn up towards the belly; the leap is higher than the courbette (q.v.).

crouper mount A method of mounting the horse; to run towards a standing horse from behind, leap towards the croup (q.v.) placing one hand on each haunch, and land seated in the saddle; used by trick and circus riders, and movie stunt people.

croup high A dressage term; said of a horse who moves heavy on the forehand and whose croup moves up on each stride instead of the quarters lowering and the hind legs being brought under the body.

crowd A racing term; said of a jockey who rides too close to another horse, forcing its jockey to pull up (q.v.) or change course.

crow hop Said of the horse; to make a short, mild jump.

crowned An antiquated term; a horse with broken knees (q.v.) from which a portion of hair has worn away.

crownpiece Also known as head piece; that part of the bridle (q.v.) that crosses over the poll (q.v.) behind the horse's ears; attached to the cheekpieces (q.v.).

CRT The acronym for capillary refill time (q.v.).

Cruciferae A family of plants including cabbage (q.v.), cauliflower, Brussel sprouts, broccoli, kale, and others; from crucifer, so called because family members bear flowers having a cross-like, four-petaled corolla; infrequently fed to horses due to the goitrogenic compounds they contain which impact iodine (q.v.) production.

crude fat The material extracted from moisture-free feeds by ether; consists of fats and oils with small amounts of waxes, resins, and coloring matter.

crude fiber The part of the feed which comes from the cellulose and lignin part of plants both of which are poorly digested by the horse.

crupper (1) *see* HARNESS CRUPPER AND SADDLE CRUPPER. (2) *see* CROUP no. 1

crupper dock Also known as dockpiece; a padded leather loop fitted under the dock (q.v.) of the horse's tail on one end, and stitched or buckled to the back strap on the other to pre-

vent the harness pad or the riding saddle from slipping forward; commonly filled with linseed which exudes a certain amount of natural oil and thus prevents friction.

crupper line *see* CROUP no. 1

crupper strap A leather strap which connects to the riding saddle or harness pad on one end and buckles to the crupper dock (q.v.) on the other; as a unit, in conjunction with the crupper dock, constitutes the harness crupper (q.v.) or riding crupper (q.v.) and prevents the saddle or harness pad from slipping forward.

crust of the hoof *see* HOOF WALL

crust of the wall *see* HOOF WALL

cry (1) *see* SPEAK. (2) Also known as voice, music, or tongue; a hunting term; the sound the hound makes when in pursuit of a fox; varies with the quality of the scent.

cryogenic That method of physics dealing with very low temperatures at which gases such as nitrogen liquefy; cryogenics are used in many applications including branding (q.v.) and preserving organic material.

cryogenic branding *see* FREEZE BRANDING

cryosurgery Selective destruction of tissue by freezing, usually with liquid nitrogen.

cryptorchid *see* RIG

cryptorchidism A developmental defect in which one or both testicles are retained above the scrotum; a genetically based disorder.

CS The acronym for chondroitin sulfates (q.v.).

Csikos Hungarian cowboys or herdsman whose primary responsibility it is to tend to herds of horses grazed on the Hungarian plains.

CT scanning *see* COMPUTERIZED TOMOGRAPHY

cub A young fox from birth, usually March through November 1, although it may be born any time between Christmas and May; the average litter size is five.

cubbing *see* CUB HUNTING

cubbing season *see* CUB HUNTING SEASON

cubes Also known as alfalfa cubes, hay cubes, or nuts; a compressed feed generally composed of grass or legume hay which is often shaped into 1 to 2 inch (25-50 mm) squares; other feeds, minerals, and vitamins are sometimes added; the hay in a cube is ground less finely than that used in pellets; cube analysis is often guaranteed and the grade is generally identified – cube grade depends on the maximum fiber and minimum protein contents; cubing eliminates the dust associated with most hays.

cub hunting Also known as cubbing; a hunting term; to hunt fox prior to the beginning of the regular hunting season (between the end of July and the end of September in the United States and the end of harvest until the end of October in the United Kingdom) to teach young, unentered (q.v.) hounds (q.v.) to hunt, and fox cubs to leave their coverts (q.v.); historically conducted to reduce fox overpopulation; a cap (q.v.) is usually not taken.

cub hunting season Also known as cubbing season; a hunting term; the period preceding the beginning of the formal fox hunting season during which time fox cubs are located and encouraged to run.

Culicoides A tiny, swarming insect which feeds overnight on the blood of its hosts by the thousands; has a relatively painless bite, although saliva may cause seasonally hyperallergic reactions in susceptible horses.

Culicoides hypersensitivity A Canadian term; sweet itch (q.v.).

cull An unwanted horse disposed of by the owner.

culture (1) The cultivation of micro-organisms, as bacteria, in an artificial medium for scientific study or medical use. (2) The product or growth resulting from cultivation.

cup (1) Also known as mark or bean; the outer visible section of the internal enamel/grinding surface of the tooth; the depth and appearance of the cup changes as the horse ages – originally oval, the cup become more oval, then flat, round, triangular, and finally disappears at about 12 years; effective in determining horse age. (2) A racing term; a trophy awarded to winning horse owners as in

stakes races (q.v.). (3) The flat or dished metal support inserted into a standard and used to support a rail to be jumped.

cup horse A racing term; a horse who performs best in races longer than 1 1/8 miles (1.8 km).

Cup of Nations *see* PRIX DES NATIONS

cuppy Also known as cuppy track; wet or moist ground into which the horse's feet could sink during competition; the surface breaks up and shows hoofprints.

cuppy track *see* CUPPY

curb (1) A thickening or bowing of the plantar tarsal ligament, approximately 4 inches (10 cm) below the point of the hock (q.v.), due to strain; not necessarily accompanied by lameness. (2) *see* CURB BIT

curb bit Also known as curb; a bit consisting of two metal cheek pieces and a ported mouthpiece which brings pressure to bear on the bars of the mouth using leverage instead of direct pressure; the reins are attached to rings on the cheek pieces; used in conjunction with a curb strap (q.v.) or curb chain (q.v.).

curb chain A small metal, metal and elastic, leather, plastic, or nylon chain attached by hooks (in English) or by buckles or a strap (in western) to the cheeks of a curb or pelham bit; passed under the lower jaw and twisted clockwise until it lies flat in the chin groove (q.v.); increased pressure on the lower rein increases the leverage and tightens the curb chain; when used with western bits must be a minimum of 1/2 inch (13 mm) in width.

curb groove Also known as chin groove; a furrow in the underside of the lower jaw just above the lower lip where the curb chain rests when put into action.

curby hocks *see* SICKLE HOCKS

curb hook A metal hook attached to the top ring on the cheeks (q.v.) of a curb or pelham bit (q.v.) to which the curb chain (q.v.) is attached; the hook portion faces away from the horse's cheek; made in pairs and vary in size from 1/2 to 2-1/2 inches (13-64 mm); the Melton (q.v.) is the most popular.

curb rein The rein attached to the lower rings of the cheeks (q.v.) of a curb bit (q.v.).

curby hocks *see* EXCESSIVE ANGULATION OF THE HOCK JOINTS

cur dog Previously known as care dog; a hunting term; any dog other than a foxhound responsible for the care of a herd of sheep and for coursing (q.v.) a fox.

curl A roping term; the upward curling action of a thrown rope as it encircles the neck of the calf, horse, etc.; a good curl indicates that the loop has been well thrown.

Curre-type A hunting term; a foxhound (q.v.), generally English-bred, having at least one strain of Welsh foxhound blood in its pedigree; developed by the late Sir Edward Curre.

curricle (1) A horse-drawn two-wheeled carriage of Italian origins popular in Britain during the late 18th and early 19th centuries; either open or headed, but usually had a falling hood, seated two, side-by-side, with a liveried groom positioned on a rearward or rumble seat, was hung on cee-springs, and was drawn by a pair of horses harnessed by means of traces and a center pole; the main hauling power was through the traces; said to correct the effects of sway or uneven motion; difficult to drive as the horses had to move together in the same pace and stride; replaced by the cabriolet (q.v.); the name derived from the Latin curriculum, meaning light chariot. 2) To put a pair of horses to a two-wheeled vehicle by means of a curricle bar (q.v.).

curricle bar A harness term; a steel bar placed horizontal to the backs of a pair (q.v.) and attached to their saddle pads; used in conjunction with a supporting strap and a curricle harness to support the pole of a curricle (q.v.) vehicle.

curry To rub the horse's coat hair with a hard or pliable curry comb (q.v.) until dirt is loosened and can be brushed off with a body brush (q.v.); stimulates circulation and helps to build muscle tone by massaging the large muscle masses.

curry comb A hand-held instrument or comb set with very short teeth on one side; used to scrape dirt and debris from a brush (metal curry comb [q.v.]) and to clean and comb a horse (rubber curry comb [q.v.]).

curved bar shoe A bar shoe (q.v.) in which the bar that connects the two heels of the shoe is curved above or below the ground surface; used to apply or to relieve frog pressure, especially when the frog is small and atrophied or large and protruding; when the bar is curved toward the frog may be used to treat contraction, and when curved away from the frog, may be used to treat thrush, corns, or sheared heels.

curvet A historical English term used by riding masters in the 16th and 17th centuries; a skirmish movement of attack similar to the present-day levade (q.v.), in which the horse rears onto deeply flexed haunches at an angle of no more than 30 degrees; marking time with the forelegs, the horse then takes a series of small leaps forward or to the left or right; the name derived from the French courbette (q.v.), a movement to which it bears no resemblance.

curtal Also spelled curtall; an antiquated 16th and 17th-century term; a horse whose tail is cut short and whose ears are sometimes cropped.

curtall *see* CURTAL

cushion A racing term; the loose top surface of a track.

cut (1) To geld or mark a horse; to castrate (q.v.). (2) To make an incision in the tissue. (3) Also known as cut out; a cutting term; to select a cow and separate it from the herd.

cut and laid A hunting term; a low fence in which thorn bushes are woven horizontally in and out of vertical positioned stakes.

cut and set tail *see* SET TAIL

cut and slash A hunting term; said of the hounds when they range too far from the field when attempting to locate a fox (q.v.).

cutaneous habronemiasis A skin disease caused in part by the larvae of stomach worms which, when they emerge feed on pre-existing wound tissue or on genitalia and eye moisture, and migrate into and irritate the tissue causing chronic lesions; symptoms include the appearance of non-healing, reddish-brown, greasy skin containing rice-grain-sized, yellow, calcified material.

cut a voluntary Hunting slang; said of the rider who chooses to fall off his horse rather than go down with it.

cut away *see* CUT SHOT

cut away coat *see* SHAD BELLY

cut away shot *see* CUT SHOT

cut back (1) *see* CUTBACK SADDLE. (2) Formerly known as a cow-mouthed or cow gulleted saddle; any English-type saddle (q.v.) in which the pommel is cut away so it will sit more easily on high-withered horses.

cutback saddle Also known as a cut back or saddle seat saddle; a long, flat saddle resting low on the horse's back which is designed to place the rider's weight over the loins of the horse; used on Saddlebred (q.v.), Tennessee Walking Horse (q.v.), and certain classes of the Arab (q.v.) and Morgan (q.v.) show divisions.

cut corners A dressage term; said of the dressage rider who fails to ride his horse into the corners of the dressage arena.

cut down A racing term; said of a horse injured in a race by the horseshoe of another horse or by striking itself with its own shoe.

cut for shape A cutting term; said of a mounted rider; to drive cattle into the center of an arena or other area, wait for them to move around the horse in an attempt to return to the herd, and to cut and work one of the remaining cows.

cutis *see* CORIUM

cut-out *see* CUT no. 3

cut out under the knees A conformation defect of the horse; when viewed from the side, the front surface of the cannon bone just below the knee has a cut or dished out appearance.

cuts A cutting term; the location of cows cut (q.v.) from the herd.

cut shot Also known as cut away or cut away shot; a polo term; any fore- or backhand stroke of the ball hit at an angle away from the horse.

cutter (1) A small sleigh drawn by a single horse or pony having a very high S-shaped front or dash which prevents snow thrown by the horse's hooves from covering the driver and passengers; joined to the runners by tall and narrow iron struts; of two primary types: the Albany cutter (q.v.) with rounded sides and the Portland cutter (q.v.). (2) A light, four-wheeled passenger vehicle drawn by a single horse. (3) A cutting term; one who separates a cow from a herd as for doctoring or branding and to hold it until the ropers arrived; now performed predominantly for sport. (4) A hunting term; a hound (q.v.) who, rather than hunt with the pack, runs on ahead hoping to locate the scent of the fox (q.v.) and thus becomes the leader.

cutter's cross A cutting term; a two-handed grip on the reins used by the rider when training a cutting horse (q.v.); the reins are held in the opposing hands, i.e., left rein to right hand and vice versa.

cutter's slump A cutting term; the posture a cutter (q.v.) assumes when working cattle; the rider sits deep in the saddle with a relaxed, slightly convexly curved back and slumped shoulders.

cutting A contest between a cow and a horse; the cutter (q.v.) guides his horse into the herd slowly and deliberately so as not to disturb the cows, and selects one calf to separate from the herd; once a cow is cleared from the herd, the rider positions himself and his horse between the cow and the herd; when the cow tries to return to the security of the herd, the cutter's horse meets it and sends it back to the cuts (q.v.); evolved on cattle ranches where riders would sort groups of cattle or single out individual cows for doctoring, branding (q.v.), sale, and the like; performed as a competition in the United States since 1898.

cutting horse Also known as a cutting pony; a cow horse; any horse used to work cattle selected from the herd; the ability is predominantly instinctive and the talent is generally developed not trained; Quarter Horses (q.v.) or Quarter Horse crosses are commonly used.

cutting horse competition An organized event in which the talent and ability of the horse and rider are demonstrated in the cutting (q.v.) of cows from a herd during a 2-1/2 minute ride; the first advertised cutting competition took place in Huskell, Texas, USA in

1898; organized as a sport in the United States in 1946 with the formation of the National Cutting Horse Association (q.v.).

cutting out *see* CUT-OUT

cutting pony *see* CUTTING HORSE

cutting saddle A western-type saddle with a relatively flat seat, a long, narrow horn that allows the rider to brace and pull with the movements of the horse, and a low cantle; is lightweight and has fenders that permit easy backward and forward motion of the legs and a feel for the horse under the leather; generally has a back cinch (q.v.).

CVA The acronym for Concours Voltige d'Amitie (q.v.).

CVF The acronym for Concours Voltige Frontière (q.v.).

CVI (1) An international vaulting event with no limit to the number of foreign nations participating. (2) The acronym for certificate of veterinary inspection (q.v.).

cyanocobalamin *see* VITAMIN B_{12}

D

D *see* DEE-RING

daiku *see* POLO

daily double Also known as a double; a racing term; a betting option in which the bettor (q.v.) attempts to select the winning horses in two nominated races, usually the first and second, buying a single ticket on the double choice; to win this bet, both selected horses must win their respective races.

daily energy requirement The amount of calories required by a horse on a daily basis to maintain weight; individual metabolic rate, air temperature, performance demands, pregnancy, lactation, and growth must be considered when establishing this base requirement.

Daily Racing Form Also known as the form; a racing term; a daily newspaper containing news, past performance data, and handicapping information on racehorses; used by bettors (q.v.) and odds makers (q.v.).

Daily Triple *see* PICK THREE

daisy-cutter Said of a horse who, when moving at the trot, appears to skirt the surface of the ground; such horses are predisposed to stumbling.

Dales Also known as Dales pony or generically as native pony (q.v.); a pony breed originating in the upper dales of North Yorkshire, England; a close, but heavier and larger, relative of the Fell pony (q.v.); descended from the Celtic pony, crossed with Welsh Cob (q.v.) blood in the 19th century and Clydesdale (q.v.) in the later 19th and early 20th centuries, to the extent that in 1917, the breed was considered two-thirds Clydesdale; stands up to 14.1 hands and most commonly has a black coat, although browns, bays, and occasionally grays occur; white markings are rare; has a small head, wide-set eyes, prominent withers, a strong back, full mane and tail, the latter being low set, tough, blue-colored hooves, and silky feathering; is tremendously strong, has a remarkable weight-carrying capacity, is calm and sensitive, and a good keeper; historically used underground in Britain's ore and coal mines, as a general farm animal, and for pack-ing; currently used under harness in competitive driving and as an all-purpose riding mount.

Dales pony *see* DALES

Dales Pony Improvement Society, The An organization founded in England in 1917 to encourage and improve the standard of the Dales pony (q.v.) and to maintain the breed registry.

Dales Pony Society, The Northern An organization founded in England in 1957 to improve and encourage breeding and use of the pure-bred Dales pony (q.v.).

dally Also known as go to the horn; a roping term; the quick turn or loop of one end of the lariat (q.v.) around the saddle horn (q.v.) to secure the rope after roping an animal.

Dalmatian Also known as coach dog; a large, 50 to 90 pounds (23-41 kg), short-haired white dog with black or brown spots historically used to accompany horse-drawn vehicles and protect cargo from theft; trained to run between the wheels of the vehicle, immediately behind the horse's heels.

Dalric cuff A German-made, glue-on (q.v.) horseshoe (q.v.) consisting of a plastic rim and 1-1/2 inch (38 mm) plastic cuff that extends upward from the rim at an angle consistent with the hoof angle; a forged shoe is riveted to the bottom surface of the plastic rim; the cuff and shoe combination is then glued to the hoof or reconstructed hoof wall using an epoxy or space-age glue; commonly used in massive reconstructions of the hoof.

dam The female parent of a horse; a colt is said to be out of the dam; listed on the bottom side of the pedigree.

dam's sire Also known as broodmare sire; the sire (q.v.) of a broodmare; used in reference to the maternal grandsire of a foal.

Damage Fund A hunting term; a small cap (q.v.) assessed by some hunts (q.v.) on a per-meet basis, to all present, including foot followers, to compensate landowners and others for damage to their property incurred during the hunt.

Damalinia equi *see* BITING LOUSE

dancing *see* CHATTER

dancing competition A mounted sport performed on the islands of Sumba and Sumbawa, Indonesia in which Sumba (q.v.) and Sumbawa (q.v.) ponies are ridden bareback in bitless bridles by young boys and are lunged by a trainer who directs their movements; bells are attached to the ponies' knees who dance in time to the beat of a tom-tom drum; are judged on elegance and lightness of the performance.

Dandi A litter (q.v.) used in India and the Middle East; suspended from a single pole and carried between two men or pack animals.

Dandy A horse-drawn railway carriage used in Cumberland, England between 1861 and 1914.

dandy brush A wooden-backed brush (q.v.) with natural or synthetic bristles used to remove heavy dirt or mud from the coat and legs of a horse. '

danglers *see* FLY TERRETS

Danish Horse *see* DANISH WARMBLOOD AND FREDERIKSBORG

Danish Sport Horse *see* DANISH WARMBLOOD

Danish Spotted Horse *see* KNABSTRUP

Danish Warmblood Previously known as the Danish Sport Horse or Danish Horse; a warmblood developed in Denmark by crossing locally bred Fredriksborg (q.v.)/Thoroughbred (q.v.) mares with pedigree Anglo-Norman (q.v.), Thoroughbred, Trakehner (q.v.), and Polish stallions; stands 16.1 to 16.2 hands and is most commonly bay, although all coat colors do occur; is naturally well balanced and excels in dressage and show jumping.

Danubian A warmblood developed during the early 1900s in Bulgaria around the Danube Plain from which the name derives; descended from Nonius (q.v.) stallions crossed with Gidran (q.v.) mares; stands approximately 15.2 hands, has a black or chestnut coat, compact body, strong neck, powerful quarters, deep body, and relatively slender legs; used for

light draft and riding, particularly jumping.

dapple Refers to coat color pattern; a coat with small spots, patches, dots, or circular markings which contrast in color or shade with the body color; may be present on horses of any color, although most visible in silver dapples (q.v.) and grays.

dapple gray Refers to coat color; a gray coat interspersed with white hairs; a progressive color, horses are born black and gray with age.

Darashomi *see* DARASHOURI

Darashouri Also known as Darashomi or Slurazi; one of two types of Persian Arab (q.v.) indigenous to Iran, specifically the Fars region of southern Iran; is elegant, strong, spirited, energetic, and athletic, stands 14.1 to 15.1 hands, and has a bay, chestnut, gray, or rarely black, coat; used for riding.

Daresbury Phaeton A horse-drawn driving carriage designed for modern cross-country competitions; has a traditional wood finished body, hollow steel undergear, shock-absorbers, hydraulic disc brakes and a spare wheel; drawn either by a pair of horses or a four-in-hand team (q.v.).

dark A racing term; said of a race track or a day on which there is no racing.

dark bay *see* MAHOGANY BAY

dark brown Refers to coat color; a shade of brown (q.v.), very close to black, smoky black, or faded black.

dark buckskin *see* SMUTTY BUCKSKIN

dark grullo *see* SMUTTY GRULLO

dark horse A racing term; an underrated horse or one about whom little is known; so named because the abilities of the horse had been "kept in the dark."

dark muzzle Refers to coat color; said of a horse having a dark nose, as in donkeys (q.v.).

Darley Arabian One of three foundation sires of the English Thoroughbred (q.v.); a purebred Kehilan Arabian (q.v.) of the Managhi (q.v.) strain imported into England in 1705 by Mr. Richard Darley for whom it was named; foaled in 1700, stood about 15 hands, and was a bay with a blaze and three white socks (q.v.); became the most famous of the Eastern sires having sired Bulle Rocke, the first Thoroughbred (q.v.) brought to the United States; all Thoroughbreds (q.v.) in the world today trace their ancestry in direct male line to the Goldolphin Arab (q.v.), Byerley Turk (q.v.), and Darley Arabian.

dart hole Known as a crew hole in England; an American term; the holes at the end of the traces (q.v.) through which the trace hook passes.

Dartmoor *see* DARTMOOR PONY

Dartmoor pony Also known as a Dartmoor or generically as a native pony (q.v.); an ancient pony breed originating in Dartmoor, a rugged mountain area in Devon, England; one of nine breeds native to the British Isles; influenced in the 19th century by the introduction of Welsh pony (q.v.), Cob (q.v.), Exmoor pony (q.v.), Arabian (q.v.), small Thoroughbred (q.v.) and Shetland pony (q.v.) blood; Shetland blood was introduced in an attempt to produce a pony for use in Britain's coal mines; this later introduction threatened breed purity and between 1941 and 1943, it nearly fell to extinction with only two males and twelve females registered; since 1899 a strict breed registry has been maintained; registry guidelines prohibit entries standing more than 12.2 hands; most commonly bay, brown, black, and gray, while chestnut is more rare; piebald and skewbald coloring is not permitted and extensive white markings are discouraged; has a relatively small head, a well-proportioned neck with a full mane, good back, and slender legs with short cannons and ample bone; is hardy, a good keeper, and is noted for its lack of knee lift having a low and long action; an ideal mount for children due to its temperament and action; used for all types of riding.

Dartmoor Pony Society, The An organization established in England to promote and encourage the breeding of pure bred Dartmoor ponies (q.v.); has maintained a strict breed registry since 1899.

dash (1) A racing term; a horse race decided in a single trial. (2) A racing term; a sprint race.

dashboard That part of a horse-drawn vehicle located in front of the driver's and passengers' legs which protects them from dirt thrown up by the hooves of the horse; made of wood or leather sewn onto an iron frame.

day rug *see* SHEET

day sheet *see* SHEET

DE The acronym for digestible energy (q.v.).

dead heat A racing term; said of two or more horses arriving at the finish line simultaneously; all prizes to which the first and second place horses would have been entitled, are divided equally between the two.

dead meat An antiquated racing term; said of a horse entered in a race whose owner(s) have no intention of allowing him to win.

deadly nightshade Also known as *Atropa belladonna*; a highly toxic, low-growing plant with spreading green stems and narrow, pointed leaves about 4 inches (10 cm) long which produce white, star-shaped flowers and round, dark fruit approximately 1/4 inch (6 mm) in diameter; has an unpleasant taste and odor, but horses will sometimes nibble at it out of boredom or hunger; the toxin acts like an addictive drug, once "hooked" the horse will seek it out, eventually ingesting enough to cause chronic poisoning (q.v.); poisoning affects each horse at a different rate and may often cause an adverse reaction days or weeks following exposure.

dead-sided Said of a horse whose sides are numb to the action of the leg, spur, or whip aids.

dead track A racing term; said of the track surface which lacks resiliency.

dead weight *see* LEAD no. 3

deafness Loss of hearing; profound deafness in both ears is relatively easy to diagnose, but partial deafness, or unilateral deafness is difficult to diagnose; may be congenital or acquired.

dealer's whip A steel-lined, long whip used by horse dealers.

Decemjugis A Roman chariot driven to ten horses abreast.

deciduous teeth Also known as temporary teeth, milk teeth or baby teeth; any tooth present at birth, appearing shortly thereafter, or gradually until the horse is approximately nine months old; in-wear (q.v.) within approximately six months following eruption; include the first, second, and third incisors and premolars (q.v.) on each side and occasionally the canine teeth (q.v.); remain until replaced by the permanent teeth (q.v.) compared to which they are usually smaller, whiter, relatively shorter, and have constricted necks, and flat roots.

declare off *see* SUSPEND

declared off *see* RACE DECLARED OFF AND BET DECLARED OFF

declaration Also known as declaration of runners; a racing term; a written statement provided by a horse owner, trainer, or a designee of either, prior to a race or competition, which declares that a specific horse will participate.

declaration of runners *see* DECLARATION

declaration to win A racing term; a public announcement made by the owner of more than one entrant in a horse race, that he will try to win with one mount but not the other(s).

declare (1) Also known as declared; a United States racing term; to withdraw a horse from a race prior to the scratch time. (2) Also known as declared; a European racing term; a horse confirmed to start in a race.

declared *see* DECLARE

declared a runner A racing term; said of a horse confirmed to run in writing prior to the race in which it is entered.

dee cheek snaffle *see* DEE-RING SNAFFLE

deep (1) A racing term; said of a recently harrowed racing surface to which top soil has been added to increase the holding quality of the footing. (2) Internal, close to the center of gravity of the horse. (3) A hunting term; said of soft or heavy footing.

deep crack *see* PENETRATING CRACK

deep cut A cutting term; a maneuver performed by the horse and rider when selecting a cow to work; a cut or movement far enough into a herd of cattle that leaves the horse completely surrounded by cows; in competition; one deep cut for each 2-1/2 minute ride is required.

deep flexor tendon A tendon (q.v.) located in the back of the foreleg between the knee and the foot and between the hock and the foot in the hind leg; functions in conjunction with the superficial flexor tendon (q.v.) to flex the pastern (q.v.) and knee in the fore and to extend the hock (q.v.) in the hind leg.

deep going Said of wet ground made heavy by rain, in which the hooves of the horse sink deeply.

deep in the girth Also known as deep through the girth; said of a horse who has well-sprung ribs (q.v.) and a good chest capacity as measured circumferentially behind the elbows and over the withers.

deep laceration An injury that penetrates all layers of the skin and in some cases to the level of the muscle or fascia, tendons, or even bone; the edges of the wound will gape apart.

deep stretch A racing term; a race position very close to the finish line.

deep through the girth *see* DEEP IN THE GIRTH

deer fly A blood-sucking fly of the genus Chrysops, considered a large solitary daytime feeder which is most voracious early and late in the day; along with the horse fly (q.v.); considered the most significant pest in North America; about the size of a house fly (q.v.) with patterned wings; painful bites cause localized swelling.

dee-ring Also known as D, D-ring, saddle dee, or dee; a metal, D-shaped fitting found on saddles, other tack, and harnesses.

dee-ring bit Any bit having dee-shaped cheekpieces (q.v.).

dee ring snaffle: Also known as a racing snaffle, dee-shaped snaffle, dee-cheek snaffle, d-ring snaffle, or Meyer's D cheek; a bit having a single-jointed mouthpiece with slightly tapered and curved arms, joined to the flat side of the rings in the shape of a D which are placed next to the lips; commonly used on racehorses and young stock; the D shape prevents the bit from slipping into or through the horse's mouth.

dees The plural of dee (q.v.).

dee-shaped snaffle *see* DEE-RING SNAFFLE

de Foix, Gaston The French author of *Le Livre de la Chasse* published in 1387, which became the textbook on hunting in France; translated into English during the same period as The Master of Game.

degenerative   joint   disease *see* OSTEOARTHRITIS

de Gogue Also known as Gogue; an advanced piece of schooling equipment; an auxiliary rein or strap used to assist the action of the bit by restricting the position of the horse's head and neck; of two types: (1) independent Gogue consisting of an arrangement of straps fastened to the chest ring or girth on one end, which pass over the poll (q.v.) pad on either side of the temples, and connect to the bit rings on the other and (2) command Gogue consisting of an arrangement of straps fastened on one end to the girth or chest ring, which pass through rings on either side of a poll pad, to the bit rings, and attach to a rein other than the snaffle rein on the other; the action is on the poll (q.v.) and may be controlled by the rider; encourages a low head set.

de la Guérinière, François Robichon (1688–1751) Also known as "The Father of Classical Equitation"; his influence changed the course of classical equitation (q.v.) and his teachings formed the basis for modern equitation; largely due to his work, two veins of classical equitation developed in Europe, one based on the French Schools of Versailles and Saumur (q.v.), and the other on the Spanish Riding School of Vienna (q.v.); developed a system of suppling and gymnastic exercises designed to cultivate and extend the natural movements of the horse, invented the shoulder-in (q.v.), made improvements on two- and four-track (q.v.) work, made extensive use of lateral work, and designed the modern saddle, still used today in the Spanish Riding School, in which the size of the pommel (q.v.) and cantle (q.v.) were reduced and knee and thigh rolls were incorporated; authored the classic book on equitation, *Ecole de Cavalerie*, published in 1733.

delayed lethal Any disease or condition genetically transmitted to the foal which generally results in foal death sometime following birth.

Deli Pony *see* BATAK

delivery document A document given to the buyer or his agent upon settlement of a sale of a horse who authorizes the buyer to take possession of the horse from the consignor at a sale or auction (q.v.).

demi-pique *see* DEMI-PIQUED SADDLE

demi-piqued saddle Also known as demi-pique; a heavy saddle with half a saddle horn used by 18th-century cavalry and travelers.

demi-pirouette *see* HALF-PIROUETTE

demipassade A classical movement performed by the horse whereby it traverses back and forth over a specified short straight track at a fast pace, making a quick reversal and return.

Demi-Sang Charollais A group of breeds consisting of the Charollais (q.v.), Bourbannais (q.v.), and Nivernais.

Demi-Sang de Centre A regional subgroup of the general heading Cheval de Selle Français of halfbred horses bred in France; include the Limousin (q.v.) and Charollais (q.v.).

demi-volte A movement in which the horse executes a half circle on two tracks (q.v.) in the volte (q.v.) or on the straight line.

demodectic mange A skin disease caused by the mite Demodex folliculorum, which lives in the hair follicles and sebaceous glands of the skin; characterized by pustular blisters, ulcers, and scabs principally around the eyes and on the forehead with lesions spreading from the face to the shoulders and ultimately the entire body; seldom diagnosed in horses.

den A hole or series of holes having underground chambers in which foxes (q.v.) live and raise their cubs.

den dog A hunting term; a hound who, when a fox goes to ground (q.v.), remains at the den (q.v.) and gives tongue (q.v.).

denerve *see* NERVE

Dennett *see* DENNETT GIG

Dennett Gig Also known as Dennett; a horse-drawn gig (q.v.) introduced in England in the early 1800s; resembled the Stanhope gig (q.v.), yet had a unique form of suspension: a crosswise set of springs and two lengthwise springs, joined by D-links; each set of springs was rumored to be named after one of three Dennett sisters, renowned on the London stage for their beauty, wit, and nimble dancing.

dental pulp The soft interior core of the tooth (q.v.) containing nerves and blood vessels.

dental star Also known as tooth stars or star; the closed distal end of the pulp cavity in the incisor teeth (q.v.); first appears as a thin line across the chewing surface when the horse is about eight years old; the filling of this cavity is of a lighter color than the body of the tooth; by about 15 years of age this mark is distinct and round appearing on the center of the table surface of the teeth; an accurate indicator of age of the horse.

dentigerous cyst Also known as an ear fistula or conchal sinus; an infrequently occurring tumor with a center consisting of a different material than surrounding tissue, e.g., hair or tooth tissue; evidenced by a draining tract located at the edge of the ear, or by a soft, painless swelling in front of the base of the ear; as long as it remains open, it will drain a sticky, saliva-like liquid; if sealed, will swell to considerable size; may be surgically removed.

deoxyribonucleic acid Also known by the acronym DNA; a protein compound found in chromosomes which determines individual hereditary characteristics; consists of a long chain molecule comprising many repeated and varied combinations of four nucleotides: subdivisions of the molecule are believed to be the genes.

de Pluvinel, Antoine (1555–1620) A horseman, trainer, and author of *Maneige Royal* (1623) and *L'Instruction du Roy, En l'Exercice de Monter à cheval* (1625); promoted the humane treatment of the horse with his method of "gentling" rather than "breaking."

Depot Wagon Also known as station wagon; a horse-drawn American family carriage popular from the 1850s to the early 1900s; drawn either by one or two horses, depending on wagon size; fitted with two or three rows of crosswise, forward-facing seating, the rear seat of which was removable to create luggage space; similar to a rockaway (q.v.), but had a straight rather than a curved undercarriage.

depressant Any substance that slows the activity of the circulatory, respiratory, or central nervous systems.

Derby (1) *see* EPSOM DERBY. (2) *see* KENTUCKY DERBY. (3) A cutting horse term; any competition for four-year-old horses.

Derby Bank at Hickstead One of the most notorious obstacles in show jumping; a bank (q.v.) that drops a full 10 feet (3 m) on the downside.

Derby, Edward, 17th Earl of (1865–1948) One of the greatest patrons of the British racing turf, and a successful owner and breeder of race horses having won 20 classics (q.v.); founded and named the Epsom Derby (q.v.).

Derby Stakes, The *see* EPSOM DERBY

derma Also known as dermis; the sensitive, blood-vessel-supplied layer beneath the epidermis (q.v.) containing the sweat and sebaceous glands; supports, nourishes, and to some degree regulates, the epidermis (q.v.) and appendages.

dermal inclusion cyst Small cystic bumps which sometimes appear along the center line of the horse's back; caused by the inward growth of hairs; the top half of each bump may be surgically severed to allow the hair to grow to the surface.

dermatitis Inflammation of the skin.

dermis *see* DERMA

de-rotation A condition of the foot in which the outer surface of the hoof wall at the toe and the face of third phalanx is greater near the coronet (q.v.) than it is near the ground; may be due to dubbing (q.v.).

demitis Inflammation of the ligament, as resulting from tearing of the ligament fibrils.

descente de main et des jambes A French term; to yield with the hand and legs, while the horse maintains the same flexion, cadence, and rhythm in the movement being executed.

destrier (1) A French war horse. (2) The side on which the squire led his master's horse; from the Latin *dextra* meaning right side.

destroy Also known as put down; to humanely kill a horse (q.v.) or hound (q.v.) due to age, illness, or injury.

developers *see* RUBBER BANDS

deviation of the metacarpophalangeal joint *see* BANDY LEGGED

devil grass *see* BERMUDA GRASS

Devonshire slipper stirrup iron A metal, slipper-shaped fitting connected to a bar attached to the stirrup leathers on which the stirrup (q.v.) revolves; used to support the rider's foot.

deworm To use anthelmintics (q.v.) to kill internal parasites in the horse; generally administered orally in paste form.

dexter Any of several driving bits.

dh The acronym for dead heat (q.v.).

DI The acronym for dosage index (q.v.).

diagnostic ultrasound The use of high frequency sound waves, above the range of the human ear, to image internal structures.

diagonal The forefoot moving in unison with the opposite hind foot at the trot.

diagonal aids To communicate instruction to the horse using aids (q.v.) applied to the opposite sides of the body, e.g., right rein used in conjunction with the left heel or alternatively, the left rein with the right heel.

diaphragmatic hernia Also known as rupture; protrusion of abdominal contents through the diaphragm.

diamond bars *see* JUMPED-IN BARS

diaphysis Also known as cortex; the shaft of a long bone including both the bone and marrow layers.

diarrhea An ailment characterized by abnormally frequent and fluid evacuation of the intestines.

Dickey Also spelled dicky; 19th-century slang; the rear seat of a horse-drawn vehicle, commonly used by a servant.

Dicky *see* DICKEY

Dicky Coach (1) A horse-drawn coach or carriage in which the box seat (q.v.) was separated, or appeared to be separated, from the main bodywork. (2) Slang; any horse-drawn passenger vehicle with a rear or rumble seat.

die in the herd A cutting horse term; said of the rider who, when in competition, rides his horse into a herd of cattle to select another cow, but fails to do so before the buzzer sounds to end the run (q.v.).

diestrus Also spelt dioestrus; the period in the mare's breeding cycle during which she will not accept the stallion; sometimes divided into two separate periods: proestrus (q.v.), the period just prior to the occurrence of estrus (q.v.), and metestrus (q.v.).

dietary essential amino acids Also known as essential amino acids or by the acronym DEAAs; any of the ten amino acids (q.v.) which make up natural proteins (q.v.) without which normal metabolic function cannot occur; are essential for the growth, maintenance, and repair of the body tissues of the horse and must be supplied by the horse's ration as they are not internally synthesized.

Digby *see* GOVERNESS CAR

digestible energy Also known by the acronym DE; the total energy produced from carbohydrates, fats, and proteins, less the energy remaining in the feces and by products formed during digestion; the value most commonly used to describe the energy content of animal feeds in the United States.

digestive system Also known as digestive tract; the system consisting of the mouth (lips, teeth, tongue, and salivary glands), the esophagus, the true stomach, the small intestine, liver, pancreas, the large intestine, rectum, and anus; the primary functions are motility, evacuation, digestion, and absorption (to convert food and drink into a form absorbable by the body tissues).

digestive tract *see* DIGESTIVE SYSTEM

digit The portion of the horse's leg below the fetlock including the coffin and long and short pastern bones.

digital cushion *see* PLANTAR CUSHION

Diligence A heavy, lumbering, horse-drawn stage coach used throughout Europe during the 19th and early 20th centuries; provided long-distance transportation with different classes of accommodation at different fares determined by location of the seats within the vehicle: (a) coupé, (b) roof, (c) intérieur (q.v.), and (d) rear; pulled by a four-horse team or, more commonly, a team of five with three horses harnessed abreast in the lead.

dimethyl sulfoxide Also known by the acronym DMSO; an organic chemical derived from wood pulp which is rapidly absorbed into the system through the skin; utilized as a carrier to help transport other substances through the skin and has anti-inflammatory (q.v.), antibacterial (q.v.), and analgesic (q.v.) properties; is administered topically to treat acute lameness, pruritis (q.v.), lacerations, and other traumas to the musculoskeletal system, to reduce pain, and intravenously as a free-radical scavenger, anti-inflammatory agent, and to treat pneumonia; has an unpleasant odor and taste.

dinks Chaps (q.v.) that extend only to the knee; frequently fringed.

dioestrus *see* DIESTRUS

dip A western roping term; the downward angle of the lariat (q.v.) achieved during the swing.

diphron A Greek war chariot with a high front shield, entered from the rear and drawn by two or more horses harnessed abreast.

diploma *see* EARN A DIPLOMA

Diploma of the Worshipful Company of Farriers Also known as dip WFC, by the acronym DWCF and previously as Registered Shoeing Smith; one of three levels of training certification awarded to practicing farriers in England by the Worshipful Company of Farriers of London (q.v.) on the basis of written, oral, and practical examinations.

dipped back Said of the horse's back (q.v.) when it has high, protruding short withers and reasonable muscling near the loins.

dip WFC *see* WORSHIPFUL COMPANY OF FARRIERS

direct flexion The longitudinal flexion (q.v.) of the horse at the poll and in the mouth.

direct rein Also known as plow reining, opening rein, open rein, or guiding rein; to use the rein (q.v.) on the side to which a turn is desired to draw the horse, specifically the nose and head, in the direction of the desired turn with the body following.

dirt track A racing term; a racetrack (q.v.) with a surface consisting of sand and soil.

discord lupus A type of lupus (q.v.); an immune-mediated disorder rarely seen in horses characterized by inflammation of the facial skin.

dish (1) A breaking away of the horny wall. (2) Any indentation appearing on the hoof wall.

dish profile *see* DISH FACED

dish face Also known as dish profile, concave face, or stag face; said of the face of the horse when concave below the eyes or forehead as formed by a depression of the nasal bones; common to Arabs (q.v.).

dishing Also known as winging or paddling; outward deviation of the foot during flight in which the foot breaks over the outside toe and lands on the outside wall; is naturally occurring in laterally gaited horses such as the Andalusian (q.v.) and Peruvian Paso (q.v.) and common in high-going or pigeon-toed (q.v.) horses or horses with a base narrow (q.v.).

dismount Also known as light or alight; to get off a horse.

disobedient Said of a horse who ignores the training or evades aids of the rider and does not perform the requested movement.

displaced fracture A break in a bone in

which the bone fragments have moved out of alignment; depending on the degree of displacement, the pieces generally require realignment for satisfactory healing to occur.

disqualify (1) To be asked to withdraw from competition due to a serious fault of either the rider or horse. (2) A racing term; to lower the actual finishing place of a horse following completion of a race by official action as due to interference with another horse in the field, carrrying improper weight, or competing under the influence of an illegal substance.

disqualification *see* DISQUALIFY

distaff Also known as distaff side; the female line or bottom line of a pedigree.

distaffer A female horse.

distaff race A racing term; any race in which only female horses are allowed to enter.

distaff side *see* DISTAFF

distal Furthest away from the center of the horse's body or center of gravity, as in "the injury was distal (below) to the knee."

distal phalange *see* THIRD PASTERN

distal phalanx *see* THIRD PASTERN

distal profusion The total circulation of blood through all tissues.

distal pulse The rhythmic beating or throbbing of the arteries in the foot caused by heart contractions which force blood to move through the vessel; taken at the lateral rear of the fetlock.

distal sesamoid ligament Also known as distal sesamoidean ligament; strong, fibrous bands of tissue consisting of fibro-elastic (yellow) and fibrous (white) types which serve to connect the bottom of the sesamoid bones to the long and short pastern bones; strengthen and limit joint range.

distal sesamoidean ligament *see* DISTAL SESAMOID LIGAMENT

distance, a *see* A DISTANCE

distanced A racing term; said of a horse so far behind the rest of the field (q.v.) that it is

unable to regain a position of contention.

distance of ground *see* ROUTE

distance, the *see* THE DISTANCE

distemper *see* STRANGLES

distillers dried grains *see* DISTILLERS GRAINS

distillers grains Also known as distillers dried grains; the substance resulting from grain or a grain mixture following removal of ethyl alcohol from the yeast fermentation of the grain; corn and rye grains are most commonly used; contain approximately 25 percent protein, 13 percent crude fiber, and a high digestible energy content; very palatable to horses.

disunited *see* DISUNITED CANTER AND DISUNITED GALLOP

disunited canter Also known as cross-canter or broken canter; said of a cantering horse who changes leg sequence taking one lead with the front legs, and the opposite lead with the hind; may be due to a lack of balance and/or back stiffness.

disunited gallop Also known as false gallop; said of a galloping (q.v.) horse who changes leg sequence; may be caused by the horse taking one lead with the fore and the opposite lead with his hind legs; the sequence of hoof beats is: off hind, near hind, near fore, off fore (leading leg) or near hind, off hind, off fore, near fore (leading leg); is very uncomfortable to ride; may lead to lower-leg injuries.

diuretic Any substance used to increase the production of urine.

dividend Also known as pay off; a racing term; the amount paid to a bettor (q.v.) who backs a winning horse or places a horse on the totalizator (q.v.).

division A racing term; a horse race divided into two different races by the track officials because the number of entries exceeds available space.

divot A piece of sod torn up by the horse's hooves in a polo, race, hunt, etc.

divot stomping Also known as earth

stomping; the tradition of replacing the mounds of earth torn up by the horse's hooves on the polo field, racetrack, and in some hunted areas and pushing them down with one's foot or heel to keep the field in good condition.

Dixon, Henry Hall (1822–1870) An English author who penned, under the pseudonym of The Druid, such equestrian works as the *Post and Paddock* (1856), *Silk and Scarlet* (1858), *Scott and Seabright* (1862), *Field and Fern* (1865), and *Saddle and Sirloin* (1870).

DMSO The acronym for dimethyl sulfoxide (q.v.).

DNA The acronym for deoxyribonucleic acid (q.v.).

DNA testing A biotechnical identification procedure now adopted by some horse registries such as The Jockey Club (q.v.) to verify parentage of a horse; is 99 percent accurate and, in many cases, has replaced blood-typing which is only 96 percent accurate; DNA strands of an offspring are compared to those of suspected parents; when matches between the strands of the offspring and parents appear in loci in a regular and consistent manner, a match is considered approved.

dobbin A British term; a workhorse used in agricultural service.

dock (1) Also known as docking or flagging; to amputate the tail bone to a length of about 6 inches (15 cm) with a docking knife or scissors and cauterize it by application of a docking iron (q.v.); commonly practiced on certain classes of horses, such as harness horses and cobs, through 1948 to yield a more neat appearance and to prevent the reins from becoming caught under the tail; illegal in most countries since 1949 and restricted in England by the Docking and Nicking Act (q.v.). (2) The solid portion or bone of the tail including both hair-covered and bare sides.

dock and set To remove part of the dock (q.v.) of the tail, cut the tendons, and set the tail so that when healed, it is carried high.

docked *see* DOCKED TAIL

docked tail Also known as docked; said of the tail of the horse when part of the dock (q.v.) has been amputated.

docker Driving slang; a whip (q.v.) used by poor class drivers.

docking *see* DOCK no. 1

Docking and Nicking act A law passed in Great Britain in 1948 which made it illegal to dock (q.v.) or nick (q.v.) the tail of the horse to improve his appearance for show purposes.

docking iron A metal iron when heated used to cauterize the amputated dock (q.v.).

dockpiece *see* CRUPPER DOCK

dock tail Also known as cocktail; a horse having a tail cut or bobbed to a length of about six inches.

doer *see* GOOD DOER

dog (1) A racing term; any obstacle (commonly rubber traffic cones) placed adjacent to the inner rail on the racetrack during workout periods to close off a portion of the track when it is muddy; prevents horses from running there or tearing up the surface during workouts. (2) A cheap horse or one that simply fails to perform; a sluggish horse.

Dog Cart *see* DOGCART

Dogcart Also known as a gig and spelled Dog Cart; an open, horse-drawn, English sporting cart used for general purposes and to carry gun dogs who were contained in a slatted compartment beneath the driver's seat; both two- and four-wheeled types existed, the latter being known more correctly as a Dogcart Phaeton (q.v.); the two-wheeled version was drawn by one or two horses, while the four-wheeled was always drawn by a pair; both derived from the 18th-century shooting gig (q.v.); seated four passengers, including the driver, back-to-back (q.v.); one passenger and the driver faced forward and two passengers faced backward; hung on sideways elliptical springs.

Dogcart Phaeton Also known as Four-wheeled Dogcart or Double Dogcart; a horse-drawn vehicle similar in use and design to a dogcart (q.v.), but having four wheels instead of two; seated four with carriage for dogs located beneath the seats; drawn by a single pair or a team of small ponies; now quite popular for FEI (q.v.) events and private use.

dog-fall A steer wrestling term; said of a steer (q.v.) thrown by the cowboy so that all four feet and the head face different directions; an illegal throw; to obtain a time, the cowboy must turn the steer over or let it stand and re-throw it legally.

dog fox A male fox (q.v.).

dogger An American term; one who purchases asses, mules, horses, and/or hybrids live on the hoof at auctions with the sole intent of slaughtering them for pet food.

dog hound A male hound (q.v.).

dog-legged whip A driving whip in which the stock is attached at a right angle to the shaft.

Døle Gudbrandsdal Also known as Gudbrandsdal, Døler pony, Dolehest or Norwegian; an ancient pony breed originating in Norway's Gudbrandsdal Valley from which the name derives; similar to the English Fell pony (q.v.) and the British Dales pony (q.v.), probably having shared similar ancestors in the Friesian (q.v.); infusions of English Thoroughbred (q.v.) in the 19th century and that of heavy draft resulted in a breed of mixed origins; has a natural trotting ability which is most developed in a lighter version of the breed known as the Døle Trotter (q.v.); stands 14.2 to 15.2 hands and weighs 1,190-1,390 lb (540-631 kg); the coat is generally bay, brown or black, with palomino and gray occurring rarely; has a heavy and rather square head, full forelock, mane, and tail, short back, broad chest, short legs with heavy feathering from the cannons to the coronet (q.v.), and broad feet; originally used for general farm work and hauling timber; now used for heavy draft, farming, and, due to its exceptional trotting ability, trotter racing; contributed to the development of the North Swedish Horse (q.v.).

Døler Pony *see* DØLE GUDBRANDSDAL

Døle Trotter Also known as a Norwegian Trotter; a light version of the Døle Gudbrandsdal (q.v.) from which it is bred using a greater input of blood from other trotter breeds; the stud book was established in 1941; registered in breed records with a T preceding the registration number.

dolls A racing term; portable wooden barricades set on some racecourses to keep the horses on track.

domador A South American term; a horse trainer (q.v.).

Don Also known as Donsky; a Soviet-bred warmblood descended from Turkmene (q.v.) and Karabakh (q.v.) stallions bred to native steppes mares during the 18th and 19th centuries; into the early 20th century, improved with Orlov (q.v.), Thoroughbred (q.v.), and Strelet Arab blood; the largest of the native breeds and the historical mount of the Don Cossacks; stands 15.1 to 15.3 hands, has a chestnut, light bay, or brown coat with a golden sheen, deep body, long straight neck, back and shoulder, and long legs; has a tendency towards calf-knees (q.v.); is hardy, frugal, energetic, and known for its great stamina; used for riding, long-distance racing, and light harness.

done Said of an exhausted horse.

donkey An ass (q.v.); derived from the English dun (the usual color) and the suffix "ky" meaning small, thus "little dun animal."

donkey foot *see* CLUB FOOT

donkey hooves *see* CLUB FOOT

Donsky *see* DON

doorman A British term; a farrier assistant responsible for trimming the feet, nailing on the shoes, and clenching the nails.

dope (1) Also known as nobble; any substance illegally given to a horse to alter its behavior or ability to perform; commonly used on the racetrack to either increase or decrease the horse's speed; an illegal practice and carries heavy penalties in all equestrian sports. (2) To administer dope to a horse. (3) A racing term; slang; information or data, as in the previous performance, of a racehorse.

doped fox A hunting term; also known as a touched up fox; said of a fox whose scent has been enhanced with synthetic scent; generally the fox's, placed at the entrance/exit of its den; used to ensure the hounds have a strong scent to follow.

dope out a race A racing term; said of one who reads or solicits information pertaining to the past performances of specific horses competing in a race.

dope test *see* DRUG TEST

doping Also known as nobbling; the process of giving dope (q.v.) to a horse; to dope (q.v.).

Dormeuse Also known as Dormeuse chariot; a closed, long distance, horse-drawn traveling chariot widely used in France and other Western European countries from the 1820s; had a forward extension of the body into which the passengers' feet could be extended when sleeping, a mattress located in the boot, the seat cushions that made up the bed; hung on cee- or sideways-elliptical springs, had a hooded rumble for servants, and a sword case built into the back of the body; entered by half-glass doors from either side; drawn by four horses in pole gear (q.v.) and often postillion (q.v.) driven; developed in parallel with the britzska (q.v.).

Dormeuse Chariot *see* DORMEUSE

dorsal (1) Relating to or situated near or on the back. (2) Situated away from or directed away from the axis.

dorsal deviation of the carpal joints *see* FORWARD DEVIATION OF THE CARPAL JOINTS

dorsal displacement of the soft palate *see* SOFT PALATE DISEASE

dorsal stripe Also known as list, ray, eel stripe, or stripe; a black, brown, red, or gold primitive mark (q.v.) running from the withers, down the middle of the back, into the tail; can occur on any coat color.

D'orsay A light, horse-drawn carriage of the brougham (q.v.) type having a high slung body set on curved springs attached to the front and back of the frame.

dos-à-dos A French term; back-to-back passenger seating in a horse-drawn carriage;.

dosage Also known as dosage system; a racing term; a system that identifies patterns of ability in horses based on a list of prepotent sires; each of the sires is placed into one of five categories: brilliant, intermediate, classic, solid, and professional, which quantify speed and stamina; each generation of sires is worth 16 points.

dosage index Also known by the acronym DI; a racing term; a mathematical reduction of the dosage profile (q.v.) to a number reflecting a horse's potential for speed and stamina; the higher the number, the more likely a horse is suited to sprinting; the average DI is approximately 40.

dosage profile A list of dosage points given prepotent sires in each of five categories: brilliant, intermediate, classic, solid, and professional; used to develop the dosage index (q.v.).

dosage system *see* DOSAGE

Double (1) Also known as double fence or double bank; a hunting term; a jumping obstacle, e.g., a fence or bank, with a ditch on both the take-off and landing sides. (2) Also known as "to double the horn"; a hunting term; a series of short, quick, staccato notes blown on a hunting horn (q.v.) indicating a fox has been found or crossed a ride. (3) Also known as doubles betting; a racing term; said of a bettor (q.v.) who selects two horses to win in two different races on the same program; if the first horse wins, the winnings and the original stake are re-invested on the second horse; both horses must win for the bettor to collect. (4) *see* DOUBLE COMBINATION. (5) *see* DAILY DOUBLE

Double One of three types of the Basque (q.v.) pony, a semi-wild, exceptionally hardy pony indigenous to the Basque region of France standing 12.2 to 14.2 hands.

double back (1) Said of the horse's back (q.v.) when the spine is arched and higher than the muscles on either side. (2) Also known as runs his foil; a hunting term; said of a fox (q.v.) who runs back along its own line to confuse the hounds (q.v.).

double bank *see* DOUBLE no. 1

double bridle Also called full bridle; a bridle (q.v.) equipped with both curb (q.v.) and snaffle (q.v.) bits attached to two sets of cheekpieces and two sets of reins; compulsory in advanced and FEI (q.v.) dressage tests; originated sometime in the 1780s or 1790s.

double combination Also known as double; any show or cross country jumping obstacle consisting of two consecutive obstacles of any type which are numbered and judged as one; may include one or two non-jumping strides between the elements (q.v.).

double cryptorchid *see* RIG

Double Dogcart *see* DOGCART PHAETON

double event A racing term

double fence *see* DOUBLE no. 1

double gaited Said of a horse who can either trot or pace with good speed.

double harness A driving term; harness for a pair of horses.

double horse A motion picture term; any horse(s) used to replace the principal horse (q.v.) in action shots or when performing stunts or tricks; only used if the principal horse is incapable of performing the required moves.

Double Klepper *see* TORIC

double muscling Said of a horse having pronounced muscling over the croup; common in heavy-horse breeds.

double oxer A jumping obstacle consisting of two oxers (q.v.) positioned with one or two strides between them; basically an in-and-out (q.v.).

double-ring snaffle *see* WILSON SNAFFLE

doubles *see* DOUBLE COMBINATION

doubles betting *see* DOUBLE no. 3

double the horn, to *see* DOUBLE no. 2

double thong A driving term; said of the thong (q.v.) of a four-horse whip when caught on the crop.

double volte A dressage term used at the Spanish Riding School (q.v.); a six-meter circle ridden twice.

douga Also spelled duga; an arched, wooden yoke used on Russian carriages, troikas, and sleighs fixed to the shafts and passed high over the horses' necks; used to separate the shafts and, in some cases, used as a bearing rein; frequently adorned with bells.

doughnut *see* SAUSAGE BOOT

doughnut boots *see* SAUSAGE BOOT

down in front Said of a horse whose conformation is such that its forehand is, when viewed horizontally, lower than the hindquarters.

Downs *see* EPSOM DOWNS

down wind To be in a position where the wind blows from an object or place towards you carrying a scent or sound; if you are downwind from your quarry (q.v.), it cannot smell you.

dq The acronym for disqualified (q.v.).

D-ring snaffle *see* DEE-RING SNAFFLE

draft (1) A hunting term; to cull a hound from the pack or to acquire one from another pack. (2) A hunting term; hounds who are not needed by the Hunt which are sold or given away. (3) *see* DRAFT HORSE. (4) A hunting term; to select the hounds for a particular day of hunting. (5) Also spelled draft; the act of pulling or drawing loads as by horses. (6) A team of horses for pulling a load.

draft horse Also known as draft and spelled draught horse; any heavy- or light-breed horse used to pull a vehicle.

drafted hound A hunting term; said of a hound removed from the pack or on loan from another Hunt (q.v.).

draft pack A hunting term; any pack of hounds purchased from another Hunt (q.v.), the hounds having been culled from the original pack.

drafty Having the heavy characteristics of a draft horse (q.v.).

drag (1) A hunting term; the line taken by a fox to its kennel. (2) A hunting term; a trail of scent, frequently artificial, left by dragging on horseback or on foot an object soaked in any of a number of types of strong-smelling liquid similar to the scent of a fox; generally laid between one and three hours before the hunt; must be of sufficient length to require at least one check (q.v.). (3) An American term; a horse who regularly lags behind the others. (4) Any awkward heavy horse-drawn vehicle. (5) Also known as park coach, private coach, or four-in-hand coach; a four wheel, horse-drawn vehicle similar to, but more elegant than, the road coach (q.v.); used for private or park driving and sporting purposes; generally painted with family colors and driven by amateurs; the box seat held the coachman and one passenger to his left; had two roof seats built to carry four passengers and a rumble seat for two grooms; the interior compartment was rarely used, although trimmed with cloth, leather, or whip cord; frequently used as a mobile grandstand at the races, polo matches, and other sporting events; drawn by four horses and either postillion (q.v.) or coachman (q.v.) driven.

dragging the goat *see* BUZKASHI

drag horse (1) A hunting term; the horse used by the dragman (q.v.) when laying the artificial scent (q.v.) used in a drag hunt (q.v.). (2) A driving term; a horse used in a team to pull a Drag (q.v.); should match other horses used in the team in both stride and color without flashy white markings; the wheelers can be slightly taller than the leaders.

drag hound A hunting term; a hound (q.v.) trained to follow a drag (q.v.) scent.

drag hunt A hunting term; a hunt (q.v.) conducted on horseback in which the hounds follow an artificial scent (q.v.) or trail laid by dragging a bag of suitable scented material across the ground to closely simulate the run of a wild fox; common in areas where foxes are scarce; is generally faster than a live hunt (q.v.).

dragman A hunting term; one responsible for laying the artificial scent (q.v.) used in a drag hunt (q.v.); may be performed mounted or on foot; lays the scent over a stretch of country (q.v.) in such a way as to simulate the line a fox would take.

drag prop *see* DRAG STICK

drag-shoe Also known as skid, skid pan, slipper, skid-shoe, vehicle skid, or wagonlock; a driving term; a tire-shaped iron shoe or plate placed under each wheel of a heavily-laden, horse-drawn vehicle before descending a steep hill; attached to the vehicle by means of a skid chain (q.v.) whether in use or not and used as a brake.

drag shoe chain A link chain by which the drag shoe is attached to a horse-drawn vehicle.

dragsman *see* COACHMAN

drag staff *see* DRAG STICK

drag stick Also known as drag prop or drag staff; a round stick or piece of wood about 3 inches (7.5 cm) thick and tipped with a sharp iron spike approximately 4 inches (10 cm) long fitted to the rear axles of most horse-drawn vehicles between the center of the axle and the rear offside wheel; used as a brake to take the weight off the horse and prevent the vehicle from running backwards, when it is not in use and on an incline; when not in use may be hung on the rear axle.

draught *see* DRAFT no. 5 AND no. 6

draught horse *see* DRAFT HORSE

draught reins The primary reins (q.v.) used in pair and team driving controlled by the coachman; attach to the outside of the bit of each horse and buckle to the coupling reins (q.v.) which are connected to the inside of the bit of the partner horse.

draw (1) *see* DRAW A COVERT. (2) The horse's position in the working order that determines in which order he will work or compete against other horses, as in "what is your draw?" (3) A hunting term; the sequence in which a huntsman (q.v.) draws his coverts (q.v.) during a day of hunt (q.v.). (4) A carriage term; said of a horse(s) when pulling a carriage (q.v.).

draw a covert Also known as draw; a hunting term; said of a huntsman (q.v.) and hounds (q.v.) when they search every part of a covert (q.v.) in search of the fox (q.v.).

draw a hound A hunting term; said of a huntsman (q.v.) or whipper-in (q.v.) when he moves the hounds (q.v.) from the kennel lodging rooms to the feeding rooms.

draw blank *see* BLANK no. 1

draw cattle A cutting term; the ability of a cutting horse to mesmerize a cow without threatening or frightening it, and to make it approach him.

draw reins Two leather or synthetic straps or ropes attached to the girth, saddle, or harness which run through the bit rings to the hands of the rider or driver; used as a training aid to encourage the horse to lower and/or set his head.

draw yard A hunting term; the yard or other area where the hounds are collected and retained prior to being drawn off by the huntsman (q.v.) to their respective kennels.

dray (1) Also known as transfer dray in North America or flat in Scotland and northern England; a heavy, low, strong, four-wheeled, horse-drawn freight vehicle first introduced during the 17th century; lacked fixed sides and, generally, springs; some had a raised seat for the driver while others were controlled from the ground; used to carry heavy loads and usually drawn by a team of draft horses (q.v.). (2) A tall, Australian, two-wheeled, heavy-duty, horse-drawn cart used on farms for general purposes. (3) To convey by means of a dray.

Dr. Bristol *see* DR. BRISTOL BIT

Dr. Bristol bit Also known as a trotting man's bit or Dr. Bristol; a snaffle bit (q.v.) in which the mouthpiece has two joints connected by a small, flat, angled plate or flat link; each end of the mouthpiece is attached to a ring to which the reins are connected; is more severe than a French snaffle (q.v.).

drench (1) Any medicine suspended in water, thin gruel, or oil and administered as a drink to a horse. (2) To administer liquid medicine to a horse through its mouth.

dress (1) A 16th-century term; to place or set in position, put into alignment, or prepare according to certain principles. (2) To apply bandages or medications.

dressage Also known as ballet on horseback; a term popular after the turn of the 19th century; the harmonious development of the physique and ability of the horse to make him calm, supple, confident, attentive, and keen, thus achieving perfect understanding with his rider; loosely, any form of ring or school riding; derived from the French dresser (q.v.), to place or put into position; an Olympic sport since 1912.

dressage arena The flat, smooth, rectangular area in which dressage tests or maneuvers are performed; in international competitions, measures 65.6 x 21.8 yards (60 x 20 m), while the smaller arena, used in lesser competitions,

measures 43.7 x 21.8 yards (40 x 20 m); many different surface types are used including grass, sand, stone chips, woodchips, plastic, and a variety of composites.

dressage d'academique A French term; advanced dressage work performed in the manège (q.v.) which leads to the haute ecole (q.v.).

dressage d'manège A French term; general schooling of the horse in the ring (q.v.) or manège (q.v.).

dressage d'obstacles A French term; schooling the horse over fences.

dressage markers Plastic, metal, or wooden, free-standing markers upon which the alphabetical letters used to mark specific points around the perimeter of a dressage arena are printed; the rider performs movements between and around these markers; in the small arena, eight markers A, K, E, H, C, M, B, and F are used clockwise around the edge of the arena starting with A at the center line and D, X, and G mark the center line; in the large arena, four additional markers, R, S, V, and P are used.

dressage test A series of dressage movements performed at specific locations and in a defined order within the dressage arena (q.v.) during competitions within a specified amount of time; are of varying standards and consist of progressively more difficult movements at each level of performance; test scores are based on the total points attained, with each individual movement receiving a score from zero (failure to perform) to ten (excellent).

dressage whip A whip (q.v.) used by dressage riders to control, correct, or punish a horse; consists of a laquered wood, thread, fiberglass, bone, plastic, metal, or leather shaft attached to leather hand grip generally made of leather; in competition, measures 32 inches (81 cm) long while a 30-42 inch (76-107 cm) whip may be used for schooling.

dressed Said of a horse trained to carry out full collection with his hocks well engaged under him, the poll raised, and the head carried in the vertical.

dresser (1) A French term; to prepare, train, or school a horse; to put into place, to raise the head and neck of the horse; from which the word dressage (q.v.) was derived. (2) One who dresses wounds.

dresseur A French term; an expert horseman or horsemaster whose living is dependent upon the Classical Art of riding.

dressing (1) The act of one who, or that which, dresses. (2) That with which something is dressed, as bandages for a wound.

dress leather An animal hide tanned into leather, smoothed and leveled, softened with oil, and, frequently, dyed.

drift (1) A cutting term; said of a horse who slowly loses his position relative to the herd (q.v.) of cattle. (2) A change from one pace to another in which there is no distinct difference between the speed or pace, e.g., medium to collected canter.

D ring *see* DEE-RING

D-ring snaffle *see* DEE-RING SNAFFLE

drive (1) Said of the rider; to push a ridden horse forward into the bit using the influence of the seat and back. (2) To force or push a herd of cattle forward in a controlled and calm manner, generally from a mounted position. (3) A racing term; all-out exertion of the horse when tired, such as on the home-stretch (q.v.). (4) A hunting term; the urge of the hounds (q.v.) to quickly follow the line of a fox (q.v.) so as not to lose the scent. (5) *see* LONG LINE

driver (1) A driving term; one who directs the speed and movements of the horse(s) from a vehicle attached to the horse(s). (2) A driving term; one with less talent than a coachman (q.v.).

driving A racing term; said of a horse running under extreme pressure from the jockey.

driving aids Any combination of natural and/or artificial aids (q.v.) used by the rider or ground driver to move the horse forward into the bit.

driving blinkers *see* BLINKERS

driving hammer Also known as shoeing hammer; a farrier's tool consisting of a solid, metal head set crosswise on a handle used to drive horseshoe (q.v.) nails and to turn over or wring off the tips of the nails after being driven into the hoof wall when attaching a horseshoe.

driving whip *see* COACHING CROP

driving with a full hand A driving term; a method of holding two sets of reins in one hand in which each rein passes through a different finger; occasionally used in tandem driving.

Droischa *see* DROSKY

Droitska *see* DROITZSCHKA

Droitzschka Also known as Russian droschki and in England as the English droitzschka (q.v.) and spelled droitska; a horse-drawn German pleasure or passenger vehicle adapted from the drosky (q.v.); a four-passenger vehicle which carried two passengers seated on a crosswise seat positioned just a few inches above the rear axle, and two seated outside on an enlarged box seat shared with the driver; had a low center of gravity, a half-hood, was hung on sideways elliptical or semi-elliptical springs, and was drawn by either one or two horses.

drooping quarters *see* GOOSE RUMPED

drop (1) Also known as face drop, face piece, forehead piece, or forehead drop; a driving term; the decorative part of the harness which lies on the horse's forehead; generally oval shaped with a pointed tip and made of patent leather emblazoned with the owner's crest or monogram; worn in show and drag harnesses. (2) *see* FOAL no. 2. (3) Said of a male horse; to relax the genital muscles and allow the penis to fall from the sheath (q.v.).

drop a foal *see* FOAL no. 2

drop down (1) A racing term; said of a horse running against lower class horses than it had previously been competed against. (2) *see* DROP ON A COW

drop fence A jumping obstacle in which the landing side of the fence is lower than the take-off.

drop noseband Also known as dropped noseband; a noseband (q.v.) in which the front nosepiece passes across the bottom of the nasal bone and the rear nosepiece passes below the bit, fastening in the chin groove (q.v.); prevents the horse from opening his mouth or shifting his jaws to escape the action of the bit; frequently used in conjunction with a snaffle bit; originated in the German cavalry.

drop on a cow Also known as drop down; a cutting horse term; said of a horse who lowers or drops down low onto the extended forehand prior to and when working a cow; the horse appears to crouch, its haunches raised significantly higher than the forehand.

dropped *see* FOAL

dropped back *see* SWAY BACK

dropped crease shoe *see* FEATHER-EDGED SHOE

dropped fox *see* BAGMAN

dropped noseband *see* DROP NOSEBAND

dropped sole Also known as pumiced foot or prolapsed sole; a condition of the hoof in which the sole has dropped to, or beyond, the level of the bearing surface of the hoof wall; the sole is flat and has no concavity; in extreme cases it may be convex; a sequel to chronic laminitis (q.v.) characterized by heavy rings in the hoof wall.

droppings *see* FECES

drop the stirrups Said of the rider; to remove one's feet from the stirrup irons (q.v.) and continue riding without them; the stirrups may be left hanging or crossed over the withers of the horse; an exercise performed to develop balance, a secure leg position, and improved seat.

Droschki *see* DROSKY

Drosky Also known as Droschki, Droischa, or Russian cab; a four-wheeled, horse-drawn passenger carriage; originally seated two passengers on an upholstered cross-plank, which was eventually changed to a well-padded bench near road level protected by a half-hood; drawn by three horses abreast, decorated with silver bells; the center horse was positioned between shafts and under a wooden arch and did most of the pulling at a trot while the outer horses cantered with outward turned heads for show.

drover One who drives herds of cattle or sheep to market on horseback (in the United Kingdom on foot); most common in the period prior to the advent of railroads and improved highways.

drug test Also known as dope test; the use of blood, urine, and saliva tests to determine if illegal substances were administered to a horse to alter its performance or mask injury.

dry lot To isolate or confine a horse in a corral or other enclosed area denuded of vegetation and to hand feed him a regulated amount as to control weight or treat a medical condition.

dry matter The portion of feed not made up of water.

dry single A jumping obstacle consisting of a constructed mound of dirt with a platform or flat top; differs from a bank (q.v.) in that there is no ditch at the base.

dry work A cutting term; to train, work, or show a cutting horse without using cattle, the emphasis being on reining; the opposite of wet work (q.v.).

dub (1) To fit the hoof (q.v.) to the horseshoe (q.v.) instead of the shoe to the hoof; accomplished by rasping down the outside wall of the hoof. (2) Also known as dump; to dress back the toe of the hoof to treat such conditions as founder (q.v.) or toe flare.

Dubai World Cup The world's richest horse race; a 1-1/4 mile (2 km) race run at Dubai's (United Arab Emirates) al Sheba Racecourse.

dubbed Also known as dumped, dumped toe, dubbed toe, or bull nose foot; said of the hoof when the dorsal (q.v.) surface has been ground off due to excessive rasping to fit the foot to a horseshoe, as a result of lameness which may cause the horse to drag its foot, or to treat such conditions as founder.

dubbed foot *see* DUBBED

dubbed toe *see* DUBBED

Duc A horse-drawn formal park or show vehicle lacking boot (q.v.) or luggage space; a cross between a Pony Phaeton and a Victoria (q.v.); driven by the sole occupant, but frequently accompanied by a gentleman outrider (q.v.) or liveried groom; usually hung on sideways elliptical springs, although a few early types were mounted on cee-springs.

Duckett's dot An imaginary point about 3/8 inch (10 mm) behind the apex of the frog at the center of the toe arc on a properly trimmed hoof.

dude Also known as greenhorn or tenderfoot; an American term; one inexperienced in the rigors of ranching, a person from the city, or an Easterner who spends a vacation on a ranch; a stranger.

dude ranch A ranch, generally cattle, in the United States which offers accommodations and riding facilities to dudes (q.v.).

duga *see* DOUGA

dumb jockey A bitting device used to train young horses to elevate the front end; consists of a wooden pole attached perpendicularly to a surcingle (q.v.) supported by a line to a tail crupper; the wooden pole is fitted with rings through which the reins pass to the bit and back to the sides of the surcingle; pressure on the backbone causes hollowing of the back and the reins hold the head up and in a collected position; frequently used in the training of Saddlebreds (q.v.).

dumb jockeying Said of the horse; hollowing of the back and carrying the weight on the haunches, pushing out the chest, and elevating the front end.

dumb rabies *see* PARALYTIC RABIES

dummy *see* ROPING DUMMY

dummy calf *see* ROPING DUMMY

dummy foal *see* BARKER

dump (1) Said of a horse who unseats his rider. (2) *See* DUB.

dumped (1) Said of a rider unseated by action of the horse. (2) *see* DUBBED

dumped toe *see* DUBBED

dumping To shorten the toe of the hoof by rasping (q.v.) the front of the hoof wall.

dumpling A carriage term; a large and comfortable box cushion found on some horse-drawn coaches (q.v.).

dun Also known as bayo or gateado; refers to coat color; a generic term; all lighter-colored horses which may or may not have black points (q.v.); more specifically, yellow horses with black points which include all shades of yellow mixed with other colors to create variations from pale, creamy gold, to a dirty tan; commonly have amber (hazel) eyes, although some have gray eyes; horses with nonblack points include red and yellow duns; variations include dusty dun (q.v.), grullo (q.v.), claybank (q.v.), coyote dun (q.v.), golden dun (q.v.), silver dun (q.v.), zebra dun (q.v.), lilac dun (q.v.), red dun (q.v.), and yellow dun (q.v.).

dun-factor horse Any horse displaying a dun (q.v.) coat and, frequently, primitive marks (q.v.).

Duncan gag Also known as Duncombe gag or Nelson gag; a gag bit (q.v.) consisting of a plain or twisted gag mouth with small upward cheeks (q.v.) fitted with two holes through which the gag reins (q.v.) pass.

Duncombe gag *see* DUNCAN GAG

dung *see* FECES

dung eating *see* FECES EATING

Duobus *see* BOULNOIS CAB

Duquesa A horse-drawn carriage of the Victoria (q.v.) type; usually drawn by a pair of horses in pole gear (q.v.), was protected by a half hood, seated two in the box seat, and frequently had a rearward or rumble seat for carriage servants; used in Spanish cities as a ladies carriage; the Spanish word for duchess.

durchlassigkeit A German dressage term; literally, "a lettingthroughness"; the energy from the hind limbs of the horse who ripples forward and backward through the body of the horse without being checked by the reins or bit.

dusty buckskin Refers to coat color; a type of dun (q.v.) or zebra dun (q.v.) with a brownish cast to the yellow coat, black points (q.v.), and a head of a similar color to the body; the color appears similar to olive grullo without the dark head.

dusty dun *see* DUSTY BUCKSKIN

Dutch A racing term; to take advantage of booking percentages by eliminating heavily bet noncontenders, and betting on other horses in exact amounts necessary to yield profit regardless of which horse wins.

Dutch collar *see* BREAST COLLAR

Dutch Draught Also known as Dutch Horse; a horse breed developed in the Netherlands around 1914 to work sand and clay agricultural lands; derived from New Zealand-type mares crossed with Brabant (q.v.) stallions and later with Belgian Ardennes (q.v.); is massively built and heavy-boned, stands up to 16.3 hands, has strong, muscular, well-feathered legs with broad joints, and solid hooves; is quite active, has a kind disposition, and great stamina; usually chestnut, bay, or gray; used for draft and farm work.

Dutch Horse *see* DUTCH DRAUGHT

Dutchman's team To hitch the larger horse of a two-horse team on the near side (q.v.); a position customarily held by the smaller horse.

Dutch triple Also known as gans; a four-beat gait similar to the rack (q.v.).

Dutch Warmblood A horse breed developed in the Netherlands by crossing the Gelderland (q.v.) and Groningen (q.v.) with English Thoroughbred (q.v.) and other French and German warmbloods; is quiet and willing, stands about 16.2 hands, has a brown, black, chestnut, or gray coat, supple and flowing action, and is used for light draft, carriage, and riding, particularly jumping and dressage; the Stud Book was established in 1958.

DVM The United States acronym for a Doctor of Veterinary Medicine; a veterinarian (q.v.).

DWCF The acronym for Diploma of the Worshipful Company of Farriers (q.v.).

dwell (1) *see* DWELT. (2) Also known as dwelling; a hunting term; said of a hound, who instead of pressing forward on the line of a fox (q.v.), runs to the rear of the pack and gives tongue (q.v.).

dwelling (1) A pause or suspension in the movement of the horse's foot whereby the stride appears to be completed before the foot reaches the ground; common in trick horses. (2) *see* DWELL no. 2

dwelt A racing term; said of a horse who is slow to break out of the gate.

dynamic exercises A vaulting term; compulsory exercises performed by a vaulter (q.v.) in competition consisting of the mill (q.v.), flank (q.v.), scissors, and all freestyle movements that are not required to be held for a specific number of strides; require the vaulter to, using the rhythm of the horse, change position to face backwards and sideways.

dysplasia of the growth plate *see* PHYSITIS

Dystrophia ungulae *see* SEEDY TOE

Dzhab One of two types of Kazakh (q.v.), an ancient pony breed originating in Kazakhstan; thought to have descended from the Asiatic wild horse (q.v.) refined by significant infusions of Don (q.v.) blood; stands 12.1 to 13.1 hands, generally has a bay or liver chestnut coat, although brown, bay, and mouse dun also occur, a coarse head, and thick neck; is frugal and possessed of great stamina and legendary hardiness; very resistant to both cold and fatigue; used for riding.

Dziggetai A species of wild ass (q.v.) inhabiting the elevated steppes of the Tartary a region of eastern Asia controlled by the Tartars in the 13th and 14th centuries.

E

each way A racing term; to bet on a horse both to win and to finish in the top three in which case the bettor (q.v.) wins no matter which of the first three positions the horse finishes in.

ear down A method of restraining a horse through twisting or biting the ear.

ear fistula *see* DENTIGEROUS CYST

early foot A racing term; said of a horse who exhibits good speed at the beginning of a race.

early to trot A dressage term; the premature execution of the transition to the trot at a marker (q.v.) as resulting from the horse's anticipation of a change of pace or gait before receiving the rider's aid to do so.

early to walk A dressage term; the premature execution of the transition to the walk at a marker (q.v.); may result from the horse anticipating a change of pace or gait before receiving the rider's aid.

ear mange *see* CHORIOPTIC MANGE

ear mark To cut a nitch in a horse's ear to identify it when turned out to graze on common land.

earmuff A solid cloth covering placed over the ears of a horse to limit or eliminate distracting sounds.

earn a diploma *see* BREAK MAIDEN

earn your tops A hunting term; said of a hunter who has ridden with a Hunt (q.v.) for the amount of time required to earn the right to wear a top boot (q.v.) – men earn cordovan or brown tops while women earn black patent leather; a status symbol; the amount of time one must ride with a specific Hunt to qualify varies between Hunts.

ear stripping To stroke the ear of the cold or tired horse, from the base to the tip, to induce circulation and provide comfort.

earth *see* FOX DEN

earth stomping *see* DIVOT STOMPING

earth stopper A hunting term; one employed to block the entrance to the den of a fox the night preceding the day of a hunt when a fox is out and to prevent its return.

earth stopping Also known as stopping earth; a hunting term; to block the den of a fox the night preceding the day of a hunt to prevent its return; generally performed by the terrier man; commonly conducted in Great Britain, but not in the United States, to control fox populations.

eased *see* EASE UP

ease up Also known as eased; to reduce the speed of the horse by gradually shortening the stride.

East Bulgarian A warmblood developed in Bulgaria during the late 19th century by crossing Thoroughbred (q.v.), English Halfbred (q.v.), Arab (q.v.), and Anglo-Arab (q.v.) horses; one of three primary horse breeds indigenous to Bulgaria; is elegant, well-built, stands 15 to 16 hands, has a chestnut or black coat, small head, straight profile, deep girth and long straight back; is energetic, hardy, fast, and versatile; used for riding, agriculture, and competitive sports from dressage to cross-country.

eastern equine encephalomyelitis Also known by the acronym EEE; one of three primary types of encephalomyelitis (q.v.).

Eastern horse That group of horses consisting of the Arab (q.v.), Barb (q.v.), Turk (q.v.), and Syrian breeds.

East Friesian Also spelled East Frisian; a German warmblood descended from Friesian (q.v.) stock crossed with Spanish, Neapolitan (q.v.), Cleveland Bay (q.v.), Anglo-Arab (q.v.), Norman (q.v.), Thoroughbred (q.v.), Oldenburg (q.v.), and, after 1940, Arab (q.v.) blood from stallions standing at the Marbach and Balbolna studs in Hungary; recent introduction of Hanoverian (q.v.) blood has produced an all-round sporting horse; developed in parallel to the Oldenburg through the 1940s; stands 15.2 to 16.1 hands, has a brown, bay, black, gray, or chestnut coat, a well-proportioned head, prominent features, a long and straight back and strong legs with broad joints; used for riding and light draft.

East Frisian *see* EAST FRIESIAN

East Prussian horse *see* TRAKEHNER

easy boot A tough, light-weight, urethane hoof-shaped boot worn on a bare (q.v.) or shod hoof to provide protection and traction, e.g., on a trailered horse, or one having thrown a shoe; covers the hoof from the ground-side surface of the hoof to the coronet (q.v.) and is held in place by means of levered cables.

easy gait Any smooth, lateral gait such as the rack (q.v.), running walk (q.v.), fox trot (q.v.), or stepping pace.

easy keeper Also known as a good keeper; said of a horse who is not prone to digestive problems and easily maintains his weight and healthy appearance from an average or less than average ration.

écart A racing term; the degree of deviation from the standard number of dosage strains; an expression used in the Vuillier Dosage System (q.v.).

ECG The acronym for electrocardiogram (q.v.).

echini Also known as a hedgehog; a spiked roller (q.v.) used on the mouthpiece of a Grecian bit.

echocardiography The use of ultrasound to evaluate the heart muscle to diagnose congestive heart failure (q.v.).

Eclipse Award A racing term; recognition given in the United States since 1971 to the North American divisional racing champions as selected by vote of the Daily Racing Forum (q.v.), Thoroughbred Racing Associations, and the National Turf Writers Association.

Eclipse Stakes A racing term; a 1-1/2 mile (2.4 km) race for three-year-old horses held every July 13th at Sandown Park, England.

Ecole de Cavalerie A book published in 1733 by François Robichon de la Guérinière (q.v.) in which he describes his training methods including suppling exercises such as the shoulder-in (q.v.), which he invented.

écuyer A French term used throughout Europe during the 16th and 17th centuries; historically, a recognized, often noble born, master of equitation who served at court; royal blood is no longer a requisite of title; when used in a title is capitalized.

Edelweiss Pony *see* HAFLINGER

edema Also spelled oedema; swelling due to excessive accumulation of fluid in connective tissue or a serous cavity.

edematous Relating to a condition of edema (q.v.).

edge splint One of four varieties of splints (q.v.); affect the back rim of the cannon bone; as due to a tear in the tissues that link the splint and the accessory carpal bone at the back of the knee; feels gravelly along the back of the splint bone and usually causes lameness after high-speed work.

EDM The acronym for equine degenerative myeloencephalopathy (q.v.).

educating *see* SCHOOL no. 2

Edwin, Landseer *see* LANDSEER, SIR EDWIN

EEE The acronym for eastern equine encephalomyelitis (q.v.).

eel stripe *see* DORSAL STRIPE

EGE The acronym for equine granulocytic ehrlichiosis (q.v.).

egg bar shoe A bar shoe (q.v.); a therapeutic horseshoe in which the heels or shoe branches are joined into an oval bar across the back of the foot; yields more heel support than a conventional shoe and prevents possible interference with the opposing limb; used on horses with low, sloping heels, or horses suffering from founder (q.v.) or navicular disease (q.v.); so called because the shoe is egg shaped.

egg butt A barrel-shaped joint hinge used to join the bit (q.v.) mouthpiece (q.v.) to the cheek (q.v.).

eggbutt snaffle The most commonly used single-jointed snaffle bit (q.v.); has slightly tapered arms that widen from the joint to the cheekpieces where they attach to barrel shaped, fixed rings; has less mobility than offered by a loose-ring bit (q.v.).

egg-link pelham A pelham bit (q.v.) having a double-jointed mouthpiece with an oval, or egg-shaped, center link.

eglentine High-quality stainless steel used in the manufacture of stirrup irons (q.v.), bits (q.v.), spurs (q.v.), and some bridles (q.v.).

eight horses, legend of the *see* LEGEND OF THE EIGHT HORSES, THE

EHRF The acronym for the Equine Health Research Fund (q.v.).

EHV1 The acronym for equine herpesvirus 1 (q.v.).

EHV4 The acronym for equine herpesvirus 4 (q.v.).

EI The acronym for epitheliogenesis (q.v.).

EIA The acronym for equine infectious anemia (q.v.).

eighth *see* FURLONG

eight-horse hitch A driving term; a heavy horse hitch consisting of eight horses; the wheelers (q.v.) are separated by the wagon pole, the body and swing teams between a swing pole, and the leaders have no pole between them; driven with eight reins, four held in each hand, with each rein corresponding to one horse.

eighth pole A racing term; a colored post located on the inside rail (q.v.) of a racetrack (q.v.) exactly one furlong (q.v.) from the finish.

eights A driving term; the fourth pair of mules from the front of the wagon in a 20-mule team.

eild A Scottish term; a barren mare (q.v.).

Einsiedler Also known as Swiss Anglo-Norman; a horse breed developed in Switzerland around 1064 by crossing native stock with Hackney (q.v.) and, in the 1960s, Anglo-Norman (q.v.) blood; throughout the 20th century French blood was systematically introduced; Thoroughbred (q.v.), Swedish, and German blood was introduced to start the Swiss Warmblood (q.v.); is docile, stands 15 to 16.3 hands, has a straight back, slightly sloping croup, prominent withers, a slightly convex or straight head, and strong, and well-jointed legs; any solid coat color is acceptable, but chestnut and bay are most common; a good all-round riding and driving horse; the name derived from the stud of its origin, Kloster Einsiedel and the town of Einsiedeln.

EIPH The acronym for exercise-induced pulmonary hemorrhage (q.v.).

EKG *see* ELECTROCARDIOGRAM

Ekka *see* EKKA CART

Ekka cart Also known as an Ekka; a two-wheeled, horse-drawn driving cart popular in India and the Far East; carries one, is driven without traces, the draft comes through the shafts to the pad which is prevented from slipping rearwards by a breast collar onto which some of the pulling power is transferred; either driven by an occupant or led by a servant; usually hooded or screened.

elastic cartilage A type of cartilage (q.v.) found in the horse's ears, neck, windpipe, and voice box; is tough, pliable and provides support to membranes and muscles.

Elberfeld horses A group of horses used by William von Osten of Berlin to prove his theories on equine intelligence; included the Russian stallion Kluge Hans (q.v.) and two Arab (q.v.) stallions; von Osten appeared to train Klug Hans to calculate by pawing the ground with his hoof, read, and differentiate colors, up to the general standard of knowledge of a 14-year-old-child; von Osten's studies gained enormous publicity, but in 1904, the German psychologist, Oskar Pfungst, demonstrated that the stallion answered to unconscious signs from von Osten; at the outbreak of World War I, the horses were disbanded; inherited by a wealthy Elberfeld manufacturer in 1900.

elbow The upper joint of the foreleg (q.v.).

elbow boots Sheepskin or felt lined open boots worn on the elbows of the forelegs to protect them from injury; used on horses having high-stepping foreleg action.

elbow hitting Limb contact in which the horse hits its elbow with the shoe of the same hind limb; common in those horses shod with weighted shoes.

electrocardiogram Also known by the acronym EKG; a graphic tracing of the electrical impulses produced by the heart muscle; does not detect valvular malfunctions, shunts, flow rates, or pressure changes, but can detect abnormal heartbeat patterns.

electrocardiograph An instrument used to record electric potentials associated with the electric currents that traverse the heart.

electrocardiography Study of the heart through graphic records of the electrical impulses produced by the heart.

electronic identification A method of horse identification adopted in some countries including the United States as a regulatory tool to thwart horse theft; ownership and breed information is encased in a transponder sealed in a glass pellet scarcely larger than a grain of wild rice which is implanted into the nuchal ligament running along the crest of the horse's neck; the microchip contained therein is encoded with a unique identification number of nine or ten digits that can be read when a scanner is passed along the neck; is permanent, unalterable, foolproof, and inexpensive; administration, registration, detection, placement of the chip on the body of the horse is not standardized and different microchip systems exist worldwide, each having its own detection system; cannot be removed, so some horses may have more than one chip; are frequently rejected by the body of the horse and abscesses may occur.

electrolytes Simple, water soluble inorganic compounds essential for many of the chemical processes of the body; include sodium chloride, sodium acetate, sodium bicarbonate, potassium chloride, and lactate; excreted from the body in sweat (q.v.) with broken down proteins, waste products, and oxidants.

electronic eye *see* AUTOMATIC TIMER

electro-acupuncture A type of acupuncture (q.v.); the stimulation of precise points along body meridians (q.v.) using a mild electric current delivered to fine needles inserted at, or to moist sponges surrounding an area to administer a current of stimulation through the skin; more intense than traditional needling; used to control pain, treat internal malfunctions, anesthetize, and reduce stress.

elements A jumping term; one jumps that make up each combination (q.v.) or treble fence (q.v.).

elephant polo *see* PACHYDERM POLO

elf's foot *see* FLIPPER FOOT

eligible Said of a horse or rider qualified to compete according to established conditions for the breed or sport.

ELISA The acronym for ENZYME-LINKED IMMUNOSORBENT ASSAY

elk lip A loose and overhanging upper lip.

El Morzillo The black horse belonging to Hernando Cortèz, conqueror of Mexico, in the 16th century; died during Cortèz's expedition to Guatemala in 1524 at which time he was deified by the natives in the form of a large stone statue which was ultimately destroyed by the Spanish Franciscan missionaries in 1697.

El Pato Also known as Pato; a mounted sport originating in Argentina around 1610 and banned in its original form in 1822; two teams of mounted riders numbering from a few dozen to more than several hundred would try to catch a live duck sewn into a piece of leather and then ride carrying the duck to the house of a beloved where it would be thrown down in front of the door; the game often lasted for many hours; since 1937, played with fixed rules in which two four-man teams play on a field measuring 98.43 x 218.7 yards (90 x 200 m) using a leather ball weighing 1/3 pound (1250 grams), with four leather hand grips, which, as in basketball, has to be thrown into the opponent's basket; play usually consists of six seven-minute periods, with one five-minute break between each period; each team member has two horses which he rides alternately.

elve's foot *see* FLIPPER FOOT

emasculate *see* CASTRATE

emasculator A stainless steel tool commonly used to remove the testicles from a

horse.

emergency grip To clamp both legs tightly into the pommels of a side saddle (q.v.) to secure one's position as when jumping.

embouchure A 16th and 17th-century French term; a mouthpiece (q.v.).

embryo The egg from conception through approximately 40 days.

embryo transfer Removal and transfer of an inseminated embryo from a donor mare implanted in a recipient mare; limited application in horses due to registration restrictions of most breed associations.

EMND The acronym for equine motor neuron disease (q.v.).

empty A racing term; said of the horse lacking the energy necessary to complete a drive to the finish (q.v.).

empty horse A vaulting term; a vaulting horse following concurrent dismounts of all vaulters; considered a fault in any freestyle program.

EMV The acronym for equine morbillivirus (q.v.).

encephalin A morphine-like neurotransmitter secreted by the brain.

encephalitis *see* ENCEPHALOMYELITIS

encephalomyelitis Also known as encephalitis, sleeping sickness, brain fever or brain staggers; a viral, epidemic disease which may be carried by birds, mosquitoes, or other blood-sucking insects, which results in inflammation of the brain and spinal cord; symptoms include high fever, drowsiness, lack of coordination, teeth grinding, partial vision loss, inability to swallow food, and possible paralysis; generally fatal, but vaccinations are available to immunize horses against attack; of three primary strains: eastern equine encephalomyelitis, western equine encephalomyelitis, and Venezuelan equine encephalomyelitis (q.v.).

Enclosure Acts *see* FOXHUNTING

endline A polo term; one of two short ends of a polo field (q.v.) measuring 160 yards (146

m) in length; in conjunction with the side lines (q.v.), define the playing area of the polo field; the ball is considered out of bounds if it passes outside of this line.

endocrine (1) Of or pertaining to any of the ductless or endocrine glands. (2) The internal secretions of a gland.

endocrine gland Any of the ductless glands such as the thyroid or adrenal, the secretions of which pass directly into the bloodstream from the cells of the gland.

endometrial Of or pertaining to the endometrium (q.v.).

endometritis A bacterial infection of the mucous membrane lining of the uterus; the leading cause of sterility in mares.

endometrium The mucous membrane lining of the uterus (q.v.).

endorphins Morphine-like proteins produced in nerve tissue to suppress pain and regulate emotional state.

endoscope A flexible medical instrument inserted through an incision in the skin or a body passage; enables a veterinarian (q.v.) to view the interior of a body cavity; many are constructed with metal tubes fitted with magnifying lenses, an eyepiece, and a light bulb; the fiber-optic endoscope (q.v.) is one version of this instrument.

endosteum A fine vascular membrane which lines the internal cavities of the long bones within which lies the bone marrow.

endotoxemia The presence of endotoxins in the blood; may cause shock.

endotoxic shock A sustained inadequacy of blood profusion in the tissue resulting from systemic toxicity as caused by an endotoxin (q.v.) from certain bacteria.

endotoxin A toxin of a micro-organism; separates from the cell body on its disintegration.

endurance The ability of the horse to withstand physical pain, adversity, or stress.

endurance riding Also known as long distance riding; a speed and endurance race over varying distances, topography, elevation, and footing; race length depends on the season with shorter races run earlier in the year and longer more difficult and strenuous events later in the year; may vary from 25 to 100 miles (40-160 km) in length and may be conducted over a period of one, two, or three days; competing horses are subject to veterinary inspections before, during, and after each event and may be withdrawn by the veterinarian at any time if deemed necessary to protect the horse.

enema Soapy water, oil, or other liquid introduced directly into the rectum of the horse for medicinal purposes by means of a pump or special apparatus.

energizer A component of an electric fence; delivers an electrical current ranging from less than 1,000 volts to more than 10,000 volts with 4,000 to 7,000 volts most effective; may emit voltage in a steady current or in pulses that last as little as 1/10,000 of a second and are spaced about one second apart.

energy A measure of heat; the actual or potential ability to do work as enabled by carbohydrates (q.v.), fats, and proteins in the diet of the horse with carbohydrates being the body's primary source of energy; use is displayed through physical activity, growth, milk production, or repair of body tissues; energy deficiency may result in weight loss, insufficient lactation, reduced performance, or slowed growth while excess energy can cause such ailments such as weight gain, founder (q.v.), and colic (q.v.); deficiency may be caused by inadequate or poor quality feed, parasite loads, and dental problems; of four types: digestible energy (q.v.), gross energy (q.v.), metabolizable energy (q.v.), and net energy (q.v.).

energy cascade A scale of feed energy value; each step represents a lower energy value than the one preceding it; includes: gross energy (q.v.), digestible energy (q.v.), metabolizable energy (q.v.), and net energy (q.v.).

engage Said of a horse who rounds his back and brings his hind legs well under his body.

engaged (1) see ENGAGE. (2) A racing term; a horse entered in a race.

engagement (1) A racing term; a Stakes (q.v.) nomination. (2) A riding commitment.

engaging the hindquarters see COLLECTION

English buggy A hooded gig (q.v.).

English Black see GREAT HORSE, THE

English Connemara Society Also known as The English Connemara Pony Society; an organization founded in England in 1947 to encourage the breeding and utilization of improved types of Connemara ponies (q.v.) in England.

English Droitzschka A heavy, low-bodied, four-wheeled, horse-drawn vehicle of the droizschka (q.v.) type; had a passenger seat situated over the rear axle and a body low at the center to accommodate the travelers' legs, in front of which was the arch in the wagon body in which the front wheels turned; was reinforced with iron plates, drawn by two ponies, or a single horse, and was driven from a two-person box seat; being low to the ground and unlikely to overturn, it was suitable for use by the elderly.

English Great Horse see GREAT HORSE

English hunting iron see HUNTING IRON

English Jockey Club, The An association of individuals and horse owners established in 1750 in England to promote and control flat racing and formulate rules for it in the area or country; limited to approximately 50 members.

English rein see GERMAN MARTINGALE

English saddle Also known as pancake; a saddle with long side bars, reinforced cantle and pommel, no horn, and a leather seat supported by webbing and stretched between the saddle bow and cantle.

English stirrup Any stirrup (q.v.) suspended from the leathers (q.v.) on an English-type saddle; may be made of stainless steel, iron, nickle alloys, or chrome-plated iron.

English Thoroughbred see THOROUGHBRED

enlarged A hunting term; to release a deer transported to a stag hunt (q.v.) where it will be pursued by mounted riders and stag hounds.

en ligne competitions A vaulting term; to be on or in a line; a vaulting style practiced in France and the United States in which the horse gallops free in a straight line while the vaulters perform six compulsory figures and four of their own choice upon his back; dates to the 18th century; an en ligne vaulting saddle (q.v.) rather than a vaulting roller (q.v.) is used.

ensilage A method of storing and preserving green fodder in silos or pits covered with plastic; the stored substance, silage (q.v.), is tightly pressed and undergoes slight fermentation in anaerobic conditions.

enter (1) Also known as enter a hound; a hunting term; to train a young hound (q.v.) to hunt fox (q.v.). (2) To nominate a horse to participate in a competition; usually on an entry form.

enter a hound *see* ENTER no. 1

entered Also known as an entered hound; a hunting term; said of a hound (q.v.) who has completed its first cub hunting (q.v.) season, usually at one and one half years of age.

entered hound *see* ENTERED

enteric fever *see* COLIC

enteritis Inflammation of the intestinal or bowel lining; may be triggered by bacteria, chemical or vegetable poisons, or moldy or damaged food containing harmful fungi.

enterolith Also known as intestinal stone or stone; a mineral formation created in the large intestine which resembles a stone commonly found in the soil or river bottom; frequently begins with the presence of a small foreign object accidentally ingested with the food, after which dietary minerals begin to crystallize in layers around the object; generally made up of magnesium, ammonium, and phosphates which are found in high levels in alfalfa; horses more than 12 to 14 years are most commonly affected; most frequently treated with surgical removal although alteration of the acidity of the digestive tract may prevent the crystallization process that leads to enteroliths.

enter the lists To enter into the enclosures or palisades in which 16th and 17th-century tilting (q.v.) exercises were conducted.

entire *see* STALLION

entry (1) A hunting term; a young unentered hound. (2) A horse placed in a competition. (3) *see* COUPLED

entry fee The amount of money a contestant or nominator pays to enter a horse in a event, competition, or race.

environmental trait Any structural or functional defect acquired by a horse after birth and during growth.

enzyme assay A blood test performed to measure blood enzyme levels.

enzyme-linked immunosorbent assay Also known by the acronym ELISA; a stall-side diagnostic tool (q.v.) which serves as the basis for the majority of stall-side kits; uses a self-checking system in which a known sample (a control) is tested at the same time as the actual sample under evaluation; when properly run is a very precise and specific method of testing; test results are conveyed in color.

eohippus The first equine ancestor in the theory of evolution of the horse.

epidemic Common to or affecting a whole population or great number in a community at the same time, as in a contagious disease.

epidermis The outer, non-vascular, non-sensitive layer of the skin, covering the true skin or cutis (q.v.); lacks blood vessel supply; produces keratin and melanin.

epidural anesthesia A pain-killing procedure in which anesthetic (q.v.) is injected into the space around the spinal cord.

epiglottis A triangular-shaped cartilage (q.v.) located at the base of the airway above the soft palate and in front of the arytenoid cartilages which covers the airway during swallowing.

epinephrine *see* ADRENALINE

epiphyseal cartilage One of six types of cartilage found in the body structure of the horse; develops at the upper and lower aspects of the long leg bones from the epiphyseal plates (q.v.).

epiphyseal plates Also known as epiphyseal cartilage, growth plates, growth cartilage, physeal plates, or physis; the upper and lower aspects of long leg bones, including the growth plate (q.v.), at which lengthening of the bone occurs; the lengthening process involves the generation of new cartilage cells which are converted into bone; an increase in cell production or failure of timely change of cartilage to bone may be associated with physitis (q.v.).

epiphysis That part of a long bone which is above, below, and including the epiphyseal plate (q.v.).

epiphysitis *see* PHYSITIS

epistaxis Also known as nosebleed or nasal hemorrhage; a bloody nasal discharge from one or both nostrils; a condition, not a disease; uncommon in horses in general, although quite common in race horses; may be caused by exercise – in which case the condition is known as exercise-induced pulmonary hemorrhage (q.v.), trauma such as a cut or puncture to the interior of the nostril, or blunt trauma to the head below the eyes; a symptom of ruptured blood vessels anywhere in the respiratory tract or guttural pouch; if a horse bleeds from one nostril only, the source of the nasal hemorrhage is most likely in the nasal passage on the same side; horses that bleed from both nostrils, usually have a problem with the nasopharynx, guttural pouches, or in the lower respiratory tract; a horse with exercised-related epistaxis is known as a bleeder (q.v.).

epitheliogenesis imperfecta Also known by the acronym EI; a genetically based, fatal disorder in which the foal is born without skin or hooves.

EPM The acronym for equine protozoal myeloencephalitis (q.v.).

Epona The Celtic goddess, protector of horses and cavalry.

Epsom Derby Also known as The Darby, The Derby, The Derby Stakes, or the Ever Ready Derby Stakes; a horse race held annually on the first Wednesday of June since 1780 at the Epsom Downs (q.v.) course located just south of London, England; run on a U-shaped, 1-1/2 mile (2.4 km) course consisting of hills, banks, and turns run counterclockwise; named by the twelfth Earl of Derby; considered the most demanding test of jockeys (q.v.) and three-year-old horses in the world.

Epsom Downs Also known as The Downs; a U-shaped, 1-1/2 mile (2.4 km) racecourse consisting of hills, banks, and turns run counterclockwise located 15 miles (24 km) south of London, England; considered the most demanding test of jockeys and horses in the world; the site of the Epsom Derby (q.v.).

Epsom salts Hydrated magnesium sulfate used in horses as a laxative, purgative, and as a general cathartic.

equestrian (1) One who rides horseback. (2) Of or pertaining to horsemen or horsemanship.

equestrian nail A nail-and-screws device used to stabilize a fractured bone; a 16 to 18 mm long nail inserted into the bone-marrow canal to bridge two broken long bone components is stabilized by four screws, two at one end and two at the other inserted perpendicular to the nail; a state-of-the-art procedure that doesn't injure as much soft tissue or impede the bone's surface blood supply as much as with the traditional plate-and-screws stabilization (q.v.) technique.

equestrienne A female equestrian (q.v.).

Equibase Company A United States partnership between The Jockey Club (q.v.) and the Thoroughbred Racing Association (q.v.) to establish and maintain an industry-owned, central database of racing records.

Equidae The family of mammals consisting of the genus *Equus* (q.v.).

equine (1) A horse; correctly including all members of the family Equidae (q.v.) consisting of horses, zebras, and asses. (2) Of, or pertaining to, the horse.

equine abortion Expulsion of the fetus (q.v.) before 300 days of gestation at which time the fetus cannot survive because of immaturity.

equine arteritis *see* EQUINE VIRAL ARTERITIS

equine asthma *see* CHRONIC OBSTRUCTIVE PULMONARY DISEASE

equine biliary fever *see* EQUINE PIROPLASMOSIS

equine contraception A population-control measure tested by the Bureau of Land Management in the United States as a means of limiting wild horse populations; ovulating mares are injected with a vaccine containing the zona pellucida protein extracted from pig ovaries; the protein prompts the mare to produce antibodies that attack her own ova (q.v.), rendering her infertile for that ovulatory cycle; a single, three-year vaccine is under development.

equine degenerative myeloencephalopathy Also known by the acronym EDM; a genetically based disease of the spinal cord and brain stem causing weakness and incoordination.

equine dysautonomia *see* GRASS SICKNESS

equine granulocytic ehrlichiosis Also known by the acronym EGE; an ailment transmitted by the Western black leg tick characterized by flu-like signs including headache, fever, chills, shaking, and nausea; can lead to fatal organ damage; cannot be passed from horses to people or vice versa.

equine grass sickness *see* GRASS SICKNESS

Equine Health Research Fund Also known by the acronym EHRF; an organization established in the United States in 1985 by the American Horse Shows Association (q.v.) to raise funds to support ongoing research in the fields of equine health and equine sports medicine for all breeds and disciplines of show horses; studies funded range from pharmacology to lameness.

equine herpesvirus Also known as herpesvirus or by the acronym EHV; a highly adaptable virus of two distinct types: EHV-4, the cause of rhinopneumonitis (q.v.) which remains in the respiratory tract and EHV-1 which travels through the bloodstream and can cause abortion (q.v.) and neurological disease; the process of infection is not understood; disarms vaccines.

equine herpesvirus 1 infection *see* EQUINE VIRAL RHINOPNEUMONITIS

equine herpesvirus 4 infection *see* EQUINE VIRAL RHINOPNEUMONITIS

equine infectious anemia Also known as swamp fever or by the acronym EIA; an untreatable viral, blood-borne disease which causes destruction of blood cells; characterized by intermittent fever, depression, progressive weakness, weight loss, edema, and progressive anemia; has a death rate of approximately 50 percent in affected horses; the causal virus may persist for months away from sunlight in urine, feces, and so on; generally transmitted by large biting insects, principally horseflies and deerflies, and reused blood-tainted equipment; is closely related to human immunodeficiency (HIV).

equine influenza An acute, highly contagious, respiratory disease characterized by respiratory inflammation, fever, muscle soreness, and often, loss of appetite.

equine leptospirosis A contagious, essentially water-borne disease of animals and man, caused by infection with various leptospiral organisms; acquired from skin or mucous membrane contact with urine, and to a lesser extent by intake of urine-contaminated feed or water; infections may be asymptomatic or may result in a variety of disease conditions including fever ($103–105°F$ or $39.4–40.5°C$) for one two to three days, depression or dullness, anorexia, chronic uveitis, and abortion several weeks post fever.

equine lupus A rare immune-mediated disorder; of two types: localized known as discord lupus (q.v.) and systemic lupus erythematosus (q.v.).

equine malaria *see* EQUINE PIROPLASMOSIS

equine monocytic erhlichiosis *see* POTOMAC HORSE FEVER

equine morbillivirus Also known by the acronym EMV; a respiratory virus of the family *Paramyxoviridae* responsible for the condition known as acute equine respiratory syndrome (q.v.); first isolated in Australia in 1994; symptoms include shallow breathing and respiratory distress, lethargy, nervous disorders, staggers, and head butting; afflicted horses ultimately die of cardiac arrest.

equine motor neuron disease Also known by the acronym EMND; a disease of the horse's nervous system; begins in the neurons of the brain and spinal cord, slowly destroying their ability to make skeletal muscles contract; as the disease progresses, characterized by weight loss, trembling and quivering muscles when standing, profuse sweating, and lying down; vitamin E (q.v.) deficiency is thought to make horses more susceptible to the factors, as yet unidentified, that trigger it; similar to Lou Gehrig's disease in people.

equine piroplasmosis Also known as piroplasmosis, babesiosis, equine biliary fever, equine malaria, Texas fever, horse tick fever, tick fever, biliary fever, or tristeza (in Latin America); a contagious, tick-borne protozoal disease of the bloodstream caused by *Babesia caballi* or *Babesia equi*; infections may be preacute, acute, chronic, or not apparent; symptoms may include fever, listlessness, red urine, jaundice, loss of appetite, constipation, and diarrhea; death may result if left untreated; is a particularly significant disease problem in the tropics and southeastern United States.

equine protozoal myeloencephalitis Also known by the acronym EPM; a disease caused by a microscopic parasitic protozoan, a single-celled animal, *Sarcoytis neurona*, ingested by horses in their food and water; protozoa may find their way into a host horse's spinal cord where inflammation and eventually nerve-cell damage often produce a vague lameness mixed with incoordination and weakness; without prompt treatment, the victims become progressively incapacitated until euthanasia becomes necessary.

equine purpura An acute, frequently fatal, noncontagious, apparently allergenic disease affecting the horse; characteristically occurs as a consequence of strangles (q.v.), 1 to 3 weeks following the initial infection; symptoms include a sudden onset of subcutaneous edema in the area of the head, eyes, lips, belly, and legs, the appearance of small red spots caused by hemorrhage in the mucous membranes, diarrhea, colic (q.v.), or in severe cases, anemia; lasts approximately 1 to 2 weeks followed by recovery in about 50 percent of the cases; relapses are common as are secondary bacterial infections; death may be rapid due to suffocation or anemia and toxemia of secondary infection in drawn out cases.

equine respiratory syndrome *see* ACUTE EQUINE RESPIRATORY SYNDROME

equine rhabdomyolysis *see* TYING UP

equine ulcerative lymphangitis *see* ULCERATIVE LYMPHANGITIS

equine variola *see* HORSEPOX

equine vesicular stomatitis A localized inflammation of the soft tissues of the mouth characterized by blisters or other lesions which are generally confined to the upper surface of the tongue, but which may involve the inner surface of the lips, angles of the mouth, and gums; secondary lesions may appear on the feet.

equine viral arteritis Also known as viral arteritis, arteritis, pink eye, or by the acronym EVA; a highly contagious disease caused by the togavirus transmitted via the respiratory tract, by veneral contact or by contamination with infected urine; characterized by fever, conjunctivitis, redness of the eyes, edema (q.v.) of the eyelids and dependent parts of the body, nasal discharge and congestion, loss of appetite, and, in mares, abortion; spread through body fluids of infected animals, e.g., respiratory secretions, urine, or semen for approximately three weeks following acute infection; can be carried by asymptomatic horses; stallions often continue to shed the virus in their semen, sometimes for their entire lifetime; occurs in sporadic outbreaks and prompts abortion storms (q.v.) in which up to 80 percent of pregnant mares may abort; mortality is low and a vaccine is available.

equine viral rhinopneumonitis Also known as rhinopneumonitis, equine herpesvirus 1 infection or by the acronym EVR; a contagious viral infection caused by equine herpesvirus 1 (q.v.) characterized by fever, nasal discharge, cough, mild respiratory infection and, in mares, abortion, or abortion storm (q.v.) in a band of mares.

equipage The horse-drawn carriage and its attendants.

equirotal A Latin term; wheels of equal size as used on coaches or carriages.

equitation The act or art of riding on horseback.

equitation class Any English riding competition in which the rider, not the horse, is judged; the rider must demonstrate good seat and hands and sufficient management of the horse to perform the prescribed tests, either over fences or on the flat, in a smooth, controlled and accurate manner; riders are classified according to their age and previous winnings in equitation classes.

equivalent odds A racing term; odds in which mutuel price horses would pay for each $1 bet.

Equus A Latin term; horse; the genus of the family *Equidae*, the technical classification for all domesticated horses and some of their closely related feral and wild counterparts including the ass (q.v.) and zebra.

Equus africanus The scientific name for the African Wild Ass (q.v.).

Equus asinus The scientific name for the ass (q.v.).

Equus burchellii quagga The scientific name for the Quagga (q.v.).

Equus caballus Latin; the progenitor of the modern-day horse; evolved about one million years ago; unlike its predecessors, was a grazing animal; spread from America over existing land bridges to Europe and Asia.

Equus ferus The scientific name for the wild horse.

Equus ferus ferus The scientific name for the Tarpan (q.v.).

Equus ferus przewalski The scientific name for Przewalski's horse (q.v.)

Equus hemionus The scientific name for a subspecies of the Asian Wild Ass (q.v.).

Equus kiang The scientific name for a subspecies of the Asian Wild Ass (q.v.).

Equus hemionus kiang The scientific name for the Kiang (q.v.).

Equus ibericus The scientific name for the Iberian horse (q.v.).

Equus lambei The scientific term for the Ice Age horse (q.v.).

Equus przewalski "Poliakov" *see* ASIATIC WILD HORSE

Equus quagga *see* QUAGGA

eridge car *see* ERIDGE CART

eridge cart (1) Also known as Eridge car; a low-slung, but well upholstered, four-wheeled vehicle of the dogcart (q.v.) type; the front wheels were placed well ahead of the body to allow for easy turning in confined spaces and the hand brake only worked the rear wheels; the fore-carriage appeared to be detached from the rest of the vehicle, yet was attached by strong, slender side irons of a skeletal structure; introduced in limited numbers during the late 19th century; hung on full-elliptical side springs throughout with an under carriage similar to that of a pony phaeton (q.v.); seated two forward and two rearward facing passengers; drawn by a single horse or large pony and usually owner driven. (2) A low-slung, two-wheeled vehicle for two.

ergot (1) The small, horny growth at the back of the fetlock joint; a vestige of the second and fourth digits found in the extinct ancestors of the horse; made of material similar to that of the hoof, it grows from the surface of the skin downward; may be nonexistent in some horses and several inches in length in others. (2) The spurs of a horse's hooves. (3) A compound of the fungus *Claviceps purpuria* which grows under warm, moist conditions; affects the seeds of small grains and grasses such as fescue, but principally rye; consumption by horses may cause ergot poisoning (q.v.).

ergot poisoning An abnormal condition of the horse produced by consumption of any of the small grains and several grasses such as fescue (q.v.), with rye being particularly susceptible, attacked by the fungus *Claviceps purpuria*; results in a hard, dark-colored fungal growth two to four times the length of the kernel; produces a compound called ergot which stimulates the smooth muscles and may cause the blood supply to the tail, limbs, and ears to be so reduced that dry gangrene develops causing the extremities to drop off; may also cause abortion in pregnant mares.

ermine marks A leg marking (q.v.); dark black or brown spots occurring near the coronary band (q.v.) in any of the white leg marking patterns; generally accompanied by a dark stripe through the hoof wall at the location of the spot.

erythrocytes Red blood cells.

escutcheon The division of hair which begins below the point of the hip and extends towards the flanks

esophagus Also known as the gullet and spelled oesophagus; the muscular passage by which food and liquid are taken into the stomach; extends from the pharynx to the stomach.

Esseda A lightly-constructed, horse-drawn chariot used by the Ancient Britons for warlike purposes; entered from the front and drawn by a pair of horses or large ponies in pole gear (q.v.) with neck yokes.

essential amino acid *see* DIETARY ESSENTIAL AMINO ACID

essential oil Commerically available volatile oil extracted from plants by means of steam distillation and containing a mixture of active constituents; highly aromatic; used in aromatherapy (q.v.).

Estonian Klepper *see* TORIC

estrous Of or pertaining to the estrus (q.v.).

estrous cycle Also spelled oestrus; the complete cyclic series of physical, biological, and chemical changes in the mare which lead to ovulation and the shedding of the egg from the ovary; consist of estrus (q.v.), metestrus, diestrus, and proestrus; averages 21 days, but may vary from 17 to 26 days.

estrus Also known as heat, in heat, in estrus, receptivity, in use, season, in season, and spelled oestrus or estrous; the phase in the mare's estrous cycle (q.v.) when the egg matures, is released, and the mare is able to conceive; signs include squatting, urinating, eversion of the clitoris, swishing of the tail, and squealing; the time of the highest excitability in the mare; from early spring through autumn, occurs at regular intervals between 17 and 26 days with increased regularity in the spring and summer; may last a few hours to five or seven days depending on the age of the mare, if she is maiden or not, seasonal conditions, feeding, and exercise level; will discontinue in the pregnant mare until approximately nine days post foaling.

EVA The acronym for equine viral arteritis (q.v.).

evade Said of a horse who avoids obeying the rider's or lunger's commands or aids (q.v.) using learned methods.

evener A driving term; a bar located between the drawbar and single bar (q.v.) used to equalize the pulling power of three, four, five, or six horses harnessed abreast in single trees (q.v.).

evening pink *see* EVENING PINK COAT

evening pink coat Also known as evening pink; the formal red hunt coat worn by members of a Hunt (q.v.) at Hunt Balls (q.v.) or dinners.

evening stable An English racing term; the evening feeding time (q.v.).

evenly A racing term; said of a horse who neither gains nor loses position during a race.

even money Also known as evens or even money bet; a racing term; a wager in which the betting odds are one to one; the person making the bet stands to win the same amount as wagered if the horse places as anticipated.

even money bet *see* EVEN MONEY

evens *see* EVEN MONEY

event (1) *see* EVENTING. (2) Each of the items in a program consisting of various contests.

eventer A horse or equestrian (q.v.) possessing the versatility and stamina to compete in combined training (q.v.) events.

eventing *see* COMBINED TRAINING

Ever Ready Derby Stakes *see* EPSOM DERBY

EVR The acronym for equine viral rhinopneumonitis (q.v.).

ewe neck Said of the horse's neck when the topline is concave and the lower line is longer, more heavily muscled, and outwardly bulging; results in an elevated head carriage making control more difficult for the rider and may cause the saddle to slip forward.

exacta *see* PERFECTA

exacta box A racing term; a bet (q.v.) in which all possible combinations for a given number of horses are placed; the total number of combinations can be calculated according to the formula x^2-x, where x equals the number of horses in the bet; the cost of the wager is obtained by multiplying the total number of combinations by the cost of one wager.

exactor *see* PERFECTA

ex aequo A Latin term; equally, as when two or more horses gain the same number of points in a competition.

excessive angulation of the hock joints Also known as sickle hocks, curby hocks, or sabre hocks; forward deviation of the lower leg from the hock to the hoof, giving the impression of a sickle when viewed from the side; results in a transfer of weight from the front of the hoof to the back; an inherited condition considered a conformation fault in riding horses, but desirable in a draft horse; may cause curb (q.v.), spavin (q.v.), and navicular (q.v.) related issues.

excrement *see* FECES

excused A racing term; a horse permitted by race authorities to withdraw (q.v.) from a race after the official scratch time.

exercise bandage Also known as a brace bandage or track bandage; a bandage (q.v.), approximately 3 inches (7.5 cm) in diameter, made of cotton flex or elasticized material, used to protect the horse's legs while the horse is at work or exercise; covers the leg between the knee or hock and the fetlock; if applied too tightly may result in a bandage bow (q.v.).

exercise boy Also known as exercise rider; a racing term; one responsible for riding race horses in workout sessions; although originally a position held by boys or young men, women have now entered the field and the more generic exercise rider is used.

exercise-induced pulmonary hemorrhage Also known as lung hemorrhage, exercise related epistaxis, or by the acronym EIPH; the occurrence of hemorrhage (q.v.) in the lungs as a consequence of mechanical stress caused by soaring capillary blood pressure in the lungs during or following moderate to strenuous exercise; evidenced by bilateral epistaxis (q.v.) occurs in many horses with normal lungs and is not breed specific although it is common in race horses and other

high-performance equine athletes; a horse suffering from this syndrome is known as a bleeder (q.v.).

exertional rhabdomyolysis *see* EXERCISE RELATED MYOPATHY

exercise related epistaxis *see* EXERCISE-INDUCED PULMONARY HEMORRHAGE

exercise related myopathy Also known as exertional myopathy, exertion myopathy syndrome, paralytic myoglobinuria, black water, Monday-morning disease, Monday-morning sickness, over-straining disease, acute rhabdomyolysis, exertional rhabdomyolysis, myositis, or incorrectly as tying up disease; a disease affecting both the skeletal and cardiac muscles of the horse occurring within a few minutes to an hour or more after the onset of physical exertion, before muscle energy depletion can occur, following a period of rest and, generally, unrestricted feed; characterized by muscle cramping and fasciculations leaving the muscles firm and painful to the touch, profuse sweat, a tucked-up appearance, a stiff, stilted gait, and a reluctance to move; urine may be coffee-colored; in severe cases, these signs are followed by recumbency and death; is different from tying up (q.v.); draft horses not worked on Sunday, but given full feed were commonly afflicted with this disease, when put to work on Monday, hence the common name of Monday-morning sickness.

exercise rider One responsible for riding race horses in workout sessions.

exertional myopathy *see* EXERCISE RELATED MYOPATHY

exertional rhabdomyolysis *see* EXERCISE RELATED MYOPATHY

exertion myopathy *see* EXERCISE RELATED MYOPATHY

exertion myopathy syndrome *see* EXERCISE RELATED MYOPATHY

exhibitor An owner, lessee, contestant, handler, trainer, and/or rider involved in the showing of horses.

Exmoor pony Also known generically as a native pony; one of nine mountain and moorland pony breeds originating in the British

Isles of which it is thought to be the oldest; found in the Exmoor Forest in southern England from which the name derived; believed to have descended from the prehistoric wild horse used by the Celts; has a heavy mane, well-proportioned head and neck, wide-set, toad eyes (q.v.), long and slightly hollow back, slightly sloping shoulder and croup, deep chest, and sturdy, well-muscled legs; generally has a bay-brown or dun coat and may have mealy coloring on the muzzle and underbelly which extends to the inside of the forearms and legs; white markings are not permitted by the breed registry; stands 11.2 to 12.3 hands, is quiet, sturdy, possessed of good speed; an excellent child's pony.

Exmoor Pony Society, The An organization founded in England in 1921 to improve and encourage the breeding of Exmoor Ponies (q.v.) of the moorland type; ponies are entered in the National Pony Stud book.

exostoses More than one exostosis.

exostosis Also known as a bony growth; any abnormal growth or deposit of bone projecting outward from the bone surface; may result from injury, conformation fault, or heredity and may cause mechanical interference.

exotic wager A racing term; any bet (q.v.) other than win (q.v.), place (q.v.), or show (q.v.).

expansion (1) The practice of fitting the posterior half of the horseshoe larger than the hoof to allow the heel to spread. (2) The act of expanding or the state of being expanded; to spread out.

Experimental Free Handicap A racing term; a year-end projection of the best two-year-old race horses of the season in North America, as selected by a panel under guidance from The Jockey Club (q.v.); selection is based on performances in unrestricted races with separate lists created for male and female horses.

expression A cutting term; the alertness of a horse in front of a cow.

extend (1) A racing term; to push a horse to his limits in a race. (2) To lengthen a pace or gait by encouraging the horse to reach up and out with his forelegs.

extended *see* EXTEND no. 1

extended canter A lengthened pace or gait in which the cantering horse covers as much ground as possible without losing rhythm, lightness, or calmness; achieved by great impulsion from the hindquarters.

extended heel Also known as an extension; a long heel, 1/4 inch (6 mm) or more beyond the heel of the horse's foot, on the outside of a hind-hoof horseshoe; usually fit parallel to the center-line of the foot and in line with the direction of travel.

extended pace A lengthening of the stride at any pace or gait.

extended-toe shoe Also known as a beaked shoe; a horseshoe in which the shoe is fitted well forward of the natural toe of the foot exposing the bottom of the hoof wall at the toe; alternately, a projection may be welded onto the center of the toe of the shoe to slow the breakover of the foot and prevent the foot from knuckling over; used on the feet of clubfooted horses or horses with contracted tendons.

extended trot A lengthened pace or gait in which the trotting horse covers as much ground as possible without losing the rhythm of his steps as achieved by impulsion from the hindquarters; the horse remains on the bit, but lowers and extends his neck.

extended walk A lengthened pace or gait in which the horse remains on the bit, but covers as much ground as possible at the walk without losing the regularity of his steps; the hind feet touch the ground in front of the marks of the forefeet.

extension (1) The lengthening of the stride at the walk, trot, or canter whereby the movement of the front legs is more forward than upward; the horse should demonstrate equal extension in both the fore- and hind legs. (2) *see* EXTENDED HEEL

extensor process disease *see* PYRAMIDAL DISEASE

extensor tendon A tendon (q.v.) that extends the knee or ankle joint, pastern, foot, and elbow.

extravagant action Said of the horse; to

have high knee and hock movement, as in the Hackney pony (q.v.).

exudate The fluid or cell discharge from a sore or wound characterized by dry, crusty, scab-like sores.

eye (1) The organ of sight. (2) The uppermost ring on the cheekpiece (q.v.) of a bit to which the bridle cheekpiece (q.v.) is attached.

eye appeal A cutting term; the ability of a horse to earn extra points in a cutting horse competition due to an attractive style of working that sets him apart from other horses.

eye for a country A hunting term; said of a huntsman who knows the location of all roads, trails, and jumpable areas in the country hunted and is capable of anticipating the line a fox (q.v.) will take.

F

FAA The acronym for Facteur d'Anglo-Arab (q.v.).

face drop *see* DROP

face fly A swarming daytime feeder occurring in large numbers around the eyes and the muzzle of the horse; feed on facial secretions such as tear fluid, nasal mucus, and saliva; do not bite, but will partake of blood from open wounds; similar in appearance to a common house fly (q.v.).

face marking Any white mark appearing on the face or head of the horse; describes the extent of white including star (q.v.), star, stripe, and snip (q.v.), star and stripe (q.v.), snip (q.v.), snip lower lip (q.v.), strip (q.v.), stripe (q.v.), stripe and snip (q.v.), blaze (q.v.), bald face (q.v.), apron face (q.v.), paper face (q.v.), race (q.v.) and white muzzle (q.v.).

face piece *see* DROP

facet syndrome pain Pain resulting from stretching of the joint capsule secondary to increased stress on the synovial joints; the associated muscles may respond by contracting to form a muscular splint of the area.

Facteur d'Anglo-Arab Also known by the acronym FAA; a French Anglo-Arab (q.v.) with less than 25 percent Arab (q.v.) blood as required by the Stud book registry.

factory-made horseshoe *see* MACHINE-MADE SHOE

fade A racing term; said of a horse who tires and drops out of contention in a race.

fade back A cutting term; a cue given by the rider to the horse to back off, yet remain hooked (q.v.), to the cow being worked.

fadge *see* HOUNDPACE

faeces *see* FECES

failing scent A hunting term; said of the scent (q.v.) of a fox (q.v.) when it gradually becomes more faint.

failure of passive transfer Also known by the acronym FPT; the reduced ability of a newborn foal to fight off infectious disease; results from failure to receive protective antibodies from the mare's colostrum (q.v.).

fair catch Also known as legal catch; a team roping term; said of a steer or calf when roped in competition if the header's (q.v.) lariat falls around his horns, head, or neck.

Fairville Cart An Australian, horse-drawn gig hung on a three spring or Dennett suspension system with detachable shafts.

Falabella A miniature horse breed developed by the Falabella family at their Recreo de Roca Ranch near Buenos Aires, Argentina; derived from a Shetland Pony (q.v.) deliberately down-bred with crosses of the smallest horses and thereafter through close in-breeding; the smallest horse in the world; is not suitable for riding, but is popular as a pet and for light harness; most colors occur with the Appaloosa (q.v.) coat being highly sought after; stands under 34 inches (86 cm), has an ample mane and tail, small head and ears, large eyes, high withers, short back, and slender legs; is quiet, intelligent, very strong for its size, and possessed of a graceful action; cowhocks (q.v.) are common.

fall (1) Said of a horse in competition when his shoulder and flank or quarters on the same side have touched the ground or an obstacle and the ground. (2) Said of a rider in competition who has separated from his horse, who has not fallen, in such a way that he must remount or vault into the saddle.

fall and a drag A stunt performed on horseback in which a rider performs a backwards roll off the hip of a moving horse on cue and drags behind it with the aid of a cable which runs from the stuntperson's harness down one pant leg to a quick-release system connected to a second length of cable attached to the D-ring of the saddle.

fallen back *see* HOLLOW BACK no. 1

fallen neck *see* BROKEN CREST

fall in Also known as lean in; said of an unbalanced or stiff horse who, at any pace, falls off the true circle by dropping his shoulder in and throwing his weight onto it; the haunches will generally fall outside of the true circle.

falling out A dressage term; said of a horse whose outside shoulder falls off the true circle on a corner, circle, or in the shoulder in by dropping his shoulder and throwing his weight onto it, or that the horse has left the original line to the outside.

falling top *see* FOLDING HOOD.

fall into the trot A dressage term; said of an unbalanced cantering horse who, when given the aid to slow up and execute a downward transition, throws his weight onto the forehand.

fallopian tube *see* OVIDUCT

false belly band A leather or sythetic band fitted over the belly band on pair and team harness horses to prevent the hame tug buckle from moving up and down when the horses are in action; buckles on one side to the hame tug buckle and on the other to the hame tug point.

false canter *see* COUNTER CANTER

false collar A flat leather pad shaped to fit under the harness collar (q.v.) to protect the shoulders of an unfit or soft horse, one new to harness work, or one who does not fit the collar.

false extension Also known as goose-stepping or toe-flipping; a trot (q.v.) performed with hyperextended forelegs so that the toes flip up in an exaggerated manner; generally a sign of tension, constraint, stiffness, or insufficient engagement and propulsion from the hindquarters.

false favorite A racing term; a horse competing in a race who is favored, despite being outclassed by the rest of the field (q.v.).

false gallop *see* DISUNITED GALLOP

false leg A driving term; an iron leg guard worn by the postillion (q.v.) on the outside of his right leg to protect it from being injured by the pole (q.v.).

false nostril An anatomical peculiarity of the horse's nostril; the top edge of the nostril

forming a blind pocket which sometimes flaps when the horse canters resulting in a noise known as high blowing (q.v.).

false martingale A strap connecting the harness collar (q.v.) to the girth (q.v.); used on pair or team wheelers to hold the collar down and the hames (q.v.) onto the collar.

false ribs Those ribs (q.v.) numbering 9 to 18 from the front of the horse which are not attached to the sternum.

false rig A completely castrated horse who demonstrates masculine behavior such as attempting to round up mares, attraction to a mare in heat (q.v.), full erection, and occasionally, ejaculation.

false quarter A horizontal crack in the hoof wall caused by disease or injury which affects the growth of the hoof wall from the coronary band (q.v.) and results in permanent hoof wall weakness; generally does not result in lameness provided the soft internal tissue of the foot is not exposed and corrective shoeing is used.

false sole *see* RETAINED SOLE

false start A racing term; said of a horse who begins a race prematurely, before receiving formal authorization to do so; an anticipatory reaction occurring seconds or splits of seconds prior to the regulation start.

falter A racing term; said of a horse who tires badly.

family (1) A specific group of related objects or living things with a common or associated characteristic, function, or origin, as in the family Equidae to which the horse belongs. (2) The lineage of a horse as traced though either the male or female, depending on the breed of horse.

fancied *see* FAVORITE

fancy curb Any single rein curb bit (q.v.) with elaborately designed cheeks (q.v.).

fancy matched A team of harness horses of distinctly different markings and coloring.

fanning (1) A rodeo term; said of a bronc rider (q.v.); to wave one's cowboy hat in the air and slap one's mount with it to encourage a heartier buck. (2) An old coaching term; light use of the whip (q.v.).

fantail *see* FAN TAIL

fan tail Also spelled fantail; the tail of a docked horse (q.v.) which is not square cut, but which is cut shorter on the sides, tapering to a longer tip.

Fantasia A mounted Moroccan sport performed using mostly gray and black horses of Berber (q.v.) descent; a mock attack performed by two opposing, weapon-bearing bands enacted in a thrilling manner.

farcy *see* GLANDERS

farm pony *see* WELSH PONY OF COB TYPE

farrier Also known as horseshoer, fireman or incorrectly as a blacksmith or smithy; one specializing in shoeing horses; formerly one who cared for all aspects of a horse's health; it is believed the word derived from the Low Latin word ferraius, meaning a worker in iron and from the old French ferrer, to shoe a horse.

Farriers (Registration) Act A law passed in 1975 in Britain which prohibits the shoeing of horses by unqualified persons and provides for the training and examining of farriers by the Worshipful Company of Farriers (q.v.) of London.

Farriers and Blacksmiths, Amalgamated Society of *see* AMALGAMATED SOCIETY OF FARRIERS AND BLACKSMITHS

farriery (1) The art of shoeing horses. (2) The place where a farrier (q.v.) works.

far side (1) Also known as off side; the right side of the horse when viewed from behind; the opposite of near side (q.v.). (2) A racing term; that portion of a race track on the side opposite the viewing boxes, stands, and club house between the curves.

Fasciola hepatica *see* LIVER FLUKE

fast (1) Swift; rapid. (2) *see* FIRM no. 2

fast cheek *see* FIXED CHEEK

Fast Heavy Draught Breton Also known as Heavy Draught Breton or previously as the Grand Breton; one of three distinct morpho-logical types of Breton (q.v.) that evolved more than 4,000 years ago in Brittany, France; descended from native Brittany stock crossed with Norfolk Roadster (q.v.), its descendant the Norfolk Trotter (q.v.), Ardennais (q.v.), Percheron (q.v.), and Boulonnais (q.v.); is selectively bred and must pass performance tests in harness to qualify for inclusion in the stud book which it has shared with the Postier-Breton since 1909; the coat is generally chestnut, but bay, gray, roan, and red roan also occur – black is not a breed color; has a well-proportioned head with a heavy jaw, broad forehead, short ears, and flared nostrils, a short, broad, and muscular neck, short and straight back, broad loins, sloping croup, and short, powerful legs with heavy joints; the tail is generally docked; stands 15 to 16 hands and weighs 1,540–1,980 pounds (699–898 kg); registered foals are branded on the left side of the neck with a cross surmounting a splayed, upturned V.

fast martingale *see* STANDING MARTINGALE

fast mouth Said of the bit mouthpiece (q.v.) fixed solidly to the cheekpiece (q.v.) of a bit; does not move in any direction up, down, or sideways.

fast track A racing term; a dry, hard dirt racing surface on which horses clock better times than on other tracks; the equivalent of a firm track on grass.

far turn A racing term; the bend of the track (q.v.) off the backstretch (q.v.).

fat *see* ADIPOSE AND ADIPOSE TISSUE

Father of Classical Equitation, The *see* DE LA GUERINIERE, FRANCOIS ROBICHON

Father of Foxhunting, The *see* WARDE, JOHN

fats Also known as lipids; soft, solid organic compounds composed of carbon, hydrogen, and oxygen; a useful, and far more concentrated source of energy for the horse than carbohydrates (q.v.) or protein (q.v.); aids in the absorption of some nutrients including the fat-soluble vitamins A, D, E, and K, and is essential for tissue function; supplies unsaturated essential fatty acids including linoleic, linolenic, and arachidonic; can be of vegetable or animal origin.

fat soluble vitamin Any vitamin that dissolves in fat or oil; can be stored in the body for later use.

fault (1) A weak point in the conformation of a horse. (2) A scoring unit used to record a knockdown, refusal, or other offense committed by a competitor and/or his mount in an event such as show jumping or eventing; the number of points assessed varies by type of competition and the severity of the infraction. (3) *see* AT FAULT

favor a leg (1) Said of a horse with an injured leg who refuses to place its full weight on it; a clear indication of lameness. (2) Said of a horse who always leads with the same front leg at the canter irrespective of the direction traveled.

favorite Also known as fancied; a racing term; the horse considered likely to win a specific race who has the shortest odds placed against it.

FBHS The acronym for Fellow of the British Horse Society (q.v.).

feather (1) Also known as feathering; a hunting term; said of a hound when he waves or moves his hindquarters and tail side-to-side while moving along the presumed line of the fox (q.v.) with its nose to the ground; indicates that the scent is faint and that the hound is uncertain if he is on the scent of a fox; the hound will not speak (q.v.). (2) Also known as feathering; the long hairs growing from the region of the fetlock, ergot, and pastern on the lower legs of some breeds such as the Clydesdale, may extend along the entire lower leg and over the foot and hoof wall. (3) A racing term; extremely light weight, as in the jockey (q.v.).

feathered whorl A hair pattern; a type of whorl (q.v.); a change in direction of the flow of the hair in which two sweeps of hair meet along a line, with the direction of flow of each sweep at an angle to the other so that together they form a feathered pattern.

feather edging A driving term; to drive a horse-drawn vehicle extremely close to anything.

feather-edged shoe Also known as an interfering shoe, speedy-cutting shoe, dropped crease shoe, or knocked down shoe; a horse-shoe (q.v.) in which the part of the shoe from the toe to the quarter, away from the point of interference, is squared off; the squared edge is feathered and rounded off by hot rasping; only nailed to the hoof on the inside.

feathering (1) *see* FEATHER no. 1. (2) *see* FEATHERING no. 2.

feather in the eye A mark across the eyeball that does not touch the pupil; may be a congenital blemish or one caused by injury.

fecal exam A type of laboratory test in which technicians quantify the horse's parasite burden by taking microscopic counts of worm eggs in manure samples.

feces Also spelled faeces and known as manure, dung, droppings, excrement, or horse shit; the solid dark brown to green discharge from the intestines of the horse; a full-grown horse will defecate eight to nine times a day, averaging a total of 40 pounds (18kg) of manure; feces from a healthy horse will be formed in well-shaped balls.

feces eating Also known as coprophagy; a vice (q.v.); said of a horse who consumes excrement.

Fédération Equestre Internationale Also known by the acronym FEI and as International Equestrian · Federation; the international governing body for officially recognized equestrian competitions including the Olympic Games; founded in 1921 by Commandant G. Hector of France, and is headquartered in Brussels; all nations must be affiliated with the FEI if they wish to participate in official international competitions.

Federico Caprilli *see* CAPRILLI, FEDERICO

fee (1) The cost of nominating or entering a horse in a race or other event. (2) The amount paid to a professional rider for competing a horse(s) in a race or other event.

feed (1) To give food to; to supply with nourishment. (2) Also known as fodder; the food fed to, or consumed by, herbivores, e.g., horses.

feed bag A generally round bag made of canvass, leather, or other material to which a long buckled strap is attached on both sides used to feed a horse; is placed over the muzzle of the horse and held onto the head by the strap which passes over the crest, just behind the ears.

feed bucket A cylindrical, hand-held container used to transport feed to a horse or from which a horse may eat; not to be confused with a manger (q.v.).

feeder (1) One whose responsibility it is to feed horses or other livestock. (2) *see* MANGER

feed stuff A nutritive substance used as food for livestock.

feeding time Also known in Britain as foddering time (obs) or fothering time (obs); the time at which a horse is provided with feed by its owner.

feet (1) More than one foot (q.v.). (2) The base of an anvil (q.v.).

FEI The acronym for the Fédération Equestre Internationale (q.v.).

FEI World Cup An annual show jumping competition governed by the FEI (q.v.) in which the world's top riders compete to determine the reigning world champion; held in a different location every year.

fell Also known as Fell Pony and generically as a native pony (q.v.); a light draft and riding pony originating in Cumbria, Britain; the name derives from the Fells, the wild and hilly moorlands of Westmorland and Cumberland on the western slopes of the Pennines; descended from *Equus celticus* (q.v.), Friesian (q.v.) horses brought to Great Britain by the Roman legionaries, and the Galloway (q.v.); genetically related to the Dales Pony (q.v.) compared to which it has a better riding shoulder; stands 13 to 14 hands, is generally black, brown, bay or gray and devoid of white markings, although a white star is acceptable; has a small, quality head, large nostrils, and small ears, luxuriant mane and tail, prominent withers, a long back, short croup, long sloping shoulder, sturdy legs with a minimum of bone of 8 inches (20 cm), considerable feathering (q.v.), and bluish, round hooves; is extremely strong, frugal, a good trotter, and quiet, but lively; for centuries used in the Pennine lead mines, to transport goods and people from the mines to the ports, and for farming; now used under harness in competitive driving and for riding.

felloe *see* FELLOW

fellow (1) Also spelled felloe or fellowe; that portion of the carriage wheel rim that holds the spokes in place and carries the tire. (2) One belonging to one of several learned societies.

fellowe *see* FELLOW no. 1

Fellow of the Worshipful Company of Farriers Also known by the acronym FWCF; the highest level of certification awarded to a farrier practicing in Britain by the Worshipful Company of Farriers of London (q.v.); recipients must have achieved the level of Associate of the Worshipful Company of Farriers (q.v.) a minimum of one year prior to application, completed a written thesis 21 days prior to certification, and oral and practical examinations.

Fell pony *see* FELL

Fell Pony Society, The An organization founded in Great Britain in 1927 to promote the breeding and registration of purebred Fell ponies (q.v.) in the National Pony Stud book; to qualify for registration as a purebred, both the dam (q.v.) and sire (q.v.) must be registered, the cannon bone must have a minimum circumference of 8 inches (20 cm), and white coloring limited to stars and minimal white on the legs.

female tail *see* DISTAFF

femur Also known as the thigh bone; the primary bone (q.v.) in the thigh of the horse extending from the hip joint (q.v.) to the stifle (q.v.).

fence (1) Any obstacle over which a horse and rider jump; of four basic types: uprights (q.v.), spreads (q.v.), water (q.v.), and combinations (q.v.); may be natural or man made. (2) *see* RAIL no. 2. (3) Also known as to fence; to jump over an obstacle.

fencing man *see* TERRIER MAN

fender (1) Also known as a sudadero or western stirrup leather; one of two wide pieces of leather attached on either side of the saddle under the western saddle seat; one on each side of the saddle. (2) An American term; the splashboard on a horse-drawn vehicle.

Fenners bit Also known as parallel bit; a

pelham bit (q.v.) with two mouthpieces (q.v.) joined by a rubber band at the center of the mouth; the upper mouthpiece slides up and down while the lower slides backwards into the mouth of the horse.

feral Any animal who lives in a self-sustained population following a history of domestication.

Fernerley, John (1782–1860) A renowned equestrian artist with specific interest in fox-hunting scenes.

ferrule A hunting term; the shaft of a hunting horn (q.v.).

fertile The ability of the stallion to produce sperm and the mare to produce ovum (q.v.) so that if mating occurs offspring will result.

fertility (1) The state of being fertile; the ability to produce offspring. (2) Also known as fertility rate; the ability of a stallion (q.v.) to produce offspring as measured by the number of mares mated and the frequency with which they are mated; the state of being fertile (q.v.); varies significantly from stallion to stallion and from the same stallion at different times.

fertility rate *see* FERTILITY

fertilize *see* IMPREGNATE

fetgangur One of five gaits of the Icelandic Horse (q.v.) used by a horse under pack.

fetlock (1) Technically, the tuft of hair located externally behind the fetlock joint (q.v.) of both the fore and hind legs. (2) *see* FETLOCK JOINT. (3) A leg marking (q.v.) consisting of white which extends from the coronary band (q.v.) and includes some of the bulge of the fetlock joint (q.v.).

fetlock boots A protective leg covering made of felt, leather, and/or synthetic materials used to protect the hind fetlock joint from strikes and blows; generally worn in pairs.

fetlock joint: Also called the ankle or metacarpalphalangeal joint; the point of junction of the cannon bone (q.v.) and long pastern including the sesamoid bones; present in both the fore and hind legs.

fetlock ring *see* FETLOCK RING BOOT

fetlock ring boot Also known as brushing ring boot, fetlock ring, or ring boot; a hollow rubber ring fitted over the fetlock of the foreleg and held in place by means of adjustable staps to protect the fetlock joint from strikes and blows.

fetus The developing embryo from 41 days after fertilization until birth.

fever in the feet *see* LAMINITIS

fever rings *see* HOOF RINGS

few spot leopard Refers to coat color pattern; a predominantly white horse with a few colored spots and areas of colored skin; has less spotting than a leopard (q.v.).

FHOD The acronym for flexible hydroactive occlusive dressing (q.v.).

Fiacre A horse-drawn French hackney (q.v.) coach used for ambulance and cab service introduced in the mid-17th century; named after St. Fiacre, an early patron of hospitals and the suffering poor; early versions seated six and were drawn by a pair of horses while later they seated four and sometimes two passengers, and were drawn by a single horse in shafts.

fiador A narrow cotton rope attached to either side of the brow band (q.v.) which passes under the throat and connects to the end of the bosal; used in conjunction with a hackamore (q.v.); functions similar to a throat latch (q.v.) and keeps the bosal from dropping below the chin.

Fiakr A horse-drawn, public cab or carriage used predominantly in Austria, Bohemia, and other parts of Central Europe; closely resembled the Fiacre (q.v.).

fiber Also known as roughage and spelled fibre; matter composed of plant filaments; provides bulk to the horse's diet required to aid and stimulate the digestive process; the primary component of feces (q.v.).

fiber optics The use of light-conducting flexible fiber bundles to deliver light to and from internal spaces.

fiber-optic endoscope Also known as fiber-optic scope; a flexible medical instrument slid through an incision in the body to enable a veterinarian to view the interior of a body cavity; constructed of a flexible tube containing light-conducting fiber bundles which reflect an image into an eyepiece.

fiber-optic scope *see* FIBER-OPTIC ENDO-SCOPE

fiber shoe *see* ROPE SHOE

fibre *see* FIBER

fibrin A protein (q.v.) present in the blood (q.v.) formed in the process of coagulation.

fibrinogen A part of the blood proteins responsible for blood clotting.

fibro cartilage A type of cartilage (q.v.) found in the nose and some supporting joints of the horse; is relatively stiff, brittle, and structured.

fibrosus Also spelled fibrous; the singular form of fibrosis (q.v.).

fibrosis An accumulation of fibrous tissue in organs where it is not normally found.

fibrous *SEE* FIBROSUS

fibula The long, slender bone of the hind leg attached to the upper and lower ends of the tibia (q.v.); situated below the stifle joint and extending to the hock (q.v.).

fiddle Slang; a whip (q.v.).

fiddle head A large, coarse, and ugly-shaped head, as of a horse.

fiddling *see* GINGERING

field (1) A racing term; the entire group of horses entered in a race. (2) *see* PARI-MUTUEL FIELD. (3) A betting term; all bets placed other than those placed on the favorite (q.v.). (4) Also known as hunting field or followers; a hunting term; the mounted followers, other than the hunt staff of a hunt (q.v.); usually led by a Field Master. (5) A piece of land suitable for tillage or pasture.

field boarder A horse maintained in a pasture for a fee.

field boots A tall riding boot made of either black or brown leather with lacing at the ankle and over the instep which enables the wearer to walk with comfort; less formal than a dress boot (q.v.).

field horse A racing term; one of a group of horses designated by the racing secretary to run in a pari-mutuel field (q.v.).

Field Master Also known as master of the pack; a hunting term; one designated to lead and control the field (q.v.), keeping them apprised of the movement of the fox and when the hounds (q.v.) are drawing (q.v.) or hunting (q.v.); the Master (q.v.) generally makes the best Field Master.

field trials A hunting term; a competitive event for foxhounds bred to hunt as individuals rather than as a pack; Walker, Trigg, and July foxhound (q.v.) strains are commonly used; in the United States, are regulated by the National Foxhunters Association.

fifth wheel A circular piece of iron attached to the underside of the front of a four-wheeled, horse-drawn carriage which forms a bearing for the front axle and the undercarriage assembly.

figging *see* GINGERING

figure (1) A racing term; said of a horse; to have a winning chance. (2) A racing term; the handicapper's (q.v.) rating number that identifies the winning chance of a horse.

figure eight (1) A dressage movement in which the horse performs two identical circles of the same diameter which do not overlap but share a common side, touching in the middle. (2) *see* GRACKLE NOSEBAND

figure eight bandage Also known as figure eight wrap; refers to the manner in which a bandage is wrapped on the leg rather than a type of bandage; the leg is encircled by the wrap once or twice below the hock or knee; next, the wrap is angled up across the front of the joint, then downward crossing the joint from the inside to the outside to form an X; this crisscross is repeated several times with stabilizing loops both above and below the joint made as necessary.

figure eight noseband *see* GRACKLE NOSE-BAND

figure eight wrap *see* FIGURE EIGHT BANDAGE

filing *see* FLOAT

filing teeth *see* FLOAT

filled leg *see* STOCK UP

fillet strap *see* FILLET STRING

fillet string Also known as rug fillet, fillet strap, or tail string; the string, strap, or braid of fabric passed under the horse's tail which connects the two rear flaps of a rug (q.v.), sheet (q.v.), or horse blanket (q.v.) to hold it in place and prevent it from slipping.

Fillis, James (1850-1900) An influential British riding master, well known authority on horses, and author of *Breaking and Riding* and other instructional works; lived most of his life in France, although in 1898 he was appointed riding master to the School of Cavalry for Officers in St. Petersburg, Russia where he remained until 1910.

Fillis method One of three methods of holding the reins of a double bridle (q.v.) in which the curb reins pass around the little fingers and the snaffle reins from above over the index finger of each hand; allows for effective use of the snaffle reins; developed by James Fillis (q.v.).

filly A young female horse under three years of age and in Thoroughbreds (q.v.) under four years of age; from the Anglo-Saxon fola meaning young horse, the feminine of which is filly.

film patrol A racing term; the crew that records a horse race on film or tape.

find (1) A hunting term; said of a hound (q.v.) who discovers the line of a fox (q.v.) or coyote and gives tongue (q.v.). (2) *see* UNKENNEL

fine punched A nail hole in a horseshoe located relatively close to the outer edge of the web (q.v.).

finish *see* FINISH LINE

finish fast A racing term; said of a horse who gains on the leader on the last stretch of a race.

finish line Also known as the finish, finish wire, or wire; an electronic beam or overhead wire spanning the width of a racetrack which marks the end of the racecourse; the first qualified horse to cross the beam or run under the wire is the winner of the race.

finishing post Also known as winning post; a racing term; the location on the racetrack where the race is concluded, that is the finish line (q.v.).

Finnish Also known as Finnish Horse; a coldblood historically bred in two types: (a) the heavy, or Finnish Draught (q.v.) and (b) the light-heavy, known as the Finnish Universal (q.v.); descended from native ponies crossed with a mixture of many warm and coldblood types imported to Finland; stands 14.3 to 15.2 hands, is strong with good bone, docile, good-natured, and hard working; has good staying power and usually has a chestnut coat with white markings, although brown, bay, or black coats are also common; a good all-round horse, being used for driving, timber hauling, riding, and trotting; the only official breed of Finland.

Finnish Draught One of two types of Finnish (q.v.); a coldblood used for heavy pulling; heavier than the Finnish Universal (q.v.).

Finnish Horse *see* FINNISH

Finnish Universal One of two types of Finnish (q.v.); a coldblood used for riding, light draft, trotting, racing, and farming; lighter than the Finnish Draught (q.v.).

Fino board Also known as pista, sounding board, or Fino strip; a 30 feet (9 m) long, approximately 2 to 3 feet (61-91 cm) wide wooden board upon which the Classic Fino (q.v.) gait of the Paso Fino (q.v.) is demonstrated; in the Classic Fino Division, the horse is required to traverse the length of the board to demonstrate its even, unbroken, and rapid footfall.

fino strip *see* FINO BOARD

fire (1) *see* FIRING. (2) A racing term; a burst of speed by a horse competing in a race.

fire brand *see* HOT BRAND

fireman (1) A farrier (q.v.) who hot shoes (q.v.) horses. (2) *see* AXLE-TREE MAKER

firing Also known as fire; to apply or insert an extremely hot needle, pin, or iron to a blemish (q.v.) or unsound area to hasten and strengthen the reparative process by increasing blood supply; treatment may be graduated from a slight puncturing of the skin to a penetration as deep as the bone; of two types: line firing (q.v.) and pin firing (q.v.).

firm track A racing term; a firm, resilient turf strip on which horses run faster than other surfaces.

first flight A hunting term; those members of the field (q.v.) who travel closest to the hound (q.v.) pack.

first incisors *see* CENTRAL INCISORS

first jockey A racing term; the principal person hired by an owner or trainer to ride his race horses in competition.

first leg A racing term; the first half of a double event.

first lock The first part of the mane located just behind the poll and ears, where the bridle path (q.v.) is cut.

first over Also known as first overland, from which the term is derived; a harness racing term; said of a horse racing on the outside of the track (q.v.) without another horse directly in front of him.

first overland *see* FIRST OVER

first phalanx That portion of the leg of the horse including the long pastern bone.

first premolars *see* WOLF TEETH

first season hound A hunting term; a hound (q.v.) hunted for the first time.

first whipper-in: One of two principal assistants to the huntsman (q.v.) from whom instructions are received; assists in control of the hounds (q.v.), maintenance of the kennels including collection of flesh (q.v.), hunt staff horses, and when out hunting, turns the hounds to the huntsman.

Fischer von Erlach, Josef Emanual An architect who, between 1729 and 1735, designed and oversaw the building of the Winter Riding Hall, the present home of the Imperial Spanish Riding School (q.v.).

fish eye *see* WALL EYE

fishmeal An animal source of high energy supplemental protein made from several different kinds of fish; an excellent source of amino acids (q.v.), calcium (q.v.), phosphorus (q.v.), and selenium (q.v.); seldom fed to horses because of cost and lack of palatability.

fissure fracture A longitudinal crack through only one side of a bone.

fistula An abnormal channel from a natural body cavity or duct in the skin to the exterior or internal surface; a drainage tract.

fistulous withers A primarily infectious inflammatory disorder of the bursae of the withers caused by the organisms *Brucella abortus* or *Actinomyces bovis*, trauma from cuts, abrasions, bites, or badly fitting tack, or worm infestation; symptoms include initial swelling, followed by the development of a fistula (q.v.) between the infected bursa and a weeping lesion on the skin; inflammation leads to considerable thickening of the bursa wall; may result in lameness; best treated if diagnosed early; the most successful treatment is the excision of the infected bursa.

fit Said of a horse in good physical condition.

five-eighths pole A racing term; a marker pole located on the inside rail (q.v.) exactly five furlongs from the finish line.

five-gaited Said of horse capable of performing two artificial gaits, the slow gait or four-beat stepping pace (q.v.) and the rack (q.v.) in addition to the walk, trot, and canter; depending on the training, pacers and gaited horses may be three- or five-gaited – most five-gaited horses must be taught to rack.

five-gaiter saddler One of three types of horse show classes for the American Saddlebred (q.v.) in which demonstration of the walk, trot, canter, slow gait (q.v.), and rack (q.v.) are required; the other two classes being light harness (q.v.) and three-gaited saddler (q.v.).

fixed cheek Also known as fast cheek; a curb bit (q.v.) in which the mouthpiece does not have any movement on the cheeks (q.v.).

fixed head *see* HUNTING HEAD

fixed race Also known as boat race; any horse race in which the winner has been determined in advance of running the race; a practice not supported by The Jockey Club (q.v.) or other racing associations, but which occurs.

fixture card *see* APPOINTMENT CARD

Fjord Also known as Fjord pony or Westlands pony; an ancient pony breed originating in Norway; has retained the primitive characteristics of its forebears such as a dun coat, black and silver mane, eel stripe (q.v.), and zebra markings (q.v.) on the legs; stands 13 to 14.1 hands, has a small head, short neck, upright mane, compact body, sloping croup, full tail, and sturdy legs with light feathering; is frugal, stubborn and tireless; used for riding, packing, light draft, and farm work; historically used by the Vikings as a war-time mount, it is believed that all present-day heavy draft breeds descended from this pony.

Fjord pony *see* FJORD

flag (1) A piece of cloth of varying size, shape, design, and color, usually attached at one edge to a staff or cord, and used as a sign, standard, symbol, or signal. (2) To place a flag on or use it to signal. (3) *see* FLARE. (4) A hunting term; the floor of a hound's kennel.

flag down A racing term; to signal an exercise rider that the horse he is riding is working too hard.

flagging *see* DOCK

flagman A rodeo official responsible for signaling the end of elapsed time in timed events or competitions.

flak jacket A protective vest worn by jockeys (q.v.) and eventers while competing to protect the kidneys, ribs, and back.

Flanders horse *see* BRABANT

flank (1) The part of the horse behind the ribs and below the loins which extends down to the belly. (2) A vaulting term; a compulsory movement (q.v.) performed in vaulting (q.v.) competitions whereby the vaulter (q.v.) starts from a sitting position, swings both straight legs forward, then backwards into an extended handstand position, then flexes the hips and rotates them, legs together, to the inside,

where the vaulter slides into a sitting position on one buttock; from this position, the vaulter swings his legs backward and again into a handstand, pushes off the grips on the vaulting roller (q.v.) and lands behind and to the outside of the horse.

flank cinch Also known as hind cinch or back cinch; the second girth (q.v.) used on western saddles; usually hangs loose approximately 1 to 2 inches (25-50 cm) beneath the belly of the horse, lies approximately 12 inches (30 cm) behind the front girth (q.v.), and is never drawn tight; used to keep the back of the saddle in place on the back of the horse.

flanking A calf roping term; said of the roper; to take the catch rope (q.v.) in one hand, reach across the back of the calf with the opposite hand to pick the calf up and lay it on its side in preparation for tying its feet.

flank strap A leather strap or rope tightened around the flank area of a horse or bull to encourage it to buck; commonly used in rodeo competitions.

flap *see* SADDLE SKIRT

flapper A racing term; a horse who runs in an unauthorized race event.

flapping Also known as flapping meeting; a racing term; an unofficial race meeting not governed by The Jockey Club (q.v.) rules of racing.

flapping meeting *see* FLAPPING

flare (1) Also known as flag; a compulsory exercise performed in vaulting competitions; the vaulter (q.v.) kneels on the back of the horse on one knee, while the other leg and opposite arm are outstretched, back and forward respectively; the hand and raised foot must be at the same height with the side of the foot facing upwards; the vaulter's spine is arched. (2) An outward distortion of the hoof wall; if left untreated may alter functional toe angle, mediolateral balance, and hoof symmetry.

flash (1) A racing term; the change of odds information on the tote board (q.v.). (2) *see* FLASH NOSEBAND.

flash noseband A hybrid noseband (q.v.) that combines a standard cavesson (q.v.) with another loop which attaches to the front of the cavesson nosepiece, passes in front of the bit, lies in the curb groove, and is buckled on the left side just below the bit; the cavesson exerts some downward pressure on the upper jaw while the dropped loop exerts closing pressure on the lower jaw; used to prevent the horse from opening his mouth.

flask *see* HUNTING FLASK

flat (1) Also known as flat work; to school or exercise a horse on the flat ground without incorporating cavaletti (q.v.) or jumps. (2) A racing term; the area around the winning post on the opposite side of the course to the grandstand and official enclosure. (3) A racing term; said of a racing surface, other than a grass or jump course. (4) *see* DRAY

flat bone The cannon bone (q.v.) which appears wide and flat when viewed from the side; the reverse of round bone (q.v.), but does not mean that the bone is actually flat; a complimentary term.

flat canter Said of a horse lacking sufficient suspension between canter strides.

flat catcher Said of a horse who looks outwardly sound and of good build, but upon closer examination, has defects.

flat foot A foot lacking normal concavity in the sole; present in some draft breeds; may be inherited and is much more common in the fore than hind feet.

flat footed Said of a horse who does not place its foot squarely or evenly on the ground striking first with the heel rather than the toe of the hoof; commonly caused by a low hoof wall and associated with a large soft frog; horses raised on soft ground are particularly prone.

flat foot walk A natural, inherited, loose, four-beat gait, slower than the running walk, in which each foot strikes the ground separately at regular intervals: left fore, right rear, right fore, left rear; the hind hooves may overstep the print of the fore by as much as 18 inches (46 cm); characterized by a bobbing or nodding of the head, flopping of the ears, and a clicking of the teeth in rhythm with the movement of the legs; the center of balance is somewhat behind so that the horse appears to squat.

flat pace A smooth, lateral gait in which both legs on the same side leave and strike the ground simultaneously.

flat race Also known as racing on the flat; a racing term; a horse race conducted on flat ground without obstacles such as hedges, hurdles, or fences.

flat-sided Also known as slat-sided or slab-sided; said of a horse whose ribs are neither rounded nor well-sprung (q.v.), resulting in the impression of a straight instead of a curved side; a conformation fault.

flat saddle An English saddle; one without a high pommel or cantle as used for hunting (q.v.), jumping (q.v.), and dressage (q.v.).

flatten out A racing term; said of an exhausted horse who stops mid-race; will often drop his head below the level of the withers (q.v.).

flatulence Also known as gas or wind; the expulsion of gases generated in the alimentary canal from the rectum; gas production generally results from indigestion.

flat work *see* FLAT

flatworm *see* TAPEWORM

flax Any plant of the genus Linum; a slender, erect, annual plant with blue flowers cultivated for its fiber and seeds.

flaxen Refers to mane and tail color; pale, yellowish, and light-colored.

flaxseed *see* LINSEED

fleabitten (1) Refers to coat color; any light-colored horse, e.g., white or gray, whose coat is covered with small, brown marks. (2) A mangy-looking horse.

fleabitten gray Refers to coat color; a horse with a gray (q.v.) coat into which small flecks of color are mixed as in brown or white.

fleaseed Also known as psyllium seed; the seed of the fleawort (q.v.); when crushed and consumed, absorbs large amounts of moisture and becomes slippery and gelatinous in the intestinal tract; used as a mild laxative and preventive for sand colic (q.v.).

fleawort Also known as psyllium; an Old World plantain, Plantago psyllium, having seeds that swell and become gelatinous when moist and that are used as a mild laxative.

flèche, à la *see* A LA FLÈCHE

flecked Refers to coat color; randomly distributed irregular collections of white hairs throughout the coat.

flecked blanket *see* BLANKET no. 1

flecked roan *see* SABINO

Flehmen *see* FLEHMEN POSTURE

Flehmen posture Also known as Flehmen; the body position of the horse in which the head and neck are outstretched and the upper lip curled upward; the upward-turned lip concentrates the airflow over the vomeronasal organ; stimulated by certain odors, pain, or sexual arousal.

Flehmen response The reaction of the horse to certain odors, pain, or sexual arousal characterized by the Flehmen posture (q.v.).

flesh A hunting term; meat upon which hounds (q.v.) are fed.

flesh hovel An antiquated hunting term; a room where carcasses were skinned and boned and the meat hung until fed to the hounds (q.v.).

flesh marks Refers to coat color; patches of skin lacking pigment or which differ in color from the rest of the body.

flexible Said of a horse capable of moving the muscles to cause the full bending of a joint between the bones and allow a supple (q.v.), fluid motion; generally refers to movement of the neck, spine, and/or leg joints; different than supple.

flexible hydroactive occlusive dressing Also known by the acronym FHOD; a generic wound cover made of a polymer that becomes a gel upon contact with wound fluids; is impermeable and blocks out contaminants and irritants to create a second skin; promotes rapid healing of difficult wounds; originally developed for human application.

flexibility *see* FLEXIBLE

flexing hocks Said of the action of a Hackney pony (q.v.); significant hock action in which the pony carries his legs quite far under his body.

flexion The act of bending in the joints; specifically the bending of the head of the horse at the poll (q.v.) and the rounding of the neck in response to the aids (q.v.); of two types: longitudinal (from back-to-front), and lateral (sideways).

flexor tendon A tendon (q.v.) that causes flexion of a joint when stimulated.

flews A hunting term; the overhanging lips of the upper jaw of a foxhound.

flier A vaulting term; a vaulter performing an exercise who is supported by other vaulters and does not contact the horse.

flies The plural of fly (q.v.).

flight (1) A vaulting term; the movement of a vaulter (q.v.) through the air when performing an exercise; starts as soon as the body is in the air and ends when some part of his body comes in contact with the ground or horse. (2) A jumping term; said of the horse after it has left the ground to jump an obstacle until it lands. (3) The act of fleeing; a hasty or precipitated departure.

flipper foot Also known as elve's foot or elf's foot; said of the hoof when the toe is extremely overgrown and flared.

float (1) Also known as floating, rasping, tooth rasping, filing teeth, or filing; to file off the sharp edges and points that develop on the outside edges of the upper molars (q.v.) and the inside edges of the lower molars using a rasp. (2) A horse-drawn American goods wagon or dray widely used during the second half of the 19th century; either sprung or dead axle with a sprung seat; drawn by a single horse. (3) An English horse-drawn, two-wheeled, low-loading vehicle, with a forward facing seat, used for both agricultural and retail delivery purposes such as for milk delivery; generally mounted on cranked axles. (4) *see* HORSE-BOX no. 1

floating (1) *see* FLOAT no. 1. (2) A racing term; to drag a flat plate or wooden implement over the surface of a wet track to help drain standing water.

floating leaders A driving term; said of lead horses in a team (q.v.) who do not move freely forward.

flog a dead horse, to To revive a feeling of interest that has died or to engage in a fruitless undertaking; it being as difficult to stir up interest in a mute issue as to try to get a dead horse to pull a load by flogging it; the phrase in French translates more literally – chercher a ressusciter un mort – to seek to resuscitate a corpse.

floorman A racing term; one responsible for placing s bookmaker's (q.v.) bets.

fluke Any of several trematode flatworms parasitic in sheep, man, and snails; two subtypes may affect horses: *gastrodiscus aegyptiacus* (q.v.) and *fasciola hepatica* (q.v.).

fluorine An element in the chlorine family; although no minimum dietary requirements have been established, it has been determined that small quantities are important for the development of bones and teeth of the horse, while excess fluorine, fifty parts/million or more in the ration, is highly toxic and can result in severe skeletal damage including thickened bones, enlarged fetlock joints, and worn down teeth.

flute bit A bit in which the front side of the straight-bar mouthpiece (q.v.) is perforated with holes; used on windsuckers (q.v.).

flutters Rapid and ineffective contractions of the heart chambers.

fly (1) Any of a large group of insects with two transparent wings including the horsefly (q.v.), blackfly (q.v.), face fly (q.v.), horn fly (q.v.), stable fly (q.v.), housefly (q.v.), deerfly (q.v.), culicoides (q.v.), and mosquito. (2) *see* BROUGHAM

fly bonnet Also known as fly cap; a single-piece crocheted hood that covers the ears and forehead of the horse and ties under the throat; the forehead piece swings freely with movement of the horse and in so doing protects the horse from flies and gnats.

fly-by-night *see* BROUGHAM

fly cap *see* FLY BONNET

fly fence *see* FLYING FENCE

flying angel A vaulting term; a freestyle exercise in which the flier (q.v.) is supported by another vaulter at the shoulders in a horizontal position with arms and legs outstretched.

flying change Also known as flying change of leg, change in the air, change of leg in the air, or change of leg at the canter; an advanced movement in which the horse changes leading legs simultaneously during the moment of suspension following the third beat of the canter (q.v.); the horse springs from one pair of leading legs (q.v.) to the other in one fluent movement with the fore and hind legs changing concurrently; may be executed in a series such as at every fourth, third, second, or first stride; the horse should remain calm and straight with lively impulsion and a consistent rhythm and balance.

flying change of leg *see* FLYING CHANGE

flying coach Any horse-drawn, high-speed, six passenger coach (q.v.) which traveled during the 17th century between London and Exeter, York and Chester, Great Britain in four days time (ordinary coaches of the period traveled at four to four and one half miles per hour).

flying fence Also known as a fly fence; a jumping obstacle; a natural or man-made bank that does not have to be jumped on or off or any fence that can be cleared (q.v.) at a gallop (q.v.).

flying mount *see* RUNNING-QUICK MOUNT

fly link A single ring located in the center of a curb chain (q.v.), set at a different angle than the other rings and through which the lip strap (q.v.) passes.

fly mask A covering for the face of the horse worn for protection from flies and gnats; generally made of fine-gaged mesh; fitted over the ears just behind the poll, connects under the throat, and covers the face of the horse from the ears to just above the muzzle.

fly net A band of strings attached to the brow band (q.v.) of the bridle; the strings fall over the forehead and eyes of the horse, the movement of which prevents flies and gnats from landing on and annoying the horse.

fly sheet Also known as a skim sheet; a thin

linen, cotton, or synthetic covering for the body of the horse; is breathable and used in the summer months to protect the horse from flies; is buckled across the chest (q.v.) and under the belly (q.v.).

fly terrets A terret (q.v.); small rings or loops attached to the browband (q.v.) of the bridle (q.v.) and/or headcollar used on heavy harness horses; used for decoration and to scare away flies in summer; of three types: swingers, danglers, and hodders.

fly wisk A switch consisting of a horse-hair thong attached to a wooden or leather handle used by the rider to remove flies from the horse; the horse hair is often gray.

foal (1) A young horse of either sex from the time of birth until weaning, a time of approximately one year; from the Anglo-Saxon fola. (2) Also known as dropped, dropped a foal, or drop; said of a mare; to give birth to a foal. (3) The offspring of either a male or female parent, e.g., He was the first foal of Doc Bar. (4) A mule (q.v.) less than two years of age.

foal heat Also known as nine-day heat; the estrus period (q.v.), occurring approximately nine to eleven days after foaling, during which the mare shows signs of heat (q.v.).

foal heat scours Diarrhea (q.v.) that commonly occurs in the mare seven to nine days after foaling.

foaling see PARTURITION

fodder see FORAGE AND FEED

foddering time see FEEDING TIME

foetus see FETUS

foil see FOILED

foiled Also known as foil the ground, foil, or stained; a hunting term; said of the scent of the quarry when obliterated by sheep, horses, cattle, etc. which cross its line; the quarry may foil its own scent by crossing over its tracks.

foiled line Also known as stained line; a hunting term; said of the line of the fox (q.v.) when obliterated by the scent of sheep, horses, cattle, etc.

foil the ground see FOILED

folacin Also known as folate and formerly folic acid; an intestinally synthesized B-complex vitamin necessary for cell metabolism and normal blood formation; although deficiency in horses is quite rare, anemia related deficiency may occur.

folate see FOLACIN

folding a whip see CATCHING A DOUBLE THONG

folding head see FOLDING HOOD

folding hood Also known as folding head or falling top; a driving term; a convertible or folding leather top found on some horse-drawn vehicles.

folic acid see FOLACIN

follicle (1) A small sac or cavity in the ovary (q.v.) containing a developing egg surrounded by a covering of cells; may be found in various stages of development and/or degeneration in the active, mature ovary at any time during the natural breeding season; contains the ovum (q.v.) which may be fertilized by the stallion's sperm. (2) A small anatomical cavity or deep, narrow-mouthed depression, as in a hair follicle.

follicle stimulating hormone A hormone formed in the anterior lobe of the pituitary gland that stimulates growth of ovum-containing follicles (q.v.) in the ovary (q.v.) and activates sperm-forming cells.

follicular stage The period during the estrous cycle (q.v.), including proestrus (q.v.) and estrus (q.v.), during which follicles (q.v.) are formed and the mare becomes receptive to the stallion.

followers see FIELD no. 4

fomentation The application of hot, moist substances to the body by some vehicle such as wool or flannel to ease pain; should not be hotter than the hand can bear.

food wagon see CHUCK WAGON

foot (1) see HOOF. (2) A racing term; speed.

foot board A driving term; the part of a horse-drawn vehicle on which the driver and passengers rest their feet; commonly attached to the wagon at an angle of 33º to the horizontal.

footboard lamp A driving term; a small lamp attached to the foot board (q.v.) of a horse-drawn coach (q.v.) to illuminate the pole head (q.v.).

footing The condition of the surface of a track, arena, course, or field; may be good, bad, wet, etc., e.g., The footing was wet and dangerous.

foot-lock *see* FEATHER

foot loop *see* VAULTING ROLLER

foot mange *see* CHORIOPTIC MANGE

foot polo A polo term; a training exercise performed by a walking polo player to work eye to ball to hand coordination; to practice polo strokes and movement of the ball down the field while walking.

foot rest A driving term; a movable foot rest used on two-wheeled horse-drawn vehicles; generally made of rubber-covered wood shaped so that the feet sit at an angle of 90 percent to the legs.

foot-stool (1) Also known as shoeing block; a block made of wood or metal upon which a farrier rests the foot of the horse to crimp the nails used in setting the horseshoe to the hoof and other processes. (2) A driving term; shallow wooden boxes placed above the front and rear boots (q.v.) of a horse-drawn carriage upon which passengers occupying the roof seats rested their feet.

forage (1) Also known as fodder; the food fed to, or consumed by, herbivores, e.g., horses; consists of the entire plant, stalk, leaves, and grain in a fresh, dried, or ensilaged state; of two types: grasses such as Timothy (q.v.), orchard grass, fescue, Bermuda grass (q.v.), etc. and legumes including alfalfa (q.v.), clover (q.v.), lespedza (q.v.), etc.; an excellent source of energy and other nutrients. (2) To wander in search of food.

forage poisoning *see* BOTULISM

forbidden substance Any stimulant, depressant, tranquilizer, or local anesthetic which might affect the performance of the horse, the use of which is illegal.

forearm That portion of the foreleg (q.v.) between the elbow and the knee; contains two bones, the radius and ulna.

forecarriage That section of a four-wheeled, horse-drawn carriage consisting of the undercarriage of the front wheels including the front axle, the lower half of the wheel plate, axle bed, sway bar, futchells, splinter bar, and associated smaller parts.

forecast A betting term; the bookmakers' odds on each horse running in a horse race as based on past performance.

forefoot Also known as front foot; either of the front feet of the horse.

forefooted A roping (q.v.) term; said of a horse, steer, or other animal roped by the front feet.

foregirth A flat strap approximately 2 inches (5 cm) wide, made of nylon or other material having two leather-covered metal projections with rearward facing hooked tops; is put on the horse in advance of the saddle, buckling behind the shoulder, slightly in front of the saddle girth; the hooks prevent the saddle from slipping forward onto the withers of a horse who is down in front (q.v.) or when riding downhill; available in different shapes and sizes.

forehand Also known as the front or incorrectly as forequarters; the part of the horse including the head, neck, shoulders and forelegs (q.v.) in front of the horse's center of gravity.

forehead That part of the face above the eyes and between the temples.

forehead drop *see* DROP

forehead piece *see* DROP

foreign body Any substance or particle present in the body of the horse that is not part of the tissues or bones, e.g., nails, glass, wood splinters, and gravel.

foreleg Also known as front leg; either of the front two front limbs of the horse below the knee.

forelimb Either of the front legs of the horse including the forearm (q.v.) and foreleg (q.v.).

forelock The part of the mane extending between the ears and that falls onto the forehead.

forequarters That portion of the body of the horse consisting of the withers (q.v.), shoulders (q.v.), and front legs (q.v.).

Forest *see* NEW FOREST PONY

Forester's pace The canter (q.v.) as performed by the New Forest Pony (q.v.); the action (q.v.) is long and low.

Forest Pony *see* GOTLAND

foretop *see* FORELOCK

forewale A driving term; the foremost rim of a collar (q.v.); generally made of leather and stuffed with straw until stiff.

forfeit (1) *see* SCRATCH. (2) A racing term; a sum of money consisting of part or all of the entry fee for a race, that is not refundable to the owner or nominator of a horse if the horse is withdrawn from competition. (3) To sacrifice an entrance fee by scratching a horse from a race after the field (q.v.) has been set.

forfeit list A racing term; a list of horses maintained by the racing authorities who are ineligible to compete until the conditions of the forfeiture are resolved.

forge (1) Also known as click, clicking, or forging; limb contact in which the hind foot hits the sole of the forefoot on the same side; recognized by the clicking noise that occurs when one shoe strikes the other; indicates the horse is moving too much on the forehand, which delays the foreleg break-over; occurs in tired, green, or immature horses, those with a short back and long legs, or when shod incorrectly. (2) Also known as a shoeing forge; a furnace in which a horse shoe or other metal is heated and wrought. (3) To shape or form a horseshoe or other metal object by heating and hammering. (4) To move with a sudden increase of speed and power, as in a horse on the homestretch.

forging *see* FORGE no. 1

forhoss Also known as forhust; an antiquated term; the leader in a team when driven at length.

forhust *see* FORHOSS

fork (1) Also known as a saddle fork; the open portion of the under-side of the saddle (q.v.) that rests upon the horse's withers (q.v.). (2) Also known as stable fork or pitchfork; a tool having a long, approximately 4 ft (1.2 m), handle attached to the head with two or more prongs; used for holding or lifting as in mucking out (q.v.) stalls or pitching hay.

Forked Slipe A primitive horse-drawn Irish slide car constructed from the forked branches of a tree or large bush, boarded across the center; attached to the harness of a draft animal by chains or leather traces.

form (1) A racing term; the past performance of a race horse (q.v.). (2) *see* DAILY RACING FORM. (3) A hunting term; an indentation or hollow in the ground in which a hare will lie.

formal season A hunting term; that part of the hunt season beginning with the opening meet, around the first of November; hunt staff and members of the field (q.v.) are required to wear formal hunting clothes during this period.

form player A racing term; a bettor (q.v.) who selects horses upon which to bet based on their past-performance records.

form sheet A racing term; a list of horses competing in a race and their past racing performances.

forrard Also known as forrard-on; a hunting term; a huntsman's cheer to the hounds to encourage chase of the hounds.

forrard on *see* FORRARD

forty horse hitch *see* SCHLITZ FORTY HORSE HITCH

forty thieves An antiquated term; gypsies and hawkers found at horse fairs.

forward deviation of the carpal joints Also known as dorsal deviation of the carpal joints, bucked knees, knee sprung, goat knees, over in the knees, or over at the knee; a conformation defect; said of a horse whose knees have a forward bend or curve and project too far forward in front of the vertical line of the leg.

forward seat Formerly known as the Italian seat; the position of the mounted rider; the rider stands in the stirrups, bends slightly forward at the waist to position his weight over the shoulders and neck of the horse; enables the rider to stay over the center of gravity more easily when jumping; re-introduced by Federico Caprilli (q.v.) in 1890, as pictorial evidence indicates the style existed during the time of Xenophon (q.v.) approximately during the mid 400s BC.

forward seat saddle *see* CLOSE CONTACT SADDLE

fothering time A corruption of foddering-time (q.v.).

foul To commit an act, e.g., dangerous, that is contrary to the rules of the game played; in the game of polo (q.v.) may be called due to charging, intimidation, foul hooking (q.v.), or crossing the line of the ball.

foul hooking A polo term; a principal infringement in the game of polo in which a player hooks (q.v.) an opponent's mallet at a level higher than the withers of the horse.

foundation mare Also known as a tap root mare; one of the original, primary mares used to establish the characteristics of a breed.

foundation pedigree option Also known by the acronym FPO; a registration option offered by the Appaloosa Horse Club (q.v.) since 1994 for non-characteristic Appaloosa (q.v.) horses; to qualify, a horse must have at least half his ancestors four generations back also registered Appaloosas (q.v.).

foundation sire One of the original, primary stallions used to establish the characteristics of a particular breed for ensuing generations.

founder A chronic condition sequel to laminitis (q.v.) with some degree of rotation to the pedal bone; internal deformity of the foot resulting from rotation of the pedal bone caused by simultaneous detachment from the hoof wall and the constant pull of the deep flexor tendon on the pedal bone; pedal bone rotation may progress to perforation of the sole just in front of the frog; may be triggered by a number of external conditions such as excess protein or water intake as in grain founder (q.v.), grass founder (q.v.), postpar-

turient founder (q.v.), road founder (q.v.), water founder (q.v.), and hypothyroidism.

founder rings *see* HOOF RINGS

founder stance The standing position sometimes assumed by a horse afflicted with acute laminitis in which the hind and forefeet are placed well forward of their usual positions; the hind feet bear an inordinate amount of the horse's body weight while the forefeet only bear weight at the heels.

four at length A driving term; a team of four farm horses put to, one in front of the other; controlled by two men who walked on the offside of the forhoss (q.v.) and the other on the offside of the lash-horse (q.v.) by means of whips placed over the necks of the horses; neither harness nor verbal commands were used.

four-beat stepping pace *see* SLOW GAIT

fourgon (1) A four-wheeled, horse-drawn luggage van or wagon used in the late 19th and early 20th centuries to carry luggage and servants to a destination in advance of a traveling carriage; well sprung and fitted with a hooded row of crosswise seats for personal servants. (2) The luggage van at the fore-end of a passenger train.

Four-H Club Also known as 4-H or 4-H Club; a rural youth organization founded in the United States by the Department of Agriculture offering instruction in agriculture and home economics.

Four Horsemen Also known as Four Horsemen of the Apocalypse; the riders of the four horses described in the apocalyptic vision in Rev. 6: 2–8, which represents the four plagues of humankind: war, famine, pestilence, and death; the figure representing death rides a white horse, war a red horse, famine a black horse, and plague a pale horse.

Four Horsemen of the Apocalypse *see* FOUR HORSEMEN

four-in-hand (1) A vehicle drawn by a hitch of four horses consisting of two pairs with one pair harnessed in front of the other and one (driver. 2) Also known as a four-in-hand team; a four horse team consisting of two wheelers (q.v.) and two leaders (q.v.).

four-in-hand coach *see* DRAG no. 5

Four-in-Hand Driving Club A horse-drawn vehicle driving club established in Great Britain in 1856; club members, who at its inception numbered 30, met twice annually for drive-to diners; the only club in Great Britain until 1870, at which time the Coaching Club (q.v.) was formed.

four-in-hand team *see* FOUR-IN-HAND no. 2

four-point trim A hoof trimming technique in which the heels are trimmed back to the widest point of the frog, the toe is beveled upward, and the quarters rasped down until they no longer bear weight on a firm surface; the weight of the horse is therefore only borne on four points: one on each side of the toe and each heel.

four time The canter (q.v.) when the footfalls occur independently of each other marked by four hoof beats at each stride.

Four-wheeled Dogcart *see* DOGCART PHAETON

Four-Wheeler A four-wheeled, one-horse-drawn cab used in London, England.

fox Also known as Charley or Charlie; any of a group of wild carnivorous mammals, genus Vulpes, of the dog family, having bushy tails, commonly reddish-brown or gray fur, and weighing 8 to 12 pounds (36-54 kg); especially noted for their cunning and speed; hunted on horseback for more than 300 years; may be released from captivity for the hunt or flushed out of hiding by hounds or terriers.

fox den Also known as a fox earth or earth; the subterranean recess used as a hiding place or lair of a fox.

fox dog *see* FOXHOUND

fox earth *see* FOX DEN

foxhound Also known as fox dog; one of the various breeds of fleet, keen-scented, keen-sighted hounds bred and trained to hunt foxes.

Foxhound Kennel Stud Book, the A breeding record of foxhounds (q.v.) first compiled in 1841 in Britain; the first volume contained a list of the King of England's buck-hounds and 46 packs of foxhounds; subsequent volumes have been issued at frequent intervals; registers two strains of foxhounds under the heading American Hounds: (1) the Penn-MaryDel and (2) the Rappahonnock River Valley strains.

fox hunt *see* FOX HUNTING

foxhunter Any generally handy horse possessed of good stamina and jumping ability ridden by a hunter (q.v.) when following hounds in their pursuit of fox and other hunted game.

Foxhunter An international show jumper (q.v.) foaled in 1940 by the Thoroughbred (q.v.) sire Erehwemos and out of Catcall who descended from a purebred (q.v.) Clydesdale (q.v.) mare; represented Great Britain and tallied 78 international wins, and was retired in 1956.

fox hunt *see* FOX HUNTING

fox hunting Also known as hunting or fox hunt; to hunt for live fox or coyote from horseback or on foot, with a pack of hounds; due to the scarcity of wild fox in many regions today, foxes released from captivity, coyotes, and fox scent are used as quarry; the national sport in Britain where it gained the height of its popularity in the 18th century.

fox hunting club *see* HUNT

Fox Hunting, The Father of *see* WARDE, JOHN

fox kennel A hunting term; a fox den located above the level of the surrounding ground.

fox sense A hunting term; the innate ability of a hound to locate a bedded fox and to recover its line after a check (q.v.).

fox terrier A small, smooth- or wire-haired dog of the terrier family formerly used to hunt small burrowing animals such as fox and rabbits (q.v.); from the French word terrier meaning the hole of a rabbit.

fox trot (1) A slow, short, unevenly spaced, four-beat gait with distinct over-striding of the hind hooves; the horse walks actively from the front shoulder trotting behind, the hind hooves stepping onto the track of the fore and then sliding forward; the left hind foot strikes the ground followed quickly by the diagonal or right forefoot, followed by a slight pause and then the right hind; accompanied by a rhythmic movement of the head; the sliding action minimizes the concussive effect of the trot; the horse can maintain this gait for long distances at a regular 5-10 miles (3-6 km) per hour; (2) A social dance, in duple or quadruple time, characterized by various combinations of short, quick steps.

FPO The acronym for foundation pedigree option (q.v.).

FPT The acronym for failure of passive transfer (q.v.).

fractions A racing term; race time taken at quarter-mile intervals in races and workouts.

fractional time A racing term; the running time taken at various points between the start and finish of the race.

fracture Also known as break; to become separated into parts as a bone and the resulting condition; may be one of twelve types: comminuted frature (q.v.), compound fracture (q.v.), condylar fracture (q.v.), fissure fracture (q.v.), metacarpal frature (q.v.), oblique fracture (q.v.), saucer fracture (q.v.), sesamoid fracture (q.v.), slab fracture (q.v.), spiral fracture (q.v.), simple fracture (q.v.), or stress fracture (q.v.).

Franches-Montagnes A small draft warm-blood originating in the Jura region of Switzerland by putting imported Anglo-Norman stallions to native, Bernese Jura mares; English half-bred hunter and Ardennes (q.v.) blood was introduced in early days of the breed; since that time, the breed has remained relatavely pure; is early developing, steady, sure footed, active, calm, powerfully built, cob-type with a rather heavy head, a full forelock falling over a broad forehead, small ears, a muscular, arched neck, short back, and slightly sloping croup; may be bay or chestnut; used for light draft, farm work, and riding.

Frederico Grisone *see* GRISONE, FREDERICO

Frederiksborg Also known as the Danish Horse and spelled Frideriksborg; a breed of horse developed in 1562 at the Royal Stud in Frederiksborg, Denmark by King Frederik II, by crossing Neapolitan (q.v.) and Andalusians

(q.v.) after contributing to the development of the Lipizzaner (q.v.) and the Orlov Trotter (q.v.), it fell into a period of decline until 1939, at which time it was further developed with the addition of Friesian (q.v.), Oldenburg (q.v.), and later, Thoroughbred (q.v.) and Arab (q.v.) blood; stands 15.1 to 16.1 hands, has a chestnut coat; has a good temperament, small foot, full and fairly deep chest, strong shoulder, straight back, and well-proportioned, although slightly convex, head; used as a military charger, school horse in the great European riding schools, under light harness, carrriage, and riding.

free action Said of a horse who has good impulsion from behind, is balanced, and moves the front feet well out in front of its body.

free handicap (1) A racing term; a race in which no nominating fees are required. (2) *see* EXPERIMENTAL FREE HANDICAP

freelance A racing term; said of a jockey who is not under contract to a stable or owner.

freemartin A filly twin of a colt.

free radical An atom lacking one or more electrons; attempts to replace the missing electron(s) by scavenging the body and robbing electrons from healthy cells; this process creates a damaging free radical chain reaction in the body that erodes the cell membranes and can alter the manner cells incode genetic information in the DNA (q.v.).

Free Roaming Wild Horse and Burro Act Legislation passed in the United States in 1971 to protect wild horses and burros from harassment, death, and capture; subsequent amendments prohibit tracking by helicopter.

freestyle exercise *see* KÜR EXERCISE

freestyle reining Reining maneuvers set to music in a format designed by each other competitor; a sanctioned National Reining Horse Association (q.v.) class since 1992.

free walk A relaxed walk (q.v.) in which the horse is allowed to lower its head, stretch out its neck, and relax its back; may be ridden on loose or long reins.

freeze brand (1) Also known as freeze mark, cold brand, or cryogenic brand; an identifying symbol, character, letter, or series of numbers, or any combination thereof, burned into the flesh of the horse using a bevel-edge iron supercooled in liquid nitrogen to 320º below zero; the length of time the iron is applied to the hide to achieve the mark depends on what material the iron is made of, the strength of the brander, the age, sex and breed of the horse, the time of year, and the strength of the horse's hide; on dark coloured horses, the iron is applied to the hide a sufficient amount of time to freeze the hair and skin, without killing the hair follicle, within the mark, the hair will grow in white; the ideal mark has a bald center surrounded by white hair; on roans (q.v.), grays (q.v.), whites (q.v.), palominos (q.v.), buckskins (q.v.), and Appaloosas (q.v.) prone to roaning, the iron is left on long enough to kill the hair follicle, leaving a pink, hairless mark; an AHSA (q.v.) rule that a horse shall not be discounted for a freeze brand, although the color-added rule may be exercised by some judges. (2) To apply an identifying symbol, character, letter, or series of numbers, or any combination thereof to the hide of the horse using an iron supercooled to 320º below zero in liquid nitrogen.

freeze brand iron A bevel-edged iron made of brass, copper, steel, or iron used to freeze brand (q.v.) a horse.

freeze mark *see* FREEZE BRAND

Freidberger A relatively new warmblood breed developed at the Avenches Stud in Switzerland based on the Franches-Montagnes (q.v.) improved with heavy infusions of Shagya Arabian (q.v.) and Norman blood; a riding horse standing 15.2 to 16 hands with an Arabian-type head, good shoulders and quarters, short back, deep girth, and strong legs with plenty of bone; is active, intelligent, and possessed of great stamina.

French Anglo-Arab Also known as an Anglo-Arab (q.v.); a breed of horse developed in 1843 by veterinarian E. Gaynot at the Le Pin and Pompadour stud farms, located in France; developed from a nucleus of broodmares of Oriental origin interbred with local horse populations to produce the Tarbes and Limousin (q.v.) breeds with the addition of other Arab (q.v.) and Thoroughbred (q.v.) blood; a solidly built horse standing 15.2 to 16.3 hands with good conformation, and powerful hindquarters; must have at least 25 percent Arab (q.v.) blood and have an absence

of pedigree of other horse breeds other than Arab, Anglo-Arab, or Thoroughbred for at least the last six generations; a solid-coloured coat dominates in bay, brown, black, and chestnut; used for riding, racing, and other competitions.

French bridoon A snaffle bit (q.v.) consisting of a jointed mouthpiece connected in the middle with a small, flat plate approximately 3/4 inch in length.

French brushing boot A light duty brushing boot (q.v.)which is shorter than an ankle boot (q.v.), protecting only the fetlock joint.

French Cavalry School at Saumur Previously known as the French School, School of Saumur, or the School of Mounted Troop Instruction; one of two riding schools established in France in the early 18th century to teach the French school of classical equitation (q.v.) which was combined with other forms of competitive sport; influenced by François Robichon de la Guérinière (q.v.); favors Thoroughbred (q.v.) and Anglo-Arab (q.v.) horses; the home of the Cadre Noir (q.v.).

French chasing boot A heavy-duty brushing boot (q.v.) which is somewhat taller than an ankle boot (q.v.), protecting the fetlock joint and part of the lower cannon bone.

French clip *see* STUD FASTENING

French Phaeton A horse-drawn carriage of the phaeton (q.v.) type; hung on front and rear sideways-elliptical springs seated two on the driving seat, with two rearward cross seats in a semi-open compartment, and was entered through side doors; had slatted compartments for gun dogs under both the passenger and driving seats; drawn by a single horse in shafts or a pair in pole gear (q.v.).

French Saddle horse *see* SELLE FRANÇAIS

French Saddle pony Also referred to as a Selle Français although that name usually pertains to the horse; a pony breed newly developed in France through the selective crossing of native mares with Arab (q.v.), Connemara (q.v.), New Forest (q.v.) and Welsh (q.v.) stallions; stands 12.1 to 14.2 hands; all colors are permitted; has a small head, long neck, straight back, a wide, deep chest, and strong legs with well-formed joints; is quiet, yet energetic; used for jumping, dressage, and under harness.

French School *see* FRENCH CAVALRY SCHOOL AT SAUMUR

French snaffle A snaffle bit (q.v.) in which the mouthpiece has two branches connected by a small, flat rounded link; is less severe than a Dr. Bristol (q.v.).

French Tilbury Tug *see* TILBURY TUG

French tie *see* MUD TIE

French Trotter Also known as the Norman Trotter; a breed developed in France in 1836; descended from Thoroughbred (q.v.), halfbred English Hunters, and Norfolk Trotters (q.v.) put to Norman (q.v.) mares; two Thoroughbreds had particular influence on the breed, Young Rattler and The Heir of Linne; 90 percent of modern Trotters trace back to five descendants of these two stallions: Conquerant, Lavater, Normand, Phaeton, and Fuschia; a tall, light-framed horse, with a fine head, prominent withers, strong back, and sloping hindquarters; lacks uniformity in conformation; stands 15.1 to 16.2 hands, with a bay, black, chestnut, dark chestnut, or occasionally gray coat; an athletic and fast horse used for trotting, riding, and cross-breeding.

fresh (1) Said of a horse that is feeling good, spirited, slightly excitable, and perhaps a little strong, as on early mornings, cool days, or when not having been worked. (2) *see* FRESH CATTLE

fresh cattle Also known as fresh or unsettled; a cutting term; cattle that have not previously been used in cutting events or competitions.

fresh-catched coachman An antiquated driving term; a newly trained driver.

freshener A racing term; to lay off an overworked horse to restore his energy.

fresh fox A hunting term; any fox, other than the one originally pursued by the hounds (q.v.) at the beginning of the hunt; the hounds may switch to the line of a fresh fox of their own accord.

fresh line A hunting term; any new scent left by a fox or other prey.

Frideriksborg *see* FREDERIKSBORG

Friendship Stakes A stakes race (q.v.) held in the United States for two-year-old, Accredited Texas-Bred Thoroughbred horses; sponsored by the Texas Thoroughbred Breeder's Association.

Friesian Also known as Harddraver meaning "good trotter" in Dutch and spelled Frisian; one of the oldest breeds in Europe indigenous to the Netherlands; has a compact and strong build, a short, but well-arched neck, straight and short back, broad chest and loins, full and long mane and tail hair, feathered legs, large, strong feet, an exclusively black coat, very rarely presenting white markings on the forehead, and stands approximately 15 hands; the leg action is characteristically high; used for carriage driving, farming, and dressage.

Friesian Chaise Also known as a Sjees; a two-wheeled, horse-drawn vehicle of the gig (q.v.) type pulled by two Friesian (q.v.) horses harnessed on either side of a pole; traditionally, the traces and reins were made of white rope and the harness decorated with white trimmings.

Frisian *see* FRIESIAN

frock coat A knee-length coat worn by members of the hunt (q.v.); staff members will wear square-skirted frock coats while members of the field will wear round-skirted ones.

frog (1) The V-shaped, elastic-like portion of the rear underside of the hoof between the bars acts as buffer to absorb impact and prevent slipping; expands laterally when bearing the weight of the horse. (2) A driving term; the single loop which connects the reins when using the Hungarian style of driving.

frog cleft The natural depression located in the center of the widest pan of the frog (q.v.).

from the horse's mouth From the original source.

front (1) *see* BROWBAND (2) *see* FOREHAND

front boot A storage compartment located between the driving seat and the front axle of most horse-drawn coaches.

front foot *see* FOREFOOT

front leg SEE FORELEG

front runner A racing term; a horse who prefers to run in the front of the field (q.v.).

frost Refers to coat color pattern; white specks of hair on a dark body; one of six symmetrical coat color patte'ms of the Appaloosa (q.v.) recognized by the Appaloosa Horse Club (q.v.).

frost nails A special horseshoe nail designed to provide temporary hard surface traction.

frosty Also known as skunk tail; refers to coat color; white hairs at the base of the tail, in the mane, and down the back, over the pelvic bones, and other bony points such as the hocks.

frozen track A racing term; a frozen running surface.

frush *see* THRUSH

full *see* STALLION

fullblood *see* HOTBLOOD

full book Said of a stallion (q.v.) when bred to the maximum number of mares allowed by his manager in any given year.

full bridle *see* DOUBLE BRIDLE

full brothers *see* BROTHERS

full cheek The vertical portion of the bit exterior to the mouth and extending above and below the mouthpiece (q.v.) to which the bridle cheekpieces (q.v.) and reins are attached.

full-cheek snaffle A bit consisting of a straight or jointed mouthpiece fitted at either end with fixed rings, arms are attached to the rings above and below the mouthpiece on the mouth-side of the bit; the rings prevent the bit from running through the mouth of a horse if he runs sideways or refuses to turn; when attached to the cheekpiece of the bridle is considered a leverage bit, acts on the sides of the mouth, the lips, and the corners of the mouth; commonly used on jumpers.

full clip Also known as body clip or clipped right out; to remove the entire coat of the horse including the head and leg hair; the mane may be clipped or left full; used mainly on horses shown or worked through the winter and spring.

full collar An adjustable, oval-shaped piece of harness equipment placed over the head of the horse and fitted around the neck and against the shoulders to support the hames (q.v.) to which the traces are attached.

full cry A hunting term; said of the pack when each hound cries on the line of a fox (q.v.).

fullered shoe A horseshoe (q.v.) having a narrow groove cut into the ground-side surface of the horseshoe; the groove fills with dirt and thus provides traction and prevents suction.

fullering (1) To cut a groove into the ground side of barstock (q.v.) before it is shaped into a horseshoe to provide traction for the shoe and a seat for the nail heads. (2) A blacksmithing term; to spread metal by forcing a wedge or similar edge tool into in. (3) *see* CREASING. (4) A two-phase process in which horseshoe stock is worked prior to the nail groove being cut so that the web is the same width before and after fullering.

full halt A complete stop of the horse achieved by the total halting of the rider's hands and bracing of the back.

full hand A driving term; a method of holding the four reins of a team, all four reins are held in the left hand, the near lead rein passes over the index finger, the off lead rein over the second finger, the near wheel rein over the third finger, and the off wheel rein over the little finger.

full horse *see* STALLION

full mouth (1) Also known as a made mouth the mouth of a horse at five years of age, when it has grown all of its teeth (40 in the male and 36 in the female). (2) A horse six years of age or older.

full pass Also known as full travers; an advanced dressage movement performed on two tracks (q.v.) in which the horse moves laterally without forward movement; can only be executed from a standstill; the horse's outside legs step over those of the inside, the hoofmarks of the fore and hind legs marking two parallel lines; introduced for military purposes to allow the riders to correct their position between one another.

full pastern *see* PASTERN

full port Also known as a high port; the portion of a curb bit (q.v.) that curves upward in the center of the mouthpiece 1/2–1 1/2 inches; can be extremely severe; presses against the roof of the mouth while the mouthpiece on either side acts on the bars.

full safe *see* BOX KEEPER

full sisters *see* SISTERS

full stocking A leg marking (q.v.); consists of white which extends from the coronet (q.v.), along the cannon bone, and includes the knee; not accepted by some horse registries such as the American Quarter Horse Association (q.v.).

full travers *see* FULL PASS

fully headed Said of any fully enclosed horse-drawn carriage.

fully mouthed Said of a horse having a full set of permanent teeth (q.v.), 36 in female horses (female horses do not have canines) or 40 in the male; usually occurs by approximately five years of age.

Fulmer snaffle *see* AUSTRALIAN LOOSE RING CHEEK SNAFFLE

funeral horse *see* BLACK BRIGADE

funk Said of a temperamental horse who gets onto its toes, breaks into a sweat, or shows other signs of nervousness.

Furioso Also known as a Furioso-North Star, a warmblood descended from two English stallions, Furioso and North Star, imported to the Mezőhegyes Stud, Hungary in about 1840; both were put to Norman (q.v.) mares but, initially, the two lines were kept separate; in 1885, the Furioso and North Star lines were crossed to create the Furioso strain; stands 16 to 16.2 hands, has a brown, bay, or black coat with white markings the exception, a muscular body, straight back, sloping hindquarters, and low-set tail; exceptionally versatile, it is a good all-round riding horse which goes equally well under harness.

Furioso-North Star *see* FURIOSO

furious driving Reckless coach racing; a chargeable offense in 19th-century England, as for coach drivers of heavy wagons drawn by four and five horses, and wagoneers.

furious rabies Rabies (q.v.) infection in which the excitative phase is predominant, the affected horse will demonstrate the classical mad-dog syndrome in which the horse becomes irrational and viciously aggressive; the facial expression is anxious and alert, the pupils dilated, all fear and caution of natural enemies lost, paralysis absent, the horse may appear extremely agitated as evidenced by rolling as with colic (q.v.) or biting or striking viciously and self-inflicted wounds may result.

furlong Also known as eighth, in slang, as panel, and historically as furrow long; a racing term; a distance of one-eighth mile; a contraction of *furrow long*, that being the length of a plowed field.

furniture Also known as horse furniture; a late 19th and early 20th-century term for the metal buckles or mountings used on harnesses or saddlery as made from a variety of metals including solid nickel, solid brass, steel, or any metal plated with silver or brass; all the buckles used in a harness should be made of the same metal and design, and match that of the vehicle fittings and lamps.

furosemide A medication used in the treatment of bleeders (q.v.); acts as a diuretic (q.v.) and reduces pressure on the capillaries; commonly known by the trade name Lasix.

furrow long The length of a plowed field; became the unit of measure in horse race distances, that being a distance of 1/8 mile.

futchell A driving term; the longitudinal pieces of wood that support the splinter bar, pole (q.v), or shaft (q.v.) at one end and attach to the axle-tree bed and to the sway bar (q.v.) on the other.

futchell stay An iron plate used to strengthen a wooden futchell (q.v.) on a horse-drawn carriage.

futurity (1) A racing term; a stakes race for two-year-old horses nominated for the race before birth. (2) A cutting event for three- and four-year-old cutting horses.

fuzztail *see* MUSTANG

fuzztail running To herd and catch wild horses or mustangs (q.v.).

FWCF *see* FELLOW OF WORSHIPFUL COMPANY OF FARRIERS

G

gad (1) *see* SPUR. (2) A racing term; a jockey's whip.

GAG The acronym for glycosaminoglycan (q.v.).

gag (1) *see* GAG BIT. (2) *see* GAG CHEEK

gag bit Also known as gag; any snaffle bit (q.v.) equipped with full or half rings into which holes or slots are cut in the top and bottom and through which rolled leather or cord cheekpieces pass; the cheekpieces are attached to gag reins (q.v.) below the bit; when the rider draws down or back on the rein, the bit slides upward along the cheekpieces, putting pressure on the poll and corners of the mouth rather than the bars; a strong bit effective for hard-to-control horses.

gag bridle A bridle (q.v.) used in conjunction with a gag bit (q.v.); consists of rolled leather or cord cheekpieces (q.v.) which pass through holes at the top and bottom of the bit rings and attach to the reins.

gag cheek Also known as a gag or gag cheekpiece; that portion of a gag bit attached on either side to the mouthpiece and through which the cheekpieces pass.

gag rein Any rein used in conjunction with a gag bit (q.v.) and gag bridle (q.v.); attached to the bit cheekpieces (q.v.).

gag runner Also known as a bradoon hanger or bearing rein drop; a small leather strap with a dee-ring on one end, buckled to each side of the crown piece on the other, and through which the bearing rein passes before connecting to the pad.

gags The two cheekpieces (q.v.) of a gag bit (q.v.).

gait (1) Also spelled incorrectly gate; any of the natural or acquired paces of the horse characterized by a distinctive rhythmic movement of the feet and legs; the four basic gaits include the walk (q.v.), trot (q.v.), canter (q.v.), and gallop (q.v.). (2) Also known as at gait, horse gait, gaited out, stint, or gisted; an outdated British term; agistment (q.v.).

gaited *see* GAITED HORSE

gaited horse Also known as gaited, any horse having three natural gaits: walk, trot, canter, or walk, jog, and lope, and at least one acquired gait or one inherent to the breed such as the stepping pace (q.v.), rack (q.v.), or single-foot; common to such breeds as Tennessee Walkers (q.v.), Fox Trotters (q.v.), Paso Finos (q.v.) and Peruvian Pasos (q.v.).

gaited out *see* GAIT no. 2

Galiceño A pony breed originating in the 15th century in the Spanish region of Galicia from which the name derived; descended from the Portuguese Garrano (q.v.) transported to Mexico in the 16th century by the conquistadors; stands 12 to 13.2 hands, usually has a bay, black, or chestnut coat with piebald, skewbald, and albino colorations not accepted; has an average head, short and muscular neck, pronounced withers, short back, narrow chest, relatively straight shoulder, strong, long legs, and a small foot; is docile, intelligent, versatile, courageous, a naturally good jumper, and possessed of speed and endurance; since 1959, popularity has spread throughout the United States where it is a favored harness and children's riding and jumping pony.

Galician pony Also known as Asturcon or Asturian in Asturia; an ancient pony breed originating in the Spanish regions of Galicia, from which the name derived, and Asturia, particularly the Asturian mountains, located in Spain; is very hardy, docile, frugal, and adept at locating forage; has a brown or black coat which becomes notably longer, thicker, and lighter colored in winter; except for a star, white markings are not permitted; has a heavy head, small ears, long neck, a thin, flowing mane, low-set tail, and tough, short legs; used for riding and light draft; recent efforts have saved the breed from extinction.

gall (1) A sore and/or swelling on the hide of the horse caused by friction as by ill-fitting or dirty tack. (2) To put a sore and/or swelling on a horse, e.g., To gall a horse.

gallop Also known as run in western terminology, true gallop, or formerly as springing; a four-beat action, in which all four feet leave the ground simultaneously, once during each stride; the stride is more extended and the moment of suspension longer than that of the canter (q.v.); the fastest of the gaits.

gallop for wind To gallop (q.v.) a horse in circles to ascertain whether he is sound in the wind (q.v.).

galloping ground of western coaches An antiquated British term; a straight stretch of road between the English towns of Hounslow and Staines along which coachmen would let their teams stretch out.

gallop up To ask a horse to gallop (q.v.) by means of the rider's aids.

Galloway (1) An ancient English Pacer bred between Nithsdale and the Mull of Galloway, Scotland extinct since the 19th century; the favored mount of the border raiders and then of the Scottish drovers; stood between 13 and 14 hands, was hardy, sure-footed, possessed great stamina and strength, and was fast under saddle and harness; had a brown, black, or bay coat and was renowned for its hard blue hooves; thought to have been part of the running horse stock which contributed to sires of the 17th and 18th centuries from which descended the English Thoroughbred (q.v.); contributed to the gene pool of the Fell Pony (q.v.). (2) A specific height class in riding and hand show classes in which horses stand 14 to 14.2 hands; smaller horses are judged as ponies while the larger horses are judged as hacks; some shows run both large and small Galloway classes, the former being in the height range of 14 to 14.2 hands and the latter 14.2 to 15 hands.

galon (1) A Mexican term; a heavy or draft horse. (2) A contraction of get along, pronounced g'long; a voice command to urge working horses into their harness collars.

galop depart A dressage term; said of a horse when it transitions from a stop, halt, or walk into a canter.

galop faux *see* COUNTER CANTER

galop juste *see* TRUE CANTER

Galton, Francis (1822-1911) A geneticist who developed the theory of genetic inheritance now known as Galton's Law (q.v.).

Galton's Law The theory of genetic inheritance developed by Francis Galton (q.v.) in which inheritance is determined 1/4 by the sire (q.v.), 1/4 by the dam (q.v.), 1/16 by each of the grandparents, 1/64 by each of the great grandparents, and so on with each ancestor contributing just 1/4 as much to the total inheritance as the generation closer to the individual; incorrectly assumes that individual heredity is completely determined by the heredity of the ancestors; the relationship between ancestor and descendant is halved with each additional generation intervening between them; often used as a stamina index by Thoroughbred (q.v.) breeders.

Galvayne's Groove Also known as Galvayne's mark; a longitudinal, dark-colored groove in the upper third incisors (q.v.) appearing when the horse is about 10 years of age; begins at the gum line of the upper corner incisor at about 10 years, moving halfway down the tooth by 15 years, covering the entire length of the tooth by 20 years, seen in the bottom half of the tooth at 25 years, and disappearing at about 30 years; is less reliable than other indicators for estimating age in the young horse, but is quite valuable in placing the age of the older horse.

Galvayne's mark *see* GALVAYNE'S GROOVE

Galvayne, Sydney A renowned British horse breaker and trainer active in the late 1800s; his technique involved using the strength of the horse against itself.

Galway Blazers BLAZERS, THE

Gambler's Choice A timed jumping competition in which each fence is awarded a point value based on the difficulty of the jump; each competitor is free to select the jumps and the course he or she will ride to accumulate the most points; normally a fence cannot be rejumped more than once in the course; the rider obtaining the most points within the time allowed wins.

game Also known as wild game; wild animals, including birds and fish, that are hunted or taken for sport or profit.

gamete A mature sex cell.

gammon board Also known as backgammon board; a coaching term; the six roof-top seats on a horse-drawn coach, the hind-roof seat in particular; named for Mr. Gammon, who in 1788, initiated an Act of British Parliament which, for safety reasons, limited the number of roof-seat passengers.

gammy legged Also known as gummy; said of a horse whose legs, when stocked up (q.v.) due to strain or hard work, do not reveal the tendons below the knee and hock.

ganted up *see* TUCKED UP

gap A racing term; an opening in the outside rail where horses enter and leave the race track (q.v.).

garden-seat bus A horse-drawn bus which succeeded the knifeboard bus (q.v.) used in London, England prior to replacement by the automobile; passengers were seated outside on double, forward-facing seats with a central gangway.

garden spot A harness racing term; a horse racing in second position on the rail (q.v.).

Gardiens The herdsmen of southern France who ride the Camargue Pony (q.v.) and are responsible for herding the famous black bulls of the region.

Garrano Also known as Minho; a pony breed originating in the Portuguese regions of Minho and Tras os Montes, located along the boarder with Spain; an ancient breed dating to the Paleolithic era, it has remained virtually unaltered in appearance for thousands of years; received selected infusions of Arab (q.v.) blood, although Arab characteristics are noticeably absent; influential in the development of the Andalusian (q.v.) and, in the 16th century, the Galiceño (q.v.); is lightly built, strong, hardy, sure-footed, and stands 10 to 12 hands; almost always chestnut in color and has a luxuriant mane and tail; used for packing, light agricultural work, riding, and trotting races.

Garrison finish A racing term; a victory from a come-from-behind horse; named for Snapper Garrison who commonly finished in such a fashion.

Garron Also known as Mainland Pony; a type of Highland Pony (q.v.) standing up to 14.2 hands; from the Gaelic, gearran, meaning gelding (q.v.).

garry *see* GHARRY

garter Also known as jodhpur strap; a narrow leather strap with a buckle on one end passed through a small loop attached to the top rear seam of a field or dress riding boot; historically used to hold the breeches constant in the boot by passing through small loops sewn onto the breeches at the front and rear, between the second and third buttons; no longer common due to the use of elasticized breech materials, but used as an appointment of taste; buckled on the outside of the leg.

gas *see* FLATULENCE

Gascoigne, Chien de A blue-mottled hound; believed to be the oldest strain of hunting hound indigenous to France.

gaskin Also known as second thigh or calf; that part of the hind leg above the point of the hock (q.v.).

gastrodiscus aegyptiacus A species of fluke (q.v.) found in the large intestine of the horse, but also of pigs and warthogs; infection is most common in the dry season because snails, the intermediate host, congregate around permanent water where the most palatable grazing also occurs; symptoms include bloody diarrhea and rapid weight loss.

gastrointestinal Relating to or affecting the stomach and intestines.

gastrointestinal tract Also known as GI tract; the tract consisting of the stomach and intestines.

Gastrophilus haemorrhoidalis One of three types of bot fly (q.v.), the other two being Gastrophilus intestinalis (q.v.) and Gastrophilus nasalis (q.v.); a small fly with a yellow and black banded body which lays its yellow and black eggs on the head hairs of the horse in the late summer and autumn in temperate climates and during spring, summer, and autumn in warmer climates; has a life cycle similar to Gastrophilus intestinalis (q.v.), but the eggs hatch spontaneously and then enter the horse's mouth where they spend approximately one month followed by eight months in the stomach; found occasionally in all countries, but is most common in Russia and parts of Asia.

Gastrophilus intestinalis One of three

types of bot fly (q.v.), the other two being *Gastrophilus haemorrhoidalis* (q.v.) and *Gastrophilus nasalis* (q.v.); the most common of the bots (q.v.), it is found in most horses; a small fly with a yellow and dark banded body, the female of which attaches her eggs to the hairs on the forelegs, shoulders, neck, and mane of the horse in the late summer and autumn in temperate climates and during spring, summer, and autumn in warmer climates; first-stage larvae are stimulated to hatch by moisture, warmth, and friction of the horse's tongue and lips when biting itself; the hatched larvae burrow into the soft tissues of the tongue and gums around the molar teeth where they remain for about one month before they are swallowed; the second- and third-stage larvae then attach to the stomach wall where they spend approximately nine months before they are passed in the feces where they develop for one month to the adult stage.

Gastrophilus nasalis One of three types of bot fly (q.v.), the other two being *Gastrophilus intestinalis* (q.v.) and *Gastrophilus haemorrhoidalis* (q.v.); a small yellow fly with a yellow and dark banded body of which the female attaches her eggs to the hairs on the head and face of the horse in the late summer and autumn in temperate climates and during spring, summer, and autumn in warmer climates; has a life cycle similar to Gastrophilus intestinalis (q.v.), but the eggs hatch spontaneously and then enter the horse's nasal cavity where they spend approximately one month followed by eight months in the stomach.

gate (1) A single vertical jumping obstacle (q.v.) consisting of spaced, horizontal slats supported by standards (q.v.). (2) *see* STARTING GATE. (3) To excuse a horse from a show competition for refusal in an over fence class, going off course, or improper or dangerous behavior of either the horse or exhibitor or both based on the rules and opinion of the judge. (4) *see* GAIT

gateado *see* DUN

gate card A racing term; a card issued by the starter which verifies that a horse is correctly schooled in starting gate procedures; required of all competing horses.

Gato One of two Criollo (q.v.) horses ridden by Aimé Tschiffely (q.v.) in his famous two and one half year, 10,000 mile (16,000 km) ride from Buenos Aires, Argentina to Wash-

ington DC, USA; died at the age of 36.

Gaucho A South American cowboy, thought by many to be world's finest roughrider (q.v.).

gay An antiquated term; a horse who carries his head and tail well and has a free and airy walk.

Gayoe *see* GAYOL

Gayol Also spelled Gayoe; a pony breed native to the Gayol Hills, Northern Sumatra, Indonesia from which the breed name derived; is less lively, heavier and has shorter and thicker legs than the Batak (q.v.).

gear (1) The equipment and accessories used in harness driving, excluding the vehicle, and in polo, excluding the bridle and saddle. (2) *see* CARRIAGE

gee Also known as heck; a voice command used on agricultural horses to indicate a turn to the right.

geld To castrate (q.v.); from the Scandinavian geld meaning barren.

Gelderland Also known as Gelderlander; a horse breed developed in the Gelderland Province of the Netherlands by crossing native mares with Andalusian (q.v.), Neapolitan, Norman (q.v.), and Norfolk Roadster (q.v.) stallions; Anglo-Norman (q.v.), Oldenburg (q.v.), and Hackney (q.v.) blood was introduced in the 19th century and English Thoroughbred (q.v.) in the 20th century; is elegant, stands 15.2 to 16 hands, has a chestnut, bay, black, or gray coat, commonly has white markings, a long and rather flat head, crested neck, high-set tail, short-coupled body, and a high-stepping trot; used for light draft, driving, riding for leisure, and jumping.

Gelderlander *see* GELDERLAND

gelding (1) A castrated (q.v.) male horse which cannot sire offspring; from the Scandinavian geld meaning barren. (2) *see* CASTRATE

gelding donkey Also known as john; a castrated ass (q.v.), one incapable of siring offspring.

Gemini Cart A two-wheeled, horse-drawn vehicle used in Switzerland to transport passengers over the Gemini Pass for which it is named; passengers traveled facing the rear on a narrow single seat fitted between the wheels; had a wind-on brake attached to the near side (q.v.) shaft (q.v.).

gene The element or unit of a chromosome which carries and transfers an inherited characteristic from parent to offspring, and determines the development of some particular character or trait in the offspring.

gene dominant A gene (q.v.) that will produce a trait in the offspring no matter what the other genes are.

gene lethal A gene (q.v.) resulting in a condition that may lead to death at or shortly after birth, or a foal with a condition which will affect its health or use in the long term.

general anesthesia An artificially produced, body-wide state of insensibility, especially to the sense of pain, achieved by putting the patient into a state of conscious sleep as with drugs.

general anesthetic Any substance that has the power to deprive feeling or sensation to the body by putting the patient into a conscious sleep.

general purpose saddle *see* ALL PURPOSE SADDLE

general service wagon Also known by the acronym GS wagon; an open, horse-drawn vehicle with a container back and a single seat for the driver used to convey goods; pulled by a pair or team on a long rein either coachman or postillion (q.v.) driven; resembled an open lorry.

General Stud Book Also known by the acronym GSB; the main stud book (q.v.) for a horse breed, originally as for Thoroughbreds (q.v.).

gene recessive A gene (q.v.) carried by both parents effective in transferring a trait to the offspring.

generous Said of a horse who gives his best when performing in a race or other competition.

genet *see* JENNET

genetics The science of heredity and the evolutionary similarities and differences of related organisms, as produced by the interaction of the genes; the inherited features and characteristics of an organism or group or type of organisms.

genotype selection Selection of breeding stock based upon the genetic makeup of the animals rather than appearance.

genotyping Verification of parentage using DNA (q.v.) testing of nasal mucous, hair, blood, etc.; considered superior to blood-typing (q.v.).

gentlemen, I leave you here An antiquated British coaching phrase; a signal from the mail coachman to his passengers to provide a monetary tip.

gentleman jockey A racing term; an amateur rider, generally in a steeplechase.

gentleman rider *see* AMATEUR

genu *see* STIFLE

George IV *see* PARK PHAETON

Géricault, Théodore (1791–1824) A noted artist of equestrian scenes.

German Coldblood *see* RHINELAND HEAVY DRAFT

German martingale An auxiliary rein consisting of two straps of leather attached to a ring on the girth (q.v.) which passes between the forelegs, one strap running from girth through the left bit ring and fastened to the left rein and the other passing through the right bit ring and connecting to the right rein; has similar action to a draw rein (q.v.); downward pressure on the mouth occurs when the horse raises its head.

German posting A method of controlling a four-horse hitch using a single postillion (q.v.); the near leader (q.v.) was rein controlled, while the off leader was not; speed of the team was maintained by the postillion using voice commands and a long whip.

German silver Also known as albata or white brass; a usually white alloy of copper, zinc, and nickel, used for making some ornamental tack and bits.

German wagon A horse-drawn vehicle introduced in Great Britain in the 1760s; a German version of the barouche (q.v.); had full undergear and lower panels, but no upper panels, a half-hood which covered the rear seat only, and a raised box seat for the driver located well above the body work.

germinal In the earliest stage of development.

germ plasm Germ cells and their precursors which bear hereditary characteristics.

gestation *see* GESTATION PERIOD

gestation period Also known as gestation; the term of the pregnancy from the time of conception to birth (approximately 335 days or 11 months); the term for colts is generally a few days longer than for fillies.

get Also known as progeny or offspring; the offspring of a stallion, e.g., a foal is the get of a stallion and the produce (q.v.) of a mare; may refer to one or more progeny (q.v.).

get a bite *see* GET HANGED

getaway day A racing term; the last day of a race meeting (q.v.).

get down A cutting horse term; the action of the horse lowering itself down to the level of the cow being worked.

get hanged Also known as get a bite; a driving term; said of the lash or thong of a team whip when it becomes caught in a part of the harness (q.v.) or on the bars (q.v.).

get into A racing term; said of a jockey, to whip a horse.

get into the ground Also known as getting down into the ground; a cutting and reining term; said of a horse who executes a good sliding stop (q.v.), setting deep onto his haunches.

getting down into the ground *see* GET INTO THE GROUND

get to the heads A hunting term; said of the whippers-in (q.v.), who, in an attempt to stop rioting (q.v.) hounds (q.v.), runs ahead and turns them rather than give chase.

get under Also known as get underneath; a jumping term; said of a horse who takes off too near to the jump.

get underneath *see* GET UNDER

get-up Also known as giddap; a voice command to go or move forward and when repeated, to increase speed.

get wood on it A polo term; to make contact with the polo ball using the mallet (q.v.).

Gharry Also spelt garry; (1) An open, four-wheeled carriage drawn by a single horse and driven from an elevated seat; frequently used as a cab or sight-seeing vehicle in parts of India and the Middle East. (2) A large, fully-headed or enclosed, oblong public carriage used by natives throughout India; driven from a roof seat; usually dead axle and designed without windows.

giddap *see* GET-UP

Gidran *see* GIDRAN ARABIAN

Gidran Arabian Also known as a Gidran or Hungarian Anglo-Arab; a horse breed developed in Hungary in 1816; the present-day breed results from crossings with Thoroughbred (q.v.) and Arab (q.v.); now of two types: Middle European and Southern and Eastern European; the Middle European Gidran (q.v.) is a stouter horse than the Southern and is often used in harness; the Southern and Eastern European Gidran (q.v.) is lighter and is an all-purpose competition horse; stands 16.1 to 17 hands, has Arab characteristics, and usually has a chestnut coat, although bay and black do occur; used for riding, light draft and is particularly suited to jumping; its name derived from the stallion Gidran, an Arab (q.v.) of the Siglavy strain.

gig (1) Historically, a two-wheeled passenger vehicle used in country districts, but later adapted for town driving; usually owner driven and noted for the ease with which it could be turned in a confined space; all types were open in the front, enclosed at the back, and had ample luggage space below the cross-seat; drawn by a single horse or pair; varieties include bagman's gig (q.v.), chairback gig (q.v.), Dennett gig (q.v.). whiskey gig (q.v.), Liverpool gig (q.v.), rib back gig (q.v.), stanhope gig (q.v.), skeleton gig (q.v.), and seven spring gig (q.v.). (2) *see* SULKY no. 1

gimp Slang; a lame or limping horse.

gimpy Slang; said of a lame (q.v.) or limping horse.

ginger *see* GINGERING

gingering Also known as ginger or figging; to insert ginger or another irritant such as cayenne pepper, into the anus of a horse, specifically Saddlebreds (q.v.), Morgans (q.v.), and Arabs (q.v.), although it is illegal in the latter breed, to achieve a high tail carriage; the irritation of the ginger causes the horse to lift its tail; considered cruelty.

gin horse A horse used for draft work and around mills.

ginney *see* GUINEA

girl *see* GROOM no. 2

girth (1) Also known as a cinch or belly band; a 3 to 4 inch (7.5-10 cm) wide strap that holds the saddle in place on the back of the horse and prevents it from slipping sideways and to some extent forward; connects the two sides of the saddle underneath the belly of the horse just behind the front legs/shoulder; may be made of leather, cotton, wool, or synthetic materials. (2) *see* HEART GIRTH

girthed Said of a saddle or other tack held in place by a girth (q.v.).

girth gall A gall (q.v.) that develops in the belly area behind the elbow of the horse where the girth (q.v.) generally passes; caused by dirty, stiff, or badly fitting girths, as those too tight or too loose; similar to a blister; horses with thin, sensitive skin are most prone.

girth-place The place on the belly of the horse just behind the forelegs, marked by a depression in the underline, where the girth (q.v.) is fitted.

girth safes Flat, single layered pieces of leather, 3 to 4 inches (7.5–10cm) in width with horizontal slots cut into them and through which the girth straps (q.v.) pass; used to protect the saddle flap from being rubbed by the girth buckles and to smooth out the buckle bulge under the rider's legs.

girth shy *see* CINCH BOUND

girth straps Narrow pieces of leather attached vertically to the English saddle tree on both sides to which the girth buckles are attached when saddling the horse; there are usually three straps on each side of the saddle, although lightweight saddles may have only one.

girth up To tighten the girth (q.v.) on a horse.

girth weight tape A measuring tape calibrated in pounds (kg) rather than inches (cm) which is placed around the girth (q.v.) of the horse to measure his weight; the margin of error may be as much as 5 percent.

gisted *see* GAIT no. 2

GI tract *see* GASTROINTESTINAL TRACT

give and take of the reins Said of the rider; to relax and tighten the grip of the fingers on the reins to remove and re-apply bit pressure on the bars of the horse's mouth to encourage him to accept the bit (q.v.).

giving tongue *see* GIVE TONGUE

give tongue Also known as giving tongue, throw tongue or throw his tongue; a hunting term; said of a hound (q.v.) when he bays or barks on the line of (q.v.) the quarry.

give with the hands Said of the rider; to relax the grip of the fingers on the reins and thus release bit pressure on the bars of the horse's mouth.

glanders Also known as farcy; a contagious and usually fatal disease caused by *Pseudomonas mallei*, characterized by a discharge from the eyes and nose and ulcerating nodules that occur most commonly in the upper respiratory tract, lungs, and on the skin; one of the world's oldest diseases, it has been largely eliminated from horse populations today; may be transmitted to man.

Glass Coach A horse-drawn vehicle of the coach (q.v.) type introduced in the 17th century, so named because the panels above the elbow line were made of glass.

glass eye *see* WALL EYE

gleet *see* NASAL GLEET

Glover, Webb, & Liversidge Ltd. A horse-drawn coach-building firm established in 1720 in London, England.

glucose One of the simple sugars formed by the hydrolysis of complete carbohydrates; the form in which carbohydrates (q.v.) are assimilated in the body.

glucose concentration A blood test performed to measure blood sugar levels.

glue on shoe A plastic horseshoe (q.v.) used on horses with reconstructed hooves, shelly feet, and fractured coffin bones; has clip-like plastic extensions on the inside and outside rims which project upwards towards the coronary band (q.v.) and a thin aluminum plate set inside the plastic rim; attached to the hoof with epoxy or space-age adhesive; on worked horses, generally lasts no longer than three to four weeks.

gluteal muscles Any of three large muscles of the rump consisting of the gluteus superficialis, gluteus medius, and gluteus profundus that extend the hip and push the body forward.

glycosaminoglycan Also known by the acronym GAG; one of the substances found in cartilage (q.v.) and in the viscous synovial fluid surrounding joints; there are nine in total of which three are chondroitin sulfates (q.v.); believed that ingested chondroitin sulfates will migrate to the joints where they inhibit destructive enzymes and contribute to cartilage repair.

goal (1) A polo term; the area, space, or object into which polo players attempt to hit the ball. (2) The act of scoring points by placing a ball in a designated area, space, or object; in the game of polo, a goal is considered scored regardless of whether a horse or a mallet hits the ball through the goal posts; to equalize wind and turf conditions, the teams change sides after each goal is scored. (3) A polo term; the value of a player to the team, not the number of goals a player is expected to score; a player may be ranked as a high-, medium-, intermediate-, or low-goal player.

goal handicap *see* POLO HANDICAP

goal posts The vertical poles located in pairs on the short ends of a polo field which define the goal (q.v.); in polo, set 8 yards (7 m) apart and should be a minimum of 10 feet (3 m) high; has no cross piece connecting the posts and are made to collapse on impact; a goal is considered to be scored if the ball passes between the posts or what would constitute the upward prolongation of such.

goal rating *see* POLO HANDICAP

goat knees *see* FORWARD DEVIATION OF THE CARPAL JOINTS

goat snatching The national game of Uzbekistan in which a mounted man, traveling at a gallop, carries a goat while others try to take it from him; played on the Karabair (q.v.), the breed indigenous to the area.

go cart A horse-drawn vehicle of the cabriolet (q.v.) type used in America; has two wheels and a cranked axle.

Godolphin Arab Also known as the Godolphin Barb; one of three Arab (q.v.) foundation sires of the English Thoroughbred (q.v.) to which all Thoroughbreds (q.v.) in the world today trace their ancestry in direct male line; a purebred Kehilan Arabian imported to England in 1728 by Mr. Edward Coke; upon Mr. Coke's death, was bought by the Earl of Godolphin for whom he was named; stood just under 15 hands, had a bay coat, and lop ears; died in 1753.

Godolphin Barb *see* GODOLPHIN ARAB

goes well into the bridle Also known as bridles well; said of a horse who accepts the bit without pulling.

going Said of the condition of a track or other surface over which a horse is expected to travel, e.g., The going was good, bad, wet, etc.

going amiss A racing term; said of a mare in training who comes into season at the time she is due to race.

going away A racing term; said of a horse who wins a race while increasing the lead.

going big A Standardbred harness racing term; said of a driver who goes as fast as possible at the beginning of the race.

going short Also known as short; said of a horse having a short, uncertain gait (q.v.); may indicate lameness or a tendency to such.

going under the wire An obsolete racing term; said of a horse who wins a race, as the finish line was originally marked by a wire which crossed the track.

go into the cow A cutting term; said of a horse who, when prompted by the rider, steps forward up to the cow.

goiter A morbid enlargement of the thyroid gland, forming a protuberance on the side or front part of the neck; may be fatal if not treated and is transmittable to unborn foals invivo; caused by dietary iodine excess or deficiency.

go large A dressage term; said of the rider, to come off the circle and proceed around the arena on the rail.

golden age of coaching The period between 1815 and 1840 during which horse-drawn mail and stage coaches reached the height of popularity.

golden age of fox hunting A hunting term; the period between 1820 and 1890 regarded as the premier fox-hunting period during which time the great estates in Britain were still intact, motorways and cars were nonexistent, and there were no fumes, fertilizers, etc. to confuse the scent.

golden age of racing A racing term; the 40-year period following the American Civil War during which horse racing in America came of age.

golden dun Also known as creamy dun; refers to coat color; a type of dun (q.v.) having yellow coat hairs mixed with white.

golden horse *see* PALOMINO

golden horse of the West *see* PALOMINO

Golden Horse Society, The An organization founded in Britain in 1947 to maintain the Palomino (q.v.) breed registry and promote interest in the breed.

Gold State Coach A custom-made, horse-drawn vehicle of the coach (q.v.) type built in 1953 for the coronation procession of Queen Elizabeth II of England.

gonad The male or female reproductive gland that produces gametes, sperm, or ovum (q.v.); a testes (q.v.) or ovary (q.v.).

Gondola of London *see* HANSOM CAB

gone away A hunting term; a call announced by the huntsman indicating the fox has left his covert (q.v.).

gone in the wind Said of a horse who has difficulty breathing normally or is unsound in the wind, due to whistling (q.v.), roaring (q.v.), or broken wind (q.v.) etc.

gone to ground Also known as go to ground; a hunting term; said of a fox or other prey who has taken refuge from the chase in the ground, drain, or other shelter.

gonitis Inflammation of the stifle joint; may be precipitated by a number of different causes, namely: persistent upward fixation of the patella (q.v.), injuries to the medial or lateral collateral ligaments of the joint or the cruciate ligaments of the menisci, erosions of the articular cartilage, and bacterial infection of the joint due to puncture wounds (q.v.); signs are variable depending on the cause and extent of the physiological changes and may include supporting- and swinging-leg lameness, the shortened forward flight of the leg, a flexed fetlock in which only the toe of the hoof rests on the ground when resting, or the leg may be carried in a flexed position.

Gooch Wagon An elegant, lightweight, under-cut, four-wire-wheeled, single-horse vehicle of the spider phaeton (q.v.) type; had a small rumble seat in the rear for a groom; designed by Mr. Vivian Gooch after whom it was named.

good bone Said of a horse; to have good bone structure which is indicative of weight-bearing ability and ruggedness; varies from breed to breed.

good bottom A racing term; a wet or dry track that is firm under the cushion (q.v.).

good cow A cutting horse term; a cow who acknowledges the horse when cut from the herd, but does not panic and bolt.

good cow sense *see* COW SMART

good curl A roping term; a well thrown lariat (q.v.) or rope.

good doer Also known as doer; said of a horse who readily eats his ration (q.v.) and is not a picky eater; may be prone to overeating.

good front *see* GOOD REIN

good hack A horse who is quiet to ride, alert, and sound in the wind (q.v.).

good hands Said of a rider whose hands are both light and sensitive on the rein and therefore on the mouth of the horse.

good head A hunting term; said of hounds who hunt fast on a wide front.

good keeper *see* EASY KEEPER

good mouth (1) Said of a horse having a soft and sensitive mouth who is responsive to the action of the bit. (2) A horse 6 -10 years of age.

good nick An antiquated term; a horse in good physical condition.

good night A hunting term; a salutation extended from the hunters to the Master at the end of a hunting day, however early that may be.

good nose Said of hay (q.v.) that smells sweet; a quality determining factor.

good outlook *see* GOOD REIN

good rein Also known as good front or good outlook; said of a horse who is well muscled in the front end and has a balanced neck on his body.

good roof Also known as a good top; an antiquated term; a good top line (q.v.).

good top *see* GOOD ROOF

good track A racing term; a racetrack that is almost a fast track (q.v.) or a turf track that is slightly softer than a firm track (q.v.).

go off feed Said of a horse who is not eating normally, as due to illness, stress, etc.

go on A racing term; said of a horse who wins at a new, longer distance.

goose-rumped Also known as drooping quarters or jumping rump; said of a horse having a short, steep croup (q.v.) that narrows at the point of the buttocks; caused by an elevation of the backbone or a lack of muscle over the top of the hindquarters.

goose stepping *see* FALSE EXTENSION

go-round *see* ROUND

Gorst Gig A horse-drawn, hooded vehicle of the gig (q.v.) type having a boot (q.v.) under the seat; hung on sideways-elliptical springs.

go short Said of a lame horse or one with restricted forward movement which shortens the stride.

Gotland Also known as Swedish Gotland, Forest Pony, or Skogsruss; one of the world's oldest and smallest horse breeds, having existed for more than 10,000 years on the Swedish island of Gotland located in the Baltic Sea from which the name derived; descended from the Tarpan (q.v.); historically served as a cavalry mount for the Goths, the Swedish Vikings, and the Swedish warrior kings; highly prized for its speed, maneuverability, endurance, and easy-keeper (q.v.) qualities; facing the extinction of the breed in the 1880s due to loss of habitat, the Swedish government placed it under strict government protection and allowed the limited introduction of Oriental blood to ensure a strong genetic base; again due to poaching resulting from World War I food shortages in the 1900s, were hunted near extinction; although still considered a rare breed, world-wide numbers are on the increase; weighs an average of 600–650 pounds (272–295 kg), stands 12 to 14 hands, and has a sturdy build somewhat more stocky than a Hackney (q.v.) and larger than a Shetland (q.v.); is long-lived, healthy, very resilient, loves water and has an intelligent, lively, and gentle temperament; all solid coat colors occur with black, bay, buckskin, and sorrel most common; most have a dorsal stripe (q.v.) and very few white markings such as a star (q.v.) or coronet (q.v.), but never spots or patches; has a broad forehead, sometimes a dished profile, wide-set eyes, muscular and crested neck, strong back, rounded croup, and a full mane and tail with light fetlock feathering (q.v.); used by both adults and children for pleasure riding, driving, and jumping; are bloodtyped and registered in the United States with the Gotland Horse Registry, administered by the American Livestock Breeds Conservancy (q.v.).

go to ground *See* GONE TO GROUND

go to the horn *See* DALLY

gouge Said of the rider; to make a quick, hard jab with a spur.

Governess car *see* GOVERNESS CART

Governess cart Also known as Avondale in North America, Digby in Northumberland or jingle in Somerset, England, governess car, tub cart, or tub car; a small, two-wheeled, pony- or donkey-drawn vehicle with a rounded or tub shape introduced around 1880; entered through an outward opening rear door, had sideways seating that followed the interior perimeter of a foot well, two midway driving positions, one on each side of the vehicle, with scooped-out wall portions to provide the driver room to twist his body for better control of the reins, and stained and grained body work; some were designed with cane basket-work and hoods; mounted on cranked axles hung with sideways-elliptical springs; designed to carry a governess and the children in her charge; often had considerable sideways motion.

grab a quarter *see* OVERREACH

grabbing slack *see* PULLING SLACK

grabbin' the apple *see* PULLING LEATHER

Grackle *see* GRACKLE NOSEBAND

Grackle noseband Also known as figure eight, cross noseband, Mexican noseband, grackle, and spelled grakle noseband; a nose-band having its own headstall and consisting of two straps which cross over the bridge of the nose diagonally at a point nearer the eyes than the nostrils; one passes in front of the bit and buckles in the curb groove, while the other passes above and behind the bit buckling behind the jaw approximately 2 inches (5 cm) below the cheek bones; the center part at the cross-over point rests on the nose bone rather than on the cartilage below it; used to prevent the horse from crossing its jaws and/or open-ing its mouth; cannot be used in dressage competitions, but may be used in jumping or the dressage phase of eventing competitions; named for the horse Grackle who wore this type of noseband when he won the British Grand National in 1931.

grade (1) *see* GRADE HORSE. (2) A show jumping term; a level of competition in which the weakest competition occurs at the lowest grade.

Grade I A racing term; the highest of three levels of premiere stakes races (q.v.) held in the United States each carrying a minimum purse of $50,000 (US); consists of all top races such as the Kentucky Derby (q.v.); always designated by a Roman numeral.

Grade II A racing term; the middle of three levels of premiere stakes races (q.v.) held in the United States, each carrying a minimum purse of $50,000 (US); consists of all middle-caliber races based on the quality of the horses competing and as designated by a panel of racing industry experts; always designated by a Roman numeral.

Grade III A racing term; the lowest of three levels of premiere stakes races (q.v.) held in the United States, each carrying a minimum purse of $50,000 (US); consists of all third best races as based on the quality of the horses competing and as designated by a panel of racing industry experts; always designated by a Roman numeral.

grade horse (1) Also known as grade; a horse who does not carry enough blood of any specific breed to meet breed registration requirements, but who shows some, although not all, specific breed characteristics; "grade" may be suffixed to the name of any breed, e.g., grade Hackney (q.v.). (2) A horse who has one registered or pure blood (q.v.) parent and the other parent of mixed or unknown breeding.

graded race Also known incorrectly as group race (q.v.) or pattern race; a racing term; a premiere stakes race held in a country as des-ignated by a panel of racing industry experts; of a higher class than non-graded stakes, carry a minimum purse of $50,000, and eligibility cannot be restricted in any way other than by sex or age; in the United States, constitute 15 percent of all stakes races and are divided into grades designated by Roman numerals: Grade I (q.v.), Grade II (q.v.), and Grade III (q.v.) as based on the quality of the competing horses; established at the request of European authori-ties in 1973 to classify select races in North America.

graduate (1) A racing term; a horse or jockey who wins his first race. (2) A racing term; a horse who has moved up into allowance, stakes, or handicap racing.

graduated-side stirrup *see* HUNTING STIRRUP

grain A single fruit or seed of a food plant or cereal grass such as wheat, oats, barley, and corn.

grain founder Also known as grain overloading; founder (q.v.) caused by the ingestion of excessive amounts of carbohydrate as found in grain which results in inflammation of the sensitive laminae (q.v.) of the hoof.

grainger martingale An auxiliary, adjustable strap attached on one end between the forelegs to the girth (q.v.) that splits into two branches and attaches to its own noseband positioned below the normal cavesson noseband (q.v.) position; used to prevent the horse from throwing up its head; may be fitted with a neck strap to keep it in place; is more severe than the standing martingale (q.v.).

grain overloading *see* GRAIN FOUNDER

grain sorghum *see* SORGHUM

grakle noseband *see* GRACKLE NOSEBAND

gram-negative bacteria Families of bacteria that do not stain blue in laboratory examination; used to help identify specific bacterial causes of infection.

Grand Breton *see* FAST HEAVY DRAUGHT BRETON

grandam Also known as second dam; the mother of a horse's dam unless otherwise specified, as in paternal grandam (q.v.).

Grand Circuit A program of harness racing on the major tracks common around the turn of the 19th century.

Grand Liverpool Steeplechase *see* THE GRAND LIVERPOOL STEEPLECHASE

Grand National, The *see* GRAND NATIONAL STEEPLECHASE

Grand National Steeplechase Also known as The Grand National, The National, and previously as The Liverpool Steeplechase; a handicap steeplechase (q.v.) conducted over the 4 mile, 856 yard (7.22 km) Aintree (q.v.) race course located in Liverpool, England since 1839; the course has 30 fences and a water jump 15 feet (4.5 m) wide.

Grand Pardubice A grueling steeplechase (q.v.) held annually in Czechoslovakia on the second Sunday in October since 1874; a 4-1/2 mile (7.2 km) course over ploughed fields with 31 fences, the most difficult of which is the 16 foot 5 inch (5 m) wide Texas ditch fronted by a natural fence 5 feet (1.5 m) high and 5 feet (1.5 m) wide.

grandsire The father of a horse's sire unless otherwise specified, as in maternal grandsire (q.v.).

granulated tissue Small, rounded masses of tissue, composed of capillaries and connective tissue cells which grow outward from the body to fill a wound opening.

grapes Characteristic fungal growth developing as a result of scratches (q.v.).

grass Any plant of the family Gramineae characterized by jointed stems, sheathing leaves, and flower spikelets upon which grazing animals pasture; when harvested and dried, is fed as grass hay (q.v.).

grass belly *see* HAY BELLY

grass burner *see* GRASS CUTTER

grass clippings The vegetative material resulting from grass mowing operations; sometimes used as a food source; crude protein levels may vary widely, with levels of 25 to 30 percent not uncommon.

grass cutter Also known as grass burner; a polo term; said of a polo ball hit with such force by the polo player (q.v.) that it travels at a higher speed than the average shot, thus grazing the surface of the grass field.

grass founder Founder (q.v.) caused by the ingestion of excessive amounts of protein found in lush pastures; results in inflammation of the sensitive laminae of the hoof; occurs most often in horses turned out to pasture following a prolonged period of feed on cured grasses, as during the winter.

grass hay Cut and dried grasses (q.v.) and grains (q.v.); are high in fiber, but have relatively low nutritional content and are generally lower in protein than legume hays (q.v.), the digestible protein content being less than 5 percent; may be fed freely with little likelihood of overfeeding, colic (q.v.), or founder (q.v.) resulting; commonly mixed with legume hays to create a hay of moderate protein content.

grass pen A hunting term; an area where bitches in season (q.v.) are confined.

grass sickness Also known as grass tetany, equine grass sickness, or equine dysautonomia; an 85 to 90 percent fatal condition of unknown origins involving a progressive degeneration of the nerves that control gut function; results in a drastic slowdown of the digestive system; victims waste away and eventually die of dehydration or malnutrition; characterized by colic-like symptoms including abdominal pain, distention, and in severe cases, rupture, loss of the ability to swallow, drooling, depression, restlessness, elevated pulse rate, patchy sweating, involuntary movement of the fine muscles over the shoulders and flanks, and food discharge from the nostrils; occurs at any age after weaning and at any time throughout the year, but the peak incidence is in spring in two- to seven-year-old horses; generally associated with horses kept solely at grass, although the condition has been reported in housed stock; death occurs within 24 hours (preacute), four days (acute), and 21 days (subacute), while chronic cases may continue for weeks or months; confirmation of grass sickness currently can be made only through a postmortem examination of the nerve cells, although a new technique is under development that uses a surgical biopsy of the small intestine to check for nerve cell damage; no diagnostic test is available; reported in Europe, Australia, Japan, England, Scotland, and the United States.

grass slip A racing term; written permission granted by the racetrack authorities to a jockey, trainer, or owner to exercise a horse on the turf course.

grass tetany *see* GRASS SICKNESS

grass yard A British hunting term; a wire-enclosed paddock where hounds and puppies may be left to exercise and to air themselves.

gravel A lay term; the supposed migration of a piece of gravel from the white line (q.v.)

towards the coronet band (q.v.); actually, a hole in the white line permits infection to invade the sensitive structures of the foot with resulting pus and gas creating intense pain; when left untreated, and because there is no drainage, gas and pus vent at the top of the coronary band; lameness occurs before drainage.

gray (1) Also spelled grey; refers to coat color; a pattern of white hairs mixed with colored body and point hairs; gray horses are born colored and become progressively more white with each shedding; the mane and tail may either remain dark or go white before the coat grays; dappling (q.v.) is common and the skin is always pigmented; graying tends to mask patterns of white on the horse as it ages. (2) Also known as graying; refers to coat color; said of the coat; to change from any color to gray.

gray fox Also known as *Urocyon cineroargenteus*, a carnivorous mammal of the dog family having a pointed muzzle, erect ears, long bushy tail, gray coat, which is noted for its cunning and alertness; native to the United States and Canada; the primary quarry of foxhounds; usually runs in circles.

graying *see* GRAY no. 2

gray overo Also known as azulejo (q.v.) in Argentina; refers to coat color; a gray (q.v.) horse with large ragged patches of white.

Grayson-Jockey Club Research Foundation A charitable organization founded in the United States in 1989 by the merger of the Grayson Foundation and The Jockey Club Research Foundation; devoted to equine medical research.

gray ticked Refers to coat color; sparsely distributed white hairs throughout the coat on any part of the body.

grazing bit A curb bit (q.v.) having backward-slanted shanks; designed to enable the horse to graze with the bit in its mouth.

grease heel *see* SCRATCHES

greased heel *see* SCRATCHES

greasy heel *see* SCRATCHES

great coat Also known as postboy's coat or

postboy waistcoat; a heavy overcoat slit to the waist worn by the postillion (q.v.) to protect him from rain and cold; the tails which hung down on either side of the saddle were pulled forward, to cover the thighs, and were tucked under the knee.

Great Horse Also known as the English Great Horse or English Black; England's medieval war horse developed in the early 8th century and used well into the middle of the 15th century; was strong enough to carry a knight in full armor bearing heavy weapons, and agile enough to move about in combat; also used for jousting (q.v.); contributed to the development of the most powerful draft breeds in northern Europe.

green (1) *see* GREEN HORSE. (2) *see* GREEN RIDER. (3) A trotter or pacer who has not previously been raced against the clock. (4) A hunter (q.v.) in its first or second year of showing over obstacles 3 feet 6 inches (1 m) or higher.

green broke A horse who has recently been broken, is inexperienced and requires further training.

green horse Also known as green; a broken, but not fully trained horse.

green hunter Any horse bred, and/or appropriate to follow hounds (q.v.) in the sport of hunting (q.v.) who still requires training.

green meat Basic horse feed consisting of hay, grass, and straw.

green rider Also known as green; an inexperienced rider.

grey *see* GRAY

grid A jumping term; a series of obstacles (q.v.).

gridiron port An oval-shaped metal tongue piece having circular ends which could be clipped around the bit mouthpiece (q.v.), on either side of the existing port (q.v.), to extend its length and action; lies along the tongue in the direction of the throat; has a metal cross in the arch to prevent the tongue from catching on it; prevents the horse from getting its tongue over the bit.

Griffen Also spelt Griffin; a Mongolian pony

breed used in China for polo (q.v.); is tough, handy, agile, and possessed of good speed.

Griffin *see* GRIFFEN

grinders *see* MOLARS

grind teeth A vice; said of a horse who rubs or grates his teeth together, as due to boredom, excitement, anger, resistance to the bit, or tension.

gripes *see* COLIC

Grisone, Frederico A 16th-century Italian nobleman who established a riding school in Naples and was one of the first to promote the use of combined aids and the leg rather than the spur (q.v.).

grissel *see* ROUNT

gizzle *see* ROUNT

grogginess *see* KNUCKLING OVER

groin Also known as lisk; the fold or hollow on either side of the body where the thigh meets the abdomen.

Groningen Also known as Groningen horse; a warmblood (q.v.) developed in the Netherlands by crossing Friesians (q.v.) and Oldenburgs (q.v.); stands 15.2 to 16 hands, has a great depth of girth, powerful quarters and shoulders, short legs, and a black, dark brown, or bay coat; is an easy keeper; nearly disappeared following World War II and is still quite rare; bred for light draft and riding.

Groningen Horse *see* GRONINGEN

groom (1) Also known as strap or in the racing industry, swipe; to curry or care for, as in horses; the act of brushing and cleaning a horse in preparation for or following exercise or work. (2) Also known in Britain as lad, girl, or in racing circles, as a guinea and spelled ginney (because winning British owners of raced stock would tip the groom a guinea); one responsible for the care of horses.

grooming kit Collectively, the brushes, combs, and other equipment used to groom (q.v.) a horse.

grooming stable rubber *see* STABLE RUBBER

groom's coat A coaching term; a single-breasted coat customarily worn by the groom (q.v.); had buttons down the front, three pairs of buttons down the rear, and no pockets,

grooving The act or process of cutting or burning a horizontal groove across the fibers of the hoof horn to alter the way in which stress, as in a crack, is transferred up the hoof wall.

gross energy The caloric content of feed defined in terms of the energy potential it contains; established by incinerating a known quantity of feed in a bomb calorimeter placed inside a defined quantity of water; the number of degrees the water temperature is raised is used to calculate the calorie content of the feed; does not establish how well the calories will be used.

gross feeder Said of a hound or horse who overeats

Grosvenor Dog Cart A horse-drawn vehicle of the dog cart (q.v.) type; had back-to-back seats for four, dash-board lamps, a built-in apron, and was hung on sideways-elliptical springs.

ground (1) *see* GROUND TIE. (2) A coaching term; the area traveled by a coachman, e.g., The coachmank's ground was the forty miles between London and Sawbridgeworth.

grounded A racing term; said of a jockey (q.v.) suspended from competition by racing authorities for rule infractions.

grounding The process of touching down on the ground after being raised in stride, as the hoof.

ground line A jumping term; an imaginary line drawn at the base of a fence from which the take-off (q.v.) spot is judged.

ground man One who, from a position on the ground, aids a mounted rider by setting fences, cavalletti, and grid lines, raising and lowering rails (q.v.), and providing instruction on riding style or technique.

ground money A rodeo term; the entry fee and purse money split equally among all contestants in an event when no individual winner has been determined.

ground pole Also known as a ground rail, guard rail, or take-off rail; a round pole approximately 10 to 12 feet (3-3.6 m) long and 4 to 6 inches (10-15 cm) in diameter laid on the ground, or a few centimeters above, along the sides or in front of a jump to assist the horse in gauging his jump take-off (q.v.); also used in constructing jumping grids and gymnastics; offer no height options and are unstable if the horse mis-steps and starts them rolling beneath his feet.

ground rail *see* GROUND POLE

ground tie Also known as ground; to let the reins drop to the ground after dismounting as an indication to the trained horse to remain standing where he is.

group race Also known as pattern race; a racing term; a method established in 1971 by racing organizations in Britain, France, Germany, and Italy to classify select stakes races run in Europe; are divided into grades designated by Arabic numerals 1, 2, or 3; capitalized when used in a race title as in Group 1 Epsom Derby; equivalent to a graded race (q.v.) in North America.

Growler Slang; a Clarence cab (q.v.), on account of the noise made by its movement.

growth cartilage *see* EPIPHYSEAL PLATES

growth rings *see* HOOF RINGS

growth plates *see* EPIPHYSEAL PLATES

grub *see* LARVA

grulla The feminine of grullo (q.v.).

grullo Also known as slate-grullo, grulla, or mouse dun or blue dun by English riders or when describing breeds from Europe; refers to coat color; slate-colored, having a slate- or tan-colored body with only slight variations of shade and a dark head; in strong sunlight may fade to an olive grullo (q.v.); commonly has wither and dorsal stripes (q.v.), stripes over the knees and hocks, and black skin; the Spanish word for a crane of the same color; an ancestral color of the Tarpan (q.v.).

grunter Also known as a bull; a horse, who when tested for wind soundness, grunts; so called because the horse will emit a grunting noise similar to that of a pig, when frightened or following excessive work; may mean the horse is overweight or that he is suffering from some type of unsoundness in the wind.

grunting Also known as grunt to the stick; said of a horse who, when threatened, and frightened by the anticipated blow of a stick to the belly, emits a grunting noise; a potential sign of wind unsoundness; if no noise is emitted, the horse may be presumed to be sound of wind (q.v.).

grunt to the stick *see* GRUNTING

GSB The acronym for the General Stud Book (q.v.).

Guaga A small, four-wheeled, horse-drawn public carriage used in the towns and cities of Cuba throughout the 19th century; entered from the rear and drawn by four ponies abreast.

Guajira A Colombian-bred Criollo (q.v.) descended from Spanish stock brought to South America by the Conquistadors in the 16th century; the name derived from the region of the same name.

guard rail *see* GROUND POLE

Gudbrandsdal *see* DØLE GUDBRANDSDAL

Guérinière, François Robichon de la (1688-1751) *see* DE LA GUERINIERE, FRANÇOIS ROBICHON

Guerney A horse-drawn vehicle of the cab (q.v.) type popular in the United States around the turn of the 19th century; patented by A. J. Guerney for whom it was named.

guide terrets Small, upright metal rings fastened onto the pads used on the team wheelers (q.v.), through which the reins of the leaders (q.v.) pass.

guiding rein *see* DIRECT REIN

guinea *see* GROOM

guinea hunter English slang; one who works as an intermediary between the seller and buyer of a horse(s) for payment; historically gypsies.

gullet *see* ESOPHAGUS

gullet plate (1) An arch-shaped iron fork attached to the front of the saddle tree (q.v.) to provide strength to the saddle. (2) The metal, generally aluminum, portion of some types of cribbing (q.v.) straps that fits on either side of the esophagus on the under side of the neck; used to prevent cribbing.

gumbo A racing term; heavy mud, as on the racetrack.

gummy legged *see* GAMMY LEGGED

Gustav Rau *see* RAU, GUSTAV

gutteral pouch One of two sacs connected to the eustachian tube (q.v.) located between the ear and throat of the horse and open to the throat; thought to function as a pressure regulator in the airway.

gymkhana Mounted competitive games which improve agility, sharpen reactions, and develop rider and horse physical fitness, particularly for youngsters; evolved from mounted exercises performed by Indian soldiers during the British colonial period; a British word derived from a combination of the word gymnastics and the Hindustani gend-Khana meaning sports ground.

gyp A female foxhound (q.v.); used instead of bitch (q.v.) which in some circles is considered indelicate.

gyp horse A regional British term; a horse having one parent a light breed and the other a heavy breed.

Gypsy Wagon An enclosed, horse-drawn, four-wheeled wagon (q.v.) used by gypsies as a road home.

H

habit (1) Historically, the clothing worn by a woman riding sidesaddle consisting of a jacket and matching long skirt or shaped panel worn over the breeches and boots. (2) A generic term; the clothing, including the boots, belts, etc., worn by an English rider, male or female.

habitat The natural locality in which a plant or animal is found.

habituation A training technique; a decrease in responsiveness of the horse upon repeated exposure to a stimulus.

Habronema Also known as stomach worm; a species of internal parasite found in the mucosa of the stomach; infection occurs by ingestion of house or stable flies which fed on habronema larvae, the free larvae that emerge from flies as they feed around the lips or open wounds on the horse, or by larvae entering through an external wound; when larvae enter a wound, habronemiasis (q.v.) results.

Habronemiasis A condition resulting from Habronema (q.v.) infestation in which good-sized, itchy nodules develop in a wound which ulcerate and weep.

hack (1) To exercise a horse lightly. (2) Any refined riding horse used for riding at an ordinary gait over roads, trails, and so on; is a recognized type, not an established breed; not to be confused with Hackney (q.v.); a contraction of Hackney from the period when carriage horses were used for riding; classifications include covert hack (q.v.), road hack (q.v.), and park hack (q.v.); from the French haquenée, meaning work worn.

Hack *see* HACKNEY COACH

hackamore (1) Also known as jaquima from which the word was Anglicized, or incorrectly as hackamore bit; a bitless bridle (q.v.) consisting of a leather headstall (q.v.) attached to a semi-oval plaited leather or rawhide bosal (q.v.) knotted under the chin of the horse to which a hair or cotton rope mecate (q.v.) is attached; a cotton fiador (q.v.) may attach to the headstall and to the mecate which acts as a throat latch (q.v.); the bosal generally sits at a 45 degree angle from the bridge of the nose to the chin; control is achieved through pressure

applied to the bridge of the nose and the poll. (2) *see* MECHANICAL HACKAMORE

hackamore bit *see* HACKAMORE

hack classes Any competition for the best hack (q.v.) held at a major horse show; may be divided into weight classes on the basis that a 10 stone (62.5 kg) hack should be able to provide a comfortable ride all day for a person of that weight; size classes include: (a) Show, Ladies: a horse larger than 14.2 hands but not exceeding 15.3 hands and capable of carrying a lady riding side saddle, (b) Show, Large: a horse between 15 and 15.3 hands to be ridden astride; and, (c) Show, Small: a horse between 14.2 and 15 hands to be ridden astride.

hacking out To ride a horse for pleasure in the field or on a trail or road as opposed to working in a *manège* (q.v.) or arena (q.v.).

hackles Erectile hairs along the neck and back of a hound commonly raised in excitement and/or anger.

hackles up Said of a hound (q.v.) when the erectile hairs along the neck and back stand upright as due to anger, excitement, and/or fear; a hound in pursuit of a fox (q.v.) will have its hackles up when close to the fox and running for blood.

Hackney Also known as Hackney Horse; a compact trotting horse breed developed in Great Britain; descended from Norfolk Trotters (q.v.) crossed with native and Arab (q.v.) horses; formerly any active riding horse used for road work, now used chiefly for driving; characterized by its high-stepping trot and far-reaching action; stands between 14.0 and 15.2 hands, are of whole colors with some white, and generally have a flat shoulder; the stud book (q.v.) was established in 1883.

Hackney Coach Also known as hack; a four-wheeled, springless, six-passenger public service vehicle drawn by a pair of horses in pole gear (q.v.) with the near-side horse sometimes postillion (q.v.) driven; used in London, Paris, and other European cities throughout the 17th and 18th centuries; were frequently the discarded coaches of the wealthy patched-up for additional years of service; smaller versions were drawn by a single horse.

Hackney Horse *see* HACKNEY

Hackney Horse Society, The An organization founded in Great Britain in 1884 to promote and encourage the breeding of Hackneys (q.v.), harness horses, cobs, and ponies.

Hackney Pony A pony breed originating in early 19th-century Great Britain; developed by crossing the Hackney (q.v.) with Fell (q.v.) and Welsh ponies (q.v.) and selected Trotters and Roadsters; the coat may be brown, black, gray or roan with white markings permitted; stands 12.1 to 14 hands (q.v.), has a light head, arched neck, pronounced withers, a long and rounded croup, slender, yet strong legs, and somewhat straight-hocked hind legs; is fiery, energetic, and fast; registered in the Hackney stud book; until the beginning of the 20th century used by tradesmen to pull delivery vehicles, now used predominantly for show.

Hackney show wagon *see* BOX WAGON

Hackney stand Any location where Hackney coaches (q.v.) assembled, waiting to be hired; the first recorded stand was established in London, England in 1634.

hack on A hunting term; to ride one's horse to a meet of hounds.

Hack Show, Ladies *see* HACK CLASSES

Hack Show, Large *see* HACK CLASSES

Hack Show, Small *see* HACK CLASSES

Haematopinas asini *see* SUCKING LOUSE

haemolysis The destruction of red blood cells.

haemolytic jaundice A condition caused by the dissolution of red blood cells and the liberation of the cell contents; jaundice (q.v.) occurring when the destruction of red cells, which rupture continuously throughout the lifespan of any individual, is increased to such an extent that the bone marrow cannot adequately produce replacement cells and the liver is unable to clear the blood of the large quantities of bile pigment; may also be caused by bacteria, virus, or parasites which occur in such conditions as equine infectious anemia (q.v.), leptospirosis (q.v.), and piroplasmosis

(q.v.), respectively.

Hafflinger *see* HAFLINGER

Haflig *see* HAFLINGER

Haflinger Also spelled Hafflinger and known as a Haflig or Edelweiss Pony; a cold-blood (q.v.) pony breed originating in the Southern Austrian Tyrol, around the mountain village of Hafling from which the name derived; the base stock descended from the now extinct Alpine Heavy Horse with infusions of Norik, Hucul (q.v.), Bosnian, and Korik (q.v.) all modern purebreds can be traced to the Arab stallion El Bedavi XXII; the breed is a fixed type with an unmistakable appearance; is always chestnut or palomino with a flaxen mane and tail, stands up to 14 hands, has a broad head, large eyes, open nostrils, small ears, long back, muscular loins and quarters, tough hooves, and short legs, a free action, and a long-strided walk; is frugal, surefooted, tough, hardy, sound, and kind; young stock raised on Alpine pastures to develop their hearts and lungs and are not worked until four years of age; often lives and remains active well into its 40s; used for packing and draft; branded with Austria's native flower, the Edelweiss with the letter H in the center; the Italian-bred version of this breed is known as the Avelignese (q.v.).

HAHS The acronym for the Hooved Animal Humane Society (q.v.).

hair A fine filament which originates in the hair follicles and grows from the skin of the horse; performs a thermoregulatory function, protecting the horse from extreme changes in air temperature.

hair color Refers to coat color; any of the five primary colors: brown, black, bay, chestnut, or white, variations of which include dun (buckskin), gray, palomino, pinto (calico or paint), and roan.

hairies More than one hairy (q.v.).

hair up Said of a horse; to grow a winter coat, e.g., The horse did not hair up much.

hairy (1) *see* HAIRY BULLFINCH. (2) Slang; any heavy-breed horse such as the Shire (q.v.); so called because of the heavy feathering (q.v.) found on the legs of such breeds.

hairy bullfinch Also known as a hairy; a jumping obstacle; a live, thin and straggly hedge jumped over not through.

half Balding gag bit A bit consisting of a jointed mouthpiece (q.v.) with large, loose-ring half-cheek gags (q.v.) used with a single rein; prevents the effect of the gag until considerable pressure is applied.

halfblood *see* WARMBLOOD

half-breed (1) A horse having mixed blood strains, as in out of different races or breeds. (2) A horse sired by, but which is not out of a Thoroughbred (q.v.); is not eligible for entry into the General Stud Book (q.v.), but may be registered in the Half-Bred stud book.

half-breed bit Any curb bit (q.v.) with a high port and a cricket (q.v.); popular in the southwest United States.

half brother A relationship of two male offspring out of the same dam (q.v.), but by different sires (q.v.); does not apply to horses who only share the same sire.

half cannon *see* SOCK

half chaps *see* LEGGINGS

half cheek The vertical portion of the bit exterior and extending below the bit mouthpiece (q.v.) to which the cheekpieces (q.v.) are attached above and the reins below.

half-cheek snaffle A snaffle bit (q.v.) consisting of a straight or jointed mouthpiece fitted at either end with fixed rings to which straight- or spoon-shaped (wider and slightly curved toward the horse's jaw at the top) arms attach; the cheeks (q.v.) may extend either above the mouthpiece as in an upper-cheek snaffle (q.v.) or below as in a lower-cheek snaffle (q.v.); the cheeks prevent the bit from running through the mouth of a horse if he runs sideways or refuses to turn.

half halt The hardly visible, almost simultaneous, coordinated action of the seat, legs, and hands of the rider performed to increase the attention and balance of the horse before the execution of any movement or transition to lesser or higher gait or pace; does not completely halt the movement of the horse, it merely restricts, diminishes, and collects it.

half-mile pole A racing term; a vertical pole located on the infield rail 4 furlongs from the finish.

half-miler (1) A racing term; a track of -1/2 mile (804 m) length. (2) A racing term; a horse who prefers running on a 1/2 mile track.

half moon bit *see* MULLEN MOUTH BIT

half moon mouth *see* MULLEN MOUTH BIT

half parade *see* SIMPLE CHANGE

half-pass A lateral dressage movement performed free of the track, in which the horse bends uniformly on two tracks throughout his body in the direction in which he is moving; the horse's shoulders move slightly in advance of the hindquarters (q.v.), the outside legs crossing in front of the inside legs; there is only slight lateral flexion.

half-pass counter change *see* COUNTER HALF PASS

half-pastern A leg marking (q.v.); white on the foot of the horse which extends from the coronary band (q.v.) half way up the pastern (q.v.).

half-pirouette One half of a pirouette (q.v.); a movement performed by the horse in which he makes a 180 degree turn, with the forehand scribing a half-circle around the inside hind leg.

half sister A relationship of two female offspring out of the same dam, but by different sires; does not apply to horses that only share the same sire.

half stocking Also known as a boot; a leg marking (q.v.) consisting of white on the leg of the horse extending from the coronary band (q.v.) to the lower half of the cannon bone just above the fetlock joint (q.v.).

half-struck Also known as set back; said of a horse-drawn carriage folding hood when positioned halfway between being fully open and completely closed.

half volte A dressage movement; one half of a 6-meter circle.

half volte and change A dressage movement in which the horse moves off the track (q.v.), haunches in (q.v.) and scribes one half of a 6-meter circle, returning to the track at a 45 degree angle traveling in the opposite direction; other volte (q.v.) movements include the renvers volte (q.v.), renvers half volte (q.v.), and half volte (q.v.).

half volte reversed *see* RENVERS-HALF VOLTE

halloo *see* VIEW HALLOO

halt To stop a horse through displacement of his weight to his quarters by driving him towards a progressively more restraining hand; of two types: a full halt (q.v.) and half halt (q.v.).

halt early A dressage term; said of a horse who, after receiving instruction from the rider, stops before the marker (q.v.).

halt late A dressage term; said of a horse who, after receiving instruction from the rider, stops after the marker (q.v.).

halter (1) Also known as a head collar; a bit-less leather, nylon, or natural fiber headstall (q.v.) with or without a detachable rope, strap, or chain by which a horse is led or tied. (2) Racing slang; to claim (q.v.) a horse. (3) To put a halter on the head of a horse.

halter break To train a horse to allow a halter to be put on and to respond to being led by a rope, strap, or chain attached to the halter.

halter broke Said of a horse trained to wear a head stall and lead.

halter man A racing term; an owner or trainer who specializes in buying horses from claiming races (q.v.).

halter puller A horse who pulls back on the halter rope when tied; a vice.

halter pulling Said of the horse who pulls against the halter rope when tied; a vice.

halter rope *see* LEAD LINE

hame A curved wood or brass-plated steel piece that fits around the harness collar (q.v.) worn by the horse; there are two hames used on each collar; may be made in one or two sections; on the top half of each hame is a terret (q.v.) through which the rein passes; transfer the draft to the collar and support the

harness tugs (q.v.), trace chains, and hame straps (q.v.).

hame chain A small-linked chain used to connect the bottom ends of the hames (q.v.).

hame rein A short rein buckled to the bit and looped over the hame horn used on heavy-horse harness to prevent the horse from excessively lowering his head..

hames The plural of hame (q.v.).

hames collar *see* HARNESS COLLAR

hame strap A leather harness strap used to hold the tops and/or the bottoms of the hames (q.v.) together; passes through the hame eyes and connects to the collar (q.v.).

ham-fisted *see* MUTTON-FISTED

hammer cloth Also spelled hammercloth; heavy woven cloth used to cover the coachman's seat in state and dress horse-drawn vehicles; often trimmed with gold braid.

hammercloth *see* HAMMER CLOTH

hammer head Said of a coarse-headed horse.

Hammock Wagon A horse-drawn vehicle popular in 11th century England; the body resembled a hammock and was hung from large hooks imbedded in posts supported by the axles between the four wheels.

hamschackle To restrain a horse by a rope or strap connecting the head to one of the forelegs.

hamstring (1) Also known as the Achilles tendon; the fibrous cord which joins the muscles of the gaskin to the point of the hock (q.v.). (2) Also known as hock; to cut the hamstring or hamstrings of the horse; to cut, cripple, or render powerless.

hamstrung Disabled by an injury to the Achilles tendon above the location of the hock (q.v.).

hand Also known by the acronyms hh and Hh; a linear measurement of a horse's height equaling 4 inches (10 cm), with fractions expressed in inches; calculated from the ground to the high point of the withers; derived from the time when the height of horses was measured by the number of spans of a man's hand, e.g., a horse who stands 16.2 hands high is 66 inches or 5 feet 6 inches (1.6 km) tall.

hand breeding Also known as hand mating; the mating of a stallion and mare as orchestrated by a handler; includes teasing (q.v.), washing, the act of coitus, and the return of the mare and stallion to their respective living quarters.

hand canter A semi-extended canter (q.v.) between a gallop (q.v.) and a promenade canter (q.v.).

hand gallop A controlled, yet extended (q.v.) canter (q.v.) in which the horse remains collected, traveling at about 18 mph (29 kmph).

hand gate *see* BRIDLE GATE

hand horse A coaching term; the farside horse when two horses are controlled by a postillion (q.v.).

handicap (1) The advantages or disadvantages of weight, distance, or time placed upon competitors to equalize their chances of winning; may be applied to either the horse or rider. (2) A racing term; to evaluate the race records of competing horses to attempt to determine the winner of a race in advance of the race and to wager on such horses. (3) *see* HANDICAP RACE

handicapper (1) A racing term; one, generally the racing secretary, responsible for assigning the weights to be carried by each horse running in a handicap race (q.v.). (2) A racing term; one who places bets on horses based on a thorough study of their past performances.

handicap race Also known as a handicap; a racing term; a race in which competing horses carry weight assigned by the racing secretary to equalize the winning chances of all entrants; the superior horse, as determined by the racing secretary's assessment of its past performance, carries high weight, while lessor competitors, as based on perceived ability, carry less.

Handicap Triple Crown A United States racing term; a mythical award to a horse who wins all three classic handicaps – the Brooklyn, Suburban, and Metropolitan – in one season.

handily A racing term; said of a horse who works or races with ease and without urging.

handiness The extent to which a horse is nimble, light-footed, and agile.

handle A racing term; the total amount bet on a race, in a day, a meeting, or a season.

handled Said of a young horse who has been touched, brushed, haltered, and led prior to breaking.

handler One responsible for handling (q.v.) of a horse.

handling The initial phase of training of a young horse; includes imprinting (q.v.), haltering, grooming, and basic socialization.

hand mating *see* HAND BREEDING

handpiece A carriage term; that part of the rein held in the hand.

hand piece That portion of the whip (q.v.) between the cap and collar (q.v.) where it is held by the user.

hand ride A racing term; said of a rider who urges a horse toward a longer, faster, more rhythmic stride without use of a whip by rolling his hands forward on the neck of the horse and lifting his head at the beginning of each stride.

hand rub To massage or rub the legs of the horse to improve circulation and prevent and/or reduce swelling.

hands (1) The extremity of the arm consisting of the palm, four fingers, and thumb; a rider may have good hands (q.v.) or bad hands. (2) The plural of hand (q.v.)

hand sale An obsolete term; to finalize the sale of a horse on the basis of a hand shake; the outstretched hand of the person making the sale is struck by the person making the offer.

handy Said of a nimble, light-footed, and agile horse.

hang A racing term; said of a horse competing in a race who is unable to produce a finishing kick and is therefore unable to improve its position on the home stretch (q.v.).

hanging on An antiquated coaching term; said of one of a pair of horses who hangs away from the other.

hang up your bars An antiquated coaching term; said of one who retires from coaching as a profession.

Hanover *see* HANOVERIAN

Hanoverian Also known as a Hanover; a warmblood (q.v.) developed in the Hanover and Lower Saxony districts of West Germany in the 17th century through the breeding of imported Spanish, Neapolitan, and Oriental stallions to local mares; at this time the breed was only suited to draft and farm work; English Thoroughbred (q.v.) blood was introduced around 1714, and in 1735 George II, Elector of Hanover, established a stud in the small town of Celle where the breed was further improved and lightened; by the end of the 19th century input of English blood was stopped to avoid further change to the breed, and after 1924, Trakehner (q.v.) and Arab (q.v.) blood was introduced to produce a riding competition horse; breed development and breeding is strictly controlled by a performance and licensing system; the modern horse stands 16 to 17.2 hands, is quiet, courageous, athletic and powerful, has impressive action (q.v.), yet little knee action, and a long stride; the coat is generally chestnut, brown, black, or gray and white markings are frequent; has a well proportioned head, long neck, pronounced withers, a long back, strong, well-muscled legs, and a tough hoof; used for show jumping, hunting, dressage, eventing, and harness; the Westphalian (q.v.) is the Hanoverian bred under another regional title.

Hans, Kluge A Russian stallion, one of a number of horses collectively known as the Elberfeld Horses (q.v.), used by William von Osten (q.v.), a Berliner, to prove his theories on equine intelligence; von Osten appeared to train the stallion to calculate by pawing the ground with his hoof, read, and differentiate colors, up to the general standard of knowledge of a 14-year-old child; von Osten's studies gained enormous publicity, but in 1904, German psychologist, Oskar Pfungst, demonstrated that the stallion answered to unconscious signs from von Osten; at the outbreak of World War I, the horses were disbanded.

Hansom *see* HANSOM CAB

Hansom cab Originally known as the Hansom safety cab and subsequently as Hansom, the gondola of London, or twowheeler; a two-wheeled, horse-drawn vehicle patented in 1834 by Joseph Hansom for whom it was named; had a closed, low-slung body, high wheels, a rearward driving seat positioned high above the back of the vehicle, and a curved dashboard at the rear of the shafts bringing the hindquarters of the horse fairly close to the vehicle for increased control; seated two forward-facing passengers on a single cross-seat, their legs protected by knee flaps, and entered from the front by a folding door with a sliding glass window; not very popular in the United States; some threewheeled versions were manufactured; from the 1890s most had solid rubber tires and were hung on semi-elliptical side springs while others were fitted with solid silver accessories and interior mirrors; seldom used by unescorted women; drawn by a single horse.

Hansom safety cab *see* HANSOM CAB

Hanoverian Cream *see* PALOMINO

hard boot An American racing term; one from Kentucky whose horse training methods are of the old school; so called for their typically mud-caked boots.

harbourer An old English stag hunting (q.v.) term; one selected by the Hunt Master to identify the stag (q.v.) to be hunted; generally a local gamekeeper or farrier familiar with the ground hunted.

hard and fast A calf roping term; said of the roper; to take a double half-hitch of the lariat (q.v.) on the saddle horn (q.v.) to secure the rope when dismounting to tie off (q.v.) the calf.

hardel An antiquated hunting term; to couple (q.v.) hounds (q.v.).

hard horse Said of a horse resistant to illness and unsoundness.

hard keeper Said of horse prone to digestive disturbances, who does not maintain his weight nor a healthy appearance from a normal diet; is difficult to fatten and train as any dietary change, including the quality of the feed, may result in weight loss or digestive problems.

hard-mouthed Said of a horse whose bars of the mouth have become callused and desensitized to the action of the bit because of continued bit pressure; most commonly caused by bad hands (q.v.).

hard palate The anterior bony arch of the roof of the mouth (q.v.) which, in conjunction with the soft palate (q.v.), separates the nasal and oral cavities.

hard pressed A hunting term; said of a fox when the distance between it and the pursuing hounds narrows.

hard track A racing term; a turf track lacking resiliency.

hare (1) A hunting term; to hunt rabbits or hare. (2) A small mammal of the genus *Lepus* in the family *Leporidea* having long ears, a divided upper lip, a short tail, and lengthened hind legs adapted for leaping.

hare foot A hunting term; said of a hound's foot when long and narrow, resembling that of fox or coyote.

hare-pied Refers to hound coat color; a cream- or fawn-colored head, legs, body, and stern with the ears and back shading into brown with lighter tips to the ears.

hark An antiquated hunting term; to listen.

Harma A hunting or war chariot of the Ancient Persians drawn by teams of two, three, or four horses harnessed abreast and entered from the rear.

harmony The balanced interrelationship of the horse and rider or the body parts to one another.

harness (1) Also known as harness tack; the combination of leather pieces and metals used to connect a horse to a wagon, carriage, cart, etc.; generally consists of a bridle (q.v.), collar (q.v.), hames (q.v.), tugs (q.v.) or traces (q.v.), back band (q.v.), belly band (q.v.), and breeching (q.v.). (2) To put a harness on a horse(s). (3) Also known as put to; to harness a horse(s) to a vehicle.

harness collar Also known as a neck collar, hames collar, or collar; an oval-shaped ring consisting of the forewale (q.v.) and afterwale (q.v.) placed over the head of the horse and fitted around the neck and against the shoulders to support the hames (q.v.) to which the traces (q.v.) are attached, and by which a vehicle is pulled; fit is essential; available in different sizes, shapes, and weights depending on the horse and the use.

harness crupper Also known as a crupper; a back strap attached on one end to a dee located on the back of harness pad and to the crupper dock (q.v.) on the other; used to prevent the pad from slipping forward.

harness hopples *see* HOPPLES

harness loops *see* KEEPERS

harness martingale A leather strap attached on one end to the girth (q.v.) and to the lowest end of the collar (q.v.) on the other; prevents the collar from riding up on the neck of the horse; similar to the standing martingale (q.v.) used on the saddle horse.

Harness Race Cart An American sulky (q.v.) of the gig (q.v.) type having small wheels and a safer, more permanent seat than an ordinary sulky; used when driving long-gaited horses for racing and other sport purposes.

Harness Race Sulky A modern, two-wheeled racing sulky (q.v.) with curved shafts in a continuous, bow-like formation from the underframe which slope in a rearward direction; mounted on wire-spoked wheels with pneumatic tires; the skeleton seat is 27 inches (69 cm) from ground level; quite popular in the United States and Australia.

harness rack An open rack made of iron, plastic-covered iron, or wood on which harness tack (q.v.) is hung when not in use; accommodates the collar (q.v.), pad, crupper (q.v.), bridle (q.v.), and reins (q.v.).

harness racing Also known as pacing or Standardbred racing; a sport in which Standardbreds (q.v.), trotters (q.v.) and pacers (q.v.), race a distance of 1 mile (1.6 km); contested on two gaits, the trot (q.v.) and the pace (q.v.); a third gait often manifests itself, running, but a horse who runs must return to his natural gait or face disqualification; competing horses are driven by drivers seated in two-wheeled carts pulled behind the horse; speeds average 25-30 mph (32-48 kmph); competing horses may not be younger than two nor older than 15 years of age; generally considered a native American sport which commenced in 1806, although it actually traces back more than 3,000 years.

harness tack *see* HARNESS no. 1

harras An enclosure or establishment in which stallions and mares are retained for breeding.

harrier A hunting term; a light-bodied hound bred to hunt hare (q.v.) from horseback; measures 18 to 21 inches (46-53 cm) at the shoulder; smaller than a foxhound (q.v.).

harrier pack A hunting term; a pack of hounds measuring 18 to 21 inches (46-53 cm) at the shoulder entered (q.v.) to hare (q.v.).

harrow (1) A tool with a long handle attached to metal pulling teeth used to rake and loosen the upper surface of the race track. (2) To rake and loosen the soil using a hand harrow or a tractor pulling a harrow attachment.

Harry Highover's pelham A curb bit (q.v.) popular at the turn of the 19th century; had a two-inch port (q.v.) attached to a bridoon (q.v.) mouth.

hat rack An emaciated horse.

hatchet blinkers A driving or harness blinker (q.v.); hatchet-shaped, leather-covered metal plates attached to the cheek-pieces of the bridle or to a hood (q.v.) used to restrict the horse's vision to the sides and rear in either or both eyes.

haunch *see* HIP

hat trick A racing term; said of a jockey who wins three races on a single program.

haunches That portion of the horse consisting of the buttocks and hips (q.v.).

haunches in *see* TRAVERS

haunches out *see* RENVERS

Haute Ecole Also known as High School; the classical school of advanced equitation where the horse is trained to a very high level of performance in dressage (q.v.) including the high and low airs (q.v.).

have a leg Said of a horse having unsoundness or swelling in one or more legs.

have a lot of cow *see* COW SMART

have one in the boot A racing term; said of a jockey who rides a horse upon which the owner or trainer has made bets including those made on behalf of the jockey.

having a handful A coaching term; said of the driver who has picked up the reins of a team (q.v.).

haw (1) A coaching term; a voice signal given by the driver of a horse-drawn vehicle to instruct the team to turn to the left. (2) *see* NICTATING MEMBRANE

hay Cut and dried grasses, legumes, and cereal crops; a primary source of roughage in the diet of non-pastured horses; high in fiber, calcium, and protein and a primary source of vitamin D if sun-cured; of two varieties: grass hay which includes cereal grass hays (q.v.) and legume hay; generally pressed into 50 to 100 pound (23-45 kg) bales strung with wire or rope, or may be stacked loose; may be stored for many months without sacrificing quality; of many types including Timothy (q.v.), Bermuda (q.v.), bluestem grass (q.v.), bromegrass (q.v.), wheat grass (q.v.), sudangrass (q.v.), Johnsongrass (q.v.), orchard grass hay (q.v.), prairie hay, and grass hay (q.v.).

hay bale Any bound bundle of grass or legume hay (q.v.); generally rectangularly shaped, bound with twine or wire, and weighing, depending on the hay's moisture content, 75 to 120 pounds (34-54 kg); large operations are now turning to larger bales, in excess of one ton, in which the hay is rolled and bound in a shape similar to a jelly roll.

hay belly Also called grass belly; said of a horse having a distended belly due to excessive feeding of bulky rations such as hay (q.v.), straw (q.v.), or grass (q.v.).

hayburner Also known as an oatburner; a racing term; said of a horse who does not win enough to pay for its feed bill.

haycock *see* HAYSTACK

hay cubes *see* CUBES

haylage Vacuum-packed hay sealed immediately following cutting and drying; little nutritional value is lost in this process; frequently fed to horses with dust allergies or a tendency to cough.

hayloft An area located above the first floor in a barn or stable, where hay and other items may be stored.

haynet A string, rope, or corded net, which holds loose hay (q.v.) or alfalfa (q.v.) and is hung to enable the horse to eat without the hay touching the ground; a common method of feeding horses in transit.

hay rack Also known as a rack; a framework, grating, or stand above ground level that holds fodder (q.v.) for horses or cattle.

haystack Also known as a haycock; a conical pile of loose hay (q.v.) or bales stacked outdoors.

haytea A beverage for sick horses made by infusing hay in hot water and allowing it to steep.

Haywick Common Riding Also known as common riding; a Scottish ceremony conducted on horseback held during the first full week in June and extending over several days; consists of many individual events, the principal one known as the Cornet's Chase (q.v.); the date of origin is unknown.

haze Said of a cowboy (q.v.) who keeps a steer or calf running in a straight line parallel to a wrestler or roper.

hazer A cowboy (q.v.) who rides on the side of the steer or calf opposite to the wrestler or roper to keep it running in a relatively straight line and prevent it from running away from the wrestler's or roper's horse.

Hb The acronym for hemoglobin (q.v.).

HCG The acronym for human chorionic gonadotropin (q.v.).

HCT The acronym for hematocrit (q.v.).

head (1) The upper part of the body of the horse attached by the neck to the body; the head and neck comprise close to 20 percent of

the horse's body weight. (2) A racing term; a measurement of the margin between horses competing in a race; the length of the horse's head, e.g., The horse won by a head. (3) *see* CARRY A GOOD HEAD. (4) *see* CARRIAGE HEAD. (5) *see* HEADSTALL

head a cow Also known as heading; a cutting term; to position a ridden horse in front of a cow to force it to change direction or stop.

head a fox A hunting term; to turn back a fox; generally performed by the hounds (q.v.), although sometimes performed by the field (q.v.).

head bumper Also known as a poll guard; a felt or sherling-lined leather cap which provides extra protection to the sensitive poll region of the horse's head during shipping; extends from the top of the neck just behind the poll to just above the eyes, with holes cut for the ears; attaches at the temples to the halter.

head cap *see* HOOD

head carriage The natural position of the head and neck of the horse; varies between breeds.

head collar *see* HALTER

head collar chain shanks *see* CROSS TIES

headed (1) A racing term; said of a horse competing in a race who loses by the length of one head (q.v.) at the finish. (2) A hunting term; said of a fox who has turned from his original line (q.v.). (3) Said of a horse-drawn vehicle with a top.

header (1) A team calf roping term; one who is most talented at, and whose responsibility it is in competition, to rope the horns, head, or neck of the horse; works in conjunction with a healer (q.v.). (2) *see* HEAD HORSE

head horse Also known as header; a stout, strong, fast mount from which a roper ropes the head of a steer; trained to accelerate and make a sharp turn to the left once the steer is roped.

heading *see* HEAD A COW

headland A hunting term; the edge of a field.

head lap *see* HOOD

head of the saddle *see* POMMEL

head of the stretch A racing term; the beginning of the straight run to the finish (q.v.) on a racetrack.

headpiece (1) *see* HEADSTALL (2) *see* CROWN PIECE

head plate A metal ornament, frequently silver, used to adorn some types of horse-drawn carriages; sometimes embossed with crests or other decoration.

heads *see* GET TO THE HEADS

headstall Also known as headpiece, bridle head, or head; the part of the bridle or hackamore placed on the horse's head for the purpose of holding a bit, bosal, or similar device in the horse's mouth or on his nose, and to which the reins are attached.

heads up (1) A hunting term; said of the hounds who, having lost the scent, raise their heads to search for it. (2) Also known as head up; a call of caution; an announcement to pay attention; may be communicated from one rider to another or to a person on the ground, as when in close proximity.

heads up, sterns down A hunting term; said of hounds (q.v.) who are running a fox (q.v.) at top speed with the scent at breast height (q.v.) in which case their heads will be held high and their hindquarters low.

head terret A coaching term; a fixed upright metal ring attached to that portion of the crownpiece (q.v.) between the ears of the wheeler's bridle through which the leader's reins pass; now generally attached to the cheekpiece at brow level.

head to the wall *see* TRAVERS

head up (1) Said of a horse who momentarily evades the action of the bit when transitioning upward from a walk to a trot or trot to canter by raising its head. (2) *see* HEADS UP no. 3.

healer *see* HEELER AND HEEL HORSE

health certificate A document issued by a licensed veterinarian (q.v.) which is evidence

that the horse has been examined and is sound and free from any contagious condition at the time of examination; such a horse is said to vet clean (q.v.).

hearse A four-wheeled, horse-drawn carriage in which coffins were transported; frequently glass sided and painted black, except those in which children were carried, which were white; pulled by horses known as the Black Brigade (q.v.).

heart (1) The hollow muscular organ which circulates blood received from the veins throughout the body by means of rhythmic contractions and dilations; consists of four cavities. (2) Said of a horse who has great courage and willingness.

heart bar shoe A therapeutic horseshoe of the bar shoe type in which the shoe branches (q.v.) are left long and welded into an arc behind and join at the center of the heels to create a heart shape; used to treat some cases of navicular by relieving pressure on the center of the frog, and founder by applying pressure slightly behind the point of the frog to prevent further coffin bone rotation.

heartbeat irregularity *see* ARRHYTHMIA

heart brasses One of four primary historic patterns of horse brasses (q.v.) used on horse harnesses to ward off the evil eye; the heart pattern was struck into brass or other metal and placed on the harness or other tack of the horse.

heart girth Also known as girth or heart room; the distance around the body of the horse as measured behind the elbows and over the withers; may be used to calculate the weight of the horse using the following equation: heart girth (in inches) x length (in inches from the point of the shoulder to the point of the hip)/241.3.

heart room *see* HEART GIRTH

heat (1) *see* ESTRUS. (2) *see* ROUND. (3) A single effort, round, bout, or trial, especially in competition, the winners of which compete in any of the preliminary rounds of a race or other competition in the final round.

heat bumps *see* HIVES

heat cramps Spasm or cramping of the

muscles as of the legs due to electrolyte and fluid imbalance.

heat exhaustion Inability of the body to maintain the normal cooling mechanism of the horse because of overheating; may be triggered by high environmental temperature, poor ventilation, high humidity, and/or overexertion in warm weather; symptoms include weakness, staggering, rapid breathing, elevated body temperature, heavy sweating, and rapid heart rate.

heat prostration A nonspecific term; prostration (q.v.) due to heat.

heatstroke Also known as sunstroke; failure of the heat regulatory mechanism at the central nervous system level caused by a severe response to overheating; the regulatory mechanism shuts down and the body quits trying to cool itself; may be triggered by elevated environmental temperature, poor ventilation, high humidity, and/or overexertion in warm weather; is more severe than, but not necessarily precipitated by, heat exhaustion (q.v.); symptoms include hot body temperature, dehydration, dry skin, rapid breathing and/or respiratory failure; may result in neurological collapse, shock, gradual physiological failure, and ultimately, if untreated, death.

heaves *see* CHRONIC OBSTRUCTIVE PULMONARY DISEASE

heavy boned Said of a horse having a large and heavy bone structure.

Heavy Draught Breton SEE FAST HEAVY DRAUGHT BRETON

heavy-headed A racing term; said of a horse who fights the reins, responds slowly to guidance, and/or prefers to run with its head low.

heavy horse Any horse possessing characteristics of the large draft breeds such as the Clydesdale (q.v.), Shire (q.v.), Suffolk Punch (q.v.), or Percheron (q.v.).

heavy top Said of a horse having a thick, coarse neck and shoulders which appear out of proportion with the rest of the body.

heavy track (1) A racing term; a racing surface that is more dry than mud, and often slower. (2) A racing term; the wettest possible condition of a turf track.

heavy transport collar A collar (q.v.) used on horses in heavy army work; ranged in size from 23 to 27 inches (58-69 cm) and were substantially larger and wider than those used on draft horses.

Hecca A two-wheeled, horse-drawn passenger cart popular in India; had a movable or canopy top and little or no metal work in the construction; the shafts met at a point above the horse's withers which gave the vehicle a pronounced rearward inclination; the driver sat cross-legged on a small platform of the forepart.

heck *see* GEE

Hedijn Any progeny (q.v.) of a Persian Arab (q.v.) stallion and non-Arab mare.

hedgehog *see* ECHINI

Heecul *see* HUCUL

heel (1) A leg marking (q.v.); a white spot (q.v.) or mark located across the heel of the foot or on one side of the heel. (2) Also known as running heel, heel way, hunting the heel line, or counter; a hunting term; said of hounds (q.v.) who run the line (q.v.) of a fox (q.v.) in the opposite direction to that the fox is traveling. (3) One of two bulb-like areas located on the rear, underside portion of the hoof (q.v.) and which consists of hoof wall and frog tissue; provides shock absorption to the leg.

heel avulsion *see* AVULSION OF THE HOOF WALL AT THE HEEL

heel boot Also known as a shin and ankle boot; a heavy-duty brushing boot (q.v.) that protects the point of the fetlock and a portion of the lower cannon bone against brushing (q.v.).

heel bulbs Also known as bulbs; the two rounded sections of the horse's foot located on either side of the back of the hoof above the coronary band (q.v.).

heel calk A calk (q.v.) located on the heel of the horseshoe; provides braking traction as the hoof lands, but no grip at breakover.

heel catch A roping term; said of a thrown rope that holds a steer from behind the shoulder and back, around the flank, or on one or both of the heels, but not by the tail only.

heel crack (1) A vertical crack in the hoof wall at the heel, starting at the bearing surface, extending a variable distance up the hoof wall, or originating at the coronary band (q.v.), and extending downward; may occur in either the fore or hind feet; more severe than toe crack (q.v.) as the sensitive laminae (q.v.) are usually involved. (2) *see* AVULSION OF THE HOOF WALL AT THE HEEL

heeler (1) Also spelled incorrectly healer; a team roping term; one most talented at, and whose responsibility it is in competition, to rope the hind legs of a calf; works in conjunction with a header (q.v.). (2) *see* HEEL HORSE

heel horse Also known as heeler and spelled incorrectly healer; a stout, strong, fast mount from which a heeler (q.v.) ropes the hind legs of a calf or steer in team roping.

heel knot The knot of the bosal (q.v.) located under the chin, to which the reins and lead rope are usually attached in a hackamore (q.v.) bridle.

heel nerve *see* NERVE

heel way *see* HEEL no. 2

heifer A young female cow.

height The tallness of the horse as measured perpendicularly from the bottom of the hoof, excluding the shoe to the highest point of the withers; defined in hands (q.v.).

hell bent for leather Also known as hell for leather or ride hell for leather; an American term popular in the early 1800s; to press a horse to its extreme speed; to move at a reckless speed regardless of the consequences, namely hell, fire, and damnation; may have derived from all of a lather, as in the condition of a horse following such a ride.

hell cart Slang; a horse-drawn passenger vehicle as called by pedestrians in the 17th century when splashed with mud or forced into the gutter when such vehicles pass.

hell for leather *see* HELL BENT FOR LEATHER

helmet (1) A lightweight fiberglass cap held onto the head of the rider by a chin strap prevents injuries to the head; designs having passed impact testing are currently required by most societies in over fence classes, exercise riders at race tracks, jockeys at race meetings, and by some combined driving, trotter, gymkhana, steeplechase, point-to-point, polo, and polocrosse competitors. (2) *see* CAP

hematinic Any agent that improves the quality of the blood by increasing hemoglobin and erythrocyte (q.v.) levels.

hematocrit Also known by the acronym HCT or as packed cell volume (q.v.).

hematoma Also known as blood blister; an abnormal collection of blood in an organ, space, or body tissue due to break in the wall of a blood vessel; generally caused by an impact related injury to the blood vessels.

hem gears The harness worn by a farm horse in the lead of a tandem (q.v.).

hemoglobin The oxygen-carrying protein pigment of red blood cells.

hemoglobinemia Excessive levels of hemoglobin (q.v.) in the blood plasma; a symptom of hemolytic anemia (q.v.).

hemoglobinuria The presence of free hemoglobin (q.v.) in the urine of the horse; a type of hemolytic anemia (q.v.); may result from poisoning, presence of a blood parasite, viral infection, antigen/antibody reaction, or severe stress.

hemolytic anemia An abnormal condition of the blood, characterized by a deficiency of erythrocytes (q.v.) which may be destroyed by poison, blood parasites, viral infection, or by an antigen/antibody reaction; symptoms include pale mucous membranes, jaundice (q.v.), lowered PCV (q.v.) and hemoglobin levels, hemoglobinuria (q.v.), hemoglobinemia (q.v.), and elevated temperature.

hemolysis A breakdown of red blood cells.

hemorrhage An excessive loss of blood.

hemorrhagic anemia An abnormal condition of the blood characterized by a deficiency of hemoglobin and/or erythrocytes (q.v.); caused by an actual decrease in the blood volume due to acute blood loss from trauma, parasites, or internal hemorrhage from ulcer, abscess, etc.; symptoms include pale mucous membranes, rapid pulse, evidence of bleeding, cold limbs, weakness, and depression.

hemp A tall annual herb, *Cannibis sativa*; hashish and marijuana are derived from the female plant, while the tough fiber of the male plant is used to make fabric and rope; historically used to make halters while individual fibers were used by saddlers for sewing.

hengest A historical term common in 476-1450 AD; a horse, generally a gelding.

hepatic jaundice Jaundice (q.v.) occurring secondary to disease of the liver.

herb Any plant or portion thereof put into culinary or medicinal use.

herbalism Also known as the simpler's art or herbal medicine; the systematic use and application of herbs and related materials for the purpose of healing.

herbalist Also known as herbal practitioner; one studied and practiced in the art of herbology (q.v.).

herbal medicine *see* HERBALISM

herbal practitioner *see* HERBALIST

herbal treatment Herbs taken orally or applied topically in poultices, oils, or tinctures to treat physical and emotional conditions.

herbology The practice of treating physical ailments and conditions using natural agents and physical means.

herd (1) Also known as band; a group of animals of one kind kept together under human control, as cows or horses. (2) A group of wild animals. (3) A racing term; to alter the course of the horse so as to prevent another from improving his position.(4) To keep together, to assemble or move animals together; to lead, gather, and drive as if in a herd. (5) *see* HERDER

herd bound (1) An animal reluctant to move away or be separated from the herd as a horse or cow.(2) *see* BARN SOUR

herder Also known as herd; one who herds (q.v.) domestic animals.

herd help A cutting term; riders who assist

the cutter (q.v.) by holding the herd together and preventing a separated cow from returning to the herd; in competition, consists of two volunteer herd holders (q.v.) and two turn back riders (q.v.).

herd holder A cutting term; one of two riders positioned close to the fence, one on either side of a contained herd of cattle, whose responsibility it is to help contain the herd when the cutter (q.v.) is driving cattle or working a cow.

herd-side leg A cutting term; the rider's leg parallel to the herd.

herdsman A manager, breeder, or tender of livestock.

heredity Also known as inheritance; the transmission of characteristics of parents to offspring through chromosomes which bear the genes.

hereditary multiple exostoses A hereditary condition in which numerous bony protrusions extend from the normal contour of affected long bones as well as the ribs and pelvis; in some cases may severely restrict movement while in other horses severe lameness rarely results.

hereditary trait Any characteristic, feature, or ability passed from the genetic make-up of either or both parents to the offspring.

heritability The extent to which a characteristic, feature, or ability is generally passed from the parents to the offspring.

Hermosillo bit A handmade Mexican curb (q.v.) having loose curved cheekpieces (q.v.) and a port provided with a cricket (q.v.); usually inlaid with a distinctive silver design on the shanks or cheek pieces.

hernia The protrusion of any internal tissue through the wall of its containing cavity; most occur in the abdominal cavity and may be any one of several types: umbilical hernia (q.v.), inguinal hernia (q.v.), direct or indirect (scrotal) hernia (q.v.), and ventral hernia (q.v.); are classified as either (1) reducible, characterized by a noninflammatory, painless, soft, elastic, compressible swelling that may vary from time to time where the protruding organ can be pushed back into the correct body cavity, (2) irreducible where the protruding organ has become attached to other body parts and because it is enlarged cannot be pushed back into the cavity, and (3) strangulated where the blood supply to the protruding section of the organ has been cut off requiring immediate surgical removal before infection or gangrene sets in.

herniae The plural of hernia (q.v.).

herpesvirus *see* EQUINE HERPESVIRUS

herring-gutted Also known as single-gutted; said of a horse whose body is flat sided, running upward sharply from the girth, and lacking depth of the flank.

heterozygote A horse who does not breed true to type because either the dam or sire contributes at least one pair of genes with different characteristics.

Heythrop Hounds, The Also known as The Heythrop; a pack of foxhounds (q.v.) – although originally harriers – used to hunt the Heythrop County located in the Cotswolds, Great Britain; the master and hunt servants of this pack still wear green livery to denote the pack's harrier origins.

hh An acronym for hands high (q.v.).

Hh An acronym for hands high (q.v.).

HH The acronym for the Hampshire Hunt, located in England.

Hickstead One of the greatest show jumping centers in the world, located in England; home to four meetings each year since 1960; built on the grounds of Hickstead Place (q.v.).

Hickstead Place The home of Douglas Bunn who, in 1960, started the All England Jumping Course there to provide a continental-style jumping facility with permanent obstacles for British horses and riders; in 1961, the British company W. D. & H.O. Wills began sponsoring what have become internationally recognized annual horse shows at the Hickstead (q.v.) facility.

hidden ride A riding technique used by the Roman cavalry and other populations subsequently whereby the rider would slip from the back of the horse and ride along its side in a prone position, supporting his weight by the mane, reins, and/or a neck grip; adopted to reduce the size of the target to the enemy.

hidebound Said of a horse whose skin is tight over its entire body resulting from dehydration (q.v.) or internal parasite infestation.

high airs *see* AIRS ABOVE THE GROUND

high blowing Also known as cracking the nostrils; a distinct sound sometimes made by a galloping horse caused by excessive flapping of the false nostril (q.v.); disappears as speed is increased.

high bow One of three classifications of bowed tendon (q.v.) identified on the basis of location, the other two being middle bow (q.v.) and low bow (q.v.); any true physiological damage to the tendon or tendon sheath, most commonly of the superficial flexor tendon of the foreleg; specifically, tearing or breaking of one or more of the tendonous fibers of the tendon just below the knee; may be precipitated by fatigue, deep going (q.v.), uneven terrain, improper shoeing, obesity, excessively tight fitting running bandages or boots, work on slippery surfaces, long, weak pasterns, sudden changes in stress loads, low heel angles, long toes; symptoms may include diffuse swelling over the tendon area, heat, and pain; lameness may or may not be present.

High Flyer *see* HIGH FLYER PHAETON

High Flyer Phaeton Also known as high flyer or spelled highflier phaeton; a four-wheeled, horse-drawn driving phaeton (q.v.) popular in the late 18th century; had extremely large wheels, those in the front being more than 5 feet (1.5 m) in diameter, while the rear may have exceeded 6 feet (1.8 m), a leather hood, and a long rear platform for two servants; the curricle-shaped body was hung from whip springs behind and elbow springs in front; drawn either by a single horse or pair, although a few might be driven four-in-hand or to a team of six – in the latter case, the nearside leader would be ridden by a postillion (q.v.).

high hook A polo term; to hook (q.v.) an opponent's mallet above the level of the withers of the horse.

Highlander Any Thoroughbred (q.v.) horse descended from the Godolphin Barb (q.v.); imported to the United States in the 1820s where they contributed to the early development of the American Saddlebred (q.v.).

Highland *see* HIGHLAND PONY

Highland Pony Also known as a Highland and generically as a native pony (q.v.); an ancient pony breed originating in the Scottish Highlands and the Scottish islands following the Ice Age; its ancestry is similar to the Fell (q.v.) and Dale (q.v.); Percheron (q.v.) blood was introduced in the 16th century, followed by Spanish and Arab (q.v.) blood in the 17th century; of two varieties: (1) the western Isles type standing 12.2 to 13.2 hands and (2) the Mainland type also known as a Garron that stands up to a height of 14.2 hands; has primitive markings (q.v.) including an eel stripe (q.v.) and zebra marks (q.v.) on the legs; the coat may be gray, palomino, mouse, dun, bay, brown, black, or liver chestnut with a silver mane and tail; has a well-proportioned head, a long, muscular neck, full mane and tail, well-muscled legs with feathering on the lower parts; used for riding, packing, light draft, and farm work; is free from heredity disease, long lived, docile, affectionate, and hardy.

Highland Pony Society, The An organization founded in 1923 in Britain to promote the general interests of the breeders and owners of Highland Ponies (q.v.); registers ponies in the National Pony stud book.

high leader The nearside leader of a 20-mule team; driven by voice commands in conjunction with a single jerk line (q.v.) which ran through the harness rings on all nearside mules to the leader.

high lows *see* PADDOCK BOOTS

high port *see* FULL PORT

high ringbone A bony growth occurring at the joint linking the long and short pastern bones.

high roller Said of a horse who leaps high into the air when bucking (q.v.).

High School *see* HAUTE ECOLE

High School horse Any horse trained in the Haute Ecole (q.v.) or classical airs (q.v.).

High School movements Any advanced action, pace, and or figure performed or executed by a horse trained in dressage (q.v.); consist of the piaffe (q.v.), passage (q.v.), pesade/levade (q.v.), and the airs above the ground (q.v.).

high weight A racing term; the top weight assigned to a jockey (q.v.) or carried by a horse in a race.

hill topper A hunting term; mounted riders who follow hounds (q.v.) at a distance behind the rest of the field (q.v.), mostly on lanes and roads, through gates, and without jumping; generally beginners or those on green horses (q.v.).

hind A hunting term; a female red deer.

hind boot Also known as a rumble; a coaching term; a straw-lined basket located over the rear axle in which passengers traveled; after the 1700s, replaced by a wooden box to which a lid and seat were eventually added.

hind cinch *see* FLANK CINCH

hind footboard A coaching term; a leather-covered, narrow platform, attached to the rear of a town carriage, on which the servant stood.

hind hunting A hunting term; to hunt female red deer from horseback; generally begins in early November, continuing until mid-March.

hind leg Also known as rear leg; the hind limb, specifically the portion of the horse's leg (q.v.) between the hock and coronary band (q.v.).

hindquarters Also known as quarters or buttocks; the rear or hind end of a horse including the croup (q.v.) to a point a few inches below the root of the tail, rump (q.v.), haunches (q.v.), gaskin (q.v.), and rear legs.

hind standard A coaching term; ornate framing located on either side of the hind footboard (q.v.) of some horse-drawn town chariots and coaches (q.v.); made of a combination of carved, wooden pillars and ornamental iron; used for decoration to balance the profile of the carriage, and to serve as mounting handles for the servants climbing onto the footboard.

hind sticker A racing term; a horseshoe (q.v.) having a cleat on the outside rather than the inside edge.

hinge joint The point of junction between two moveable bones where the joint (q.v.) may be extended, as in the knee joint.

hinny Also known as bardot or jennet in England; the hybrid progeny of a male horse or pony and a female ass (q.v.); looks more like a horse with the body of an ass having a light head, short ears, and a full tail (the head and tail of a hybrid inherit the characteristics of the sire); often difficult to differentiate from a mule (q.v.); bred more rarely than mules because the dam throws offspring that mature smaller and because asses do not conceive as readily to stallions as they do to jacks (q.v.); males are generally castrated.

hip Also known as the haunch; the side of the pelvis including the hip joint (q.v.) and the upper part of the thigh with their fleshy covering parts.

hip brand An identifying mark, symbol, number or any combination thereof, applied to the hip of a horse using a flame-heated, red-hot iron in hot branding (q.v.), cryogenics when freeze branding (q.v.), or acid.

hip down Said of a horse having a healed fracture (q.v.) of the point of the hip (q.v.) in which the healed point of the hip may appear lower than customary.

hip joint *see* ACETABULUM

hip number An identification number sprayed onto the hip of horses presented at Thoroughbred (q.v.) sales.

hipogryph *see* HIPPOGRIFF

Hipparchikos Also spelled Hopparchikos; a treatise on Xenophon's (q.v.) duties as a cavalry commander and the training of cavalry mounts; the earliest known written work on the subject of cavalry training written in 365 BC.

Hipparion An early Pliocene mammal with three toes; in the theory of evolution it is believed to be one of the earliest ancestors of the horse.

Hippike The treatise on horsemanship written by Xenophon (q.v.) in 365 BC in which he describes the classic principles of horse training; a different work than the *Hipparchikos* (q.v.).

hip, point of *see* POINT OF THE HIP

hippocrene *see* HORSEWELL

hippology The study of the horse.

hippodrome (1) In ancient Greece and Rome, a course for horse and chariot races. (2) Any arena (q.v.) or structure in which equestrian or other events were conducted.

Hippodrome de Vincennes The leading French raceway; a 1-1/4 mile (2 km) track recognized as the supreme test for both harness and saddle trotters; begins downhill, then levels out until the last 1,000 yards (900 m), which have a severe uphill gradient.

hippogriff Also spelled hipogryph; a mythological animal having the body and hind parts of horse and the wings, claws, and head of a griffin.

hipposandal Thought to be the oldest type of horseshoe (q.v.) used by the Romans sometime during the 1st and 4th centuries AD; consisted of a metal sole tied to the horse's hoof with leather straps.

hip strap *see* BEARING STRAP

hireling A hunting term; a horse who is rented for a day or season of hunting (q.v.).

hirsutism Abnormal hair growth.

Hispano Also known as Spanish Anglo-Arab, Spanish Arab, or Hispano Arabian; a horse breed indigenous to Spain which descended from Arab Spanish mares put to English Thoroughbred (q.v.) stallions; is quiet, but energetic, agile, intelligent, and has great courage and spirit; has more pronounced Arab characteristics than the Anglo-Arab (q.v.), stands 14.3 to 16 hands, and usually has a bay, chestnut, or gray coat; is versatile, being well suited to many types of equestrian events including jumping, dressage, and to test the fighting spirit and stamina of young bulls bred to be fought in the bullring.

Hispano Arabian *see* HISPANO

histamine A substance produced by the body in response to an allergy or infection which causes pruritis (q.v.), urticaria (q.v.), and bronchoconstriction (q.v.); neutralized by antihistamines (q.v.).

hitch (1) To tie a horse to an object as in, Hitch the horses to a rail.(2) Also known as hitch up, put to, hook up, or hitch to; to harness or yoke and secure one or more horses to a coach or carriage it is to pull. (3) The connection between the horse(s) and the horse-drawn vehicle. (4) The connection between the horse trailer and the vehicle pulling it. (5) A gait defect noted in the hind legs, whereby the horse seems to skip at the trot; results from uneven stride length between the hind legs. (6) A generic term; the horses used to pull a horse-drawn vehicle, e.g., The draw chain is used in multiple draft hitches.

hitch and hop Slang; said of the action of a Hackney (q.v.) when he momentarily breaks his trotting stride to a half-canter, hesitates as he puts in a short stride, and continues with an elevated cadence and pace.

Hitchcock gag A gag bit (q.v.) with fast action consisting of a single- or double-jointed loose ring mouthpiece with a smaller, second ring attached at right angles to the bit cheekpiece; a rounded leather or cord gag rein runs from the rider's hands, through holes in the secondary ring, up to and through a pulley attached to the bridle cheekpiece, and back down to the bit.

hitching (1) *see* HITCH no. 1. (2) *see* HITCH NUMBER no. 5

hitching bar *see* HITCHRACK

hitching post Also known as horse post; a fixed and sometimes elaborate vertical standard to which a horse or team (q.v.) can be tied to prevent it from straying.

hitching rack Also known as hitching rail; a fixed horizontal rail supported by two or more vertical posts to which a horse or team can be tied to prevent it from straying.

hitching rail *see* HITCHING RACK

hitch up *see* HITCH no. 2

hitch to *see* HITCH no. 2

hit off the line A hunting term; said of the hounds (q.v.) when they return to the line of a fox (q.v.), particularly after having lost the scent.

hit the hay To go to bed; to sleep.

hit the line A hunting term; said of the hounds when they pick up the scent of the quarry and begin to give tongue (q.v.).

Hittie Handbook for the Treatment of the Horse The earliest known treatise on the care and use of the horse for battle and chariot racing; inscribed on six clay tablets around 1360 BC.

hives Also known as urticaria, nettle rash, protein bumps, heat bumps, or sweet feed bumps; a skin ailment characterized by multiple, small, round elevated eruptions which are flat topped, and approximately 0.5 mm in diameter; may be produced by toxic irritating products of plants, insect stings or bites, the inhalation or ingestion of allergens, sensitivity to food stuffs, change of diet, bedding, intestinal parasites, or an allergic reaction to foreign proteins including serums, vaccines, antibiotics (particularly penicillin), and bacterins; welts may appear within a few minutes or hours following exposure; can develop on any part of the body, but occur mainly on the neck, back, flanks, eyelids, and legs; in advanced cases, may occur in on the mucous membranes of the mouth, nose, conjunctiva, rectum, and vagina.

hobble (1) To bind a horse's forelegs together to restrain its movement using hobbles (q.v.). (2) One half of a set of hobbles (q.v.).

hobbles Straps made of leather, rope, chain, or other material which encircle the pasterns (q.v.) or fetlock joints (q.v.) of the forelegs of the horse and are connected by a short strap or chain which fasten the forelegs together and restrict movement; designed to allow the horse sufficient leg movement to graze, but not to run away.

hobble strap Any strap component of hobbles (q.v.).

hobby (1) A generic term used since the 12th century; any strong, active, rather small riding horse standing less than 14 hands; a slightly different breed than the Irish Hobby (q.v.). (2) *see* HOBBY HORSE no. 3

hobby-horse (1) A figure of a horse fastened about the waist of performers in a morris-dance or pantomime. (2) A dancer wearing a hobby horse (q.v.). (3) Also known as hobby; a stick having an imitation horse's head at one end that a child pretends to ride as in a horse. (4) *see* ROCKING HORSE

Hobday Also spelled Hobday'd and known as laryngeal ventriculotomy (q.v.).

Hobday'd *see* HOBDAY

Hobday, Sir Frederick (1870-1939) A distinguished veterinary surgeon who practiced in London, England during the late 19th and early 20th centuries; authored several surgical books and developed the surgical procedure for relief of roaring (q.v.) known as laryngeal ventriculotomy (q.v.).

hock (1) Also known as tarsus; the large joint (q.v.) or region of the horse's hindlimb which connects the gaskin to the cannon bone when raised from the ground, appears as if bent backward. (2) *see* HAMSTRING

hock boot A protective covering of the hock (q.v.) used to provide support; may be constructed of leather or synthetic materials; straps around the front of the hock.

hockey on horseback *see* POLO

hock spavin A generally hereditary bony growth occurring at the back inside of the hock (q.v.) caused by a blow or strain; less serious than a knee spavin (q.v.).

hocks, well let down Said of a horse's hocks (q.v.) when relatively low to the ground, a preferred conformation characteristic; indicates a short cannon bone.

hoddlers *see* FLY TERRETS

hog To remove the entire mane with clippers.

hog back *see* ROACH BACK

hog backed *see* ROACH BACK

hogged back *see* ROACH BACKED

hog mouth *see* UNDER SHOT JAW

hogged mane Said of the horse's mane when completely removed by shaving or cutting.

hog's back Any show or cross-country, single-element jumping obstacle consisting of three rails; the first and last rails being set at

the same height with the middle rail positioned higher than the other two.

hogtied An American term; to bind all four feet of the horse or cow together to prevent him from standing or getting up.

hoick *see* YOIKE

Hoick Holloa A hunting cheer voiced to draw the attention of the huntsman or hounds to a fox.

hoicks *see* YOIKES

hold (1) *see* HOLD HOUNDS ROUND. (2) A hunting term; a covert (q.v.) in which a fox rests.

holder A frequently tasseled or ornamented braid or webbing strap attached by staples to the back of a horse-drawn carriage onto which servants riding on the footboard (q.v.) would hold.

hold hard A hunting term; a warning of the huntsman (q.v.) to the field (q.v.) to take care not to override the hounds (q.v.).

hold hounds round Also known as hold; a hunting term; said of the huntsman when he makes a cast (q.v.)

holding A racing term; said of a soft or heavy track.

holding scent A hunting term; said of the fox's scent (q.v.) when good enough to enable the hounds (q.v.) to follow his line.

holding up Also known as hold up; a hunting term; to turn a fox cub back into his covert (q.v.) when he attempts to run into the open.

hold up *see* HOLDING UP

hold your horses To take it easy, be patient, control one's temper, or slow down; an admonition tracing back to the American country fair of the 1800s where racing was a favorite pastime; harness races were especially difficult to initiate because the horses, sensing the eagerness of the drivers, were constantly breaking from the line and had to be called back; the restraint of the horses was figuratively transferred to refer to human restiveness and the restraint thereof.

holloa A hunting term; a cry of the hunter, commonly the whippers-in (q.v.), to indicate he has sighted a fox.

hollow back (1) Also known as sagging back or fallen back; a dressage term; a fault in which the horse drops his back resulting in a concave top line (q.v.) as opposed to convex one; may result when the horse fails to move from behind and/or evades the action of the bit by raising its head above the vertical. (2) *see* SWAY BACK

hollow backed *see* SWAY BACKED

hollow wall *see* SEEDY TOE

holly Trees or shrubs of the genus *Ilex,* a wood from which some whip (q.v.) shafts are made.

Holstein Also known as Holsteiner; a German-bred warmblood developed in the early 14th century as a war horse; infusions of Oriental, Spanish, and Neapolitan blood made the horse lighter, while Thoroughbred (q.v.) and Cleveland Bay (q.v.) blood refined the conformation and improved the gallop, and Yorkshire Coach Horse blood gave the breed its high, wide action and excellent temperament; in the 19th century used exclusively as a harness horse; since 1945, Thoroughbred blood has been used to produce a lighter, competition horse with greater speed and scope; stands 16 to 17 hands and generally has a bay, brown, black, chestnut, or gray coat; historically used under harness, yet now used for dressage, show jumping, and eventing; of a heavier build than the Hanoverian (q.v.).

Holsteiner *see* HOLSTEIN

Holyhead Mail, The A 19th-century British mail coach which regularly completed its 260-mile (418 km) route in less than 20 hours, stopping 27 times to change horses.

homebred (1) A racing term; a horse foaled in the state where it races. (2) Said of a horse bred by its owner.

homeopathic aggravation *see* HOMEO-PATHIC HEALING EVENT

homeopathic healing event Also known as homeopatic aggravation; a condition resulting in the first few weeks of homeopathic (q.v.) treatment, in which patients experience an intensification of their physical symptoms or emotional status or a return of previous symptoms; an indication the body is responding to the homeopathic remedy (q.v.) and is working to eliminate the disease process that is at the root of all the symptoms.

homeopathic preparation *see* HOMEO-PATHIC REMEDY

homeopathic remedy Also known as a homeopathic preparation; a medicament prepared from various plant, mineral, and animal sources using a process of serial dilution; more than 2,000 such formulations exist; frequently described by the use of the old Latin name of the drug, substance, or composition employed, followed by a designation of the dilution: X or D for decimal dilution, c or cH for centesimal dilution, and O for mother tinctures (q.v.).

homeopathic treatment To treat a horse using homeopathy (q.v.).

homeopathy A highly systematic, scientific method of therapy based on the principle of stimulating the organism's own healing process to accomplish cure; each creature is evaluated as a whole being, mental, emotional, and physical, and the prescribed remedy (q.v.) is based on the unique patterns found on all three levels; this means each creature is given the remedy that will stimulate its particular organism to heal itself at that particular moment recognizing that each organism possesses its own mechanisms for healing including chemical and physiological processes in addition to many more subtle ones that are yet to be understood; the dynamic healing energy in the organism is known as the vital force (q.v.); it is the vital force which is stimulated by the homeopathic remedy; the system was devised and verified by Samuel Hahnemann, a German physician, nearly 200 years ago; offers a safe, effective and natural way of healing by activating the body's own natural defenses and releasing the inner power of self-healing.

homestretch A racing term; the straight part of the racetrack (q.v.) between the final turn and the finish.

honda A western term; a small eye or loop in the end of the lariat (q.v.) through which the balance of the rope is passed to form a larger loop.

honest Said of a kind and reliable horse.

honest hound A hunting term; said of a dependable and trustworthy hound (q.v.).

honey bay *see* SANDY BAY

honey roan Refers to coat color; a roan (q.v.) pattern on a light sorrel alazán (q.v.) or blond sorrel.

honor (1) A cutting term; a cow who acknowledges and looks at the horse and rider. (2) A hunting term; said of the pack (q.v.) when it runs to an individual hound who has located the line of a fox (q.v.) and has given tongue (q.v.).

honor a line A hunting term; said of a hound when it gives tongue (q.v.) on a scent.

honorary huntsman A hunting term; the Master or an amateur when hunting.

honorary whipper-in Also known as an amateur whippers-in; a whipper-in (q.v.) who, unlike a professional whipper-in, does not receive payment for his services.

hood Also known as head cap or head lap; a fabric covering for the head, ears, and/or part of the neck when used in cold or wet weather for protection and the just head when blinkers (q.v.) are used on competition horses such as racehorses.

hooded gig *see* BUGGY no. 1

hooded port A bit port (q.v.) covered with copper.

hooey A calf roping term; the half-hitch put into the piggin string (q.v.) by the cowboy when tying off the feet of the calf; completes the tie.

hoof (1) Also known as horse hoof or foot; the horny covering of the distal end of the horse's leg including the third phalanx, navicular bone, tendons, ligaments, digital cushion, sensitive laminae (q.v.), and pedal joint; absorbs and reduces shock to the leg resulting from foot impact with the ground; averages 40 to 45 percent moisture; the single remaining toe on the leg of the horse, the vestigial toes include the chestnut and the splint bones. (2) The entire foot of the horse.

hoof angle Also known as toe angle; the degree of slope at which the dorsal line of the hoof intersects with the plane of its solar or ground-side surface.

hoofbeat The sound of a hoof (q.v.) striking the ground or other hard surface.

hoofbound Said of a horse having a dry and contracted hoof that occasions in pain and lameness.

hoofed Having hooves (q.v.).

hoofer (1) One who travels on foot. (2) A professional dancer.

hoof gauge A farrier tool used to determine hoof angle (q.v.).

hoof head The area where the hoof joins the leg at the coronary region.

hoof horn The horny, tough, insensitive parts of the hoof, such as the hoof wall.

hoof knife A wood-handled, 2-1/2 to 3 inch (6-7.5 cm) knife with a slightly curved, wide blade and upturned end used to pare away the dead sole from the hoof, remove ragged parts from the frog, to relieve pressure on corns and cracks, and remove foreign bodies from the foot; available in right- and left-handed styles.

hoofless Lacking hooves (q.v.).

hooflike Resembling a hoof (q.v.), especially having a horny texture as a hoof.

hoof nippers A pritchel-type farrier tool having long handles and a wide cutting tip; used to remove the surplus growth of the hoof wall; available in a variety of sizes.

hoof oil Any of a variety of lubricants applied to the hoof to moisturize and maintain pliability.

hoof-pick A hooked metal or plastic hand-held tool used to remove dirt, stones, and other debris from the ground-side surface of the horse's hoof.

hoof print An impression or hollow made by a hoof (q.v.).

hoof rasp *see* RASP

hoof rings Also known as growth rings, founder rings, laminitic rings, or fever rings; any horizontal distortion of the exterior hoof wall, which is visible the entire circumference of the hoof; reflects the dynamic ability of the hoof to adapt to internal or external forces; may be caused by any local injury, abrupt change in the quantity, quality, and/or type of nutrition, other metabolic insults such as a change in environment or season, or body-wide illness that compromises circulation to part or all of the foot; generally appear on all four feet.

hoof sealant Also known as sealant; any number of artificial varnishes applied to the exterior hoof wall which limit moisture loss from the hoof surface.

hoof tester A long, thin-handled instrument with a large, pincher-type tip, used to apply leveraged pressure to the walls and sole of the hoof to detect bruises or punctures, or to diagnose foot bone diseases or injuries.

hoof wall Also known as horn, wall, wall of the hoof, crust of the hoof, or crust of the wall; the horny portion of the hoof visible when the horse is standing with his feet flat on the ground consisting of the toe, quarters (q.v.), and the heel.

hook (1) A small curve appearing on the exterior surface of the upper corner incisor teeth of the seven-year-old horse; generally disappear when the horse is nine, returning when he is 11, and are often present until 17 or 18 years; an unreliable means of estimating the age of a horse, but may be used to strengthen an estimate; are generally removed by floating. (2) A polo term; to spoil an opponent's shot by placing one's mallet in the way of his striking mallet; of two types: cross hook (q.v.) and high hook (q.v.).

hooked A cutting horse term; a horse whose total attention is focused on the cow he is working.

hook fastening *see* STUD FASTENING

hook up *see* HITCH no. 2

Hoor Progeny (q.v.) of two Persian Arabs (q.v.).

hooved Having hooves.

Hooved Animal Humane Society Also known by the acronym HAHS; an organization founded in 1971 in the United States to investigate animal cruelty and neglect and perform animal rescue, education, and legislation benefiting the humane treatment of hooved animals.

hooves The plural of hoof (q.v.).

hop A racing term; to illegally drug a horse.

Hopparchikos *see* HIPPARCHIKOS

hopped A racing term; said of an illegally drugged horse.

hopples Originally known as Indiana pants; leather straps used to restrain and/or retrain the movement of the legs on trotting and pacing horses so that they maintain their desired gaits, e.g., to keep pacers from trotting and trotters from pacing; consist of a pair of leather straps with semicircular loops hung on hopple hangers from a crupper (q.v.) and neck straps; the straps are placed on the gaskin and forearm, connecting the fore and hind legs of the same side in pacers, and connect the diagonal fore and hind legs in trotters; developed in 1885 by railroad conductor John Browning.

hormone A secretion of the endocrine gland distributed through the blood stream or in bodily fluids; affects the action of tissues, glands, and organs other than the endocrine gland, e.g., growth, digestion, and reproduction; synthetic or man made hormones are often used to overcome deficiencies.

hormone assay A blood test performed to assess hormone levels in the blood.

horn (1) *see* HUNT HORN. (2) *see* HOOF HORN. (3) *see* COACH HORN. (4) *see* SADDLE HORN. (5) *see* BEAK

horn basket Also known as horn case; a leather case or basket historically strapped to the right rear of a horse-drawn coach where it was in reach of the head groom and which stored the guard's horn.

horn case *see* HORN BASKET

horn fly A blood-sucking fly (q.v.) most common in Europe in the waning days of summer and early fall; feed almost exclusively on the head, neck, and belly of horses and cattle; a swarming daytime feeder similar in appearance to a stable fly (q.v.), although more slender and about half the size; they burrow into the skin, where they may take as many as 24 blood meals per day; common in Europe, North Africa, Asia Minor, and the Americas.

horn neck Also known as horn; the vertical shaft upon which the saddle horn of a western saddle sits on one end and which inserts perpendicular to the pommel (q.v.) on the other.

horny laminae *see* INSENSITIVE LAMINAE

horny sole The layer of hard horn (q.v.) approximately 3/8 inch (9.5 mm) thick secreted by the sensitive sole; composed of variable-length horn tubules, is concave on the ground surface, and attaches to the frog towards the rear of the hoof; protects the sensitive inner part of the foot from impact and assists in providing support.

horse (1) Historically known as a prad; a large, solid-hooved, herbivorous mammal, *Equus caballus*, domesticated by man since prehistoric times and used as a beast of draft and burden and for carrying a rider; distinguished from the other existing members of the genus *Equus* and family *Equidae* by the long hair of the mane and tail, the usual presence of a callosity on the inside of the hind leg below the hock, and other less constant characteristics. (2) To ride horseback. (3) To give a person a horse to ride. (4) To control by brute force. (5) Said of a mare; to be in season (q.v.). (6) Large or coarse of kind. (7) Hauled or powered by a horse, e.g., horse barge. (8) The male of a horse; a stallion (q.v.). (9) A racing term; a stallion four years or older.

Horse & Hound A weekly periodical first published in 1884; includes stories and show/race information on racing, hunting, and showing.

horse-and-buggy (1) Of or relating to the era before the advent of the automobile and other socially revolutionizing major inventions. (2) Clinging to outworn attitudes or ideas, e.g. the horse-and-buggy city planners.

horse apples Horse droppings or manure (q.v.).

horseback (1) To ride astride a horse. (2) The back of a horse. (3) Given thorough consideration as in a horseback opinion.

horsebacker A person on horseback (q.v.).

horse bee *see* HORSE BOT

horse blanket Also known as blanket, clothes, or rug; a covering worn by the horse to provide warmth, refuge from biting insects, protection from the weather, and to keep clean; available in a variety of designs, weights, and materials as dictated by the use for which it is intended.

horse block *see* MOUNTING BLOCK

horse boat A boat for conveying horses and cattle.

horse bot Also known as horse bee, bot larvae, or bot; the larval stage of the horse botfly (q.v.) which occur in the stomach of the horse where they may live for months; most horses are affected.

horse botfly Also known as botfly; any of several botflies (q.v.) chiefly attacking horses; a fly with a yellow and dark banded body which lays tiny yellow eggs on the leg, shoulder, nose, and throat hair of horses during the summer months whence they are ingested and passed into the digestive tract where they hatch into larvae and feed on the stomach lining; of three types: *Gastrophilus intestinalis* (q.v.) (the most common), *Gastrophilu nasalis* (q.v.) (abundant, but not found in colder climates), and *Gastrophius haemorrhoidalis* (q.v.) (found occasionally in most countries, but is common in Russia and parts of Asia).

horse-box (1) Also known as box or in Australia as float or horse float; a truck equipped to carry and transport horses; the horse compartment is positioned over the vehicle axles rather than pulled behind the vehicle. (2) A square-shaped, well-sprung vehicle used to transport horses; usually headed, with a crosswise driver's seat located at roof level with an angled footboard; drawn by a single horse or pair; horses were loaded by means of a rear ramp which formed the tailboard.

horseboy *see* HOSTLER

horse brass Historically, a protective amulet (q.v.) worn by people and attached to the harnesses of draft horses and oxen to distract and ward off evil spirits; these shiny, hammered brass, nickel plate, or other metal amulets were thought to repel the evil eye with their images of the pagan gods; it was believed that the evil eye was most powerful when the potential victim was triumphant, therefore horses were decked out with protective amulets at all festivals and important events; there are approximately 3,000 different known patterns, but all are of four basic patterns: sun circle or sunflash brasses (q.v.), crescent brasses (q.v.), heart brasses (q.v.), and horseshoe brasses (q.v.); today used solely for decoration and show; in the late 1800s and early 1900s were often struck for special events and to denote specific trades, e.g., an anchor for dock teams.

horsebreaker *see* TRAINER

horsebrush Any of several plants of the genus *Tetradymia*, family *Compositae*, occurring on the rangelands in the western United States which are a major cause of bighead disease (q.v.), particularly in sheep.

horsecar (1) Also known as streetcar; an American term; a horse-drawn vehicle operated over a street tramway or light railway, frequently on a channel rail; invented in 1831. (2) A vehicle equipped to transport horses.

horse cassia An East Indian cassia plant of the genus Cassia marginata, having long pods containing a black cathartic pulp used as a horse medicine.

horse cavalry Cavalry troops mounted on horseback as distinct from mechanized cavalry.

horse chestnut A large Asian tree, *Aesculus hippocastanum* of the family *Hippocastanaceae*, the horse-chestnut family, that has palmate leaves and erect conical clusters of showy flowers; is widely cultivated as an ornamental and shade tree.

horse-coper *see* HORSE DEALER

horsecorser An archaic term; a dealer in horses, particularly a tricky one.

horsecourser *see* HORSECORSER

horsecouper *see* HORSE DEALER

horse dance (1) A dance performed by many North American Indians in which a rearing horse is imitated. (2) A dance executed on either a live horse or hobby-horse (q.v.).

horse dealer Also known as horse trader or in Britain as a coper, horse-coper, or horsecouper; one who buys, sells, and/or trades horses and ponies for profit or commission.

horse devil Also known as tumbleweed; a wild indigo, *Baptisia lanceolata*, common to the southern United States that when dried and withered is rolled around by the wind sometimes frightening horses.

horse doctor *see* VETERINARIAN

horse drawing A competition in which the pulling power of draft horses is tested.

horseface Any person having a long and homely face.

horse-fall A movie industry term; a fall performed on cue by a stunt horse, e.g., in battle scenes, cavalry charges, and race-horse accidents.

horsefeathers Slang; nonsense.

horseflesh (1) Also known as horsemeat; the flesh of the horse especially when slaughtered for food. (2) A generic term; horses, especially those used for driving, racing, or riding.

horse float *see* HORSE-BOX no. 2

horsefly (1) Any large, stocky, swift-flying, two-winged insect of the family Tabanidae having in the female a piercing, blade-like proboscis with which the blood of animals such as horses is sucked inflicting painful bites which result in swelling; range in size from less than 1/3 to 1-1/4 inches (8.5-32 mm) long and have clear wings; up to 1/2 mm (two drops of blood) may be extracted with each bite; along with the deer fly (q.v.), considered the most important pest in North America; the life cycle can last from one to two years depending upon the species and location in which it is found; the larvae are aquatic or semiaquatic; males of the family feed on flowers and vegetable juices; difficult to control with fly-control compounds. (2) Any of several flies that annoy the horse.

horse gait *see* GAIT no. 2

Horse Guards A hand-picked group of cavalry riders, especially the English Household Cavalry from which guards for the sovereign are selected.

horsehair (1) The hair of the horse, particularly of the mane and tail. (2) Cloth made of horsehair.

horsehide (1) The hide of the horse. (2) The leather made from a horsehide. (3) The ball used in the game of baseball.

horse hinny A male hinny (q.v.).

horse hoe A horse-drawn surface cultivator.

horse hoof *see* HOOF

horse identification Any of several methods used to permanently mark a horse including hot brands, acid brands, freeze brands (q.v.), tattoos (q.v.), and microchips (q.v.) to prove ownership.

horse in hand *see* LONGE

horsekeeper One who has charge of horses.

horse knaker *see* KNACKER

horse latitudes Either of two belts or regions in the area of 30 degrees N and 30 degrees S latitude characterized by high pressure, calms, and light, baffling winds.

horse laugh A loud and boisterous laugh.

horseleech An aquatic sucking worm, of great size and sucking capability, with which veterinary surgeons historically used to remedy common diseases of the horse; the worm was used to suck the bad blood from the horse.

horseless carriage An automobile, especially earlier models.

horselike Resembling a horse.

horse louse *see* LOUSE

horseman (1) A man on horseback. (2) One skilled in riding horses. (3) One who raises, manages, trains or tends to horses. (4) *see* CAVALRYMAN

Horseman's Benevolent and Protection Association A trade association consisting of the owners and trainers of race horses.

horsemanship The art of riding on horseback; equestrian skill.

Horseman's Sunday Service A religious service originating in 1949 in Britain and held annually at Tattenham Corner, Epsom Downs (q.v.); to bless all horses, ponies, and donkeys, whether ridden or driven; now held at other locations throughout the world.

Horse Marines *see* TELL THAT TO THE HORSE MARINES

horsemastership A generic term; the care, maintenance, and use of a horse in all pleasure and commercial activities.

horse meat *see* HORSE FLESH

horse mule Also known as a john mule; a male mule (q.v.); generally gelded, since stallions, although sterile, are sexually active.

horse nail *see* HORSESHOE NAIL

horse opera A novel, story, motion picture, or broadcast dealing with life in the western United States, especially during the latter half of the 19th century, and usually having cowboys as the principal characters.

horse parlor A place where betting on horses is conducted.

horse pistol A large pistol formerly carried by horsemen (q.v.).

horseplay (1) Rough or rowdy play or practical jokes. (2) To engage in horseplay.

horseplayer One who habitually bets on horse races.

horseplaying Betting on horse races.

horse post (1) *see* HITCHING POST. (2) A mail carrier who makes his deliveries on horseback. (3) Mail service performed by a horse post.

horsepower The power that a horse exerts in pulling; technically speaking, the rate at which work is accomplished when a resistance (weight) of 33,000 pounds is moved one foot in one minute, or 550 pounds is moved one foot in one second; a term conceived in the 18th century by Scottish engineer James Watt to explain the work rate of his new machinery, steam engines; calculated as the average rate of power of dray horses used in London breweries multiplied by 1.5, e.g., to be 10 horsepower an engine had to have the power of 15 muscular dray horses.

horsepox Also known as equine variola; a viral disease of horses related to cowpox and marked by a vesiculopustular eruption of the skin, especially on the pasterns.

horsepower hour The work performed or energy consumed by working at the rate of one horsepower hour for one hour; equal to 1,980,000 foot-pounds.

horse race *see* RACE

horse racer (1) One who keeps horses for racing. (2) *see* JOCKEY

horse racing Also known as sport of kings; a racing term; the racing of horses for sport.

horse rake A horse-drawn rake.

horse-riding *see* RIDING

horse room A bookmaker's (q.v.) establishment where information on horse races is provided and where bets are placed on them.

horses Also known in slang as cattle; the plural of horse (q.v.).

Horses and Ponies Protection Association An organization founded in Great Britain in 1937 to improve conditions for the slaughter horse, encourage more strict supervision of slaughter houses, and to protect native pony breeds at fairs, sales, and in transit.

horse's ass A stupid or incompetent person; considered vulgar.

horse sense Practical good sense; common sense.

horse shit (1) *see* FECES. (2) Nonsense, bunk; considered vulgar.

horseshoe (1) Also known as shoe; a metal, U-shaped plate which follows the outline of the horse's foot to which it is attached to provide protection from rough surfaces; prior to 70 AD, consisted of broom slippers, while in the 1st through 4th centuries AD, consisted of a metal plate fitted to the hoof with leather strapping (Roman hipposandal [q.v.]); nailed types were first used in the 9th century AD and became widely known sometime after 400 AD; during the Dark Ages and Medieval times, the horseshoe was crescent-shaped and resembled a snake which was thought to be divine and keep witches away. (2) 18th century slang; the female genitals. (3) A form of quoits played by tossing horseshoes over a peg. (4) *see* SHOE. (5) Shaped like a horseshoe.

horseshoe brasses A shiny, hammered brass, nickle plate, or other metal amulet struck with the a horseshoe pattern; were attached to the harness and other tack to ward off the evil eye and bring good luck; the heels of the horseshoe generally pointed up, although brasses for towns or districts near the sea always had the heels pointing down to protect against the dangers of water; other patterns include sunflash brasses (q.v.), crescent brasses (q.v.), and heart brasses (q.v.).

horseshoe nail Also known as a horse nail or nail; a thin, pointed, soft steel nail with a heavy flaring head used to fix a horseshoe (q.v.) to the hoof; generally four-sided, with a tapered shaft, and a tip beveled on the inside; a pattern or trademark is stamped on the inside face of the head to make it possible to determine the inside from the outside of the nail.

horseshoe pad Also known as a pad or shoe pad; a leather, plastic, or rubber lining cut in the shape of the ground-side surface of the hoof which is placed between the horseshoe and hoof to provide protection and padding to the sole.

horseshoer *see* FARRIER

horse show Also known as show; a meeting at which competitions are held to test or display the qualities and capabilities of horses and their riders, drivers, or handlers; may take place on one day or over many; prizes are awarded depending on performance or the judge's selection.

horsesickness *see* AFRICAN HORSESICKNESS

horse standard *see* MEASURING STICK

horse tail *see* TAIL

horse-tailing To take charge of a herd of horses, as in drovers (q.v.) when herding horses, cattle, or sheep over long distances.

horse-tamer *see* TRAINER no. 1

horse tick Any tick that feeds on a horse.

horse tick fever *see* EQUINE PIROPLASMOSIS

horse trade (1) A commercial negotiation conducted to buy and sell a horse(s). (2) Any negotiation accompanied by shrewd bargaining and reciprocal concessions.

horse-trade To engage in horse trade.

horse trader *see* HORSE DEALER

horse trading The act; practice; or instance of making a horse trade (q.v.).

horse-trainer *see* TRAINER no. 1

horse trials Also known as militaire, military trials, or combined training event; an event consisting of show jumping, cross country, and dressage phases conducted over a period of one, two, or three days; differs from a Three-Day Event (q.v.) in its exclusion of the endurance phase.

horse tripping Any Mexican competitive event as performed at charreadas (q.v.) in which a horse is herded, lassoed (q.v.), and toppled to the ground; include piales en el lienzo (q.v.) and the mangana (q.v.); now illegal in a number of states within the United States.

horsewell Also known as Hippocrene; the mythical fountain or stream which sprung from Mount Helicon following a swift blow of Pegasus' (q.v.) hoof.

horsewhip (1) *see* WHIP. (2) To flog with, or as if with, a whip made to be used on a horse.

Horse Whisperers Also known as whisperers; a school of horse trainers which emerged in the United States in the 19th century known for their technique of training and calming horses by breathing into their nostrils; the most famous was John Rarey, who, in the mid-1800s, demonstrated the technique around the world.

horse with the fine walk *see* PASO FINO

horsewoman: (1) A woman on horseback. (2) A woman knowledgeable in riding and maintaining horses; a woman possessed of a good sense (q.v.) of the horse.

horsey (1) Also spelled horsy; associated with the nature or quality of horses; engrossed with horses, as with their breeding or racing. (2) Characteristic of horsemen (q.v.) and horsewomen (q.v.). (3) Relating to or resembling a horse.

horsily In a horsey manner.

horsiness The quality or state of being horsey (q.v.).

horsing: (1) Said of a mare in heat (q.v.) who demonstrates signs of estrus (q.v.). (2) To engage in horseplay (q.v.).

horsing stone *see* MOUNTING BLOCK

horsy *see* HORSEY

Hosteiner *see* HOLSTEIN

hostler Also known as a horseboy and spelled ostler; a British term; a man in charge of the stabling of horses and other stock at an inn.

hot (1) Said of a horse whose body temperature has risen above normal levels due to exercise or illness. (2) A racing term; a stable or jockey on a winning streak or expected to win. (3) Said of an easily excitable horse.

hotblood Also known as fullblood; a fine-boned, high-spirited horse, generally of Arab (q.v.) or Thoroughbred (q.v.) extraction; so called because of the temperament exhibited and because the original stock came from the hot regions of the Middle East and North Africa.

hot-blooded (1) Of Eastern or Oriental blood. (2) A horse possessed of a fiery, high-strung, or excitable temperament.

hot brand (1) Also known as fire brand or hot iron brand; an identifying mark, symbol, number or any combination thereof, applied to the hide of a horse using a flame-heated, red-hot metal iron; generally found on the hip and for some breed registrations on the shoulder or neck; does not hold up in a court of law as proof of ownership as is easily altered; now used predominantly to identify breed registration; identified on the basis of location, i.e. hip brand (q.v.). (2) To apply an identifying mark, symbol, or number to the hide of a horse using a shaped, flame-heated, red hot iron; the hot iron burns the hide sufficiently to create scar tissue in the shape of the mark, symbol, or number.

hot fit Also known as hot set; to hold a hot shoe against the prepared bottom of the foot until it scorches it sufficiently to identify high spots on the horn which must be removed to make the surface of the hoof level; also used to seat clips; generally performed when hot shoeing (q.v.).

hot horse *see* HOT

hot iron brand *see* HOT BRAND

hot nail A horseshoe nail when driven too close to the white line resulting in a condition known as nail bind (q.v.).

hot quit A cutting term; said of the cutter (q.v.) who lifts his hand or pulls off (q.v.) a cow in competition while the cow is still facing him and is actively trying to return to the herd; a three-point penalty; a cutter may only quit a cow when that cow is obviously turned away from his horse or when he comes to a dead stop in the arena.

hot set *see* HOT FIT

hot shaping To modify the shape of a horseshoe to fit the hoof after heating it in a forge (q.v.).

hot shoe (1) A long-heeled machine-made horseshoe. (2) A horseshoe made or shaped as in a forge (q.v.). (3) *see* HOT SHOEING

hot shoeing To shoe a horse with horseshoes shaped and fitted to the hoof using the heat of a forge (q.v.); often accompanied by hot fitting (q.v.).

hot shoer A farrier (q.v.) who, using a forge, hot fits (q.v.) horseshoes to a horse.

hot shot An electrical charge given to a horse ridden in bucking, bronc, or jumping events administered by the rider to shock the horse into bucking more strongly, to improve scores, or encourage him to jump when he might otherwise refuse; is illegal.

hot up Said of a horse who becomes easily excited.

hot walk To walk a horse to cool him down after a work out.

hot walker (1) One employed to walk horses to cool them out. (2) An electrical walking machine to which one or more horses are attached and led around the machine, which has varying speeds, in a circular direction; used to either exercise or cool down a horse.

hound A dog used for hunting as in sight hounds (q.v.) or scent hounds (q.v.).

hound couples A hunting term; a harness consisting of two hound collars connected by a piece of chain and swivel used to connect two hounds (q.v.).

hound gloves A hunting term; gloves made of horse hair worn by a handler to massage hounds (q.v.).

hound hunt A hunting term; a fox hunt in which the hounds pursue the fox with little scent and no sightings.

hound jog *see* HOUNDPACE

houndpace Also known as hound jog or fadge; the pace at which hounds normally travel on the road, about 6 mph (9.5 kmph); a jog (q.v.), neither a trot nor a walk.

Hounds Please A hunting term; a verbal warning to the field (q.v.) to be aware of the hounds (q.v.) and to move the horses out of the way.

hounds will meet *see* MEET

hound trot *see* JOG

housefly Also known as *Musca domestica*; a two-winged, swarming, nonbiting, daytime feeding insect; a fly; prefers the interior of buildings.

housing *see* SHABRAQUE

hovel Any three-sided shed located in a field or meadow used to shelter horses turned out to pasture.

hub Also known as nave or wheel hub; the thick center piece of a wheel into which the spokes attach and the axle is inserted.

Hucul Also known as Carparthian Pony and

spelled Huzul and Heecul; a pony breed native to the Carpathian region of Poland where it descended from the Tarpan (q.v.) with later infusions of Arab (q.v.) blood; ranged wild for thousands of years; has been formally bred since the 19th century in both Poland and Great Britain; stands 12 to 13 hands and all coat colors are seen, with dun (q.v.) and bay (q.v.) occurring most often; has a short head and a low-set tail, is very hardy, frugal, calm, sure-footed, and has good endurance; used for pack and draft.

huick *see* YOICKS

hull *see* SADDLE

hulled peanut meal A high protein, high energy concentrate produced from the residue of peanuts hulled before oil extraction and processing; contains 40 percent more protein and energy than unhulled peanut meal (q.v.).

human chorionic gonadotropin Also known by the acronym HCG; a hormone found in the urine of women during the first 50 days of pregnancy; sometimes used to stimulate ovulation in mares.

hummel *see* NOTT STAG

humor *see* HUMOUR

humour Also spelled humor; a historical British and 18th-century American term; any edematous swelling of the leg; now known as stock up (q.v.).

hung A racing term; said of a horse who does not advance its position in a race when encouraged by its jockey.

Hungarian Arabian *see* SHAGYA ARABIAN

Hungarian Shagya *see* SHAGYA ARABIAN

hunt (1) Also known as hunting; the sport of following, chasing, or searching, whether mounted or on foot, fox, stag, hare, or drag line behind a pack of hounds; to be held separately from shooting (q.v.). (2) *see* HUNT A COW

Hunt (1) Also known as hunt club or fox hunting club; a hunting term; an organization or group of hunters (q.v.) having complied with the standards of, and recognized and registered by, the governing association of the area – in the United States, this being the Mas-

ters of Foxhounds Association of America; is always capitalized. (2) Also known as hunt country; a hunting term; a geographical area delineated by a mixture of historical precedent, and in the case of dispute, arbitrated by the Master of Foxhounds Association (q.v.), hunted by a specific pack of foxhounds; is always capitalized.

hunt a cow Also known as hunt; a cutting term; said of a horse who follows the movement of a cow with its eyes.

hunt ball A hunting term; a black tie gala generally held during the hunt season or in conjunction with some formal event to raise money for the Hunt (q.v.) and to involve the community in the Hunt.

hunt boots Also known as hunting boots or jockeys; tall black riding boots worn by participants in a Hunt (q.v.); may have mahogany, flesh, or patent leather (q.v.) tops, the former being worn with a pin coat and the latter with a black.

hunt button A hunting term; a brass, silver, or black button engraved with a design, monogram, or distinctive lettering representative of a particular Hunt (q.v.); staff and members of the field invited to do so by the Master of the Hunt are authorized to wear the buttons with an appropriately colored hunt collar, both in the hunting field and with hunt evening dress; award of buttons is purely subjective; a brass or silver button is worn on a pink coat (q.v.) and a black bone button with a white design is worn on the black coat.

hunt cap (1) Also known as a hunting helmet or hunting cap; a hard-shell helmet (q.v.) historically covered with black velvet and worn only by Masters (q.v.), ex-Masters, Field Masters, hunt Secretaries, hunters, and children when on the hunt; adopted by women for hunting and riding in the 1940s. (2) A black helmet worn by English riders in competition and practice in hunting, eventing, jumping, and dressage.

hunt club *see* HUNT

hunt coat A coat worn by members of the Hunt (q.v.) when hunting; generally made of wool; men wear scarlet or black coats, while gray, black, and dark blue are acceptable for women.

hunt collar A fawn- or cream-colored fabric jacket collar presented to members of the Hunt (q.v.) when awarded hunt buttons (q.v.).

hunt colors The coat color worn by participants in a Hunt, e.g., a green coat denotes harriers (q.v.) while yellow coats are worn by the Berkeley Hunt (q.v.) in Great Britain.

Hunt Committee A hunting term; the annually elected Board of Directors of a Hunt (q.v.); hold title to all Hunt property including land, buildings, hounds (q.v.), horses, tack (q.v.), staff clothes, and miscellaneous equipment; has two primary responsibilities: (1) appointment of a Master (q.v.) or Joint Masters (q.v.) for a fixed term of office and (2) collection of funds to finance the Hunt.

hunt country *see* HUNT no. 2

hunter (1) A type, not a breed; any horse bred, trained, and/or appropriate to follow hounds (q.v.) in the sport of hunting (q.v.); is largely influenced by the nature of the country over which it is used; possess stamina and jumping ability and are generally Thoroughbred (q.v.) or Thoroughbred crosses. (2) A hunting term; one who rides in a hunt (q.v.). (3) *see* SHOW HUNTER

hunter clip To remove the coat of the horse leaving the hair on the legs up to the height of the elbows and thighs, and a saddle patch on the back; the coat is left on the legs to protect the horse against cold, mud, and cracked heels, and the saddle patch saves a sore back under the saddle.

hunter pace An American sport developed and first conducted by the Blue Ridge Hunt and run at Woodly Farm in Berryville, Virginia, USA in March 1954; two-person teams compete over lengthy courses in pursuit of an undisclosed goal within a predetermined ideal time; courses are 4 to 10 miles (6-16 km) long, include a number of obstacles ranging in height from 2-1/2 to 3-1/2 feet (76-107 cm), and at least one, three to ten-minute rest stop; teams set off from the starting area at three- to five-minute intervals, with competitors timed out when they leave the start and in at the finish; placings are determined by how closely a team's time matches the predetermined course time; time is meant to reflect the pace of an actual hunt over the same course.

hunter's bumps Also known as sacroiliac desmitis; acute and severe strain of the sacroiliac ligaments; occurs when the tuber sacrale is pushed upward and forward because of torn ligament attachments; symptoms include pain in the pelvic area, hindlimb lameness, shortened stride, quarters asymmetry, and, in some cases, a reluctance to jump; commonly seen in horses used for hunting and jumping.

hunter, show *see* SHOW HUNTER

Hunters Improvement and National Light Horse Breeding Society An organization founded in Great Britain in 1885 to improve and promote the breeding of hunters (q.v.) and other horses used for riding and driving.

hunter trials A hunting term; a competitive event for horses and ponies held by most Hunts (q.v.) and associated organizing bodies during the hunting season in which horses are ridden over a course of obstacles, preferably natural, made to look like those encountered in a natural hunt field within a specified amount of time.

Hunter-Type Pinto One of four Pinto (q.v.) conformation types developed with specific breed goals and standards in mind; an English horse of predominantly Thoroughbred (q.v.) conformation and breeding, although a running-style Quarter Horse may also be found in this classification; may be medium to tall and display refinement, quality, substance, and balance required for under saddle and over fences classes.

hunt field *see* FIELD no. 4

hunt horn Also known as a horn or hunting horn; a cylindrical instrument, usually 9 to 10 inches (23-25 cm) long and made of copper with a silver or nickel (German silver) mouthpiece, ferrule, and bands; carries only one note D or A; the quality of which is affected by the length and diameter of the tube; carried by the Master, Huntsman, or whippers-in and used to signal the hounds (q.v.) and the field (q.v.).

hunting *see* HUNT no. 1 AND FOX HUNTING

hunting boots *see* HUNT BOOTS

hunting box A hunting term; a small house occupied primarily during the hunting season.

hunting bow A black gossamer ribbon tied

in a bow which adorns the back of the hunt cap (q.v.); the tails or feathers of the bow are worn pointing upward by the Hunt Master (q.v.), while all others wear the tails of the bow pointing downward.

hunting cap *see* HUNT CAP

hunting flask A hunting term; also known as a flask; a small flattened container, usually of metal, used to carry liquor while hunting; may be carried on the person, in a leather holster, or in a sandwich case, either being attached by short leather straps to the dees (q.v.) on the saddle.

hunting gate *see* BRIDLE GATE

hunting head Also known as a fixed head, near head, near pommel, top pommel, or second pommel; the higher of the two padded pommels or horns on the side-saddle (q.v.); sits above the leaping head (q.v.) and supports the rider's right leg.

hunting helmet *see* HUNT CAP

hunting horn (1) *see* HUNT HORN. (2) *see* LEAPING HEAD.

hunting iron Also known as a plain hunting iron, swaged-side stirrup iron, English hunting iron, or graduated-side iron; the most common English-style stirrup (q.v.) having symmetrical tapered and slightly rounded sides and a perpendicular eye (q.v.) located at the top and center of the arch through which the leathers (q.v.) run; usually made of stainless steel, although may be constructed of nickle alloys or chrome-plated iron, depending on the desired function.

Hunting Phaeton *see* BEAUFORT PHAETON

hunting saddle *see* CLOSE CONTACT SADDLE

hunting season Also known as season; a hunting term; the period during which time organized hunts (q.v.) are conducted; in most countries, when both cub-hunting (q.v.) and formal seasons are considered, runs from late August through late March.

hunting seat *see* HUNT SEAT.

hunting the circle A reining term; said of the rider in competition who follows prior competitor's pattern, rather than creating his own; may also be said of the horse who follows a previously ridden track.

hunting the heel line *see* HEEL no. 2

hunt livery A hunting term; the distinctive coat, collar, and buttons of a particular Hunt (q.v.) worn by the staff and/or members of that Hunt.

Hunt Master *see* MASTER

hunt races *see* POINT-TO-POINT

hunt seat Also known as hunting seat; the traditional position of the rider in the saddle in which he sits back into the saddle with feet and legs pushed forward; no longer considered correct; superceded by the two-point position (q.v.).

hunt seat saddle *see* CLOSE CONTACT SADDLE

Hunt Secretary A hunting term; one responsible for maintaining the notes, files and records of the Hunt (q.v.), collecting cap (q.v.) money, and maintaining relations with landowners of the property over which the hunt is conducted.

hunt servant (1) A hunting term; any salaried employee of a Hunt (q.v.), e.g., the huntsman (q.v.), kennel huntsman, or whippers-in (q.v.). (2) *see* PAD GROOM

huntsman A hunting term; one in charge of the hounds (q.v.) during the hunt (q.v.), unless the Master is hunting his hounds as an amateur huntsman in which case the responsibility is assumed by the Master or his appointee; supported by assistance from the whippers-in (q.v.); normally lives in residence at the hunt kennels (q.v.).

huntsman's pocket, in the A hunting term; said of member(s) of the field (q.v.) who ride too close to the huntsman (q.v.) and interfere with his hunting the hounds (q.v.).

hunt staff A hunting term; the Master or Joint Master(s) (q.v.), huntsman (q.v.), and whippers-in (q.v.) responsible for the management of the hounds (q.v.) and conduct of the hunt; some authorities do not include the Master.

Hunt subscription A hunting term; the

annual fee paid by each member of a Hunt (q.v.) for the right to participate in all hunts identified on the appointment card (q.v.); varies according to the number of days normally hunted each week and is generally paid in advance every May 1st.

hunt terrier A small, short-legged terrier such as a Jack Russell Terrier, used by a Hunt (q.v.) to spook foxes from the earth, drains, or other hiding places inaccessible to the hounds (q.v.).

hunt tie *see* STOCK

Hunt Treasurer A hunting term; one of three officers of the Hunt (q.v.) responsible for maintaining the financial records/accounts of the Hunt (q.v.).

hurdle Any one of a series of wattle fences over which a horse must jump in hurdle racing (q.v.); constructed of brush in the United States.

hurdle race A race conducted on horseback in such countries as England, France, New Zealand, and Australia in which participants race over a flat cross country course having four to six, and sometimes more, low hurdles in the first mile, with an additional jump generally added every quarter mile thereafter.

hurdle racing To race horses over a course of hurdles (q.v.).

hurried Said of a horse who rushes through the paces (q.v.) without demonstrating rhythm.

Huzul *see* HUCUL

hyaline cartilage One of three types of cartilage (q.v.) found in fetuses, newborns, elk antlers, etc.; can ossify into bone.

hyaluronate sodium *see* ACID

hyaluronic acid The thick, lubricating fluid within a joint.

hybrid The offspring of two animals of different species or races; in the horse world, the offspring of any two species of the genus *Equus* which includes the ass, horse, zebra, and onager; all species within this genus will mate with each other with the resulting progeny a hybrid; is generally normal in all respects except that it may be infertile due to the different chromosome numbers of the different species; e.g., the mule (q.v.) is a hybrid of a horse and ass.

hydrochloric acid An aqueous solution of hydrogen chloride, HCl, a strong, fuming, highly corrosive acid used in industry, research, medicine, and to brand (q.v.).

hydrocortisone *see* CORTISOL

hyperimmune plasma A blood product exposed to an antigen (q.v.) to stimulate immunity above those levels required for protection; used to create harvestable blood levels of antibodies.

hyperkalemic periodic paralysis Also known by the acronym HYPP; a genetically transmitted muscular disorder characterized in some horses by muscle tremors, sweating, respiratory difficulty, weakness, and recumbency; affected horses have a defect in the channel that regulates the amount of sodium entering the muscle cell with an excess of sodium causing the muscle fibers to depolarize and the muscles to twitch involuntarily; serum blood levels are generally, but not always, elevated during attacks; the sodium channel defect is due to a genetic mutation inherited from one or both parents; began as a point mutation in a single horse which has been linked to, but not absolutely proven to have come from, the Quarter Horse halter sire Impressive (q.v.); a serious issue for Quarter Horse (q.v.), Paint (q.v.), and Appaloosa (q.v.) horse owners.

hyperlipemia A recently identified disease affecting plump donkeys and ponies, particularly mares in foal; is rare in horses; characterized by an excess of fat molecules, primarily triglicerides, in the blood; obesity, stress, pregnancy, gastrointestinal problems (usually from parasitism), malnutrition, a lack of appetite, or an insensitivity to insulin interfere with the amount of carbohydrate fuel in blood; the body responds by flooding the bloodstream with fat, which the liver and kidneys are unable to process and therefore shut down; symptoms include a loss of appetite, lethargy, and depression followed by a reluctance to move, lack of coordination, weakness, mild and intermittent colic (q.v.), diarrhea, head pressing, circling, convulsions, and death; is fatal in 65 percent of all cases within six to ten days; treatment is difficult.

hypermobility Increased motion in a motor

unit (q.v.); results in stress to the ligamentous components and associated structures due to the pathologically increased range of motion; may indicate facet syndrome pain (q.v.).

hyperparathyroidism *see* BIG HEAD DISEASE

hypersensitivity An overreaction to any substance such as shampoo, equipment cleaning solutions, or plant secretions that contact the skin; characterized by tenderness, heat, weeping sores, and pitting edema; symptoms will generally subside within one to three days following removal of the irritant.

hyperthermia Also known as elevated body temperature or raised body temperature; elevated body temperature above the normal range as caused by disease, overexertion, or high environmental temperature or humidity; exhibited in heat exhaustion (q.v.) and heatstroke (q.v.).

hyperthyroidism A treatable condition caused by abnormally high secretions of the hormones triodothyronine (T_3) and thyroxin (T_4) from the thyroid gland; symptoms include an increased metabolic rate, weight loss, vomiting, diarrhea, increased feces volume and appetite, enlargement of the thyroid gland, heart murmurs, and congestive heart failure.

hypomobility Joint fixation or lack of motion in the motor unit (q.v.) causing a joint or vertebra to lose function over all joint surfaces; evidenced by decreased range of motion in the affected area which is seen as a disruption of spinal movement including lateral bending and the inability to flex at the poll; when occurring in one motor unit usually results in hypermobility (q.v.) in adjacent motor units as the body attempts to maintain a normal level of vertebral function; unresolved fixations result in local muscle atrophy from disuse or from decreased nerve supply to the muscles.

hypomagnesemia A disease caused by inadequate levels of magnesium (q.v.) in the diet or absorption thereof; symptoms include muscle incoordination and nervousness.

hypothalamus An organ in the brain responsible for the regulation of body processes through the production of hormones or by direct control of the nerve cells.

hypothermia A state of abnormally low body temperature as caused by viral infection, internal bleeding or substantial external bleeding, and/or low environmental temperatures; symptoms include chills, disorientation, pale (loss of circulation) or muddy gums (circulation static), and loss of energy.

hypothyroidism A treatable hormonal condition caused by abnormally low secretions of triodothyronine (T_3) and thyroxin from the thyroid gland; characterized by decreased metabolic rate, weight gain, and development of a crested neck.

hypovolemic shock Circulatory collapse characterized by a progressively diminishing circulating blood volume relative to the capacity of the vascular system, leading to acute failure of perfusion of vital organs; caused by decreased blood volume through either blood loss or dehydration; symptoms include increased capillary refill time (q.v.), pale mucous membranes, ataxia (q.v.), low pulse pressure, irregular respiratory rate, low body temperature.

HYPP The acronym for hyperkalemic periodic paralysis (q.v.).

hyracotherium A lower Eocene mammal the size of a fox having four toes; thought to be an ancestor of the horse.

I

IAD The acronym for inflammatory airway disease (q.v.).

IAHA The acronym for the International Arabian Horse Association (q.v.).

Iberian Horse Also known as *Equus ibericus*; an ancient horse breed that contributed to the development of the Barb (q.v.).

ice Also known as icing; to anesthetize and/or reduce swelling and inflammation in the feet or legs of a horse by standing or packing them in ice; commonly practiced on the racetrack (q.v.).

Ice Age horse Also known as *Equus lambei*; a species of horse who roamed the tundra steppes of Eurasia until about 8000 BC, at which time the climate changed dramatically and the breed became extinct; stood about 14 hands, had a coat consisting of short, blackish-brown hair above the hoof becoming chestnut further up the leg, a long, flaxen mane and dorsal stripe (q.v.); the jaw and tooth structure were markedly different than that of *Equus caballus* (q.v.).

Icelandic Also known as Icelandic Horse or Icelandic Pony; a pony breed descended from ancient English Pacers (q.v.) taken to Iceland by the Norsemen who settled there between 860 and 935 AD; in 930 AD, laws were passed that prevented the importation of horse stock, thus keeping the breed pure for more than 1,000 years; selectively bred since 1879 to maintain the quality of its five gaits which include the *fetgangur* (q.v.), *brokk* (q.v.), *stökk* (q.v.), *skied* (q.v.), and *tølt* (q.v.); is small, stocky, has a deep girth, short back and legs, large head set onto a short, thick neck, an abundance of mane and tail hair, and feathering on the heels; stands up to 13.2 hands; is extremely intelligent, docile, hardy, and surefooted, has great endurance and is noted for its homing instinct; although usually gray or dun, there are 15 recognized coat color combinations; often kept in semi-feral conditions; used for mining, farming, transportation, racing (since 1874) and as a food source for the Icelanders who depend upon it as a staple of their diet.

Icelandic Horse *see* ICELANDIC

Icelandic Pony *see* ICELANDIC

ice skid A drag shoe (q.v.) used to hold a horse-drawn carriage/coach on an icy slope; a 2 to 4 inch (5-10 cm) iron link with protruding teeth placed under a tire of a hind wheel and attached by a floating ring to the axle.

ICF The acronym for Intern Classification Farrier (q.v.).

ichthamol An ointment made from a coal-tar base used to treat bacterial infections including abscesses.

icing *see* ICE

icterus *see* JAUNDICE

Ideal Pinto Driving class A Pinto (q.v.) performance event in which horses are shown pulling two- or four-wheeled carts; are judged 50 percent on performance and manners, 25 percent on conformation, and 25 percent on color.

identical twin *see* MONOVULAR TWIN

ileocolonic aganglionosis Also known as lethal white syndrome; a genetically based, fatal disease in which the foal is born without part of his intestine; colics (q.v.) soon after birth.

ilium Also known as wing or shaft; the bone of the ilia or flank which extends up and above the base of the pelvis and sacrum, the internal angles of which form part of the croup and the point of the hip (q.v.).

IM The acronym for intra-muscular (q.v.).

immune stimulant Any natural or synthetic substance which provokes the body's immune and inflammatory responses to defend the horse against illness and/or injury.

immune system A body-wide group of tissues including, but not limited to, the lymph system, spleen, bone marrow, and intestinal tissues, which are responsible for identifying and combating foreign substances.

immunomodulation An ill-defined chronic

soft-tissue soreness which does not respond to nonsteroidal anti-inflammatory drugs such as bute (q.v.) and which may result from a defective immune response.

impact The contact or striking of one object against another, as in the hoof to the ground.

impaction An obstructive lodging of food or food matter in the intestines.

imperial Also known as lunch box; a box positioned between the roof seats of a drag (q.v.), traveling coach, or chariot in which lunch for the passengers was stored.

imperial mercury An unusual, 16 passenger, horse-drawn vehicle patented in 1780 by Crispus Claggett; divided into four compartments by doors and glass.

Imperial Spanish Riding School of Vienna Also known as the Spanish School, Spanish Riding School, Spanish Riding School of Vienna, or Imperial Riding School of Vienna; a riding school founded in Vienna, Austria in 1572 to instruct nobility in classical equitation; originally, a wooden arena located adjacent to the Imperial Palace; the present location, the Winter Riding Hall, was built in 1735; so called because of the high percentage of Spanish and/or Andalusian (q.v.) horses used there; now, Lipizzaner (q.v.) stallions are used exclusively to ensure preservation and development of the natural paces of the breed which is specifically suited to the steps and movements of dressage (q.v.), including the airs above the ground (q.v.): the *levade* (q.v.), *courbette* (q.v.), and the *capriole* (q.v.); only Austrian male citizens are admitted and training may last from four to eight years; considered the home of classical riding.

Imperial Riding School of Vienna *see* IMPERIAL SPANISH RIDING SCHOOL OF VIENNA

import To transport a horse from one country to another; all registered imported horses are identified by either an asterisk in front of the name (e.g., *Flarisco [Ger]), or by the abbreviation Imp. in front of the name, and the country of export (e.g., Imp. Flarisco [Ger]).

impost A racing term; the weight carried by a horse in a race.

impregnate Also known as fertilize; to make pregnant by means of artificial (q.v.) or natural insemination.

Impressive The most successful halter sire in Quarter Horse (q.v.) history; responsible for passing the genetic defect hyperkalemic periodic paralysis (q.v.) to his descendants.

imprinting The initial act of socializing the foal performed by a knowledgeable handler shortly after initial contact of the foal with the mare following birth; includes the constant handling of the foal's body, lifting his feet, insertion of a rubber glove finger in the anus and another rubber glove finger in both nostrils until resistance to this type of activity is nullified.

improved Maremmana A modern Maremmana (q.v.) breed crossed with Thoroughbred (q.v.) to increase the stature and refine the appearance; the cross resulted in a loss of hardiness and the exceptional stamina which characterized the breed.

improver A European term; a farrier whose professional status is between that of an apprentice and journeyman.

impulsion The energy generated by the hindquarters (q.v.) which causes the horse to move forward actively and vigorously which, when unrestrained, becomes speed.

in and out A jumping obstacle consisting of two or three jump elements in which the individual elements are separated by one or two strides.

in-and-outer Also known as runs hot and cold; a racing term; a horse who runs inconsistently.

inattentive Said of a horse who does not listen to the aids of the rider due to distraction.

in-blood A hunting term; said of hounds (q.v.) having made a recent kill.

in-bred Said of the progeny (q.v.) of a closely related dam and sire.

in-breeding Mating of closely related horses such as mother-to-son, sister-to-brother, and father-to-daughter; seldom practiced in horse-breeding operations because of the high risk of producing offspring with poor dispositions and faults.

incisor teeth Also known as incisors or pincers; the 12 front (six upper and six lower) teeth of the horse consisting of four central incisors (q.v.), four lateral incisors (q.v.), and four corner incisors (q.v.); used for cutting rather than grinding; begin to erupt at 2-1/2 years with the appearance of the central incisors erupt followed by the lateral and corner incisors at one year intervals.

incisors *see* INCISOR TEETH

Incitatus Also known as Caligula or Porcellus the latter meaning little pig; Emperor Julius Caesar's racing stallion; when the horse began to win races, his name was changed to Incitatus meaning swift and speeding; was ultimately appointed a citizen of Rome and a Senator.

incomplete fracture A fracture (q.v.) which does not extend completely through the bone.

independent Gogue One of two types of de Gouge (q.v.); an advanced piece of schooling equipment consisting of an arrangement of straps fastened to the chest ring or girth on one end which split and run through the poll (q.v.) pad on either side of the temples, and to the bit rings on the other; used to assist the action of the bit by restricting the position of the horse's head and neck.

independent seat Said of a rider whose balance and body position on the horse are maintained without relying on the reins or stirrups as an aid.

index A racing term; a number that identifies a specific results chart; when printed in racing papers, directs the player to a chart of a horse's most recent race.

Indian broke A horse trained to allow mounting from the off side.

Indian martingale (q.v.) An auxiliary rein or strap used to assist the action of the bit by restricting the position of the horse's head and neck; consists of a strap fastened to the girth at one end which forms a noseband on the other that tightens around the nose of the horse as he raises his head.

Indian pony *see* PINTO

Indian style (1) Also known as swing up; a method of mounting a horse in which the rider stands at the shoulder of the horse facing the haunches, grabs hold of the horse's mane with both the left and right hands, and swings up on the back of the horse with the right leg. (2) *see* BARE BACK RIDING

Indiana pants *see* HOPPLES

indirect rein Also known as a bearing rein or opposite rein; to use the rein to apply pressure to the neck of the horse on the side opposite to which a turn is required, e.g., to signal the horse to turn to the right, the rider applies pressure to the left side of the neck using the left rein.

indoor polo *see* ARENA POLO

in estrus *see* ESTRUS

infectious arthritis Arthritis (q.v.) involving inflammation of the joint capsule caused by the introduction of infectious organisms into the joint through a wound or via the blood or lymph systems; the joint capsule appears distended and hot to the touch; the infection destroys the joint cartilages and underlying bone and causes new bone growth which ultimately results in ankylosing arthritis (q.v.) or osteoarthritis (q.v.).

inferior check ligament The direct continuation of the posterior ligament of the knee which provides support to the deep flexor tendon (q.v.); located below the knee.

infertile Inability to conceive.

in-field A racing term; the area inside of the inside rail of a racetrack where the grass and jump races are held and the tote board (q.v.) is located.

infield rail *see* INSIDE RAIL

inflammatory airway disease Also known by the acronym IAD; an irritative airway disease thought to be associated with persistent viral infection or the chronic pulmonary stress and inhalation of particulate matter associated with training and racing; normally strikes two- and three-year-old performance horses; symptoms include a slight nasal discharge and occasional light coughing early in exercise.

influenza *see* EQUINE INFLUENZA

in foal Said of pregnant mare.

in front of the vertical The horse's head carriage when he carries his muzzle (q.v.) in front of, e.g., towards the sky, an imaginary line drawn perpendicular to the ground; the opposite side of the vertical line from behind the vertical (q.v.).

in full cry A hunting term; said of a pack of hounds in strong pursuit of a quarry (q.v.) and giving tongue (q.v.).

infundibulum The funnel-like depression in the biting surface of the incisor teeth (q.v.) which becomes the cup.

infusion The introduction of fluid other than blood, e.g., a mare's uterus is sometimes infused with a sterile saline solution post-foaling to clean it out.

ingesta Food or drink consumed by the horse.

inguinal Pertaining to the groin area located between the leg and pelvis.

inguinal hernia A hernia (q.v.) occurring in the groin area; a condition where tissue descends into the inguinal canal leading to the scrotum in the male horse but does not enter it; surgical correction almost invariably leads to simultaneous castration.

in hand (1) To lead or work a horse from the ground. (2) A racing term; said of a horse running under restraint. (3) see IN-HAND CLASS

in-hand see IN-HAND CLASS

in-hand class Also known as in-hand or, incorrectly, in hand; any show class in which livestock is led, usually in a show bridle or halter, unsaddled and without harness, in and around the show ring through various paces and patterns; horses are judged on conformation, condition, and/or movement; draft horses are shown in saddle or harness.

in-hand line A cotton or synthetic rope or piece of webbing 6 feet (1.8 m) long and approximately 1 inch (2.5) wide, which is attached to the bridle by a hook and snap or buckle; used in dressage when training a horse such movements as *piaffe* (q.v.) and *passage* (q.v.) from the ground; the horse is worked in a straight line or in a fixed position, not on the circle.

in heat see ESTRUS

inherited lethal Any condition or disease genetically transmitted to the foal which may affect its lifespan or future productivity; of three types delayed lethal (q.v.), partial lethal (q.v.), and true lethal (q.v.).

in light A racing term; said of a horse competing in a race who is carrying relatively little weight.

inositol A B-complex vitamin necessary for proper metabolism and which may function as a coenzyme, although the exact function and daily dietary requirements of the horse have not been determined; produced by intestinal synthesis and deficiency is unlikely to occur.

inquiry (1) An official investigation into a competition to determine if a rule infraction occurred; initiated by an objection (q.v.) lodged by an official or competitor. (2) A racing term; a sign flashed on the tote board (q.v.) to indicate there is an inquiry on a specific race.

in rut Said of a deer or stag during rut (q.v.)

in season Also known as season; estrus (q.v.).

insecticide A commonly toxic substance or preparation used to kill insects and to suppress and/or control insect populations in and around the stable; potentially ineffective or even harmful if not used correctly.

inseminate To inject, to impregnate, as in semen (q.v.) into the mare.

insemination The act of inseminating.

insemination, artificial see ARTIFICIAL INSEMINATION

insensitive laminae Also known as horny laminae; the layer located just under the hoof wall which attaches the hoof wall to the coffin bone; does not contain blood vessels.

in shape (1) A racing term; said of a horse (who is ready to win. (2) Said of a well-conditioned horse.

inside (1) The side of the horse on the inside

of the movement, e.g., when on a right circle the inside is the right side of the horse. (2) Also known as inside position; a racing term; the racing position closest to the rail (q.v.). (3) A racing term; anything or anyone located to the left side of a horse during a race.

inside car A horse-drawn vehicle popular in Ireland; not unlike a governess car (q.v.) in construction; the driver sat upon an exposed seat in the front of the vehicle.

inside leg The leg of the rider or horse on the inside of the movement, e.g., in a circle to the right, the rider's inside leg would be the right leg.

inside position *see* INSIDE no. 2

inside rail Also known as an infield rail, running rail or fence; a racing term; the inside rail or fence separating the racing strip (q.v.) from the infield (q.v.).

inspection Visual examination of the horse to evaluate quality and/or condition for registration, breeding, health, sale, etc.

inspector One authorized or designated by an individual or organization to visually inspect a horse to gather data both in report and pictorial form; may be authorized to tattoo any horse which has passed breed registry inspection.

insulin A hormone secreted by the pancreas; controls blood-sugar levels and the utilization of sugar by the body.

Institute of the Horse and Pony Club, Ltd. An organization founded in 1925 in Great Britain; the authoritative center of information on all matters related to the training and management of the horse; absorbed by The British Horse Society (q.v.) in 1947.

Institut du Cheval An organization founded in Pompadour, France to register French-bred horses and maintain complete computerized files on such horses including ancestry, offspring, and track performance records.

intercostal Situated between the ribs (q.v.) as in cartilage (q.v.) or muscle (q.v.).

interdigitate (1) To interlock, as the fingers of both hands or the insensitive and sensitive

laminae (q.v.) within the hoof. (2) Collision between two pair of legs.

interfere (1) A racing term; said of a horse who impedes another horse in a race. (2) *see* INTERFERING

interfering Also known as interfere; limb contact occurring in both the fore- and hind feet of a horse in motion anywhere between the coronary band (q.v.) and the cannon, by the opposite foot.

interfering shoe *see* FEATHER-EDGED SHOE

intérieur Also known as the body; a class of accommodation offered on diligence (q.v.) horse-drawn vehicles during the 19th and 20th centuries in Europe; accommodated six or eight passengers seated vis-à-vis (q.v.) between the rear (q.v.) and coupé (q.v.).

Intermediate A jumping term; a second-level jumper (q.v.) between Preliminary and Open stages of development.

intern Also spelled interne; an advanced student gaining practical experience under supervision of one more experienced.

International American Albino Association, Inc. Also known by the acronym IAAA; an organization that superseded the American Albino Association, Inc. (q.v.) in 1985; maintains breed registries for the American Cream (q.v.), and American White (q.v.), and acts as the National Recording Club (q.v.) for horses, ponies and miniature horses.

International Arabian Horse Association Also known by the acronym IAHA; an organization founded in 1950 in Westminster, Colorado, USA to register Anglo-Arab (q.v.) and Half-Arab Horses and to regulate competition and exhibition of Arab Horses, including establishment of the criteria for showing and judging Arab (q.v.), Half-Arab, and Anglo-Arabian horses, at events across the United States and Canada; acquired the official stud book for Half-Arabian and Anglo-Arabian horses from the American Remount Association in 1951.

International Equestrian Federation *see* FEDERATION EQUESTRE INTERNATIONALE

International Federation of Pony Breeders, The An organization founded in Great

Britain in 1951 to develop international markets for different pony breeds and to serve as a liaison between breeders and buyers.

International Horse Show *see* ROYAL INTERNATIONAL HORSE SHOW

International Horse Show, Royal *see* ROYAL INTERNATIONAL HORSE SHOW

International Horse Show, Royal (CHI) *see* ROYAL INTERNATIONAL HORSE SHOW (CHI)

International Horse Show, Royal (CHIO) *see* ROYAL INTERNATIONAL HORSE SHOW (CHIO)

International Society for the Protection of Mustangs and Burros Also known by the acronym ISPMB; an organisation established in the United States in 1965 by Mustang Annie to register and campaign for the protection of wild horses and burros in North America.

International Union of Journeymen Horseshoers of the United States and Canada Also known by the acronym IUJH, as Platers Union, or formerly as Journeyman Horseshoers National Union; an association of farriers (q.v.) organized in Philadelphia, USA in 1874, membership being based on a comprehensive forging and practical horseshoeing tests; evolved from draft horse shoers to include racetrack horseshoers.

International Veterinary Acupuncture Society Also known by the acronym IVAS; an international association of veterinarians who use acupuncture to treat horses organized in the United States in 1974; trains and certifies veterinarians worldwide in the use of acupuncture.

Intern Classification Farrier Also known by the acronym ICF; a level of ability of student and novice farriers awarded by the American Farriers Association (q.v.) on the basis of written examination; is not a certification.

interne *see* INTERN

interosseous splint A splint (q.v.) occurring between the cannon and splint bones at the mid-splint bone area characterized by a telltale bump which is usually not accompanied by lameness.

interphalangeal arthritis *see* RINGBONE

interstitial Within the spaces between the tissues.

intestinal stone *see* ENTEROLITH

intertrack wager A racing term; a bet placed at one racetrack on a horse(s) running in a horse race at another track.

intertrack wagering A racing term; to place a wager at one racetrack on a horse(s) running in a horse race at another track.

interrupted stripe A face marking; any long, narrow white marking on the face of the horse which runs in a relatively straight line from the forehead, at eye level to, or almost to, an imaginary line which connects the top of the nostrils; is no wider than the width of the nasal bone.

in the book Said of a horse; accepted for, or entered in, the General Stud Book (q.v.) for the breed.

in the bridle *see* ON THE BIT

in the can A racing term; said of a horse who does not finish in the money (q.v.).

in the cheek Also known as plain cheek; said of the reins (q.v.) when attached to the mouthpiece (q.v.) rings of a bit such as a Liverpool (q.v.).

in the money Also known as run in the money; a racing term; technically, said of any a horse competing in a race who finishes in the top four positions; however, the bettor (q.v.) is only paid if the horse places in first through third position.

in the plate An antiquated term; said of a rider seated on the saddle on a horse.

in the soup A historical hunting term; said of a rider having fallen from the horse into water.

in the white Said of a horse-drawn carriage following construction, but before painting and trimming.

in tough A racing term; said of a horse racing against a field (q.v.) he is unlikely to beat.

intra-articular Within the joint (q.v.) space.

intracytoplasmic sperm injection Also known by the acronym ICSI; to take a sperm sample and inject it into the egg which is then implanted in a mare.

intradermal Administered directly into the skin, as in an injection.

intradermal injection To inject a liquid substance directly into the skin.

intramuscular Also known by the acronym IM; administered directly into the muscle, as in an injection.

intramuscular injection To inject a substance directly into the muscle tissue.

intravenous Also known by the acronym IV; administered directly into the bloodstream through a vein, as in an injection.

intravenous injection To inject a substance directly into a vein or artery as with a needle.

intussusception The telescoping of one section of the intestines by an adjoining section.

in use *see* ESTRUS

in velvet Said of a stag (q.v.) during the period April through July or August during which the antlers are covered by velvet (q.v.).

invitational Any competitive event in which participating horses and riders must be invited to attend and participate.

in vitro fertilization Also known by the acronym IVF; a laboratory method of fertilizing an ovum (q.v.); the ovum, surgically removed from the mare, is fertilized in a test tube with sperm from a donor male, then returned to the uterus of the original female donor or a surrogate mother to complete the gestation period; effective in humans and most other animal species, but historically difficult to implement in horses.

involuntary muscle Any muscle (q.v.) not controlled by will, as that which operate in such involuntary movements as breathing and digestion.

involution The process by which an organ

returns to its former size and cellular state, as in the return of the uterus and mammary glands to normal state following pregnancy or lactation.

in wear Said of teeth (q.v.) newly erupted from the gums that have grown out sufficiently to be used in the normal chewing action of the horse.

in whelp A hunting term; the state of a bitch (q.v.) when carrying young.

iodine A mineral component of the hormone thyroxin, produced in the thyroid gland; essential for reproduction and normal physiological processes, influences the metabolic rate and oxygen consumption, increases the uptake and utilization of glucose by the cells, and increases protein synthesis; dietary requirements for the horse have not been established, although estimates indicate rations containing 0.1 parts per million are satisfactory for the mature horse, a level generally achieved in the normal diet; deficiency may result in an enlarged thyroid gland (goiter), high foal death rate, or poor growth; levels in excess of 40 milligrams per day, may be toxic.

iodine deficiency Lack of sufficient levels of systemic/tissue iodine as required for normal body function; may result in goiter (q.v.).

Iomud Also known as Jomud or Yomud; a Russian warmblood developed by the Iomud Turkoman tribe from the ancient Turkmene (q.v.); previously popular as a cavalry mount and today excels at long distance races; similar to the Akhal-Teké (q.v.) in its stamina, but is not as fast and is smaller and more high strung; has Arab (q.v.) characteristics, standing about 15 hands with a compact, sinewy body, and long legs; generally has a gray coat although bays and chestnuts do occur; is exceptionally resistant to heat and able to survive without water for long periods and is particularly well-suited to cross country racing due to its stamina, speed, and natural jumping ability; used for riding and racing.

iris The pigmented, muscular eye structure located behind the cornea; dilates and contracts the pupil to regulate the amount of light reaching the retina.

Irish car *see* JAUNTING CAR

Irish Cob A type rather than a breed bred in Ireland since the 18th century established by crossing Connemara (q.v.), Irish Draft (q.v.), and English Thoroughbred (q.v.); breed characteristics are not stable and it often exceeds the height limits for cobs (q.v.); stands 15 to 15.3 hands, has a short neck and back, powerful, but short legs, and may have a bay, brown, black, gray, or chestnut coat; used for riding and light draft.

Irish Draft *see* IRISH DRAUGHT

Irish Draught Also known as Irish Draft; an all-purpose breed developed in Ireland; of uncertain origin, although it is thought to have resulted from upsizing of the Connemara (q.v.) with Clydesdale (q.v.) crosses during the 19th century; stands 15 to 17 hands, has sound, strong legs with little hair on the fetlocks, a strong, yet heavy-looking shoulder, free and straight natural action, and a brown, bay, chestnut, or gray coat; the stud book was established in 1917; a natural jumper and when put to Thoroughbred (q.v.) stallions results in top Irish Hunters (q.v.).

Irish Halfbred *see* IRISH HUNTER

Irish hobby A 16th and 17th-century Irish term; any equine sport including racing.

Irish Hunter Also known as an Irish Halfbred; a horse breed developed in Ireland by crossing Thoroughbred (q.v.) with Irish Draught (q.v.); stands 16 to 17.1 hands, is quiet and docile, has a slightly convex head profile, a short back, slightly sloping croup, and a bay, brown black, gray, or chestnut coat; although considered a halfbreed, the name is capitalized and listed with other breeds due to constancy of the physical characteristics; bred for hunting, show jumping, and eventing.

Irish Jaunting Car *see* JAUNTING CAR

Irish martingale Also known as Irish rings or spectacles; an auxiliary rein consisting of two metal rings connected by a short leather strap through which the bridle reins run and connect to the bit rings; positioned between the chest and chin of the horse; prevents the reins from entangling or being thrown over the head of a raucous or nervous horse.

Irish rings *see* IRISH MARTINGALE

Irish Slide Car A wheeless, horse-drawn cart popular in Ireland through the early 1900s; had two poles which formed the shafts to the rear of which a large, laundry basket was fixed and a load transported; the ends of the poles dragged along the ground on one end and were attached to the collar (q.v.) by means of rope traces on the other; pulled by a single horse.

Irish Sport Horse A relatively new horse breed developed in Ireland by crossing Irish Draught (q.v.) with Thoroughbred (q.v.); has great bone due to the limestone in the grass upon which they are raised; bone density is passed on at least through two generations in horses bred outside of Ireland; the breed registry is maintained by the Irish Horse Board in Dublin, Southern Ireland.

iron (1) An essential mineral in the nutrition of the horse; a constituent of hemoglobin contained in red blood cells which is responsible for transporting oxygen throughout the body; also contained in some enzymes responsible for utilization of food components by the horse; deficiency causes anemia; the dietary requirement of iron is low, estimated at approximately 40 parts per million. (2) *see* STIRRUP. (3) *see* BRANDING IRON

iron cart A waterproof, two-wheeled, box-shaped, horse-drawn cart constructed of bolted and cemented cast iron plates; had an outlet hose, valve, and pump with which to spread the contents; used to cart water and/or liquid manure for agricultural purposes.

iron gray Refers to coat color; a gray (q.v.) horse with little dappling.

iron horse A locomotive.

iron shot A cutting term; spurring, as to a horse.

irregular Said of the horse when one or more strides differ in rhythm, being shorter or longer than the others.

irregular pacing walk A walk (q.v.) in which both legs on the same side move forward almost together, the natural four-beat gait of the walk almost becoming two beats; results from tension and stiffness and is considered a fault.

Isabella Also spelled Y'sabella; refers to coat color; a very light, cream-colored shade of palomino (q.v.); the horse will have nonblue eyes and white, flaxen, or ivory mane and tail; in Europe, refers to all palominos (q.v.).

Isabella quagga Also known by the scientific name *Asinus isabellinus*; an extinct wild ass of a pale yellow color; roamed in large herds throughout Africa until the late 1800s.

ischaemia *see* ISCHEMIA

ischemia Also spelled ischaemia; a temporary or permanent, localized body tissue anemia (q.v.) due to blocked blood supply.

isolation barn A facility where sick horses are stabled separate from healthy ones.

ISPMB *see* INTERNATIONAL SOCIETY FOR THE PROTECTION OF MUSTANGS AND BURROS

Italian Heavy Draft A medium-sized cold-blood draft horse originating in 1860 at which time it was developed at the Deposito Cavalli Stalloni stud farm in Ferrara, Italy; descended from the Brenton (q.v.) crossed with Ardennes (q.v.) and Percheron (q.v.); historically bred for farm work, but due to mechanization is increasingly bred for human consumption.

Italian Saddle *see* CLOSE CONTACT SADDLE

Italian seat *see* FORWARD SEAT

itchy heel *see* CHORIOPTIC MANGE

itchy leg *see* CHORIOPTIC MANGE

IUJH The acronym for International Union of Journeyman Horseshoers of the United States and Canada (q.v.).

ITW The acronym for intertrack wagering (q.v.).

IV The acronym for intravenous (q.v.).

IVAS The acronym for the International Veterinary Acupuncture Society (q.v.).

ivermectin A generic name for an antiparasitic agent.

IVF The acronym for in vitro fertilization (q.v.).

J

jab (1) To poke or prod as with a spur. (2) *see* JOBBING THE MOUTH

jaca A Spanish term; a nag or pony.

jack (1) Also known as jackass or, in Britain, as stallion donkey; a male donkey (q.v.) or ass (q.v.). (2) *see* BONE SPAVIN. (3) *see* HORSE MULE

jackass *see* JACK no. 1

Jack Cart A primitive, flat, horse-drawn cart made in horse, cob, and pony sizes used in the hilly regions of southwest of England; had hoop-raves above the wheels and no side-planks or spindles.

jack-knifing Also known as straight bucking; a rodeo term; said of a bronc (q.v.) when he clicks his fore and hind legs together beneath his body when in mid-air, or when he crosses them so that their positions are reversed.

jackpot Prize money consisting of all entry fees collected for a particular event and to which no purse money is added.

jack sores *see* CUTANEOUS HABRONEMIASIS

jack spavin Any hard swelling on the lower front of the inside of the hock.

jack stock More than one American mammoth jack (q.v.) or jennet (q.v.).

jade Also known as jadey; a worthless, uncontrollable, or worn-out horse; from the Icelandic jalda meaning mare and the Scottish yaud, meaning an old mare.

jadey *see* JADE

Jaf One of two breeds derived from the Persian Arab (q.v.) indigenous to Kurdistan; is more highly regarded than the Darashouri (q.v.), being accustomed to harsh desert conditions; is spirited but gentle, hardy, tough, wiry, possessed of great stamina, and particularly noted for its tough, hard hooves; has Arab (q.v.) characteristics, stands about 15 hands, and will generally have a bay, chestnut, or gray coat.

jagger (1) A peddler's pack horse (q.v.). (2) *see* JAGGER WAY

jagger way Also known as jaggin way or jagger; an antiquated term; a path traveled by pack ponies and horses which carried coal or lead ore.

jaggin An antiquated British term; any small pack load carried by a pack pony or horse.

jaggin way *see* JAGGER WAY

jail A racing term; said of the first month a claimed horse is in a new barn when racing law requires it to run at a 25 percent higher claiming price or remain idle as in "the horse is in/out of jail."

jaivey *see* JARVEY

jam Also known as traffic jam; a racing term; a bunching up of horses on the racetrack when they are competing in a race.

James Pollard *see* POLLARD, JAMES

James Todhunter Sloan *see* SLOAN, JAMES TODHUNTER

jammed heel Said of the heel of the horse's foot when pushed up into the foot, as by an incorrectly fitted horseshoe; the heel bulb and coronary band are correspondingly distorted.

japan A coating put on leather to give it the shiny surface known as patent leather (q.v.).

japanned leather *see* PATENT LEATHER

japanner One employed to glaze and work leather specifically to patent and enamel it for use in carriages and harness.

japanning The process of applying japan (q.v.) to leather.

jar Extra sharp calks (q.v.) used on horseshoes.

jarvey Also known as jaivey; an Irish term; the driver of a Hackney carriage (q.v.) or jaunting car (q.v.).

jaundice A symptom, not a disease; a yellowness of the skin, sclera of the eye and mucous membranes of the mouth, vagina, and eyelids due to the accumulation of bile pigment which is normally excreted by the liver into the intestines; if the liver is incapable of clearing the bloodstream of the pigment, its concentration increases until it finally spills into the tissues to stain not only the skin, but muscles, brain, and other organs; of three types: hemolytic jaundice (q.v.), obstructive jaundice (q.v.), and that caused by liver damage.

Jaunting Car Also known as Irish Car, Irish Jaunting, Jaunty Car, Side Car, or Outside Car; a, traditional, horse-drawn, two-wheeled passenger vehicle popular in Ireland where it first appeared in the streets of Dublin as a means of public transportation around 1813; evolved from the Trottle Car; hung on shallow, sideways, semi-elliptical springs, the driver's seat was positioned above the outward-curving shafts, higher than passenger seating, it had two parallel passenger seats running front to rear which shared a common backrest, and footboards; some versions had a parcel storage area located between the driver's and passenger's seats; drawn by a single horse.

Jaunty Car *see* JAUNTING CAR

Java A pony breed indigenous to the island of Java, Indonesia; influenced by Arab (q.v.) blood, is similar in conformation to the Timor (q.v.), but is slightly taller and stronger; is docile, willing, strong and hardy, stands approximately 12 hands, and may have a coat of any color; has a heavy head, short, thick and muscular neck, a straight, long back, and long, well-muscled legs; used to pull sados (q.v.).

JBM The acronym for just beat maiden (q.v.).

jennet (1) Also known as a she ass, nontechnically as a jenny, as a mare donkey in Britain, and spelled gennet; a female ass (q.v.). (2) A small Spanish horse bred in Granada, Spain by the Berbers from the upland regions of Andalusia thought to have descended from the Andalusian (q.v.); very popular in the Middle Ages.

jennet jack A male of the ass (q.v.) species used to breed females of the ass species to produce stock.

jenny *see* JENNET no. 1

Jenny A small open carriage, either two- or four-wheeled, drawn by a small pony or donkey; usually hung sideways on semi-elliptical springs.

Jenny Lind A horse-drawn, light, four-wheeled American buggy named for the Swedish opera singer of the same name, by whom it was frequently driven when in the United States; had a forward-facing seat protected by a canopy placed in the center of the box-shaped body which was only 2 feet 6 inches (76 cm) wide; hung on transverse springs and a perch.

jerk (1) To lead a string of pack animals from horseback. (2) A western roping term; the abrupt stop of the roped calf by the horse.

jerking slack *see* PULLING SLACK

jerk line (1) A western American term; a team of horses, ranging in number from six to 20, strung out two abreast. (2) Also known as a jerk-line string; a driving term; a single rein fastened to the brake handle of a wagon or coach that runs through the driver's hand, passes through rings on the harness of all near-side horses or mules to the bit of the near side lead horse; the driver directs the team to turn to the right with jerks on the rein, and a turn to the left by a steady pull on the same rein. (3) A roping term; a long soft rope which is attached to the bridle bit, passed through a ring or pulley attached to the swell of the saddle, and tucked into the roper's belt which when the roper dismounts the horse and runs to the calf, is pulled loose from the roper's belt and signals the horse to step backwards to keep the rope taut.

jerk-line string *see* JERK LINE no. 2

Jerky A small, low, one-horse, four-wheeled, topless American vehicle of the buggy (q.v.) type; when fitted with a hood (q.v.), known as a surrey (q.v.).

jet black Refers to coat color; a pure black (q.v.) body with same-colored points, even when viewed in strong sunlight.

JHNU The acronym for the Journeyman Horseshoers National Union (q.v.).

JHU The acronym for the International

Union of Journeymen Horseshoers of the United States and Canada (q.v.).

jib *see* BALK

jibbah The bulge between the ears and down across the first third of the nasal bone in Arabs (q.v.) as formed by the frontal and parietal bones of the forehead; is most pronounced in foals up to the second year, modifying with maturity, and is rounder and more pronounced in mares.

jibbing *see* JIB

JIC A very severe, patented driving bit, the mouthpiece of which protrudes through the cheekpiece and terminates in a small ring to which the driving lines are attached.

jig An irregular, four-beat jog trot performed by some horses in lieu of walking (q.v.); is generally the behavioral by-product of discomfort, anticipation, or insecurity.

jigging Said of a horse who jigs (q.v.) rather than trots (q.v.).

jiggle (1) *see* JOG. (2) Said of the rider; to shake the reins in short, visually imperceptible movements to encourage the horse to pick up, release pressure on, or stretch into the bit.

Jineteada A South American rodeo; usually includes two competitions, one for amateurs and one for professional riders and such events as bronco riding.

jingle (1) Any horse-drawn cart having long shafts. (2) An Irish, public-hire, vehicle, pulled by a single horse. (3) *see* GOVERNESS CART

jinked back Also known as chinked back; a condition of the vertebra of the back due to injury or normal activity in which one of the bony processes of a vertebra becomes caught or hooks over another process; may result in pinched nerves and atypical movement; realignment may be achieved with chiropractic (q.v.) treatment or massage.

jinked neck A condition of the vertebra in the neck due to injury or normal activity in which one of the bony processes of a vertebra becomes caught or hooks over another process; may result in pinched nerves and atypical movement; realignment may be achieved with chiropractic (q.v.) treatment or massage.

Jinker A headed or open, horse-drawn driving cart produced in both horse and pony sizes popular in the towns and cities of Victoria, Australia.

jinking A condition of the vertebral column caused by injury or, in some cases, normal movement; in which part of the vertebral column becomes dislocated or dislodged, specifically, one of the bony processes of a vertebra becomes caught or hooked over another process; symptoms include malalignment of the vertebral column and atypical or unusual movement; may be located in the neck or back where the condition is known as jinked neck (q.v.) or jinked back (q.v.), respectively.

job *see* JOBBING THE MOUTH

jobbing the mouth Also known as job or jab; said of the rider; to intentionally or involuntarily jerk the bit in the mouth of the horse through the reins.

job horse *see* RENTAL HORSE

job master An antiquated term; one who offers horses, vehicles, and/or harness for hire for riding or driving by the season, month, etc.

jockey (1) Also known as a horse racer or, in slang, as boy; an amateur or professional rider of a horse competing in a horse race will generally weigh anywhere from 94 to 116 pounds (43-53 kg); originally from jack, a general term for any unidentified peasant, and the Scottish jock, a groom, the juvenile of which is jockie; by the 17th century, jockie widely applied to young horse dealers from which the first hired riders were drawn for racing. (2) An antiquated term; an unreliable person, or one with a poor reputation who deals in horses. (3) *see* JOCKEY FOR POSITION. (4) A thin sheet of metal molded to the shape of the front and rear tops of riding boots; used to guide the boot over the lower edge of the breeches when putting them on.

jockey agent A racing term; one who helps riders to obtain mounts to ride in horse races; generally charges a fee of 20 percent or more on the rider's earnings.

jockey apprentice *see* APPRENTICE JOCKEY

Jockey Club, The (1) An association or group of individuals and horse owners which promotes and controls horse racing and formulates rules for it in an area or country; the New York, United States organization was incorporated in 1894 and maintains the American stud book and registry and approves all registered Thoroughbred (q.v.) names; limited to approximately 75 members. (2) An area of a racetrack reserved for club members and consisting of box seats, a restaurant, and lounges.

jockey fee A racing term; a sum paid to a rider for riding a horse in a sanctioned horse race.

jockey for position Also known as jockey; a racing term; said of a jockey who attempts to maneuver his mount into a favorable position in a race.

jockeys *see* HUNT BOOTS

Jockeys' Guild An association of race riders established in the United States.

jockey's race A racing term; a horse race in which the outcome is determined by the strategic planning of the jockey (q.v.).

jockey's room A racing term; a room at a racetrack where competing jockeys store their tack and prepare for or unwind from a race.

jockey stick A driving term; a stick fastened to the hame of the near horse and the bit of the off horse controlled by a single rein; prevents the horses from crowding each other.

jodhpur boots *see* PADDOCK BOOTS

jodhpur breeches *see* JODHPURS

jodhpur curb Also known as cap curb; a bit consisting of two metal cheek pieces and a mouthpiece with a large center link; eliminates pressure on bars of the mouth using leverage instead of direct pressure; the reins are attached to rings on the cheek pieces (q.v.); used in conjunction with a curb strap (q.v.) or curb chain (q.v.).

jodhpurs Also known as jodhpur breeches; a traditional riding pant cut to flare at the thigh and fit tight over the lower leg to the ankle; with the advent of stretch fabrics, they have taken on a sleek, slim fit; worn with jodhpur boots (q.v.) or in some cases shoes; always

considered informal; developed by British officers stationed in Jodhpur, India from which the name derived.

jodhpur strap *see* GARTER

jog (1) Also known as hound trot, houndpace, hound jog, jiggle, or jog trot; an antiquated hunting term, now used by western riders; a relaxed, slow trot with a shortened length of stride in which the rider remains seated and does not post; usually performed on a loose rein; evolved as a gait as hounds (q.v.) exercised on the road travel about 6 mph (10 kmph), an awkward speed halfway between a walk and trot. (2) A racing term; a slow warm-up exercise in which the horse is exercised for several miles on the track, but traveling in the opposite direction to that in which races are run.

Jog Cart Also known as jogging cart; a low-slung, horse-drawn exercise cart used for training and exercising trotting horses; is longer and heavier than a racing sulky.

Jogging Cart A light, two-wheeled, horse-drawn, American-made vehicle used for exercising trotting horses; had one seat for one or two passengers and a slatted floor.

jog trot *see* JOG

john *see* GELDING DONKEY

john mule *see* HORSE MULE

John Rarey *see* HORSE WHISPERERS

Johnsongrass A tall perennial grass, *Sorghum halepense*, used for horse and cattle feed.

Johnsongrass hay A cut and dried grass hay made from Johnsongrass (q.v.) related to the sorghums; common grown in the Southern United States and is generally cut at the early-bloom stage to yield two to three cuttings; contains approximately 3 percent digestible protein.

joint (1) The point of junction of two moveable bones; named in accordance with location, e.g., the gaskin and cannon bones meet at the hock joint; of two types: hinge joint (q.v.) and ball and socket joint (q.v.). (2) *see* BATTERY

joint capsule The sac-like membrane enclosing the joint space and which secretes synovial fluid (q.v.).

joint cartilage *see* ARTICULAR CARTILAGE

jointed bit The mouthpiece (q.v.) of the bit which connected in one or more places; a single joint as in a snaffle bit (q.v.) is most common; the action applies pressure to the tongue as in a nutcracker.

jointed snaffle Also known as a plain jointed snaffle; any snaffle bit (q.v.) having a jointed rather than a straight mouthpiece; the mouthpiece consists of two arms which taper down and interlock in the center of the bit; has a nutcracker action on the tongue and lips; mouthpiece varies in severity considerably depending on mouthpiece size, arm shape, and the looseness of the joint; the greater the curve of the arms and the tighter the joint, the less sharp the nutcracker action on the tongue.

joint evil *see* JOINT ILL

joint fluid *see* SYNOVIAL FLUID

joint ill Also known as joint evil, navel ill or navel infection; a serious and often fatal disease of foals up to six months of age in which foals may be born dead or die shortly after birth; caused by the bacteria *Actinobacillus equuli* which enters the umbilical opening shortly after birth; symptoms include a breakdown of the joint surfaces which results in painful swelling of the joints, particularly in the legs, fever, anemia, and an elevated white blood cell count.

Joint-Master A hunting term; one appointed by the hunt committee to share the responsibilities of the Master (q.v.); responsibilities are generally defined in writing and vary from Hunt to Hunt.

joint oil *see* SYNOVIAL FLUID

Jomud *see* IOMUD

Josef Emanual Fischer von Erlach *see* FISCHER VON ERLACH, JOSEF EMANUAL

jostle A racing term; said of a jockey (q.v.) or horse competing in a race; to make physical contact with or bump another horse during a race.

jostling stone An antiquated term; a mounting block (q.v.).

journeyman (1) A racing term; a professional jockey (q.v.). (2) *see* JOURNEYMAN FARRIER

journeyman farrier Also known as a journeyman; a farrier who, having completed an apprenticeship, is free to sell his labor to a farrier shop; due to the mobile nature of most farriers today, the traditional journeyman farrier is rare.

Journeyman Horseshoers National Union Also known by the acronym JHNU; an association of draft horse farriers (q.v.) organized in Philadelphia, United States in 1874; in 1893, the name was changed to International Union of Journeyman Horseshoers of the United States and Canada (q.v.).

joust A combat between two mounted knights clad in armor and bearing lances.

jowl That portion of the head contained within the branches of the jaw bone.

Judge Monitor An auxiliary judge used at all National Cutting Horse Association events held in the United States, whose responsibility it is to review any run (q.v.) on video tape for which there is a discrepancy between the judges concerning a major penalty.

jughead (1) A stupid horse. (2) A horse with a large, ugly head.

jugular vein One of two large veins located on either side of the horse's windpipe (q.v.) in the underside of the neck which transport blood from the head and neck to the chest.

Jules Charles Pellier *see* PELLIER, JULES CHARLES

jump Said of a horse who springs clear of the ground or other support by a sudden muscular effort.

jump blind Said of a horse; to jump through an untrimmed hedge, or over an overgrown ditch or obstacle for which the landing side (q.v.) is not visible by the rider from the point of take off.

jumped A historical American cowboy term; said of a herd of wild horses which, when warned by a neigh from the stallion, gallop off.

jumped-in bars A therapeutic horseshoe of the bar shoe (q.v.) type consisting of a bar welded between the heels of an open keg shoe or a shoe with calks or other projections on both heels; so called because the bar is placed (using a forge), or jumped-in between the heels of an existing shoe; the bar may be created in a variety of patterns and named accordingly, e.g., butterfly bars, diamond bars, etc.

jumper (1) Any horse breed or size trained to compete over jumps; in competition, must be able to negotiate obstacles ranging in height from 3 feet 6 inches to 5 feet (1-1.5 m) or more with spreads (q.v.) of up to 6 feet (1.8 m), depending on the division in which they compete. (2) A racing term; a horse who runs in steeplechases or hurdle races. (3) One who rides a horse over jumping obstacles.

jumper's bump An obvious enlargement at the point of the croup erroneously thought to increase a horse's power when jumping; considered a conformation fault.

jump clean *see* CLEAR

jump flat Said of a horse who jumps over an obstacle with a flat back and head held high.

jump free Also known as free jumping; to exercise a horse over jumps without a rider.

jump jockey A racing term; a jockey (q.v.) specializing in races over hurdles (q.v.) or steeplechase (q.v.) obstacles (q.v.).

jumping chute Also known as a jumping lane or weedon; a narrow chute, commonly the width of a jump, designed with high walls on either side, through which a horse may be ridden or free jumped over one or a series of obstacles; generally used to train horses to jump.

jumping derby A jumping event in which the horse jumps natural fences over a longer course than in show jumping (q.v.), as in the Hickstead and Hamburg Derbys.

jumping lane *see* JUMPING CHUTE

jumping on the lunge To jump a horse over obstacles guided by a lunge line (q.v.) attached to the side ring of a lungeing cavesson (q.v.); the horse is encouraged to jump through the use of rein, voice, and whip aids.

jumping order Also known as starting order; a jumping term; the sequence in which a horse is placed to participate in a competition, e.g., first, second, fifth, twelfth, etc.; determined in advance of an event by drawing; gives each rider an equal chance of attaining a favorable position – riders near the end of the starting order have the advantage of seeing how the first riders complete the course (q.v.).

jumping rump *see* GOOSE RUMP

jumping powder *see* STIRRUP CUP

jumping saddle Also known as a jump-seat saddle; a variation of a close contact saddle having a deeper seat and slightly more pronounced knee blocks (q.v.).

jump into the canter Said of a horse who, when transitioning from the trot to the canter, strides as if about to jump; the front legs are higher off the ground than the hind and the head and neck are usually raised.

jump off Also known as barrage or against the clock; a show-jumping term; a round (q.v.) held in which all riders having previously completed the course without faults, compete over a final, timed, and shortened course to decide the winner; the competitor with the least number of jumping faults in the fastest time is the winner.

Jump Seat Carriage *see* JUMP SEAT WAGON

jump seat saddle *see* JUMPING SADDLE

Jump Seat Wagon Also known as shift seat wagon or jump seat carriage; a four-wheeled, horse-drawn American vehicle of the wagon (q.v.) type; had a canopy over the two forward-facing seats, and could be converted into a single seat vehicle by folding the front seat down and jumping the rear seat forward.

jump standard *see* STANDARD

jump stand *see* STANDARD

Junky A two-wheeled, horse-drawn vehicle used in some parts of Australia.

junior Any rider competing in an event who is under 18 years of age; an American Horse Shows Association (q.v.) distinction of competitors determined by age.

Just Beat Maiden Also known by the acronym JBM; a racing term; a horse who has only won a maiden race (q.v.) and no other and who is given a small chance against more experienced runners he meets in open competitions.

Justin Morgan A small, 14 hand bay (q.v.) foaled in the United States in 1790; the foundation sire of the Morgan (q.v.) who was sired by a Thoroughbred (q.v.) and out of a mare of mixed Arab (q.v.) Welsh Cob (q.v.), Harddraver (q.v.) and Fjord (q.v.) blood; named after his second owner, Justin Morgan; all Morgans trace to his three sons: Sherman, Woodbury, and Bullrush; the Morgan played an important role in the evolution of American breeds such as the Standardbred (q.v.), Saddlebred (q.v.), and the Tennessee Walking Horse (q.v.).

Jutland An ancient medium to heavy cold-blood developed on Jutland Island, Denmark where it has existed for thousands of years, and from which the name derived; used in the Middle Ages for jousting (q.v.) and carrying heavily armored knights into battle; the modern breed was strongly influenced by Suffolk Punch (q.v.), specifically Oppenhein LXII in 1860, Cleveland Bay (q.v.), and more recently, Ardennes (q.v.) blood; bears a marked resemblance to the Schleswig (q.v.); has a heavy, common head, great depth of chest and girth, short and heavily feathered legs, and stands 15.2 to 16 hands; a chestnut coat with flaxen mane and tail is most common, although roan, bay, and black coats also occur; has tremendous endurance and is strong, docile, and gentle; numbers are on the decline due to mechanization; used for heavy draft and farm work.

jute The glossy fiber of either of two East Indian tiliaceous plants, genus *Corchorus olitorius* and *Corchorus capsularis* used in the manufacture of coarse cloths such as burlap, twine, etc. used in some horse blankets and sheets.

juvenile A two-year-old horse.

K

Kabachi A Russian equestrian sport similar to tiling (q.v.); the rider, while galloping, throws his spear with the intent of placing it through a small hoop placed atop a post 3.2 yards (3 m) tall.

Kabarda *see* KABARDIN

Kabardin Also known as a Kabarda; a Soviet-bred warmblood originating in the Caucasian mountains in the 15th century; descended from indigenous mountain stock crossed with Arab (q.v.), Turkmene (q.v.), and Karabakh (q.v.) blood; is well suited to steep, mountainous terrain, and is gifted with a well-developed sense of direction and long life span; is sure-footed, agile, strong, and possessed of great endurance; a popular sport horse used for riding and packing as well as the improvement of other breeds such as the Tersky (q.v.); has strong Oriental features, stands 14.1 to 15.1 hands, and usually has a bay, brown, or black coat with gray occurring less often; has a long neck, strong legs, and excellent feet, but the quarters tend to be a bit weak and sickle hocks (q.v.) prevalent; the ears have a distinctive inward turn.

Kadir Cup, The A mounted pig-sticking competition held annually at the Meerut Tent Club, India where it was first conducted in 1874; breaks in the annual competition occurred in 1879 and 1890 for the Afghan war and from 1915 through 1918 for World War I; the name derived from the rough terrain surrounding the Ganges-Kadir country which historically teamed with wild boar.

Kalesch *see* CALECHE

Kamsat *see* ASSIL

Karabair An ancient warmblood indigenous to the Central Asian mountains, specifically those in Uzbekistan; although the exact origins of the breed are unknown, its Oriental appearance suggests Mongolian and Arab (q.v.) descent; bred in three different sizes standing 14.2 to 15 hands; is very resistant to cold and fatigue, extremely sure-footed, agile, and fast, resembles a stocky Arab (q.v.), and generally has a gray, bay, or chestnut coat; used for light draft, driving, packing, riding, and mounted sports such as goat snatching (q.v.).

Karabakh A Soviet-bred warmblood originating in the mountains of Karabakh separating northwest Iran from Azerbaijan; of Oriental origins influenced by Arab (q.v.), Persian, and Turkmene (q.v.) blood; stands 14 to 14.1 hands and generally has a golden dun coat, but chestnut, bay, and gray do occur; is tough and sure-footed, has a small, fine head having the dished profile typical of the Arab, low-set tail, and good feet; is calm, energetic, strong, enduring, and has good action; used for riding, equestrian games, racing, and limited harness work; numbers appear to be reducing.

Karacabey A warmblood developed at the beginning of the 20th century at the Karacabey Stud, Turkey; descended from local mares crossed with Nonius (q.v.) stallions; is tough, versatile, has good conformation, stands 15.1 to 16.1 hands, may have a coat of any solid-color; previously used by the Turkish cavalry, it is well suited to saddle and light draft work; the only Turkish breed to display uniformity of type and consistent transmission of characteristics.

karozzin A four-wheeled, horse-drawn passenger carriage drawn by a single horse or large pony used in Malta; seated four passengers vis-à-vis (q.v.), under a high canopy or roof, and was hung on four sideways-elliptical springs with high clearance above road level.

kasen A Japanese term; sweet itch (q.v.).

Kathi *see* KATHIAWARI

Kathiawari Also known as a Kathi; a pony breed indigenous to the western Coast of India, in the former princely state of Kathiawari; descended from small (about 13 hands), frugal native ponies crossed with Arabs (q.v.); a tough, hardy, tenacious, and unpredictable breed which thrives on little feed; stands approximately 14 to 15 hands, is very light and narrowly framed, having a weak neck and quarters, low-set tail, sickle hocks, and ears that curve distinctively inwards, almost touching at the tips; all coat colors occur including skewbald (q.v.) and piebald (q.v.); used for riding, packing, farming, light draft, and the best ones, racing; virtually identical to the

Marwari (q.v.).

kave Also known as port or porting; the pawing, scraping, or stomping action of the horse with its front legs, especially in stall bedding.

Kazakh An ancient pony breed originating in Kazakhstan; thought to have descended from the Asiatic wild horse (q.v.) refined by significant infusions of Don (q.v.) blood; stands 12.1 to 13.1 hands and has good hard limbs and feet; is bred in two distinct types: the Dzhabe (q.v.) and the Adaev (q.v.); is willing, quiet, frugal, strong, and possessed of great stamina and legendary hardiness; the young are often fattened and the mares produce milk both of which are used for human consumption.

keep *see* PASTURE

keep a horse at grass To maintain a horse in a pasture (q.v.) where it feeds exclusively off pasture grass; a minimum of 1 acre (4,047 sq m) per horse, but preferably 3 acres (1.2 hectares), is necessary.

keepers Also known as runners or harness loops when used on harness tack; fixed, or in some cases sliding, leather loops used on saddlery, particularly bridles, through which the ends of the straps pass to keep them in place.

keep the horse to the track Said to the rider; to make one's horse follow a previously path made.

keg shoe *see* MACHINE-MADE SHOE

kehilan An Arabic term; a purebred Arab (q.v.).

Keiger Horse *see* KEIGER MUSTANG

Keiger Mustang Also known as Keiger Horse; a dun-factor wild horse first discovered in the Steens Mountains of Southern Oregon, USA, in 1978 at which time it was identified by the US Bureau of Land Management as a distinct type; although commonly believed to have descended from the Spanish horses brought to North America by the conquistadors, it is now believed that the strain may be much older; stands 14 to 15.2 hands, is short-backed, has durable legs, strong hooves, a willing disposition, and is extremely sure-footed; zebra and dorsal striping is common with fawn-colored inner ears and ear coat hair

that is darker on the upper one third than the lower two thirds; protected by the Wild Horse and Burro Act (q.v.) and the Keiger Mesteño Association (q.v.); named for the range developed for the original band in the Keiger Gorge, located in the Steens Mountains..

Keiger Mesteño Association An organization founded in Burns Oregon, USA in 1987 to protect and preserve the Keiger Mustang (q.v.) from extinction and dilution by other breeds.

kelshie Also spelled kelsie; a woven basket hung on either side of a klibber (q.v.) used to carry peat in the Shetland Islands north of Scotland.

kelsie *see* KLIBBER

kendrick girth A 1-1/2 inch (38 mm), double-folded strap used to hold an English saddle in place, preventing it from slipping sideways and to some extent forward on the back of the horse; connects the two sides of the saddle underneath the horse just behind the forelegs/shoulder; may be constructed of leather, cotton, wool, or synthetic materials.

kennel (1) Also known as kumel; a hunting term; a fox bed located above, rather than in, the ground. (2) The buildings and/or yards where hounds (q.v.) are maintained, i.e., bred or boarded.

kennel coat A hunting term; an ankle-length white cotton or linen coat worn by hunt staff (q.v.) or hound handlers to keep the hunting or day clothes of the wearer clean when in the kennel (q.v.).

kennel huntsman A hunting term; one employed by the Hunt (q.v.) to oversee the care and maintenance of the hounds (q.v.); is generally assisted by an amateur huntsman (q.v.) who actually manages the hounds and acts as a first whipper-in (q.v.) on hunt days.

kennel man A hunting term; one who works in the hunt kennels under the supervision of a huntsman (q.v.) or kennel huntsman (q.v.).

Kentucky Derby A 1-1/4 mile (2 km) race for three-year olds established in 1875 at Churchill Downs, Louisville, Kentucky, USA and run annually since; in 1896 the distance was reduced from 1-1/2 to 1/4 miles (2.4-0.4 km); one of three classic races (q.v.) comprising the American Triple Crown (q.v.) to be established, the other two being the Belmont Stakes (q.v.) and the Preakness Stakes (q.v.); the last of the three races to be established.

Kentucky Saddlebred *see* AMERICAN SADDLEBRED

Kentucky Saddler *see* AMERICAN SADDLEBRED

kept-up To maintain a horse during the summer months in a stable rather than at pasture (q.v.).

keratoma A rare tumor developing in the deep aspect of the hoof wall; lameness may or may not be present.

Kerry Pony A robust and hardy pony native to Ireland, specifically the county of Kerry for which it was named; used for riding and driving during the 19th century.

Kersey A usually coarse and ribbed woolen or woolen and cotton cloth historically used for ankle boots (q.v.) and trousers.

Kersey protection boots *see* ANKLE BOOTS

key bugle A copper wind instrument similar to a cornet in appearance, but having keys instead of valves, historically used by stage coach (q.v.) guards.

key horse A racing term; a single horse used in multiple combinations in an exotic wager (q.v.).

keys Also known as bit keys or players; pieces of shaped metal attached to the mouthpiece of some bits such as breaking bits (q.v.) to encourage the horse to accept the bit; the horse will play with the keys using its tongue.

Khamsa *see* ASSIL

Khis-Kouhou An equestrian sport popular in Russia; known as the "bride hunt" of the Mongols, young men ride after the girls and attempt to kiss them; the girls retaliate fiercely with their whips.

kiang Also spelled kyang; a wild variety of ass (q.v.), *Equus hemionus kiang*, inhabiting Tibet and Mongolia; may have dorsal stripes (q.v.), but no shoulder or leg stripes; stands 12.2 to 14 hands, has a coat of variable color

varies, ears longer than those of horses, but shorter than those of the true ass, and long, narrow hooves with long heels; in the natural state is generally found in valleys 12,000-15,000 feet (3,660-4,570 m)above sea level.

Kibitka A roughly made, horse-drawn posting wagon used in Russia and other parts of Europe beginning in the late 15th century; consisted of a wooden framework held together by strands of rope which supported hay-filled cushions or bundles of straw for passenger seating; sometimes protected by a canvas sheet secured over tilts or bows; pulled by teams of various numbers.

kick (1) Said of the horse when he strikes out with either of his hind legs; a defense mechanism used by the horse as for protection when his space has been invaded, out of meanness, anger, fear, etc.; in hunting, the tail of a horse who kicks is tagged with a red ribbon. (2) To win as in a wager, competition, or bet (q.v.).

kicking strap A wide leather strap attached on one end to the left shaft (q.v.) which passes over the loins of the horse, through a loop on the crupper (q.v.), and connects to the right shaft on the other; keeps the quarters (q.v.) down if a harness horse is prone to kicking.

kick over the traces A driving term; said of a cart or coach driver; to release control of the traces (q.v.) to avert an accident such as when a horse gets a leg over a trace.

kidney link A jointed, kidney-shaped metal link which takes the place of a bottom hame strap or hame chain in some pair and team harnesses; sometimes opens at the center top, so that it may pass through the bottom hame eyes.

kidney link ring A metal ring attached to the lower side of the harness kidney link to which the pole strap or pole chain is fastened in pair and team harness.

kill (1) Also known as a worry; a hunting term; the raw meat fed to the hounds as a reward following the hunt as in the quarry, e.g. fox; now horse or other meat is individually fed to each hound or buried in a natural hole, drain pipe, etc. to allow the pack to seek it out. (2) To deprive of life in any manner; cause the death of; slaughter; to destroy.

kilocalorie *see* CALORIE

kimbelwicke *see* KIMBLEWICK

kimberwick *see* KIMBLEWICK

kimblewick Also known as Spanish snaffle or Spanish jumping bit and spelled kimbelwicke and kimberwick; a pelham (q.v.) bit requiring one instead of two reins (q.v.), having a straight, low-ported mouthpiece (q.v.), and short cheeks (q.v.) with dee-rings (q.v.) topped with a square eye running the full length of the cheeks; when the rider's hands are held in a standard position, the bit acts as a snaffle (q.v.), but when lowered, or when used in conjunction with a martingale (q.v.), the resulting action is similar to that of a curb (q.v.); of five types: the true kimblewick, uxeter kimblewick (q.v.), Whitmore kimblewick (q.v.), mullen-mouth true kimblewick (q.v.), and single-jointed true kimblewick (q.v.).

kinesiopathy The functional pathology of movement that can manifest as hypomobility (q.v.) or hypermobility (q.v.) of the motor unit (q.v.).

Kineton noseband Also known as Puckle noseband or lever noseband; a severe noseband (q.v.) used on hard-pulling, soft-mouthed, horses; consists of a headstall and nosepiece joined by semi-circle metal loops which fit around the cheeks of the bit; the nosepiece is generally adjustable on both sides; when fitted correctly, the metal pieces touch, but do not apply pressure to the bit unless aided by rein action; use of the reins, applies pressure to both the bridge of the nose and the bit causing the horse to lower its head at which point the action of the bit can be implemented; named for the village of Kineton in which the inventor Puckle lived.

King George V Cup An annual individual show jumping competion held under FEI (q.v.) rules at the Royal International Horse Show in London, England.

kinked tail Said of the tail of the horse when, as due to injury, a twist or bend in the tail bone develops; may be corrected by rebreaking and splinting.

Kinsey splint A splint used to stabilize fractured bones while preserving the health of the arteries preventing preoperative circulation trouble; invented in 1980 to replace the air cast.

Kiplingcotes Race Also known as the Yorkshire Derby; the oldest known horse race in the world run on a 4-mile (6.4 km) course over old tracks and roads in the Yorkshire Wolds, England on the third Thursday of every March; founded by a group of foxhunters in 1619.

Kirgiz *see* NOVOKIRGHIZ

Kirghiz *see* NOVOKIRGHIZ

Kirgis *see* NOVOKIRGHIZ

kiss the eighth pole A racing term; said of a horse who finishes far behind the field.

kitchen A racing term; a horseman's restaurant located in the backstretch (q.v.) area.

Kladrub *see* KLADRUBER

Kladruber Also known as a Kladrub; a warmblood developed in 1572 at the Royal Stud in Kladruby, Czechoslovakia, using Andalusian (q.v.) stallions; Neapolitan blood was periodically used and, in the 1920s, Shagya Arabian (q.v.); breeding is strictly controlled; historically used as a carriage horse and stood at an average height of 18 hands; recent breeding has resulted in a more active horse standing 16.2 to 17 hands which is still used for harness work, but also for riding, particularly dressage; is black or gray in color and is similar in appearance to the Andalusian from which it derived.

Klepper A native pony breed believed to have descended from native Latvian and Estonian mares crossed with Norfolk Roadster (q.v.); stands 13 to 15 hands, possess great strength and endurance, and has a good trot; instrumental in development of the Toric (q.v.).

klibber Also known as a kelshie or kelsie; a wooden saddle specifically designed for use on Shetland ponies (q.v.), historically used in the Shetland Islands located north of Scotland.

Kluge Hans *see* HANS, KLUGE

Knabstrup Also known as the Danish Spotted Horse or Knabstruper; a Danish horse breed which traces back to a spotted mare called Flaebehoppen, who in 1808 was put to a Frederiksborg (q.v.) stallion and founded a line of spotted, lighter-built horses argued by some to be a type rather than a true breed; stands about 15.3 hands, with spotted Appaloosa (q.v.) patterns on a roan body; used predominantly for circus; the current breeding accent is on coat pattern rather than conformation.

Knabstruper *see* KNABSTRUP

knacker Also known as a horse knacker; a British term; one who buys and slaughters old and/or worn out horses for pet food rather than human consumption.

knackery Also known as a knacker's yard; a British term; a horse slaughter yard.

knacker's yard *see* KNACKERY

knee *see* CARPUS

knee block *see* KNEE ROLL

knee boots *see* KNEE CAPS

knee caps (1) Also known as knee boots, knee protectors, or knee pads; a protective covering for the knees of the horse; provide support and/or protection in the eventing, jumping, bred, or shipped horse; may be made of felt, neoprene, or leather. (2) *see* KNEE GUARDS

knee guards Also known as knee caps; full-front padded leather covering that buckles behind the polo player's knee, used to protect the knee from bruises and abrasions resulting from impact with other riders, horses, and mallets (q.v.).

knee-narrow conformation *see* MEDIAL DEVIATION OF THE CARPUS JOINTS

knee pad *see* KNEE GUARDS

knee protectors *see* KNEE CAPS no. 1

knee roll Also known as a knee block; a pad of varying length or thickness attached to the underside of the saddle-flap (q.v.) at about knee height; provides the rider with improved grip and security in the saddle.

knees and hocks to the ground Also known as well to the ground or near to the ground; a British term; said of a horse having short cannon bones (q.v.).

knees narrow *see* MEDIAL DEVIATION OF THE CARPUS JOINTS

knee spavin A bony growth occurring at the back inside of the knee caused by a blow or strain; more serious than a hock spavin (q.v.), but unlike the latter, it is not hereditary.

knee splint One of four types of splints (q.v.); affects the nerve-packed joint capsule between the tops of the splint and cannon bones; the most serious of the splints, usually appearing as a small, but supersensitive bump coupled with marked lameness.

knee-sprung *see* FORWARD DEVIATION OF THE CARPAL JOINTS

knees wide *see* LATERAL DEVIATION OF THE CARPAL JOINTS

knifeboard bus An early horse-drawn bus used in London, England having outside, roof-top passenger seating back-to-back on long benches; succeeded by the garden-seat bus (q.v.).

knobber *see* BROCKET

knobbler *see* BROCKET

knocked-down shoe *see* FEATHER-EDGED SHOE

knocker Also known as collier's horse; a horse trader's term; a horse with cow (q.v.) and/or sickle hocks (q.v.).

knock in A polo term; to initiate play by hitting the polo ball into play from the back or sidelines; the opposite of throw-in (q.v.).

knock knees *see* MEDIAL DEVIATION OF THE CARPAL JOINTS

knot head A disparaging term; a problem horse, one who is unintelligent, or potentially a threat to himself or his rider.

knots *see* SIDEBONES

knuckling at the fetlock *see* KNUCKLING OVER

knuckling over Also known as grogginess, overshot fetlock, knuckling over at the fetlock, or knuckling at the fetlock; a condition in which the fetlock joints, fore and hind, project forward in the resting horse or collapse forward when it is in action due to chronic lameness of the flexor tendon; also a condition occurring in older horses in which the pastern joints protrude backwards in the horse in motion causing the horse to falter in stride or in newly born foals with weak extensor tendons and young foals in which case the condition is genetically inherited and may not be correctable.

knuckling over at the fetlock *see* KNUCK-LING OVER

Kocklani *see* ASSIL

Koheil *see* ASSIL

Kohuail *see* ASSIL

Konik A pony breed originating in Poland; descended from the Tarpan (q.v.), which it closely resembles, refined by infusions of Arab (q.v.) blood; is hardy, willing, frugal, has great endurance and power for its size, is long lived, extremely resistant to hunger and cold, stands 12 to 13.3 hands, may have a dun, palomino (with occasional zebra markings [q.v.] on the legs), or bay coat, has a slightly heavy head, long mane and tail, and a short straight back; bred selectively at two state studs in Popielno and Jezewice; is similar to the Hucul (q.v.); several native breeds are referred to generically as Konik meaning small horse, with each breed having its own name, e.g., the Bilgoraj Konik (q.v.) and Mierzyn (q.v.).

Kornokoff iron *see* OFFSET STIRRUP

Kossiak A breeding herd of Russian Steppe Horses (q.v.).

KryoKinetics Associates, Inc. A United States company which developed a method of permanently identifying horses using an unalterable freeze marking (q.v.) system known as the international Alpha System; developed in the 1960s at Washington State University, the system uses a series of six to eight (always eight in the United States and in most European countries) angles and alpha-symbols to identify the breed, state or country of registration, year of birth, and breed registration or state number; all wild burros (q.v.) and horses (q.v.) under the protection of the United States government who are given up for adoption, are registered using this technique; many breed associations including the Thoroughbred (q.v.), Arab (q.v.), Saddlebred (q.v.), Standardbred (q.v.), Morgan (q.v.), Quarter Horse (q.v.), etc., also endorse use of this system.

Kuhailan *see* ASSIL

kumel A hunting term; a fox bed located above the ground.

kumiss A Mongolian drink made from mare's milk.

kür exercises Also known as freestyle exercises; a vaulting term; any optional exercise performed by the vaulter (q.v.) of which there are more than 250 types; may include compulsory exercises (q.v.), but they will not be scored.

kür program A vaulting term; an event consisting of kür exercises (q.v.).

Kustanair Also known as a Russian Steppe Horse; an ancient oriental breed from Kazakhstan; now evolved into two distinct types: one which is light and elegant, having been crossed with Thoroughbred (q.v.), and the other more solid, resulting from Orlov (q.v.) and Don (q.v.) crosses; stands 14 to 15.1 hands and may have any solid-colored coat; has long, well-muscled legs and a light head; used for riding and light draft.

kyang *see* KIANG

L

labor birth *see* PARTURITION

laced reins Leather reins (q.v.) the outer edges of which are laced with 1/8 inch (3 mm) leather strands; provide improved grip particularly when wet.

lacing *see* ROPE WALKING

laceration Any injury that penetrates the skin, as superficial laceration (q.v.) and deep laceration (q.v.).

lacking impulsion Said of a horse who lacks sufficient energy to move forward at a regular gait or pace.

lacking collection Said of a horse who performs a movement with insufficient shortening of the gait or pace.

lacking rhythm Said of a horse whose gait, pace, or movement lacks regular, even steps.

lactate To secrete milk from the mammary glands.

lactating mare Any mare producing milk; generally has a foal at foot.

lactation (1) The secretion of milk; averages 30 gallons (113.56 liters) per day. (2) The period of milk production by the mare.

lactational anestrus The period of sexual inactivity in the nursing mare during which there is an absence of observable heat (q.v.) or acceptance of the stallion.

lactic acid A by-product of the breakdown of stored carbohydrates normally present in the body in small, harmless quantities; occurs in excess when there is insufficient oxygen supply to the cells, especially muscle cells as during strenuous exercise; an increase in lactic acid may result in muscle fatigue, inflammation, pain, and, in severe cases, azoturia (q.v.).

lactic acidosis A condition resulting from excess lactic acid (q.v.) circulating in the bloodstream; a common result of overexertion and the source of stiffness following exercise.

lad *see* GROOM no. 2

Lady Suffolk sulky An American, two-wheeled, metal-framed, horse-drawn exercise cart; named after the famous trotting mare Lady Suffolk.

Lady's Basket Phaeton *see* BASKET PHAETON

Lady's Phaeton *see* PARK PHAETON

large standard donkey A donkey (q.v.) standing 48 to 56 inches (1.2-1.4 m) tall.

lame Also known as unsound; said of the horse when his ability to perform is in some way impaired due to disease or injury of the bone, tendon, ligament, muscle, or other tissues or structures in one or more of the limbs; impairment may result in a change in the gait or stance and may be accompanied by pain; symptoms may range from limping to an inability to walk and include a characteristic bobbing of the head of the horse as the affected foot strikes the ground.

lame hand Also known as spoon; and antiquated driving term; a poor coachman.

lameness *see* LAME

lamina The singular of laminae (q.v.).

laminae Layers of membranes containing from 500 to 600 (depending on the size of the hoof) fine, leaf-like projections and tubules which originate on the inside of the hoof wall at the coronary cushion and extend to the lower edge of the pedal bone (q.v.); bind the hoof wall to the pedal bone; of two types: (a) sensitive laminae (q.v.) which contain blood vessels and cover the external surface of the pedal bone and the lateral cartilages, interlocking with the insensitive laminae and (b) insensitive laminae (q.v.) which originate in the hoof wall and do not contain a blood supply.

laminitic condition *see* LAMINITIS

laminitic rings *see* HOOF RINGS

laminitis Also known as fever in the feet and laminitic condition; a painful inflammation of the sensitive laminae (q.v.); precipitated by a number of factors including (a) ingestion of excessive amounts of grain, lush pasture, and/or cold water, (b) allergic reaction to the proteins in highly concentrated foods, (c) retained placenta at parturition, (d) over use on hard surfaces, (e) standing for long periods during transport or recovery from injury, or (f) obesity; characterized by heat and pain at the coronary band, a pounding digital pulse, muscular trembling, accumulation of blood in the laminae, increased systolic pressure, sweating, and uniform tenderness in the feet; may occur in the forefeet, all four feet, or very occasionally, only the hindfeet; broadly classified as acute laminitis (q.v.), subacute laminitis (q.v.), or chronic laminitis (q.v.), and may result in founder (q.v.).

lampas Also known as lampers or palatitis; a condition, not a disease, in which the mucosa covering the hard palate (q.v.) becomes inflamed; occurs in young horses during eruption of the permanent incisors (q.v.) and in horses of any age as a result of stomatis (q.v.); is self limiting and requires no treatment.

lampers *see* LAMPAS

lancer bit A plain-cheek curb bit (q.v.) with two vertical slots located in the cheekpieces (q.v.) below the mouthpiece; may be used with one or two reins.

Landais A pony breed indigenous to the Landes region around Barthais de l'Adour in southeast France; thought to have derived from the Tarpan (q.v.) crossed with Arab (q.v.) as early as 732 AD, and Welsh (q.v.) blood, after 1970; stands 11.1 to 13 hands and may have a brown, black, bay, or chestnut coat; has a small head, short, pointed ears, straight profile, a long neck that is thick at the base, short back, hard hoof, and a thick and silky mane and tail; is independent, hardy, an easy keeper, and resistant to harsh weather conditions; used for riding and light draft.

Landau Also known as sociable landau; a four-wheeled, open or semi-open horse-drawn carriage designed and first used in the late 16th century in Landau, Bavaria from which the name derived; usually had two half-hoods made of harness leather which, when necessary, could be brought together to form an enclosed compartment; had opposite cross seats for four passengers seated vis-à-vis (q.v.); evolved into two primary types: (a) square roofed with angular bodywork and (b)

more elegant rounded or canoe-shaped; both were hung on cee springs, but later on sideways elliptical and semi-elliptical springs or a combination of both; usually drawn by a pair of horses in pole gear (q.v.), although a few smaller types were pulled by a single horse in shafts; most were driven from a box seat, with the larger versions postillion (q.v.) controlled; varieties include the Landau Barouche (q.v.) and the landaulet (q.v.).

Landau barouche *see* BAROUCHE LANDAU.

Landaulet A coupe version of the landau (q.v.); a four-wheeled, horse-drawn carriage seating two forward-facing passengers with the rear protected by a falling hood (q.v.); drawn by either a single horse in shafts or a pair in pole gear (q.v.); hung on sideways-elliptical and semi-elliptical springs; named for the city of Landau, Bavaria where the Landau was first used.

landing (1) A vaulting term; that part of the exercise following the vaulter's (q.v.) dismount from the horse to land standing on the ground. (2) A jumping term; the contact made by a horse with the ground on the far side of an obstacle (q.v.).

landing side The far side of any obstacle (q.v.) onto which a horse lands after clearing the obstacle.

lane creeper *see* NEW FOREST PONY

Lane Fox saddle *see* CUTBACK SADDLE

landship *see* BARCO-DE-TIERRA

Landseer, Sir Edwin (1802–1873) A popular Victorian artist specializing in animal, including horse, portraits.

lap-and-tap (1) A western roping competition; a race run without using a starting gate. (2) A steer wrestling and calf roping term; a timed competition in which the cattle are not given the 10 to 30 foot (3-9 m) headstart over the horse and rider as is customary in smaller arenas.

lapped on A harness racing term; said of a horse whose nose is at least opposite the hindquarters of the horse ahead of it at the finish.

lapping traces *see* LAP TRACES

lap traces Also known as lapping traces; a driving/coaching term; to cross the traces (q.v.) of a four-in-hand team to keep the horses close together; the trace of one leader crossing over to the other and returns to its own bar.

large colon The section of the large intestine located between the cecum and small colon where, together with the cecum, digestion and absorption occur; in the horse, measures 8 to 18 inches (20–46 cm) in diameter and 10 to 12 feet (3–36 m) in length.

large metacarpal *see* CANNON BONE

large metacarpal bone *see* CANNON BONE

large roundworm Also known as equine ascarid or parascaris equorum; a stout, whitish worm up to 1 foot (30 cm) in length which infects the horse, foals being most susceptible; in heavy infections respiratory signs, unthriftiness, loss of energy, and, occasionally, colic (q.v.) may result; infective eggs may persist for years on contaminated soil.

large strongyle Also known as blood worm, red worm, palisade worm, or sclerostome; a class of parasitic roundworm affecting all ages of horse; of three different species: *Strongylus vulgaris*, up to 25 mm, *Strongylus edentatus*, up to 45 mm, and *Strongylus equinusis*, up to 50 mm; the most destructive of all equine internal parasites; have a six-month life cycle; the eggs, laid in the large intestine, are passed in the feces; the infected larvae live on the grass, then, when ingested, travel to the large intestine where they burrow into the gut wall and migrate through the body where they may be found in the liver, peri-renal tissues, flanks, pancreas, and cranial artery; eggs may live outside the horse on pasture for considerable time and are resistant to low temperatures; can permanently damage intestinal blood vessels and walls resulting in lameness (q.v.), verminous colic (q.v.), hemorrhage, and/or death; mixed infections of large and small strongyles are the rule.

lariat Also known as a lasso, reata, or rope; a long rope made of rawhide, hemp (common through the 1970s), horsehair, or polyethylene strands with a running noose; used for catching horses, cattle or other animals; from a contraction of the Spanish el lazo which became lasso and la reata from reatar (to bind again) which became riata and ultimately lariat.

lariat neck ring Also known as a neck ring; a relatively rigid circle of rope placed around the base of the horse's neck used by the rider to turn a trained horse without the aid of a bit or reins.

lark A hunting term; said of members of the field who jump fences unnecessarily, as when the hounds (q.v.) are not running or on the return from the hunt.

laryngeal Relating to or used on the voice box.

laryngeal hemiplegia Also known as roaring or whistling; a disease of the larynx (q.v.) caused by partial or total paralysis of the nerves enervating the muscles which elevate the arytenoid cartilages and open and close the larynx; affected horses make an abnormal inspiratory noise – typically a whistle or roar when exercising; in 90 percent of the cases, the left side of the larynx is left paralyzed; may be surgically corrected with a laryngoplasty (q.v.).

laryngeal ventriculotomy Also known as ventricle stripping, Hobday or spelled Hobday'd; a surgical operation performed on the larynx to alleviate roaring (q.v.); the mucosal lining of the afflicted laryngeal saccule, usually the left, is stripped and allowed to heal as an open wound, a process that takes about three to five weeks; the horse must be stalled for 2 to 2 1/2 months during recovery; if surgery is performed soon after the horse is diagnosed as a roarer (q.v.), chances of recovery are approximately 70 percent; named for the veterinary surgeon who originated the operation, Sir Frederick Hobday (q.v.) (1870-1939).

laryngoplasty Also known as tie-back surgery; a surgical procedure performed on the larynx (q.v.) to correct laryngeal hemiplegia (q.v.) in which a suture is inserted through the arytenoid cartilage (q.v.) to hold it out of the airway and allow the horse to breath freely.

larynx Also known as voice box; the organ found in the upper respiratory track at the back of the lower jawbone which fits in a small hole in the soft palate forming an air-tight, food-tight seal; functions to keep unwanted substances out of the airway and to produce voice; equivalent to the human Adam's apple.

larva Also known as worm, grub, or caterpillar; the stage which follows the egg in the life cycle of an insect.

larvae The plural of larva (q.v.).

laserpuncture A type of acupuncture (q.v.); stimulation of precise body points along the horse's body meridians (q.v.) using a low-intensity laser beam to control pain, treat internal malfunctions, anesthetize, and reduce stress; 100 percent noninvasive; quite popular for treating horses, particularly to stimulate the points on the leg, where needles are sometimes difficult to insert.

lash Also known as whiplash; a silk or braided horse-hair attachment to the whip thong (q.v.) which is in turn connected to the crop (q.v.).

lasix A drug used to lower blood pressure in horses; often used to treat bleeders (q.v.).

lasso (1) *see* LARIAT. (2) To catch a horse or other animal using a lariat (q.v.).

late behind Also known as late change; said of a horse performing a flying change (q.v.) during which, at the moment of suspension in the canter, the horse changes the lead correctly with the foreleg, the hind leg changing a full or half stride later.

late change *see* LATE BEHIND

late double A racing term; a second daily double (q.v.) offered during the later part of a race program.

lateral Outside, away from the center line of the body.

lateral aids The rider's hand and leg on the same side of the horse as used to communicate instruction.

lateral deviation of the carpal joints Also known as bow legs, carpus varus, bandy-legs, or knees wide; closely set feet and an outward deviation of the knees; may be accompanied by a base-narrow, toe-in conformation; the term may have been coined in the 17th century by a comparison of the legs to a curved stick called a bandy used in the game of hockey.

lateral deviation of the metacarpal bones Also known as offset knees or bench knees; a congenital condition of the cannon bone offset to the lateral side which does not follow a straight line from the radius; medial splints (q.v.) are a common result.

lateral flexion The suppleness and development of the muscles that allow the horse to bend uniformly from poll to croup.

lateral gait A gait in which two feet on the same side make contact with the ground simultaneously, or nearly simultaneously.

lateral incisors Also known as laterals or second incisors; four of the horse's 12 incisor teeth (q.v.) located on either side of the central incisors (q.v.) top and bottom; appear between four to six weeks after birth.

lateral movements *see* LATERAL WORK

laterals *see* LATERAL INCISORS

lateral work Also known as lateral movements, work on two tracks, or side steps; any movement in which the sequence of steps in the walk, trot, or canter remains unchanged, the hind feet do not follow in the path of the forefeet, and the horse moves forward and sideways; the legs involved in the movement cross over in front of those that are on the ground.

lateral wedge shoe A horseshoe which is thicker on the left than the right side or vice versa; used to alter the mediolateral balance of the foot.

lather An excessive discharge of salt or broken-down protein structures emitted in the process of perspiration by a horse in poor condition and stressed or a horse in good condition and heavily stressed; so called because it is white and frothy.

lathered up Also known as a proteinaceous sweat or soaping; said of a horse who discharges a white, frothy substance composed of fluids containing emitted salts, potassium, sodium, electrolytes, water, and broken-down protein structures following a period of exercise or stress.

latigo A leather strap, 4 to 5 feet (1-1.5 m) long on the near side and 1 to 1-1/2 feet (20-46 cm) on the off side, attached on one end to the metal rigging ring in a western saddle (q.v.) and to which the cinch is attached on the other; on the off side of new saddles, the latigo generally buckles to the cinch (q.v.), while on others, it is threaded through the cinch ring and back to the rigging until the slack is taken up and the latigo tied off; there are two latigos on each saddle, one on each side.

Latvian Also known as a Latvian Harness Horse; a warmblood descended from the ancient forest horse of northern Europe; the modern breed dates from the 17th century when warmbloods, including the Oldenburg (q.v.), were crossed with native Latvian stock; to add substance, coldblood crosses were also made to such breeds as the Finnish Draught (q.v.) and the Ardennes (q.v.); firmly established as a breed in 1952; an all-purpose draft horse which may also be used for harness or under saddle; is strong, with good endurance and a docile and calm attitude; stands 15.1 to 16 hands, has rather short legs, with good bone, some feathering, and a bay, brown, or chestnut coat.

Latvian Harness Horse *see* LATVIAN

Latvian Heavy Draft The name by which the Lithuanian Heavy Draft (q.v.) horse is known when bred in Latvia.

lavage Therapeutic flushing with a large volume of fluid.

lavender roan *see* LILAC ROAN

law A hunting term; said of the huntsman who holds the hounds (q.v.) for a short while before putting them onto the line of the fox (q.v.) to give the fox a sporting chance.

lawn clippings Also known as turf grass clippings; the cut remnants of fresh grass (q.v.); may cause colic (q.v.) and, as such, are not generally used as horse feed unless absolutely necessary.

lawn meet A hunting term; any meet of a Hunt (q.v.) held at a private estate or house by invitation of the owner.

Lawton gig A horse-drawn vehicle; a superior type of Liverpool gig (q.v.) manufactured by the English firm of Lawton during the second half of the 19th century.

lay (1) A racing term; said of a jockey who occupies a certain running position deliberately while waiting to make a strategic move, e.g., to lay third off the pace. (2) *see* BET no. 2

lay off A racing term; to reduce the net amount of a bet (q.v.) placed by hedging a bet the other way as the odds (q.v.) change.

lay-up To allow a horse to recuperate from an injury or illness or to rest.

lazy back The back rest of a seat in a horse-drawn vehicle such as a coach (q.v.); may be folded down.

lazy walk A four-beat gait executed in four-time in which the horse drags its toes, lacks engagement, balance, and forward swing of the striding leg.

lead (1) To guide or conduct a horse from one place to another by showing the way; the rider may show the way either on foot or from a mounted position on another horse. (2) *see* LEADING LEG. (3) Also known as dead weight or weight; a racing term; blocks, normally made of lead, which may be placed in pockets in a lead pad (q.v.) to make up the difference between the actual weight of the jockey (q.v.) and the weight the horse has been assigned to carry in the race. (4) *see* LEAD LINE

lead bag *see* LEAD PAD

lead change *see* CHANGE OF LEAD

leader Also known as lead horse; either of the two head horses in a tandem (q.v.), or one driven horse which leads one or more other horses to pull a vehicle.

leaders The head team consisting of a pair of horses harnessed in front of a four-, six-, or eight-horse hitch pulling a vehicle.

lead harness A combination of leather pieces and metals used to connect the lead horses (q.v.) to a wagon, carriage, cart, etc. which they are to pull; generally consists of a bridle (q.v.), collar (q.v.), hames (q.v.), tugs or traces (q.v.), back band (q.v.), belly band (q.v.), and breeching (q.v.).

lead horse (1) *see* LEADER. (2) The highest ranking stallion or mare in a herd.

lead hounds A hunting term; hounds (q.v.) who run in front of the pack when running a fox (q.v.).

leading leg Also known as the lead; the front leg that leads the gait, striking the ground in front, and independent of, the other three at the canter (q.v.) or gallop (q.v.); will either be a right lead (q.v.) or left lead (q.v.).

leading rein A single, long rein (q.v.) attached to the bit (q.v.), generally with a quick-release attachment, by which is guided the bridled horse from the ground.

lead line Also known as lead rope, lead, or halter rope; a leather or webbing strap, chain, or rope, or any combination thereof, attached to the halter and used to lead the horse.

lead pad Also known as lead bag or weight cloth; a racing term; a saddle pad equipped with small pockets in which thin slabs of lead (q.v.) are placed to achieve the minimum weight required in a race, as when the jockey does not meet the minimum weight requirements the horse has been assigned to carry.

lead pony *see* PONY no. 3

lead rope *see* LEAD LINE

leak A cutting term; the action of a horse during or after a turn that causes him to move forward towards the cow he is cutting instead of staying back; often results in the horse losing the working advantage (q.v.).

leaky roof circuit A racing term; a geographical grouping of minor racetracks.

lean head Said of the horse's head when the muscles, veins, and bony projections are clearly visible.

lean in *see* FALL IN

lean on the bit Said of an off-balance horse who attempts to balance himself by leaning against the rider's hands for support through the bit and reins; there is too much weight on the forehand.

leaping head Also known as lower pommel, leaping pommel, or hunting horn; the lower of two padded pommels or horns on the sidesaddle (q.v.); used as an emergency grip to prevent the side saddler's left knee from rising up; is detachable, being screwed into a socket on the sidesaddle tree, may be adjusted to fit the size of the rider's leg, and curves outwards over the rider's left thigh; replaced the top pommel which made it difficult and unsafe to jump fences; invented in 1830 by Jules Pellier at which time it revolutionized sidesaddle riding and entirely altered the concept of cross-country riding.

leaping pommel *see* LEAPING HEAD

leash *see* LEASH OF FOXES

leash of foxes Also known as leash; a hunting term; three foxes (q.v.).

leather (1) The skin of animals, especially that of cattle, dressed and prepared for use by tanning or similar processes; the best hides for tack come from slow-maturing cattle such as Aberdeen Angus; the slower the growth, the more the hide's substance has a chance to develop and the greater the resulting hide strength. (2) *see* WHIP no. 2

leathers (1) Also known as stirrup leathers, stirrup straps, or straps; adjustable straps by which the stirrup irons (q.v.) are attached to the English saddle (q.v.) at the bars; historically, made of leather hence the name, but may now be purchased in a variety of synthetic materials and in a variety of lengths and widths. (2) A type of riding breech (q.v.) made of leather.

leave it A polo term; a call from one team member to another meaning do not touch the ball, immediately ride off an opposing player, and continue up the field for a pass.

left diagonal Said of the horse when the left foreleg and forefoot move in unison with the right hind foot at the trot.

leery An antiquated term; a horse lacking energy and heart when working, the cause being attitudinal, not physical.

left half pass A lateral dressage (q.v.) movement performed free of the track, in which the horse bends uniformly throughout his body in movement to the left; the horse moves forward and to the left on two tracks (q.v.) with his shoulders slightly in advance of the hindquarters (q.v.); the right legs cross in front of the left.

left-hand course A racing term; a racetrack (q.v.) in which the horses run counter clockwise.

left lead Said of the horse when his left fore and hind legs lead at the canter or gallop.

left rein (1) To move to the left. (2) The rein attached to the near-side bit ring. (3) To use the left rein to communicate direction to the horse.

leg (1) The portion of the fore or hind limb of the horse below the knee or hock. (2) The portion of a tall riding boot between the ankle and the knee; may be lined, unlined, or partially lined and is sometimes cuffed.

leg aids Also known as lower aids; the rider's legs when employed to communicate direction to the horse, e.g., to produce forward movement and to shift or hold the haunches of the horse in the same manner.

legal catch *see* FAIR CATCH

legal hook A polo term; any hook (q.v.) of an opponent's shot conducted below the level of the withers of the opponent's horse.

leg barring *see* ZEBRA STRIPES

leg brace (1) *see* SURGICAL LEG BRACE. (2) Any brace (q.v.) applied to the horse's legs.

leg em up *see* LEG UP no. 4

Legend of the Eight Horses, The An ancient Chinese legend originating in the 9th century BC; the Emperor of the Chow Dynasty, full of wanderlust, wanted to travel the world; to do so he collected eight horses: Wah Lau, Luk Yee, Chik Kee, Pak O, Ku Wong, Yu Lung, Du Lee, and Sam Chee, who could travel 30,000 li (Chinese miles) in one day; while traveling he climbed the Kun Lun mountains where he encountered a goddess, Si Wong Mu; during his extended visit with her, the Baron of Chu attempted to seize the Emperor's throne; had it not been for the stamina of his eight horses, he would have been unable to rush home to suppress the efforts of the Baron and save his throne.

legging A roping term; said of a roper; to lift a calf's front leg thus tipping him onto his side in preparation for the tie (q.v.); an alternative move to flanking (q.v.).

leggings Also known as half chaps or historically as Richmonds; smooth or rough-out leather (q.v.), canvas, or synthetic material used to protect the lower leg of the rider from rubbing and to obtain a better grip in the saddle, closes on the outside of the leg with velcro, zippers, lacing, or buckles; a modern adaptation of the original chaps (q.v.) which covered the entire leg; worn with paddock boots (q.v.) or any low shoe.

leg lock A racing term; an illegal maneuver performed by a jockey to impair performance of another jockey's horse, as by hooking legs.

leg mange *see* CHORIOPTIC MANGE

leg marking Any white mark on the horse's leg defined by the pattern, location of the pattern, and the limb marked; the skin under these marks is unpigmented; may be used as a means of identification; include white spot (q.v.), heel (q.v.), coronet (q.v.), pastern (q.v.), half pastern (q.v.), fetlock (q.v.), sock (q.v.), stocking (q.v.), half stocking (q.v.), and ermine (q.v.) marks.

legs out of the same hole Said of a horse having a very narrow chest; generally such horses will stand wide at the base (q.v.).

leg swing *see* CARPITIS

legume Any species of plant of the legume family, Leguminosae, that bear pod-like fruits which split along two seams, as a pea pod; plants of this family are used for fodder and fertilizer.

legume hay A cut and dried hay made from legumes such as alfalfa (q.v.) and clover (q.v.); a good source of vitamins A, B, and D, and are higher in calcium (q.v.), phosphorus (q.v.), nitrogen, and protein (q.v.), but lower in fiber and also richer, generally higher yielding, and more laxative than grass hays (q.v.); contain a higher nitrogen content because the roots of these plants are covered with a bacteria known as rhizobia which converts gaseous nitrogen to fixed nitrogen.

leg up (1) To assist a rider to mount a horse from the ground by lifting up his bent left leg, and thus his body, at the same time the rider jumps upward off his right foot. (2) A racing term; to increase the speed and stamina of a horse with work. (3) A racing term; a jockey's riding assignment. (4) Also known as leg em up; to bring a horse back to fitness following a period of inactivity.

leg yield A lateral movement performed on two tracks, forward and sideways, in which the horse moves away from the rider's leg applying pressure, i.e., if the rider applies pressure with his off-side (q.v.) leg just behind the girth (q.v.), the horse will move in the direction of the near side (q.v.).

Le Livre de la Chasse *see* DE FOIX, GASTON

Le Maneige Royal *see* DE PLUVINEL, ANTOINE

length A racing term; a horizontal measurement of 8 or 9 feet (2.4-2.7 m), roughly the distance from the nose of the horse to his tail; a unit of measure by which the margin of the winning horse in front of other competing horses is measured as in fractions or numbers of lengths.

lengthening insufficient A dressage term; said of a horse who does not demonstrate sufficient difference between two paces, e.g., collected to working trot, working trot to extended, etc.

leopard A horse exhibiting a leopard spotting (q.v.) coat pattern.

leopard marking *see* LEOPARD SPOTTING

leopard spotting Also known as leopard marking; refers to coat color pattern; a white or colored body with an extensive blanket (q.v.), having colored spots on the white which extend over the entire body; spots can vary from a few to several centimeters in diameter; the leopard gene is dominant and rarely skips a generation; of three types: patterned leopard (q.v.), unpatterned leopard (q.v.), and few-spotted leopard (q.v.); one of six symmetrical coat color patterns of the Appaloosa (q.v.) recognized by the Appaloosa Horse Club (q.v.).

lespedeza Any one of several herbs or shrubs of the genus Lespedeza, in the legume family, cultivated as forage or as a soil binder.

lespedeza hay A legume hay (q.v.) made from cut and dried lespedeza (q.v.); contains a digestible protein content ranging from 11.7 percent in a pre-bloom second cut, to 7.5 percent in a full-bloom second cut; drought resistant and grows well in poor soil.

lethal dominant white A dominant gene that produces a white foal with blue or hazel eyes; homozygous foals die in utero and all white horses with the dominant white gene are heterozygotes which when mated, 25 percent of the embryos will be homozygous.

lethal white syndrome *see* ILEOCOLONIC AGANGLIONOSIS

leucocyte *see* WHITE BLOOD CELL

leukocyte *see* WHITE BLOOD CELL

leucoderma *See* LEUKODERMA

leukoderma Also spelled leucoderma; an aquired, permanent whitening of previously pigmented skin or hair as a result of trauma from badly fitting harness, saddlery, bits, cryogenic surgery, etc.; the resulting destruction of the pigment cells is permanent and adventitial marks (q.v.) result.

leu-in A hunting term; to put the hounds into a covert (q.v.).

levade A classical air (q.v.); a movement in which the horse's forehand is elevated on deeply bent hind legs, the hocks lowered to 8 to 10 inches (20-25 cm) above the ground; the longer the levade is held, the more difficult it is to perform; the horse does not raise his body quite as high and does not balance himself on his haunches for quite as long as in the pesade (q.v.); the base for the courbette (q.v.).

leve Also spelled levée; a 16th and 17th-century term; to raise, as in the lance which the knight used when tilting (q.v.).

levée *see* LEVE

level *see* LEVEL PACK

level mover Said of a horse who moves evenly and in a balanced manner with legs swinging freely and toes pointed forward.

level pack Also known as level; a hunting term; said of a pack of hounds matched in color, size, conformation, and working ability.

lever noseband *see* KINETON NOSEBAND

LHLT The acronym for low heel, long toe (q.v.).

liberty Said of a horse who moves freely.

Liberty horse A circus horse that, in a group and without a rider, carries out movements on command.

Libyan *see* BARB

Libyan Barb *see* BARB

lice (1) Also known as pediculosis; the plural of louse (q.v.). (2) Also spelled lise or list; a 16th and 17th-century French term; the walls or other barriers which enclosed a space established for tilting (q.v.).

lift *see* LIFT HOUNDS

lift hounds A hunting term; said of the huntsman (q.v.) when he takes the hounds (q.v.) off of the line of the hunted fox (q.v.) and moves them forward to a location where he believes the fox has run.

ligament A strong, fibrous band of tissue consisting of fibro-elastic and fibrous types which connect one bone to another, provide support, strengthen the joints, and limit joint range.

light *see* DISMOUNT

light brown Refers to coat color; a shade of brown (q.v.) less red than bay (q.v.) with which it is easily confused.

light harness One of three types of horse show classes for the American Saddlebred (q.v.) in which demonstration of the walk and animated park trot are required.

light horse Any horse, other than a heavy horse or pony, used or suitable for hack (q.v.) or hunting (q.v.).

light of bone Said of a horse lacking sufficient measurement of bone to support his body weight and that of the rider without strain.

light seat Also known as crotch seat; the position of the mounted English rider when posting the trot; his weight is on his thighs rather than on his seat.

lilac dun Refers to coat color; a rare variation of dun (q.v.); a lilac or dove-colored body with chocolate points; the skin is light brown or pink and the eyes are amber.

lilac roan Also known as lavender roan; refers to coat color; a roan (q.v.) pattern with white hairs uniformly mixed into the coat of a dark or liver chestnut (q.v.); the points and head will be dark or liver chestnut with no white hairs.

limb The leg and the structures above it which join it to the trunk of the horse.

limited-age event A cutting horse (q.v.) event restricted to horses between the ages of three and six years of age.

limited partnership An agreement of two or more individuals who cooperatively purchase a horse for racing, showing, or breeding purposes, the costs and profits of which are distributed according to the agreed terms.

Limousin Also known as Limousin Half-Bred; a heavy-weight halfbred horse of English blood indigenous to the Limousin area in France from which the name derived; descended from native mares crossed with Thoroughbred (q.v.), Arab (q.v.), Anglo-Arab (q.v.), and Anglo-Norman (q.v.) stallions; is large boned, stands 16 to 17 hands, and generally has a chestnut or bay coat; of the group Cheval de Selle Français and the regional group Demi-Sang du Centre as is the Charollais (q.v.).

Limousin Half-Bred *see* LIMOUSIN

linchpin A pin passed through the end of the axle tree of a horse-drawn vehicle to keep the wheel in place.

line (1) The ancestors of a horse on the male side; define the relationship between horses by blood. (2) The profile of a horse. (3) The direction of travel. (4) *see* LINE OF THE FOX

lindell Also known as a side pull; a soft latigo leather headstall with a stiff lariat nosepiece to which the reins are attached used to start young horses or encourage mature horses who overcollect to relax and lengthen; may be used in conjunction with a snaffle bit and as a transition to a neck ring (q.v.).

line *see* LINE OF THE FOX

linear whorl A hair pattern; a whorl (q.v.); a change in direction of the flow of the hair in which two opposing sweeps of hair meet from diametrically opposite directions along a line.

line-back Refers to coat color pattern; said of a horse having a dark dorsal stripe (q.v.) which continues and darkens into the tail; may be black, brown, red, or gold; a primitive mark (q.v.).

line-breeding Mating of horses of common ancestry, several generations removed; presents the same dangers inherent to in-breeding programs, but slightly less intensified.

line drive *see* LONG LINE no. 1

line firing To insert, in a series of vertical lines, hot needles and/or pins in a blemish or unsound area, most commonly the legs, as a treatment to hasten and strengthen the reparative process by increasing blood supply.

line gaited Said of a horse who trots with each hind foot following directly in line with its lateral forehoof.

line of the ball A polo term; the concept governing traffic on the polo field during play: the player(s) established in the imaginary line created by the travelling ball, whether behind or in front, have the right of way.

line of the fox Also known as line; a hunting term; the scent trail of an animal.

lines *see* LONG LINES no. 2

linseed Also known as flaxseed; the small, flat, and shiny seed of flax (q.v.); has a high protein and fat content; usually fed as a hot or cold mash, jelly, or tea; must be soaked and then boiled to split the seeds.

linseed meal Also known as linseed oil meal; a high protein, high energy concentrate produced from the residue of the flaxseed following extraction of the oil; contains 30 to 32 percent protein and from 1 to 5 percent fat; lower in protein quality than soybean meal because it is low in several amino acids and has a low-palatability factor; credited with producing a nice finish on the hair coat.

linseed mash A wet mash made with linseed meal (q.v.) or linseed (q.v.) combined with bran (q.v.) and water; must be fed within 24 hours to avoid spoiling; also used as a poultice (q.v.).

linseed oil The oil obtained by pressing the flaxseed (q.v.); is not used as an equine supplement.

linseed oil meal *see* LINSEED MEAL

L'Instruction du Roy, En l'Exercice de Monter à cheval A book written in 1625 by Antoine de Pluvinel (q.v.) on the subject of training riding horses.

Lippizzan *see* LIPIZZANER

Lipizzana *see* LIPIZZANER

Lipizzaner Also known as Lippizzan and formerly as Lipizzana; an Austrian-bred warmblood named for the village of Lipizza, now part of northwest Yugoslavia, where Archduke Charles II founded the Imperial Austrian Stud and the breed in 1580; descended from Andalusian (q.v.) stock put to a nucleus of native Karst horses; succeeding generations were crossed with Neapolitan (q.v.), Arab (q.v.), Kladruber (q.v.), and Frederiksborg (q.v.); a sturdy, late developing horse standing 14.2 to 16 hands; born with a dark, black-brown, brown, or mousy-gray coat which gradually lightens to white or gray between the ages of six and ten; has a lavish head, small ears, crested neck, compact body, and full mane and tail; action is high rather than low and long; used extensively at the Imperial Spanish Riding School of Vienna (q.v.), and is well suited to the airs above the ground (q.v.), pleasure riding, carriage, and light farm work; considered a rare breed.

lip marking Any colored marking on the lip of the horse

lips the bars Said of a horse who plays with the bit shanks with his lips when bitted (q.v.).

lip strap Also known as bridle lip strap or curb strap; a narrow leather or nylon strap buckled to the bit ring on one side, threaded through a special link in the curb chain (q.v.), and buckled on the other side to the other bit ring; softens the effect of the curb chain, keeps it from overhanging the lower lip, and the cheeks of the bit from turning.

lip tattoo A registration tattoo (q.v.) placed on the inside lip of a horse, as in race horses.

lise *see* LICE no. 2

lisk *see* GROIN

list (1) *see* DORSAL STRIPE. (2) *see* LICE no. 2

listed race A racing term; a stakes race (q.v.) of less quality than group or graded races (q.v.).

Lithuanian Heavy Draft A coldblood originating in Lithuania in the late 1890s; descended from the local Zhmud (q.v.) put to the Finnish Horse (q.v.) and Swedish Ardennes (q.v.); registered and breeding has been strictly controlled since 1963 with all breeding stallions undergoing rigorous performance tests; is massively built and medium-sized with short, lightly feathered legs and good bone; the neck is quite short, thick, muscular and arched, and the mane full; sickle hocks (q.v.) are common, but the action is free, fast, and attractive; has a quiet temperament, stands 15 to 16 hands, is quite strong, and has enormous powers of traction, and a chestnut coat with black, roan, bay, and gray also occurring; used for heavy draft; when bred in Latvia, it is known as a Latvian Heavy Draught (q.v.).

litter (1) A group of young born to the same mother at the same time, as in a litter of puppies or cubs. (2) *see* BEDDING. (3) A wheelless carriage on shafts supported either between horses or mules in tandem (q.v.) or on the backs of human bearers which support a single passenger in a seated or reclined position; later versions were box shaped with a semi-open or headed top.

live foal guarantee A provision in a breeding contract which guarantees the owner of the bred mare to a live, standing, nursing foal as a result of a purchased breeding; generally gives the owner of the mare the right to re-breed to the same stallion in the following season in the event the mare fails to produce a live foal as a result of the initial breeding.

live hunt A hunting term; any hunt in which the hounds pursue the trail or scent left by a live animal; the opposite of a drag hunt (q.v.).

liver (1) A large, reddish-brown glandular organ positioned in the upper right-hand side of the abdominal cavity; divided by fissures into several lobes, secretes bile, and performs various metabolic functions such as controlling erratic swings in blood sugar, fluid, protein, and electrolyte levels and the accumulation of body toxins; when it malfunctions, the body becomes poisoned by its own metabolic toxins and diminishes the appetite and thirst mechanisms. (2) *see* LIVER CHESTNUT

liver chestnut Also known as liver; refers to coat color; one of the darkest of the chestnut (q.v.) or red shades; the coat consists of a mixture of red and black hairs with similar-colored points.

liver chestnut alazán Refers to coat color; one of the darkest of the red shades; the coat consists of a mixture of red and black hairs with red or dark flaxen points.

liver chestnut tostado Refers to coat color; one of the darkest of the red shades; the coat consists of a mixture of red and black hairs with legs that become progressively lighter towards the hoof.

liver chestnut ruano Refers to coat color; a dark red shade; the coat consists of a mixture of red and black hairs with light flaxen points.

liver fluke Also known as *fasciola hepatica*; a trematode flatworm parasitic in man, sheep, and snails and occasionally horses; the amphibious mud snail is the intermediate host; horses become infected when they graze in poorly drained or marshy pastures in common with infected sheep or cattle; may cause abdominal pain, anemia, and poor performance.

Liverpool A jumping obstacle consisting of a small, shallow water hole over which a bar (q.v.) supported by two standards (q.v.) is suspended; the rail and water hole are jumped and scored as a single element.

Liverpool bit A circular-cheeked driving bit with a straight bar mouthpiece smooth on one side and corrugated on the other having a sliding, pivot action; the part of the shank below the mouthpiece is flat and has two rein slots; above the top rein slot is a circle bisected by a perpendicular bar to which the mouthpiece is attached by sliding action.

Liverpool gig A fully enclosed, square-sided, elegant yet sturdy, horse-drawn vehicle of the gig (q.v.) type; provided no rearward access to the luggage space, but had a large buck under the cross seat; first made and used in the mid-19th century in Liverpool, England, although its use later spread throughout Great Britain.

Liverpool horse Any horse capable of jumping the Grand National hurdle course at Aintree (q.v.).

Liverpool Steeplechase, The *see* GRAND NATIONAL STEEPLECHASE

live weight A racing term; the weight of a jockey excluding his tack, as contrasted with dead weight (q.v.).

livery (1) A horse boarded at a facility other than the horse owner's for which a fee is paid. (2) A hunting term; clothing worn by professional members of the Hunt (q.v.). (3) The care and feeding of a horse for a set fee. (4) *see* STABLE

Livery Company Also known as livery guild; one of several trade associations in London, England, that sprang from the medieval guilds; concerned with the standards and traditions of work within respective guilds as well as the welfare of the members; now predominantly associated with equestrian-related trades such as saddle and harness makers, farriers, coach builders, etc.

Livery Guild *see* LIVERY COMPANY

livery man (1) A British term; one entitled to wear livery (q.v.), especially a freeman of the City of London. (2) Any owner or employee of a livery stable (q.v.).

livery stable (1) A stable where horses and carriages are tended or kept. (2) *see* STABLE

live stock Domestic animals, such as cattle and horses, bred or maintained on a farm for use and/or commercial profit.

Llanero A Venezuelan-bred Criollo (q.v.); a warmblood descended from Spanish stock brought to South America by the Spanish conquistadors in the 16th century; has a lighter and less solidly built frame than the Argentine Criollo (q.v.), a head similar to a Barb (q.v.) with a rather convex profile, stands approximately 14 hands, and may have a dun, yellow with a dark mane and tail, white, yellow cream, or pinto (q.v.) coat; used for ranch work and riding.

loaded shoulder Said of the shoulder of the horse when excessively thick due to either muscle or fat.

loafer A racing term; a horse who is unwilling to race well without hard urging by the rider.

loafing hound A hunting term; a hound when he leaves the work of hunting to the rest of the pack.

lob A racing term; a cooler (q.v.).

lobbing and sobbing Said of a horse so exhausted following hard work that he is not in full control of his actions or coordination.

lobo dun Refers to coat color; a grullo (q.v.) of the color group dun (q.v.) in which the slate-colored body hairs are mixed with black resulting in a darker coat color especially along the topline (q.v.).

local anesthesia An artificially produced, localized insensibility, especially to the sense of pain.

local anesthetic Any substance that deprives feeling or sensation to a specific area in the body; generally administered by injection.

lock (1) Also known as a sure thing; a racing term; a guaranteed win, e.g. "that horse has a lock on the race". (2) The amount of turn possible in the forecarriage and front wheels of a horse-drawn vehicle, e.g., The coach had a quarter distance lock.

lockjaw *see* TETANUS

lock the stable door after the horse is stolen To take belated precautions; dated to the Romans as quoted from Plautus' Asinaria "Ne post tempus proedoe proesidium parem" (After the time of plunder one provides protection); English use is found in John Gower's Confessio amatis (1390): "For whan the grete Stiede [steed] is stole, thenne he [Negligence] taketh hiede, and maketh the door fast."

loco (1) To poison with loco weed. (2) Crazy.

loco disease *see* LOCOISM

locoism Also known as loco disease; a disease of horses, cattle, and sheep caused by loco weed (q.v.) poisoning characterized by a loss of sense, and, ultimately, death.

loco weed Any of various plants of the legume family, genera Astragalus and Oxtropis, found in the southwestern United States that when ingested by horses or cattle, produces locoism (q.v.).

lodging rooms A hunting term; the rooms in a hunt kennel (q.v.) where the hounds (q.v.) sleep and are kept.

loft An area in some barns, usually a second floor, in which hay is stored.

log headcollar A solid block of wood with a hole drilled through the center, through which a rope is passed and knotted; the other end being passed through a ring in the manger; allows limited head movement for a horse kept in a tie stall.

loin The body part(s) on either side of the vertebral column between the false ribs and the hip bone.

loin cloth A waterproof cloth fitted over the loins of cart or carriage horses when standing in wet weather.

loins More than one loin (q.v.).

Lokai A warmblood of mixed ancestry which originated in southern Tadzhikistan on the western side of the Pamir mountain range; for many centuries local stock was crossed with Karabair (q.v.), Arab (q.v.), and Iomud blood by the Lokai people, for which the breed is named; from the 16th century, stock was improved with crosses to Akhal-Teke (q.v.), Karabair, and Arab blood; stands 14 to 14.2 hands, has a long neck, short back, sloping croup, notably tough hooves, and a chestnut coat with golden highlights, although bay, or gray and rarely black or dun also occur; used for riding, packing, and mounted competitive sports.

lolls the cricket A western term; said of the horse when he plays with the bit roller (q.v.) with his tongue.

London Cart Horse Parade Society An organization founded in London, England in 1890 to improve the general condition and treatment of cart horses.

London color A light shade of brown

tanned leather, from which saddlery is made.

London International *see* ROYAL INTERNATIONAL HORSE SHOW

London tan A slightly darker shade of brown tanned leather than London color (q.v.) used to make saddlery.

London Van Horse Parade Society An organization founded in Great Britain in 1904 to improve the general condition and treatment of van and light draft horses used for commercial purposes.

long *see* LONG ON A COW

long-coupled Said of a horse who has more distance between the last rib and the point of the hip than average or preferred.

longe *see* LUNGE

longeing cavesson *see* LUNGEING CAVESSON

longeing whip *see* LUNGE WHIP

longe line *see* LUNGE LINE

longer *see* LUNGER

longe rein *see* LUNGE LINE

longe whip *see* LUNGE WHIP

long in the tooth Said of an old horse.

longitudinal flexion The bending of the horse's joints from back-to-front, e.g., flexion at the poll or flexion throughout the body.

long line (1) Also known as long rein, line drive, or drive; to move a horse between two long lines (q.v.), one attached to either side of the cavesson (q.v.) or bit (q.v.), to introduce hand aids, supple, and improve impulsion from behind; the long liner walks or jogs behind the horse. (2) Also known as long rein, lines, or in driving terms as reins; one of two 39 to 46 foot x 1 inch (12-14 m x 25 mm) long reins used to long line a horse; may be made of leather or synthetic straps, webbing, or rope with approximately 5 feet (1.5 m) of halyard ending in snap hooks or buckles on one end; two reins are required, with one rein attached to each bit ring; the total length allows one to maintain a distance of 6-1/2 to 7-1/2 yards (6-

6.4 m) from the horse and to scribe circles of 16.4 to 21.9 yards (15-20 m) in diameter.

long liner One who drives a horse between two long lines (q.v.).

long on a cow Also known as long; a cutting term; said of a horse who moves ahead of the cow being worked instead of remaining across from his shoulder or head; may result in the cow gaining the working advantage (q.v.) and cutting back to the herd.

long pastern *see* PASTERN BONE

long pastern bone *see* PASTERN BONE

long rein (1) *see* LONG LINE. (2) *see* LONG LINE no. 2

long rein, on a To ride a horse with the reins as long as possible without losing contact with the bit to allow the horse to stretch his neck freely.

long shafted cart *see* BREAKING CART

long side One of two long sides of a rectangular arena or *manège* (q.v.).

long sloping pastern Said of the pastern when too long for the length of the limb; characterized by a normal or subnormal angulation of the forefoot (45 degrees or under).

Long Wagon Also known as a whirlicote or medieval long wagon; a horse-drawn, dead-axle traveling carriage used throughout Britain and Europe in the 13th and 14th centuries; was headed with rich embroidery work and had inner seats slung on the hammock principle; drawn by teams of six or more horses controlled by postillons (q.v.).

Lonsdale Wagonette A luxurious horse-drawn vehicle of the wagonette (q.v.) type having a low-hung, rounded body, and falling hood; introduced by the fifth Earl of Lonsdale after whom it was named.

look A cutting term; the expression of the horse when facing a cow.

looker An antiquated British term; one who, for a reward or fee, watches horses or cattle grazing on unfarmed marsh land surrounded by dykes to ensure their well-being.

look for a hole in the fence A racing term; said of a horse who would rather run back to the barn than continue running in a race; a quitter.

look of eagles A racing term; said of a good horse with a proud look in his eyes, as though he knows he is good.

loops not equal A dressage term; circles scribed in the arena by the horse under saddle that are not equal in size or shape; only used when the rider performs movements of three or more loops.

loose jumping Said of a horse who jumps over obstacles in an enclosed arena without a rider; the horse is controlled from the ground by voice commands or long lines (q.v.).

loose box *see* STALL

loose mount Said of a horse who continues to race or jump a course after losing its rider.

loose rein (1) Reins that have been dropped by the rider to give them extra length to allow slack and eliminate contact between the rider's/driver's hands and the bit. (2) A cutting term; said of the rider in competition; to drop the reins to allow the horse to work an isolated cow; points are deducted from the score if the reins are used to guide the horse during this part of the contest.

loose rein, on a To ride a horse with the reins as long as possible in the rider's hands to allow the horse to stretch his neck freely.

loose-ring The cheekpiece of a bit; a variably sized ring passed through a hole in the end of the bit mouthpiece.

loose-ring snaffle A snaffle bit (q.v.) having ring cheeks which pass through the ends of the mouthpiece.

loose seat The position assumed by the English rider in the saddle; the thighs and knees are relaxed, not tense or gripping, the rider staying in the saddle by balance rather than grip.

lope A smooth, slow, three-beat gait in which the horse's head and neck hang lower than at a gallop (q.v.); the hind legs drive and the forelegs reach out allowing the horse to stretch; the western equivalent of a slow gallop, is a less collected gait than the canter (q.v.) and slower than the hand gallop (q.v.).

lop ears Said of the ears of the horse which flop and hang down in a pendulous fashion; does not affect hearing and may be surgically corrected; a conformation defect.

lop-neck *see* BROKEN CREST

loriner One who makes the metal parts of saddle and harness tack such as bits (q.v.), curb chains (q.v.), and stirrup irons (q.v.).

Loriners Company, The A livery company (q.v.) organized in England sometime around 1245 to represent loriners (q.v.).

Lorry Also known as Lurry; any open, horse-drawn dray, truck, or trolley used for general hauling and delivery; common in the country districts of Northern England; frequently unsprung with equirotal or near equirotal wheels, and drawn by a single horse in shafts, or more frequently by teams of chain horses which could pull up to 8 tons; driven from the fore-end of the platform in a standing position.

Los Caballos de Paso Fino *see* PASO FINO

lose a cow A cutting term; said of a cutter when the cow being worked returns to the herd before he has had the opportunity to quit it; in cutting horse competitions, a five-point penalty.

losing flesh Said of a horse losing weight, as due to parasite infestation, bad teeth, insufficient feed or water, etc.

lose the working advantage, to A cutting term; said of the horse when he loses the attention of the cow being worked; the cow controls the actions of the horse instead of the horse holding and controlling the movements of the cow.

loss A hunting term; said of the hounds (q.v.) when they are unable to follow the line of the fox (q.v.).

lost a horseshoe 18th-century German slang; said of a seduced girl (Sie hat ein Hufeisen verloren).

lost shoes A antiquated British term; said of an exhausted horse.

lot of horse in a little room A British term; a short-coupled (q.v.), short, compact, horse having good bone.

lots of color Refers to coat color; said of an Appaloosa (q.v.) who shows a lot of white.

louse Also known as horse louse; an external, biting and sucking parasite; demonstrates a high degree of host specificity and two different species may infest the horse: the biting louse (q.v.) and the sucking louse (q.v.); although less than 1/10 inch (2.5 mm) in length, are visible to the naked eye as small or light-gray objects; may be detected by inspecting the mane, root of the tail, inside the thighs, or on the underside of the saddle blanket following exercise; is not communicable to people.

low airs Formalized posture or movements of the horse performed near the ground; include the passage (q.v.), piaffe (q.v.), gallopade, change of hands (q.v.), volte (q.v.), demi-volte (q.v.), passade (q.v.), pirouette (q.v.), and terre à terre (q.v.).

low bow One of three classifications of bowed tendon (q.v.) identified on the basis of location; any true physiological damage to the tendon or tendon sheath, most commonly of the superficial flexor tendon of the foreleg; specifically, tearing or breaking of one or more fibers of the lower third of the tendon; may be precipitated by fatigue, deep going, uneven terrain, improper shoeing, obesity, excessively tight fitting running bandages or boots, work on slippery surfaces, long, weak pasterns (q.v.), sudden changes in stress loads, low heel angles, and long toes; symptoms may include diffuse swelling over the tendon area, heat, and pain; lameness may or may not be present.

Lowe Figure System *see* BRUCE LOWE FIGURE SYSTEM

lower aids *see* LEG AIDS

lower-cheek snaffle A half-cheek snaffle bit (q.v.) consisting of a straight or jointed mouthpiece (q.v.) fitted at either end with fixed rings and a straight- or spoon-shaped (wider and slightly curved toward the horse's jaw at the top) arm attached to the rings below the mouthpiece on the mouth-side of the bit; used on driving horses to prevent the bit from running through the horse's mouth if he runs sideways or refuses to turn; acts on the corners and sides of the mouth and the lips.

lower pommel *see* LEAPING HEAD

low heel, long toe Also known by the acronym LHLT; a condition of the hoof of the horse in which the heels are excessively low due to trimming, wear, or underrun growth and the toe often long, as in a flare; may precipitate navicular disease (q.v.).

low ringbone A type of ringbone (q.v.); a bony growth developing inside the hoof in the joint connecting the short pastern (q.v.) and pedal bone (q.v.); not to be confused with sidebone (q.v.) which is a different condition.

low scenting hounds A hunting term; said of hounds (q.v.) who follow the line of the fox (q.v.) with their noses to the ground; are especially useful when the scent is light.

Lowther bit *see* ARKWRIGHT BIT

Lowther riding bit *see* ARKWRIGHT BIT

low wither Said of a horse whose croup (q.v.) is higher than his withers.

lozenge *see* BIT GUARD

lucerne *see* ALFALFA

lug Said of a horse who leans on the bit when ridden or driven.

lugger A horse who leans on the bit when ridden or driven.

lug in *see* BEAR IN

lug out *see* BEAR OUT

lumbar muscles The muscles of the loins adjoining the lumbar vertebrae.

lunch box *see* IMPERIAL

lung Either of two sac-like respiratory organs located in each thoracic cavity (q.v.).

lunge Also known as roping and spelled longe; to exercise or train the horse on a single long line (q.v.) attached to the bridle, lungeing cavesson (q.v.) or halter (q.v.) in a circle around the trainer on the flat or over jumps.

lungeing cavesson Also known as a breaking cavesson, breaking head collar, or training cavesson and spelled longeing cavesson; a specially designed halter or head collar with an adjustable throat latch (q.v.), noseband (q.v.), and headpiece to which long lines (q.v.) or a lunge line (q.v.) may be attached; generally has three ring attachments on the noseband and two on the brow band; a long line (q.v.) may be attached to the center ring to permit lungeing either to left or right without changing gear; the side and brow rings may be used in conjunction with two long reins (q.v.) to drive or long line (q.v.) the horse.

lunge circle The track scribed by the horse as he is worked around the lunger (q.v.); in vaulting (q.v.) this circle must be at least 42 feet (13 m) in diameter.

lunge line Also known as lunge rein, and spelled longe line; a cotton or synthetic rope or piece of webbing 20 to 30 feet (6-9 m) long and approximately 1 inch (25 mm) wide, attached to the halter, bridle, or lungeing cavesson (q.v.) by a hook and snap or buckle; used to train or exercise the horse from the ground; customarily the horse is worked in a circle.

lunger Also spelled longer; one who lunges (q.v.) a horse.

lunge rein *see* LUNGE LINE

lunge whip Also spelled longe whip; a whip (q.v.) approximately 4 feet (1.2 m) long, with a leather lash at least 4.4 yards (4 m) long, and a short handle which enables the lunger to reach the horse as much as 6-1/2 yards (6 m) away while working him in a circle; a shorter dressage whip (q.v.) may be used for lunge work up close.

lung hemorrhage *see* EXERCISE-INDUCED PULMONARY HEMORRHAGE

lungworm An internal parasite, *Dictyocaulus arnfieldi*, which lives in the air passages of the lungs (q.v.); the male worm may reach approximately 1 inch (25 mm) and the female 2 inches (50 mm) in length; has a direct life cycle in the horse; may be found in many countries throughout the world, particularly those with temperate climates; may result in bronchitis, pneumonia, or both.

lungworm infection An infection of the lower respiratory track caused by the internal parasite, *Dictyocaulus arnfieldi*; symptoms include coughing, increased respiratory rate, bronchitis or pneumonia or both; the clinical signs of infection in foals and donkeys, the latter being prone to carry large populations, are few, while in older horses, unthriftiness is common; it is advisable to treat horses pasturing with donkeys for this parasite.

Lurry *see* LORRY

Lusitano A horse breed of unknown origins indigenous to Portugal believed to have a history similar to the Andalusian (q.v.) which it closely resembles; historically used for military purposes and as a carriage horse, while today it is used for light farming, light draft, riding, and in the bullfighting ring by the rejoneadores (q.v.); is intelligent, frugal, agile, and docile; has a fine, small head, thick, well-set-on neck, substantial girth depth, short back, rounded croup, powerful shoulders, and stands 15 to 16 hands; most solid coat colors occur with gray, brown, and chestnut most common; numbers are in decline.

lymph The yellow, nutritive liquid exuded from the blood vessels into the tissue spaces and drained back into the veins via the lymph vessels; important in fighting infection and maintaining the body's fluid balance.

lymphatic Relating to the lymph (q.v.).

lymphangitis Also known as lymphangitis of horses; an inflammation of the lymph vessels and nodes primarily affecting one or, in some cases, both of the pelvic limbs; develops following infection of streptococcus (q.v.), and less frequently by staphylococcus or corynebacterium bacteria; lack of exercise may be a contributing factor; the onset of symptoms is abrupt and pain is severe; symptoms include fever, anorexia, increased pulse and respiration rates, a hot, spreading, painful swelling that may involve the entire limb, swollen lymph ducts, and the exudation of fluid at areas including the hock and the medial aspect of the thigh; severe lameness accompanies the swelling; recurrent attacks are not uncommon; observed more frequently in horses in good condition.

lymphangitis of horses *see* LYMPHANGITIS

Lynwood Palmer *see* PALMER, LYNWOOD

M

machine *see* BATTERY

machine-made shoe Also known as a keg shoe, or factory-made shoe; any factory-made, preformed horseshoe; available in a variety of sizes.

Mackintosh (1) A cloth coat made waterproof by means of India rubber. (2) Cloth made waterproof by means of a India rubber coating.

macs A British term; riding breeches made of Mackintosh (q.v.); sometimes worn by jockeys when racing in wet weather.

mad-dog syndrome The classic irrational and aggressive behavior demonstrated by a horse in which the excitative rabies (q.v.) phase is predominant.

made Said of a horse whose education and training are complete.

made field hunter Any fully trained horse bred, and/or appropriate to follow hounds (q.v.) in the sport of hunting (q.v.); the type is largely influenced by the country over which it shall be used.

made pack A hunting term; said of the pack of hounds (q.v.) when the young entries (q.v.) and the older entered (q.v.) hounds have begun to work as a team.

made mouth *see* FULL MOUTH no. 1

mad woman An antiquated coaching term; an empty stage coach.

madrina *see* BELL MARE

Magenis snaffle Also, yet incorrectly spelled, McGuinness; a bit (q.v.) with a straight or jointed mouthpiece having slits into which revolving rollers are fitted; attached to the ring cheeks on either side and used with one set of reins; acts on the tongue, the bars (in the straight snaffle), the sides of the mouth (in the jointed snaffle), the lips, and corners of the mouth.

magnesium An essential mineral required by horses in small amounts for proper bone and tooth development; the requirement for growing horses is estimated to be 0.1 percent of the diet and 0.90 percent for mature horses; most feeds contain adequate dietary amounts; and deficiency may result in hypomagnesemia (q.v.).

magnesium sulfate *see* EPSOM SALTS

magnetic therapy A physical therapy technique utilizing magnetic fields to treat soft tissue and bony injuries in which opposing polarity magnets are used to create a low-energy electrical field which results in dilation of the blood vessels and stimulation of the tissue to increase circulation, reduce inflammation, and expedite healing.

mahogany bay Also known as dark bay; refers to coat color; a variation of bay (q.v.); a red coat mixed either with black hairs or red hairs with black tips; black is more abundant along the topline and particularly around the croup and withers; may be confused with seal brown.

maiden (1) Also known as maiden mare or primigravida; a mare who has never been bred or produced a foal or a mare in foal who has not yet delivered. (2) Also known as a maiden horse; a racing term; a horse or jockey of any sex, who has not won a race of any distance on a recognized racetrack (q.v.). (3) *see* MAIDEN RACE. (4) A show horse who has not previously won an event.

maiden allowance A racing term; authorization for a horse to carry reduced weight if it has not previously won a horserace.

maiden class Any horse show class for maiden (q.v.) horses exclusively.

maiden horse *see* MAIDEN no. 2

maiden mare *see* MAIDEN no. 1

maiden race Also known as maiden; a racing term; any race for horses of either sex who have not previously won a race of any distance on a recognized track; competing horses must be maidens when race entries are placed, but not necessarily at the time of the race.

mail cart A light, two-wheeled, horse-drawn cart used to collect and deliver mail; manufactured in horse, pony, and cob sizes, but sometimes drawn by a donkey; hung on sideways-elliptical springs.

Mail Coach A horse-drawn public coach used in England during the 18th and early 19th centuries to carry both the Royal Mail and passengers, the latter as a secondary consideration only; introduced to replace mounted postboys (q.v.); originally ran between London, Bath, and Bristol, England, but was later extended as a system to other parts of the country; originally hung on elbow springs and braces and carried inside passengers only, with the guard and driver sharing a box seat; eventually suspended by a combination of crosswise and sideways semi-elliptical springs connected by D links known as telegraph springs (q.v.); by 1829, 94 mail coaches were in operation; the number of each coach was painted on the rear of the vehicle and the Royal Coat of Arms painted on the body panels; drawn by four-horse teams which worked in stages of 7 to 10 miles (11-16 km) between inns and posting houses traveling at an average speed of approximately 11 mph (18 kmph).

Mail Phaeton A massive, horse-drawn vehicle of the phaeton (q.v.) type popular in the 1820s; resembled a mail or stage coach without an enclosed passenger compartment; frequently used for exercising coach horses, leisure driving, and mail delivery; drawn by two or more horses harnessed in pole gear (q.v.), using chain rather than leather traces; had mail hubs and axles, a strong underperch, and was hung on sideways, semi-elliptical or telegraph springs (q.v.); the high front seat was hooded while the rear groom's seat was contained in an open compartment entered through side doors by means of iron steps.

main bar The largest of three bars hanging from the swingle tree (q.v.) of a horse-drawn vehicle to which the traces are connected.

Mainland Pony *see* GARRON

maize *see* CORN

major penalty A cutting term; a three- or five-point penalty infraction.

make a check A racing term; said of a horse who places first through fifth, as in Sisters Aliby made a check, the owner of which receives a check for monies won.

make and break To break (q.v.) a young horse.

make a run A racing term; said of a horse who increases his speed and moves up in the field.

Malapolski A recently-developed Polish warmblood bred mostly in southern Poland; descended from Oriental stock crossed with Thoroughbred (q.v.), Furioso (q.v.), and Gidran Arabian (q.v.); characteristics vary by region, but are similar to those of the Wielkopolski (q.v.); stands 15.3 to 16.2 hands, has a solid-colored coat of any color, and a calm, well-balanced temperament; used for riding and light draft and jumping.

male tail *see* TAIL no. 2

malignant histiocytoma A giant cell tumor of the soft parts; is slow to spread and rare in horses.

mallenders An antiquated term; a condition of the skin involving an eruption on the back of the knee joint of the foreleg, characterized by a scurfy thickening of the skin, watery discharge, and loss of hair; may be caused by injury or infection.

mallet *see* POLO MALLET

mameluke bit Also known as a turkey bit or turkey curb; a curb bit (q.v.) having a ported mouth in the center of which is attached a large ring.

mammoth jack stock A donkey (q.v.) or jennet (q.v.) standing 54 inches (1.3 m) or taller or a jack (q.v.) 56 inches (1.6 m) or taller.

manada A South American term; a herd of wild mares led by a mustang (q.v.); often number in excess of 50 mares to one stallion.

Mancha One of two Criollo (q.v.) horses ridden by Aimé Tschiffely (q.v.) in his famous 2-1/2-year, 10,000 mile (16,000 km) ride from Buenos Aires, Argentina to Washington DC, USA; died at the age of 40.

manchero A Spanish term; one who travels on horseback, his primary consideration being the safety, well-being, and schooling of his

horse.

Manchester team *see* TRANDEM

mane The hair growing along the neck of the horse between the poll and withers (q.v.).

mane and tail comb A hand-held metal or plastic toothed instrument used to untangle or remove debris from the mane and tail.

mane drag *see* PULLING COMB

manège (1) Also spelled maneige and incorrectly menege; any enclosed or open arena which is usually rectangular, but may be circular, where horses are schooled or dressed (q.v.); originally of French derivation and meaning horsemanship. (2) Historically, the exercises performed in the manège; the training of the horse in the low and high airs (q.v.), including lateral and vertical suppling exercises.

manège figures *see* SCHOOLING FIGURES

maneige *see* MANEGE

Maneige Royal, The *see* DE PLUVINEL, ANTOINE

Mangalarga One of three types of Criollo (q.v.) found in Brazil, the other two being the Criollo of Rio Grande Do Sul and the Campolino (q.v.); a warmblood descended from Spanish stock brought to South America by the conquistadors in the 16th century crossed with Andalusian (q.v.), Altér-Real (q.v.), and Argentine Criollo (q.v.); has a distinctive gait between a trot and canter known as the marcha (q.v.).

mangana A Mexican rodeo event; one of nine scored events in a charreada (q.v.) in which targeted mares retained in a circular arena are hazed (q.v.) and herded by mounted or walking charros (q.v.) around the perimeter of the ring; of two types: the mangana a pie (q.v.) and the mangana a caballo (q.v.); the objective is to snare the front legs of the mare and bring her down to a shoulder roll; now illegal in many states in the USA.

mangana a caballo A Mexican rodeo event; one of nine scored events in a charreada (q.v.) in which targeted mares retained in a circular arena are hazed (q.v.) and herded by mounted charros (q.v.) around the perimeter of

the ring, while the mounted competitor prepares to throw his rope from horseback; the objective being to snare the front legs of the mare and bring her down to a shoulder roll; now illegal in many states within the United States.

mangana a pie A Mexican rodeo event; one of nine scored events in a charreada (q.v.) in which targeted mares retained in a circular arena are hazed (q.v.) and herded by walking charros (q.v.) around the perimeter of the ring, while the competitor prepares to throw his rope from a standing position on the ground; the objective being to snare the front legs of the mare and bring her down to a shoulder roll; now illegal in many states within the United States.

manganese A mineral required in trace amounts by the horse, although no exact dietary requirements have been established; utilized by enzymes in the formation of cartilage; although deficiency is uncommon, symptoms include shortened or crooked limbs, deafness due to improper development of the bones of the inner ear, and the birth of deformed foals.

mange Also known as acariasis; a contagious skin disease caused by the presence of mites (q.v.); may be spread by contact with diseased animals or their attendants or from contaminated objects or quarters; transmission occurs when larvae, nymphs, or fertilized females are transferred to a susceptible host; causes incessant and increasing itching of the affected skin; of four types: sarcoptic mange (q.v.), chorioptic mange (q.v.), demodectic mange (q.v.), and psoroptic scabies (q.v.).

manger Also known as crib or feeder; a container designed to hold food; may be free standing or built into or attached to the wall of a stall, barn, etc.

manier (1) A 17th-century French term; to school or handle a horse. (2) A 17th-century French term; to put a horse into the low and high airs (q.v.).

Manipur *see* MANIPURI

Manipuri Also known as a Manipur; an ancient pony breed indigenous to India where it descended from the Asiatic Wild Horse (q.v.) and Arab (q.v.); thought to have been introduced into India by the invading Tartar tribes sometime before the 7th century; stands 11 to 13 hands, has a light, well-proportioned head, almond-shaped eyes, full mane and tail, and sturdy legs; is strong, fast, energetic, and hardy; may have a bay, brown, gray, or chestnut coat; used for riding.

manners Said of a horse willing and obedient to the desires of his rider.

Man O'War Also known as Big Red; a chestnut Thoroughbred (q.v.) believed by many to be the finest American-bred racehorse of all time; foaled in 1917 in Kentucky, USA; beaten only once in 21 starts.

manure *see* FECES

manure spray An insecticide (q.v.) sprayed over stored manure to control fly populations in and around stabling facilities by killing fly larvae; only used when manure cannot be removed from the premises on a weekly basis; sprayed manure may be toxic to certain crops, mammals, and birds.

marathon A racing term; any horse race longer than 1-1/4 miles (2 km).

marathon phase *see* COMPETITION B

marcha Also known as marchador; the distinctive gait, between a trot and canter, of the Mangalarga (q.v.).

marchador *see* MARCHA

Marchioness Emily Mary Salisbury *see* SALISBURY, MARCHIONESS EMILY MARY

mare (1) Any female horse more than four years of age, at which point she is considered sexually mature; in Thoroughbreds (q.v.), any horse five years or older; an Anglo-Saxon word derived from mearth, meaning horse, the feminine of mearth being mere, pronounced mare. (2) Any female horsee who has borne a foal.

mare donkey A British term; a jennet (q.v.).

mare hinny A female hinny (q.v.).

Maremmana A horse breed indigenous to Italy; used as a light draft or farm horse and as a mount for the Italian police and the butteri (q.v.) of the Maremma region of Tuscany and Latium, from which the name derived; is

solidly built, adaptable to every type of terrain, able to withstand bad weather conditions, very hardy, and an economical feeder; stands 15 to 15.3 hands, and any solid coat color is acceptable with bay, brown, chestnut, and black occurring most often; currently crossed with Thoroughbred (q.v.) to improve stature and refine the appearance, but at the expense of the hardiness and exceptional stamina that characterized the breed; historically bred in the wild.

mare mule Also known as a molly mule; a female mule (q.v.).

Marengo The gray Arab stallion, a favorite charger of Emperor Napoleon, who Napoleon rode during his Austrian and Italian campaigns and at the battle of Waterloo in 1815; his skeleton is preserved and on display at the Royal United Service Institution, London, England.

mare's month A racing term; the month of September which, in theory, is the month mares who did not run well during the summer improve their performance.

mare's nest A discovery or accomplishment found to be bogus or worthless.

Mareyeur One of two sub-types of the Boulonnais (q.v.); is smaller and stands less than 16 hands; the name means horse of the tide, as the breed was used to transport fish from Boulogne to Paris, France; has almost died out.

mark (1) *see* CUP no. 1. (2) *see* CASTRATE

marked to ground Also known as mark the fox to the ground; a hunting term; said of the hounds (q.v.) when they run a fox (q.v.) so that it takes refuge in an earth (q.v.); they identify the hiding spot of the fox in the ground, or mark it, by giving tongue (q.v.) and digging.

Market Harborough *see* GERMAN MARTINGALE

mark the fox to the ground *see* MARKED TO GROUND

Marocco A performing horse active in Europe during the late 16th and early 17th centuries who, on command from his owner Thomas Bankes, would rap out the numbers on a rolled dice with his hoof, lie down, sit up, rear, and dance; having attributed his powers to black magic, the Italians ordered Marocco and his owner to be burned at the stake; although Bankes returned safely to England, the fate of his horse remains a mystery.

Marshall, Benjamin (1767–1835) An acclaimed artist whose subjects included hunters, racehorses, hacks, and sporting groups.

martingale Any auxiliary rein or strap used to assist the action of the bit by restricting the position of the horse's head and neck; consists of a strap, or arrangement of straps, fastened to the girth at one end, passed through the forelegs, and depending on the type, attached on the other end to the reins, noseband, or directly to the bit; include the German martingale (q.v.), Irish martingale (q.v.), running martingale (q.v.), standing martingale (q.v.), Cheshire martingale (q.v.), continental martingale (q.v.), chambon (q.v.), grainger martingale (q.v.), harness martingale, Indian martingale (q.v.), Market Harborough martingale (q.v.), purgi martingale (q.v.).

martingale pulley A pulley or wheel used in conjunction with a running martingale (q.v.) to allow the split auxiliary rein to move freely as the horse moves its head; eliminates any pressure to the outside of the bit which may result when using a running martingale; the martingale is attached between the forelegs to the girth (q.v.) at one end, splits into two branches which connects to the bit rings; the two split reins are joined together by a cord which moves around the pulley.

Marwari A pony breed indigenous to the state of Jodhpur, India; descended from small (about 13 hands), frugal native ponies crossed with Arabs (q.v.); is tough, hardy, tenacious, and unpredictable, thrives on little feed, stands approximately 14 to 15 hands, and may have a coat of any color including skewbald (q.v.) and piebald (q.v.); is very light and narrowly framed, and has a weak neck and quarters, low-set tail, sickle hocks, and ears that curve distinctively inwards, almost touching at the tips; used for riding, packing, farming, light draft, and the best ones, racing; virtually identical to the Kathiawari (q.v.).

Maryland Hunt Cup One of the oldest and most celebrated steeplechases (q.v.) in the United States; run annually since 1896 in Glyardson, Maryland, USA over a permanent course built in natural hunt country; the fences are constructed of solid timber up to 5 feet 6 inches (1.7 m) in height.

mascot A companion for a pastured horse, the most common of which include ponies, dogs, goats, cats, and chickens.

mash Steamed or cooked grains or the outer shell of the grain which, when cooled, are fed to the horse; used as a laxative, poultice, and, when mixed with sweeteners, to administer medications; bran mash (q.v.) is most common.

mask A hunting term; the head of a fox.

massage The act or art of treating the body by rubbing or kneading to stimulate circulation and healing and/or increase suppleness.

Master Also known as Master of Foxhounds, The Master, and by the acronym MFH; a hunting term; one appointed by the hunt committee (q.v.) to, either solely or with joint Masters, organize and manage all aspects of the hunt including the hiring and firing of professional members of the hunt staff such as the huntsman (q.v.), kennel huntsman (q.v.), and whippers-in (q.v.) and appointment of honorary whippers-in, the Field Master (q.v.), and the hunt Secretary; the term of appointment is determined by the hunt committee; normally provided with a sum of money by the committee collected from followers, subscriptions, capping fees (q.v.), and Hunt social functions; required to make any shortfall of funds necessary to hunt the country (q.v.); may also hunt hounds as an amateur huntsman.

master (1) To become adept at or expert in. (2) One skillful or experienced enough to train others and to independently pursue his own trade.

Master of Foxhounds *see* MASTER

Master of Game, The *see* DE FOIX, GASTON

Master of Hounds Also known by the acronym MH; one responsible for management of hounds used in the hunt including stag hounds, drag hounds, harriers, beagles, bassett, or otter hounds.

Master of the Foxhounds Association of America An organization founded in 1907 to promote the sport of fox and drag hunting (q.v.) in the United States and Canada, improve foxhound (q.v.) breeds, register and annually recognize Hunts (q.v.) which have met its standards, and assign and record the boundaries of the individual Hunt counties (q.v.) in North America.

Master of the pack *see* FIELD MASTER

mastership A hunting term; the period of time during which a Master (q.v.) reigns over a specific Hunt (q.v.).

mastitis Inflammation of the mammary gland; almost always due to bacteria-related infection.

Masuren Any East Prussian (q.v.) horse left in East Prussia following the German retreat from Poland in 1945; crossed with the Poznan to create the Wielkopolski (q.v.).

match (1) Also known as match race; a racing term; a race between two horses the terms of which are agreed upon in advance by the owners of the horses and for which there is no prize. (2) *see* POLO MATCH

match race *see* MATCH

maternal grandsire The sire of a horse's dam (q.v.).

mating hobbles *see* BREEDING HOBBLES

mating posture The position assumed by the mare in preparation to receive the stallion during breeding in which her forelegs are positioned in front of the vertical, her back is slightly arched, and her hind legs slightly spread and extended slightly behind the vertical.

matron A mare who has produced a foal.

mature horse A horse of either sex who has reached five years of age, at which time his mouth is said to be made or full.

maturity A racing term; a horse race for four-year-old horses entered to compete before their birth.

maxim of Guthrie The propensity for any animal to respond to a stimulus in the same manner in which it responded to the same stimulus when last used; the primary consideration in training.

McGuinness *see* MAGENIS SNAFFLE

ME *see* METABOLIZABLE ENERGY

meal A cooked porridge or pudding (q.v.) of corn or oats, generally mixed with meat, fed to the foxhounds.

mealy bay *see* SANDY BAY

mealy nose Said of the nose of the horse when oatmeal colored.

measuring stick Also known as horse standard; an instrument by which the height of the horse is determined; a straight, generally rigid stick, calibrated in inches, centimeters, and hands (q.v.) which is fitted at right angles with a sliding arm; the stick is placed parallel to the forelegs while the arm is slid upward along the stick shaft until it rests upon the withers (q.v.) where the measurement is read; both the shaft and right-angle arm generally contain a spirit level (q.v.).

measuring tape A long cloth, metal, or paper tape marked in inches or centimeters and hands used to measure the height of the horse.

meat for manners *see* MEAT FOR WORK

meat for work Also known as meat for manners; an antiquated term; the free keep of a horse in exchange for the use of the horse for work.

meat and bone meal A high energy supplemental protein made from mammalian tissues, exclusive of hair, hoof, horn, hide trimmings, manure, and stomach contents; although a good source of protein (q.v.), calcium (q.v.), and phosphorus (q.v.) it is not commonly added to rations as it appears to be unpalatable to horses.

mecate The rope rein attached to the heel knot of a bosal (q.v.).

mechanical hackamore Originally known as a brockamore or hackamore bit or in Europe as a Blair bridle; a bitless bridle consisting of a leather headstall with any type of nose piece, on either side of which is attached a long metal shank to which the reins are connected; control is achieved through pressure applied to the bridge of the nose and, when used in conjunction with any type of curb chain or strap, on the bridge of the nose (q.v.) and the chin groove (q.v.); historically used by the Egyptians on their war chariot horses.

Mecklenburg A German warmblood once prized as a carriage horse; although smaller than the Hanoverian (q.v.), has many similar characteristics; after 1945, the breed was revived in East Germany where stallions were controlled by the state and mares generally belonged to individual breeders; is strong and courageous, stands 15.3 to 16 hands, may have a brown, bay, chestnut, or black coat, and is used as a riding and cavalry mount.

meconium The blackish contents of the intestines of the newborn foal, its first feces.

medial Relating to the middle or inner portion of a body or to any position close to the axis (q.v.).

medial deviation of the carpal joints Also known as knock knees, carpus vulgus, knee-narrow conformation, or knee narrow; a conformation abnormality in which the knees deviate towards each other, breaking the vertical line from the shoulder to the hoof; results in increased strain on the medial collateral ligaments.

medial deviation of the hock joints Also known as cow hocks or tarsus valgus; a conformation abnormality in which the hocks (q.v.) are too close, point toward one another, and the feet are widely separated; when viewed laterally, the horse may be sickle-hocked (q.v.).

medication list A racing term; a list maintained by the track veterinarian and published by the track and Daily Racing Forum which identifies those horses competing under the influence of legally prescribed medications.

medicine Any substance used to treat disease or relieve pain.

medicine ball Also known as medicine pill, physic ball, or ball; a medicinal compound encapsulated in gelatin and administered into the horse's mouth using a balling gun (q.v.), balling iron, or by hand; a somewhat antiquated method of administering medicine and drugs to horses.

medicine pill *see* MEDICINE BALL

medicine hat Refers to a coat color pattern; an arrangement of colored areas on a predominantly white horse, specifically a colored spot that covers both ears and the poll; colored patches on the chest, flank, and base of the tail are common.

mediolateral balance The distribution of loading over the medial and lateral halves of the hoof.

medium Breton *see* POSTIER-BRETON

medium canter A pace between the working and extended canter (q.v.); the horse moves forward on the bit with free, balanced, and moderately extended strides with impulsion (q.v.) from the hindquarters; the strides are as long and even as possible, the whole movement being balanced and unconstrained; the head may come slightly in front of the vertical (q.v.).

medium trot A pace between the working and extended trots (q.v.), which is more round than the latter; the horse moves forward on the bit with free, balanced, and moderately extended strides with impulsion from the hindquarters; the strides are long and even as possible, the whole movement being balanced and unconstrained; the head may come slightly in front of the vertical.

medium walk A free, regular, and unconstrained walk (q.v.) of moderate extension; the horse walks energetically, but calmly, with even steps, the hind feet touching the ground in front of the imprints of the forefeet; the horse is on the bit, but the head may come slightly in front of the vertical.

meet (1) A racing term; a race meeting. (2) A hunting term; the location where the hunt servants (q.v.), hounds (q.v.), and field (q.v.) assemble before the hunt (q.v.); a contraction of hounds will meet from the days when several neighboring landowners would bring their own hounds to the meet where they would be combined and hunted as one pack. (3) A hunting term; the hunt itself.

megrim *see* STAGGERS

melanoma Also known as black cell tumor; a tumor of the pigment-producing skin cells appearing in hairless areas around the muzzle or ears, under the tail, or in the anus or perineal area, the fresh or cut surface of which is characteristically jet black; the hard, dome-shaped, hairless, small bumps appear benign at the onset, but may turn malignant and spread rapidly without warning; malignant melanomas are usually larger and softer than benign growths; single, rapidly growing melanomas on young horses are generally malignant from the onset; occur in 80 percent of gray horses beyond the age of 15.

Melbourne Cup One of the most prestigious horse races run in Australia; a handicap race (q.v.) run over a distance of 2 miles (3 km).

melton (1) Also known as a circle curb hook; a circular curb hook (q.v.) to which the curb chain (q.v.) is attached; consists of a hook fitted inside the circle of a ring. (2) A smooth, strong, tightly woven wool having a short nap, used for overcoats and other outdoor garments; popularized in the town of Melton Mowbray, England, for which it is named.

Melton Mowbray The center in Leicestershire, England, for hunt meets of the Belvoir, Cottesmore, and Quorn Hounds.

melts into the ground A reining term; said of a horse who digs into and slides low to the ground when performing a sliding stop (q.v.).

membrana nictans *see* NICTITATING MEMBRANE

menege *see* MANEGE

Mèrens Also known as Ariègeois, cheval de Ariègeois, or cheval de Mèrens; an ancient horse breed originating some 30,000 years ago in the Pyrenean mountain chain dividing France from Spain; originally named for the Ariège river which flows through the region; is very similar to the Fell (q.v.) and a near duplicate of the Dale (q.v.); has a solid black coat with reddish highlights appearing in winter; white markings are rare, although white hairs on the flanks do occur; stands 13 to 14.1 hands, has a relatively coarse head framed by a heavy mane and forelock, small ears, a short neck which is thick at the base, a long back, well-muscled croup, long, full tail, and short legs; cow hocks (q.v.) are common; is sure-footed, an easy keeper, and well adapted to mountainous terrain and long harsh winters, but is intolerant of heat; used for farm work, riding, and packing.

Merlins *see* WELSH PONY

meridians Twelve paired and two unpaired pathways through the body that connect internal organs with external features, such as joints and sense organs; each meridian bears an organ name, e.g., heart meridian, bladder meridian, etc.; traditional Chinese medicine such as acupuncture (q.v.) and acupressure (q.v.) utilizes trigger points along these meridians.

mesair *see* MEZAIR

mesenteric artery A vessel which supplies blood to the intestine; passes through the tissues connecting the intestines to the back abdominal wall.

mesentery A fold of the abdominal lining from which the intestine and associated organs are suspended from the backbone.

metabolizable energy *see* METABOLIZABLE ENERGY VALUE

metabolizable energy value Also known by the acronym ME or metabolic energy; the digestible energy (q.v.) content of the feed consumed by the horse less the energy lost to gas and urine, but not to body heat production; measured in calories; only useful for describing the amount of energy available in a feed for metabolic processes at the tissue level.

metacarpal Of or pertaining to the metacarpus (q.v.); a metacarpal bone (q.v.) such as the large metacarpal (q.v.) or small metacarpal (q.v.).

metacarpal bone Either of the splint bones (small metacarpal) or the cannon bone (large metacarpal) of the foreleg.

metacarpal fracture A break in any of the three metacarpal bones located in the foreleg such as the cannon and splint bones.

metacarpalphalangeal joint *see* FETLOCK JOINT

metacarpus The part of the foreleg between the knee and fetlock including the cannon and splint bones.

metal curry comb A metal, hand-held instrument or comb set with very short teeth on one side used to scrape dirt and debris from a brush.

metal horse *see* VAULTING BARREL

metaphysis The part of the bone beyond the growth plate (q.v.) which includes the zone of trabeculae projecting from the growth plate.

metatarsal Belonging to the metatarsus (q.v.); a bone of the metatarsus.

metatarsal bone Either the cannon bone or splint bones of the hind leg.

metatarsus The part of the hind limb, especially the bony structure, between the tarsus (q.v.) and the fetlock including the cannon and splint bones.

methylsulfonylmethane Also known by the acronym MSM; an oral crystalline dietary derivative of DMSO (q.v.) with the same anti-inflammatory (q.v.) properties, but without the unpleasant odor; patented in 1986.

Métis Trotter A Russian warmblood developed in the early 20th century and officially recognized as a breed in 1949; descended from Orlov (q.v.) crossed with imported American Standardbreds (q.v.); has a flowing, far-reaching action and slightly knock-kneed (q.v.) limbs, particularly in the hind, which result in dishing (q.v.); much faster than the Orlov, but less so than American and European trotters; stands 15.1 to 15.3 hands and usually has a gray, black, or chestnut coat.

Metropolitan Drinking Fountain and Cattle Trough Association An organization founded in England in 1865 to build and maintain drinking fountains for people and water troughs for stock; now defunct.

metritis Inflammation of the muscular and endometrial (q.v.) layers of the uterus (q.v.) caused by the introduction of contaminants during parturition (q.v.); acute metritis occurs following abnormal parturition and is often accompanied by retention of the fetal membrane; symptoms include a fetid discharge from the uterus, fever, depression, anorexia, and laminitis (q.v.); if left untreated sterility will result.

mewing Said of a stag (q.v.) when shedding his antlers

mews A British term; stables or coach houses, usually with living quarters, situated around a court, alley, or back lane; from the French muer, meaning a place where molting falcons were confined; in the 1537, the royal stable at Charing Cross was built on a site where the royal hawks were kept and the name derived.

Mexican noseband *see* GRACKLE NOSE-BAND

Meyer's D cheek *see* DEE-RING SNAFFLE

mezair Also spelled mesair. (1) A dressage term; a High School movement (q.v.) in which the horse conducts a series of *levades* (q.v.) in succession, between which the forefeet touch the ground simultaneously and the horse moves forward a short step. (2) A dressage term; one half a *courbette* (q.v.).

MF The acronym for Master of Hounds (q.v.).

MFH The acronym for Master of Foxhounds (q.v.).

microchip *see* ELECTRONIC IDENTIFICATION

middle bow One of three classifications of bowed tendon (q.v.) identified on the basis of location, the others being low bow (q.v.) and high bow (q.v.); any true physiological damage to the middle third of the tendon or tendon sheath, most commonly of the superficial flexor tendon of the foreleg; specifically, tearing or breaking of one or more of the tendon fibers; may be precipitated by fatigue, deep going (q.v.), uneven terrain, improper shoeing, obesity, excessively tight fitting running bandages or boots, work on slippery surfaces, long, weak pasterns, sudden changes in stress loads, low heel angles, and long toes; symptoms may include diffuse swelling over the tendon area, heat, and pain; lameness may or may not be present.

middle distance A racing term; a horse race longer than 7 furlongs (q.v.), but less than 1–1/8 miles (3.4 km).

middle distancer One of three morphological types of Thoroughbred (q.v.); has a sloping croup and shoulder and a rather short back.

Middle European Gidran One of two types of Gidran Arabian (q.v.); a Hungarian breed developed in 1816 from an Arab (q.v.) of the Siglavy strain crossed with Thoroughbred (q.v.); is heavier than the Southern and Eastern Gidran (q.v.), and is thus used predominantly in harness.

medieval long wagon *see* LONG WAGON

midsection That portion of the horse's body between the forehand (q.v.) and the hindquarters (q.v.), e.g., from the withers to front portion of the flanks (q.v.).

Mierzyn One of several pony breeds native to Poland; essentially a medium-sized Konik (q.v.); is an easy keeper (q.v.), resistant to cold and hunger, and possessed of amazing power and endurance for its size; stands about 14 hands.

mildew Any of numerous minute parasitic fungi producing a whitish coating or discoloration on plants and grains.

mile pole A racing term; a colored post located on the infield rail (q.v.) exactly 1 mile (1.6 km) from the finish line (q.v.).

militaire *see* HORSE TRIALS

military boots White canvass, non supporting, decorative boots worn on all four lower legs of the horse when in formal or ceremonial dress, as for parades.

military trials *see* HORSE TRIALS

milk protein An animal source of high energy supplemental protein derived from several products such as dried skim milk, dried buttermilk, dried whole milk, dried whey, and casein; contains an excellent combination of amino acids, plus vitamins, and a good balance of calcium and phosphorus.

milk teeth *see* DECIDUOUS TEETH

mill Also known as round the world; a vaulting (q.v.) term; a compulsory exercise (q.v.) in which the vaulter (q.v.) performs a complete circle above the horizontal line of the withers by swinging one leg at a time over the horse's back or neck; in competition, the vaulter must move each leg every four canter strides.

miller's disease *see* BIG HEAD DISEASE

milling A coaching term; said of a kicking horse.

milo *see* SORGHUM

minerals Any inorganic compound, containing no animal or vegetable matter, some of which are necessary for proper body growth and function; constitute components and building materials of body tissues and catalytic compounds that help trigger reactions within the body; excess intake may be as harmful as deficiencies; the exact equine requirements are still undetermined, but there are at least 16 minerals which are considered essential because they normally occur in the body tissues; the essential minerals are sodium (q.v.), chloride (q.v.), phosphorus (q.v.), calcium (q.v.), potassium (q.v.), magnesium (q.v.), manganese (q.v.), iodine (q.v.), copper (q.v.), iron (q.v.), zinc (q.v.), chlorine (q.v.), cobalt (q.v.), sulfur (q.v.), fluorine (q.v.), and selenium (q.v.).

Minho *see* GARRANO

miniature donkey A donkey (q.v.) standing 28 to 36 inches (71–91 cm) tall which descended from the Miniature Mediterranean Donkey (q.v.); native to, but now thought to be nearly extinct in, Sicily and Sardinia; extensively bred in the United States where more than 10,000 exist today; weighs 250 to 450 pounds (113–204 kg), has a life expectancy of 30 to 35 years, body hair that ranges from flat to curly to long and shaggy and in texture from smooth to wiry, is thrifty, an easy keeper, and adaptable to any climate or altitude; most will show a cross (q.v.).

Miniature Landau A horse-drawn vehicle of the Landau (q.v.) type; is small, easy to enter, suitable for invalids and the elderly, and generally drawn by a pair of ponies.

Miniature Mediterranean Donkey A donkey breed native to the Mediterranean islands of Sicily and Sardinia; of two types identified as either Sicilian (q.v.) or Sardinian (q.v.) according to their ancestry; nearly extinct in the land of their origin, but are extensively bred in the United States as miniature donkeys (q.v.).

Miniature Sardinian Donkey *see* SARDINIAN

Miniature Sicilian Donkey *see* SICILIAN no. 2

minor penalty A cutting term; a one-point penalty infraction.

minus pool A racing term; a pool (q.v.) provided by the racetrack (q.v.) from its own funds to cover insufficient funds in pari-mutuel betting (q.v.) when so much money is bet on a horse (usually to show), that the pool is insufficient, i.e., after deduction of state tax and commission, to pay winning ticket holders the legal minimum odds of 1 to 10 or 20.

mise en main A French dressage term; to flex the horse's jaw; literally, "put in hand."

misfit Said of a horse who is not representative of his breed and/or is unsuitable for the purpose for which he is being used.

miss (1) A polo term; said of a polo player who takes a stroke on the ball and fails to make contact. (2) A cutting term; said of the horse; to overrun a cow; results in a loss of working position (q.v.) and a one-point penalty; often a horse will have a miss prior to losing a cow. (3) A roping term; to fail to lasso the calf, steer, or other animal with a thrown rope.

Missouri Fox Trotter Also known as a Missouri Fox Trotting Horse; a warmblood established around 1820 in the Ozark Mountains of Arkansas and Missouri, USA; descended from Spanish Barb (q.v.) stock put to Morgans (q.v.) and Thoroughbreds (q.v.) followed by infusions of Saddlebred (q.v.) and Tennessee Walking Horse (q.v.); is plain, compact, sure-footed, and moves in a smooth, broken, four-beat gait known as the fox trot (q.v.); walks from the shoulder in front and trots behind, the hind hooves stepping onto the track of the fore hooves and sliding forward; this sliding action minimizes the concussive effect and produces a very smooth ride which can be maintained for long distances at an average speed of 5 to 10 mph (8–16 kmph); the canter is halfway between the fast, long-rein lope (q.v.) of the cow pony (q.v.) and the high, slow gait of Walkers and Saddlebreds; the breed society prohibits the use of artificial aids to achieve leg height; has a strong, compact body, intelligent head, tapered muzzle, long neck, low-set tail, and stands 14 to 16 hands; all coat colors occur including skewbald (q.v.), piebald (q.v.), chestnut, bay, black, gray, and occasionally roan; usually ridden in western tack; the stud book was established in 1948.

Missouri Fox Trotting Horse see MISSOURI FOX TROTTER

mistetched Also known as mistaught; said of an improperly or badly broken horse who, as a result of such training, possesses a vice(s).

mitbah The angle at which the neck of an Arab (q.v.) attaches to the head; at the crest, the neck angles gently towards the head, creating an arched neck set.

mites Also known as acari; any of several species of small external parasites that cause mange (q.v.).

mixed gait Said of a horse who will not stick to any one true gait at a time.

mixed lameness Lameness evident when the horse's limb is in motion and when supporting weight.

mixed meeting A racing term; a horse race in which both flat and steeplechase or hurdle races are conducted on the same day.

mixed pack A hunting term; a group of hounds consisting of both bitches (q.v.) and dog hounds (q.v.).

mixed sale A horse sale in which only one breed, such as Thoroughbred (q.v.), is offered; consists of different classifications within the breed: mares, yearlings, horses in training, etc.

mixed stable A racing term; a stable where both flat and National Hunt Horses are kept.

mob (1) An Australian term; a herd of cattle. (2) see MOB A FOX

mob a fox Also known as mob; a hunting term; said of the hounds when they surround a fox without giving it a chance to run.

model horse Any authentic, small-scale reproduction of a horse, generally made in plastic, i.e., a Breyer horse (q.v.); may be used as a toy or collected by hobbyists.

modern A large, well-developed Stock-Type Pinto (q.v.).

Mohammed's Ten Horses Ten horses who, according to legend, formed the foundation stock of the Prophet Strain (q.v.); it is believed that in the days of Mohammed only horses with superior intelligence and obedience were used for war purposes, such horses were trained to follow the bugle; when the

Prophet Mohammed required horses he selected a herd from which he would make his selection; the herd was fenced off from the river until their thirst became excessive at which time he ordered the fence removed; when the horses rushed to the river to quench their thirst, a bugle was sounded, and only ten of the horses obediently responded to the bugle call; those ten horses comprised the foundation of the Prophet Strain.

mohawk attachment A straight bar fitted with rubber ball washers that attaches by means of two up-turned hooks to the eyes of the cheeks of a pelham bit (q.v.); anchored above and in the center to the pelham mouthpiece by means of a rubber ring; increases the bearing surface of the bit on the tongue and bars of the mouth.

molars Also known as grinders, cheek teeth, or molar teeth; 12 permanent grinding teeth, numbering three on each side of each jaw top and bottom, located behind the premolars (q.v.); the first of the permanent teeth (q.v.) to erupt; do not replace deciduous teeth (q.v.); first appear between six and 12 months while the second and third molars appear at one to one and one-half year intervals thereafter; the normal chewing action on the molars produces sloping instead of horizontal surfaces; because of the sloping wear on these teeth, the outside edge of the upper molars and the inside edge of the lower molars develop sharp points which catch on the tongue and cheek membranes and cause painful ulcers to form; removal of these sharp points requires floating (q.v.).

molar teeth *see* MOLARS

molasses A by-product of sucrose refined from sugar cane, sugar beets, dried citrus pulp, or from grain starch, the fermentation of which produces yeast, an excellent source of B vitamins; supplies little or no protein or phosphorus; may be fed dried or wet although wet is preferred; often added to rations to improve taste and decrease dust; molasses from cane sugar is an excellent source of energy and contain significant amounts of calcium;

molly mule *see* MARE MULE

moment of suspension The moment when the horse has all four feet off the ground whether on the flat or jumping.

Monday morning complaint *see* STOCK UP

Monday morning disease *see* EXERCISE RELATED MYOPATHY

Monday morning evil *see* STOCK UP

Monday morning leg *see* STOCK UP

Monday morning sickness *see* EXERCISE RELATED MYOPATHY

money rider A racing term; a jockey who excels in high-stakes races.

Mongolian An ancient pony breed originating in Mongolia; has had great influence on all Asiatic breeds due to its widespread use by the Mongols as a war mount; is found in a number of different types which evolved according to greatly differing environmental factors; stands 12 to 14 hands, may have a brown, black, mouse dun, or palomino coat, has a heavy head, short ears, thick forelock, mane, and tail, short withers, strong back, and sturdy, well-boned legs; is hardy, frugal, and active; used for riding, packing, light draft, and farm work.

Mongolian wild horse *see* ASIATIC WILD HORSE

monkey A British racing term; a bet of less than £500.

monkey crouch Also known as monkey-on-a-stick; a racing term; a riding position popularized by jockey Tod Sloan; the jockey rides with short stirrups and his body bent forward over the withers of the horse.

monkey-on-a-stick *see* MONKEY CROUCH

Monte Foreman bit A bit having extra rings attached to the headstall which prevents the curb chain or lip strap from pinching the corners of the horse's mouth; designed by horseman Monte Foreman.

monorchid A horse in which one of the testes has failed to descend normally into the scrotum.

monovular twin Also known as identical twin; one of two young brought forth at birth resulting from the fertilization of one egg which splits in two; the young will be identical; an extremely rare occurrence in horses.

moon blindness Also known as periodic ophthalmia, night blindness, or equine recurrent uveitis; one of the most common inflammatory conditions affecting the eyes of horses, donkeys, mules, or ponies; a cloudy and/or inflamed condition which may involve one or both eyes and lead to blindness; the condition disappears and returns in cycles that are often completed within a one-month period thus the name; many causes have been proposed, including vitamin A deficiency, but few verified.

Morgan An American bred warmblood descended from a cross of Thoroughbred (q.v.), Arab (q.v.), Welsh Cob (q.v.), Harddraver (q.v.), Fjord (q.v.) blood; contributed to development of the Standardbred (q.v.), Saddlebred (q.v.), and Tennessee Walking Horse (q.v.); stands 14.1 to 15 hands, may have a bay, chestnut, or black coat with white markings, a short, broad back, strong shoulders, short, strong legs, well-crested neck of medium length, and a full mane and tail; the gaits are comfortable, long, and elastic; is versatile, tough, and even-tempered; used for hunting dressage, park classes, western and pleasure riding, driving, and trail riding.

morning glory Also known as morning horse; a racing term; a horse who clocks good times in the morning workouts or training gallops, but fails to live up to the same potential when racing.

morning horse *see* MORNING GLORY

morning line A racing term; the forecast of probable odds for each horse in a given race as calculated by an experienced track handicapper; usually printed in the program and posted on the totalizator (q.v.) prior to betting.

morning stable An English racing term; the morning feeding time (q.v.).

Morocco saddle *see* BURFORD SADDLE

Morochuco One of three types of Criollo (q.v.) or Salterno (q.v.) horses bred in the Andes Mountains of Peru, the other two being the Costeño (q.v.) and the Chola (q.v.); descended from Spanish stock brought to South America by the conquistadors in the 16th century; occasionally has a protruding forehead and smaller ears.

mort A hunting term; a horn signal or yell signifying the death of the fox or other hunted prey at the end of the hunt.

mosquito Any of various dipterous insects of the family *Culicidae*; a tiny, swarming, dusk, dawn, and overnight feeder, being the most common of the blood sucking insects; there are more than 3,000 species worldwide with about 150 in the United States; most species avoid bright sunlight; males do not bite while females have a long proboscis which they use to puncture the skin and suck blood from their hosts; the bites are annoying, but leave no lasting traces unless exposure is extreme; may be dangerous transmitters of disease.

mother tinctures The concentrated form of a medicament used in homeopathic remedies (q.v.).

motor nerve Any of the whitish fibers extending from the brain and spinal cord and spreading throughout the body which enervate muscles and when stimulated cause muscle function.

motor unit Two adjacent vertebrae (q.v.) and their associated structures.

mottled Refers to a coat color pattern; small white spots appearing on the muzzle, genitalia, and around the eyes of some horses, most commonly those with symmetrical patterns of white.

mottled skin Also known as parti-colored skin; a speckled pattern of pigmented skin consisting of small, round, dark spots characteristic to the Appaloosa (q.v.); appears in the anus region, on the udder and sheath, and on the muzzle; differs from mottled (q.v.) which is a coat color pattern.

mount (1) To get on a horse in preparation to ride. (2) The act of the stallion straddling the mare to breed. (3) A riding horse. (4) An American term; a number of cow ponies used by one man.

Mountain Bashkir Also known as Mountain Bashkir Curly; one of two distinct types of Bashkir (q.v.), a centuries-old pony breed originating in Bashkiria, around the southern foothills of the Urals in the former Soviet Union; due to the introduction of Don (q.v.) and Budonny (q.v.) blood, is smaller and lighter than the Steppe Bashkir (q.v.); stands

13.1 to 14 hands, has a distinctive thick, curly winter coat and thick mane, tail, and forelock that enables it to survive in sub-zero temperatures; is kept outdoors where it can withstand winter temperatures of -22 to 40° F (-30 to 40°C); the coat is usually bay, chestnut or palomino; has a short and long neck, low withers, elongated and sometimes hollow back, a wide and deep chest, short and strong legs, and a small foot for its size; the breed standard quotes a bone measurement of 8 inches (20 cm) below the knee and a girth measurement for stallions of 71 inches (1.8 m); is docile, strong, quiet, and hardy; used for packing, light draft, riding, and to provide meat, milk and clothing for human consumption and use; in a seven- to eight-month lactation period a mare can yield as much as 350 gallons (1,590 liters) of milk; the long winter coat hair is spun into cloth; due to the exceptionally hard hoof, is generally left unshod.

Mountain Bashkir Curly *see* MOUNTAIN BASHKIR

Mounties *see* CANADIAN MOUNTED POLICE, THE ROYAL

mounting block Historically known as a horsing stone, jostling stone, horse block, or pillion post; any stepped block or platform approximately 2 to 2-1/2 feet (61–76 cm) high on which a rider stands to facilitate mounting a horse.

mount money A rodeo term; the money paid to a rodeo competitor who rides, ropes, and/or bulldogs in an exhibition, but not in a competition.

Mounty *see* CANADIAN MOUNTED POLICE, THE ROYAL

mouse dun *see* GRULLO

moustache *see* MUSTACHE

mouth (1) The opening through which man or animals intake food and liquid; the cavity containing the teeth (q.v.), bars (q.v.), tongue, etc. (2) *see* MOUTHPIECE

mouth a horse *see* MOUTHING no. 1

mouthing (1) Also known as mouth a horse; to determine the age of the horse by examining the teeth (q.v.) for wear and eruption. (2) Said of a horse who chews or plays with the bit in his mouth. (3) To accustom a young, unfamiliar horse to the bit.

mouthing bit *see* BREAKING BIT

mouthpiece Also known as a mouth and historically as embouchure or in Spanish as bocado; that portion of the bit (q.v.) which rests on the tongue and bars (q.v.) of the horse's mouth and which attaches to the cheekpieces (q.v.).

mouthy (1) A hunting term; said of a hound who babbles. (2) Said of a horse who is active with his mouth, e.g., licking, biting, nibbling, etc.

movement The act of moving; the course, process, or result of change involving position.

movements off the ground *see* AIRS ABOVE THE GROUND

movements on the ground A dressage term; any of the classical airs (q.v.) performed by the horse on the ground; consist of simple and flying changes (q.v.), turns on the forehand (q.v.) and haunches, side steps, shoulder in (q.v.), shoulder out (q.v.), haunches in (q.v.), haunches out (q.v.), *passage* (q.v.), *pirouette* (q.v.), *piaffe* (q.v.), *levade* (q.v.) or *pesade* (q.v.), and *mezair* (q.v.).

move off To move the horse forward from a standing position.

move off the leg Said of a horse who responds by moving away from the rider's leg pressure; may be a forward or lateral movement.

move up (1) A racing term; to gain ground. (2) A racing term; said of a horse who runs in a higher-class race than previously entered.

moxibustion A type of acupuncture (q.v.); the stimulation of precise points along body meridians (q.v.) by burning a herb known as moxa, and more commonly mugwort, over those points; delivers penetrating heat with amazing effectiveness; frequently used to alleviate pain and muscular problems.

MSM The acronym of methylsulfonylmethane (q.v.).

Mtidaudaschweba A professional, long-distance race conducted in the Caucasus mountains, Russia; the course covers 3 to 4 miles (5–7 km) and the competitors, who ride bareback, are mostly herdsmen and workers on stud farms.

muck *see* MUCK OUT

muck out Also known as mucking out, muck, or skepping out which is derived from skep, a box on wheels used to haul away soiled bedding; the process of removing droppings and soiled bedding from a stall and replacing it with fresh bedding.

mucking out *see* MUCK OUT

mucosa *see* MUCOUS MEMBRANE

mucous (1) Covered with or as if with mucus (q.v.). (2) To secrete or contain mucus (q.v.).

mucous membrane Also known as mucosa; a membrane rich in mucous (q.v.) glands, specifically, one who lines body passages and cavities which communicate directly, or indirectly, with the exterior; produces mucus (q.v.) which moisturizes and protects the lining.

mucus The viscid, slippery secretion that is usually rich in mucins and is produced by mucous membranes (q.v.) which moisturize and protect the lining of all body passages and cavities.

mudder Also known as mud runner, webfoot, or mudlark; a racing term; a horse who runs well on a wet, muddy, or sloppy track.

muddy dun Refers to coat color; the darkest of the red dun (q.v.) shades; the body hair is a light brownish red or brownish yellow, the points (q.v.) chocolate brown, and the head usually brown; resembles grullo (q.v.) except that brown and a light brownish red replace the black and slate.

muddy track A racing term; said of a wet racetrack which does not contain standing water.

mud fever *see* SCRATCHES

mudlark *see* MUDDER

mud runner *see* MUDDER

mud sticker *see* CALK

mud tie Also known as French tie; to fold up and tie the tail of the horse to prevent it from entangling in the harness or collecting brush and other debris; commonly used on draft horses.

Mug's horse A horse who is easy to ride although it looks hot (q.v.) and difficult.

mule The progeny of a jack (q.v.) and a mare (q.v.); although a sterile hybrid, a small percentage of female mules may produce foals; looks more like a donkey with the body of a horse (heavy head, long ears, and fine-boned legs with small hooves); the horse contributes a horse-like tail, size, speed, and strength; generally more robust than a hinny (q.v.); the female of the species is known as a mare mule (q.v.) and the male as a horse mule (q.v.).

muled heels A horseshoe (q.v.) with both heels extended beyond the posterior limit of the hoof.

mule ears *see* RAT TAILS

mule feet *see* MULE FOOTED

mule footed Said of a horse having a long, narrow hoof with high heels, and a narrow hoof wall between the toe and quarters.

mule jack A male of the ass (q.v.) species used to breed mares to produce donkeys (q.v.).

mule shoeing contest A timed contest in which farriers (q.v.) trim mules' feet and pre-shape the shoes; judged principally on speed times which are often less than five minutes to trim and shoe all four feet; a common component of Mule Days competitions held in the United States.

mullen mouth *see* MULLEN MOUTH BIT

mullen mouth bit Also known as a half moon bit, half moon mouth, mulling mouth, or mullen mouth; a snaffle bit (q.v.) with a straight bar mouthpiece that is slightly bent or curved to accommodate the shape of the tongue; acts on the lips, tongue, and bars (q.v.); appropriate for horses with a low palate and/or those who do not like tongue pressure; also a good transition bit when changing from a snaffle (q.v.) to the double bridle (q.v.); the mouthpiece may be rubber coated.

mulling mouth *see* MULLEN MOUTH BIT

multi-jointed snaffle A snaffle bit (q.v.) in which the mouthpiece has more than one joint, as in a Dr. Bristol (q.v.); is more severe than a regular snaffle as, the more joints, the more severe the bit; applies more pressure to the tongue than the roof of the mouth.

Muniqi *see* ASSIL

Murakosi *see* MURAKOZ

Murakoz Also known as a Murakosi or Murakozer; a coldblood developed in the town of Murakoz, Hungary from which the name derived during the 20th century by crossing native Mur-Insulan mares with Percheron (q.v.), Belgian Ardennes (q.v.), and Noriker (q.v.) stallions; in the 1920s one fifth of all horses in Hungary were Murakoz; stands about 16 hands, usually has a chestnut coat with a flaxen mane and tail, although bay, brown, and black coat colors do occur, a strong frame, small withers, hollowed back, round hindquarters, and some feathering (q.v.); is swift-moving and possessed of a good temperament; used for draft and agricultural work.

Murakozer *see* MURAKOZ

Murgese Also spelt Murghese; a warmblood indigenous to Italy which descended from Arab (q.v.) and Barb (q.v.) crosses more than 200 years ago; selective breeding of the modern breed began in 1926; the name derived from the famous horse breeding region of Murge near Puglia, Italy; reared in the wild to produce a hardy nature; stands 14 to 16 hands, has a prominently jawed head, broad neck, full mane, pronounced withers, straight and occasionally hollow back, large leg joints, and a docile, but lively nature; coat color is usually chestnut, although brown, black, and gray with a black head occur; used for riding, particularly cross country, farm work, and light draft.

Murghese *see* MURGESE

muscle Tissue consisting of elongated fibers, generally in the form of sheets or bundles, that contract on stimulation and produce bodily motion; of three types: striped muscle (q.v.), smooth muscle (q.v.), and cardiac muscle (q.v.).

muscle atrophy A reversible diminution in the volume of muscle (q.v.) due to a decrease in the size of individual muscle cells; occurs when a muscle is not subjected to sustained periods of tension.

musculoskeletal Relating to, or involving both the musculature and skeleton, including the bones, muscles, ligaments, tendons, and joints of the body.

musculoskeletal system The structure of the horse including musculature and skeletal components.

mushroom bar shoe A bar shoe (q.v.) in which the shoe is bent in at the quarters and frog (q.v.) with the edges welded together; a hole(s) is generally punched in the stem to rivet pads or leather wedges to the bar; used to apply pressure to the frog and relieve pressure from the heels, especially in horses with sore heels or corns (q.v.).

music *see* CRY no. 2

mustache Also spelled moustache; hair growing near the mouth of the horse.

Mustang Also known as fuzztail or incorrectly as wild horse; a small, warmblooded, wild horse of western North America and Mexico descended from European-bred horses including the Andalusian (q.v.) introduced by the Spanish conquistadors in the 16th century; served as the foundation stock for a large number of the American breeds; stands 13.2 to 15 hands, is sturdy, tough, has a lightweight frame, good bone, notably tough feet, a common heavy head, may have a coat of any color, and is highly adaptable; at the beginning of the 20th century numbers exceeded two million, herds are now reduced to less than 30,000; the name derived from the Spanish mesteña, meaning wild and untamed, as in a horse; protected by the Free Roaming Wild Horse and Burro Act (q.v.) of 1971.

muster An Australian term; a cattle round-up.

mute (1) A hunting term; said of the hounds (q.v.) when they hunt the line of a fox (q.v.) without giving tongue (q.v.). (2) *see* PACK

mutton-fisted Also known as ham-fisted; said of a heavy-handed, but not necessarily rough, rider.

mutton-withered A horse with a low wither (q.v.) and a heavily muscled shoulder.

mutuel pool *see* PARI-MUTUEL POOL

muzzle (1) The lower end of the horse's nose including the nostrils, lips, and chin. (2) A protective covering for the nose which may be made of leather, netting, or synthetic fabrics; used to prevent the horse from biting, eating such things as dung, fencing, or bedding, or tearing at wound coverings, wraps, and blankets; held in position by a single strap which rests on the bridle path (q.v.) behind the ears. (3) To put a muzzle on the horse.

muzzle in a pint pot An antiquated term; said of a horse, such as an Arab (q.v.) with a muzzle so refined and small it would fit in a pint-sized pot.

myopathy Damage to the muscle cells.

myositis *see* EXERCISE RELATED MYOPATHY

N

nag Also known as a yaboo; an antiquated term; a saddle horse; now, any aged, slow, worthless horse; derived from the Anglo-Saxon *knegan* meaning to neigh.

nagging The process of training and schooling a horse for hunting or riding.

nagsman An English term popular in the 19th and 20th centuries; a man who made his living breaking and schooling horses used for road hacking and hunting.

nail (1) *see* QUICK. (2) *see* HORSESHOE NAIL. (3) To attach a horseshoe to the horse's hoof by means of nails.

nail cutter Also known as a nail nipper; a long-handled, pritchel-type tool made of metal used to cut off clinched, turned-over, and wrung-off nails to an equal length.

nail bind Also known as close nail or shod too close; to place a horseshoe nail too close to the white line (q.v.) when fitting a horseshoe to the hoof; results in pressure on the sensitive laminae (q.v.) causing pain, shortened stride, or temporary lameness; generally less serious than nail prick (q.v.).

nail nipper *see* NAIL CUTTER

nail prick *see* QUICK

nail quick *see* QUICK

name A racing term; to enter a horse in a race.

Nangqen horse An exotic horse breed indigenous to that part of western China which was once part of greater Tibet; a small, dun-factor horse with a black mane, small head, thin neck, enlarged lungs, and strong bones; written record of the breed dates as early as 366 AD.

nap (1) A horse who demonstrates any form of resistance; may include rearing, bucking, running away, failure to obey the aids (q.v.), e.g., failing to move forward off the leg. (2) A racing term; a good betting tip.

nape *see* POLL

Napoleon shoe *see* BACKWARDS SHOE

nappy Said of a horse who refuses to obey the aids (q.v.), e.g., to refuse to leave the stall when led.

NARHA The acronym for the North American Riding for the Handicapped Association (q.v.).

Narragansett Pacer A fast pacing horse descending from Norfolk Trotters (q.v.), Galloway (q.v.); and Hobby Horses (q.v.) brought to North America in 1625 by English colonists; developed by commercial breeders in Rhode Island and Virginia and named for the Narraganset Bay of Rhode Island, USA; became a major commercial product in the 1650s at which time hundreds were sold to the Canadians and Spanish plantation owners in the West Indies; due to losses from export and cross-breeding the Narragansett (q.v.) had disappeared from the United States by 1820; when Narraganset mares were put to Thoroughbred (q.v.) stallions in the early 1700s, the generic American Horse was created from which the American Saddlebred (q.v.) ultimately evolved; also contributed to the gene pool of the Morgan (q.v.), Paso Fino (q.v.), and Standardbred Pacer (q.v.).

narrow behind Said of the horse when the croup, quarters, and thighs lack muscle.

nasal gleet Also known as gleet; a colored discharge from the nostrils.

nasal hemorrhage *see* EPISTAXIS

NASFHA The acronym for North American Selle Français Horse Association, Inc. (q.v.).

nasogastric tube A long tube capable of reaching from the nose to the stomach of the horse.

natal Of or pertaining to birth.

National Cutting Horse Association Also known by the acronym NCHA; an organization founded in 1946 in Fort Worth, Texas, USA, by a group of ranchers to develop a standard format for cutting horse (q.v.) contests, including rules for judging.

National Equestrian Federation The national governing body of equestrian events and activities in any country; affiliated with the FEI (q.v.).

National Horse Association of Great Britain An organization founded in Great Britain in 1922 to further the welfare of the horse and pony and the interests of horse and pony owners and breeders; subsumed into the British Horse Society (q.v.) in 1947.

National Horse Show Also known as The National or The Garden; a premier horse show first organized in the United States in 1883; held annually in Madison Square Garden, New York, USA.

National Master Farriers and Black-smiths Association An organization founded in Great Britain in 1905 to promote the welfare of farriers (q.v.) and blacksmiths (q.v.).

National Pony Society An organization founded in 1893 in Great Britain to promote the breeding and registration of polo and riding ponies and to encourage the breeding and use of British pony breeds.

National Quarter Horse Association An organization founded in the early 1940s in the United States to establish breed specifications and a registry for the Quarter-type horse; merged into the American Quarter Horse Association (q.v.) in 1949.

National Recording Club Auxiliary Also known by the acronym NRC; an auxiliary registry of the American White (q.v.) and American Cream (q.v.) registries for off-colored foals of American White or American Cream Horses, or any grade horse, which carries white or cream genes who can be used for future breeding of whites or creams; horses brought into the breed for good cross-over may also be registered.

National Reining Horse Association Also known by the acronym NRHA; a non-profit organization founded in Ohio, USA in 1966 to organize, promote, and establish purses for shows, develop rules for showing and judging, create a forum and guidelines for breeders and trainers, and to promote the use of the reining horse (q.v.); is open to all breeds.

National Road Transportation Federation An amalgamation of local associations organized in Great Britain; membership was originally restricted to operators of horse-drawn vehicles.

national sire A state-owned stud horse.

national stud A state-owned stud farm.

National Trotting Association of Great Britain An organization founded in Great Britain in 1952 to promote the sport of trotter (q.v.) racing.

NATRC The acronym for North American Trail Ride Conference (q.v.).

National Veterinary Medical Association of Great Britain and Ireland An organization founded in Great Britain in 1881 to promote and oversee the interest and practice of veterinary medicine in Great Britain and Ireland.

Nations Cup Also known as the Prix des Nations, Cup of Nations, or Coppa Delle Nazione; an international show jumping event open to four male and female riders from each participating country, each riding one horse; open to female competitors since 1953.

native pony Any pony breed indigenous to Great Britain, including the Welsh Pony (q.v.), Shetland Pony (q.v.), Dartmoor (q.v.), New Forest (q.v.), Highland Pony (q.v.), Exmoor (q.v.), Fell (q.v.), Dales (q.v.), and Connemara (q.v.).

natural aids The means by which the rider communicates instruction to the horse, including legs, hands, and the influence of the body, seat, and voice; the opposite of artificial aids (q.v.).

natural allures Any untaught gait or pace of a horse, e.g., walk, trot, and canter.

natural cover Impregnation of the mare by a stallion under natural rather than orchestrated conditions; the most commonly used method of breeding; differs from artificial insemination (q.v.) or embryo transplant (q.v.).

natural fence Any naturally occurring jumping obstacle found in the environment such as fallen logs, stone walls, gates, hedges, etc.

natural paint marking Refers to coat color; a predominant hair color with at least one contrasting area of solid white hair with some underlying pink, or unpigmented skin present in the prescribed zone (q.v.) on the horse at the time of its birth; on a predominantly white horse, at least one contrasting area of colored hair with some underlying dark pigmented skin must be present in the prescribed zone on the horse at the time of its birth; in both cases, the marking must extend beyond the perimeter of a 2 inch (5 cm) diameter ring and be in the prescribed zone.

naturopathy A method of treating and healing emotional and physical conditions using natural agents and physical means.

nave *see* HUB

navel ill *see* JOINT ILL

navel infection *see* JOINT ILL

navicular (1) Also known as a navicular bone; the small, flat, boat-shaped bone located behind the coffin joint in the hoof; regulates the angle at which the deep flexor tendon attaches to the coffin bone (q.v.). (2) *see* NAVICULAR DISEASE

navicular bone *see* NAVICULAR

navicular bursitis *see* NAVICULAR DISEASE

navicular disease Also known as podotrochlitis, navicular, or navicular bursitis; a chronic degenerative condition of the navicular bone which may involve the flexor surface of the bone and the overlying deep digital flexor tendon; essentially unknown in donkeys and ponies; the exact cause is unknown; the condition is both chronic and degenerative although it may be managed in some horses through corrective shoeing and in some cases nerving (q.v.) of the affected limb; symptoms include stumbling, shortened stride, and a characteristic pointing of the toe of the forefoot when the horse is resting, whereby the pressure of the deep flexor tendon on the painful area is relieved; if both forefeet are affected, the horse points alternately.

NCHA The acronym for the National Cutting Horse Association (q.v.).

Neapolitan An ancient, extinct warmblood similar to the Andalusian (q.v.).

near horn *see* HUNTING HORN

near head *see* HUNTING HEAD

near horse Also known as near leader; a driving term; the horse on the left of a tandem (q.v.).

near leader *see* NEAR HORSE

near pommel *see* HUNTING HEAD

near side Also known as the nigh side; the left side of the horse when viewed from the rear of the horse and the right side when facing it from a standing position on the ground; evolved from two situations: (a) in the days when horsemen wore swords, the sword hung to the left side, if the rider mounted from the right side, the sword would have interfered by hanging between the rider's legs and (b) in England, traffic keeps to the left; therefore, the coachman stood on the left side of the horse to be on the side of the road and out of traffic.

nearside backhand shot A polo term; a stroke on the ball; the swing of the mallet (q.v.) from right to left over the neck of the horse to strike the ball in a backward direction, e.g., opposite to the direction of travel.

nearside forehand shot A polo term; a stroke on the ball; the swing of the mallet (q.v.) from right to left across the neck of the horse to strike the ball in a forward direction, e.g., in the direction of travel.

nearside horse The left-hand horse in a pair used to pull a horse-drawn vehicle.

near to the ground *see* KNEES AND HOCKS TO THE GROUND

neck (1) That portion of the horse's body connecting the head to the shoulders; conformation types include ewe neck (q.v.), bull neck (q.v.), and swan neck (q.v.). (2) A racing term; a measure of distance; approximately one quarter length (q.v.) which is accepted as the length of the horse's neck including the head.

neck clip *see* BELLY CLIP

neck collar *see* HARNESS COLLAR

neck rein To guide or direct the horse using rein contact against the neck rather than bit action, e.g., to turn the horse to the right, or offside, pressure with the nearside rein is applied to the neck with the supporting hand (q.v.); commonly used in western riding.

neck reining To neck rein (q.v.) a horse.

neck ring *see* LARIAT NECK RING

neck rope A western roping term; the rope that encircles the neck of the horse halfway between the poll and withers, through which the tail of the catch rope (q.v.) is passed and tied to the saddle horn (q.v.); keeps the trained horse straight on the calf and prevents him from turning away from the calf while the roper is flanking or tying.

neckshot A polo term; a shot on the polo ball (q.v.) in which the polo player strikes the ball by reaching under the neck of the horse from either side.

neck strap A narrow, adjustable leather strap which fits around the base of the horse's neck, through which the martingale (q.v.) passes, and by which the martingale is held in place.

neck stretcher An elastic cord attached between the horse's forelegs to the girth (q.v.), which passes through the left bit ring, over the poll, through the right bit ring, and connects back to the girth between the legs; adjusts to apply pressure to the horse's poll when he is above the bit (q.v.) by encouraging him to lower his head and stretch his neck.

negative reinforcement Negative reward used to modify behavior; a punishment.

neigh *see* WHINNY

neonatal maladjustment syndrome Also known by the acronym NMS; a condition of foals characterized by gross behavioral disturbances; foals appear normal at birth with signs including loss of affinity for the mare and sucking reflex, apparent blindness, aimless wandering, and emission of a barking noise developing within 12 hours of birth; mortality is approximately 50 percent.

neonate A foal (q.v.) less than three or four days old.

Neapolitan School A classical riding school founded in Naples, Italy in 1532 by Federico Grisone (q.v.) who, after Xenophon (q.v.), is considered the first of the classical masters.

Nelson gag *see* DUNCAN GAG

nerve (1) Any of the cord-like fibers connecting the body organs with the central nervous system and parts of the nervous system with each other, and carrying impulses to and from the brain or a nerve center to convey sensation and originate motion. (2) Also known as denerve, nerving, unnerve, or neurectomy; to cut a nerve (q.v.) or nerve group surgically using cryosurgery to eliminate normal nerve response to the targeted area; performed for pain-reduction purposes, i.e., to eliminate feeling to the navicular bone (q.v.) in which case the two posterior digital nerves serving the heels are cut, and for cosmetic purposes in show horses whereby the tail nerve is cut to achieve a quiet tail; is not always an effective way to treat pain and may result in the development of neuromas (q.v.). (3) A hunting term; said of a hunter; to display courage in the hunting field.

nerve block Also known as block; to anesthetize a nerve (q.v.) to eliminate feeling to the area it supplies.

nerves A hunting term; said of a hunter; to display fear while on the hunt.

nerving *see* NERVE

net energy value The energy (q.v.) remaining after subtracting waste energy from the total energy content of a specific food; measured in a calorimeter and is described in calories for a specific amount of feed; the energy of feed actually utilized by the horse to maintain life or which is incorporated into the tissue; differs from digestible energy (q.v.).

nettle rash *see* HIVES

neurectomy *see* NERVE

neuroendocrine Pertaining to the interaction between the nervous and endocrine systems (q.v.).

neuroma A benign tumor appearing on the nerve sheath due to repeated trauma on the severed stumps of cut nerves

neuropathy Nerve pathology or nerve interference due to hypermobility (q.v.); may occur directly or indirectly in the spine; of two types: facilitation and inhibition.

neurotransmitters Chemical messengers in the nervous system responsible for conveying electrical impulses across the space between the cells.

Newcastle, William Cavendish, Duke of (1592–1676) A celebrated 17th-century cavalryman and horse trainer noted for his sympathetic treatment of the horse; established the famous riding school at Antwerp, Belgium and published there a number of books on horsemanship including, but not limited to, *Methode et Invention Nouvelle de Dresser les Chevaux* and *A New Method and Extraordinary Invention to Dress Horses and Work With Them According to Nature*.

New Forest *see* NEW FOREST PONY

New Forest Hunt Club A group founded in 1789 in Great Britain to organize and monitor hunting of the New Forest region in Great Britain.

New Forest Pony Also known as the Forest, New Forest, native pony (q.v.), or lane creeper – so called because it leaves the forest for the villages in winter in search of food and shelter, devouring gardens and decorative shrubbery; a pony breed originating in the heavily wooded New Forest region of southern England; domesticated as early as 1079 by William the Conqueror; efforts to improve the breed began as early as 1016 with the passing of Canute's Forest Law (q.v.), followed by the introduction of Welsh (q.v.) mares in 1208, Thoroughbred (q.v.), Arab (q.v.) and Barb (q.v.) stallions in the 18th and 19th centuries, and subsequently other pony breeds including Welsh (q.v.), Fell (q.v.), Dale (q.v.), Dartmoor (q.v.), Exmoor (q.v.), and Highland (q.v.); presently, mares are crossed with standard-size horses to produce stock suited to light draft, polo (q.v.), and other equestrian sports; all coat colors except piebald (q.v.), skewbald (q.v.), and blue eyed creams occur with bays and browns predominating; for the most part studbred; stands 12 to 14 hands, has a long and sloping shoulder, long, and low action, and is intelligent, cunning, and easily trained; the stud book is maintained by the New Forest Pony Breeding and Cattle Society (q.v.).

New Forest Pony Breeding and Cattle

Society An organization formed in Great Britain in 1938 following the amalgamation of earlier societies to promote development of the New Forest Pony (q.v.) and to maintain the breed registry; the stud book (q.v.) was opened in 1960.

Newhouse, Charles B. (1805-1877) A British artist known for his coaching and road scenes.

New Kirgiz *see* NOVOKIRGHIZ

Newmarket The center of racing in England since the reign of Charles II; is renowned for the racehorses bred and trained there; the location of The National Stud and numerous other Thoroughbred (q.v.) studs, the headquarters of the Jockey Club (q.v.), and two primary racecourses, the Round Course and the Summer Course where the 2,000 and 1,000 Guineas, and the Cesarewitch and Cambridgeshire handicap races are run.

Newmarket boots A tall riding boot, the foot and sole of which are made of leather, while the leg is made of a waterproof canvas.

Newmarket breast girth *see* AINTREE GIRTH

Newmarket girth *see* AINTREE GIRTH

Newmarket plate A horse race first run on the Round Course at Newmarket (q.v.) in 1666; open to female riders only.

New Zealand cobb coach A horse-drawn vehicle of the concord coach (q.v.) type used for long-distance passenger transport and mail delivery in New Zealand until the arrival of the railway; seated 14 passengers.

New Zealand Horse Society Also known by the acronym NZHS; an organization founded in New Zealand to organize and oversee amateur equine sports.

New Zealand rug An extremely durable, traditionally waterproof, partially lined, canvas rug (q.v.) used to cover and protect a turned out horse from the elements of weather.

niacin A B-complex vitamin; a component of two coenzymes: nicotinamide adenine dimecleotide and nicotinamide adenine dinucleotide important for normal metabolism; deficiency is uncommon in horses as normal dietary levels are synthesized in adequate quantities by bacterial flora of the cecum and colon and in the tissues from the amino acid tryptophan.

nibble Mutual grooming as by small bites, particularly on the shoulder or withers.

nick (1) Also known as nicking; to surgically sever the small tendons and muscles under the tail of the horse to achieve a more elevated tail set (q.v.) or carriage; a crupper is used to set the tail; performed almost exclusively on American Saddlebreds (q.v.). (2) An exceptional horse, the product of two different blood lines.

nicker Also known as whicker; a low-pitched, vibrating sound emitted by the horse denoting pleasurable anticipation.

nicking (1) *see* NICK no. 1. (2) A breeding term; the mating of two different bloodlines to produce certain desired results, i.e., greater speed, improved bone, better size, etc.

nictitating membrane Also known as the third eyelid, haw, or *membrana nictans*; one of three eyelids found in the horse, dog, and certain other animals; a thin sheath of tissue that underlies the upper and lower eyelids.

nigh side *see* NEAR SIDE

nightcap A racing term; the last horse race listed in a racing program.

night eyes *see* CHESTNUT no. 1

night roller A roller (q.v.) when used to hold a night rug (q.v.) in place.

night rug *see* STABLE RUG

Nightingale, Basil (1880–1910) A noted painter of hunting portraits and scenes and some racehorses.

nisakinetum A Russian equestrian sport in which spear-bearing participants mounted on galloping horses attempt to knock balls from atop several wooden posts arranged in a line.

nit The egg of a louse (q.v.) or other parasitic insect; a louse in the immature stage; generally white or yellow in color, about the size of a pin head, and laid in the hair of the horse.

Nivernais *see* CHAROLLAIS

NMS The acronym for neonatal maladjustment syndrome (q.v.).

nobble *see* DOPE no. 1

nobbling *see* DOPING

noble science A hunting term; the art and science of hunting a pack of foxhounds (q.v.).

nod (1) Said of a horse who lowers and raises his head, as to denote lameness or unacceptance of the bit. (2) A racing term; to give permission to a jockey to dismount following a race. (3) A racing term; said of a horse who lowers and extends his head, his nose reaching the finish ahead of a close competitor.

nodding Said of the lame horse; the action of the head dropping down when the horse places his weight on the good leg and jerking his head up when weight is placed on the bad leg.

noisy A hunting term; said of mouthy (q.v.) hounds.

Nom de Course A racing term; the stable name, or a name adopted by an owner or group of owners for racing purposes.

nominate To propose, offer, or pay a fee to make a horse eligible to compete in an event.

nomination Also known as noms; the act of nominating; the state of being nominated.

nomination fees An amount of money paid to make a horse(s) eligible to compete in an event; are part of the prize money.

nominator A racing term; one who owns a horse at the time it is nominated to compete in a stakes race.

noms *see* NOMINATION

non-articular fracture A break in a bone which does not involve a joint.

non-articulating ring bone A ring bone (q.v.) condition where the bony growth has not attached to the joints between the long and short pastern or the short pastern and the pedal bone; may not result in lameness.

non-characteristic registration A registration category for horses who do not represent recognizable characteristics of a specific breed; both the dam and the sire must be registered within a common registry for color-type breeds such as the Appaloosa (q.v.), Pinto (q.v.), and Paint (q.v.).

noncontender A racing term; said of a horse running in a race who is not expected to win.

nondescript horse A movie industry term; a plain-looking horse used by extras or for background action in a film.

nondisplaced fracture A break in a bone in which the bone fragments remain in alignment.

non-essential protein Any one of the 14 of the 24 known amino acids (q.v.) produced in the gastro-intestinal tract of the horse from the ten essential amino acids (q.v.) and other food components and which are not necessary for growth, maintenance, or repair of body tissues.

non-hand-fed mare Said of a New Forest Pony (q.v.) mare who has never been off the forest except to participate in an annual New Forest Pony horse show.

nonleading leg *see* TRAILING FORELEG

Nonius A warmblood breed developed at the Mezőhegyes stud, Hungary, in the early 1800s; descended from the French stallion Nonius (sired by an English Halfbred and out of a Norman [q.v.] mare) put to Andalusian (q.v.), Arab (q.v.), Kladruber (q.v.), Norman, and English Halfbred mares; the smaller type stands 14.2 to 15.2 hands, while the larger stands 15.2 to 16.2 hands; has a bay, black, or brown coat, elegant head, long neck, and strong back; is strong, hardy, and of docile, but lively temperament; used for harness and riding.

non-pro The contraction of nonprofessional (q.v.).

nonprofessional Also known as non-pro; said of a rider who does not accept payment for work or prize money for events in any equestrian event, including monies for the training of the horse or rider, competing of the horse, or buying and selling of horses; the opposite of a professional (q.v.).

nonprogressive color pattern Refers to coat color pattern; coat color remains the same from birth through old age; the opposite of progressive color pattern (q.v.).

non-steroidal anti-inflammatory drug Also known by the acronym NSAID; any drug which intercepts the chemicals that trigger and maintain inflammation by blocking prostaglandin activity and the blood-clotting effects of thromboxane; reduces the perception of pain without impeding healing.

non-sweater Said of a horse whose sweating mechanisms fail, a condition known as anhydrosis (q.v.).

Norfolk cart A two-wheeled, horse-drawn vehicle of the dogcart (q.v.) type developed and used in the English county of Norfolk beginning in the mid-19th century; frequently slat-sided with a grained and varnished finish; hung on sideways semi-elliptical springs with either curved or straight shafts; carried four dos-a-dos (q.v.).

Norfolk Roadster *see* NORFOLK TROTTER

Norfolk Trotter Also known as a Norfolk Roadster or Roadster; an extinct pony breed native to Norfolk, England from which the name derived; its bloodlines are rooted in Yorkshire and Arab (q.v.) stallions; was a short-legged, strong trotter, possessed of exceptional speed, fortitude, and endurance; served as foundation stock for most trotting breeds, as well as many riding horses; the closest surviving relation is the Hackney (q.v.).

Noric Horse *see* NORIKER

Noriker Also known as Pinzgauer, Pinzgauer Noriker, Oberlander, Noric Horse, or South German Coldblood; a horse breed developed by the Romans in the province of Noricum which corresponds roughly to present Austria; thought to have descended from tough Haflinger Ponies (q.v.) crossed with Neapolitan, Burgundian, and Andalusian (q.v.) blood in the 16th century; a sure-footed, heavy draft horse standing 15.1 to 16.1 hands; the coat is generally bay, chestnut, or spotted, while dapple (q.v.) and gray are rare; has a slightly heavy head with a straight or slightly convex profile, a short neck, flowing, wavy mane, broad withers, a long, slightly-hollow back, and well-muscled legs with broad joints and feathering (q.v.); used for heavy draft and farm work and is well-suited for work in the mountains; stallion selection is carefully controlled with weight pulling, walking, and trotting trials mandatory before a horse can stand at stud.

normal shoeing *see* PHYSIOLOGICAL SHOEING

norman A hoof shape pattern in which the hoof is generally round with the widest part of the hoof located midway between the toe and heels.

Norman Also known as Anglo-Norman, Norman Horse, or French Saddle Horse; an ancient horse breed originating more than 1,000 years ago at which time it was used as a heavy draft war horse; descended from a mix of German, Arab (q.v.), and Barb (q.v.) blood which produced a sturdy saddle horse which was crossed with English Thoroughbred (q.v.) and Norfolk Trotter (q.v.) in the 18th and 19th centuries; more recent introductions of Thoroughbred blood have resulted in a hunter-type horse known as the Selle Français (q.v.) whose stud book is a continuation of that for the Norman; stands about 16 hands and usually has a bay or chestnut coat; is used for riding and jumping.

Norman Horse *see* NORMAN

Norman-Percheron Association An organization founded in the United States in 1876 to maintain the stud book and promote breeding and use of Percheron (q.v.) horses; the first pure-breed stock association formed in the United States; in 1877 the name was changed to the Percheron Association.

Norman Trotter *see* FRENCH TROTTER

North American Riding for the Handicapped Association Also known by the acronym NARHA; an organization founded in the United States in 1981 to organize equine events, facilities, and programs for handicapped individuals.

North American Selle Français Horse Association, Inc. Also known by the acronym NASFHA; an organization formed in Winchester, Virginia, USA in early 1990 to promote and register Selle Français (q.v.),

Anglo-Arab (q.v.), and other French breed horses in the United States under official agreement with the French Ministry of Agriculture, National Stud Farms Division, and the Institut du Cheval; all registered horses are automatically entered in the appropriate French stud book and issued a French passport and identification documents.

North American Trail Ride Conference Also known by the acronym NATRC; an organization founded in the United States in 1961 to sanction competitive trail rides in which horse and rider are judged separately; the riders are evaluated on horsemanship skills, safe riding practices, and a safe camp environment while the horses are judged on soundness, manners, conditioning, and way of going; such events are not races, although there is a specific time limit for completion of the event; horses must be at least four years old to compete.

Northern Dales Pony Society, The An organization founded in Great Britain in 1957 to encourage and improve the purebred Dales Pony (q.v.).

Northern Hackney Horse Club An organization founded in Great Britain in 1945 to further interest in Hackney (q.v.) horses, cobs, and ponies.

north-hestur *see* NORTH SWEDISH TROTTER

Northlands A relatively rare pony breed indigenous to Norway; descended from the Asiatic wild horse (q.v.) and the Tarpan (q.v.); since the 1920s, selection criteria for breeding stock has been loosely standardized; is strong, frugal, quiet and energetic, stands about 13 hands, may have a chestnut, bay, brown, or gray coat, has a well-proportioned head, short neck, long back, rounded croup, sturdy, well-muscled legs, and full forelock, mane and tail; used for riding and light draft.

North Swedish *see* NORTH SWEDISH HORSE

North Swedish Horse Also known as the North Swedish; an active, heavy, medium-sized cold blood originating in Sweden; descended from an amalgam of breeds based on ancient Scandinavian stock and is most closely related to the Døle Gudbrandsal (q.v.); is powerful, has a large head, short neck, long, deep body, short, strong legs with plenty of bone, a special aptitude for trotting, lively striding action, is an easy keeper, long lived, and is notably resistant to disease; possesses a kind temperament, and tremendous pulling power; stands 15.1 to 15.3 hands and commonly has a dun, brown, chestnut, or black coat; used for heavy draft and farm work; the breeding program is systematic and includes hauling tests and regular veterinary inspections.

North Swedish Trotter Also known as the North-Hestur; the same breed, but a lighter version of the North Swedish Horse (q.v.); bred by careful selection to develop its natural trotting ability; has a long and active stride and is a popular harness racehorse.

Norwegian *see* DØLE GUDBRANDSDAL

Norwegian Trotter *see* DØLE TROTTER

nose (1) That portion of the horse's head including the muzzle (q.v.) and mouth. (2) Also known as short head in Britain; a racing term; the narrowest possible winning margin in a race being less than a neck as, "the horse won by a nose" (q.v.). (3) A hunting term; the ability of the hound (q.v.) to follow and remain on the line (q.v.) of a hunted fox (q.v.) regardless if the scent (q.v.) is breast high (q.v.) or faint.

noseband Also known as cavesson or cavesson noseband; tack, separate from, but used in conjunction with, the bridle; consists of a slip head to which is attached a round nosepiece that lies across the bridge of the nose and buckles under the jaw, approximately 2 inches (5 cm) below the cheek bones, yet above the bit; types include the grackle noseband (q.v.), drop noseband (q.v.), flash noseband (q.v.), Australian noseband (q.v.), and Kineton noseband (q.v.); from the French cavecon meaning to curb or restrain.

nosebleed *see* EPISTAXIS

not between hand and leg A dressage term; said of a horse who is not sufficiently under control of the leg and hand aids of the rider.

not enough collection Said of a horse who does not demonstrate sufficient engagement of the hindquarters, resulting in steps that are too long and movement on the forehand (q.v.).

not enough extension Said of a horse who does not show sufficient lengthening of stride.

no time (1) A rodeo term; said of a rider; to fail to qualify in a timed cattle event by exceeding the time allowed; signaled by the flagman (q.v.) waving his flag. (2) A team sorting (q.v.) term; called if any calf crosses the foul line out of numerical order or passes across the foul line and then retreats to the original side.

Nottingham cart Also known as a Nottingham cottage cart; a light, two-wheeled, horse-drawn vehicle of the dogcart (q.v.) type; had hood-protected rear seats and was frequently flat-sided; popular beginning in the mid-19th century in Nottingham, England, from which the name derived.

Nottingham cottage cart *see* NOTTINGHAM CART

nott stag Also known in Scotland as a hummel; a British term; a stag (q.v.) who does not grow antlers.

novice An inexperienced horse or rider; a beginner.

Novokirghiz Also known as a Kirghiz, Kirgiz, New Kirgiz, or Kirgis; a Russian warmblood indigenous to the mountains of Soviet Central Asia and China; descended from old Kirghiz (q.v.) stock bred by nomadic tribesmen, the modern breed was developed between 1930 and 1940 through introduction of Thoroughbred (q.v.) and Don (q.v.), and later half-bred Anglo-Don, blood; is ideally suited to working at high altitudes, sure-footed and tough, has a longish back, straight shoulder, short, strong legs with good bone, and strong feet; stands 14.1 to 15.1 hands and may have a coat of any solid color although bay occurs most often; is good tempered and active; used for riding, harness, and packing.

NRC The acronym for the National Recording Club (q.v.).

NRHA The acronym for the National Reining Horse Association (q.v.).

NSAID The acronym for non-steroidal anti-inflammatory drug (q.v.).

NT *see* NO TIME

numb A cutting term; a cow who is not threatened or challenged by a horse and shows little desire to return to the herd.

number A hunting term; the number appearing after the name of a hound (q.v.) in a show catalogue; refers to the year in which a hound (q.v.) was entered (q.v.), which is usually one year after the hound was born.

number 1 *see* THE PROP

number ball Also known as a pill; a racing term; a small, numbered ball selected in a blind draw from a number box (q.v.) to determine post positions (q.v.) of the horses.

number board A racing term; an electronic board upon which post positions (q.v.) are identified after the number balls (q.v.) are drawn; includes the name of the horse and jockey for a given race, as well as any pertinent information such as if a horse will be wearing blinkers.

number box A racing term; a box containing numbered balls (q.v.) used to assign post positions (q.v.).

number cloth Also known as a saddle cloth; a racing term; a square, white linen cloth cut slightly larger than the saddle which bears the number corresponding to the horse's program number; given to the jockey at the time of weighing out, is included in the jockey's weight, and is placed under the saddle so that the number is visible; the jockey may opt to wear an armband bearing the same number.

number four A polo term; the player in the number four position (q.v.).

number four position Also known as number four or the back; a polo term; one of four positions on a polo team (q.v.) the responsibility of which it is to protect the goal (q.v.) and guard the number one position (q.v.) on the opponent's team.

number one A polo term; the player assuming the number one position (q.v.).

number one position Also known as number one; a polo term; one of four positions on a polo team (q.v.); the most forward offensive player.

number three A polo term; the player assuming the number three position (q.v.).

number three position A polo term; one of four positions on a polo team (q.v.); is usually the team captain or quarterback; along with the number two position (q.v.), is the highest rated and the most experienced player on the team; the pivot player between offense and defense.

number two A polo term; the player assuming the number two position (q.v.).

number two position A polo term; one of four positions on a polo team (q.v.) usually played by the highest rated and the most experienced player on the team; responsible to push both the offensive and defensive play; is played as aggressively as the number one position (q.v.), yet deeper and harder.

numnah Also incorrectly known as a saddle cloth; a saddle-shaped pad (q.v.) cut slightly larger than the saddle, placed between the saddle and the back of the horse to absorb sweat and provide protection; may be made of felt, sheepskin, or cloth-covered foam or rubber.

nursery handicap A racing term; a race for two-year old horses usually run after September 1.

nutcracker A horse who grinds his teeth.

nutraceutical Any food supplement reputed to have health benefits as reducing or relieving symptoms such as inflammation; a word coined in 1989 by The Foundation for Innovation in Medicine to describe feed; little is known about how the active ingredients in these products – chondroitin sulfates (q.v.), methylsulfonylmethane (q.v.), yucca (q.v.), etc. – although it is thought they may scavenge free radicals, change joint fluid viscosity, affect circulation, boost or otherwise alter metabolic pathways, and/or provide dietary supplements whose functions are yet unknown.

nutritional anemia A type of anemia (q.v.); an abnormal condition of the blood characterized by a deficiency in the production of red blood cells; may be caused by a deficiency in protein (q.v.), minerals (q.v.), and/or vitamins in the diet of the horse.

nutritional hyperparathyroidism *see* OSTEODYSTROPHIA FIBROSA

nutritional muscular dystrophy *see* WHITE MUSCLE DISEASE

nuts (1) *see* CUBES. (2) slang; testes (q.v.).

NZHS *see* NEW ZEALAND HORSE SOCIETY

O

Oaks A racing term; a 1-1/2 (2.4 km) mile stakes race for three-year-old fillies run annually at the Epsom Downs (q.v.) course in London, England since 1779; is conducted at the same meeting as the Derby (q.v.).

oakum A farrier term; medicated hemp used for packing the hoof; usually used in conjunction with a horseshoe pad (q.v.).

oatburner *see* HAYBURNER

oat grass Any wild species of oat; any of certain oat-like grains.

oat hay A cut and dried grass hay (q.v.) made from oat grass after harvesting the grain; first- and second-cuts average 4.3 percent digestible protein and 33 percent fiber.

oats (1) A cereal grass, *Avena sativa*, cultivated for its edible grain used as a feed for animals. (2) The edible grain of the cereal grass, *Avena sativa*; supplies about 75 percent of the TDN (q.v.); higher in fiber content than corn (q.v.), barley (q.v.), or rye (q.v.) and higher in protein content than corn, contains between 12 and 13 percent protein and 11 to 12 percent fiber as calculated by weight with weight being an important factor in judging the quality of oats – the higher the weight per bushel, the greater the proportion of kernel to husk; the average weight per bushel is 32 pounds (16.5 kg); best fed by weight and not by volume; may be fed either whole or processed, e.g., clipped (q.v.), rolled, crushed, or crimped to improve digestible energy content; processing results in some loss of nutritional quality and may result in grain fermentation and/or deterioration.

obedience Said of the horse; the act or habit of obeying; submission.

Obel Lameness Grades A system of rating degrees of lameness resulting from laminitis (q.v.); developed by Niles Obel in 1948.

Obel Grade I A degree of lameness resulting from laminitis (q.v.) as defined by the Obel Lameness Grades (q.v.); the horse frequently shifts weight between the feet, demonstrates no discernible lameness at the walk, but bilat-eral lameness at the trot.

Obel Grade II A degree of lameness resulting from laminitis (q.v.) as defined by the Obel Lameness Grades (q.v.); the horse will not resist having one leg lifted nor walking, but does show lameness at the walk.

Obel Grade III A degree of lameness resulting from laminitis (q.v.) as defined by the Obel Lameness Grades (q.v.); the horse will resist having one leg lifted and is resistant to walk.

Obel Grade IV A degree of lameness resulting from laminitis (q.v.) as defined by the Obel Lameness Grades (q.v.); the horse will walk only if forced.

Oberlander *see* NORIKER

obesity The condition of being fat; overweight.

objection Also known as a protest; a complaint submitted to an event organizing body against another competitor or about an official call or rule infringement.

objection flag A racing term; a red flag raised on the number board (q.v.) following completion of a race indicating an objection (q.v.) has been filed.

objection overruled To rule or decide against an objection (q.v.); in racing denoted by the raising of a white flag on the number board (q.v.) to replace the objection flag (q.v.).

objection sustained To rule in favor of an objection (q.v.); in racing denoted by the raising of a green flag on the number board (q.v.) to replace the objection flag (q.v.).

oblique fracture A break of a bone at an angle.

oblique shoulder *see* SLOPING SHOULDER

obstacle course *see* COMPETITION C

obstructive pulmonary disease *see* CHRONIC OBSTRUCTIVE PULMONARY DISEASE

obstructive jaundice A jaundice (q.v.)

condition caused by obstruction of the flow of bile from the liver to the duodenum; results in increased pressure in the bile duct which causes a backflow of bile pigment into the blood with the concentration of pigment increasing until it becomes deposited in the tissues and the signs of jaundice (q.v.) is seen, e.g., yellowing of the eyeballs, skin, and urine; may be caused by inflammation of the duodenum, bot larvae entering the bile duct, tumors, roundworm (q.v.) migration through the liver, or certain types of impaction of the large or small intestines.

occipital crest *see* POLL

occult spavin Arthritis (q.v.) of the lower joint of the hock (q.v.) caused by development of a growth between the two bones of the hock (q.v.) just below the joint on the inner side; difficult to detect because of the lack of visible signs.

odd board *see* TOTALIZATOR BOARD

odd colored Refers to coat color; a coat consisting of large irregular patches of more than two colors which may merge into each other at the edges of the patches.

odds A racing term; an equalizing advantage given by a bettor or competitor in proportion to the assumed chances in his favor; a betting quote on a horse running in a race (q.v.).

odds man A racing term; an employee responsible for calculating the changing betting odds and numbers and amounts of bets staked in any given horse race; employed at tracks where totalizators (q.v.) are not used.

odds on A racing term; betting odds of less than even money (q.v.).

oedema *see* EDEMA

oesophagus *see* ESOPHAGUS

oestrus *see* ESTRUS

oestrus cycle *see* ESTROUS CYCLE

off (1) Also known as the off; a racing term; the time of the start of a race. (2) A racing term; the difference between the track record and the final time of a race. (3) Said of a lame horse, e.g., "He's off in the right front." (4) A racing term; the slowness of a horse as expressed in a time or lengths comparison (q.v.) between what it should run, or what other horses have run. (5) Said of a horse who has passed a certain year of his age, e.g., in his fifth year, the horse is said to be five off. (6) A racing term; to begin a race, e.g., "They're off."

off course bet *see* OFF SIDE BET

off horse Also known as off leader; a driving term; the horse on the right of a tandem (q.v.).

official (1) A racing term; a notice displayed when the results of a race are confirmed. (2) An individual invested with authority at a equine event.

off leader *see* OFF HORSE

off its feed Said of a horse who is not eating normal quantities of food as due to illness or injury.

offset knees *see* LATERAL DEVIATION OF THE METACARPAL BONES

offset stirrup Also known as a Kornokoff iron; a modification of the hunting iron (q.v.) in which the mounted rider positions his foot for stability; has an off-center eyelet positioned toward the outside of the stirrup and forward-sloping sides; the foot tred is inclined upward to encourage correct leg position, forcing the heels down and the toes in.

off side (1) *see* FAR SIDE. (2) Said of a horse/player in illegal territory, or ahead of the ball, as in mounted games such as polo (q.v.).

offside horse The right-hand horse in a pair used to pull a horse-drawn vehicle.

off the bit Said of a horse who fails to carry himself easily, is unbalanced, does not move from behind, and resists the aids (q.v.); may be due to the horse being behind the bit (q.v.) or above the bit (q.v.).

off the board (1) A racing term; said of a horse who fails to finish in the money (q.v.). (2) A racing term; a horse so lightly bet that his odds exceed 99 to 1.

off the pace A racing term; said of a horse who trails the early leaders.

off the top A racing term; the practice of deducting a fixed sum or percentage from the mutuel pool (q.v.) before paying off winning ticket holders.

off track (1) *see* OFF-TRACK BETTING. (2) A racing term; said of a racing surface that is not fast.

off track bet Also known as an off-course bet; any wager made at a site other than the racetrack where the race(s) bet on is being run.

off-track betting Also known as off-track or by the acronym OTB; a racing term; betting conducted at legalized betting venues other than the racetrack; may be operated by the tracks, management companies specializing in pari-mutuel wagering, or by independent corporations authorized by individual states; money wagered is usually commingled with on-track betting pools.

off-track betting site A racing term; a legal location where bets, other than those placed at the track at which the race is run, are placed.

old scent *see* STALE SCENT

oil (1) Any of a large class of substances typically unctuous, viscous, combustible, liquid at ordinary temperatures, and soluble in ether or alcohol, but not in water; used for food, moistening, lubricating, etc.; those used for food are generally derived from oilseed grains. (2) To moisten, smear, lubricate, or condition with oil, as in leather or hooves.

oil cake A mass of seeds or pulp remaining after the extraction of oil from cottonseed, linseed (q.v.), or coconut fruits; used as a feed for livestock and as a fertilizer.

oiled Said of a horse given mineral oil through a nasogastric tube (q.v.) to relieve gas or to help the horse pass an intestinal blockage.

oiling To administer mineral oil to a horse through a nasogastric tube (q.v.) to relieve gas or help the horse pass an intestinal blockage.

oilseed Also known as oilseed grains; any seed grown as a source of oil (q.v.), such as linseed (q.v.), cottonseed, and soybean.

oilseed grains *see* OILSEED

oilseed meals The edible part of any oilseed grain remnant following extraction of the oil; include cottonseed meal (q.v.), linseed meal (q.v.), and soybean meal (q.v.); fed in conjunction with grain to offset protein deficiencies and balance rations; the fat and protein content varies slightly depending on the extraction method used.

Oldenburg The heaviest of the German warmbloods; derived from the Friesian (q.v.) during the 17th century for use as a strong carriage horse; over the years, Spanish, Neapolitan, Cleveland Bay (q.v.), Anglo-Arab (q.v.), Norman (q.v.), and Thoroughbred (q.v.) blood was introduced; due to reduced requirements for carriage horses, Thoroughbred, Hanoverian (q.v.), and Norman blood was later introduced to develop an all-purpose riding and competition horse; stands 16.2 to 17.2 hands, has a bay, brown, black, or gray coat, rarely chestnut, relatively short legs for its size, a high-set tail, broad croup (q.v.), pronounced withers, straight back, and a wide and deep-set chest.

old heavy *see* STAGE COACH

Oleander A Thoroughbred stallion foaled in 1924; one of Germany's greatest racing stallions.

olive dun *see* OLIVE GRULLO

olive grullo Also known as olive dun; refers to coat color; a grullo (q.v.) of the color group dun (q.v.); the coat hair is a yellowish grullo color, the points black, and the head dark; sometimes included in the buckskin (q.v.) group.

omnibus A horse-drawn, four-wheeled, single or double-decked public service bus originally developed by French philosopher Blaise Pascal in the second half of the 17th century; reintroduced again in Paris during the 1820s; drawn by a pair of horses or three horses abreast; used predominantly in the inner suburbs and city centers; earlier types were entered from the rear, with either longitudinal or crosswise seating for six with luggage generally carried on a railed roof.

onager *see* ASIATIC WILD ASS

on course bet *see* TRACK BET

one-day event A three-phase eventing

(q.v.) competition consisting of dressage (q.v.), show jumping (q.v.), and cross country phases conducted over a period of one day with all three phases performed by the same rider/horse team; in some cases, if the number of entries is high, the cross country phase may be conducted on a second day.

on-edge Said of a nervous horse.

one healed *see* CAUGHT ONE

one run A racing term; said of a horse who expends all his energy in a single burst of speed, usually on a stretch (q.v.).

one-sided (1) Said of a horse who bends more easily to one side than the other, as due to unbalanced muscle development, injury, etc. (2) Also known as one-sided mouth; said of the horse; the horse's mouth when only responsive to the action of the bit on either the left or right side.

one-sided mouth *see* ONESIDED no. 2.

one-sidedness The state of being one-sided (q.v.).

One Thousand Guineas A 1-mile (1.6 km) horse race for three-year old horses first run at the Newmarket (q.v.) meet in England in 1809.

one two *see* QUINELLA

on foot A hunting term; said of a fox (q.v.) when the hounds (q.v.) have located his line (q.v.) in a covert (q.v.) and he begins to move.

on its toes Said of a fidgety horse who is eager to move forward.

on-site diagnostic test *see* STALL-SIDE DIAGNOSTIC TEST

on terms A hunting term; said of hounds able to continue hunting because the scent remains strong.

on the aids Also known as between hand and leg; said of a horse framed between the rider's hands and legs and who is fully responsive to the actions of the rider including natural and artificial aids (q.v.).

on the Bill Daly Said of a jockey who, in a race, uses the riding style promoted by Bill Daly (q.v.), i.e., to take the lead as soon as possible out of the gate, set the pace, and remain in the lead to the finish (q.v.); commonly used prior to the turn of the 20th century.

on the bit Also known as in the bridle; said of a horse who takes a light, but gentle contact on the bit and is responsive to any slight change in the pressure applied to the bit through the reins; the horse carries himself easily, is well balanced, moves from behind, and does not resist application of the aids (q.v.).

on the board A racing term; a horse who finishes a race in one of the first three positions.

on the chin strap A racing term; said of a horse who wins by a wide margin.

on the flags (1) A hunting term; the manner in which hounds (q.v.) are exhibited at hound shows. (2) A hunting term; the exhibiting of hounds (q.v.) at the kennel for visitors; so called because the hound kennels were historically faced with flagstone and when the hounds were exhibited they were lined up in front of this stone.

on the forehand Also known as too low or on the hand; said of a horse who places most of his weight on its shoulders and front legs with little engagement of the hindquarters; the forehand of the horse will be lower than it should be and the horse will be unbalanced, the gaits short, the paces off, and he will frequently lean on the bit (q.v.) using the rider's hands for support.

on the ground A racing term; a jockey suspended from competition.

on the hand *see* ON THE FOREHAND

on the leg Also known as showing too much daylight; said of a horse disproportionately long in the leg; a tall horse.

on the muscle (1) Said of a fit horse. (2) Said of a strong horse who pulls against the bit.

on the nose A racing term; to bet a horse to win a race.

on the rail A racing term; said of a horse who runs close to the infield rail.

on the right rein (1) To move to the right as in a horse under saddle. (2) A dressage term; said of a horse when the right rein is the outside rein.

on top A racing term; said of a horse running in the lead.

on track bet *see* TRACK BET

on two tracks The movement of the horse's fore and hind legs in parallel tracks as in lateral movements (q.v.).

oozing A slow leak or trickling of fluid such as blood or serum (q.v.) from a wound.

open (1) Also known as an open event; any competition in which any rider, professional, or nonprofessional, is eligible to perform. (2) Also known as open on a fox; a hunting term; said of the hounds (q.v.) when they first speak (q.v.) on the line of a fox (q.v.) in a covert (q.v.). (3) A jumping term; an advanced jumping division in which competitors are not restricted from entering by previous winnings. (4) A hunting term; a fox's earth that is not stopped.

open bridle A bridle (q.v.) without blinds or blinkers (q.v.) covering the eyes.

open ditch A jumping obstacle consisting of a short slant rail, followed by a shallow ditch not more than 6 feet (1.8 m) wide, and a bush fence or hedge.

open event *see* OPEN no. 1

open fracture *see* COMPOUND FRACTURE

open-hocked Said of a horse who is wide at the hocks and narrow between the hooves.

opening meet A hunting term; the first meet (q.v.) of the formal hunting season.

opening rein *see* DIRECT REIN

open knee An immature knee; a stage of development in the one- to three-year-old horse in which the distal end of the radius growth plate is still cartilaginous.

open mare Also known as yeld; a brood mare who was not bred during the previous breeding season.

open on a fox *see* OPEN no. 2

open race A racing term; a horserace with lenient terms of eligibility in which a wide variety of horses are allowed to enter and compete.

open rein *see* DIRECT REIN

open toe eggbar shoe *see* BACKWARDS SHOE

open tug That part of the harness used on a single horse through which the shafts (q.v.) pass; a stout, oval-shaped leather band which buckles at the top to the backband and which passes through the top of the saddle.

open top collar Any harness collar (q.v.) that can be spread open at the top to facilitate slipping it over the head of the horse; once in place, it is closed and held together with a housing strap before the hames (q.v.) are put on; used on a horse with a wide head and narrow neck; may lose rigidity with use and is liable to produce shoulder sores and/or pinching.

Opera Bus A small, single-decker, privately owned, horse-drawn bus used for theater-going; first used in the 1870s; had longitudinal seating reached through a rearward opening door, folding steps, and was drawn by a single horse in shafts.

opposite rein *see* INDIRECT REIN

opthalmia An inflammation of the eye and associated membranes characterized by pain and discharge.

optic nerve The nerve (q.v.) that transmits electrical impulses from the light-sensitive retina of the eye to the brain.

optimum take-off zone A jumping term; the ideal area in which a horse must take off to clear a jump; size varies according to the height and type of jump to be cleared as well as the stride and jumping ability of the horse.

optional claimer A racing term; a race for horses to be claimed (q.v.) for a fixed price, at a price within a limited range, or for horses who previously ran at such a price, but which are not entered to be claimed.

option fence Any jumping obstacle consisting of two upright fences positioned side-by-side facing the rider; the rider has the option to jump either the left or right fence; the fences may be of different types and/or difficulty and may present different distances to the next fence.

orange dun Refers to coat color; a light red dun (q.v.) coat with red or light red points.

orchardgrass hay A cut and dried grass hay (q.v.) made from orchardgrass which is grown throughout the United States; contains a digestible protein content of approximately 4.2 percent; generally cut at the early-bloom stage to insure palatability and satisfactory nutritional levels.

ordinary hack *see* ROAD HACK

ordinary walk *see* WALK

original *see* RIG

Orloff Trotter *see* ORLOV TROTTER

Orlov *see* ORLOV TROTTER

Orlov-Rostopchin *see* RUSSIAN SADDLE HORSE

Orlov Trotter Also known as a Russian Trotter, Orlov, and spelled Orloff Trotter; a Russian-bred warmblood developed in the 1780s from an Arab (q.v.) stallion put to Danish and Dutch mares; considered one of the world's best trotting breeds and is the most widely known and commonly used breed in Russia; named after Count Alexis Orlov who founded the Krenov Stud in 1778 where the breed was developed; through a process of strict selection and introduction of Danish, Dutch, English, Russian, Polish, and Arab mares, together with important contributions from Thoroughbred (q.v.) stallions, a breed of distinctive characteristics was developed; the stud book was founded in 1865 and was originally open to any horse who could run 914 yards (1 km) in less than two minutes; now, the registry is only open to those horses with both the dam and sire listed in the Stud Book; the coat is most commonly gray, although black and bay do occur, stands 15.1 to 17 hands, has a light, powerful build, elegant conformation, long back, and a long, swan neck; is docile, but energetic; used for trotting races, harness, and riding.

orra horse The progeny of a Highland (q.v.) mare and a draft horse.

orthopedic Pertaining to the skeletal system.

osmosis The tendency, when two solutions of differing concentrations are separated by a semipermeable membrane, for the solution of higher density to pass through the membrane until the two solutions are equalized in pressure.

os pedis *see* PEDAL BONE

osselets Also known as arthritis of the fetlock joint and spelled osslets; a bony growth occurring on the fetlock or ankle joint; results from inflammation of the enveloping membrane of the bone caused by injury such as a wound, bruise, sprain, etc., and the repeated strain and trauma of hard training in young horses; symptoms include a short choppy gait, pain when the ankle is flexed, and a soft, warm, sensitive, swelling of the front and sometimes the side of the fetlock joint.

ossification The formation of bone in the connective tissue of chronically traumatized or inflamed muscles.

osslets *see* OSSELETS

osteoarthritis Also known as secondary joint disease or degenerative joint disease; inflammation and degeneration of one or more joints due to excessive wear or joint weakness; characterized by a progressive loss of articular cartilage, and bone; most commonly seen in older horses and is frequently associated with chronic joint problems; in working horses, results from trauma associated with continued use of a horse suffering from serous arthritis (q.v.).

osteodystrophia fibrosa Also known as miller's disease, bran disease, bighead, bighead disease, or nutritional hyperparathyroidism; a generalized bone disease primarily caused by dietary calcium deficiency with phosphorus excess resulting from diet or parathyroid problems; signs include symmetric enlargement of the mandible and facial bones, loosening of the teeth, and in advanced cases, flattening of the ribs with fractures and detachment of the ligaments if the horse is worked; horses of both sexes and all ages are susceptible, with lactating mares, foals and mules more at risk; is relatively uncommon, but if left untreated, may result in death.

osteomyelitis An infection of the bone caused by microorganisms which may gain access through broken tissue resulting from comminuted or compound fractures (q.v.)

osteoporosis Demineralization of the bones that may cause fracture (q.v.); uncommon in horses.

ostler *see* HOSTLER

OTB The acronym for off-track betting (q.v.).

Our Dumb Friends League An organization founded in England in 1897 to promote animal welfare; now defunct.

outcross *see* CROSS-BREEDING

outcrossing *see* CROSS-BREEDING

outfit (1) A ranch (q.v.) including all the equipment and employees. (2) A western term; the personal equipment of a cowboy (q.v.), i.e., tack.

outlaw A renegade horse, one who cannot be broken; a rogue.

outline The profile of the horse.

outlier A hunting term; a fox (q.v.) found in the open rather than a covert (q.v.).

out of Said of a horse's maternal parentage, e.g, The foal was out of the mare Ziva.

out of blood Also known as short of blood; a hunting term; said of hounds who have not killed hunted prey for some time.

out-of-bounds A polo term; said of a ball that crosses the side or end lines, or goes over the sideboards thus requiring stop of play (q.v.); necessitates a throw-in by the umpire.

out of position A cutting term; said of a horse who is unable to respond quickly enough to the movements of the cow being worked to maintain control over it and who will lose the working advantage.

out of the money A racing term; said of a horse who, technically, finishes in any position

other than first, second, or third.

outrider A racing term; a mounted employee who escorts horses competing in a race to the post (q.v.).

outside The side of the horse on the outside of the movement, e.g., when riding a horse on a right circle the outside is the left side of the horse.

outside car *see* JAUNTING CAR

outside leg The rider's leg on the side opposite the movement.

outside mare A mare not owned by the facility which boards or breeds her.

outsider A racing term; a racehorse (q.v.) given long odds by the odds maker because his chances of winning are slim.

outspanners A driving term; the two horses put to the outside in a troika (q.v.).

out to walk *see* WALK no. 2

ova The plural of ovum (q.v.); eggs.

ovary One of two female reproductive glands in which ova (q.v.) and sex hormones are produced; connected to the uterus by the oviducts (q.v.).

overalls (1) Tight dress riding pants with a stirrup through which the foot passes; worn with a silk hat and tail coat (q.v.) in hack classes. (2) Loose, stout trousers, usually with a part extending over the chest and supported by shoulder straps.

over and under A western term; to use the long ends of the split reins of a western bridle to slap the belly of the horse as a reprimand or to encourage movement, the ends being whipped from side to side, or from over to under the horse.

over at the knee *see* FORWARD DEVIATION OF THE CARPAL JOINTS

overbent *see* BEHIND THE BIT

overbite *see* OVER-SHOT JAW

over carted Said of a horse or pony pulling a vehicle too large, but not necessarily too heavy, for its size.

overcheck *see* CHECK REIN

over collected Said of a horse moving with too much collection (q.v.); the horse is on the bit, although the head position may be behind the vertical (q.v.).

overface (1) Also known as overfacing; to encourage a horse to jump a fence that is either too large or too difficult for it to jump. (2) To provide a horse with excessive quantities of feed.

overfaced Said of a horse asked to jump an obstacle that is clearly beyond his capabilities.

over facing: *see* OVERFACE

overgirth *see* SURCINGLE

over horsed (1) Said of a riding horse who is too much for the rider to handle, whether that be due to size, speed, training, etc. (2) Said of a rider whose size relationship to his/her mount is disproportionate, e.g., a small framed rider on a very large horse.

over in the knees *see* FORWARD DEVIATION OF THE CARPAL JOINTS

overland Also known as scenic route; a racing term; a horse who runs wide on the turns, thus losing ground.

overlay A racing term; said of a riding horse posting higher odds than expected when based on past performance.

overnight *see* OVERNIGHT RACE

overnight race Also known as overnight; a racing term; any race in which the entries close 72 hours (exclusive of Sundays) or less before the post time (q.v.) for the first race on the day the race is to be run.

overnights A racing term; a printout available from the racing secretary's office the day prior to that on which a race is to be run which identifies entries in the next day's races.

overo Refers to coat color pattern; a basic solid base coat with large, asymmetrical patterns of horizontally arranged white patches where the definition between the white and colored areas is ragged; white body patches

occur in the middle of the sides of the body, neck, and occasionally the belly, rarely extending to the topline (q.v.); the white is irregular, rather scattered or splashy, and is often referred to as calico; head markings are distinctive, with bald-face (q.v.), apron-face (q.v.), or bonnet-face (q.v.) common; the eyes are frequently, but not always, blue and one or more legs may be colored; a bald face (q.v.) and a small white spot on the side of the horse is the minimum extent; small spots frequently have a butterfly shape; may be predominantly dark or white, but rarely all white; the tail is usually one color; the result of the influence of a recessive gene.

overreach Also known as grab a quarter; minor limb contact to the heel bulb (q.v.) and adjoining area of the foot caused by the toe of the hind foot when it catches the forefoot on the same side; the hind foot advances more quickly than in forging (q.v.); may occur as a consequence of jumping or galloping, particularly on muddy, slippery, or wet ground; the heel can be protected with over-reach boots (q.v.).

over-reach boots Also known as bell boots, racking boots, or over-reaching boots; a bell-shaped protective covering for the hoof and coronary band (q.v.) made of leather, rubber, and/or synthetic materials used to protect the heels of the forelegs from injury by the toe of the hind shoe or hoof.

overreaching boots *see* OVER-REACH BOOTS

over-ride (1) A hunting term; said of the rider; to ride too close to the hounds (q.v.). (2) A cutting term; to push a horse and not wait for him to react instinctively to a cow. (3) To ride a horse at an excessive pace or speed for too long a period of time without regard for his physical condition.

over-run Also known as over run the line; a hunting term; said of the hounds when they run past the line of the fox (q.v.) because the scent has been diverted by a change of course or foil (q.v.).

over run the line *see* OVER-RUN

overshot fetlock *see* KNUCKLING OVER

over-shot jaw Also called brachygnathism, overbite, parrot mouth, parrot jaw, or overshot mouth; a congenital malformation of the mouth in which the upper jaw is longer than the bottom jaw and the teeth in the top jaw overshoot or protrude beyond the teeth of the lower jaw; thought to be inherited; may cause the horse to have difficulty eating.

over-shot mouth *see* OVER-SHOT JAW

over-straining disease *see* EXERCISE RELATED MYOPATHY

over the bit *see* ABOVE THE BIT

over the bridge A horse dealer's term; a horse with a weak back.

over the odds A racing term; said of a backer when he or she obtains a longer price than that offered at the start of the race.

over the sticks Said of a horse; to jump over an obstacle.

overtrack Said of a horse at the walk or trot when the hind foot steps in front of the corresponding forefoot print.

overweight (1) A racing term; said of a jockey who exceeds the weight assigned his mount; a jockey may be a maximum of 5 pounds (2.3 kg) overweight, a situation that is either posted on an information board or announced over the public address system prior to the race. (2) A racing term; extra pounds carried by a horse, in excess of officially assigned weight, because the jockey is too heavy.

oviduct Also known as Fallopian tube; the duct connecting the ovary (q.v.) to the uterine horn.

ovulation Release of the ovum (q.v.).

over the bit *see* OVERBENT

ovum An egg; the female reproductive cell produced in the ovary (q.v.).

owlhead A horse who is impossible to train.

own brothers *see* BROTHERS

owner One named on the certificate of regis-

tration or bill of sale for a horse; one to whom a horse belongs.

ownership brand *see* RANCH BRAND

owns *see* OWN THE LINE OF A FOX

own sisters *see* SISTERS

own the line *see* OWN THE LINE OF A FOX

own the line of a fox Also known as owns or own the line; a hunting term; said of a hound (q.v.) who has given tongue (q.v.) on the line of a fox (q.v.).

ox A suffix to the name of any pure-bred Arab.

oxbow stirrup A stirrup (q.v.) with a round bottom, and slightly curved sides made of metal, plastic, leather, or other material; connected to a western saddle by stirrup leathers (q.v.); used to support the rider's foot.

oxer Also known as post and rails or ox fence; a parallel fence utilizing two sets of standards and any combination of poles, angles, or spreads which is jumped as a single unit; the term evolved in England where the trails in and out of town were originally lined with posts and rails set wide enough apart to allow passage of oxen without difficulty; hunters traveling through these towns would jump the posts and rails at an angle perpendicular to the trails used by the oxen.

ox fence *see* OXER

Oxford cart *see* OXFORD DOGCART

Oxford Dogcart Also known as bounder or Oxford cart; a light, fast, horse-drawn vehicle of the dogcart (q.v.) type suspended on a pair of high wheels with red-painted spokes, hung on semi-elliptical springs, and seating four, dos-a-dos (q.v.); named after the city of its origins; frequently driven by sporting undergraduates attending Oxford University.

oyster feet Said of the horse's hooves when rather flat, white, and displaying horizontal rings; occurs naturally as a condition of laminitis (q.v.).

P

P1 *see* PASTERN BONE

P2 *see* SHORT PASTERN BONE

PI *see* PASTERN BONE

PII *see* SHORT PASTERN BONE

PIII *see* THIRD PASTERN

pace (1) The sequence of steps at any gait. (2) A two-beat lateral gait with suspension performed in two time in which the hind and foreleg (q.v.) on the same side move forward simultaneously; is smooth and fast, ranging from 12 to more than 30 mph (19–48 kmph); results in more rotation of the spine from side-to-side and less lateral bending than the trot (q.v.); an inborn affinity. (3) A racing term; the speed of the leaders at each stage of a race.(4) Also known as passe; a herd of asses (q.v.).

pacemaker *see* PACE SETTER

pace not true Said of a horse who does not perform a pace (q.v.) or gait in the correct time, e.g., a walk should be performed four time, trot two, and canter three time.

pacer Also known as a wiggler, sidewheeler, or sandshifter; any horse bred and naturally gaited to pace (q.v.).

pace setter Also known as pacemaker; a racing term; a horse who takes the lead and sets the pace/speed for the other horses in the field (q.v.).

pachyderm polo Also known as elephant polo; a mounted game consisting of two 10 minute chukkers (q.v.) with a 15-minute break at half-time played on elephants ranging from 20 to 40 years old, although some younger, and faster, elephants are used; small elephants are played in the offensive positions and each elephant is ridden by two individuals, a mahout and the polo player; developed in 1982 by Jim Edwards and James Manclark in southern Nepal; has similar rules to equine polo (q.v.), with a few exceptions: (a) one player from each team must remain on his side of the midfield at all times, (b) only two players from each team may be within the boundaries of an arc marked around the goal,

(c) riding off (q.v.) and hooking (q.v.) are not permitted, (d) played on a 120 x 70 yard (110 x 64 m) field, and (e) mallets (q.v.) are 98 to 110 inches (2.5–2.8 m)in length depending on the size of the elephant and are made of a bamboo upper and cane lower shaft; the sport is officially recognized by the Nepal Sports Council and the Nepal Olympics Association; at the beginning of each season, the teams in the World Elephant Polo Tournament are divided into two leagues by a handicapping committee; each team plays the other teams in its league with finalists competing for the championship on the last day of the tournament.

pacing *see* HARNESS RACING

pack (1) Also known as pack of hounds or previously as mute; a hunting term; a group of dog hounds (q.v.) who cooperatively hunt a fox (q.v.), coyote (q.v.), stag (q.v.), etc. (2) A bundle, parcel, or bale for transport on the back of a animal.

pack animal Any animal used to carry burdens for conveyance to another location.

packed cell volume Also known as hematocrit or by the acronym PCV; the ratio of red blood cells to total blood volume, expressed as a percentage; an indicator of dehydration, anemia, and other disorders.

packer One who works packing goods and supplies onto the backs of livestock (horses, mules, donkeys, burros, llamas, etc.) and who is responsible for transporting such goods to another location.

pack horse Also known as a somer or sumpter; a horse used to carry burdens for conveyance to another location.

Packington Blind Horse A black horse with white feathering (q.v.); the foundation sire of the Shire (q.v.) who stood at stud 1755 through 1770.

pack of hounds *see* PACK

pack pony A pony used to carry burdens for conveyance to another location.

pack saddle A saddle designed to carry burdens for conveyance by pack animals.

pack string Also known as a string; a number of livestock carrying burdens for conveyance to another location tied together and following one behind the other; so called, because the animals string behind the packer (q.v.).

pad (1) *see* SADDLE PAD.(2) The foot of a fox or hound. (3) That part of the harness tack bridging the horse's back. (4) *see* HORSESHOE PAD. (5) *see* ANCIENT ENGLISH PACER. (6) *see* SADDLE no. 4. (7) The central part of a carriage step. (8) *see* STIRRUP PAD

pad cloth *see* QUARTER SHEET

paddling *see* DISHING

paddock (1) Also known as field; an enclosed, fenced area used for tgrazing or exercising horses. (2) Also known as a race-course paddock; a racing term; the area adjacent to a racecourse used for saddling, mounting, and viewing of horses prior to the race.

paddock boots Also known as high lows or jodhpur boots; low boots no taller than 1 to 2 inches (2.5–5 cm) above the ankle bone made of leather or synthetic materials and available in laced, zipper, and pull-on styles.

paddock judge A racing term; one responsible for all activity in the paddock (q.v.) and saddling areas.

paddock sheet *see* SUMMER SHEET

pad groom Also known as the second horse man or hunt servant; a special groom responsible for riding a lady's hunter to a hunt meeting and returning with the covert hack (q.v.) or to ride the fresh hunter to a check (q.v.) in the hunt and return with the tired horse.

pad horse An antiquated term; a road hack.

pad saddle An outer covering that fits on top of and across a sidesaddle (q.v.) which is fitted with stirrups (q.v.) on either side; allows the rider to sit astride the horse saddled with a sidesaddle.

pad scent *see* STALE LINE

pad tree A wooden or metal frame to which harness pads are attached.

Pahlavan A warmblood indigenous to Iran which descended from Plateau Persian (q.v.) crossed with Arab (q.v.) and Thoroughbred (q.v.); stands 15.2 to 16 hands, may have a coat of any solid color, and is strong and elegant; used for riding.

paint (1) Refers to coat color; an asymmetrical pattern of white patches on any base color; the patches are generally well defined and there are no white hairs mixed into the colored areas; several specific patterns occur, namely tobiano (q.v.), overo (q.v.), sabino (q.v.), and splashed white (q.v.). (2) *see* PAINT HORSE. (3) A spotted cow. (4) A counter-irritant used to increase blood circulation to the leg area and promote healing; a mild blister (q.v.).

Paint Horse An American-bred warmblood of a stock-type whose breeding is based upon bloodlines of registered American Paint Horses, Quarter Horses (q.v.), or Jockey Club (q.v.) or Jockey Club recognized organization registered Thoroughbreds (q.v.) who meet minimum color requirements; must have a definite natural paint marking, white leg markings extending above the knees and/or hocks, glass, blue, or wall eyes (q.v.), an apron (q.v.) or bald face (q.v.), white on the lower jaw or lower lip, a blue zone around a natural paint marking, a two-color mane with one color being natural white, dark spots, or freckles in the white hair on the face or legs, white areas completely surrounded by a contrasting color in the nonvisible zone, excluding the head and a contrasting area of another color in the non-visible zone including the head; the spectrum of colors ranges from almost total color with minimal white markings to almost total white with minimal dark markings; overo (q.v.), tobiano (q.v.), and tovero (q.v.) coat patterns occur with piebald (q.v.), skewbald (q.v.), or medicine hat (q.v.) coloring; most can be double registered as Pintos (q.v.) and as either Stock- or Hunter-Type horses, but not every Pinto is a Paint.

pair (1) Two horses hitched and driven abreast. (2) Two horses ridden side by side, or competing in an event as one entry, as in pair classes. (3) Two things similar in form and situated close to one another.

pair jumping A show-jumping event in which two riders ride a course, and jump all obstacles, side by side.

pairs More than one pair (q.v.).

palate The roof of the mouth; separates the nasal and oral cavities and consists of the hard palate (q.v.) and soft palate (q.v.).

palatitis *see* LAMPAS

palfrey *see* ANCIENT ENGLISH PACER

palisade worms *see* LARGE STRONGYLES

palmar Also known as volar; relating to the rear or lower surface of the foreleg below the knee, including the knee, fetlock, pastern, and hoof.

palmar deviation of the carpal joints *see* BACKWARD DEVIATION OF THE CARPAL JOINTS

palmar digital neurectomy Also known as heel nerving; to cut a portion of the palmar digital nerve in the fore-feet to relieve pain related to navicular disease (q.v.); to nerve (q.v.) the palmar digital nerve.

Palmar, Lynwood (1868–1941) A British equestrian artist and leading authority on horsemanship, driving, and shoeing.

palmar process The rearmost portion of either side of the third pastern (q.v.).

palomino Refers to coat color; a horse having a golden coat which may vary from pale yellow to dark cream, white, or flaxen (q.v.), with an ivory mane and tail; white markings are only permitted on the face and the lower legs; may have pink skin and blue eyes; found in many horse and pony breeds, but does not appear in purebred Thoroughbreds (q.v.) or Arabians (q.v.).

Palomino Also known as Palomino horse, golden horse, buttermilk horse, golden horse of the West, Café-au-Lait in France, Royal Hanoverian Cream, Hanoverian Cream in England, or previously as Isabella, Y'sabella, and Golden Horse of the Queen; a color breed developed by Queen Isabella of Spain in the 15th century for her personal use; originally of Arab (q.v.) stock; believed to have been brought to America by the Spaniards, the name being derived from Juan de Palomino who received a horse of this color type from the explorer Cortez; in America, has been selectively bred since the mid 1930s; progeny must have one registered Palomino parent and the other of Quarter Horse (q.v.), Arab, or Thoroughbred (q.v.) blood; cannot show draft, pony, or Paint (q.v.) breeding; the eyes should be dark or hazel and both of the same color; white markings are permitted on the face and are limited to a blaze (q.v.), snip (q.v.), or star (q.v.) and on the legs below the knees or hocks; the coat must be golden, but may vary from pale yellow to dark cream, with a white, flaxen (q.v.), or ivory mane and tail containing no more than 15 percent dark (black, sorrel, chestnut), or off-colored hair; the skin must be dark colored without pink spots; zebra marks, dorsal striping, and/or white hairs interspersed within the coat associated with gray, roan, or rabicano patterns are unacceptable; stands 14 to 17 hands; physical characteristics vary and does not breed true to type; used for riding, parades, stock work, and driving.

Palomino Horse *see* PALOMINO

Palomino Horse Association, Inc. An organization established in the United States in 1936 to perpetuate and improve the Palomino Horse (q.v.) through recording of blood lines and issuing of certificates of registration to qualifying horses.

Palomino Horse Breeders of America, Incorporated Also known by the acronym PHBA; an organization established in the United States in 1941 to collect, record, preserve the blood purity and improve the breeding of Palomino horses (q.v.); primarily a color registry with pedigree a secondary requirement.

Palouse Pony *see* APPALOOSA

Palousy *see* APPALOOSA

palpate To examine using the sense of touch.

pancake *see* ENGLISH SADDLE

pancreas A gland located in the area of the stomach which secretes digestive enzymes into the intestine and insulin into the blood.

panel (1) Racing slang; one furlong (q.v.). (2) A hunting term; two thin, flat pieces of wood, generally oak, 16 feet (4.8 m) long or less, placed horizontally, onto triangular frames on either end positioned at right angles over the top of barb wire fences; the height of the panels may vary from 3 to 3-1/2 feet (91 cm–1 m) with a spread at the bottom (on the ground) from 5 to 5-1/2 feet (1.5–8.5 m); used to enable hounds and hunters to cross fence lines safely. (3) Also known as saddle panel; the padded part of the saddle (q.v.) between the saddle tree and the back of the horse; there is one panel on each side of the horse's spine, separated by a channel (q.v.); distributes the weight of the rider evenly over the back of the horse; made in various sizes and shapes and stuffed with different materials including felt and horse hair.

pangaré Refers to coat color pattern; the area over the muzzle, eye, and on the inside of the legs and flanks when a lighter shade than the body color; coloring effect does not change the descriptive name, that is, a blond sorrel is also a pangaré; a Spanish word meaning mealy muzzle.

pannier A wicker basket often used in pairs and carried over the back of a beast of burden; a pack consisting of two bags or cases for carriage by an animal.

pantothenic acid A B-complex vitamin; bacterial synthesis in the intestinal tract is thought to be sufficient to meet the daily dietary requirement of approximately 15 PPM; a component of coenzyme A, which is integral to the metabolism of fat, carbohydrates, and some amino acids; deficiency is uncommon in horses fed good quality hay or pasture.

Papach-oinu A ten-minute Russian equestrian sport conducted on a playing field, during which each rider attempts to snatch as many caps as possible off the heads of the other riders without losing his own.

paper Also known as shredded paper; a substance manufactured from rag, wood, or other vegetable fiber reduced to a pulp, shredded, and used as bedding (q.v.) material; is absorbent, dust free, and the carbon content in the ink reduces odors; may be pelletized to improve manageability.

paper face A face marking (q.v.); said of a horse with a completely white head; different than a bonnet (q.v.).

parabola The figurative arc made by a horse from the point of takeoff to the point of land-ing when he jumps an obstacle.

parallel *see* PARALLEL BARS

parallel bars Also known as a parallel; a jumping obstacle consisting of two sets of posts and rails jumped as a single element.

paralytic myoglobinuria *see* EXERCISE RELATED MYOPATHY

paralytic rabies Also known as dumb rabies; a rabies (q.v.) condition characterized by early paralysis of the throat and masseter muscles, profuse salivation, inability to swallow, a lack of aggression or viciousness, paralysis progressing rapidly to all body parts, coma, and death within a few hours.

Paranoplocephala mamillana A species of tapeworm (q.v.) varying in length from 3 to inches (8-15 cm) and found in the small intestine and the stomach; in light infestations, no signs of disease are present, while in heavy infestations digestive disturbances may occur.

parasite A plant or animal living in or on a living organism, often injuring the host.

parasitoid Predators that feed on flies (q.v.); tiny, non-stinging members of the wasp family which lay their eggs in fly pupae, the juveniles of which consume the pupae before they are able to develop wings and fly; used in biological fly control.

parasympathetic nervous system That section of the autonomic nervous system (q.v.) made up of nerves (q.v.) arising in the sacral and cranial regions of the body; responsible for slowing the heart beat, contracting the pupils, dilating the blood vessels, and in general functions in contrast to the sympathetic nervous system (q.v.).

parcel carter *see* VANNER

parcours A show-jumping or driving course.

pariani *see* ALL PURPOSE SADDLE

parier mutuel *see* PARI-MUTUEL

parietal bones Those bones which comprise the top of the horse's skull.

pari-mutuel Previously known as parier

mutuel or Paris mutuals; a racing term; the French equivalent of the English tote or totalizator (q.v.) developed in 1865; a system of betting on a horse race in which those who bet on the winning and placing horses divide the total money wagered in proportion to their bet, less a small percentage for track management and taxes; in many countries, this system is the only legal form of government-controlled, oncourse betting on races.

pari-mutuel field Also known as field; a racing term; said of two or more lightly regarded horses grouped in a single, parimutuel (q.v.) betting entry; occurs when there are more starters than there are betting units provided by the pari-mutuel equipment.

pari-mutuel pool Also known as mutuel pool or pool; a racing term; the total amount bet to win (q.v.), place (q.v.), or show (q.v.) in a horserace or the amount bet on a daily double (q.v.), exacta (q.v.), quinella (q.v.), etc.

Paris mutuals *see* PARI-MUTUEL

park coach *see* DRAG

park course An antiquated British term; any steeplechase course in Britain other than Aintree (q.v.).

parked out A harness racing term; said of a trotter (q.v.) or pacer (q.v.) when the positions of his rivals prevent him from reaching the inside rail, thus forcing him to the outside where he must cover more ground; such a horse rarely wins a race.

park hack A classification of hack (q.v.) competed in hack classes; comes as close as possible to having perfect conformation, gaits, manners, and behavior when compared with other hacks.

park phaeton Also known as lady's phaeton, George IV, or Peter's phaeton; a light, elegant, open, horse-drawn vehicle of the phaeton (q.v.) type adapted for park driving; frequently had a rumble seat and a falling hood and was drawn by a single horse in shafts or a pair in pole gear (q.v.).

park trot A balanced, showy trot (q.v.) having collection and high action; the forelegs are raised until the forearm is horizontal, if not higher; the hind legs are active and flexed as much as the forelegs.

parlay Also known as accumulator bet or parlay bet; a racing term; a multi-race bet in which the winnings earned on the first race are subsequently wagered on each succeeding race.

parlay bet *see* PARLAY

parallel bars *see* SQUARE OXER

parallel bit *see* FENNERS BIT

parrot jaw *see* OVER-SHOT JAW

parrot mouth *see* OVER-SHOT JAW

Part A racing term; a word used by the International Cataloguing Standards Committee to separate races held in different countries for sales cataloguing purposes; races held in Part I countries (q.v.) are accepted for graded (q.v.) and black-type (q.v.) purposes; races held in Part II countries (q.v.) are accepted for black-type purposes only, without group or grade designations; races held in Part III countries (q.v.) are not accepted for cataloguing purposes.

Part-Bred Arab Any Arab (q.v.) having a minimum of 25 percent and as much as 50 percent Arab blood, the balance being blood of any breed other than Thoroughbred (q.v.).

Part I countries A racing term; a group of countries consisting of Argentina, Australia, Brazil, Canada, Chile, France, Germany, Great Britain, Ireland, Italy, New Zealand, Peru, South Africa, United States, and Hong Kong (the International Cup only), and Japan (the Japan Cup only) which the International Cataloguing Standards Committee groups to separate horse races held in different countries for cataloguing purposes.

Part II countries A racing term; a grouping of counties consisting of Belgium, Hong Kong (except the Hong Kong International Cup), India, Japan (except the Japan Cup), Malaysia, Mexico, Panama, Puerto Rico, Scandinavia, Singapore, Spain, Uruguay, and Venezuela which the International Cataloguing Standards Committee groups to separate horse races held in different countries for cataloguing purposes.

Part III countries A racing term; a grouping of countries consisting of all countries not included in Part I (q.v.) or Part II (q.v.) which the International Cataloguing Standards Committee groups to separate horse races held in different countries for cataloguing purposes.

part color Refers to color; any coat consisting of more than one color, e.g., piebald (q.v.), skewbald (q.v.), or spotted.

Parthian shot To shoot an arrow backwards from the the back of a galloping horse, as in pretend retreat; said of the Parthians – considered the most expert horsemen of the ancient world – who, during the middle of the 3rd century BC, won many victories using this technique.

partial lethal Any disease or condition genetically transmitted to the foal which rarely results in death of the foal at any time after its birth, but which may result in restricted use or a shortened life span.

parturition Also known as foaling, labor birth, or confinement; the process of giving birth including labor and delivery; occurs in four stages: a few days before foaling softening of the bones (q.v.) and waxing (q.v.), the night of foaling, the mare will look for a spot to foal, milk begins to run, and uterine contractions begin pushing the two front legs and nose of the foal to the vaginal opening, the water breaks and the foal is forced out of the vaginal canal, and the foal is fully delivered, but the umbilical cord remains intact.

part wheel A racing term; to use a key horse(s) (q.v.) in different, but not all possible, exotic betting combinations.

pas de deux A dressage term; a freestyle dressage program ridden by two riders.

paso A natural, four-beat, lateral gait unique to the Peruvian Paso (q.v.) in which the forelegs arc, or dish, to the outside as the horse strides forward with the fore and hind legs moving simultaneously; the hind legs take very long, straight strides with the quarters held low and the hocks well under the body; can produce a top speed of 11 to 15 mph (18–24 kmph); the three gait divisions include: the paso corto (q.v.), paso fino (q.v.), and paso largo (q.v.); unlike the lateral movements of other gaited breeds; from the Spanish paso, meaning step.

Paso *see* PERUVIAN PASO AND PASO FINO

paso corto (1) One of three distinct forward speeds of the Paso Fino (q.v.); a natural evenly spaced, easy-traveling four-beat lateral gait with moderate forward speed and extension; collection varies with class requirements; must be performed at a definite change of speed from the Paso Largo (q.v.). (2) One of three divisions of the paso (q.v.) gait unique to the Peruvian Paso (q.v.); the normal easy traveling gait in which the forelegs arc out to the side with each stride.

paso de la muerte One of nine scored events in a charreada (q.v.) in which a charro (q.v.) leaps from the back of his mount to that of a bareback mare who is galloping alongside his mount.

paso fino Also known as paso fino gait; the slow, collected, and elevated display gait unique to the Peruvian Paso (q.v.) in which the forelegs arc out to the side with each stride; one of three divisions of the paso (q.v.).

Paso Fino Also known as America's 500 year old new breed, Paso Fino Horse, Los Caballos de Paso Fino, Paso, or horse with the fine walk; a warmblood descended from the crossing of Barb (q.v.), Andalusian (q.v.), and Spanish jennet breeds; brought to the Dominican Republic by Columbus in the 15th century; used as remount stock for the conquistadors in the early 16th century; selectively developed in Columbia, the Dominican Republic, Puerto Rico and Venezuela before introduction to the United States; is not related to the Peruvian Paso (q.v.); has a naturally occurring, lateral, four-beat gait performed at three speeds with varying degrees of collection: classic fino (q.v.), paso corto (q.v.), and paso largo (q.v.); the gait is unique to the breed and requires strong hock action; footfall is up and down and performed in the same sequence as a natural equine walk, i.e., left rear, left fore, right rear, right fore; the breed is never shown at the trot; stands 13 to 15.2 hands with 13.3 to 14.2 most common; full size is frequently not reached until five years of age; all coat colors occur, with bay, chestnut, gray and black most common; white markings may be present.

paso fino gait *see* PASO FINO

Paso Fino Horse *see* PASO FINO

Paso Fino Horse Association, Inc. An organization founded in the United States to promote, protect, and improve the Paso Fino (q.v.); superseded the Paso Fino Owners and Breeders Association (q.v.) in 1973.

Paso Fino Owners and Breeders Association An organization founded in the United States in 1972 to promote, protect, and improve the Paso Fino (q.v.) breed; superseded by the Paso Fino Horse Association, Inc.(q.v.) in 1973.

paso lano The distinctive high-stepping gait of the Costeño (q.v.).

paso largo (1) One of three distinct forward speeds of the Paso Fino (q.v.); an evenly spaced four-beat lateral gait with rapid forward motion obtained by quickened footfall and some lengthening of the stride; performed at a definite change of speed from the paso corto (q.v.); although speeds of 15 to 20 mph (24–32 kmph) are not uncommon, forward speed varies with each horse. (2) One of three divisions of the paso (q.v.) gait unique to the Peruvian Paso (q.v.); an extended, fast gait in which the horse may achieve speeds up to 16 mph (26 kmph); the normal easy traveling gait in which the forelegs arc to the outside with each forward stride.

pass *see* TWO TRACK

passade A movement performed on two tracks (q.v.) in which the horse, traveling on a straight line, makes a small demi-volte (q.v.) and changes leads (q.v.).

passage Also known as the Spanish step; a shortened, very elevated, cadenced, and collected trot (q.v.) with accentuated flexion of the knees and hocks and an extended moment of suspension as each pair of diagonal legs is raised; the hindquarters (q.v.) are more engaged than at other trots; a low air (q.v.) High School movement (q.v.) taught under saddle; has more impulsion and balance than the piaffe (q.v.); from the Italian passagiare meaning to walk or promenade.

passe *see* PACE

passing gaited Said of a horse who trots with his hind feet trotting wider than the fore.

passive immunity Resistance to disease or infection provided by antibodies (q.v.) produced in an immune animal and transferred to one which was not previously immune, e.g., the immunity provided to a foal by the mare through the colostrum (q.v.) in her milk.

passive transfer Movement of existing antibodies (q.v.) from one animal to another, as by means of injection.

pasteboard track A racing term; an exceptionally fast racing surface; a thin, hard, exceptionally fast racing surface; generally results in faster track times than other surfaces.

past mark of the mouth *see* AGED HORSE

pastern (1) The portion of the leg between the fetlock joint and the coronary band (q.v.) of the hoof. (2) *see* PASTERN BONES. (3) Also known as white pastern or full pastern; a leg marking (q.v.) consisting of white extending from the coronary band (q.v.) to just below the fetlock (q.v.).

pastern bone Also known as P1, PI, first phalanx, long pastern bone, long pastern, or os suffraginis; the long bone forming the bottom half of the fetlock joint (q.v.).

pastern bones The long pastern (q.v.) and short pastern (q.v.) bones which provide structural support between the fetlock and hoof.

pastern joint The joint (q.v.) between the long and short pastern bones (q.v.).

pasture (1) Also known as keep; ground covered with native or cultivated grasses and grass-legume mixes upon which animals graze. (2) Also known as at pasture; to maintain a horse in a fenced area on ground covered with native or cultivated grasses and grass-legume mixes, as in "the horse is at pasture."

pastured Said of a horse at pasture (q.v.).

patch Refers to coat color; a well-defined irregular area of coat hair differing in color from the body.

patent leather Also known as japanned leather; a high-gloss leather made from specially treated, tanned, varnished hides.

patent infundibulum A painful infection in the cup of the incisor which ultimately leaves the tooth with an open center.

patent safety Said of a hunter (q.v.); to

carry the rider safely.

paternal grandam The mother of a horse's sire.

pathological shoe *see* THERAPEUTIC SHOE

pathological shoeing Any specialized shoeing technique used to correct or remedy a disease or injury of the foot or leg, e.g., founder (q.v.) or bruised heels (q.v.).

pathology The science dealing with the nature of diseases, their causes, symptoms, and effects on the organism.

pato *see* EL PATO

patrol judge A racing term; any of a number of officials who monitor the progress of a horserace from different locations around the track.

patten shoe (1) Also known as rest shoe; a bar shoe (q.v.); the heels are left high and connected at the base by a solid bar that raises the heel of the foot and prevents it from sinking into the ground as the tendon heals; the heels of the horseshoe may be lowered; used in the treatment of damaged flexor tendons; functions as an extreme wedge shoe. (2) *see* STIFLE SHOE

patterned leopard Refers to coat color pattern; a distinct type of leopard (q.v.) spotting in which the spots flow out of the flank and over the entire body of the horse.

pattern race *see* GROUP RACE

pay off *see* DIVIDEND

pay for a dead horse Also known as work for a dead horse; to perform work for which payment has already been made.

PCV The acronym for packed cell volume (q.v.).

peacock A horse possessed of style, color, and presence who thus attracts attention.

peacock neck Said of a horse having a very high neck carriage, the head being bent strongly at the poll.

Peacock safety iron A commonly used children's stirrup (q.v.); designed to release the foot in the event of a fall; a standard hunting iron design in which the outer metal side is replaced with a thick rubber band hooked to the top and bottom of the iron; in an emergency, the rubber band disconnects from the iron and releases the foot.

peanut meal A high protein, high energy concentrate produced from the residue of peanuts after oil extraction; although the protein content is equivalent to that of soybean meal, it is more expensive and has only half the lysine content; has a short shelf life and may go rancid or become moldy within six to eight weeks; available as hulled peanut meal (q.v.) or unhulled peanut meal (q.v.).

peanut skin The outer, protective layer of a peanut; although a good source of nitrogen, it is of limited nutritional value and palatability to most horses due to the high tannin content.

peas A variable annual leguminous vine, *Pisum sativum*, cultivated for its round, smooth, or wrinkled edible protein-rich seeds; have a high energy content and are fed split, crushed, or micronized.

peck Said of a horse who stumbles, as before a jump.

peck at a jump Said of a horse who jumps slowly over an obstacle, to the extent of almost falling.

pedal American slang; a stirrup (q.v.).

pedal bone *see* THIRD PASTERN

pedigree A record of the ancestry of an animal; lineage; generally recorded in a stud book with the male pedigree identified on the top line (q.v.), the female on the bottom line (q.v.).

pedigree breeding To breed horses selected on the basis of individual merit and ancestry.

peel Also known as peeling; a cutting term; said of a cow; to split away from the rider to return to the herd as the rider drives through it.

peeling *see* PEEL

Pegasus The mythical winged horse, made from the body of Medusa, who caused the stream Hippocrene to spring from Mount Helicon with a single blow of his hoof; after he created the stream, he was captured and ridden off by Bellerophon who used a golden bridle; later, Pegasus threw Bellerophon and flew into outer space where he became the northern constellation bearing his name; a Greek word meaning strong.

pegs *see* STUDS

Pegu Pony A small, hardy Indian pony.

Pelethronius The former King of Lapithae, Thessaly, said to have invented bridles and saddles.

pelham *see* PELHAM BIT

pelham Arabian *see* ALCOCK ARABIAN

pelham bit Also known as pelham; a single-piece bit with cheeks that combines the action of a snaffle (q.v.) and a curb (q.v.) in one bit; designed to be used with either one or two sets of reins, a curb chain, and sometimes a lip strap; the snaffle reins are always heavier than the curb reins; the snaffle action of the bit acts on the lips, bars, and tongue to guide the horse and lift the head while the curb action acts on the poll (q.v.) for control and to achieve the head set; if the mouthpiece has a port (q.v.), the curb action will also act on the roof of the horse's mouth; differs from a curb bit in that it has a dee-cheek on either end of the bit to which the snaffle reins are attached

pelham bridle Any bridle fitted with a pelham bit.

pelleting The process by which moistened supplements and processed roughages are heated (to 40 to 230° F) and forced through dies that create uniformly shaped nuggets which are used as feed.

pellets A compressed, usually cylindrically shaped, commercial feed available in four basic types: (1) pelleted single ingredient such as alfalfa, (2) pelleted grain mixture, (3) pelleted supplement containing high levels of protein, minerals, and vitamins, and (4) pelleted ration containing roughage and grain in a mixture that meets all of the nutritional requirements of the horse; reduces feed storage requirements, decreases the cost of transportation due to reduced bulk, reduces dust, may greatly reduce the appearance of hay belly (q.v.), prevents the horse from sorting out its feed, and reduces the possibility of over or underfeeding supplements.

Pellier, Jules Charles A Parisian riding master active in the 1830s who invented the leaping head (q.v.) which revolutionized the sidesaddle (q.v.).

pelt The skin of an animal with the hair or wool attached.

pelvic Of, relating to, or located in or near the pelvis (q.v.).

pelvic girdle The bony, cartilaginous arch that supports the hind limbs.

pelvic limb Either of the two hind limbs.

pelvis A basin-shaped structure in the skeleton of the horse formed by the pelvic girdle (q.v.) and adjoining bones of the spine which rests on the femurs.

penalty (1) A handicap or punishment assessed for committing an offense. (2) *see* POLO PENALTY

Penalty 1 A polo penalty (q.v.); a handicap assessed for committing an offense in a polo match; an automatic goal for the fouled team; the ends of the field are not changed following penalty award.

Penalty 2 A polo penalty (q.v.); a handicap assessed for committing an offense in a polo match; a free hit from the center of the 30-yard line, nearest the fouling team's goal, or if preferred by the team captain, from the point the foul occurred, to an undefended goal; all of the fouling team are positioned behind their end-line (q.v.)

Penalty 3 A polo penalty (q.v.); a handicap assessed for committing an offense in a polo match; a free hit from the center of the 40-yard line to an undefended goal.

Penalty 4 A polo penalty (q.v.); a handicap assessed for committing an offense in a polo match; a free hit from the center of the 60-yard line to a defended goal for the fouled team; no member of the fouling team shall be closer than 30 yards to the ball when the umpire says "play."

Penalty 5 A polo penalty (q.v.); a handicap assessed for committing an offense in a polo match; a free hit on the goal for the fouled team from the point of the infraction or from midfield.

Penalty 6 Also known as safety; a polo penalty (q.v.); a handicap assessed for committing an offense in a polo match when a defending player hits the ball across his own backline; a free hit from a point on the 60-yard line opposite where the ball crossed the line for the fouled team; both teams are free to position themselves anywhere on the field, except no member of the fouling team shall be closer than 30 yards to the ball when hit.

Penalty 7 A polo penalty (q.v.); a handicap assessed for committing an offense in a polo match; removal of a player from the fouling team whose handicap is nearest above that of the player disabled by a foul; the removed player is selected by the Captain of the fouled team.

Penalty 8 A polo penalty (q.v.); a handicap assessed for committing an offense in a polo match; a mount of the fouling team is ordered off the field.

Penalty 9 A polo penalty (q.v.); a handicap assessed for committing an offense in a polo match; forfeiture of the match.

Penalty 10 A polo penalty (q.v.); a handicap assessed for committing an offense in a polo match in which the Umpire may exclude a player for all or any portion of the remaining periods of the game.

penalty goal A polo penalty; awarded when a player commits a dangerous or deliberate foul in the vicinity of his team's goal box to prevent a score by the opponent; the team fouled is given a goal and the ball is thrown in 10 yards in front of the fouled team's goal; the teams do not switch ends.

penalty point Any point(s) deducted from a competitor's score for assessed infractions.

penalty zone The rectangular area surrounding a cross country obstacle in a Combined Training Event (q.v.); extends 33 feet (10 m) before the jump, and 66 feet (20 m) after the jump and to a width of 33 feet (10 m) on each side of the boundary flags marking the limits of the obstacle; only faults occurring within the penalty zone are marked against the competitor.

pendulous lip Said of the lip of the horse when it hangs low and lifeless.

Peneia One of three remaining pony breeds indigenous to Greece, bred in the district of Eleia in the Peloponnese; more refined than the Skyros (q.v.) or Pindos (q.v.) which may indicate Arab (q.v.) influence; stands 10.1 to 14 hands, may have a bay, black, chestnut, or gray coat, is an easy keeper, frugal, hardy, and quiet; used for riding, light farm work, and packing

penetrating crack Also known as a deep crack; any fissure or crack in the hoof that exposes the sensitive laminae or results in lameness.

penis The male copulatory organ formed primarily of erectile tissue which also serves as the male organ of urination.

penning (1) The annual roundup of wild horses to remove yearling colts and old stallions to reduce the risk of interbreeding. (2) *see* TEAM PENNING

Penn-Marydel Foxhounds, Inc. An organization incorporated in Pennsylvania, United States in 1934 to promote and preserve the strain of foxhounds (q.v.) bred and hunted for generations in the southeastern sections of Pennsylvania, Maryland, and Delaware; the name of the strain and association derived from a contraction of these three states.

perch (1) The main timber in the undercarriage of a horse-drawn carriage; runs from the front of the vehicle to the rear and curves slightly downward. (2) Said of the rider; to ride in the English saddle with the weight borne on the pubis rather than the seat bones; the result of an arched back.

perch bolt A pin connecting the perch (q.v.) to the fore axle and transom and thus to the horse-drawn vehicle.

Percheron A coldblood breed originating in the Le Perche region of Normandy, France, from which the name derived; descended from ancient indigenous heavy-draft breeds crossed with Norman (q.v.) and Oriental blood sometime around the 8th century AD; is well-proportioned, heavy, stands 15.2 to 17.2 hands, and most commonly has a gray, typically dappled, coat although black and roan occur rarely; has a full mane and tail, fine head, straight profile, slightly arched neck, short legs with broad joints and no feather (q.v.), powerful hindquarters, and hard, blue-horn hooves; has great freedom and grace of movement; is quiet and docile, but energetic; the French-kept stud book, maintained by the Société Hippique Percheronne, goes back to 1883; since 1911 the stud book has been restricted exclusively to horses from registered parents; is used for draft and farm work and has recently been crossed with Thoroughbred (q.v.) and Thoroughbred-type horses to produce hunter, jumper, and dressage mounts.

Percheron Association An organization founded in the United States in 1876 as the Norman Percheron Association (q.v.) and renamed to its present name in 1877; chartered to maintain the stud book and promote breeding and use of the Percheron Horse (q.v.).

Percheron Horse Association of America An organization founded in the United States which superseded the Percheron Society of America (q.v.) in 1934; chartered to promote and preserve the Percheron (q.v.) breed and maintain a national stud book.

Percheron Society of America An organization founded in 1905 in the United States to establish registration standards for the Percheron (q.v.); continued until 1934, at which time it was subsumed by the Percheron Horse Association of America (q.v.).

perfecta Also known as exacta or exactor in Canada; a racing term; a betting option in which the bettor (q.v.) selects the first two horses under the wire (q.v.) in the exact order.

Performance Thoroughbred Registry Also known by the acronym PTR; a registry established in the United States in 1994 by The Jockey Club (q.v.) to recognize Thoroughbreds (q.v.) and Thoroughbred crosses which compete off the racetrack and to document the performance and pedigree records of non-racing Thoroughbreds and mixes.

period *see* CHUKKER

periodic ophthalmia *see* MOON BLINDNESS

periople A thin, varnish-like tissue produced by the horn-producing cell layer of the perioplic ring (q.v.); generally extends about 3/4 to 1 inch (19-25 mm) down the wall from the coronet, except at the heel where it blends in with the frog; protects the sensitive coronary

band (q.v.) at the junction of the skin and hoof and has the same consistency as the horny frog; the underside flakes off and is carried down as the hoof wall grows out to produce hoof varnish.

perioplic band *see* PERIOPLIC RING

perioplic ring Also known as perioplic band; a narrow ring located just above the coronary band (q.v.) and next to the hair line of the coronet which secretes the periople (q.v.); composed of papillae like those of the coronary band, but smaller in size.

periosteum A thin, tough, fibrous membrane which covers the entire length of the bone; overlays cells capable of becoming bone-forming cells and attaches tendons and ligaments to the bone.

periostitis An inflammation of the periosteum (q.v.) resulting from a direct blow to the periosteum (q.v.) or a lifting of the periosteum away from the underlying bone; the bone-forming cells respond by creating new bone; when the inflammation subsides, a bony lump generally remains; commonly occurs in the small and large metatarsal and metacarpal bones.

periplantar shoe *see* CHARLIER SHOE

peristalsis A series of wave-like contractions of the smooth muscles of the gut, moving the contents of these organs through the body to be processed.

peritonitis Inflammation of the membrane lining of the abdominal walls and covering the abdominal organs; difficult to diagnose.

perlino Refers to coat color; a nearly white or cream-colored coat having slightly red or blue points; the horse will have blue eyes.

permanent premolars *see* WOLF TEETH

permanent teeth Any of the teeth that supplant the deciduous teeth (q.v.); include the first, second, and third molars (q.v.), wolf teeth (q.v.), first, second, and permanent third incisors (q.v.), and the second, third, fourth, and permanent second premolars (q.v.); in place when the horse is about five years old.

permanent white A registry classification for the American White (q.v.); a white horse produced from a dam and sire of registered stock of any breed; proof of reproducibility of color is not a requirement.

Persian *see* PERSIAN ARAB

Persian Arab Also known as a Persian; an Arab (q.v.) bred and raised in Iran; a strong, athletic horse standing 14.1 to 15.1 hands and having a bay, chestnut, or gray, rarely black, coat; more robust than other Arab strains, but has a similar head and body lines; protected from the introduction of other than Persian Arab blood and as such, a stud book separate from other strains is maintained; two breed types are derived from the Persian Arab, the Jaf (q.v.) from Kurdistan and the Darashouri (q.v.) from the Fars region.

Persian Horse *see* PLATEAU PERSIAN

Peruvian Paso Also known as the Caballo Peruano de Paso, Paso, or the Peruvian Stepping Horse; a warmblood originating in Peru in the mid-1500s; descended from Spanish stock put to Barb (q.v.), Friesian (q.v.), jennet (q.v.), and Andalusian (q.v.) mares; to systematically develop its characteristic gait, known as the paso, the breed has been very selectively bred and no outside blood has been introduced for several centuries; the only naturally gaited breed in the world that can guarantee its gait to 100 percentage of its offspring; the gaits are not induced or aided in any way by artificial training or devices and include the paso (q.v.), paso corto (q.v.), paso fino (q.v.), and paso largo (q.v.); the action of the breed is known as termino (q.v.); shown without shoes and with a short, natural hoof; can reach speeds up to 16 mph (26 kmph), stands 14.1 to 15.1 hands, and may have a coat of any solid color, as well as gray, and roan with bay and chestnut coats most common; has great stamina, a naturally low-set tail, a well-sprung and very deep rib cage, medium head, short to medium-length back, and a fairly short, well-muscled neck; is not related to the Paso Fino (q.v.).

Peruvian Stepping Horse *see* PERUVIAN PASO

pesade A High School (q.v.) movement performed in place in which the total mastery of balance and the ultimate in collection are achieved; the horse raises his forelegs off the ground and folds them at a sharp angle while lowering his hocks under his center of gravity

(q.v.); the body is maintained at an angle of 45 degrees for several seconds while the hind legs are held firmly on the ground so that the horse does not mark time with his haunches.

petechial fever *see* PURPURA HEMORRHAGICA

petechial hemorrhage *see* PURPURA HEMORRHAGICA

Peter's Brougham A horse-drawn carriage of the Brougham (q.v.) type designed with angular lines.

Peter's phaeton *see* PARK PHAETON

phaeton A comfortable, swift, light, four-wheeled, horse-drawn buggy used in 18-century Western Europe for exercising and driving purposes; at first characterized by large wheels, a driver's seat protected by a falling hood, high bodywork, and seated one or two passengers; drawn by a single horse, pairs, or teams of four and six and hung on cee or elbow springs; later models were both smaller and more substantial, adapted for pony draft, with rearward, crosswise seating and improved suspension; many versions evolved including the basket phaeton (q.v.), pill box phaeton (q.v.), high-flyer phaeton (q.v.), park phaeton (q.v.), mail phaeton (q.v.), stanhope phaeton (q.v.), and spider phaeton (q.v.); the name derived from phaeton, who drove the sun chariot in classical mythology.

phalange *see* PHALANX

phalanges More than one phalanx (q.v.).

phalanx Also known as phalange; any of the primary digital bones of the foot.

phenylbutazolidan *see* PHENYLBUTAZONE

phenylbutazone Also known as phenylbutazone, butazolidin, butazone, or bute; a non-steroidal anti-inflammatory analgesic drug (q.v.); reduces pain and inflammation in the treatment of traumatic or inflammatory musculoskeletal disorders and lameness; may cause gastrointestinal irritation and is banned for use in most competition horses.

PHF The acronym for Potomac horse fever (q.v.).

phill horse *see* SHAFT HORSE

phosphorus A solid, non-chemical element, the second most important mineral in the body of the horse; in conjunction with calcium (q.v.), is required for the mineralization of bone including bone formation, growth, maintenance, and repair and comprises 75 percent of the minerals in the horse's body and approximately 90 percent of the minerals in the skeleton; high levels inhibit calcium availability.

photo finish A racing term; said of a race that is so close it is necessary to review film shot by a narrow-field-of-vision camera located at the finish line to determine the winner; first used to record a photo finish in 1890 at Sheepshead Bay, United States.

photosensitization Also known as blue nose; sensitivity of the horse to the sun resulting from a systemic chemical reaction; a more painful and chronic problem than sunburn (q.v.); excessive amounts of a chemical found in most legumes (q.v.), especially clovers and some weeds, are converted to photosensitive (q.v.) chemicals in the liver of the horse which circulate through the bloodstream, and when exposed to sunlight through unpigmented white skin, react and destroy the tissue; affected areas turn purple prior to the skin sloughing off, after which painful and persistent scabs and scars develop.

photosynthetic Pertaining to the synthesis of chemical compounds with the aid of radiant energy as a source of hydrogen (as water) in the chlorophyll-containing tissues of plants exposed to light, and in the formation of carbohydrates from carbon dioxide.

physeal plates *see* EPIPHYSEAL PLATES

physeal dysplasia *see* PHYSITIS

physes Plural of physis (q.v.).

physic ball *see* MEDICINE BALL

physiology The science dealing with the normal function of animal organisms or their organs, e.g., the function of the body.

physiological shoeing Also known as normal shoeing; to balance the hooves and attach horseshoes (q.v.) taking into account the physiological movements of the foot.

physis *see* EPIPHYSEAL PLATE

physitis Also known as epiphysitis, physeal dysplasia, or dysplasia of the growth plate; pain associated with abnormal activity in the growth plates (q.v.) of certain long bones in rapidly growing young horses, commonly involving the distal (q.v.) ends of the radius, tibia, third metacarpal/metatarsal bones, or the proximal aspect of the first phalanx; is most common in yearlings; characterized by slight swelling and heat around the growth plate, boxy looking affected joints, and in some cases, lameness; may be due to malnutrition, conformational defects, faulty hoof growth, fetal malpositioning, compression of the growth plate, and toxicosis (q.v.).

piaffe A ground movement in which the horse performs a cadenced trot (q.v.) in place; the trot has no forward movement and has moments of suspension between each diagonal step; the forelegs are light and elevated higher than the hind feet; involves less leg elevation than at the passage (q.v.); the most collected of all dressage (q.v.) movements and the foundation of all High School movements (q.v.).

piales *see* PIALES EN EL LIENZO

piales en el lienzo Also known as piales; a Mexican rodeo event; specifically, a type of horse tripping (q.v.); one of nine scored events in a charreada (q.v.) in which a mare is goaded out of a pen into a long, wide chute leading to a circular arena; before she reaches the end of the chute, a mounted charro (q.v.) gallops up behind and lassos (q.v.) her hind legs; the charro then takes a wrap of the lariat around the saddle horn and attempts to stop the mare within a specified distance after she leaves the chute; points are awarded based upon the difficulty of the throw; now illegal in some states in the United States.

pic A wooden-handled lance used by a picador (q.v.) in a corrida de toros (q.v.); is approximately 17 feet (5 m) long having a sharp point and a 4 inch (10 cm) crusetta attached at right angles to the distal end; the point is about the size of a little finger and 3 inches (7.5 cm) long; the crusetta prevents the point from penetrating the shoulder muscles of the bull too deeply.

picador A participant in a corrida de toros (q.v.) mounted on a heavily padded horse; responsible to poke the heavy shoulder muscles of the bull with a pic (q.v.) to weaken them sufficiently to cause the bull to lower its head and, therefore, be fought more easily; historically used Lusitano (q.v.) mounts, but in today's modern bullrings the Andalusian (q.v.) and Lusitano are almost used equally with Thoroughbred (q.v.), Azteca (q.v.), and Quarter Horses (q.v.) also used.

pick A racing term; a multi-race bet in which the bettor (q.v.) selects winners of all included races; the most common wagers of this type are pick three (q.v.), pick six (q.v.), and pick nine (q.v.).

pickaxe *see* PICK AXE TEAM

pick axe team Also known as pick axe; a team of horses consisting of three leaders and two wheelers (q.v.) or two leaders and one wheeler used to pull a horse-drawn vehicle.

pick up a lead Said of the horse; to initiate a lead with either the right or left foreleg as appropriate.

pick up his face A western term; said of a rider, to ask the horse for increased collection and more contact with the bit.

pick up hounds A hunting term; to move the hounds onto a new line (q.v.).

pickup man A rodeo term; a mounted arena official who assists bareback and saddle bronc (q.v.) competitors in dismounting from their horses when the required ride time ends.

pick nine A racing term; a wager in which the bettor (q.v.) attempts to select the winners of nine consecutive races.

pick six Also known as pic six or five-ten; a racing term; a wager in which the bettor (q.v.) attempts to select the winners of six consecutive races; if no bettor selects all six winners, a small percentage of the pool may be distributed to those who picked five winners out of the six with the balance of the pool carried over to the following day's pick six.

pick three Also known as daily triple; a racing term; a wager in which the bettor (q.v.) attempts to select the winners of three consecutive races.

pick up (1) A hunting term; to obtain the attention and regain control of the hounds (q.v.). (2) To obtain the use of a horse(s) for use in competitions, as in "to pick up a ride."

picnic races Race meetings held in Australia's Outback in which amateur riders and their mounts compete for small prizes on primitive bushland racetracks (q.v.)

pic six *see* PICK SIX

piebald Refers to coat color; a black horse with tobiano (q.v.), overo (q.v.), sabino (q.v.), or splashed asymmetric patterns of white; the lines between the black and white are well-defined.

Piebald One of three types of the semi-wild Basque (q.v.) indigenous to the Basque region of France; stands 11 to 13 hands and is very hardy.

pied Refers to hound (q.v.) coat color; an asymmetric pattern of color on a cream or fawn-colored body, head, legs, and stern; characteristic of English-bred hounds; differs from badger-pied (q.v.) and hare-pied (q.v.).

pigeon-toed Also known as pin toes, toed in, or toe in; a congenital condition in which the toes of one or both of the horse's forefeet are turned towards each other when viewed from the front; usually accompanied by base narrow (q.v.) condition; may cause the forelegs to swing out during movement as in paddling (q.v.) resulting in stress on the outside and inside of the fetlock and pastern joints respectively.

pig-eyed Said of a horse having small, deep-set, narrow, squinty eyes with thick lids.

piggin' string *see* PIGGING STRING

pigging string Also known as pigging string or pigging strap; a roping term; a length of twisted nylon or cotton with a loop woven in one end, used by calf ropers to tie the feet of the calf; available in different strengths and lengths.

pigging strap *see* PIGGING STRING

pig-mouthed Also known as swine chopped; a hunting term; a hound with an undershot (q.v.) lower jaw.

pigskin The skin of the pig or hog, leather made from it; used in the manufacture of some saddles.

pig sticking The sport of hunting wild boar

from horseback using a spear; developed by British officers stationed in India in the early 1800s.

pigtail The small rope by which horses strung in a pack string (q.v.) are connected to one another; is fastened to the rear end of the saddle of the horse or mule in front and to the halter of the animal following, and so on.

piker A driver who contrived to bypass a toll-gate without paying.

pill (1) A small, usually globular or rounded, mass of medical substance designed to be swallowed.(2) *see* NUMBER BALL

pillar reins *see* CROSS TIES

pillars Heavy posts set wide enough apart to accommodate a horse, between which the horse is tied; used for centuries to increase balance and rhythm and to teach levade (q.v.) and other airs above the ground (q.v.), a practice used more commonly in Europe than Britain or the United States.

pillars of the stud book The three Arab (q.v.) sires to which all Thoroughbreds can trace their lineage: Byerley Turk (q.v.), Godolphin Arabian (q.v.), and Darley Arabian.

Pill Box Slang; a small, horse-drawn vehicle of the phaeton (q.v.) or chariot (q.v.) type used by a doctor on his daily rounds during the 18th century; drawn by a single horse in shafts.

Pill Box Phaeton A horse-drawn vehicle of the phaeton (q.v.) type; a larger and sturdier version of the pill box (q.v.), having room for one passenger; commonly used in the Atlantic coast states of North America during the 18th century to transport and sell pills and potions.

pillion (1) A cushion or pad placed behind the saddle on a horse upon which another rider sits, especially a woman. (2) To ride on a pillion.

pillion post An antiquated term; a mounting block (q.v.); so called because it was used by ladies who rode in pillion (q.v.) saddles.

pincers *see* INCISORS

pinched back A racing term; said of a jockey caught in a jam of horses who is forced to fall back during the horse race.

Pindos One of three remaining ancient native pony breeds indigenous to Greece, the others being the Skyros (q.v.) and Peneia (q.v.); evolved from native mares put to Oriental stallions; bred in the mountain regions of Thessaly and Epirus; stands 12 to 13 hands, generally has a dark gray coat although bay, black, and brown also occur, is strong, hardy, possessed of exceptional stamina for its size, and is very frugal; used for light farm work, packing, and riding.

pin firing Also known as point firing; to insert extremely hot pointed pins and/or needles into a blemished or unsound area to stimulate circulation and tissue growth; treatment may be graduated from a slight puncturing of the skin to a penetration as deep as the bone; when applied in line pattern, is known as line firing.

pinhooker A racing term; one who buys a racehorse(s) with the intention of reselling him at a profit.

pink (1) A hunting term; the traditional scarlet or red color of the coats worn by huntsmen. (2) *see* PINK COAT

pink coat Also known as scarlet coat or pink; a hunting term; the traditional scarlet or red hunt coat worn by huntsmen (q.v.) and competitors participating in the upper level jumper show ring.

pinkeye *see* EQUINE VIRAL ARTERITIS

pinto (1) Refers to coat color; an asymmetrical pattern of well-defined white patches on any base color; no white hairs are mixed into the colored areas; several specific patterns occur: tobiano (q.v.), overo (q.v.), sabino (q.v.), splashed white (q.v.), with overo and tobiano occurring most commonly. (2) *see* PINTO

Pinto Also known as Indian pony; an American-bred warmblood of a color type which is selectively bred and recognized as a distinct breed; descended from Barb (q.v.) stock brought to America by Spanish conquistadors in the 16th century crossed with native Mustangs (q.v.); of two patterns: tobiano (q.v.) which occurs most commonly and overo (q.v.); according to legend, considered by the American Indian to have magical powers, possessed of natural camouflage, and especially capable in war; height varies, but registered horses must stand more than 14 hands, ponies 8.5 to 14 hands, and miniatures under 8.5 hands or 34 inches (86 cm); coat coloring is either piebald (q.v.) or skewbald (q.v.); has a sparse mane and tail, the result of selective breeding to prevent entanglement in the undergrowth, pink skin, blue eyes, and white or multi-colored hoof markings; four conformation types are accepted: Stock-type Pinto (q.v.), Hunter-type Pinto (q.v.), Pleasure-type Pinto (q.v.), and Saddle-type Pinto (q.v.); breed characteristics apart from the coat color are poorly defined; an Appaloosa (q.v.) or a horse with Appaloosa ancestry cannot be a Pinto; recognized as a breed in 1963; used for riding and light draft; a Spanish word meaning painted.

Pinto Horse Association of America, Inc., The Also known by the acronym PtHA; an organization founded in Ellington, Connecticut, USA in 1947 and officially incorporated in 1956 to maintain color registries for Pinto (q.v.) horses, ponies, and miniature horses, to improve conformation and breeding, and to increase public interest in the breed; the stud book was started by the American Paint Horse Association (q.v.) in 1963; recognizes four conformation types: Stock-type Pinto (q.v.), Hunter-type Pinto (q.v.), Pleasure-type Pinto (q.v.), and Saddle-type Pinto (q.v.); to qualify for entry in the registry, a horse must have at least one registered parent, with the other parent either Quarter Horse (q.v.) or English Thoroughbred (q.v.); the registry maintains both Breeding Stock and Color Divisions.

Pinto Horse Breeding Stock Division A division of the PtHA (q.v.) registry which records the bloodlines of solid-colored horses with color in their pedigrees or horses who lack sufficient body markings to be registered in the Color Divisions of the registry.

pin toes *see* PIGEON TOED

pinworm A small nematoid worm; of two species in the horse: (1) the relatively harmless and small, *Probstmayria vivipara*, which infests the large intestine and (2) the large white pinworm, *Oxyuris equi*, which is 50 times larger than the small pinworm and may cause anal itching, yet which is also relatively harmless; so called because its slender body terminates in a point.

Pinzgauer *see* NORIKER

Pinzgauer Noriker *see* NORIKER

pipe A hunting term; a branch or hole of a fox's den.

pipe loop *see* BOX KEEPER

pipe collar A harness collar (q.v.) reshaped with a hollow to accommodate the windpipe; used on horses prone to choking.

pipe opener A sharp, short gallop (q.v.) to stimulate the circulatory system and clear the lungs of the horse before extended or fast work.

pipe stall An open enclosure constructed of pipe rails used to contain a horse; vary in size and generally provide a covered manger.

piroplasmosis *see* EQUINE PIROPLASMOSIS

pirouette A High School (q.v.) dressage movement similar to the volte performed in a circle in one place; the horse's forehand and outside hind leg make a 360 degree turn around the inside hind leg; the radius of the circle equaling the length of the horse; ridden in collected walk (q.v.), collected canter (q.v.), or piaffe (q.v.); lightness of the forehand is essential.

pirouette sur le centre *see* TURN ON CENTER

pirouette sur les haunches A movement in which the horse turns around his inner hind leg; the hind leg remains on the spot or scribes a small circle, and a larger outer concentric circle cut with the other legs; the smallest of the turns; corresponds to the half pirouette (q.v.) at the canter; taught and executed at the walk.

pista *see* FINO BOARD

pitch fork *see* FORK no. 2

pit pony Also known as pitter or collier; a British term; the common name for ponies (Shetland [q.v.], Welsh [q.v.], Fell [q.v.], Dartmoor [q.v.], Exmoor [q.v.], Icelandic [q.v.], etc.) used in coal mines to retrieve and haul coal to the surface; used in this capacity for the last three centuries, the last four pit ponies were put into retirement in February, 1994; lived in stables as much as 4 miles (6.4 km) underground during the work week and were turned out to pasture on the weekends.

Pit Ponies' Protection Society An organization founded in Great Britain in 1927 to improve the conditions under which pit ponies (q.v.) or other animals were worked underground; now defunct.

pitter *see* PIT PONY

pivot (1) Also known as pivot on the hindquarters; a western term; a half-turn on the haunches performed at either the canter (q.v.) or gallop (q.v.); the horse swings its forelegs around its stationary inner hind leg. (2) *see* TURN ON THE FOREHAND. (3) *see* TURN ON THE HAUNCHES

pivoted Said of a horse who fails to pick up one of his hind legs when performing a walk pirouette (q.v.).

pivot on the hindquarters *see* PIVOT no. 1

place (1) A racing term; said of a horse, to finish in second position in a race. (2) *see* PLACE BET. (3) A position won in a competition, as to win first place.

place bet Also known as place; a racing term; any wager placed on a horse to finish a race in first or second position.

placed A racing term; said of a horse to finish second or third in a race; not to be confused with place.

placenta Also known as afterbirth or caul; the fetal membranes which develop in the uterus (q.v.) in early pregnancy; connect the unborn fetus to the lining of the mare's uterus by the umbilical cord, nourishes the fetus, and removes waste products from it; formed within the first 15 days of fetal life by the fusion of two embryonic membranes, the chorion and the allantois; within 90 days of fertilization, attaches to the uterine wall; is passed by the mare at foaling.

placentation Development of the placenta (q.v.) and attachment of the fetus (q.v.) to the uterus during pregnancy.

place pool A racing term; the sum of money wagered in a horse race for second place finishers.

placing judge A racing term; one who posts

the order in which horses finish in a race.

plain cheek *see* IN THE CHEEK

plain horseshoe A machine-made or hand forged horseshoe (q.v.) without calks (q.v.) or special features other than creasing through the nail holes.

plain hunting iron *see* HUNTING IRON

plain jointed snaffle *see* JOINTED SNAFFLE

plait (1) To braid; to interweave, as in the locks or strands of the mane or leather. (2) A braid.

plaited reins A rein (q.v.) in which the handpiece and/or the entire length of rein is made of braided or plaited leather; offers improved grip over a smooth rein (q.v.).

plaiting (1) *see* ROPE WALKING. (2) *see* PLAIT

plank A component of a jumping obstacle; a flat, wide piece of wood, painted or natural, supported by standards (q.v.), over which a horse jumps.

plank jump *see* BOARD FENCE

plantar Pertaining to the sole of the hoof or the back of the hind limb from the hock (q.v.) to the hoof.

plantar cushion Also known as digital cushion; a mass of fibro-fatty tissue, filling the space behind the coffin bone and separating it from the frog, which forms the bulb of the heel; functions as a shock absorber for the foot.

Plantation Walking Horse *see* TENNESSEE WALKING HORSE

plate (1) A shallow circular vessel, from which food may be served; used as a prize for winning an equestrian event; generally made of silver or silver plate; usually less valuable than a cup. (2) *see* RACING PLATE

plate-and-screws stabilization A method of stabilizing a fractured leg bone in the horse; a metal plate is placed the length of the bone over the break and attached both above and below the break with screws inserted into the stable portion of the bone; the recovery rate in adult horses using this technique is approximately 6 percent; in some cases now replaced by the state-of-the-art equestrian nail (q.v.).

Plateau Persian Any Arab-type horse indigenous to the plateau regions of Iran; an amalgamation of breeds including the Jaf (q.v.), Darashouri (q.v.), Arab (q.v.), Shiragazi (q.v.), Quashquai (q.v.), Basseri (q.v.), Yamoote, and Bahhtiari; stands about 15 hands, generally has a gray, bay, or chestnut coat, good action, and is strong and surefooted.

plater (1) A farrier who specializes in shoeing race horses, specifically flat track (q.v.) or Thoroughbred (q.v.) and Quarter Horse (q.v.) running horses. (2) Also known as selling plater; a racing term; a horse who runs in cheap claiming races (q.v.); so called because of the silver plates formerly awarded to winners of such races.

Platers Union *see* INTERNATIONAL UNION OF JOURNEYMAN HORSESHOERS OF THE UNITED STATES AND CANADA

play *see* BET

players (1) *see* KEYS. (2) *see* BETTOR

pleasure class A horse show class in which horses or mules are shown at the walk, trot, canter, and backing.

Pleasure-Type Pinto One of four Pinto (q.v.) conformation types developed with specific breed goals and standards in mind; of predominantly Arab (q.v.) or Morgan (q.v.) breeding and build displaying conformation qualities to enable it to be used for a variety of both English and western events; of medium size, has a comparatively horizontal croup, a naturally high tail carriage, and a well-muscled thigh and gaskin.

pleurisy Also known as pleuritis; inflammation of the membrane lining the chest and covering the lungs; characterized by fever, painful and difficult breathing, and fluids in the chest cavity.

pleuritis *see* PLEURISY

pleuropneumonia A debilitating and possibly deadly inflammation of the lungs which causes or is closely followed by pleurisy.

Pleven A warmblood developed in the late 1800s in Pleven, Bulgaria, from which the name derived; descended from Russian Anglo-Arab (q.v.) stallions crossed with purebred Arabs (q.v.) or local halfbred mares; until breed characteristics were fixed, around 1938, only Arab (q.v.) and Gidran (q.v.) stallions were used; after that time Thoroughbred (q.v.) blood was selectively introduced; stands about 15.2 hands, has a chestnut coat, and Arab-like features; a good all-round horse equally suited to light agricultural work, riding, and competitive sports; a natural jumper.

plough (1) *see* PLOW. (2) *see* PLOUGHLAND

ploughland Also known as plough; a hunting term; the fields over which a hunt is conducted.

plow (1) Also spelled plough; to make furrows or turn up the soil. (2) To work with a plow. (3) An agricultural implement for cutting furrows in and turning up the soil.

plow rein *see* DIRECT REIN

plow reining *see* DIRECT REIN

plug (1) A horse of common breeding and poor conformation. (2) A slow moving and tired horse.

PMU The acronym for pregnant mare urine (q.v.).

PMU farm Any facility where mares are maintained for the purpose of urine production and collection from which estrogen is extracted; during the period October through March, the time of highest estrogen levels in the urine of pregnant mares, mares are hooked up around the clock to a harness attached to a funnel that collects the urine from the urethra and carries it down a tube into a one-gallon container; when estrogen levels decrease in the mare's urine prior to birth of a foal (q.v.), around April, the mare is put to pasture (q.v.) at the same facility; following birth she is reimpregnated while pastured with her foal and on October 1 is returned to the collection line; water intake is often restricted to raise urine estrogen concentrations.

pnemo-puncture A type of acupuncture (q.v.); stimulation of precise body points along body meridians (q.v.) of the horse achieved by injection of air into those points; used to control pain, treat internal malfunctions, anesthetize, and reduce stress.

poached A hunting term; said of the footing in front of a jump when cuppy (q.v.), muddy, or cut-up.

pocket (1) A barrel racing (q.v.) term; the turning area between the horse and the barrel; (varies between individual horses. (2) *see* HUNTSMAN'S POCKET, IN THE

pocketed A racing term; said of a horse competing in a race who is surrounded by other horses and unable to increase his speed until an opening presents itself.

podotrochlitis *see* NAVICULAR

point (1) *see* POINT TEAM. (2) A hunting term; the location to which the whippers-in (q.v.) is sent to watch for a fox (q.v.) breaking a covert (q.v.). (3) Also known as point of a run; a hunting term; the distance, as the crow flies, between the two most widely separated points traveled by the hounds (q.v.) while running a fox. (4) Any external area on the horse's body, e.g., hock, nose, flank, etc.

point a cow A cutting term; said of the cutting horse (q.v.) when he focuses on the cow being worked with its ears forward.

point firing *see* PIN FIRING

pointing (1) Said of a resting horse who stands with one foreleg placed further forward than the other; the horse assumes this position to relieve the weight and therefore pressure on the pointed foot; usually indicates there is something wrong with the forward leg, although the horse may alternate the pointed leg if both forefeet are affected; a sign of navicular disease (q.v.). (2) Refers to the action in any gait, but generally the trot, when the horse places the toes of his forefeet on the ground before the heels; normally the horse would strike the ground with the entire flat surface of the foot (toe and heel together); may relieve heel pressure common in navicular disease. (3) A perceptible extension of the stride with little flexion in the leg; a condition common in Thoroughbreds (q.v.), Standardbred (q.v.), and long-strided horses bred and trained for speed.

pointing your leaders *see* POINT THE LEADERS

point of a run *see* POINT no. 3

point of call A racing term; the position of a horse running in a race as noted at different locations on the racetrack (q.v.) and posted on a chart; the point at which the racing position is noted varies with the distance of each race.

point of the croup *see* POINT OF THE HIP

point of the hip Also known incorrectly as point of the croup; the bony prominence and highest spot on the croup (q.v.) of the horse; is located approximately 4 inches (10 cm) behind the last rib and formed by the internal angles of the ileum (q.v.).

point of the shoulder The bony prominence formed by the scapula and humerus of the forearm.

points (1) Also known as points of the horse; the tail, ear rims, mane, tail, and lower legs of the horse; grouped on the basis of color, e.g., black points or nonblack points. (2) Ready-knitted tips for a whip (q.v.).

points of the horse *see* POINTS no. 1

point team Also known as the point; the team (q.v.) of horses positioned in back of the leaders (q.v.) in an eight-horse hitch.

point the leaders Also known as pointing your leaders; said of the coachman (q.v.) when he indicates to the lead horses of a team that a change of direction to the right or left is about to occur by looping or pointing the rein.

point-to-point Also known as hunt races; a mounted competition first held in Great Britain several centuries ago where it still remains popular as an amateur sport; competitors race from one place, or point, to another over open fields and paddocks rather than on a race or steeple course, the average distance being 3-1/2 miles (5.6 km); generally restricted to horses which have been regularly hunted with a recognized pack of hounds and for which the owner has obtained and registered a Master of Hounds' certificate.

poison (1) Any agent that chemically destroys health or life upon contact or absorption by an organism; may be slow acting, occurring over a period of days or weeks, or fast acting. (2) To destroy by means of poison. (3) To put poison on or into.

Poitevin Also known as Cheval du Poitou or

Mulassier meaning mule breeder; a heavy draft breed from the Poitiers regions of France from which the name derived; descended from local mares crossed with a variety of breeds and types of horses imported by the Dutch from the Netherlands, Norway, and Denmark who used them in land reclamation work; now principally used in the production of Poitue mules (q.v.); is lethargic, well balanced, and strong with good endurance; stands 15 to 17 hands and weighs 1,540 to 1,980 pounds (699-898 kg), has a heavy head, a short, straight neck, long, broad back, sloping quarters, thick, short legs with some feather, broad feet, and a dun, bay, gray, black, or palomino coat; was in danger of extinction in the 1950s, but its numbers are now on the increase; the genealogical registry dates back to 1884; used for heavy draft, farming, and in the production of mules.

Poitue mule Also known as Poitue ass; an exceptionally large mule standing more than 16 hands and having short, stout legs and wide hooves; developed in the province of Poitue France from which the name derived; a cross between the large Poitue jackass and Poitevin (q.v.) mares; historically used for heavy agricultural work as performed by Shires (q.v.); no longer a working breed, but raised by enthusiasts.

polarization stress analysis A technique used to determine whether or not cryogenic (q.v.) alteration of a brand or area of hair has occurred.

pole (1) see RAIL no. 1 (2) A racing term; markers placed at measured distances around the track which indicate the distance to the finish, e.g., the quarter pole is located 1/4 mile (400 m) from the finish. (3) A piece of wood attached to and projecting from the undercarriage of a horse-drawn vehicle on either side of which the wheelers (q.v.) are harnessed. (4) A training aid used on pacers (q.v.) and trotters (q.v.); a pointed pole, generally made of wood, placed on the side opposite that to which the horse pulls; buckled to the saddle pad and extends through a ring on the headpiece, protrudes a few inches beyond the nose of the horse.

pole chains Short chains used in double harness of owner-driven coaches and phaetons (q.v.); attached to the pole head (q.v.) on one end and to the kidney link of the hames collar on the other.

pole head A moveable steel fitting on the pole (q.v.) of a horse-drawn coach and some other vehicles to which the pole chains (q.v.) or pole pieces are attached.

pole hook Also known colloquially as swan neck; a hook on the end of the coach pole (q.v.) from which the bars in a harness are hung.

pole race *see* BENDING RACE

pole pieces Short leather straps used in double harness on coachmen driven vehicles; attached to the pole head (q.v.) on one end and to the kidney link of the harness collar (q.v.) on the other.

pole pin A steel pin securing the pole (q.v.) between the futchells on a horse-drawn vehicle.

poling Also known as poling-up or pole-piecing; to attach the pole chains (q.v.) or pole pieces (q.v.) to the hames collar.

polish (1) To make smooth and glossy, usually by friction. (2) The shine of the horse's coat when clean and groomed. (3) A substance used to impart a gloss.

Polish Warmblood *see* WIELKOPOLSKI

poll Also known as the nape or occipital crest; the highest point of the horse's head, just between the ears.

poll evil An inflammatory disorder of the bursae of the poll (q.v.); is primarily infectious in origin, caused by the organism *Brucella abortus* or *Actinomyces bovis*, but may also be caused by worm infestation or trauma from cuts, abrasions, bites, or badly fitting tack such as halters, headstalls, and bridles; symptoms include initial swelling, followed by the development of a fistula (q.v.) between the infected bursa, a weeping lesion on the skin, and sensitivity about the head and poll.

Pollard, James (1772–1867) A noted English artist of hunting and sporting scenes, particularly coaching and driving subjects.

poll guard *see* HEAD BUMPER

polo Historically known as hockey on horseback, chaugán, daiku, or pulu; a mounted ball game originating around 521 to 486 BC in

Persia played by two teams of four mounted players, on a field where the goals can be no more than 250 yards (228 m) apart and the width of the field cannot exceed 200 yards (183 m); consists of six, 7 1/2 minute chukkers (q.v.) or periods during which mounted players attempt to move a polo ball down the field and through the goal posts by means of a polo mallet (q.v.); played on bicycles, elephants (pachyderm polo [q.v.]), and camels; arena polo (q.v.) has also gained popularity in recent years.

polo ball A white sphere, 3-1/4 inches (8 cm) in diameter and weighing 5-1/2 ounces (156 g) used by polo players to play polo (q.v.); originally made of bamboo root, most are now made of either a light wood or plastic.

polo boards see BOARDS

polo boots Any knee-height, unlaced brown leather boot worn by a polo player.

polo cart see POLO GIG

polo club An organization of polo teams and players defined on the basis of region or association; simple polo clubs were established in Manipuri Indian villages during the mid 1800s; the first polo club in the Western world was officially established in London in 1873 and was controlled by the Hurlingham Polo Association.

polocrosse A mounted game originating in Australia; a horseback version of lacrosse in which the riders scoop up a ball in a small net attached to the distal end of a long stick, throw or carry it down the field to score by putting the ball between the goal posts.

polo field Also known as polo ground; a 10-acre (4 hectares) grass field, 300 x 200 yards (274 x 183 m) wide, unless boards (q.v.) are used to keep the ball in play in which case it is only 160 yards (146 m) wide, upon which the game of polo is played; has two sets of goal posts (q.v.), positioned 8 yards (7 m) apart, on each end of the field and penalty lines marked in white chalk at 30, 40, and 60 yards (27, 36.5, and 55 m) from each back line (q.v.); the center line is similarly marked; the object is to score goals by hitting a polo ball through goal-posts.

polo game see POLO MATCH

polo gig Also known as polo cart; a horse-drawn sporting gig (q.v.) popular in the late 19th century; used to exercise or drive a polo pony to a match; had crude disc brakes and a wickerwork basket to hold polo mallets (q.v.).

polo ground see POLO FIELD

polo handicap Also known as goal rating, polo rating, goal handicap, or handicap; a rating awarded each polo player, male or female, on the basis of general mastery of the fundamentals of the game, horsemanship, sense of strategy and conduct, and pony quality; expressed in number of goals, e.g., a ten goal player; ratings range from C (minus 2 goals) to 10, with 10 being the best rating; the system was instituted in 1888; player handicaps are revised annually by the USPA (q.v.); about two-thirds of the rated players carry a rating of 2 goals or less and ratings of 5 goals and above generally belong to professional players; team handicaps (q.v.) are also awarded.

poloist see POLO PLAYER

polo mallet Also known as mallet, polo stick, or stick in Britain; a shaft made from a bamboo cane with a hand grip and leather loop on one end and a hard wooden head made from bamboo root or a hard wood such as maple attached at a right angle to the shaft on the other; the shaft is more narrow and flexible towards the mallet head; varies in length from 48 to 52 inches (1.2-1.3 m); more narrow and flexible towards the mallet head; used by polo players to strike and move the ball down the field to the goal; the ball is struck broadside of the mallet head, not on the narrow ends; for safety reasons, the mallet is held in the right hand.

polo match Also known as polo game and match; a game lasting approximately 1 1/2 hours and divided into six, seven and one half minute chukkers (q.v.); when played on the flat, reflects the score as goals are made, and when played by the handicap, the sum total rating of the players on the team is subtracted from that of the opposing team, any difference being awarded to the lower rated side in goals on the scoreboard, e.g., a 26-goal team will give two goals to a 24-goal team.

polo mount see POLO PONY

polo penalty Also known as penalty; a

handicap imposed for infringement of the rules in the game of polo (q.v.); there are 10 penalties: penalty 1 (q.v.), penalty 2 (q.v.), penalty 3 (q.v.), penalty 4 (q.v.), penalty 5 (q.v.), penalty 6 (q.v.), penalty 7 (q.v.), penalty 8 (q.v.), penalty 9 (q.v.), and penalty 10 (q.v.), six of which are awarded as free hits toward the goal from a set distance and four as non-stroke penalties; generally assessed to prevent play which may be considered dangerous to either the horse or rider; the severity of the foul committed and the position on the field where it occurred, determines the penalty award.

polo player Also known as a poloist; a person who plays polo (q.v.).

polo pony Also known as polo mount; any horse ridden by a polo player in the game of polo (q.v.); commonly of Thoroughbred (q.v.) blood although the tougher Argentine polo ponies (q.v.) with their better bone and inbred talent for the sport dominate the game; stands 15 to 15.3 hands and is distinctly Thoroughbred in appearance; has speed, stamina, courage, good balance, and a bold, lively temperament; the mane is usually roached (q.v.) to prevent interference with the mallet (q.v.) and the tail tied; referred to as ponies due to the height limit imposed on them until early this century; each player uses an average of six horses per match and rides a different one in each chukker (q.v.); no pony may play more than two chukkers per match; credited with being 75 to 80 percent of the player's game.

polo positions *see* POLO TEAM

polo rating *see* POLO HANDICAP

polo spur A blunt spur (q.v.) with a flattened shank on the horse-side.

polo stick *see* POLO MALLET

polo stroke A polo term; a technique of striking the polo ball with the mallet (q.v.) used by the polo player (q.v.); there are four principal strokes: offside forehand (q.v.), offside backhand (q.v.), nearside forehand (q.v.), and nearside backhand (q.v.) and eight subsidiary strokes: under the neck shots (q.v.), nearside and offside, under the tail shots (q.v.) nearside and offside, forehand cuts (q.v.), offside and nearside, backhand cuts (q.v.), offside and nearside.

polo team A polo term; one of two opposing sides in a polo game; consists of four players each; each team is designated by a different shirt color; players wear jerseys numbered 1 to 4 which correspond to their assigned positions; the number one position, the forward, is an offensive player; the number two and number three positions are usually the highest rated and the most experienced, with number two position responsible to push the play both on offense and defense and the number three position being the quarterback or field captain; the number four position, the back, is primarily responsible for protecting the goal; in defense each player is assigned a man to cover, no. 1 usually covering the opposing no. 4 and no. 2 cover the opposing no. 3.

polo widow A polo term; a wife of a dedicated polo player (q.v.).

polycythemia A blood disease caused by overproduction of red blood cells; thickens and slows the blood's flow, which delays the delivery of oxygen and energy to the muscles and other tissues resulting in loss of stamina; occurs spontaneously in certain Standardbred (q.v.) families; manifested almost exclusively in stallions and is aggravated by intense training; the concentration of red cells in an exercising polycythemic horse's blood can run over 80 percent, well above the normal range of 55 to 60 percent.

polysulfated glycosaminoglycan Also known by the acronym PSGAG; a glycosaminoglycan (q.v.), a category of joint-lubricating substances chemically similar to the components of cartilage; when injected intramuscularly or directly into a joint, stimulate synovial-fluid production and quality.

pommel (1) Also known as head of the saddle; the protuberant part of the front and top of the saddle formed by the saddle bow (q.v.). (2) The knob or ball on the hilt of a sword or dagger.

pommel blanket *see* POMMEL PAD

pommel pad Also known as a wither pad or pommel blanket; a small, oval sheepskin, wool, or other material pad positioned under the pommel (q.v.) of the saddle to protect the withers (q.v.) from chafing; used on horses with prominent withers.

pony (1) A horse of either sex and any age who does not exceed 58 inches (14.2 hands) in height (except for an Arab (q.v.) which is always a horse); in some countries the height limit is set at 14 hands; from the Latin *pullus*, meaning foal and *pullanus*, meaning colt which in old French became *poulain* and *poulenet* (pronounced pool-ney) and in 1700 Scotland the word was subsequently modified to *powney* (pronounced poo-ney) where it became strongly associated with the small Scottish horses found in the Shetlands; pooney was ultimately shortened to the present-day spelling of pony. (2) To lead a horse while mounted on horseback. (3) Also known as lead pony; a racing term; a quiet horse used to lead young or unpredictable racehorses to and from the training track or to the post. (4) In gambling, the sum of $50.00.

pony break A light, horse-drawn break used in Australia for exercise purposes; drawn by four or more small ponies.

Pony Club, The An organization founded in 1928 in England to help farmer's children with their ponies; now an international organization with branches in more than 21 countries dedicated to encouraging young people, under the age of 21, to ride, to instruct them in all aspects of horsemanship, and to encourage sportsmanship.

Pony Club Mounted Games Previously known as the Prince Philip Mounted Games; a mounted games competition first organized by Prince Philip in 1957 in Great Britain, the purpose being to provide Pony Club (q.v.) members with an opportunity to hone their equestrian skills through various skill-based competitions such as gymkhanas (q.v.); limited to riders under the age of 15 mounted on ponies at least four years old and 14.2 hands tall; zone finalists compete in the Horse of the Year Show held every October where they compete for the Prince Philip Cup.

pony express A postal system operated through the western United States during the period 1860 to 1861 in which mail was carried by mounted relay riders; replaced by the telegraph.

pony express mount A method of mounting a horse; to run along side a galloping (q.v.) horse and, using the saddle horn, swing into the saddle without the aid of the stirrup; so called because it was readily used by pony express riders in the 1860s to quickly mount their horses; now used by trick riders and movie stunt people.

pony goal A polo term; a goal scored when the polo ball (q.v.) is deflected across the goal line by the feet or legs of a polo pony (q.v.).

Pony of the Americas A pony breed developed in 1956 in the United States; has conformation between an Quarter Horse (q.v.) and Arab (q.v.) and the coat color pattern of an Appaloosa, stands 11.1 to 13.1 hands, has a nice head, prominent withers, short and straight back, well-muscled croup and loins, wide and deep chest, strong legs, and a hard, vertically striped hoof; all Appaloosa coat patterns are acceptable including snowflake (q.v.), leopard (q.v.), frost (q.v.), marble, spotted blanket, and white blanket; is versatile, docile, and fast; an all purpose pony and children's mount used for trotting, jumping, flat racing, distance riding, and trekking.

pony roach *see* ROACHED MANE

pony speed test An Australian horse race in which ponies ridden by light boys are raced around a 1/4 mile (400 m) circuit at showgrounds.

pony tail (1) A human, long-hair style in which the hair is pulled to the back of the head, gathered with a rubberband or clip, thus resembling a pony's tail. (2) The tail of a pony or horse.

pool Also known as stake money; a racing term; the total amount bet in any race by all bettors (q.v.) to win, place, or show.

poor doer Also known as poor keeper; a horse having a picky appetite who goes off his feed easily; may be undernourished; generally influenced by psychological causes.

poor keeper *see* POOR DOER

pop-eyed Said of a horse with prominent or bulging eyes.

popped a splint *see* SPLINT

popped knee *see* CARPITIS

popped sesamoid *see* SESAMOIDITIS

Porcellus *see* INCITATUS

port (1) The portion of a curb bit (q.v.) that curves upward in the center of the mouthpiece under which the tongue fits; permits the mouthpiece of the bit, on either side of the port, to act on the bars (q.v.); if high, acts on the roof of the mouth. (2) *see* KAVE

port de bras A vaulting term; a warm-up exercise performed by vaulters (q.v.) to stretch the hamstring and quadriceps muscles and spine; the straight arms are raised up, above the head, forward towards the ground, and then backward as high as possible, passing on either side of the hips; the body bends only at the waist.

ported Said of a curb bit when designed with a port (q.v.).

porting *see* KAVE

Portland cutter A small horse-drawn sleigh having straight or nearly straight lines and a very high S-shaped front or dash to prevent snow, thrown by the horse's hooves, from covering the driver and passengers.

position (1) To flex or bend the horse to either the left or right. (2) A situation, place, or location especially with reference to other objects as a horse in position to an obstacle.

positive reinforcement Positive reward for behavior.

positive identification system Any system used to identify a horse using methods such as photographs, tattooing (q.v.), brands (q.v.), identifying scars, and face, leg, and coat markings.

post (1) A racing term; the starting and ending positions on a racetrack. (2) A racing term; to record a win, e.g., "he posted 12 wins in 13 starts." (3) *see* POST POSITION. (4) Also known as taking the bump or trotting light; the movement of the rider rising from and returning to the saddle with the rhythm of the trot.

post and rails *see* OXER

post betting A racing term; betting (q.v.) in which wagering does not begin until the numbers of all competing horses are posted.

postboy (1) *see* POSTILLION. (2) *see* POST CHAISE

postboy waistcoat *see* GREAT COAT

postboy's coat *see* GREAT COAT

post chaise Also known as yellow bounder or post boy; a four-wheeled, two-door, closed, horse-drawn traveling carriage or chariot used for public hire between inns and post houses where fresh horses and drivers could also be engaged; driven either to pairs in pole gear (q.v.) or four-in-hand (q.v.) teams guided by a postillion (q.v.) riding the near-side horse (q.v.); outfitted with a large luggage rack between the front and rear wheels, a smaller luggage space on the roof, a sword case for dress or ceremonial swords attached to the rearward part of the bodywork, no driver's box seat, and was hung on either whip or cee springs; a system of cross-country travel using this vehicle was introduced in England in 1743.

post entry Nomination of a horse to participate in a competition, usually on an entry form, on the day immediately prior to the event.

posterior Situated behind or towards the rear.

posterior digital nerve One of two nerves (q.v.) that run behind, and slightly to each side of the center of the pastern (q.v.); provide sensation to the back half of the foot and the entire sole.

Postier *see* POSTIER BRETON

Postier-Breton Also known as a medium Breton or Postier; a coldblood originating in Brittany, France; one of three distinct morphological types of Breton (q.v.) which descended during the Middle Ages from native Brittany stock crossed with Norfolk Roadster (q.v.) and its descendant the Norfolk Trotter (q.v.); is heavier and larger than the Bidet Breton (q.v.) and has shared the same stud book with the Fast Heavy Draft Breton (q.v.) since 1909; is selectively bred and must pass performance tests in harness to qualify for inclusion in the book; the coat is generally chestnut, but bay, gray, roan, and red roan also occur – black is not a breed color; has a well-proportioned head, heavy jaw, broad forehead, short ears, flared nostrils, a short, broad, muscular neck, short and straight back, sloping croup, and short, powerful legs with heavy joints; the tail is customarily docked; stands 15 to 16 hands and weighs 1,540 to 1,980 pounds (699-898 kg); registered foals are branded on the left side of the neck with a cross surmounting a splayed, upturned V.

post horse A horse led or ridden by a postboy (q.v.) or postillion (q.v.) which pulled hired carriages over specified distances, usually about 10 miles, depending on the nature of the country after which they were either worked back pulling a vehicle traveling in the opposite direction or ridden back by a postboy (q.v.).

postillion Also spelled postilion and known as postboy; one who drives a team of horses from a saddle or near leader (q.v.) when four or more horses are used to draw (q.v.) a carriage (q.v.), or one who rides the near horse when only one pair is used with a driver in the box (q.v.).

posting (1) see POST. (2) A method of travel of the wealthy using hired vehicles of various types including the post chaise (q.v.), which afforded a level of privacy unavailable in stage coaches (q.v.); pulled by a post horse (q.v.).

post master An antiquated term; the owner of a post horse(s) (q.v.).

post mortem (1) Subsequent to death, as in an examination of the body. (2) see POST-MORTEM EXAMINATION

post-mortem examination Also known as autopsy or post mortem; examination of the body made after death.

post-operative myopathy Also known by the acronym POM; a condition in which the muscle, surrounded by tough fibrous tissue, is injured; the subsequent swelling, having nowhere to go, leads to increased pressure which further injures the muscle; reduced muscle blood flow, exercise, and malignant hyperthermia are associated with its occurrence.

post parade A racing term; movement of horses from the paddock to the starting gate (q.v.) in front of the stands.

postparturient founder Inflammation of the sensitive laminae (q.v.) of the mare's hoof caused by retention of the placental membranes in the uterus following foaling.

post position Also known as post; a racing

term; the position of the horse in the starting gate (q.v.) as determined from the inner rail (q.v.) of the course outward, i.e., position number 1 is nearest the rail; may be drawn by ballot or selected by the handicapper using a number ball (q.v.) at the close of entries the day prior to the race.

post race A racing term; a flat race in which one may enter, for a flat fee, two or more horses and may compete one or all of them.

post time A racing term; the time at which all horses are required to be at the starting gate (q.v.) and ready to start a race.

potash alum see COMMON ALUM

potassium An essential electrolyte (q.v.) for the horse responsible for maintaining proper acid-alkali balance and osmotic pressure within the cells and works in conjunction with sodium to control nerve and muscle commands; foals require up to 1 percent potassium in a purified diet, while mature horses only require about 0.4 percent; dietary requirements are satisfied by a diet containing at least 35 percent roughage; potassium loss can result from high fluid excretion following strenuous exercise, exercise in high heat, or in cases of serious intestinal disturbances such as diarrhea or kidney failure; deficiency impairs transmission of nerve impulses which may trigger muscular paralysis or heart arrhythmias.

Potomac horse fever Also known as equine monocytic erhlichiosis or by the acronym PHF; an often fatal disease resulting from infection by *Ehrlichia risticii*, a member of the same family of organisms responsible for Rocky Mountain tick fever (q.v.); a higher risk is found in pastured horses as they are more likely to be exposed to the PHF causative agent, insect predation throughout the dawn, daylight, dusk, and night-time feeding cycles; despite evidence linking insects to infection, the specific vector responsible for the unpredictable transmission of the disease remains unknown; named after the Potomac River Valley in the United States where the disease was first recognized in 1979; symptoms include fever, diarrhea, mild to severe colic (q.v.), and laminitis (q.v.).

Pottock see BASQUE

Pottok see BASQUE

poultice Any hot or cold, soft, moist substance that holds moisture next to the skin; applied to the feet, limbs, or the body to cleanse wounds, draw inflammation from an area, or to alter temperature; historically cabbage leaves, cow manure, and bread were used as poultice materials, now fine clay, mud, and gels containing antiphlogistics (q.v.) such as camphor, mint, and eucalyptus are common; ingredients vary with intended use.

poultice boot A boot constructed of plastic, leather, canvas or other materials filled with a poultice or into which a poulticed hoof is put to treat hoof-related ailments.

poulticing An ancient and versatile treatment method designed to relax tissues and draw out swelling, infection, and local soreness through application of a poultice (q.v.) to cleanse wounds, draw out inflammation, or to alter temperature.

powder A racing term; slight physical contact between horses during a horserace (q.v.).

Powrys Cob An ancient pony breed indigenous to Wales which evolved in the 12th century from Welsh Mountain Ponies (q.v.) put to imported Spanish and Barb (q.v.) stock; used as a remount of the English armies; the base stock for the modern Welsh Cob (q.v.).

prad A Victorian term; a horse (q.v.).

prairie hay A cut and dried grass hay (q.v.) made from a mixture of wild native grasses the quality of which varies widely depending on the variety of grasses included, with good quality containing a digestible protein content of as much as 4.2 percent if cut in the early stages of growth; popular in the western United States.

prairie schooner Also known as a ship-of-the-plains or covered wagon; a horse-drawn American emigrant wagon of light or medium weight and dimensions which first came into popularity during the gold rush period of the 1820s; headed by a canvas top supported on bow-shaped hoops; either sprung or dead axle, could carry up to three tons (3 tonnes), had lever brakes which acted on both rear wheels, and was drawn by either two or four horses in pole gear (q.v.); not to be confused with the much larger Connestoga wagon (q.v.).

PRCA The acronym for Professional Rodeo Cowboys Association, Inc. (q.v.).

Preakness *see* PREAKNESS STAKES

Preakness Stakes Also known as the Preakness; a 1 mile, 1-1/2 furlong (302 m) race for three-year-olds run annually in May since 1873 on the Pimlico course in Baltimore, Maryland, USA; one of three American classic races comprising the American Triple Crown (q.v.).

preferred A racing term; said of a horse given priority entry for a specific race; is usually a previous winner or horse bred or foaled in the area.

preferred list A racing term; a list of horses having placement in a horse race in the event the race draws more entries than the racetrack (q.v.) can accommodate; usually consists of horses previously entered in races that were not filled with the minimum number of starters, previous winners, and/or horses bred or foaled in the area.

pregnant mare urine Also known by the acronym PMU; urine collected from pregnant mares standing in production lines on PMU farms (q.v.) from which the estrogen contained in the drug Premarin (q.v.) is extracted; collected from October through March, the period of highest estrogen (q.v.) production in the mare; mares are hooked up around the clock to a harness attached to a funnel that collects the urine from the urethra and carries it down a tube into a one-gallon container; when estrogen levels decrease in the mare's urine prior to birth of a foal (q.v.), around April, the mare is put to pasture; following birth she is reimpregnated while pastured with her foal and, on October 1, returned to the collection line; water intake is often regulated to raise the urine estrogen concentration with higher concentrates more valuable; one mare will produce an average of 100 gallons (455 liters) of salable urine annually; no permits or laws control this industry and it is aggressively contested by animal rights activists.

Preliminary A jumper term; a horse at the first level of development as a jumper who has won less than $3,000.

preliminary canter A racing term; the short warm-up canter (q.v.) from the paddock to the gate (q.v.) immediately prior to a horse race.

premarin An estrogen supplement used to counteract the effects of menopause, osteoporosis (q.v.), and heart ailments in humans; estrogen contained in this drug is extracted from pregnant mare urine (q.v.) from which the name is a contraction.

Premium Cream A registry classification of the American Cream (q.v.) having registered stock of any breed on both sides; reproducibility of color is not a requirement.

premolars Deciduous teeth (q.v.) located in the back of the jaw which are adapted for grinding; consist of the first, second, and third premolars.

prepotent The breeding power of a stallion or mare as measured by the degree to which inherited characteristics are transmitted to its offspring at a percentage better than the industry average.

prep race A racing term; a workout or race in which a horse is trained or prepared for a future competition.

prescribed zone Anywhere on the body or legs of a Paint Horse (q.v.) behind an imaginary line from the base of the ear forward horizontally to the corner of the mouth, or from the corner of the mouth under the chin, to the other corner of the mouth, or above a level line around the leg midway between the center of the knee and the front of the chest, or the point represented by a level line around the leg midway between the point of the hock and the center point of the stifle.

presentation The appearance of the horse and/or rider including grooming, riding habit (q.v.), and tack in terms of appropriateness and cleanliness.

press off A cutting term; to use the pressure of the rider's cow-side (q.v.) leg to move the horse away from the cow.

press up A cutting term; to use the pressure of the rider's herd-side (q.v.) leg to move the horse toward the cow being cut.

pressure bandage A wrap used on the lower leg to relieve swelling and provide support to an injured or damaged area; should be applied to both legs front or rear firmly, yet not too tightly; the injured leg is bandaged to relieve the injury while the sound leg is bandaged to provide support as it will carry more weight until the other leg is healed.

price A British term; the odds quoted by a bookmaker (q.v.) on a particular horse scheduled to compete in a race.

prick *see* QUICK

prick ears Said of the ears of the horse when sharp, pointed, and forward facing.

pricker An antiquated hunting term; one who follows hounds on horseback.

pricker pad A bit burr (q.v.) studded with sharp points on the cheek side; is slit from one outside edge to the center and fits around the bit mouthpiece just inside the cheekpiece (q.v.); irritates the corner of the horse's mouth; used to prevent the horse from leaning to, and assist in turning from, the side; the stud side is placed facing the skin; generally used on only one side of the bit.

pricket A buck (q.v.) in his second year having straight, unbranched antlers.

primary arthritis Inflammation of a joint resulting from direct trauma such as penetration of a foreign body or a physical blow to the joint.

primary corpus luteum A mass of endocrine cells formed from the ruptured ovarian follicle immediately following release of the unfertilized egg; secretes progesterone.

primitive marks Refers to coat color pattern; any marking on the horse including dark-colored stripes along the spine and over the withers, knees, and hocks; most commonly seen on dun-colored horses; traceable to ancient horse breeds.

primigravida *see* MAIDEN

Prince of Wales spurs Also known as a dropped spur; a spur (q.v.) having a sloping neck and offset shanks, the longer side being worn on the outside of the foot; the neck is worn pointing downward and may be blunt ended, pointed, or fitted with a rowel (q.v.).

Prince Philip Mounted Games *see* PONY CLUB MOUNTED GAMES

prince seat A vaulting term; a position assumed by the vaulter on the horse's back in which the vaulter (q.v.) kneels on one knee and places the other foot on the roller (q.v.)

with both arms outstretched from his sides.

principal horse *see* CAST HORSE

pritchel A sharply pointed tool used by a farrier (q.v.) to make nail holes in a hot shoe (q.v.).

pritcheling The act of making nail holes in a horseshoe (q.v.).

private auction Any auction (q.v.) restricted to invited participants.

private coach *see* DRAG

private pack A hunting term; a pack of hounds, the expense of which is borne solely by the Master (q.v.).

Prix des Nations *see* NATIONS CUP

prize money Any sum paid to a competitor as a reward for victory or superiority.

Probstmayria vivipara *see* SMALL PINWORM

produce (1) The progeny or offspring of a mare; a foal is the produce of a mare and the get (q.v.) of a stallion; may refer to one or more progeny. (2) Horse foodstuff available at a produce store.

producer A racing term; said of a mare who has at least one offspring who has won a race.

produce race A racing term; a flat race for the progeny (q.v.) of mares and/or stallions, the entry of which is posted before foaling.

proestrus The two-day period in which the mare becomes increasingly receptive to mating; proceeds estrus (q.v.).

professional One who receives payment for his participation in a sport which others engage in as a pastime, e.g., a horse trainer.

professional whipper-in A hunting term; a whipper-in (q.v.) who receives payment for his or her services.

progenitor *see* SIRE

progeny The offspring or descendants of either a mare or stallion horse; may refer to more than one descendant.

progesterone The female hormone secreted by the corpus luteum (q.v.) of the ovary prior to the implantation of the egg; maintains pregnancy by stopping the estrous cycle (q.v.).

prognathism *see* UNDER-SHOT JAW

progressive color pattern Refers to coat color pattern; a coat pattern that changes as the horse ages, as in Andalusians (q.v.).

prolapsed sole *see* DROPPED SOLE

promethazine *see* ACETYLPROMAZINE

prop (1) A racing term; a horse who refuses to break (q.v.) at the start of the race. (2) A racing term; said of a horse who suddenly stops by planting its front feet. (3) *see* THE PROP

Prophet Strain A line of horses selected, according to legend, by the Prophet Mohammed as the foundation stock of his horses used for war purposes; the ten horses which established the strain were known as Mohammed's Ten Horses (q.v.).

Prophet's thumb Also known as thumb print of the Prophet; a pronounced dimple or indentation in the shoulder muscles of Arabs (q.v.); believed to be a sign of good luck as legend has it that the mark was made by the thumb of the Prophet Mohammed.

propping *see* SCOTCHING

proppy Said of the horse; having short action and gait as due to a straight shoulder, lack of flexibility in the knees, and/or straight pasterns.

proprietor A historic coaching term; one who owns his own team and drives his own coach.

proprioception The reception of stimuli produced within the organism enabling the horse, especially when moving over obstacles, to know the position of his legs in relation to his body and the object jumped; a natural sense.

proprioceptor Any of the sensory organs in the muscles, tendons, etc. sensitive to the stimuli originating in these tissues by movements of the body, or its parts; functions in proprioception (q.v.).

prostaglandins A group of hormone-like, fatty-acid substances active in many physiological processes including inflammation (q.v.), reproduction, and the lowering of blood pressure.

prostation Complete physical or mental exhaustion.

protein A chain of amino acids; one of a class of complex chemical compounds containing hydrogen, sulfur, carbon, nitrogen, and oxygen and responsible for growth, maintenance, and repair of body tissues; consists of 22 amino acids of which ten are considered essential (dietary essential amino acids [q.v.]) and must be supplied by the ration because horses are incapable of synthesizing them internally; the other 12 amino acids can be synthesized from any source of nitrogen available to the horse; the requirement of foals is as much as 18 to 20 percent, 13 to 16 percent for yearlings, 12 to 14 percent for two-year olds, and approximately 12 percent for the mature horse; the growing, pregnant, lactating, or performance horse may require supplementation; unused, excess protein is converted into alternative energy; rations containing 30 percent or more total protein may cause metabolic stress and digestive disturbances.

protein bumps Hives (q.v.) triggered by excess systemic protein levels, as found in some feed.

protein supplements Any animal or plant souce of protein fed to a horse to compensate for dietary deficiency; plant proteins are more commonly fed than those from animal sources, and are usually seeds following oil extraction as in soybean meal (q.v.), cottonseed meal, peanut meal (q.v.), linseed meal (q.v.), rapeseed meal (q.v.), and sunflower meal; animal sources include meat and bone meal (q.v.), fishmeal (q.v.), and milk protein.

protest *see* OBJECTION

protrusion of the nictitating membrane A condition of the eye in which the third eyelid, interior to the true eyelid, protrudes from the eye; may be caused by severe pain associated with eye disease, the presence of a foreign body, tetanus (q.v.), dehydration (q.v.), or a tumor; the underlying cause of the protrusion must be diagnosed and treated for the condition to be corrected.

proud flesh Excessive granulated tissue (q.v.); rounded masses of flesh composed of capillaries and connective tissue cells which grow outward to fill a wound defect often beyond the skin's surface; brought about by the use of excessively strong antiseptics or by continual movement of the injury which retards complete healing; inhibits healing and must be removed; so called because the tissue is swollen, as if by pride.

provinces A hunting term; hunt country located anywhere in England, Scotland, or Wales, except in the Midlands and Shires (q.v.).

proximal Nearest the point of attachment or insertion as the extremity of a bone or limb.

proximal sesamoid bones *see* SESAMOID BONES

proximal sesamoids *see* SESAMOID BONES

pruritis Itchiness resulting from the systemic release of histamine (q.v.).

Przewalski's Horse Also known by the scientific name *Equus ferus przewalski*; one of two subspecies of wild horse found in Eastern Europe and Asia discovered in 1876 by Russian explorer Przewalski for whom the breed was named; found at that time throughout the Gobi desert and the steppes of Mongolia; intermediate in character between the equine and asinine groups having calluses on all four limbs as in the horse and a tail only half of which is covered with hair as in the ass; generally has a dun coat with a yellowish tinge on the back, becoming lighter towards the flanks and almost white under the belly, a dark brown, short and erect mane, and no forelock; presumed extinct in the wild since 1968; it has bred well in captivity and a stud book is held at the Prague Zoo, Czechoslovakia; total world count is less than 1,000 animals; being reintroduced into the wild in Mongolia and in China.

psalion A classical Greek cavesson (q.v.) resembling a hackamore (q.v.).

PSGAG The acronym for polysulfated glycosaminoglycan (q.v.).

psoroptic scabies One of four types of mange (q.v.) affecting horses; a skin condition caused by a species of mite called *Psoroptes ovis* characterized by lesions in sheltered body areas such as the forelock, mane, root of the tail, under the chin, between the hind legs, and sometimes in the ears; lesions are similar to those resulting from sarcoptic mange (q.v.), but involve larger and thicker crusts on the skin with less severe itching, and the mites may be more easily found in the crusts; these mites are surface dwellers and do not burrow; a quarantinable disease not reported in horses in the United States for many years.

psyllium *see* FLEAWORT

psyllium seed *see* FLEASEED

PTR The acronym for Performance Thoroughbred Registry (q.v.).

public auction Any open auction (q.v.) for which invitation is not required.

public stable A racing term; a stable housing horses belonging to more than one owner; horses under training are generally handled on a freelance basis.

public trainer A racing term; one who trains horses for more than one owner or stable, usually on a *per diem* or flat fee basis.

Puckle noseband *see* KINETON NOSEBAND

pudding A hunting term; a mixture of meal (q.v.) and meat cooked in the kennel (q.v.) and fed to the hounds (q.v.).

puddle The shuffling action of the horse in motion.

puffer *see* SHILL

puffing the glims An antiquated practice; to make an aged horse appear less so by making a small incision in the skin of the hollow above the eye and blowing air through a quill inserted therein to fill the hollow with air.

pughree *see* PUGHRI

pughri Also spelled pughree or incorrectly as purgi; a woven cotton cloth used by Indian men for their turbans and by some polo players as a pughri martingale (q.v.).

pughri martingale Also spelled pughree martingale or incorrectly as purgi martingale; standing martingale (q.v.) used on some polo ponies (q.v.) consisting of a length of colored pughri (q.v.) cloth, such as used to make turbans in India, tied on one end to the girth and to the underside of the noseband (q.v.) on the other.

Puissance Previously known as potenza; a non-timed show jumping competition in which competitors jump a course consisting of six to eight obstacles ranging from 4.6 to 5.3 (1.4–1.6 m) in the first round, the height and width being progressively increased in each successive round until only one competitor remains.

pull (1) To thin, shorten, or improve the appearance of the mane or tail by removing individual or groups of hairs by hand or with the aid of a pulling comb, knife, etc. (2) *see* THROW A RACE. (3) *see* PULL UP. (4) To draw blood, e.g., The vet pulled 3 cc of blood from the horse.

pulled suspensory *see* SUSPENSORY DESMITIS

pulled tail Said of the tail when the hair on the side of the dock (q.v.), from the base to the tip, and any excessive growth on top is pulled by hand to give a tidy and trimmed look.

puller A horse who leans on the bit, thus drawing the reins from the rider's hands; may be difficult to stop.

pulley bit A bit with pulleys for the gag rein (q.v.).

pulling comb Also known as a mane drag; a metal-toothed comb (q.v.), frequently attached to a handle used to trim and thin the mane or tail.

pulling leather Also known as grabbin' the apple; a rodeo term; said of a bronc rider who touches any part of the saddle with his free hand during his eight-second ride in competition.

pulling slack Also known as grabbing slack or jerking slack; a roping term; said of a roper; to take hold of the lariat (q.v.) with the hand after the loop has settled on the target so as to pull the loop tight.

pull in the weights A racing term; said of a horse who runs with a weight advantage, i.e., less weight than other competing horses.

pull off Also known as pinchers; a pritchel-type farrier's tool with knobs on the ends of the handles which distinguish them from hoof nippers (q.v.) used to remove horseshoes, nail stubs, and improperly driven nails and to turn the clinches.

pull off a cow *see* QUIT A COW

pull up Also known as pull; to intentionally slow or stop a horse or horse-drawn vehicle; as in a race.

pulmonary Of or pertaining to the lungs.

pulse The rhythmic beating or throbbing of the arteries caused by contractions of the heart which force blood to move through the vessels.

pulu *see* POLO

pumiced foot *see* DROPPED SOLE

pump handles Two curved metal handles attached to the rear body of a horse-drawn coach (q.v.) used as a handhold when entering.

punch (1) *see* BRAND no. 2. (2) An English horse having short legs and a barrel body.

Punch Carriage A four-wheeled, horse-drawn carriage drawn by a single horse popular during the 19th century; seated two, rear-facing passengers, had a coupé body mounted in reverse protected by a falling hood, and a driving apron; used by passengers averse to draughts and who were allergic to the odor of horses, as well as doctors, the infirm, and the elderly.

puncture (1) Known as puncture wound; any cut deeper than it is wide; deceptively dangerous and accounts for roughly 10 percent of all equine injuries; does not drain well and enables bacteria to flourish in an anaerobic (q.v.) environment; deep-seated infections and abscesses often result. (2) The act or action of pricking or perforating as with a pointed insturment or object.

puncture wound *see* PUNCTURE

punter *see* BETTOR

puppy show A hunting term; a competition for young, unentered (q.v.) hounds evaluated on the basis of conformation, gait, and training.

puppy walker A hunting term; one responsible for the care of hound puppies from about ten weeks of age until returned to the kennels for entering (q.v.).

purebred (1) Relating or pertaining to an animal bred from a strain of generations of pure, unmixed ancestry. (2) A horse from a strain of generations of pure, unmixed ancestry.

purebred Arab One of three basic types of Arab (q.v.) resulting from the crossing of the three primary sub-breeds of the Assil (q.v.): the Kuhailan (q.v.), the Siglavy (q.v.), and the Muniqi (q.v.).

purebred percentage The percentage of pure blood present in a horse who is the progeny (q.v.) of a purebred (q.v.) stallion and an unregistered mare or mare of another breed.

pure trot *see* TROT

purgative Also known as a cathartic; any substance or medicine that brings about a bowel movement.

purge To produce evacuations of the bowel by means of a cathartic (q.v.).

purgi *see* PUGHRI

purgi martingale *see* PUGHRI MARTINGALE

purple corn *see* CORN no. 3

purple roan Refers to coat color; a uniform mixture of red, white, and black hairs or red hairs with black tips and white hairs, with black more abundant along the topline (q.v.) and around the croup and withers; the head and points will be colored.

purpura hemorragica Also known as petechial fever or petechial hemorrhage; an acute, noncontagious, potentially fatal disease characterized by a sudden onset of fever, depression, edema of the lower limbs, hemorrhages of the skin and mucous membranes and, in some cases, colic (q.v.); thought to be an allergic-hypersensitive reaction to bacterial antigens circulating in the bloodstream; the walls of small blood vessels are damaged allowing blood and plasma to escape into the surrounding tissues.

pur sang Purebred (q.v.).

purse A racing term; prize money consisting of nomination and entry fees, and any added money, generally paid to the first five finishers; the owners of horses competing in the race do not contribute; originally, prize money was contained in a purse hung on a wire which crossed the finish line, a system from which the present name derived.

pus A yellowish-white, more or less viscid inflammation product; consists of liquid plasma in which leukocytes are suspended; of two types: sterile and infected; the latter being of inconsistent texture, contains bacteria, is darker than sterile pus, and often has a strong odor.

push button horse Said of a well-trained horse who is extremely sensitive to a rider's signals and who serves as a good mount (q.v.) for a novice rider.

pus pocket *see* ABSCESS

puss *see* HARE no. 2

put a rein on him A western term; to train a horse to respond to neck reining (q.v.).

put down *see* DESTROY

put him on his head To be bucked off a horse as in, "that horse really put him on his head."

put to (1) Said of a stallion bred (q.v.) to a mare. (2) *see* HARNESS no. 2. (3) A hunting term; a fox earth (q.v.) closed with a fox inside on the morning of a hunt.

putting to (1) The act of harnessing a horse to a vehicle. (2) A hunting term; the process of closing an earth (q.v.).

pyre Refers to foxhound coat color; a lighter tan than the belvoir tan (q.v.).

pyridoxine Originally known as vitamin B_6; a B complex vitamin (q.v.) synthesized in the lower intestines of the horse and required for the metabolism of protein (q.v.) and fat; abundant in whole grains; deficiency is unlikely.

pyramidal disease Also known as buttress foot or extensor process disease; a condition of the foot involving new bone growth in the region of the extensor process of the distal phalanx; may result from fracture of the extensor process caused by excessive pull of the tendon insertion; an advanced form of low ringbone (q.v.); symptoms include pointing with the affected foot, a shortened stride with a tendency to land heavily on the heel, heat, pain, some swelling in the early stages, lameness in all gaits, and with secondary arthritis a likely complication; horses such as the Paso Fino (q.v.) with high heels and short toes and horses that move with limbs lifted high in a short and rapid manner appear to be predisposed; prognosis is unfavorable in most cases.

Q

quad Cockney slang; a horse.

Quadrille An orchestrated ride to music generally performed by teams of four riders or groups of four who execute dressage and/or High School figures or movements on horseback; derived from the formal dance of the same name which consists of five figures or movements executed by four couples each forming one side of a square.

Quagga Also known by the scientific name *Equus quagga*; an extinct South African mammal closely related to the zebra, but only having stripes on the head, neck, and shoulders.

Qualifying Race A racing term; a horserace for which there is no purse (q.v.) nor betting, used to determine the ability, manners, and eligibility of a horse.

quality The element of refinement in the appearance of horse breeds and types; generally due to Thoroughbred (q.v.) or Arab (q.v.) influence.

quarantine barn (1) Any building equipped with stalls in which infected horses are isolated from the general horse population until no longer contagious. (2) A facility equipped to isolate horses for a short period of time following transportation across international borders to ensure they are not carrying disease; requirements vary by country; frequently located at an airport, racetrack, or other designated location.

quarry A hunting term; that which is hunted, generally stag, coyote, or fox, or people as in the sport of blood hounding (q.v.).

quarter (1) The portion of the hoof between the toe and the ground-side hoof surface and coronary band on either side. (2) *see* HINDQUARTERS. (3) A racing term; a distance of two furlongs (q.v.).

quarter blanket *see* QUARTER SHEET no. 1

quarter boot A flexible boot that cups the heel bulbs (q.v.) and coronet (q.v.) on the rear-portion of the hoof; may or may not have an open front where it is closed by means of buckles or Velcro; worn on the forefeet to protect the quarter of the front heel from the toe of the hind.

quarter clip A V-shaped metal extension of the horseshoe (q.v.) located on the left and/or right sides between the toe and heel to fit the shoe more securely to the hoof.

quarter crack A fissure on either the medial or lateral sides of the hoof wall, starting at the bearing surface and extending a variable distance up the hoof wall, or originating at the coronary band (q.v.), and extending downward; may occur in either the fore or hind feet; more severe than toe cracks (q.v.) it may involve the sensitive laminae (q.v.); in severe cases, affected horses are usually lame and may hemorrhage following exercise.

Quarter Horse An American-bred horse breed developed in the 17th century by settlers in Virginia and Carolina, USA by crossing Spanish-type mares with imported English Thoroughbred (q.v.) stallions; has massively muscled large, rounded hindquarters, is compact, agile, fast, well-balanced, and possessed of quick reflexes, stands 14.1 to 16 hands, and may have a coat of any solid color although chestnut is most common; has a short-coupled body, a short and wide head, a long neck, and well-defined withers; subsequent breed selection was based on performance in sprint races over 1/4 mile (400 m) stretches from which the name derived; the breed registry was established in 1940; bred in three specialized types: racing Quarter Horse consisting of Thoroughbred (q.v.) with some ranch horse blood, the show and halter Quarter Horse of the old bulldog (q.v.) type with more refinement, smaller bones, and longer legs, and the stock-type Quarter Horse; used as a trail mount, cutting horse, hunter, show jumper, polo mount, pleasure horse, and for racing; an elite sprinter may reach speeds of 54 mph (87 kmph) within four or five strides.

quartering To quick groom a horse; traditionally performed first thing in the morning to make the horse look tidy before exercising.

quarter marks Patterns placed or made, by modifying the direction of the hair on the horse's hindquarters (q.v.) for appearance, as by means of a stencil.

quarter pole A racing term; a colored post located adjacent to the infield rail (q.v.) exactly 2 furlongs (q.v.) from the finish.

quarters *see* HINDQUARTERS

quarters falling out Said of a horse who moves with the forehand in the correct position on the line, but whose quarters have left that line, falling out either to near or offside.

quarter sheet (1) Also known as a padcloth or quarter blanket; a natural fibre or synthetic blanket which covers the horse's quarters and tucks under the rider's legs or the saddle flap; keeps the horse warm when exercising in cold weather, preparatory to competition, in dress parade, etc. (2) *see* SUMMER SHEET

quarters in *see* TRAVERS

quarters leading A dressage term; said of the horse whose quarters (q.v.) lead the forehand in the lateral movement when performing a half pass (q.v.).

quarters not engaged Said of a horse whose hind legs are not sufficiently brought under its body; the horse may be on the forehand and have a hollowed back.

quarters trailing A dressage term; said of a horse performing a half pass who has insufficient bend in his body leaving the quarters (q.v.) behind the movement; the horse will not cross his hind legs.

quarter strap (1) That portion of the harness passing over the quarters of a horse which connects to the breeching. (2) *see* BEARING STRAP

quarters out *see* RENVERS

Quashquai A horse breed indigenous to Iran which contributed to the development of the Plateau Persian (q.v.); stands approximately 15 hands.

queen of saddles *see* SIDESADDLE

Queensland itch An Australian term; sweet itch (q.v.).

question *see* ASK A QUESTION

quick (1) Also known as nail prick, nail quick, or prick; to penetrate the sensitive structures of the foot with a horseshoe nail; traces of blood may be apparent on the nail when removed and generally results in lameness; more serious than nail bind (q.v.). (2) Any of the sensitive structures within the hoof.

quicking *see* QUICK

quick-response diagnostic test *see* STALL SIDE DIAGNOSTIC TEST

quick-stop A western training bridle that exerts significant pressure under the jaw of the horse; used sparingly to train a horse to stop quickly on its haunches.

quiddor A horse who drops food from its mouth while chewing.

quinela *see* QUINELLA

quinella Also spelled quinela, quinela, or known as one two; a racing term; a betting option in which the bettor (q.v.) selects the first and second place horses in any order in any race.

quinsy Any abscess in the throat such as strangles (q.v.).

quintain *see* QUINTAINE

quintaine Also spelled quintain; an object to be tilted (q.v.) at, especially a post with a revolving figure, tree trunk, post, pile, or shield, against which to break one's lance.

quirt (1) A small riding crop with a short handle and a braided or plaited lash. (2) To strike with a quirt.

quit *see* QUIT A COW

quit a calf *see* QUIT A COW

quit a cow Also known as pull off a cow or quit a calf; a cutting term; to stop working a cow; in National Cutting Horse Association competitions, is permissable without penalty if the cow has obviously stopped, turned away from the cutter, or if it is behind the time line.

quittor Also known as coronary sinus; a pus-forming chronic inflammation of the collateral cartilages of the foot in which pus is discharged above the coronary band (q.v.); rare today, although was once quite common in draft horses; results from an injury to the coronet or pastern or puncture to the sole of the foot; symptoms include inflammatory swelling over the area of the lateral cartilage, followed by abscessation, and ultimately lameness.

R

rabbit A racing term; a fast horse entered in a race with a stablemate who sets a fast pace to aid his stablemate in placing.

rabicano Also known as squaw tail; refers to coat color; a white color pattern occurring in a number of breeds including the Quarter Horse (q.v.), Arab (q.v.), Noriker (q.v.), Brabant (q.v.), and North American Spanish; may consist of a few white hairs on the flanks and at the base of the tail or a pattern of white hair extending out from the flanks and numerous white hairs at the base of the tail; strongly marked horses may be confused with roans (q.v.).

rabid Affected with rabies (q.v.).

rabies An acute fatal viral infection of the central nervous system affecting warm-blooded animals; transmitted from animal to animal by means of a bite from a rabid (q.v.) animal who introduces the virus-bearing saliva; is rarely transmitted by viral contamination of fresh, pre-existing wounds; the incubation period is variable, but is generally 15 to 50 days and in rare cases, as long as six months; death usually occurs within ten days of appearance of the symptoms; the clinical course occurs in three phases: the prodromal, the excitative, and the dumb or paralytic; general symptoms include an insignificant change in body temperature, an inability to retain saliva may not be noted, a loss of appetite and thirst, isolationistic behavior, irritation of the urinary tract as evidenced by frequent urination, erection and sexual desire in the male, and a change in behavior which may be indistinguishable from a digestive disorder, injury, a foreign body in the mouth, poisoning, or an early infectious disease; following the early warning or prodromal period of one to three days, horses may show signs of paralysis or become vicious, biting other animals or people at the slightest provocation; in some horses the excitative phase is predominant, in which case the term furious rabies applies (q.v.); in others paralytic rabies (q.v.) may dominate; the pre-exposure vaccine is 96 percent effective; the virus dies quickly in a warm and/or dry environment.

rabies vaccine A modified microorganism of the rabies (q.v.) virus used for preventive inoculation; is 96 percent effective.

race (1) Also known as horse race; a contest of speed between horses as in running, jumping, driving, or the like run over a set course where the result is determined by speed and time. (2) A meeting at which several races are held. (3) Also known as rache, reach, or rase; a face marking; any long, narrow white marking on the horse's face which runs from the forehead to, or almost to, the muzzle, and which diverges to the near or off side of the face; differs from a stripe (q.v.). (4) A breeding stock of animals.

race card Also known as a card or race program; a racing term; the printed program of a race meeting (q.v.) including the name and time of each race and the names of all horses, their owners and trainers, and the weights to be carried.

racecourse (1) *see* TRACK. (2) A racing term; the race track including all relevant facilities such as grandstands, paddock, stables, offices, etc. which are maintained by appointed officials.

racecourse paddock *see* PADDOCK no. 2

race declared off A racing term; any horse race announced as no longer valid or canceled by the race stewards as due to (a) failure of most of the field to start a race, (b) the gate is opened prematurely, before all the horses are at their posts; stakes races canceled will generally be rescheduled at a later date, while normal races will not be re-run.

race de trait Belge *see* BRABANT

racehorse *see* RACE HORSE

race horse Also known as a bang tail, racer and spelled incorrectly racehorse; any breed of horse bred or kept for racing either on the flat or over hurdles; normally applies to Thoroughbreds (q.v.), but which is sometimes extended to trotters (q.v.), pacers (q.v.), and sprinters.

race horse cross A cutting term; a two-handed grip on the reins sometimes used by the rider during the training of a cutting horse (q.v.) in which the left rein is crossed over the withers and gripped by the right hand and the right rein crossed over the wither and gripped by the left.

race meeting (1) A racing term; the place at which a fixed number of horse races are held. (2) A racing term; the specific period during which a race program is conducted.

Race of Champions Also known by the acronym ROC; the premier endurance race in the United States; competing teams are assembled geographically and consist of three to 15 riders per team; half of the team members must finish the race; the times of those competitors finishing the race are averaged with the team with the lowest average to declare the winner; to qualify, horses must have completed five or more 100-mile (160 km) races with at least two top-ten finishes, while qualifying riders must have completed at least one 100-mile race.

race position A racing term; the location of the horse in the field of horses competing in a race.

race program *see* RACE CARD

racer (1) *see* RACE HORSE. (2) A riding boot worn by jockeys when racing on the flat.

race track *see* TRACK

racetrack *see* TRACK

race-track *see* TRACK

race tracker One who frequents a racetrack (q.v.).

raceway A track (q.v.) upon which harness races (q.v.) are conducted.

rache *see* RACE no. 3

racing *see* RACE no. 1

Racing Biga An ancient Roman racing chariot drawn by a pair of horses harnessed in curricle gear (q.v.); noted for its forward, inclined, bow-shaped front, and wooden wheels which usually had eight spokes each.

racing blinkers A blinker (q.v.) consisting of a hood fitted over the head of the horse which allows the ears to protrude and has

leather cups which shield the eyes; restrict the horse's vision to the sides and rear in either or both eyes; fit is very important; use or disuse must be approved by the race stewards and the change reported on the official program.

racing breastplate *see* AINTREE GIRTH

racing cap *see* RACING HELMET

racing calendar Also known as the sheet calendar; a racing industry publication in which upcoming races, advertisements for sales breeding, weights and acceptances for handicaps, forfeit notices and lists, names registered, racing colors, etc. are noted; may be published weekly, monthly, quarterly, etc.

racing colors *see* COLORS

racing form A racing term; an information sheet used by bettors (q.v.) which contains the details of a race horse's past performance.

racing gallop A regular, balanced, and extended gallop (q.v.) with speeds ranging from 30 to 45 mph (48-72 kmph); faster than a hand gallop (q.v.).

racing girth *see* AINTREE BREAST GIRTH

racing iron A very small, light-weight, yet sturdy, and commonly aluminum stirrup designed to lend stability to the jockey when mounted; generally custom-made to fit the jockey's feet and generally only accommodate the toes.

racing helmet Also known as crash skull, racing cap, or generically as helmet (q.v.); protective headgear fitted with anti-concussive pads and a chin strap worn by a jockey and upon which the jockey's colors (q.v.) are worn.

racing on the flat *see* FLAT RACING

racing plate Also known as plate; a very lightweight horseshoe, usually made of aluminum, used on competing race horses.

racing saddle A saddle (q.v.) used on race horses (q.v.); of two types: light, used for flat racing which generally weigh less than 2 pounds (90 g) and heavy; used for hurdling and steeplechasing.

racing seat A racing term; the position assumed by the jockey in the saddle when riding a race horse whether in competition or workout; the leathers (q.v.) are adjusted very short, so that the knee of the jockey, when seated, is approximately parallel to the height of the withers; the jockey stands in the stirrups and rides well over the neck and shoulders of the horse.

racing secretary A racing term; one responsible for prescribing track conditions and sometimes for assigning weights to entrants in handicap races.

racing silks *see* COLORS

racing snaffle *see* DEE-RING SNAFFLE

racing sound A racing term; said of a horse who, although not in perfect health, is able to compete in a horse race.

racing strip *see* TRACK

racing trot A maximally extended trot (q.v.) which has a longer stride than an extended trot (q.v.); the diagonal pair of legs may separate with the hind leg grounding (q.v.) first; and the head and neck are high and extended; common to racing Standardbreds (q.v.).

rack (1) Also known as a single-foot because only one foot strikes the ground at the time; a smooth, bi-lateral, four-beat, natural gait in which each foot strikes the ground separately, at equal intervals, and at a high speed; there is no head movement and the entire body drops slightly; a gait midway between a pure trot (q.v.) and a flat pace (q.v.) with the sequence of footfalls similar to, but more distinct than, the slow gait; characteristic to the five-gaited American Saddle Horse (q.v.); is very comfortable to ride. (2) To travel at a rack (q.v.) as in a horse. (3) A hunting term; a break in the bush or hedge caused by the repeated passage of deer. (4) The antlers of a deer or stag inclusive of the crown. (5) *see* HAY RACK

racking To put fodder for horses or cattle in a hay rack (q.v.).

racking boots *see* OVERREACH BOOTS

Racking Horse A horse breed developed in the United States out of the Walking Horse (q.v.); is possessed of a unique natural gait, attractive and graceful build, with a long sloping neck, full flanks, good bone, smooth legs, and finely textured hair; stands approximately

15.2 hands and is considered a light horse; coat colors may include black, bay, sorrel, chestnut, brown, and gray; recognized as a breed in 1971 and named the official state horse of the state of Alabama in 1975.

Racking Horse Breeders' Association of America Also known by the acronym RHBAA; an organization established in 1971 in Alabama, USA to create and maintain the registry for and to protect and perpetuate the Racking Horse (q.v.) breed.

rack up (1) A racing term; said of a jockey who interferes with other horses running in a race so severely that they all slow down. (2) To tie a horse, as to a ring attached to the wall.

racy Said of a horse; to have a body suited for racing.

radion carpal joint *see* CARPUS

radiograph An image or picture on film produced by the action of X-rays (q.v.) or rays from other radioactive substances.

radiography The art or process of producing radiographs (q.v.).

rag Also known as a rake; a herd of young horses.

ragged hips Said of a horse having prominent hips (q.v.), as in those that are poorly fleshed and/or muscled.

rail (1) Also known as pole; a round wooden bar generally 12 feet (3.6 meters) in length, although shorter poles, 10 feet (3 meters), also occur, used to create a jump when horizontally supported in cups between two standards (q.v.), or as a guide to teach a horse to jump, in which case it is known as a ground rail (q.v.). (2) Also known as fence; a racing term; the barrier located on either side of the racing strip between which race horses run when competing or working out; referred to specifically as either the inside rail (q.v.) or outside rail (q.v.).

rail runner A racing term; said of a horse who prefers to run along the inside rail (q.v.).

railway crossing A jumping obstacle; two winged gates, in the center of each being a red circle.

rainrot *see* RAIN SCALD

rain scald Also known as rainrot or strep-tothricosis; a painful, infectious skin inflammation caused by the organism *Dermatophilus congolensis* which lives without consequence in the equine coat and gains entry into the skin when it is saturated by prolonged rain; slow-drying, humid conditions enable the organism to multiply, which irritates the hair follicles and skin of afflicted horses; the hair appears matted and tufted and with gentle pulling, will lift off revealing a green-gray pus stuck to the ends; lesions generally follow the water run-off pattern over the horse's back, belly, and lower limbs where the condition is known as scratches (q.v.); without treatment will run its course in one to four weeks; most common in the fall and winter during extended periods of rain; spread mechanically by biting and non-biting flies; prolonged wetting and a dirty coat appear to be predisposing factors.

rake (1) Also known as rake him up; a rodeo term; said of the spurring action of the rider on roughstock (q.v.) in which the rider drags the spur from the shoulders to the flanks through a swinging action, rather than jabbing; bareback and saddle bronc riders are required to spur throughout the duration of their ride, although bull riders are not, but they may score higher when they do. (2) see RAG. (3) An agricultural implement with teeth or tines for gathering together hay or leaves, or breaking and smoothing the surface of the ground.

rake him up see RAKE no. 1

Ralli car Also known as clothes basket or incorrectly as Ralli cart; a small, light two-wheeled, horse-drawn, open English passenger car with crosswise seating for two, back-to-back, first introduced at the end of the 19th century; had curved sides, with the rearward extremities of the shafts attached to the body-work rather than the undercarriage, was hung on sideways semi-elliptical springs, and pulled by a single horse, cob, or large pony; named after the family by whom it was originally designed.

Ralli cart see RALLI CAR

Ralph A hoof shape pattern in which the hoof is generally asymmetric, with the widest part of the hoof located in the rear third.

ram headed Said of a horse having a convex head profile; commonly used to describe a Barb (q.v.).

ranch Also known as rancho; an established tract of land for raising and grazing livestock, especially in the western United States.

ranch brand Also known as a vanity brand or ownership brand; a brand (q.v.), an identifying mark applied to the hide of a horse to identify the owner or ranch to which he belongs; usually applied to the hip with a hot iron; duplicate brands may exist as the ranch branch is only valid in the state or country or to the individual or ranch to which it is registered.

rancher Also known as a ranch man; one who owns or is employed on a ranch.

ranchero In the southwestern United States, South America, and Mexico, one who owns, manages, or is employed on a ranch (q.v.).

ranch house The ranch owner's house or principal building on a ranch (q.v.).

ranch man see RANCHER

rancho (1) see RANCH. (2) A hut, building, or groups thereof inhabited by ranch and/or farm workers.

randem Also spelled random; three horses hitched in single file, usually to a dog cart (q.v.).

random see RANDEM

range horse (1) Any horse foaled and raised on the range, having never been handled until brought in from the range to break. (2) see COW PONY

range the quarters Said of the rider, to move the haunches of the horse either to the left or right.

rangy Said of a slender and long-limbed horse.

rank A racing term; said of a horse who refuses to submit to a jockey during a race, running in a headstrong manner without respect to pace.

rape Also known as rapeseed; a European herb *Brassica napus* of the mustard family grown as a forage crop for sheep and pigs and for its seeds which yield oil.

rapeseed (1) The seed of the rape (q.v.). (2) *see* RAPE

rapeseed meal A high energy protein supplement produced from the residue of the rapeseed after extraction of the oil; contains 36 percent digestible protein, 2 percent lysine, and a fiber and calcium content double that of soybean meal; early varieties contained high levels of goitrogenic factors, but new varieties and processing methods have reduced this factor; recently the term canola meal has been used for products from varieties of rapeseed containing less than three milligrams of glucosinotate per gram of seed.

rapping A training practice; to use a rapping pole (q.v.) to encourage a horse to lift his feet when jumping.

rapping pole A training device; a usually wooden pole approximately 10 to 12 feet (3-3.6 m) in length either suspended in the cups of the jump standards or held on either end by ground support (q.v.) which is raised as the horse jumps, so that his hind feet hit the pole; encourages the horse to lift its feet higher on subsequent jumps to avoid the pain of striking the pole; may be set with tacks.

Rarey, John A 19th-century American who demonstrated the technique of horse whispering (q.v.) to calm and train horses around the world.

rase *see* RACE no. 3

rasp (1) *see* TOOTH RASP. (2) To scrape or abrade with a rough instrument as in the teeth or the hoof. (3) Also known as hoof rasp; a long-handled, coarse file having separate, point-like teeth used to level the bearing surface of the hoof after trimming.

rasper A hunting term; any large, untrimmed hedge, that when jumped, scratches the horses and riders.

rasping *see* FLOAT

ratcatcher (1) A hunting term; an informal riding outfit worn during cub hunting (q.v.) before the official start of the foxhunting season. (2) A formal long- or short-sleeved riding shirt with a standing banded collar worn by English rather than western riders; the name and design were adopted for riding in the 18th century from a garment worn by Eng-

lish street urchins in which they collected and carried live rats and door mice to the merchants who sold them for food; the jacket was made of lisle or corduroy, was closed at the wrist and waist, and had a high, banded collar which could be buttoned to prevent the rodents from escaping; worn over a heavy shirt which protected the rat catchers from being bitten; the design and name was adopted for use by the rider because of its warmth and ability to keep out the damp.

rat catcher An antiquated English term; historically, one whose vocation it was to catch mice and rats for sale as food.

rate (1) A cutting term; the action of a horse when he paces his actions with those of a cow; the ability of the horse to stay in the correct cutting position, parallel with the cow being worked. (2) A roping term; the action of the horse as he moves behind the calf maintaining an even speed with it while the roper swings the lariat (q.v.) and prepares the throw. (3) A barrel racing term; a maneuver in which the horse shortens or adjusts his stride to turn around a barrel. (4) A racing term; to restrain a horse early in a race to save his energy for a push later, as at the finish. (5) A hunting term; to scold a hound.

rated A racing term; said of a horse restrained by the jockey early in a horse race to save its energy for a push later on.

rat tail Said of the horse's tail when sparsely covered with hair.

rat tails Also known as mule ears; leather or fabric loops or ears stitched to the inside lining of a tall riding boot used by the rider to pull on the boot; may be used with or without boot hooks (q.v.).

rattle (1) A racing term; said of a horse who prefers to run on a firm track (q.v.). (2) Also known as rattle a fox; a hunting term; said of the hounds when they press hard on the trail of a fox forcing him to hurry along. (3) A hunting term; the note sounded on the hunt horn at a kill.

rattle a fox *see* RATTLE no. 2

rattlers Also known as rollers; weights, links of chain, or wooden, rubber or plastic balls strung on a cord or strap which are placed around the fetlock, usually of the forefeet, to encourage the horse to increase action and step higher at the trot.

Rau, Gustav (1880m–1954) A famous German hippologist.

ray *see* DORSAL STRIPE

razor backed Said of a horse having a prominent and sharp backbone.

reach *see* RACE no. 3

read a cow *see* READ CATTLE

read cattle Also known as read a cow; a cutting term; said of a horse or rider who is able to anticipate the movements of a cow.

ready To prepare a horse to participate in an event.

ready-made shoe Also known as cold shoe; a short-heeled machine-made version of a cowboy shoe (q.v.); usually manufactured in a compromise pattern where the shoe may be adapted to either the fore or hind feet; has open, graduated nail holes from toe to heel that do not require pritcheling (q.v.), and cut and rounded heels; available in sizes O, OO, 1, 2, 3, 4, and so on; nail holes are punched perpendicular to the shoe instead of corresponding to the slope of the hoof.

reagent Any substance which, by the reaction it produces, may be used in chemical analysis.

rear (1) A vice; said of a horse who rises up onto its hind legs with his forelegs raised off the ground and frequently pulled in close to his chest. (2) A class of accommodation offered on diligence (q.v.) horse-drawn vehicles during the 19th and 20th centuries in Europe; two to three rearward-facing passengers were situated over the rear boot (q.v.) and were protected by a hood.

rear boot A receptacle located on the rear portion of a coach or carriage used to contain luggage.

rearing Said of a horse who rears (q.v.); a vice.

rear leg *see* HIND LEG

reata A Spanish term; a lariat (q.v.).

reata strap A short strap used to secure a lariat (q.v.) to a western saddle.

receiving barn A racing term; a barn in which horses shipped in for a race which do not have a stall at the racetrack are stabled.

receptivity *see* ESTRUS

recessive Pertaining to or exhibiting a hidden characteristic, as opposed to a dominant characteristic.

recessive character *see* GENE RECESSIVE

recessive gene *see* GENE RECESSIVE

recognized hunt A hunting term; a Hunt (q.v.) having received permanent status from the hunting association governing hunt activity in the area.

recover A hunting term; said of the hounds; to pick up the scent again following a check (q.v.).

recovery The act or power of regaining; said of the horse after it regains its normal balance and resumes its forward gait following a fall, trip, clearing an obstacle (q.v.), etc.

recurrent uvetis *see* MOON BLINDNESS

red bay *see* BAY

red blood cells *see* BLOOD no. 1

redboard (1) A racing term; one who claims to have selected the winning horse in a horse race, but who always does so following the race; a derogatory term. (2) A racing term; an antiquated method of declaring a race official; a red flag or board was posted on the tote board (q.v.).

red corn *see* CORN no. 3

red dun Also known incorrectly as claybank dun (q.v.); refers to coat color; a variety of dun (q.v.); a washed out red or yellow coat color with brown, red, or flaxen points, and commonly primitive marks (q.v.); the lower legs are usually a darker red than the body.

refit *see* RESET

red flag A red piece of cloth of varying size, shape, design, and color, usually attached at one edge to a staff or cord, and used to mark the right side of a jumping obstacle.

red fox Also known as a red fox, *Vulpes fulva* in the United States, and *Vulpes vulpes* in Britain; a carnivorous mammal of the dog family, especially of the genus *Vulpes*; has a reddish coat, pointed muzzle, erect ears, and a long bushy tail; noted for its cunning and alertness; originally native to Canada, Alaska, and the northern United States and now found in all but the desert regions of the latter; the primary quarry of foxhounds.

red hot scent *see* BURNING SCENT

red ribbon A narrow strip of red silk, satin, or other material; when tied around the tail of a horse, indicates he is a known kicker; may also mark an endurance or cross country course when tied to bushes or trees.

red roan *see* BAY ROAN

red worm *see* LARGE STRONGYLES

referee *see* THIRD MAN

refuse A jumping term; said of a horse who declines to attempt to jump an obstacle.

refusal (1) Said of a horse who refused (q.v.) to attempt to jump an obstacle, e.g., the horse had one refusal on the course. (2) A racing term; said of a horse who fails to break the start in a race.

regional anesthesia An artificially produced state of insensibility, especially to the sense of pain, to an area of the body.

regional anesthetic Any substance possessing the power to deprive feeling or sensation to a region of the body, as in the lower or upper body.

registered hunt A hunting term; a Hunt (q.v.) which meets Association standards, but which has not been granted permanent status; the status is provisional and the Hunt is expected to improve its facilities and performance before being identified as a recognized hunt (q.v.).

Registered Shoeing Smith Also known by the acronym RSS; one of three levels of training certification awarded to practicing farriers in Britain awarded by the Worshipful Company of Farriers (q.v.) on the basis of written, oral, and practical examinations; now known as Diploma of the Worshipful Company of Farriers (q.v.).

regular Refers to the evenness with which the horse puts each foot on the ground, i.e., the horse must take each step at a regular speed and rhythm and an even length.

regulator Any device used on a harness race horse to prevent side pulling.

Reiki An ancient system of hands-on healing believed to have originated in Tibet thousands of years ago in which cosmic energy flows into the attuned practitioner through the crown chakra located at the top of the head, down through the body, expands the auric field, and flows through the practictioner's hands to the recipient; energy is drawn through the practictioner's body in direct proportion to the amount of energy required by the recipient; 15 hand positions corresponding to the chakras, glands, and energy meridians are used to treat everything from minor ailments and accidents to chronic disease by working on physical as well as psychological issues; speeds up and enhances the healing process when used alone or in conjunction with other modalities such as chiropractics, alleopathic medicine (including veterinary), TTEAM (q.v.), TTOUCH (q.v.), massage, etc.

rein (1) To direct or maneuver and control a horse by means of the reins (q.v.). (2) *see* REINS

rein aids The use of the reins to impart instruction to the horse; include direct rein (q.v.), neck rein (q.v.), indirect rein (q.v.), etc.

rein back (1) A dressage movement in which the horse steps backwards at an even two-time pace with diagonal feet touching the ground simultaneously; the horse must remain straight in the walk; only two hoof beats are heard. (2) Also known as backing up or back; a movement in which the horse steps rearward in a diagonal pattern; the foreleg set down slightly before the hind leg resulting in four distinct beats (1) right fore, (2) left hind, (3) left fore, and (4) right hind.

rein back crooked Said of the rein back (q.v.) movement when the horse swings its haunches to the in- or outside, moves with uneven strides, drags its feet along the ground, or breaks the two-stride beat.

rein billet The point of the rein (q.v.) that passes through and around the bit cheekpiece (q.v.) and back to itself where it is buckled or attached.

reiner One that participates in the sport of reining (q.v.).

reining A western, judged, non-timed event in which the athletic ability of a ranch-type horse is demonstrated in the confines of a show pen through execution of any of nine patterns; all reining patterns include small circles, large fast circles, flying lead changes, roll backs over the hocks, 360 degree spins in place to the left and to the right, and the sliding stop.

reining horse Any horse trained for reining (q.v.) maneuvers; most commonly a Quarter Horse (q.v.).

reining pattern Any of nine courses a reining horse must complete when reining; each pattern includes small circles, large fast circles, flying lead changes, roll backs over the hocks, 360 degree spins in place to the left and to the right, and the sliding stop.

reining point A cutting term; a one-point penalty assessed to a rider who picks up his left hand and the reins while working a cow in competition.

rein lame Also known as bridle lame; apparent lameness due to a lack of engagement of the haunches and uneven acceptance of the bit.

rein on him A western term; said of a horse responsive to neck reining (q.v.).

reins (1) Also known as ribbons in coaching vernacular; straps of rope, leather, or synthetic material attached to the cheekpieces (q.v.) of the bit or to the bridle on one end and held in the rider's hands on the other; used to guide and control the ridden horse. (2) *see* LONG LINE no. 2

rejoneo The art form of bull fighting from horseback in which the bull is never killed; originated in Portugal.

rejoneador The mounted participant in a rejoneo (q.v.); historically used Lusitano (q.v.) mounts, but in today's modern bullrings the

Andalusian (q.v.) and Lusitano are almost used equally; use of Thoroughbred (q.v.), Azteca (q.v.), and Quarter Horses (q.v.) also occur

relieved A horseshoe beveled or depressed on the inner half of the web (q.v.) on the hoof-facing surface, except for the heels; prevents the shoe from applying pressure to the hoof sole.

remedy *see* HOMEOPATHIC REMEDY

remount (1) A fresh horse(s) used to replace tired or lame horse(s), as those formerly used by the Pony Express, cavalry, etc. (2) To mount a horse again.

remouthing The process of correcting or attempting to correct a spoiled mouth (q.v.); to resensitize the horse's mouth to the bit; may involve the use of a more gentle bit and soft hands.

remuda A group of riding horses used on a roundup; a relay of mounts.

rental horse Historically known as a job horse; any horse let for hire or "jobbed" out.

renvers Also known as haunches out, tail to the wall, or quarters out; a dressage movement performed on two tracks where the horse's head, neck, and shoulders follow a straight track about 1 yard (91 cm) off the wall or line at an angle of approximately 30 degrees, while the loins and quarters are bent around the rider's outside leg and remain on the track; the horse's head is flexed in the direction of the movement.

renvers half volte Also known as a half volte reversed; a dressage movement in which the horse moves off the track haunches out (q.v.), scribes one half of a 6-meter circle haunches out, and returns to the track traveling in the opposite direction.

renvers-volte A volte (q.v.) movement performed in dressage; the horse performs a 6-meter circle with the haunches out (q.v.).

rep A cowboy employed to search for and round up stray cattle from a specific ranch.

repository An auction yard where horses are sold.

re-ride A rodeo term; a second ride awarded to a bronc or bull rider in the same go-round when either the cowboy or animal is not afforded a fair opportunity to perform, as when the animal fights in the chute and cannot be mounted, if the animal falls, if the animal is impossible for the rider to mount, or if the animal falls or drags the rider off in the chute gate.

resciant *see* BLISTER no. 2

reserve The minimum amount a consignor will sell a specific horse for at public auction; the consignor can either register the reserve with the sales company which will not let the horse be sold unless the price exceeds that amount, or the consignor can bid on the horse himself until the reserve is reached.

reserved (1) A racing term; said of a horse held for a particular race. (2) A racing term; said of a horse held off the pace in a race.

reserve not achieved Also known by the acronym RNA; when the reserve (q.v.) amount a consignor will sell a specific horse for at public auction is not reached.

reset Also known as shift or refit; said of the farrier (q.v.); to remove a horseshoe from the hoof, trim the hoof, and reattach the same shoe.

resin A substance from certain plants and trees used in varnishes and laquers.

resin back *see* ROSINBACK

resist A dressage term; the horse's actions to evade any or all of the rider's aids (q.v.) including opening of the mouth, crossing the jaw, handing the tongue out, swinging the hindquarters, and tossing of the head, etc..

resisting Said of a horse who resists (q.v.).

respiration The act of breathing; the inhalation and exhalation of air.

respiratory system The system of organs that enable the horse to breath and which consist of the nostrils, nasal passages, pharynx, larynx, trachea, and lungs.

rest (1) A metal projection on a suit of armor located four fingers above the waist, upon which a knight or tilter (q.v.) would rest his lance while tilting (q.v.). (2) Cessation or temporary interruption of motion, exertion, or labor.

rest horse Also known as a spare; an antiquated coaching term; an extra coach horse(s), kept at the change (q.v.) station along the coach route which replaces a tired or spent horse(s) in the team.

rest shoe *see* PATTEN SHOE

resting leg The leg of the horse not bearing weight when at a halt; the horse may bear its weight evenly on all four legs, or alternatively, on three legs, with one leg free of weight.

result chart Also known as chart; a racing term; a chart upon which the numerical results of a given race, including the names of competing horses, the names of the riders or drivers, fractional and final times, and odds and payoffs, are posted.

retained placenta Afterbirth (q.v.) that is not expelled within six hours of foaling.

retained sole Also known as false sole; said of the horse's hoof when it does not exfoliate normally; although not a normal condition, provides extra protection for the internal structures of the foot.

retainer (1) An advance fee paid to a jockey or rider of a competed horse(s) to secure the rights to the rider's services for a predetermined amount of time. (2) One who retains the riding services of a professional.

retina The sensory membrane lining the back surface of the eye's interior; receives the focused image and transmits it to the optic nerve.

reverse field A hunting term; to change the direction traveled in pursuit of a fox.

reverse shoe *see* BACKWARDS SHOE

reverse wedge shoe A horseshoe graduated in thickness from a thick toe to a thin heel; elevates the toe of the hoof and thus lowers the hoof angle (q.v.).

RHBAA The acronym for the Racking Horse Breeders' Association of America (q.v.).

Rhenish *see* RHINELAND HEAVY DRAFT

Rhineland *see* RHINELAND HEAVY DRAFT

Rhineland Heavy Draft Also known as Rhenish, Rhineland, or German Coldblood; a coldblood developed in 19th-century Germany (Rhineland, from which the name derived); descended from the Ardennes (q.v.), Ancient Forest Horse (q.v.), and the Flanders Horse (q.v.); stands 16 to 17 hands, weighs around 2,200 pounds (998 kg), is strong, has massive quarters and shoulders, a deep, broad back, crested neck, and short, and strong legs with heavy feathering; matures early; coat colors include bay chestnut or red roan (q.v.) with flaxen (q.v.) or black mane and tail; used for heavy draft and farm work; the stud book was established in 1876.

rhinopneumonitis *see* EQUINE VIRAL RHINOPNEUMONITIS

rhythm The regularity and evenness of the hoof beats.

rib One of 18 slender curved bones that attach on each side of the horse's vertebral column, enclosing the thoracic cavity, and protecting such organs as the heart, lungs, and liver.

rib bar Refers to coat color pattern; a primitive mark (q.v.); dark hair markings appearing over the ribs of the horse.

ribbed up Also known as well ribbed up; said of a horse whose back ribs are well arched and incline well backwards, bringing the ends closer to the point of the hip and making the horse short coupled.

ribbon A strip of silk, satin, or other material awarded to signify a place winner in a competition; different colors are used to identify the contestants placing in the competition: blue (1st), red (2nd), yellow (3rd), white (4th), pink (5th), green (6th), purple (7th), brown (8th), blue/red/yellow (champion), and red/yellow/white (reserve champion).

ribbons *see* REINS

riboflavin Formerly known as vitamin B$_2$ spelled riboflavine; a B-complex vitamin essential for proper energy release and nervous system function; synthesized in the small intestine of the horse and found in good quality hay and/or pasture which provide more than sufficient amounts to meet the daily

dietary requirement; highly resistant to destruction by heat and air; deficiency is uncommon, but causes stunted growth, hair loss, etc.

rice bran The outer layer of the rice kernel removed during the rice milling process to produce white rice; fed to horses to facilitate weight gain by increasing energy and calorie intake without increasing bulk; stabilized at high temperatures to prevent spoilage; has a shelf life of up to one year, and a fat content of 18 to 24 percent.

rice hulls The husk, shell, or outer covering of a rice grain; used as a bedding (q.v.) material by horsemen; is highly absorbent, dust free, attractive, difficult to store, and in some areas difficult to obtain.

Richmonds *see* LEGGINGS

ridable (1) Capable of being ridden, as a horse. (2) Capable of being ridden through or over, as a wooded area.

ridden out A racing term; said of a horse who wins a race because of the jockey's careful pacing and strategy, but who has no energy remaining at the finish.

ride (1) Also known as horse riding; to sit on the back of a horse and manage him in motion through the use of natural and artificial aids. (2) A hunting term; a wide path or trail in a wooded area.

rider One who rides.

ride and tie A sport born in the United States in 1971; a highly strategized cross country horse race between teams consisting of two runners and one horse in which the partners alternate turns running and riding a minimum of six times; the first rider rides up the trail a predetermined distance, dismounts, ties the horse to a tree and continues on foot; when the first runner reaches the tied horse, he mounts, and rides to catch his partner running in front of him; this process of riding and tying continues until all three team members have crossed the finish line; races range from 20 to 100 miles (32-160 km) in length and an average 10,000 feet (3,048 m) elevation change with top teams averaging a sub-six-minute-mile pace; 90 percent of the competing horses are Arabs (q.v.).

Ride and Tie Association, The Also known by the acronym TRTA; an organization founded in the United States in 1989 to organize and promote the sport of ride & tie (q.v.) in the United States.

ride for a fall, to Said of a competitor; to lose intentionally or to embark upon an undertaking that seems doomed to fail; originated in horse racing, particularly the steeplechase, in which the rider with the favored mount would deliberately ride in such a way as to disqualify himself by being thrown from the horse.

ride for hire To receive payment, directly or indirectly, for riding in a race or other competition as a professional.

ride hard Said of the rider; to push the horse to his physical limits without riding him into the ground (q.v.).

ride hard to the hounds A hunting term; said of a member of the field; to push one's horse hard, riding close to the hounds.

ride hell for leather *see* HEEL BENT FOR LEATHER

ride in the Master's pocket A hunting term; said of a green rider (q.v.) who, not wishing to fall behind the pack, follows closely on the heels of the Field Master.

ride into the ground Said of the rider; to ride a horse to the extent of its physical limits so that it is unable to continue.

ride off A polo term; said of a polo player who rides up upon his opponent from an acute angle and applies pressure of his body, except the elbows, and/or that of his horse against his opponent to move the opponent off the line of the ball (q.v.) and prevent him from striking it; charging at an angle greater than about 45 degrees is not allowed.

rider One who rides a horse, mule, or the like.

ride short A racing term; to ride with short stirrups.

ride to a blue Said of a rider in competition who, on the basis of the performance or ride, wins the blue ribbon or first place.

ride to hounds Also known as riding for hounds; a hunting term; to hunt or follow the hounds (q.v.) on horseback.

ridgeling *see* RIG

riding *see* RIDE

riding coat A dense, wind- and rain-resistant coat made of natural or synthetic fabric including melton wool, light-weight wools, or cotton, worn by a mounted rider; originally long enough to cover and protect the upper leg, is vented in the back to accommodate the cantle (q.v.) of the saddle, and has slanted and flapped pockets for easy hand access and to protect the contents from the weather.

riding crupper *see* SADDLE CRUPPER

riding fee A sum of money paid to a professional to show or compete a horse.

riding for hounds *see* RIDE TO HOUNDS

riding horse Any horse suitable for use as a riding mount.

riding instructor One that teaches others the art of horsemanship (q.v.).

riding on the lunge A training exercise for a mounted rider; the rider rides a horse lunged (q.v.) in a circle to gain balance, learn leg and seat aids, etc; may be performed hands-free, with or without stirrups.

riding out *see* HACK

riding pony (1) A type rather than a breed; of relatively recent creation in Great Britain where it was derived from small Thoroughbred (q.v.) and Arab (q.v.) stallions put to native pony mares including the Welsh (q.v.), Dartmoor (q.v.), and Exmoor (q.v.); all coat colors are permitted; of three size categories: up to 12.2 hands, 12.3 to 13.2 hands, and 13.3 to 14 hands. (2) Any pony (q.v.) ridden for pleasure or competition.

riding school A facility where people are taught the principles and practices of riding by a trained instructor.

rig (1) Also known as cryptorchid, double cryptorchid, ridgeling, or original; a male horse with improper, bilateral or unilateral testicular descent; the retained testicles may lie within the inguinal canal, but external to the body wall, or within the abdomen internal to the inguinal canal; will demonstrate masculine behavior including attempting to round up mares, attraction to a mare in heat (q.v.), full erection, and occasionally, ejaculation; is infertile, except in the case of a unilateral cryptorchid, which will be fertile from the scrotal testis (q.v.); may result from incorrect castration, even though both testicles may have been removed, or where one or both testicles have not descended, the latter being an inherited genetic feature classified as a partial lethal (q.v.). (2) Slang; any horse-drawn or mechanical vehicle; a truck.

right diagonal Said of the horse when the right foreleg moves in unison with the left hind at the trot.

right lead Said of the horse when the right foreleg and right hind leg lead at the canter (q.v.) or gallop.

right of way A polo term; a governing law in the game of polo which entitles the player having hit the ball to follow the line of that ball from the offside of his pony and to take a further shot; play will flow backward and forward, parallel to an imaginary line of the ball extended ahead of, and behind, the ball.

right price A racing term; the point at which mutuel odds are high enough to warrant bettors (q.v.) risking a bet on a particular horse.

right rein *see* ON THE RIGHT REIN

rim firing A rodeo term; to place a burr or other irritating object between the saddle blanket and the back of the horse to make it buck more purposefully.

rim shoe Any horseshoe (q.v.) with a long cleat on the outer edge; occasionally used correctively for horses with bad tendons.

ring bit *see* TATTERSAL BIT

ringbone Also known as interphalangeal arthritis; formation of new bone in the area of the first or second phalanx of the pastern; evolves slowly and may result from faulty conformation such as too upright pasterns, improper shoeing, repeated concussion through work on hard ground, working a young horse (under three years of age) too hard too quickly, bruises, sprains, strains, injuries to ligaments, tendons, or joints, or may follow trauma, infection, or wire-cut wounds; may or may not result in lameness; more common in the fore than back feet; produces a characteristic bell-shaped pastern; of two types, high ringbone (q.v.) and low ringbone (q.v.).

ringbone, high *see* HIGH RINGBONE

ringbone, low *see* LOW RINGBONE

ringbone, non-articulating *see* NON-ARTICULATING RINGBONE

ring boots *see* FETLOCK RING BOOT

ringer (1) Also known as ring in; an American racing term; a horse entered in a race under a false name to obtain more favorable betting odds; to enter the ringer in a race below its class where it is almost certain to win; a dishonest practice. (2) An Australian term; a station hand on a large property, generally those in the wetter areas of Australia; appears to have originated in the days when cattle ranged on large, unfenced properties and gathering would take many months at a time; at night, one of the men would ride around the herd to keep them from escaping to their previous grazing territory; the act of riding around the herd was always performed in a circle or ring, and thus, the rider was a ringer. (3) Also known as ringing fox; a hunting term; a fox who runs in circles, twisting and doubling back in covert (q.v.), rather than running in a straight line.

ring in *see* RINGER

ringing fox *see* RINGER no. 3

ringmaster *see* RING STEWARD

rings *see* RUNNING MARTINGALE

ring sour Said of a horse who, because it is ridden continuously in an enclosed area such as a riding ring, becomes disinterested and difficult to work in that environment, i.e., the horse is bored; easily treated by varying the work schedule and location.

ring steward Also known as a ringmaster; one responsible for oversight of competitive activity in the riding or show ring or arena including assisting the judge, but not advising him.

Ring, The A racing term; bookmakers, collectively.

ringworm Also known as dermatophytosis; a fungal infection of the skin and hair resulting in hair loss and lesions; the affected area is generally circular in shape; most commonly transmitted by contaminated grooming equipment, saddle blankets, and harnesses.

riot A hunting term; said of the hounds (q.v.) when they hunt quarry (q.v.) other than that selected, e.g., a rabbit instead of a fox.

risen clinch Said of a clinch (q.v.) which rises and pulls away from the hoof wall, an indication the horseshoe is loosening.

rising The age of the horse when close to, but less than a specific year, e.g., a horse rising eight will not be eight years old.

rising trot *see* POSTING

risling *see* RIDGELING

RNA The acronym for reserve not achieved (q.v.).

roach To cut or shear the mane 1 to 3 inches (2.5-7.5 cm) long leaving a few long wisps of hair at the withers for a hand hold; used on polo ponies to ensure that the mallet does not become entangled and in breeds such as the cob, to highlight his muscular neck structure.

roach back Also known as a hog back or hogged back; said of the spine of the horse when convexly curved between the withers and loins; a conformation defect.

roach backed Also known as hog backed; said of a horse having a convex curvature of the spine between the withers (q.v.) and loins; gives the appearance of an arched back; the opposite of hollow back (q.v.); a conformation defect.

roached mane Also known as a pony roach; a mane cut or sheared, but left 1 to 3 inches (2.5-7.5 cm) long and tapered so that it stands upright; the outside hairs of the mane are shorter than the inside hairs; not as short as a clipped or hogged mane.

roaching The process by which the horse's mane is sheared or roached (q.v.).

road cart A two-wheeled, horse-drawn passenger vehicle drawn by a single horse or pony.

road coach A horse-drawn multi-passenger, public transportation vehicle which gained popularity during the last quarter of the 19th century; generally weighed in excess of one ton (1 tonnes), seated 12 outside passengers as well as the guard and coachman, was brightly colored, had small-paned windows, a folding ladder secured under the boot (q.v.), and was strongly built to withstand the heavy, daily mileage.

road founder Inflammation of the sensitive laminae (q.v.) of the hoof caused by excessive concussion over hard surfaces.

road hack Also known as an ordinary hack; a horse who, due to gaits and conformation, would not be suitable for a park hack (q.v.), but who is good for pleasure riding outside of competition.

road hunter A hunting term; a hound particularly proficient at following the line of a fox (q.v.) along a hard, dry road where the scent does not stick well.

roading hounds A hunting term; to exercise hounds down a road rather than through the country.

road puff *see* WINDPUFF

Roadster *see* NORFOLK ROADSTER

road wagon A four-wheeled, horse-drawn open wagon suited for carrying merchandise.

roan Refers to coat color; a specific color pattern consisting of a uniform mixture of colored and white body hairs and a colored head and points; a non-progressive seldom dappled color pattern; scarred areas will grow in colored and the coat color changes throughout the year being lightest in the spring and darkest in the winter; are further described by the base color of the horse followed by the term roan as in bay roan (q.v.), strawberry roan (q.v.), honey roan (q.v.), purple roan (q.v.), and lilac roan (q.v.).

roan blanket *see* BLANKET no. 1

roarer A horse with paralysis to one or both sides of the larynx due to the obstruction of the larynx by the arytenoid cartilage and vocal fold, resulting in a characteristic roaring noise during inhalation.

roaring *see* LARYNGEAL HEMIPLEGIA

ROC The acronym for Race of Champions (q.v.).

rock 'n' roll A vaulting term; a freestyle exercise in which the vaulter (q.v.), standing on the back of the horse, assists a partner in an aerial forward roll dismount using a wrist grip.

Rockaway Also known as Rockaway Coupé or station wagon; an American two-passenger, horse-drawn, vehicle used throughout the 19th century; manufactured in a variety of types and sizes, was usually headed (q.v.), had semi-open sides protected by curtains or roll-down blinds, hung on crosswise springs in the style of an American buggy, and had a driver's seat sheltered by a forward extension of the roof canopy; drawn either by a horse in shafts or a pair in pole gear (q.v.).

Rockaway Coupé A cut-down version of the rockaway (q.v.), sometimes used as a station wagon (q.v.).

Rockaway Landau A type of rockaway (q.v.); a horse-drawn vehicle popular during the late 19th century; combined the best features of the rockaway and the landau (q.v.); a half-hood protected the rear seats and a standing top the fore and the driver's seat.

rockered toe shoe *see* ROCKER-TOE SHOE

rocker shoe *see* ROCKER-TOE SHOE

rocker-toe shoe Also known as a roller-motion shoe, rockered-toe shoe, rocker shoe, or set-toe shoe; a horseshoe (q.v.) with thick quarters, beveled or rolled from the center third up onto the toe of the hoof; the hoof surface is left flat; used to treat arthritic conditions of the forelegs, chronic bowed tendons, to speed breakover and/or relieve stress of breaking over the toe, and, in some cases, founder (q.v.).

rocking-chair canter Said of the Tennessee Walking Horse's (q.v.) canter; a smooth, collected gallop involving a high rolling movement.

rocking horse Also known as a hobby horse; a toy horse suspended by springs from a frame upon which a child rides.

rodeo (1) Also known in Australia as a cattle men's carnival; a public performance of cowboy (q.v.) skills including bronc riding (q.v.), steer wrestling (q.v.), calf roping, etc.; from the Spanish rodear meaning to go round. (2) *see* ROUND UP

rodeoin Slang; to compete in a rodeo (q.v.).

rogue A consistently fractious horse or one who demonstrates a fierce disposition.

rogue's badge *see* RACING BLINKERS

rollback Also known as set and turn; a western term; said of the galloping horse which stops, lifts its forelegs, turns 180 degrees, and starts again at the gallop in the same direction from which it came.

rolled toe A horseshoe rounded on the outer edge of the ground surface at the toe while the hoof-side surface of the shoe remains flat.

roller (1) Also known as body roller; a girth (q.v.) or surcingle (q.v.) of leather or webbing with pads attached to the underside that fit on either side of the withers used to prevent pressure and rubbing and to hold a rug or blanket in place. (2) Also known as a bit roller, cherry roller, or in western circles as a cricket; a round, bead-shaped, stainless, blue steel, or copper ball(s) which rotates freely about the mouthpiece or port (q.v.) when played with by the horse using his tongue; encourages salivation and prevents a puller (q.v.) from setting his jaw.

roller bolt Also known as a bollard; an upright, metal projection from the end of the splinter bar (q.v.) to which the traces of a pair, or coach wheelers (q.v.) attach.

roller-motion shoe *see* ROCKER-TOE SHOE

roller pad A rectangular piece of felt, wool, cotton, or other material 1 inch (2.5 cm) thick, placed under a roller (q.v.) to provide protection and absorb sweat.

rollers (1) *see* RATTLERS. (2) The plural of roller (q.v.).

rolling Excessive lateral shoulder movement common to horses with protruding shoulders.

Romanic (1) Descended from, inheriting civilization etc., of the Romans. (2) Also known as Romanic style; a riding style inherited from the Roman period; implies a highly collected, agile style of riding based on lightness and dexterity of hand.

Romanic school A type of riding based on the Romanic style (q.v.)

Romanic style *see* ROMANIC no. 2

Roman nose Also known as Roman profile; said of a horse having a convex face from poll (q.v.) to muzzle; the nasal bone protrudes when the head is viewed from the side; considered undesirable for aesthetic reasons, and is a definite conformation defect in some breeds such as the Arab (q.v.); associated with cold-blood heavy-horse breeds.

Roman profile *see* ROMAN NOSE

romp A racing term; an easy race.

rompre en lice A 16th and 17th-century French term; in a competition, to break one's lance in the lice (q.v.), on a pile, revolving figure, tree trunk, or opponent's shield.

roof A class of accommodation offered on diligence (q.v.) horse-drawn vehicles used in 19th and 20th-century Europe; driver and guard seats were situated above the coupé (q.v.).

rooster pull A mounted game performed in the United States in the 18th and 19th centuries in which a mounted rider traveling at high speed, would lean out of the saddle, reach down and pull loose a rooster previously buried neck-deep in the ground, and complete the competition by racing the other competitors in a circle.

root crops Any of a number of vegetables fed to the horse either as a dietary supplement or a treat including carrots, rutabagas, mangels, sugar beets, and turnips.

roots A hunting term; a field of tuberous plants such as carrots, turnips, potatoes, etc.

rope (1) A thick, long cord of twisted or braided fibers, as hemp, wire, nylon, or other material. (2) *see* LARIAT. (3) To catch, tie, or fasten as with a rope.

rope bag Also known as a rope can; a western roping term; a soft or hard container in which a lariat (q.v.) is packed or stored for traveling.

rope can *see* ROPE BAG

rope horse *see* ROPING HORSE

rope shoe Also known as fiber shoe; a traction horseshoe (q.v.) now replaced by the St. Croix rim shoe (q.v.) and studs (q.v.); has a groove along the entire ground-side surface in which a tarred rope is set; used to prevent the horse from slipping on smooth pavements; special long-headed nails were used.

rope walking Also known as plaiting, lacing, or crossing feet; a gait defect in which the horse moves in such a manner that the hooves are placed in front of each other through a twisting of the striding leg around the supporting leg in a manner similar to a person climbing a rope or plaiting two pieces of rope together; common to horses wide at the base or having broad chests, or in the hind legs of pacers; a severe example of paddling (q.v.); may be corrected with shoeing.

roping A racing term; to lunge (q.v.).

roping dummy A roping term; any target a roper uses to practice throwing a loop, including a plastic calf's head.

roping horse Also known as a rope horse; any specially trained horse, such as a Quarter Horse (q.v.) or Quarter Horse cross, from which the rider is able to rope cattle and/or horses.

rosadera The parts of a jaquima (q.v.) that contact the lower jaw and the shanks.

rose gray Refers to coat color; a mixture of black and white; such horses are born either chestnut or sorrel and never have a true gray appearance, or become progressively whiter with age; the most common shade of gray (q.v.).

rosette (1) *see* BOSS. (2) A silk or cloth ribbon gathered to resemble a rose; awarded to placing competitors in an equestrian event.

rosin (1) A resin (q.v.) formed from the oil of turpentine when distilled from crude turpentine; used by vaulters to provide traction.

(2) To rub or cover with rosin.

Rosinante (1) The trusted mount of Don Quixote de la Mancha, the protagonist in Miguel de Cervantes' book of the same title. (2) A horse who has reached the end of its usefulness.

rosinback Also known as a resin back; a circus term; a generally wide or flat-backed horse on which one or several vaulters (q.v.) perform; the term derived from the use of rosin (q.v.) applied to the back of the horse, mainly around the quarters, to prevent performers from slipping.

rosinback riding machine A crane-like device used in the circus to train bareback riders; a safety line, suspended from the crane, attaches to a waist belt worn by the rider; in the event of a fall, the crane and safety line support the rider.

rough country Difficult terrain to ride through, e.g., heavily wooded, steep, etc.

roughing off Also known as roughing up; the process of preparing a stabled horse for turn out to grass or pasture by reducing and ultimately removing grain from the diet and allowing its natural coat to fill in.

roughing up *see* ROUGHING OFF

rough out Also known as rough-out leather; the rough side of a tanned hide when worn to the outside, as in chaps and some types of cowboy boots.

rough-out leather *see* ROUGH OUT

rough rider Also known as a rough stock rider; one who rides rough stock (q.v.) including saddle broncs (q.v.), bareback broncs, and bulls.

rough shod *see* COWBOY SHOD

rough stock A rodeo term; untrained stock, horses, or bulls used in mounted bucking competitions such as saddle bronc, bareback bronc, and bull riding.

rough stock rider *see* ROUGH RIDER

rough transition *see* TRANSITION ROUGH

rouncy *see* COB

round Also known as go-round or heat; in competitions, the individual performances in which the rider and/or horse compete and are scored.

rounded back Also known as arched back; a dressage term; the horse's back when the hollow between the withers and croup is reduced, the loin more horizontal, the tail swinging, and the back relaxed.

rounding A hunting term; the antiquated process of cutting off the tips of puppy's ears for appearances.

round pen (1) *see* BULL PEN. (2) A round training arena usually between 100 and 200 feet (30-61 m) in diameter with 6 to 8 foot (1.8–2.4 m) walls in which the horse is worked or trained.

round the world *see* MILL

round turn A cutting term; said of a horse who, when working a cow, walks through the turn rather than planting his hind legs and spins on his hocks.

round up Also known as catch up or rodeo; the driving together of cattle or other animals for inspection, branding, and the like, generally from pasture.

round-up wagon *see* CHUCK WAGON

roundworm, large *see* LARGE ROUNDWORM

rount Also known as grizzle or grissel; an early English term; a horse with a roan (q.v.) coat mixed with white or peach.

rouse A hunting term; to drive from cover as in a stag (q.v).

route A racing term; a horse race in excess of 1 1/8 miles (1.8 km) in length.

router A racing term; a horse who runs best in races of 1 1/8 miles (1.8 km) or longer.

rowel The revolving wheel-like attachment of the neck of a spur (q.v.); of many varieties including smooth-edged, notched, or having sharp points or projections.

Royal College of Veterinary Surgeons The governing body of the veterinary profession in Great Britain and Ireland organized in 1844.

Royal Hanoverian Cream *see* PALOMINO

Royal International *see* ROYAL INTERNATIONAL HORSE SHOW

Royal International Horse Show Also known as the London International, the Royal International, and formerly as the International Horse Show; an international horse show first held in 1907 in London, England and continued there annually except during the years of 1915 to 1919, 1933, and 1940 to 1944; from 1945 on, held at White City, London; classes are open to Hunters, Hacks, Cobs, and Ponies under saddle, Hackneys, and jumpers; granted the prefix of Royal in 1957.

Royal International Horse Show (CHI) Any horse show which includes competitions open to one or more international riders who participate as individuals as authorized by their National Federation, at the invitation of the hosting National Federation, or by personal invitation; no team or individual competitor is ever officially sent to such shows.

Royal International Horse Show (CHIO) Any international horse show which, being authorized by its National Horse Show Federation, and having obtained consent from the FEI (q.v.), is entered into the FEI Calendar; riders are sent to such shows officially by their National Horse Show Federations and with the approval of any concerned government departments.

Royal Society for the Prevention of Cruelty to Animals An organization founded in Great Britain in 1824 to encourage kindness and prevent cruelty to animals.

RSHANA The acronym for the Russian Sport Horse Association of North America (q.v.).

RSS The acronym for Registered Shoeing Smith (q.v.).

ruano Refers to point color; a Spanish term; light flaxen points; sometimes used in combination with other color distinctions for greater color specificity, e.g., chestnut (q.v.) ruano.

rubber band Also known as developer; a band made of elastic; a resilient cohesive solid made from the sap of certain tropical trees and shrubs used to hold show braids in the mane and tail.

rubber curry comb An oval, round, or square-shaped, hand-held instrument made of rubber and having rows of short rubber teeth or indentations on one side and a loop through which the hand is passed on the other; used to massage the horse, clean dirt and debris from the horse's coat, and to clean grooming brushes.

rubber shoe A horseshoe (q.v.) popular for use on horses employed in slow road work; are clipped, thicker than conventional shoes, and manufactured of rubber with a steel center; are fitted cold.

rub-down To rub the horse with a rough towel, usually following exercise, to promote circulation, lessen fatigue, and dry the coat.

rubefacient Any substance applied externally to the body of the horse which produces mild to moderate heat and skin redness without a blister (q.v.) to reduce pain and heal trauma; normally applied 36 hours following an injury.

rug *see* HORSE BLANKET

rug fillet *see* FILLET

rugged up Said of a horse wearing a rug (q.v.).

ruined Said of a spoiled horse, or one who does not obey the aids; generally due to rider, owner, or trainer error.

rule off *see* SUSPEND no. 2

rump *see* CROUP no. 1

Rum Pony An ancient strain of Highland Pony (q.v.) found on the island of Coll, Scotland; limited numbers remain; is small, sturdy, and generally has a mouse dun or chestnut coat with a pale mane.

run (1) *see* HUNT. (2) Also known as running; a hunting term; the period of time when the hounds are actually on the line of the fox (q.v.). (3) A western term; also known as gallop; a fast, four-beat gait in which each foot strikes the ground separately, the sequence being near hind, off hind, near fore, and off fore. (4) A cutting term; the 2-1/2 minute time period allotted to each cutting (q.v.) contestant participating in a competition during which the cutter attempts to cut and work as many calves as possible from the herd. (5) A racing term; the position a horse takes at the finish line, as in to run fourth. (6) *see* RUN OF THE FOX

run a hole through the wind A racing term; said of a very fast horse.

runaway (1) Said of a horse who escapes control of the rider and runs dangerously fast, often without concern for his safety or that of his rider. (2) A race or event decisively or easily won.

runcy *see* COBB

run down A racing term; said of a horse who scrapes the flesh off his heels on the track surface while racing; may be associated with weak pasterns.

run-down bandage A 3 to 6 inch (7.5-15 cm) bandage wrapped around the lower leg and fetlock to provide support and to avoid abrasive injury when the fetlocks sink toward the ground during weight-bearing in races or workouts.

run-down boots *see* TENDON BOOTS

run heel A hunting term; said of the hounds (q.v.) when they hit the line of the fox (q.v.) and run it backwards.

run his foil *see* DOUBLE BACK

run in A racing term; said of a horse who wins unexpectedly.

run in the money *see* IN THE MONEY

run mute A hunting term; hounds who run after the quarry (q.v.) so fast that they are unable to speak (q.v.).

runner (1) A racing term; one who runs to and from the mutuel windows to place bets for those seated in club boxes. (2) A racing term; any horse entered to compete in a horse race. (3) *see* KEEPERS

running (1) The act of one who runs. (2) *see* RUNNING DOWNHILL. (3) *see* RUN no. 2. (4) To compete in a contest. (5) Having a chance to win a contest, e.g., Secretariat was in the running.

running a train scent A hunting term; a drag hunt dating to late 16th and early 17th-century England; the predecessor of drag hunting (q.v.) in which a drag (q.v.) was laid in a pattern closely simulating the run of the wild fox, hounds were put on the line (q.v.) to run it at racing pace; the horse in the lead at the end of the drag was declared the winner.

running downhill Also known as running; said of a horse when he takes quick hurried strides with little or no balance or rhythm, very little suspension, and too much weight on the forehand.

running heel *see* HEEL no. 2

running iron The predecessor of the modern branding iron (q.v.); a one half inch wide iron rod slightly curved at one end.

running loose A racing term; said of a horse who runs unbacked (q.v.) in a horserace due to the owner's or stable's lack of confidence in his ability.

running martingale Also known as rings or training yoke in racing circles; a Y-shaped, split, auxiliary rein which begins as a single adjustable strap attached at one end to the girth (q.v.) passes between the forelegs and divides into two branches at the base of the neck; each branch ends with a ring through which the left and right reins pass; used to assist the action of the bit by restricting the position of the horse's head and neck.

running out (1) *see* RUN OUT. (2) Said of a horse turned out to grass.

running over a horse *see* RUN THROUGH

running-quick mount Also known as flying mount; a method of mounting a horse; to run towards a standing horse, jump with the left foot into the left stirrup, and swing the right leg over the saddle; requires a quiet horse.

running rail *see* INSIDE RAIL

running rank A racing term; said of a horse who refuses to be restrained or rated (q.v.) early in the race to conserve its energies for a push later on.

running reins Two separate leather straps attached on one end to the girth which pass between the horse's legs at which point one rein passes through the left bit ring and one through the right bit ring; the reins then return to the surcingle (q.v.) or roller (q.v.) where they are attached; used to control the head position of the horse; differ from draw reins (q.v.) in that they are not held by a rider or driver.

running up light Said of a poorly muscled horse, particularly over the haunches.

running w A discouraged and outdated method of tumbling a horse headfirst to the ground used by the movie industry; superseded by a toe tapper (q.v.); the cable runs from screws placed between the horseshoe and hoof of both front feet to a ring on a surcingle, where the two cables run into a single cable which is drawn off the horse at an slight angle and anchored to a bull prick; the length of cable attached to the bull prick determines the distance the horse can travel before the end of the cable is reached and the fall triggered.

running walk A natural, inherited, loose, four-beat gait, intermediate in speed between the walk and the rack (q.v.), in which each foot strikes the ground separately at regular intervals: left fore, right rear, right fore, left rear; the hind hooves may overstep the print of the fore by as much as 24 inches (61 cm) and the speed varies from 9 to 20 mph (14-32 kmph); is characterized by a bobbing or nodding of the head, flopping of the ears, and a clicking of the teeth in rhythm with the movement of the legs; the center of balance is somewhat behind so that the horse appears to squat and there is no suspension; a faster-paced gait than the flat-foot walk.

run of the fox Also known as run; a hunting term; the route traveled by a fox (q.v.).

run out (1) A racing term; said of a horse who finishes out of the money (q.v.). (2) A racing term; said of a horse who prefers to run along the outside rail. (3) Also known as running out; a jumping term; said of a horse who deliberately avoids jumping an obstacle by running to one side or the other of it.

run-out-bit A racing bit designed to give the rider extra leverage on one side; used to prevent the horse from bearing out (q.v.) to the left or right.

runs hot and cold *see* IN-AND-OUTER

run through Also known as running over a horse; a cutting term; said of a cow who tries to run under a horse in an attempt to return to the herd.

run-under heels *see* UNDERRUN HEELS

run up a stirrup iron To slide the stirrup iron (q.v.) to the top of the stirrup leather (q.v.).

run wide A racing term; said of a horse who runs far from the inside rail (q.v.) and therefore covers extra ground.

rupture *see* HERNIA AND HERNIA, DIAPHRAGMATIC

rushing A dressage term; said of a horse whose pace (q.v.) is too fast and hurried, lacking balance and rhythm.

Russian cab *see* DROSKY

Russian Droschki *see* DROITZSCHKA

Russian Heavy Draft A heavy-draft breed gradually developed in 1850 in Russia for agricultural work; descended from local mares put to a variety of heavy draft breeds including the Swedish Ardennes (q.v.), Belgian Draft (q.v.), Percheron (q.v.), and Orlov Trotter (q.v.); is strong, hardy, quiet and energetic, and stands 14.1 to 15 hands; may have a chestnut, roan, or bay coat, is well balanced and muscular, has well-sprung ribs, full mane, tail, and forelock, short, lightly feathered legs, and a short, straight back.

Russian Saddle Horse Also known as an Orlov-Rostopchin; a breed of horse descended from the Orlov Trotter (q.v.) crossed with the Rostopchin, a horse of English Thoroughbred (q.v.) and Arab (q.v.) extraction.

Russian Sport Horse Association of North America Also known by the acronym RSHANA; an organization formed in the United States in 1994 to cultivate a U.S. market for Russian-bred horses and those from other republics of the former Soviet Union; horses eligible for registration include the Orlov-Rostopchin, Orlov Trotter (q.v.), Russian Trakehener, Budyonny (q.v.), Ukrainskaya, Akhal-teke (q.v.), Don (q.v.), Latvian (q.v.), Russian Hannoverian, Tersky (q.v.), and crosses of these native breeds.

Russian Steppe Horse *see* KUSTANAIR

Russian style *see* TROIKA

Russian Trotter *see* ORLOV TROTTER

rut (1) The noise emitted by a stag (q.v.) when desiring to mate. (2) Sexual arousal of deer, stag, and some other animals due to hormone changes, as during the mating season.

rutting season The period during which deer, stag, and other animals experience sexual arousal associated with mating.

rye A hardy annual grass *Secale cereale*, widely grown for grain and as a cover crop; neither the grass nor grain is a popular feed for horses as the only available rye products for livestock are mill by-products such as rye middlings which are relatively low in fiber, a poor source of vitamins or minerals, and not particularly palatable; have a digestible protein content of 12 to 13 percent; grain mixtures should never contain more than one third rye which should be processed rather than whole; susceptible to the fungus *Claviceps purpuria* which produces the compound ergot (q.v.).

rye grass *see* RYE

rye grass hay A cut and dried grass hay made from rye (q.v.) following harvest of the grain; is generally low in palatability and contains a fiber content of about 38 percent and an incomplete digestible protein content of around 4 percent.

rye straw Any of several rye grasses which have been dried; highly prized as a stuffing for horse collars.

S

sabino Also known as flecked roan, buttermilk roan, or calico paint; refers to an asymmetrical coat color pattern in which the white patches are variable ranging from distinct, sharp patches to small spots of white on the background color; a pattern of both white patches and flecks which usually cover the belly is common; the head is usually white, the upper lip pigmented, and the legs white, although a dark leg is not uncommon; minimum acceptable markings consist of three or four white stockings (q.v.) and a bald (q.v.) or apron (q.v.) face; predominantly white sabinos will have colored ears, a colored chest patch, and in some cases, a colored patch on the flank and base of the tail; solid white sabinos will have colored ears, but are uncommon.

Sable Island pony A Canadian pony breed descended from French stock imported from New England during the early 18th century; indigenous to the Sable Island located off the coast of Nova Scotia; due to the lack of natural vegetation and harsh climate, evolved into an extremely hardy, frugal pony standing about 14 hands; the coat may be bay, brown, black, gray, or chestnut, has a heavy head, large ears with turned in tips, a short neck which is broad at the base, short back, full girth, strong legs, and small hoof; live in small groups consisting of one stallion and six to eight mares; used for riding and light harness; less than 500 remain today.

sabre hocks *see* EXCESSIVE ANGULATION OF THE HOCK JOINTS

saber-legged *see* SICKLE HOCKED

sacrum The five sacral bones located below the lumbar that fuse by birth and constitute the posterior pelvis.

sack out A breaking technique; to rope a horse, snub (q.v.) him to a post and let him struggle against an unbreakable halter as the handler flaps a burlap sack over his body; the horse ultimately submits out of exhaustion.

sacroiliac desmitis *see* HUNTER'S BUMPS

saddle (1) Also known as hull; a girthed (q.v.) and usually padded, leather or synthetic covered seat for a rider of a horse usually straddled; preceded by a girthless cloth placed on the horse's back; treed saddles came into use by the cavalry soldiers of the Roman Empire; of various designs according to the purpose for which it is required. (2) To put a saddle upon a horse. (3) To mount a saddled horse. (4) A pad used under harness.

saddle airer Also known as a saddle stand; a wooden or metal stand upon which a saddle is placed to be aired when not in use.

saddle back *see* SWAY BACK

saddle backed *see* SWAY BACKED

saddle bag One of a pair of covered pouches laid across the back of a horse behind the saddle to which it is attached by the saddle strings.

saddle bars *see* STIRRUP BARS

saddle blanket Also known as blanket; any square or rectangular wool, cotton, or synthetic covering placed between the back of the horse and the saddle to absorb sweat, provide padding, and prevent galling (q.v.); sometimes confused with a saddle pad (q.v.).

saddle bow The arched front part or bow of a saddle, the top of which is a pommel (q.v.).

saddle bracket *see* SADDLE RACK

Saddlebred *see* AMERICAN SADDLEBRED

saddle bronc riding A standard rodeo event in which a bronc rider (q.v.), using a regulation saddle, rides a bronco (q.v.); the rider is only allowed to use one rein attached to a halter (q.v.), may not touch or hold onto the saddle, the horse, or himself with the free hand, and must remain mounted for at least ten seconds; the rider is judged on how hard the horse bucks, in addition to spurring action and how well the horse was ridden.

saddle chamber *see* CHANNEL

saddle channel *see* CHANNEL

saddle cloth (1) *see* NUMNAH. (2) *see* NUMBER CLOTH

saddle crupper Also known as a riding crupper or crupper (q.v.); riding tack consisting of a back strap attached on one end to the saddle skirt by means of metal dees and, on the other, to the crupper dock (q.v.) which is fitted under and around the base of the tail; used to prevent the saddle from slipping forward onto the withers (q.v.).

saddle dee *see* DEE-RING

saddle fall A movie industry term; a maneuver performed by a stuntperson; to fall from a moving or standing horse on cue.

saddle flap Also known as a flap; that part of the English saddle on either side of the seat upon which the rider's leg rests.

saddle fork *see* FORK no. 1

saddle gaits Gaits of the horse including the lateral gaits, slow gait (q.v.), and the rack (q.v.).

saddle horn Also known as horn; a horn-like prolongation of the pommel (q.v.) of a stock saddle (q.v.) which has an enlarged, flat-topped head; constructed of metal, fiberglass, or wood covered with leather or rawhide.

saddle horse (1) A horse suited or trained for riding. (2) A wooden, trestle-like stand upon which one or more saddles may be placed when not in use.

saddle leather Vegetable-tanned leather made of the hide of cattle used in saddlery.

saddle linen A linen covering sewn over the serge (q.v.) panel for cleanliness and to protect the serge from wear.

saddle marks An acquired mark (q.v.) in which pigment of the hair or skin is altered due to abrasion or damage to the hair follicle as from a poorly fitted saddle or saddle blanket.

saddle pad Also known as pad; a piece of felt, cotton, wool, sheepskin, or synthetic material placed between the saddle and the horse to protect the back of the horse, provide padding, and absorb sweat; may be thin or thick, square, rectangular, or shaped to fit the contour of the saddle.

saddle panel *see* PANEL no. 3

saddle patch The area of body hair slightly larger than the shape of an English saddle, left after clipping the horse; an alternative to a body clip (q.v.).

saddle patch clip To remove the horse's winter coat except for the area beneath the English saddle; an alternative to a full body clip (q.v.).

saddler One who makes, repairs, or deals in saddlery and other furnishings for horses.

saddle rack Also known as a saddle bracket; a metal or wooden shelf-like support attached to a wall upon which a saddle rests when not in use.

saddlery (1) The tack consisting of the bridle, saddle, etc. used on a horse which is to be ridden, not driven. (2) The shop and manufactured products of a saddler (q.v.). (3) The trade or craft of a saddler (q.v.).

saddle seat saddle *see* CUTBACK SADDLE

saddle skirt Also called bastos, wings, and incorrectly flaps; the part of the stock saddle (q.v.) on either side of the seat which covers the stirrup bars.

saddle soap A mild soap used for cleansing and conditioning leather.

saddle sore (1) A gall (q.v.) or open sore developing on the back, belly, or haunches of the horse at points of pressure from an ill-fitting or ill-adjusted saddle. (2) An irritation or sore on the parts of the rider chafed by the saddle.

saddle stand *see* SADDLE AIRER

saddle strings Narrow strips of leather attached to the front and rear skirts of a stock saddle (q.v.) used to tie objects to the saddle.

saddle tree A form or frame around which the saddle is built; may be made of wood, metal, or synthetic materials reinforced with steel plates.

Saddle-Type Pinto One of four Pinto (q.v.) conformation types developed with specific breed goals and standards in mind; an English horse of predominantly Thoroughbred (q.v.), Saddlebred (q.v.), Hackney (q.v.), or Tennessee Walking Horse (q.v.) breeding and conformation; displays the high head carriage and animated, high action necessary for standard gaited and parade events; may range from a fine medium-sized animal to a tall, slightly heavier animal suitable for carrying heavy silver tack.

sado A two-wheeled, horse-drawn taxi used on the island of Java, Indonesia to transport people and goods; generally pulled by a Java (q.v.).

safe Leather lining of some tack such as saddles, girths, etc. that prevents tack fittings such as buckles and bars from rubbing on the hide of the horse and causing chafing or galling or against other portions of the tack to cause wear.

safed A horseshoe in which the ground-side surface of the medial branch is beveled; decreases the chance of the shoe being pulled off by the opposite foot or injury if the horse interferes (q.v.).

safety *see* PENALTY 6

safety chain A heavy-link chain used in case either one or both drag shoes (q.v.) used on a horse-drawn vehicle is displaced; one end of the chain was affixed to the front axle alongside the drag shoe chain (q.v.) while the other was attached to a leather-covered hook secured to the fellowe (q.v.) and iron tire.

safety stirrup A material fitting connected to the saddle by stirrup leathers (q.v.) used to support the rider's foot when seated in the saddle; designed to enable the rider to remove his foot quickly in the case of an accident or other emergency; available in a number of designs including those that break away from the rider's foot when torque is applied.

sagging back *see* HOLLOW BACK no. 1

sainfoin Also spelled saintfoin; a European leguminous herb, *Onobrychis viciaefolia,* cultivated as a forage plant; grows best in chalk or limestone soil and is drought resistant.

Saint Christopher The patron saint of all travelers, and thus of horsemen.

saintfoin *see* SAINFOIN

Saint Hubert The patron saint of the Hunt (q.v.).

sais (1) Also spelled syce; an Indian groom. (2) An ancient Russian equestrian game played by mounted herdsmen; a duel in which each rider attempts to grab his opponent by the hands or arms and pull him off his horse; participants are divided into classes on the basis of weight.

Salerno A warmblood native to the Maremma and Salerno districts of Italy; descended from the Neapolitan breed popular in the Middle Ages, crossed with Spanish and Oriental blood; the breeding program was suppressed in 1874 and it wasn't until the beginning of the 20th century that the breed was restored with the systematic introduction of Thoroughbred (q.v.) blood; the modern horse is quiet, balanced, and energetic, stands 16 to 16.2 hands, and may have any solid-color coat, with bay, black, and chestnut occurring most commonly; has a light head, long neck, pronounced and muscular withers, short loins, and a deep girth; historically a popular cavalry mount, now used as an all-purpose riding horse, particularly suited to jumping.

saline Consisting of or containing salt.

saline solution A 0.9 percent solution of salt in water.

Salisbury, Marchioness Emily Mary (1749–1835) Believed to be the first female Master of Foxhounds (q.v.) having held that position for the Hertfordshire Hunt in Great Britain from 1793 to 1819 at which time she retired on her 70th birthday.

saliva The watery, slightly viscid, acid fluid, produced in and secreted by the salivary glands of the mouth; serves to correct the pH of the food to neutral or slightly alkaline so that it can be readily absorbed further down the intestinal tract and to moisten the mouth and food; contains the enzyme ptyalin, which starts the digestive process before the food reaches the stomach; horses may secrete up to 7 or more gallons (30 liters) per day depending on the moisture content of the feed – the larger the portion of hay, chaff, and grain in the ration, the greater amount of saliva will be produced.

saliva test A chemical analysis of the horse's saliva (q.v.) performed to detect the presence of drugs or other prohibited substances; routinely conducted on those race horses who finish in the money (q.v.).

sallenders An antiquated term; a sub-acute or chronic condition of the skin involving an eruption on the front of the hock joint of the hindleg, characterized by a scurfy thickening of the skin, a watery discharge, and loss of hair; may be caused by injury or infection.

salmon marks An antiquated term; refers to coat color pattern; white hairs found on the quarters and back.

Salisbury gag bit A gag bit (q.v.) consisting of a single thin jointed mouthpiece with large loose-ring gags (q.v.); differs from the Balding gag bit (q.v.) in that the mouthpiece is thinner; used with a single rein.

salt A chemical compound consisting of equal parts of sodium (q.v.) and chloride (q.v.) discovered in 1700.

salt block Also known as a salt lick; a natural or man-made block or irregularly shaped chunk of salt upon which horses lick; may be mineralized; available in weights from 1 to 50 pounds (450 g-23 kg) or more.

Salterno A Criollo (q.v.) raised in Peru; of three subtypes: the Chola (q.v.), Morochuco (q.v.), and Costeño (q.v.); descended from Spanish stock brought to South America by the conquistadors in the 16th century.

salt lick (1) A place where animals lick an exposed natural or artificial salt deposit. (2) *see* SALT BLOCK

salute To bow or otherwise show homage or courtesy; to greet or hail, as by means of a nod of the head or tip of the cap, both of which are used to indicate to the judge(s) that a performer is ready to begin an event, give a sign of greeting, or, as in racing, to indicate a request to dismount.

salve A soothing ointment applied to wounds or sores.

Sandalwood A pony breed indigenous to the islands of Sumba and Sumbawa, Indonesia; named for the island's principal export of the same name; resembles the Batak (q.v.) due to the common influence of the Arab (q.v.); stands 12 to 13 hands, has a small, well-shaped head, a full forelock, mane, and tail, wide chest, deep girth, and strong, hard legs;

the coat may be any color and is generally quite fine; is quiet and energetic, quite fast for its size, and possessed of good endurance; used for bareback (q.v.) racing, riding, packing, light draft, and farm work.

sand colic Digestive distress resulting from the casual and inadvertent consumption of sand while grazing or eating hay rations directly from the ground; precolic symptoms include mild discomfort accompanied by diarrhea; in full colic, sand accumulated in the intestine may harden and form an enterolith (q.v.) which traps intestinal gases and stretches the bowel wall.

sand bath (1) A natural or artificial hollow or depression, generally denuded of vegetation, in which a horse will roll. (2) Said of a horse when he rolls in sand or dirt.

sand crack Also known as crack; a vertical crack in the hoof wall that begins at the ground level of the hoof and moves upward following the line of the tubules to the coronary band (q.v.); may occur in any part of the hoof wall, although generally on the front of the hoof where they are called toe cracks (q.v.) or on the side of the hoof where they are known as quarter cracks (q.v.); can result from genetics, dry hooves, injury to the coronet, excessive hoof length, fungal infection, uneven weight bearing, concussion from work on hard ground, and excessive rasping; although lameness is usually not present, deep sand cracks can result in severe lameness and when unattended may result in false quarter (q.v.) and damage to the laminae (q.v.).

sandshifter *see* PACER

sandy bay Refers to coat color; the lightest shade of bay (q.v.); a light red coat that appears yellow.

San Fratello A breed of horse indigenous to Sicily where it is bred in the wild; descended from native stock crossed with Spanish Anglo-Arab (q.v.), Anglo-Arab (q.v.), Salerno (q.v.), and, recently, Nonius (q.v.) blood; breeding stock is carefully selected; a strong and powerful breed with tremendous resistance, stands 15 to 16 hands, weighs 1,100 to 1,300 pounds (499-590 kg), has a brown, bay, or black coat, a slightly heavy head, sloping croup, wide and deep chest, and prominent withers; used for riding, light draft, and packing.

sanitary ride A racing term; said of a horse who did not give his all in a race, or of a jockey who rode a race so safely as to diminish his chances of winning.

sarcoptic mange The most severe type of mange (q.v.) caused by a species of mite, *Sarcoptes scabiei* var. *equi*; spreads quickly over the infested horse with adult mites feeding on tissue fluid and skin cells to produce small red blisters, severe itching, and eventually hair loss; other symptoms include scaling, crusting, and balding of the skin, emaciation, general weakness, and loss of appetite; early lesions appear on the head, neck, and shoulders; areas covered by long hair or the extremities are not usually involved.

Sardinian Also known as a Miniature Sardinian Donkey or Sardinian Donkey; a type of Miniature Mediterranean Donkey (q.v.) native to the Mediterranean island of Sardinia, Italy; an ancient pony breed which lives in the wild at about 2,000 feet (600 m) above sea level where it survives on sparse vegetative growth; females stand 12.1 to 12.2 and males 12.2 to 13 hands; the coat is generally bay, brown, black, or liver chestnut (q.v.); has a square head, heavy jaw, long neck, full mane, tail, and forelock, slightly hollow back, slender legs, and a small foot; cow hocks (q.v.) are common; is lively, high strung, rebellious, frugal, and agile; used for farm work and riding.

Sardinian Anglo-Arab A horse breed indigenous to Sardinia, Italy; developed from Arab (q.v.) stallions put to native mares; in the early 16th century, the breed was improved with Andalusian (q.v.) stallions; in the beginning of the 18th century, the breed went into a period of decline, but was revived in the early 20th century with the input of Arab and ultimately,Thoroughbred (q.v.) blood; stand 15.1 to 16 hands plus, has a light square head, pronounced withers, straight or slightly hollow back, short loins, full tail, broad chest and full girth, thinly cannoned, but strong legs, and a gray, chestnut, or bay coat; is hardy, swift and has good staying power; used for riding and makes a good jumper.

Sardinian Donkey *see* SARDINIAN

satchel A small pouch containing a watch carried by a coach guard.

saturation theory A unsubstantiated principle of breeding; it is believed that the offspring of a mare repeatedly put to the same stallion will increasingly resemble the stallion.

saucer fracture Small fissure fractures (q.v.) of the bone caused by stress or fatigue, the result of repetitive loading of the bone; occur more frequently in the United States than Britain, probably due to the different training and racing conditions; almost unique to young Thoroughbred (q.v.) racehorses.

Saugor The Indian Army Equitation School located in central India, closed in 1939.

Saumur A town in western France where the School of Mounted Troop Instruction known as the French Cavalry School of Saumur (q.v.) was established in the early 18th century; now the home of the Cadre Noir (q.v.).

sausage boot Also known as a doughnut or doughnut boot; a well-stuffed ring of leather or rubber with an adjustable strap, placed around the pastern of a horse prone to capped elbow (q.v.).

savage A vice; (1) A mean horse, particularly one who attempts to bite another horse or person. (2) Said of a horse; to bite or attempt to bite another horse or person.

savaging A vice; said of a horse; the act of attempting to bite another horse or person.

Savanilla Phaeton A light, horse-drawn carriage or phaeton (q.v.) widely used in Thailand and Bangkok from the 19th century; a semi-open cab hung on sideways elliptical springs in the front and sideways semi-elliptical springs in the rear; drawn by a single horse or large pony in shafts.

save ground A racing term; to cover the shortest distance in a race by hugging the inside rail on the turns and running straight on the stretches (q.v.).

sawdust bedding (q.v.) consisting of small bits and other particles of wood produced by the operation of a saw; is finer than wood shavings (q.v.), inexpensive, and easy to obtain, but like shavings, is difficult to store; also contain wood chips and splinters and has a high dust factor which makes it unsuitable for horses with allergies or other respiratory ailments; in some cases, combined with shavings to improve absorbency.

sawhorse stance The position assumed by a horse afflicted with tetanus (q.v.); both fore and hind legs are extended, forward and rearward respectively, and spread.

scab A crust formed over a wound when healing.

scabies *see* PSOROPTIC SCABIES

scale *see* SCALE OF WEIGHTS

scale of weights Also known as the scale; a racing term; an official tabulation of the correct weights for horses of different age groups, for all distance races, and at all times of the year.

scale weights A racing term; the extra pounds carried by the horse in a weight-for-age race (q.v.).

scalping Limb contact in which the toe of the fore hoof hits the hairline at the coronary band (q.v.) or above, on the hind hoof of the same side as it breaks over.

scarlet coat *see* PINK COAT

scenic route *see* OVERLAND

scent The odor of the fox or other quarry (q.v.) given off by the glands under the tail and from the pads; generally left on the ground, thus leaving a trail or line for the hounds (q.v.) to follow; dry hard ground does not hold a scent well, while vegetation such as grass and shrubs does.

scent hound A hunting dog who uses its nose instead of sight to pursue quarry (q.v.); include stag hounds, buck hounds, foxhounds, coon hounds, basset hounds, beagles, and harriers.

schaukel Also known as see saw; a German dressage term; a prescribed sequence of backwards and forward steps performed on a straight line with the hooves leaving the ground distinctly and without a halt in between; the backwards movement is performed in two time while the forward movement is performed in four time.

Schleswig horse *see* SCHLESWIG HEAVY DRAFT

Schleswig Heavy Draft Also known as

Schleswig horse; a coldblood originating in Schleswig-Holstein, Germany in the 19th century from which the name derived; descended from the Jutland (q.v.) to which Yorkshire Coach Horse, Thoroughbred (q.v.), Norfolk Punch (q.v.), and more recently Boulonnais (q.v.) and Brenton (q.v.) blood was introduced; stands 15.1 to 16.1 hands and may weigh upwards of 1,700 pounds (771 kg); has a well-proportioned head, small eyes, a short, arched neck, low broad withers, a strong, short back, short and muscular legs with feathering (q.v.), and large round hooves; the stud book was established in 1891; historically used for drawing omnibuses (q.v.), farm work, and transportation; due to mechanization its numbers are on the decline, although it is still used for draft.

Schlitz 40-horse hitch Also known as 40-horse hitch; a hitch of 40 chestnut Belgian Draft horses (q.v.) with white blazes and light-colored manes and tails first debuted in 1972 by the Schlitz Beer Company in the United States; is driven by one man and has an overall length of 135 feet (41 m), including wagon and horses; the driver holds five reins in each hand; the hitch is accompanied by outriders to assist in case of emergency.

school (1) Any area, open or enclosed, in which the horse is exercised, ridden, or trained. (2) To train or educate a broken horse, with or without a rider; involves teaching the horse movements and gaits required for future use or refining those movements and gaits previously taught through specific exercises; schooling techniques differ for each riding style. (3) To warm up a horse prior to competition.

schooled Said of a horse trained, generally at home, to do what is required in competition or races.

school figures Also known as school exercises, schooling figures, or manège figures; any exercise performed on horseback to improve the balance, rhythm, timing, and use of aids of the rider, the rider's control over the horse, and the flexibility, rhythm, and smoothness of gaits of the horse including serpentines, figure eights (q.v.), changes of rein, transitions, and turns and circles.

school horse Any horse used by a trainer or riding school as a mount (q.v.) upon which individuals are taught to ride.

schooling The act of training or educating a broken horse.

schooling figures *see* SCHOOL FIGURES

schooling list A racing term; a list of horses eligible to train at the starting gate (q.v.) before being allowed to race.

school master An experienced and well-trained horse whose ability generally exceeds that of the rider; is generally better trained than a school horse (q.v.).

school movements A dressage term; any action, pace, and/or figure performed to supple the horse and improve his versatility for riding; depending on the venue, may consist of shoulder-in (q.v.), renvers (q.v.), travers (q.v.), half-pass (q.v.), flying changes (q.v.), and pirouettes (q.v.).

School of Mounted Troop Instruction, The *see* FRENCH CAVALRY SCHOOL AT SAUMUR

School of Saumur *see* FRENCH CAVALRY SCHOOL AT SAUMUR

school rider One trained or specializing in dressage (q.v.).

school riding Riding exercises from the Classical School.

schools above the ground *see* AIRS ABOVE THE GROUND

school work *see* SCHOOL no. 2

scintigraphy A technique used to diagnose lameness; distribution of intravenous injection of a radioactive isotope in the bones and soft tissues of the limbs is evaluated.

scissors A vaulting (q.v.) term; a movement in which the mounted vaulter shifts between forward and reward facing positions; the vaulter (q.v.), starting from a basic seat (q.v.), swings both legs forward and then backward high above the croup of the horse and, when almost in a handstand, he rotates his hips 90 degrees to the inside, continuing the rotation until the legs straddle the horse; the vaulter at this point shall be facing backwards at which point, he performs the same movement in the opposite direction, ending the movement in a basic seat, facing forwards; a compulsory movement (q.v.) performed in competitions.

sclera The dense, fibrous, opaque, white outer coating of the eyeball which is contiguous with the cornea; characteristic of the eye of the Appaloosa (q.v.).

sclerostomes *see* LARGE STRONGYLE

scope The athletic ability of the horse.

score (1) A rodeo term; the distance the lead the calf or steer is given from the chute opening to the score line (q.v.); is usually determined by the arena size, with 8 to 15 feet (3.6–7 m) average. (2) A roping term; to hold the horse in the box (q.v.) to train him not to anticipate the release of the calf. (3) The aggregate of points accumulated by an individual or team in competition. (4) A racing term; to win a bet or a race. (5) A harness racing term; a lap of the racetrack's circumference.

scoring (1) A harness racing term; the number of preliminary, warm-up laps taken before beginning the race; generally no more than three score (q.v.) are permitted. (2) The act of evaluating, on a points basis by one or more judges, the ability of a rider or team to ride within the rules of the competition.

score line A rodeo term; the line that marks the distance of the predetermined head start the steer or calf is given before the roper leaves the box (q.v.); varies depending on arena conditions.

score well A roping term; said of a roping horse who does not anticipate release of the calf from the chute, waiting instead for a signal from the roper.

scorpion A cutting term; an athletic, agile, quick, stylish-moving horse.

scotch collar The housing over the collar (q.v.) of draft show harness.

scotched Said of a horseshoe in which the outer edge slopes outward from the hoof surface towards the ground; commonly used on draft horses to create a greater support base and the appearance of a larger foot.

scotching Also known as propping; a reining term; said of a horse who bounces in a slide (q.v.) rather than setting his rear feet and walking with the front; the engagement of the hocks (q.v.) is restricted.

scrambler A horse who, when trailered and in motion, overreacts to anything touching his sides; he feels as though what is touching him is trying to push him over and he reacts by pushing back, and in some cases falling over.

scraper Also known as a sweat scraper or water scraper; any hand-held, thin metal, plastic, or wooden tool used to remove liquid such as sweat or water from a horse's coat and to gently massage the main muscle masses; usually concave in appearance and approximately 6 to 12 inches (15–30 cm) long.

scratch (1) Also known as forfeit; to withdraw a horse from an equestrian event after it has been officially entered. (2) A rodeo term; to spur a horse vigorously in a continuous raking motion from front to back; compulsory in all rodeo events.

scratched Said of a horse formally withdrawn from an event or competition.

scratches Also known as greasy heal, grease heal, greased heel, mud fever, cracked heels, or *dermatitis verrucosa*; a dermatophilus infection of the lower limbs, specifically the pastern and fetlock, involving the skin and its glands in the hollow of the heel; caused by the organism *Dermatophilus congolensis* which gains entry into the skin when dirty and/or saturated by prolonged rain; most common on the hind legs and/or in horses with feathers (q.v.) or heavy hair growth; the skin in the affected area becomes moist, sensitive to the touch, thickens, develops grapes (q.v.), and has an offensive odor; lameness may or may not result.

scratch sheet A racing term; a daily publication listing graded handicaps, tips, and scratches at a specific racetrack.

screaming scent *see* BURNING SCENT

screw An inferior, unsound, or worn-out horse.

screw fixation A procedure in which steel-alloy screws are surgically inserted into a fractured bone to hold it together.

screwworm Larvae (q.v.) of the screwworm fly, one of many species of blow fly which lays 200 to 400 eggs on edges of wounds, cuts, bites, navels of newborns, and other locations on the skin; after 12 to 21 hours, the larvae hatch, crawl into the wound and burrow into the flesh where they feed on wound fluids and live tissue; in five to seven days they exit the wound, drop to the ground, and burrow into the soil; infested wounds characteristically contain a number of screwworm larvae, are usually foul smelling, and contain copious amounts of a reddish-brown fluid.

scrotal hernia Descent of intra-abdominal tissue through the inguinal canal into the scrotum, resulting in an enlarged scrotal sac; may or may not correct itself in foals and requires immediate surgical attention if occurring in older horses.

scrotum The sac containing the testes (q.v.) which hangs between the thighs of the male horse.

scrub (1) A low-grade horse. (2) A racing term; said of the action of the jockey's hands, legs, and whip at the finish of a race; the act of riding a finish in a horse race.

scrub bashing Also called scrub dashing; an Australian term; to chase cattle, often semi wild, through timbered country during roundup.

scrubbing *see* SCRUB no. 2

scrub dashing *see* SCRUB BASHING

scurry A show jumping contest conducted over a course consisting of fences up to, but not exceeding, 4 feet (1.2 m) high; the event is scored on the basis of time and faults with a refusal carrying no penalty; the rider with the fastest time and least number of faults wins.

scut The tail of a hare.

scutch grass *see* BERMUDA GRASS

SDF The acronym for synchronous diaphragmatic flutter (q.v.).

sealant *see* HOOF SEALANT

seal brown Refers to coat color; a shade of brown (q.v.) close to black, but distinguishable by the brown or yellow areas on the muzzle, eyes, flanks, and inner legs; in coats of dark seal brown, the lighter shades are not visible.

season (1) *see* ESTRUS. (2) A racing term; the period during which racing is conducted on a particular circuit or track. (3) *see* HUNTING SEASON. (4) A hunting term; the number of years a hound (q.v.) has been hunted since being entered (q.v.).

seat (1) The posture of the rider in the saddle, on the horse. (2) The part of the saddle upon which the rider sits; located between the pommel (q.v.) and cantle (q.v.).

seat bones The two prominent points of the rider's pelvis upon which his weight is balanced when mounted.

seating out To slope the inner, hoof-side portion of the horseshoe web away from the hoof to prevent the shoe from applying pressure to the sole of the foot.

seborrhea A skin disease which may result from the abnormal production of keratin; usually a secondary disease in horses following dermatitis (q.v.) or eczema.

secondary arthritis Inflammation of a joint resulting from poor conformation that predisposes a horse to joint trauma, bone disease, and localization of a systemic infection in a joint.

secondary call A racing term; a second mount used by a jockey in the event that his primary mount is scratched (q.v.).

secondary corpora lutea A mass of endocrine cells formed in follicles other than the ovarian, about one month after conception.

secondary joint disease *see* OSTEOARTHRITIS

second dam *see* GRANDAM

second horse A hunting term; an extra horse used by a participant in the hunt when a change of mount is necessary; may be ridden to the change by a pad groom (q.v.).

second horse man *see* PAD GROOM

second incisors *see* LATERAL INCISORS

second leg A racing term; the second half of a double event (q.v.).

second phalanx That portion of the horse's leg including the short pastern (q.v.).

second pommel *see* HUNTING HEAD

second season hound A hunting term; said of a hound hunted for the second year since being entered (q.v.).

second sire The paternal grandfather of a horse.

second thigh *see* GASKIN

second wind Also known as comes again; said of a horse who, although evidently tired and falling back, finds renewed energy and strength to move forward again or work with enthusiasm.

second whipper-in One of two principal assistants to the huntsman (q.v.) from whom instructions are received; provides the huntsman with an extra set of eyes and is usually positioned at the far end of a covert (q.v.) to view a fox while drawing that covert (q.v.).

Secretariat Also known as Big Red; a large, powerful chestnut Thoroughbred (q.v.) with three white socks hailed as the greatest race horse of all time.

Section A pony *see* WELSH MOUNTAIN PONY

Section B pony *see* WELSH PONY

Section C pony *see* WELSH PONY OF COB TYPE

Section D pony *see* WELSH COB

sediola A large, round-backed, horse-drawn gig (q.v.) of the dead-axle type having high wheels and suspended from long, highly flexibly shafts; popular in France and Italy during the 18th century.

seed *see* SPERM

seed hay *see* CEREAL GRASS HAY

seedy toe Also known as hollow wall or *dystrophia ungulae*; generally affects the hoof wall in the toe region, although it may also occur elsewhere on the hoof; characterized by a separation of the hoof wall from the sensitive laminae (q.v.); a symptom of chronic laminitis (q.v.); the outer surface of the hoof wall appears sound, but the inner surface is mealy and there actually may be a cavity due to loss of horn substance; lameness is infrequent, but will accompany the occasional infection and abscessation.

seeling An obsolete term; the growth of white hairs in the horse's eyebrows.

see saw *see* SCHAUKEL

selby cape A short, loose, double-breasted, sleeved cape made out of box cloth (q.v.) and worn by coachmen outside the apron in bad weather.

selenium A non-metallic element chemically resembling sufur and tellurium; identified as an essential mineral in the diet of the horse in 1950; acts in combination with vitamin E (q.v.) to prevent muscle degeneration and dystrophy as in white muscle disease (q.v.) which is common in foals and less so in mature horses; used as a treatment for azoturia (q.v.) or tying-up disease (q.v.); increased levels may produce improved performance, reduced respirations, and a better general condition in race horses; can be administered by injection or added to feed; toxicity is most likely to occur in alkaline or desert climates where the levels in forage are extremely high; symptoms of toxicity include loss of vitality, anemia, joint stiffness, rough hair coat, loss of mane and tail, development of a ring around the hoof, hoof deformities or loss, and death due to respiratory failure; two ppm a day is considered the upper level of safe consumption; deficiency is a problem in all or part of 42 of 50 states in the United States.

selenium accumulator Any plant containing high levels of selenium (q.v.); emits an unpleasant garlic-sulfur odor which discourages horses from consuming it if other forage (q.v.) is available.

self carriage *see* COLLECTION

self-colored Refers to coat color; said of the mane and tail when the same color as the body coat.

sell at halter To sell a horse without a veterinary check (q.v.) and no guarantee other than title.

Selle Français (1) Also known as a French Saddle horse; a horse breed descended from the Norman (q.v.) horse, influenced by introduction of Arab (q.v.) and Thoroughbred (q.v.) blood; the stud book, a continuation of the Anglo-Norman (q.v.) book, was established in 1950; selected, but not necessarily purebred mares, and Thoroughbred, Arab, Anglo-Arab (q.v.), and French Trotter stallions have contributed to the present day breed; stands 15.2 to 16.3 hands, has a robust frame, powerful shoulder, strong and long back, deep girth, and a smallish head; the predominant coat color is chestnut, but brown and bay, and rarely roan or gray, occur; used for riding and competitions including show jumping and eventing. (2) *see* FRENCH SADDLE PONY

selling plater *see* PLATER

selling plate race *see* SELLING RACE

selling race A racing term; an antiquated claiming race (q.v.) in which the rules required the winning horse to be auctioned off following the race and any other competing horse to be offered for claiming.

Semaituka *see* ZEMAITUKA

semen A thick, white-colored secretion of the testes (q.v.) and the accessory gland of a stallion; contains the spermatozoa (q.v.) for fertilization of the egg; each ejaculation of semen is estimated to contain 4 to 18 billion sperm with 500 million sperm per ejaculation required for fertilization of one egg.

send A racing term; to enter a horse in a race.

send away A racing term; said of the official starter who opens the starting gate (q.v.) and begins a horse race, thus sending the horses away.

send on A hunting term; said of the hunters (horses) when sent to a meet (q.v.) in advance of their riders.

sensitive frog That portion of the hoof covering part of the plantar cushion (q.v.) which projects beneath the coffin bone (q.v.); composed of very small, short papillae much like those of the perioplic ring (q.v.) of which it should be considered a continuation; nourishes the *stratum germinativum* (q.v.) that produces the horny frog.

sensitive laminae Also known as the quick; the blood-engorged area of the hoof between the hoof wall and coffin bone; interlocks with the insensitive laminae (q.v.).

sensitive sole That part of the hoof covering the crescent-shaped bottom of the coffin bone composed of small, short papillae; nourishes the horn-producing layer of cells that produces the horny sole (q.v.).

sensory nerve Any of the whitish fibers extending from the brain and spinal cord and spreading throughout the body to different organs, e.g., the skin which they enervate; when stimulated trigger sensations including pain, pressure, temperature, etc.

sepsis A poisoned state of the system due to a spread of infection throughout the blood.

septicaemia *see* SEPTICEMIA

septicemia Also spelled septicaemia and known as blood poisoning; the presence in the bloodstream of infectious microorganisms and/or their toxins.

sequela The consequence of a disease.

serous Resembling serum (q.v.); of a thin, liquid nature; containing or secreting serum.

serous arthritis Inflammation of a joint resulting from trauma and characterized by excessive accumulation of serous (q.v.) fluid in the joint space; the synovial membrane is inflamed, but the bony structures are uninvolved; often seen in poorly conformed horses; onset may be acute or recur on a chronic basis.

serpent tail Said of the tail of the horse when the curve of the dock is concave rather than convex.

serum (1) A clean, pale yellow liquid which separates from the clot in coagulation of blood. (2) A fluid obtained from the blood of an animal which has been rendered immune to some disease by innoculation.

service Said of the stallion; to mate a mare, e.g., The stallion serviced the mare.

serviceably sound Said of a horse who has no defect, ailment, or illness that will impair his value for the intended use.

serving hobbles *see* BREEDING HOBBLES

sesamoid bones Also known as proximal sesamoids, proximal sesamoid bones, or sesamoids; two small, pyramid-shaped bones (medial and lateral) located above the back of the fetlock joint (q.v.) held in place by ligaments which form part of the suspensory apparatus; attach to the cannon bone above at the back of the knee and to the long pastern below by ligaments; the deep and superficial flexor tendons pass over the back of these bones.

sesamoid boots *see* ANKLE BOOTS

sesamoid fracture A break (q.v.) in one or all of the bones comprising the fetlock joint including the two proximal sesamoids and the distal sesamoid; may consist of small chips or involve the entire bone.

sesamoiditis Also known as popped sesamoid; a term loosely applied to several inflammatory conditions involving the sesamoid bones or sesamoidian ligaments; generally a tear of the insertion of some of the ligaments which hold the sesamoids (q.v.) in place as caused by stress placed on the fetlock during fast exercise; symptoms include swelling and varying degrees of lameness; despite a variety of treatments, the prognosis for recovery is poor.

sesamoids *see* SESAMOID BONES

set (1) To attach a horseshoe to the foot, as in, "he set the shoe." (2) Four horseshoes. (3) Also known as set the head; to position the horse's head so that the horse is on the bit; his head will be bent at the poll and perpendicular to the ground.

set-and-turn *see* ROLLBACK

set back *see* HALF-STRUCK

set down (1) A racing term; to suspend a jockey, horseman, or stablehand from racing for a specific period of time generally for a rule infraction. (2) A racing term; to shake up a horse and urge it for increase speed or effort in a workout or race.

set fair An antiquated term; said of a horse when bedded down and settled in for the night.

set fast *see* TYING UP

set for the stop A cutting term; the position a cutter (q.v.) assumes in the saddle when cutting; he pushes forward on the horn with his right hand, slumps into the saddle, and drops his heels into the stirrups; allows the horse to stop and prevents the rider from bouncing in the stirrups or moving forwarding on the horn during the stop.

set tail Also known as cut and set tail; a tail which is intentionally broken, or in which the tendons on the underside have been nicked (q.v.), and set so that it heals in an elevated position; performed on gaited horses including Saddlebred (q.v.) and Tennessee Walking horses (q.v.); the horse is left with no control of its tail.

set the head *see* SET no. 3

settle (1) Also known as settle to service; said of a brood mare who has conceived as a result of mating. (2) *see* SETTLE CATTLE

settle cattle Also known as settle; a cutting term; said of a mounted cutter who quietly calms a contained herd of cattle by moving back and forth in front of them prior to cutting.

settled A cutting term; said of cattle that are familiar enough with a horse and rider to not spook from them, but not so overly familiar to have lost their curiosity.

set toe *see* ROCKER TOE SHOE

settle to service *see* SETTLE no. 1

seven-eighths brothers The male offspring of a horse and his son produced by the same dam.

seven-eighths sisters The female offspring of a horse and her daughter produced by the same dam.

seven spring gig *see* TILBURY

sex allowance A racing term; a weight concession given to mares or fillies competing in races against males except handicaps or where conditions state otherwise; mares and fillies are allowed weight below the scale (q.v.): usually 3 pounds (1.3 kg) for two-year-old fillies and 5 pounds (2.3 kg) for fillies and mares three years and older prior to September 1, and 3 pounds (1.3 kg) thereafter.

shabrack *see* SHABRAQUE

shabraque Also known as housing or shadrack; an ornamental cloth or leather covering for the saddle and horse.

shadbelly (1) Also known as a cut-away coat or tail coat; a formal black coat cut to waist length in the front and with long, weighted tails; the tails may be lined with leather or faux leather; primarily worn by competitors in advanced competitions. (2) *see* HERRING-GUTTED

shadow roll A racing term; a rolled piece of sheepskin or cloth secured over the bridge of the horse's nose to prevent him from seeing the ground and shadows thereon.

shadrack *see* SHABRAQUE

shaft One of two long, round pieces of wood between which a horse is harnessed and by which he is connected to a vehicle; an extension of the vehicle which may be attached to either the vehicle body or frame.

shaft horse Also known as a thill, thiller, phill horse, or thill horse; a driving term; the horse to which the shafts (q.v.) are connected in a horse-drawn vehicle.

Shagya Arabian Also known as a Hungarian Arabian or Hungarian Shagya; a relatively rare breed developed after 1816 at Austro-Hungarian military stud farms, primarily in Hungary at Babolna and Radautz; developed for cavalry and carriage purposes, as well as to supply prepotent breeding stallions as improvers for other breeds; the foundation sires were original desert-bred Arab (q.v.) put to Arab-type mares; English Thoroughbreds (q.v.) and Lipizzaners (q.v.) were also used to increase size and improve movement; the name and predominant cream-colored coat color derived from an Arab stallion, Shagya, a horse of the Kehil/Siglavi strain, born in Syria in 1830 and imported to the stud in 1836 for restocking purposes; stands 15 to 16 hands and should have a minimum cannon bone circumference of 7 inches (18 cm); the coat is generally gray and rarely black; breeds consistently true to type; is taller, has a bigger frame, longer hip, and possesses better riding horse qualities than a purebred Arab and has 17 ribs, five lumbar bones, and 16 tail vertebrae in comparison with the 18–6–18 formation of other breeds; used for riding and driving; numbers less than 2,000 worldwide.

shaker foal syndrome *see* BOTULISM

shake up A racing term; said of the jockey, to strike a horse with a whip in an effort to make him run faster.

Shan *see* BURMESE

Shandrydan A two-wheeled sprung cart used in Ireland.

shank (1) *see* CHEEK no. 1. (2) Also known as metatarsal, metatarsal bone, shannon, or shannon bone; the principal bone of the hind-leg located between the hock and the fetlock; the corresponding bone in the foreleg is known as the cannon bone (q.v.). (3) A chain attached to a lead rope (q.v.).

shannon *see* SHANK

shannon bone *see* SHANK

Shan Pony *see* BURMESE

shape cattle A cutting term; to manipulate a herd of cattle so they move in a specific direction.

shaping A conditioning technique; to reward behavior that comes close to that required, gradually altering or modifying the behavior by reducing the realm of acceptable rewarded behavior.

shaping a cow A cutting term; to separate and move a cow away from the center of the herd to the middle of the arena to begin work.

shaps *see* CHAPS

shavings *see* WOOD SHAVINGS

shay The colloquial name and spelling of chaise (q.v.).

sheared heels A structural breakdown of the hoof occurring between the heel bulbs (q.v.); characterized by a disproportionate use of one heel; the degree of lameness and resulting damage is proportional to the duration and degree of the foot imbalance.

sheath The fleshy pocket located in front of the scrotum (q.v.) which contains the genital organs of the male horse and has the anterior end open.

shedding coat *see* SHEDDING OUT

shedding out Also known in England as casting coat or shedding coat; said of a horse who loses his coat due to change in weather or season; generally occurs twice a year, in the spring and autumn the exact time of which is contingent on the condition of the horse's nutrition, if a mare is in foal, and stabling conditions, e.g., at grass, kept in a box stall with or without lights, and blanketing.

shed row A racing term; racetrack barns generally located in the backstretch (q.v.).

she-ass *see* JENNY

sheep knees *see* BACKWARD DEVIATION OF THE CARPAL JOINTS

sheet calendar *see* RACING CALENDAR

sheet Also known as day sheet or day rug; a light-weight cotton or linen covering for the body of the horse used to prevent the sun from fading black or dark coats of turned-out horses, to keep a horse clean, and to shield him from insects.

sheets A racing term; a handicapping tool which assigns a numerical value to each race run by a horse; enables different horses running at different tracks to be compared objectively.

Shelborne Landau *see* SHELBURNE LANDAU

Shelburne Landau Also known as a Square Landau, Angular Landau, and spelled Shelborne Landau; a four-wheeled, heavy, horse-drawn town carriage with a square or angular profile, two doors, and a double folding hood; seated four vis-à-vis; was usually pulled by a pair of horses and coachman driven.

shell cordovan *see* CORDOVAN no. 4

shelly cordovan *see* CORDOVAN

shelly The hollow center of a newly cut incisor (q.v.).

shelly feet Said of the horse's hooves when thinly soled and brittle walled.

shelt A Highland pony used by deer hunters to carry game (q.v.).

Shetland pony Also known as a Sheltie;

the smallest of Great Britain's nine native breeds, indigenous to the Orkney and Shetland Islands, Scotland; believed to have originally migrated from Scandinavia around 8000 BC; registered stock must not exceed a height of 40 inches (101 cm) at two years nor 42 inches (106 cm) at four years or under; may have a piebald (q.v.), skewbald (q.v.), brown, chestnut, gray, or black coat with the latter being the foundation color; the coat is smooth in the summer, but thick and wiry in the winter; is hardy, strong, lively, and possessed of a quick, free action; typically has a well-shaped but small head, crested neck, broad chest, short back with heavily muscled loins, considerable depth around the girth, broad quarters, short legs with sharply defined joints, light feathering, and an exceptionally thick mane, forelock, and tail; has extra large nasal cavities that enable the air to warm before entering the lungs; historically to haul and carry peat and seaweed and for mining; now used for riding and light draft.

Shetland Pony Stud Blood Society An organization founded in Great Britain in 1891 to encourage the breeding of registered Shetland Ponies (q.v.).

Sheltie *see* SHETLAND PONY

shift *see* RESET

shifting seat wagon *see* JUMP SEAT CARRIAGE

shill Historically known as a bonnet (q.v.), chaunter, puffer, or trotter; one posing as a horse buyer to run up the price of a horse at auction and to decoy onlookers into participating in the bidding, yet who has no intention of buying.

shim A wedge (q.v.) that is thicker at the toe than at the heel which is placed between the horseshoe and hoof.

shin and ankle boot *see* HEEL BOOT

shin bone *see* CANNON BONE

shinbuck *see* BUCKED SHINS

shin sore *see* BUCKED SHINS

ship To transport a horse, as by truck, rail, ship, or plane.

ship-of-the-plains *see* PRAIRIE SCHOONER

shipping boots Also known as traveling boots; padded, often fleece lined, boots which provide protection and support to the legs of the horse during shipping; extend from just below the knee to well beyond the coronary band while the rear boots extend above the hock.

shipping fever Also known as transit fever; a severe respiratory ailment generally occurring in younger animals following shipping.

Shire A heavy draft breed descended from the Great Horse (q.v.) with some contributions of Flemish, Friesian (q.v.), and Oriental stock; stands 16.1 to 17.3 hands, and in some cases as tall as 19 hands, weighs 1,760 to 2,688 pounds (798–1,219 kg), and may have a bay, brown, black, chestnut or gray coat with white markings – a black coat with white feathering, reminiscent of the foundation sire, is the most popular color; has a small head relative to its body size with a wide forehead and long ears, a long, arched and muscular neck, a short back, powerful croup, clean, relatively short legs with heavy, silky feather and is large boned; is docile and good natured; the foundation sire was the Packington Blind Horse (q.v.); the stud book was established in 1878; historically used as a carriage or omnibus (q.v.) horse and for agriculture, is now used for heavy draft and farm work; so called because it was raised in Great Britain's Midland regions of Lincolnshire, Leicestershire, Staffordshire, and Derbyshire.

Shiragazi A breed of horse indigenous to Iran; contributed to the development of the Plateau Persian (q.v.).

Shires, The (1) An area in Britain hunted by a group of fashionable packs including the Quorn, Beaver, Pytchley, Cottesmore, and Grafton; covers prime grazing land located in the counties of Leicesteshire, North Hamptonshire, and Rutland; the country is strongly fenced with cut and laid hedges. (2) An area in England consisting of Leicestershire, Rutland, Warwickshire, Northamptonshire, and parts of Lincolnshire.

shiver To shake involuntarily or tremble as with cold, fear, or excitement.

shock Circulatory collapse characterized by a progressive diminishing circulating blood volume relative to the capacity of the vascular system, leading to acute failure of perfusion of vital organs; of three primary types: (1) cardiac shock caused by damage to the heart pump, (2) hypovolemic shock (q.v.) due to decreased blood volume, or (3) vasculogenic shock in which the blood volume is normal but blood is pooled in dilated peripheral vessels a condition which may be caused by the presence of endotoxins or trauma; associated conditions include accident trauma, severe diarrhea, massive hemorrhage, colic (q.v.), and acute coliform mastitis; symptoms include lengthened capillary refill time (q.v.), pale mucous membranes, ataxia, low pulse pressure, increased/decreased respiratory rate, diminished cardiac output, temperature, and cold, clammy skin.

shock condition Any circumstance leading to a tissue fluid imbalance and the onset of shock (q.v.).

shod Said of a horse who has had horseshoes (q.v.) put on, e.g., When was the horse last shod?

shod too close *see* NAIL BIND

shoe (1) Also known as horseshoe; to fit horseshoes to the hooves of a horse. (2) *see* HORSESHOE

shoe board A racing term; a sign which identifies the type of horseshoes (q.v.) each horse entered to race wears; may be included as a panel on the totalizator board (q.v.).

shoe boil *see* CAPPED ELBOW

shoeing *see* SHOE

shoeing block *see* FOOT STOOL

shoeing chaps *see* APRON no. 1

shoeing forge *see* FORGE

shoeing hammer *see* DRIVING HAMMER

shoe pad *see* HORSESHOE PAD

shooter A cutting term; a cow who bolts from the herd for no apparent reason and interferes with the performance of a cutter (q.v.).

shooting To hunt for and kill game using a gun; to be held separately from hunting (q.v.).

Shooting Brake Also known as body brake; a light, horse-drawn vehicle of the brake (q.v.) type having a dog cart (q.v.) body which extended forward to a high box seat and a sloping dashboard; had two boots (q.v.): a large one located under the driver's seat and another, a smaller, ventilated one, centered under the passenger seats used to carry hunting dogs; popular in the mid-19th century with shooting parties; carried six to eight people on crosswise or lengthwise seating, was hung on sideways-elliptical or semi-elliptical springs, and drawn by a single horse in shafts or a pair in pole gear (q.v.).

Shooting Phaeton A four-wheeled, horse-drawn vehicle of the phaeton (q.v.) type popular in the late 18th century; noted for its tray-like body and strong underperch, which made it suitable for driving over rough tracks; had a large boot (q.v.) above the rear axle, an elevated driving seat with room for two, rearward cross seats for passengers seated vis-à-vis, and a half hood which protected the rearward seat; originally hung on whip springs, but later on sideways semi-elliptical springs; usually drawn by a pair of horses in pole gear (q.v.).

shooting your wheelers A coaching term; to move the wheelers (q.v.) into their collars to draw the weight of the load.

short (1) *see* SHORT ON A COW. (2) A racing term; said of a horse who drops out of contention in the home stretch or close to the finish in a horse race. (3) *see* GOING SHORT

short-coupled Also known as close-coupled; said of a short bodied horse in which the distance between the last rib and the point of the hip (q.v.) is short, i.e., not more than 4 inches (10 cm) wide.

short head *see* NOSE no. 2

short of a rib *see* SHORT OF RIB

short of blood *see* OUT OF BLOOD

short of bone *see* TIED IN BELOW THE KNEE

short of rib Also known as short of a rib; said of a horse in which the distance between the last rib and the point of the hip is greater than normal; indicative of a long-backed horse.

short on a cow Also known as short; a cutting term; a horse who, when moving parallel to a cow, is out of position or too far behind it to influence its movements.

short pastern *see* SHORT PASTERN BONE

short pastern bone Also known as P2, PII, second phalanx, short pastern, or coronary bone; the small bone located between the pastern bone (q.v.) and hoof and comprising the ankle.

short price A racing term; a small mutuel payoff in pari-mutuel (q.v.) betting.

short side The two short ends of a rectangular arena or manège (q.v.).

short Tommy A coaching term; a short, stiff, leather thong approximately 3 feet (91 cm) long, used on the wheel horses pulling a coach to encourage their forward movement; frequently used by the passengers.

shot-gun chaps A chaps (q.v.) worn by western enthusiasts; full-length, straight, and narrow leather leggings which close around the leg with zippers or buckles; held onto the body by a belted waistband.

shot on goal A polo term; said of a player who strikes the polo ball in an attempt to make a goal.

shoulder That part of the horse's body to which the forearm (q.v.) is attached; inserts into the chest.

shoulder atrophy *see* SWEENEY

shoulder falling out Also known as shoulder out; a dressage term; said of the horse; the shoulders move to the outside of or break the true line of a curve or straight line; indicates that the rider has lost control of the forehand.

shoulder hang A vaulting term; an exercise performed by a vaulter (q.v.), in which he hangs inverted, with a straight body, against the shoulder of the horse supporting his weight by his arms by which he holds onto the grips of the vaulting roller (q.v.).

shoulder-in A lateral movement performed on two tracks in which the horse travels forward while bent uniformly from head to tail away from the direction in which he is traveling; correctly executed, the angle should not exceed 30 degrees.

shouldering the pole An antiquated coaching term; said of a wheeler (q.v.) when he pushes the center pole against his partner.

shoulder out *see* SHOULDER FALLING OUT

shoulder paralysis *see* SWEENEY

show (1) A racing term; said of a horse, to (finish third in a race. (2) *see* HORSE SHOW. (3) To present, exhibit, or compete, as in a horse show (q.v.).

show bet A racing term; a wager on a horse to finish in the money (q.v.), third place or better; the show pool (q.v.) is split three ways and results in the lowest payoff.

show bridle *see* DOUBLE BRIDLE

show buggy Also known as show ring buggy; an extremely light, four-wheeled, single seat, horse-drawn American buggy (q.v.); has a full under-cut forecarriage, wire-spoked wheels and equally sized bicycle or rubber tires; used for showing trotting horses or ponies such as Hackneys (q.v.); popular from the late 1890s to present.

show circuit A calendar of horse shows within a defined geographic region.

show class Any competition held at a horse show (q.v.) in which participating horses are judged on conformation, condition, action and/or suitability for whatever purpose they are or will be used.

shower *see* CHATTER

shower down on one *see* CHATTER

shower the ground *see* CHATTER

show horse Any horse used, presented, exhibited, or competed in equestrian events.

show hunter Any hunter-type horse shown in classes in which he is judged on style, pace, manner and way of going on the flat and/over fences, coupled with faults.

showing too much leg *see* ON THE LEG

show jumper Any horse competed in show

jumping (q.v.) competitions.

show jumping Historically known in France as lepping or lepping contest; a jumping contest in which the horse and rider jump a series of man-made jumps in an enclosed area, in a predetermined order, and within a set time; may be conducted in indoor or open-air arenas which usually have 10 to 12 jumps, and at least one combination; the start and finish of the course are clearly marked and all jumps are numbered or flagged; originated in Paris, France in 1866, in 1912 it was first introduced as an Olympic sport, and in 1921, standardized regulations were established.

show jumping phase *see* SPEED AND ENDURANCE PHASE

show pony Any pony (q.v.) presented, exhibited, or competed in equestrian events.

show pool A racing term; a sum of money set aside by the track from wagers placed on horses to show in a specific race; winning to show ticket holders are paid from this pool.

show wagon *see* BOX WAGON

show wear A racing term; said of a horse whose fetlocks are swollen from overwork.

shredded paper *see* PAPER

shuffle A racing term; a style of riding assumed by some jockeys whereby the hands are pumped and the feet moved in rhythm with the stride of the horse.

shuffled back A racing term; said of a horse who loses ground or racing position because of a jam up of horses on the track.

shut off A racing term; said of a jockey who crosses in front of another horse during a race, forcing another jockey to pull back or go around.

shut out A racing term; said of a bettor (q.v.) who arrives at a betting window after wagering for a particular race has closed and is refused the opportunity to bet.

shut the stable door after the horse has bolted *see* LOCK THE STABLE DOOR AFTER THE HORSE IS STOLEN

shy Said of a horse; to start, recoil, or rear in fright or revulsion from something seen,

heard, or imagined.

shy feeder Said of a horse or hound with a poor appetite.

Sicilian (1) An Anglo-Arab (q.v.) indigenous to Sicily; stands 14.3 to 15.2 hands, has long legs, a short back, prominent withers, small ears, is spirited, and has good stamina; the coat may be dapple gray (q.v.), bay (q.v.), black (q.v.), or chestnut (q.v.); used for riding and light draft. (2) Also known as a Miniature Sicilian donkey and Sicilian donkey; a Miniature Mediterranean donkey (q.v.) native to the Mediterranean island of Sicily.

Sicilian Donkey *see* SICILIAN no. 2

sickle hocks *see* EXCESSIVE ANGULATION OF THE HOCK JOINTS

sickle hocked Also known as sabre-legged or sickle-legged; said of a horse afflicted with excessive angulation of the hock joints (q.v.).

sickle-legged *see* SICKLE HOCKED

side boards *see* BOARDS

side bones Also known as knots; ossification of one or both of the lateral cartilages of the pedal bone; most common in the forefeet of heavy horses, mules, hunters, and jumpers and is rare in Thoroughbreds (q.v.); symptoms include heat and the appearance of hard lumps on the coronet (q.v.) on either side of the heel; may be due to genetics, improper shoeing, repeated concussion of the quarters of the foot causing trauma to the cartilages, traumatic lesions, and poor conformation; lameness may or may not be present depending on the degree of ossification.

side car A shafted, but wheeless horse- or mule-drawn vehicle similar to a travois (q.v.) consists of two shafts, one attached to either side of the animal the ends of which drag on the ground and between which was a large box or wicker basket; eventually fitted with rollers or disc-wheels and was the prototype of all carts (such as the jaunting car [q.v.]), wagons, and carriages.

sideclaws Sharp projections on the inside of the bit cheekpieces which cause sores on the lateral lips and corners of the mouth.

side clip A clip (q.v.) placed on the shoe near the middle of the quarter (q.v.) on either side of the foot.

side jockey Also known as western side jockey; the portion of leather on a western saddle attached to the left and right sides of the saddle seat upon which the rider's thigh rests and which covers the insertion of the fender (q.v.) into the saddle tree.

side line A polo term; the two 300 yard long (274 m) sides of a polo field (q.v.) which, in conjunction with the end lines (q.v.), define the playing area of a polo field; previously identified by boards (q.v.), are now marked by chalk; the ball is considered out of bounds and play is stopped if the ball passes outside of this line.

sidelines Two equal lengths of rope connecting the pasterns of the fore and hind legs on each side used as a breaking or training tools; are shorter than the distance between the feet in a normal stance, yet long enough to enable the horse to stand; when the horse attempts to strike or kick, he pulls the other leg on the same side from underneath and falls over.

sidepass The horizontal movement of the horse without forward or rearward movement.

sidepiece *see* CHEEK

side pull *see* LINDELL

side puller A horse who pulls harder on one side of the bit than the other.

side reins Two rigid, elasticized, and/or adjustable auxiliary reins (q.v.) attached on one end to the roller, training surcingle (q.v.), or girth and to the bit rings on the other to teach the horse head carriage; may be attached as high as the withers (q.v.) or low as behind the shoulder.

sidesaddle Also known as the queen of saddles; a saddle (q.v.) designed for women which enabled them to ride without sitting astride the horse; use dates back well into the 12th century although it was not formally introduced into England until the early 1300s at which time the saddle was based on the pack saddle design fitted, on the nearside (q.v.), with a foot rest and only one pommel; in 1580, Catherine de Medici, Queen of France, added a second pommel below the first and was revolutionized in 1830 by the addition of the leaping head (q.v.); the rider sits with both feet on the near side (q.v.) of the

horse with her right leg hooked over the upper of two padded, diagonally placed projections, while her left leg fits under and against the lower one, the leaping head, with the foot resting in the stirrup.

side saddler One who rides sidesaddle (q.v.).

side steps *see* LATERAL WORK

side stick A device historically used on horses prone to biting to enable grooming without danger; a strong, yet narrow stick attached on one end to the bit and on the other to the surcingle (q.v.) that prevents and ultimately conditions the horse against bringing his head around to bite.

side step *see* TRAVERSE AND TWO TRACK

sidewheeler *see* PACER

side wheeling The side-to-side roll of a pacer (q.v.) when moving at the pace (q.v.).

sifting A technique used by some horse show judges to evaluate large show classes; the class is divided into smaller, more manageable groups from which the judge(s) selects the top performers; the top performers are then judged together as a single class, the balance of the horses being excused from the ring.

sight The power or faculty of seeing; the sense whereby objects are perceived by the eye.

sight hound A hunting dog who uses his eyes to pursue the quarry (q.v.); include Grayhounds, Whippets, Borzois, and Salukis.

Siglavy *see* ASSIL

sign Any objective indication of animal disease or ill health; a horse may show signs of illness, pain, etc.

silage A brown colored, wet material produced by the controlled fermentation of high moisture herbage such as grasses and legumes under anaerobic conditions; the production of lactic acid eventually stops the fermentation process; commonly fed to ruminants such as cattle and sheep and less so to horses because of possible unpalatability, the likelihood of spoilage, and the need to feed quickly to prevent same; should be introduced to the horse's diet slowly.

silent heat The estrus (q.v.) period in which the mare ovulates, but fails to show behavioral signs of heat (q.v.).

silks *see* COLORS

Silky Sullivan, a A racing term; said of a horse who makes a big run from far back in the field to the finish; named for the horse known as Silky Sullivan, who once made up 41 lengths to win a race.

silver buckskin Refers to coat color; of the color group buckskin (q.v.); creamy yellow coat hair with black points and no primitive marks (q.v.).

silver dapple Refers to coat color; sepia brown coat hair with light dapples (q.v.), which may be somewhat subdued, and flaxen or nearly white points; unique to Shetland ponies (q.v.) in the United States, but in a variety of breeds throughout Europe; may be confused with chestnut (q.v.).

silver dun Refers to coat color; of the color group dun (q.v.); creamy yellow coat hair with primitive marks (q.v.) and black points.

silver grullo Refers to coat color; a grullo (q.v.) of the color group dun (q.v.); the lightest of the grullo colors; a cream-colored body with slate blue, instead of black, points and head, and blue eyes.

silver ring An antiquated racing term; the cheap and secondary betting enclosure at a racetrack (q.v.) where small bookmakers conduct business.

simple change Also known as a half parade, simple lead change, simple change of leg at the canter, or change of leg through the trot; a movement in which the cantering horse is brought back to the trot for two, and at the most three strides, before resuming the canter (q.v.) on the new lead; in training of the horse precedes the flying change (q.v.).

simple change of leg at the canter *see* SIMPLE CHANGE

simple dismount A compulsory vaulting exercise performed in competitions; from a sitting position, the vaulter (q.v.) swings the outside leg up in a semi circle, bends forward at the hip, brings the outside leg together with the inside leg, and pushes away from the grips to land, feet together.

simple whorl A hair pattern; a whorl (q.v.) created by a change in direction of the flow of the hair in which hairs converge from different directions.

simple lead change *see* SIMPLE CHANGE

Simulium *see* BLACK FLY

simple fracture A break of the bone along a single line which does not penetrate the skin.

simpler's art *see* HERBALISM

simulcast A simultaneous live television transmission of an event, generally a horse race, to other tracks, off-track betting offices, or other locations for the purpose of placing wagers.

sinew *see* TENDON

singeing An antiquated practice; to trim the mane and tail hair of the horse using a gas flame or lamp; now replaced by clippers (q.v.).

single a jump An Irish term; said of the horse; to touch and clear a bank (q.v.) with only one step of each foot.

single bank A jumping obstacle (q.v.); a bank (q.v.) having a ditch on only one side.

single break *see* BREAKING CART

single foot *see* RACK

single-gutted *see* HERRING-GUTTED

single-jointed true kimblewick One of five types of kimblewick (q.v.) bit (q.v.); a type of pelham (q.v.) requiring one instead of two reins (q.v.), having a straight, jointed mouthpiece (q.v.), short cheeks (q.v.) with dee rings running the full length, and a square eye on the upper end of the cheeks.

single-tree *see* SWINGLE TREE

sinker A grave case of founder (q.v.) in which laminitis (q.v.) has destroyed so much of the laminae (q.v.) that the bone is no longer supported and begins to sink or descend into the foot.

sinking fox A hunting term; said of a hunted fox (q.v.) who begins to tire after a hard hunt.

sinuous whorl A hair pattern; a whorl (q.v.) created by two opposing sweeps of hair which meet along an irregular curving line.

sire (1) Also known as progenitor; the father or potential father of a horse; a colt is said to be "by" his sire; appears on the top side of the pedigree (q.v.). (2) To beget foals.

sired by *see* BY

sire stake A racing term; a stakes race (q.v.) restricted to the progeny (q.v.) of stallions standing at stud in a given state or province.

sisters Also known as full sisters or own sisters; a relationship of female horses "by" the same sire (q.v.) and "out" of the same dam (q.v.).

sitfast A hard and painful swelling on the back; a gall (q.v.).

sit-still A racing term; said of a jockey who loses a race due to failure to use the whip.

sitting trot Said of the rider; to ride the trot without rising from the saddle to post (q.v.).

sixteenth pole A racing term; a vertical post located on the infield rail exactly one furlong (q.v.) from the finish.

Sjees *see* FRIESIAN CHAISE

Sjurpapach A Russian equestrian sport similar to the Argentinian game of pato (q.v.) in which two teams compete to score points by throwing a stuffed, long-haired sheepskin hat through the opponents' ring fixed on top of a high post; the rings are located on opposite ends of a randomly shaped field.

skate A horse of marginal or poor quality.

skeebald *see* SKEWBALD

skeleton The total bony framework which sustains the softer body parts of the horse.

Skeleton Brake A horse-drawn vehicle of the brake (q.v.) type; a training and exercising vehicle used by professional horsebreakers, especially during the second half of the 19th century; consisted of an open platform with an elevated box located directly above the fore-wheels; horses, usually one older and more experienced in harness work than the other, were driven in pairs, harnessed to pole gear (q.v.); a groom generally stood behind the driver, who when necessary could jump from the platform and aid the novice horse.

skeleton bridle A harness bridle without blinkers (q.v.).

skep Also known as skip; a wicker or plastic basket used in stables for the collection of manure.

skepping out *see* MUCKING OUT

skewbald Also known as skeebald; refers to coat color; a nonblack horse with tobiano (q.v.), overo (q.v.), sabino (q.v.), or splashed asymmetric patterns of white; the lines of separation between the colors are well defined; from the Anglo Saxon scuwa meaning shadow which may be related to the Latin *obscurus* meaning dark shadowed, a coat shadowed by another color.

skiboy A competitor in a skijoring (q.v.) event.

skid *see* DRAG-SHOE

skid boots Protective leg wraps fitted below the hocks and covering the fetlocks of the hind legs of the horse.

skid pan *see* DRAG-SHOE

skid-shoe *see* DRAG-SHOE

skied One of five gaits of the Icelandic Horse (q.v.) used to cover short distances at great speed.

skijoring A mounted winter sport in which a rider pulls a skier by means of a long rope attached to the stock saddle (q.v.), on a straight-away or counterclockwise around a 250-yard (229 m), roughly circular course consisting of four wedge-shaped jumps and about six knee-high rubber gates around which the skier weaves; the skier wears standard downhill ski gear while western tack is used on the mostly Quarter Horses (q.v.), mounts sharp-shod with an alloy of tungsten and brass welded onto their shoes, snowball pads (q.v.) are optional; derived from the Finnish sport of the same name in which competitors ski behind reindeer or dogs.

skim sheet *see* FLY SHEET

skin (1) A racing term; to make a racetrack faster by rolling and hardening the surface. (2) To strip of money or belongings; to fleece. (3) The anatomical boundary and principal organ of communication between the horse and its environment; the largest body organ, constituting 12 to 24 percent of the horse's total body weight depending on age; consists of a variety of cellular and tissue components: the epidermis (q.v.), appendageal system (q.v.), dermis (q.v.), arrector pili muscle, panniculus carnosus, and panniculus adiposa (a fatty subacute layer).

skip *see* SKEP

skirt (1) *see* SADDLE SKIRT. (2) A hunting term; said of a hound who cuts corners and does not follow the true line when following the scent of the fox. (3) *see* APRON no. 2

skirter A hunting term; a hound (q.v.) who runs wide or skirts (q.v.) the pack (q.v.) hoping to be the first to pick up the line of the fox (q.v.) after it has made a sharp turn.

skittish Said of a horse who is easily frightened, shy, or timid.

skiving The process by which the flesh is shaved from a cured hide; to split or cut a hide into layers or slices.

Skogsruss *see* GOTLAND

skunk tail *see* FROSTY

Skyros A pony breed indigenous to the Greek island of Skyros from which the name derived; is the smallest and is believed to be the oldest of the Greek breeds bearing some resemblance to the Tarpan (q.v.); stands 9.1 to 11 hands and may have a gray, bay, brown, or palomino (q.v.) coat; has a small head, short back, poorly developed croup and chest, and slender legs; cow hocks are common; is quiet and trustworthy; used principally for packing and as a child's mount.

slab fracture A break (q.v.) in the bone in a joint that extends from one articular surface to the other; occurs most commonly in the third carpal bone of the knee.

slab-sided *see* FLAT-SIDED

slack (1) Not drawn tightly, loose, as in a rope or reins. (2) A British term; a depression between hills in a hillside or on the surface of the ground. (3) A British term; a boggy or wet hollow.

slack in the loins Said of a horse who has weak loins.

slaframine toxicosis *see* SLOBBER FACTOR

slate grullo *see* GRULLO

slat-sided *see* FLAT-SIDED

SLE The acronym for systemic lupus erythematosus (q.v.).

sleeper A racing term; an underrated horse whose performance exceeds expectations.

sleeping sickness *see* ENCEPHALOMYELITIS

slicing A barrel racing term; said of a horse who attempts to turn a barrel too soon and either strikes it or turns improperly so that he is out of position for the next barrel.

slick Said of a flat horseshoe.

slicker A long, loose, oilskin or waterproof outer coat; a raincoat.

slide *see* SLIDING STOP

sliding stop Also known as slide; an abrupt stop performed by a galloping horse in which he sets his hind feet, engages his hocks, rounds his back, sits down low on his haunches, walks with his front feet and slides to a stop on his hind feet, tucking them well under his body.

slip *see* TICKET no. 2

Slipe A horse-drawn vehicle; a shaftless version of the Irish side car (q.v.) attached to a horse or mule by means of a crude harness and dragged along the ground.

slip head That part of the bridle supporting the bit; positioned behind the horse's ears or that part of a nose band, including the cheeks and headpiece, which fits behind the horse's ears.

slipped Said of a mare who aborts a pregnancy naturally.

slipped shoulder *see* SWEENEY

slipper (1) *see* DRAG-SHOE. (2) *see* TIP SHOE

slipping a point An antiquated jumping term; the point at which the rider begins to time a horse to put him into stride for a jump.

slip rein To secure a rein to something, such as a head collar, so that it can be released quickly by letting go of one end.

slip the reins To allow the reins to slide through one's fingers to their maximum length.

slitting the nostrils A practice dating back to ancient Egypt, 1350 BC, whereby the nostrils of equids were slit in belief that it would make them breathe more freely; may have also begun in an effort to compensate for impaired breathing caused by pressure from a drop noseband; still practiced.

Sloan, James Todhunter (1874-1933) An American jockey who popularized the crouched-style of flat racing in which the rider is positioned well over the shoulders of the horse riding with very short leathers (q.v.).

slobber factor Also known as slaframine toxicosis; a noninfectious disease affecting both horses and cattle, although horses are particularly susceptible; caused by the ingestion of forages such as clovers, infected with the fungus *Rhizoctonia leguminicola* which produces a toxic alkaloid called slaframine; symptoms include profuse salivation and, in some cases, frequent urination and defecation; is not deadly, and removal of the infected forages results in rapid recovery.

sloping shoulder Also known as oblique shoulder; said of the shoulder of the horse when the humerus is the desired length and the scapula is long and slanting.

sloppy track A racing term; said of a racing strip (q.v.) covered with puddles, but not yet muddy, the surface remaining hard.

slot (1) A racing term; a post position (q.v.). (2) The track or trail of a deer or other animal.

slow gait Also known as stepping pace or four-beat stepping pace; the slow, four-beat,

broken gait performed by five-gaited horses including the American Saddlebred (q.v.) at a speed less than 10 mph (17 kmph) with an emphasis on precision and form; there is a slight break in cadence from the pace, in which the near fore and the near hind feet leave the ground simultaneously, followed with an interruption, by the off fore and off hind; primarily a show gait producing a characteristic sideways swinging motion of the rider; is very comfortable to ride; a collected form of the rack (q.v.).

Slow Heavy *see* STAGE COACH

slow pace STEPPING PACE

slow track A racing term; a slightly wet, but not muddy race track.

slug A lazy or slow horse, who requires urging to move forward.

Slurazi *see* DARASHOURI

small metacarpals *see* SPLINT BONE

small metacarpal bones *see* SPLINT BONE

small pinworm Also known as *Probstmayria vivipara*; a relatively harmless species of pinworm (q.v.) found in the horse, specifically in the large intestine.

small station wagon *see* BROUGHAM

small strongyle One of many species of round worm found in the cecum and colon of the horse; many are appreciably smaller than the large strongyle (q.v.), but some may be as large as *Strongylus vulgaris* (q.v.); is much less destructive than large strongyles, feeds superficially on the intestinal mucosa, and has a three-week life cycle; migrate to the small intestine and may remain dormant in nodular enlargements on the wall of the large intestine; in temperate areas may cause acute diarrhea and death in young horses and ponies in the late winter and spring.

smart money (1) A racing term; an insider's bet. (2) A racing term; those who give inside information or tips on future races.

smithy (1) *see* FARRIER. (2) The building or shop in which a farrier (q.v.) or blacksmith works and keeps his tools.

smoke eye *see* WALL EYE

smoky black Refers to coat color; the body coat color is a lighter black than the points (q.v.).

smooth *see* UNSHOD

smooth-mouthed Said of a horse whose teeth have been worn smooth due to use; indicates the horse is at least 12 years old.

smooth muscle Any nonstriated, involuntary muscle (q.v.) which operates in such involuntary movements as breathing and digestion, the principal exception being the heart, which consists of involuntary, but striated muscle.

smooth rein Any strap attached to the bit cheekpieces on one end and held in the rider's hands on the other; made of leather or synthetic materials without lacing or plating.

Smudish An ancient breed of horse indigenous to the Baltic states, specifically the former Lithuania; generally had a dun (q.v.) coat with a light mane and tail, although mouse dun and bay also occurred; had a dark dorsal stripe (q.v.), small head, muscular neck, strong forehand, and strong, lean, small-boned legs; stood 13 to 15 hands; a highly regarded horse.

smutty buckskin Also known as dark buckskin; refers to coat color; any horse with a yellow coat into which black hairs are mixed; will have black points and a head of a color similar to the body.

smutty grullo Also known as dark grullo; refers to coat color; a grullo (q.v.) of the color group dun (q.v.); any grullo color where black is mixed into the body color, the points are black, and the head dark.

smutty palomino Also known as sooty palomino; refers to coat color; of the color group palomino (q.v.); a yellow coat and sometimes tail hairs evenly mixed with black; may be as dark as some chestnuts (q.v.).

snaffle *see* SNAFFLE BIT

snaffle bit Also known as snaffle; the simplest and most commonly used of all bits; primarily a straight or jointed mouthpiece with a ring on either end to which one pair of reins is attached; acts on the tongue, the bars (in the straight snaffle), the sides of the mouth (in the jointed snaffle), the lips, and the corners of the mouth; types include the upper-cheek snaffle (q.v.), lower-cheek snaffle (q.v.), full-cheek snaffle (q.v.), and half-cheek snaffle (q.v.); derived from the Dutch word snavel and the German schnabel, meaning to mouth or break.

snaffle bridle A bridle (q.v.) used in conjunction with a snaffle bit (q.v.).

snatch *see* STRINGHALT

snip A face marking (q.v.); an isolated white marking located between, in the region of, or extending into the nostrils, but not extending above the nostrils.

snip lower lip A face marking (q.v.); any marking found on the lower lip.

snorter An excitable horse.

snowball hammer A farrier's tool; a hoof pick (q.v.) and hammer combined into the head of one instrument; used to breakup and remove packed snow and ice from the underside of the horse's hooves.

snowball pad A horseshoe pad (q.v.) inserted between the ground-side surface of the hoof and the horseshoe to prevent balling (q.v.).

snowflake Also known as snowflake marking; refers to a coat color pattern; one of six symmetrical coat color patterns of the Appaloosa (q.v.) approved by the Appaloosa Horse Club (q.v.); a solid body color with dominant spotting over the hips; spots may range in size from 3/8 to 1-1/4 inches (1–3 cm); may not show until the horse is three to five years of age and can increase with age until the pattern stabilizes, after which time, on some horses, the white spots can disappear; in the advanced pattern, called speckled, the horse appears almost white with small colored spots throughout the coat.

snowflake marking *see* SNOWFLAKE

snub To tie short to restrict head and neck movement, as in "he snubbed the colt to the patience post."

soaping *see* LATHERED UP

sociable *see* SOCIABLE BAROUCHE

Sociable Barouche Also known as sociable or vis-à-vis; a horse-drawn, four-wheeled open carriage popular in the 19th century; had seating for four passengers seated vis-à-vis, and double or two half hoods protecting both the front and rear of the vehicle; drawn by a pair of horses and driven from a high box.

Sociable Landau *see* LANDAU

Société Hippique Percheronne An organization founded in France to maintain the stud book (q.v.) for the Percheron (q.v.), a duty it has performed since 1883.

sock Also known as half cannon; a leg marking (q.v.); white on the foot of the horse which extends from the coronet (q.v.) along the pastern to the middle of the cannon bone.

sobre pass A Spanish term; a gait in which the horse canters with his fore- and trots with his hind legs.

sodium *see* SODIUM CHLORIDE

sodium chloride Also known as common salt; a crystalline compound important in maintaining osmotic pressure, acid-base equilibrium, water metabolism, and in regulating body temperature; is not stored in the body tissues and is therefore required in the daily ration with a mature horse requiring approximately 60 grams of salt per day; the requirement increases in working horses and lactating mares; excess salt in the diet is not toxic if sufficient water is available, and may cause digestive disturbances, weakness, loss of coordination, paralysis of the hind limbs, and even death.

sodium hyaluronate *see* ACID

soft (1) Said of an out-of-condition horse who fatigues easily. (2) A team penning and roping term; said of a cow who has little play and is easily tired.

soft bone *see* CARTILAGE

softening of the bones Said of the mare in the first stage of parturition (q.v.) during which the central joint of the pelvic girdle expands to allow for passage of the foal; concurrently, the muscles drop in over the bones of the hindquarters to protect the foal during birth.

soft mouth Said of a horse who requires minimal bit and rein action to achieve the desired response; the opposite of hard mouth (q.v.).

soft mouthed Also known as soft-mouthed hound; said of a hound who has a low voice or bark.

soft-mouthed hound *see* SOFT MOUTHED

soft palate The muscular tissue at the posterior part of the roof of the mouth; in conjunction with the hard palate (q.v.) separates the nasal and oral cavities.

soft palate disease *see* CHOKING UP

soft track A racing term; said of a racing surface which contains a large amount of moisture and into which horses sink.

Sokolsky A Polish-bred warmblood developed during the 1800s; influenced by the Norfolk Trotter (q.v.), Belgian Heavy Draft (q.v.), Belgian Ardennes (q.v.) and the Anglo-Norman (q.v.); stands 15 to 16 hands, has a chestnut, brown, or gray coat, a large head, sturdy frame, short and straight back, short legs, and large, round feet; is patient, hardworking, particularly well suited to heavy draft and farm work; a very economical keeper.

soil To feed a stall-bound horse sufficient quantities and types of feed to fatten it.

solar The bottom aspect of the horse's hoof.

sold at halter *see* SELL AT HALTER

solid blanket *see* BLANKET no. 1

solid color Refers to coat color; a coat consisting of only one color and no black or white markings.

solid horse A racing term; said of a horse who is a contender in a race.

somer *see* PACK HORSE

sonogram *see* ULTRASOUND

sooty palomino *see* SMUTTY PALOMINO

sophomore A racing term; a three-year-old horse; so called because he is in his second year.

sore (1) A place on the body where the skin or flesh is bruised, cut, infected, or painful; a wound. (2) Stiff and tender, as from physical exertion.

sore back Said of a horse who is sore (q.v.) along the topline (q.v.) in the general area of the saddle; generally caused by back strain, lameness in the hind legs, or primary back muscle stiffness due to underlying spinal problems.

sore kidneys Tenderness along the topline of the back in the general area of the saddle; rarely an indicator of true kidney soreness unless other signs of urinary problems are present.

sore knee *see* CARPITIS

soreing To cut the forehooves of the Paso Fino (q.v.) horse intentionally short to make them sore and thus encourage the horse to pick up his feet quickly; an unacceptable practice.

sore shins *see* BUCKED SHINS

sorghum A low-growing cereal plant well adapted to semiarid climates cultivated for fodder, grain, and juice; has an extensive root system and modest leaf area; varieties include milo, kafir, hergari, feterita; a high energy, high carbohydrate feed (approximately 75 percent), low fiber, (less than 3 percent), low fat (less than 3 percent), and having a protein content ranging from 8 to 16 percent, but averaging 9 percent in most cases; although a yellow grain, contains less carotene than corn; not a good source of vitamins or minerals; a heavy feed which can result in founder or severe or fatal digestive disturbances such as enterotoxemia if overfed.

Sorraia *see* SORRAIA PONY

Sorraia Pony Also known as Sorraia; an ancient pony breed originating in western Spain in the area bordering the Sorraia river from which the name derived; Spain's only native pony; thought to have descended from the Tarpan (q.v.) and Asiatic Wild Horse (q.v.) which it resembles; stands 12.2 to 13 hands and may have a dun, gray, or palomino coat, with zebra markings (q.v.) on the legs and an eel stripe (q.v.); has a large head, long ears with black tips, a slender and long neck, high withers, poor hindquarters, low-set tail, and long, solid legs; is independent, an easy

keeper, frugal, resistant to both heat and cold, and has good endurance (q.v.); historically used for agricultural work and presently for riding and packing; its numbers are on the decline.

sorrel Refers to coat color; a clear light red coat with non-black points; sometimes confused with chestnut (q.v.), the difference between the two colors depending largely on the breed under consideration; variations include sorrel tostado (q.v.), sorrel alazán (q.v.), sorrel ruano (q.v.), and blond sorrel ruano (q.v.).

sorrel alazán Refers to coat color; of the color group sorrel (q.v.); a clear light red coat with a lighter mane and tail than the body but not near the white of the ruano.

sorrel roan *see* STRAWBERRY ROAN

sorrel ruano Refers to coat color; of the color group sorrel (q.v.); a clear light red coat with a flaxen mane and tail and lower legs lighter than the body; may look similar to a palomino (q.v.).

sound Said of a horse free from illness, disease, physical or conformation defect, injury, or blemish that may affect his future performance or ability to work.

soundness The state or condition of being sound (q.v.).

soundness examination *see* VETERINARY INSPECTION

sounding board *see* FINO BOARD

soup plate A horse having disproportionately large, round feet for its body size.

sour Also known as stale; an over-trained or over-competed horse who has become lethargic and uninterested in work; to become bored, as in cattle.

sour cattle Also known as stale cattle; a cutting term; said of cattle that have been used for cutting (q.v.) too often and no longer respond well to the horse when used for training or cutting; inactive cattle.

Southern and Eastern Gidran One of two types of Gidran Arabian (q.v.) a Hungarian breed developed in 1816; descended from an Arab (q.v.) of the Siglavy strain crossed with Thoroughbred (q.v.); is lighter than the Middle European Gidran (q.v.) and is thus used for all-purpose competition.

Southern Plantation Walking Horse *see* TENNESSEE WALKING HORSE

South German Coldblood *see* NORIKER

Soviet Heavy Draft A heavy-draft breed developed in Russia between 1890 and 1930 by putting native mares to imported Percheron (q.v.) stallions; breed characteristics were firmly established by the 1940s; has a massive build, weighs 1,430 to 1,720 pounds (649–780 kg), stands about 15 hands, has a well-proportioned head with pronounced jaws, relatively short neck, low and broad withers, deep chest, short legs with mild feathering, and a chestnut, roan, or bay coat; is quiet, energetic, strong, and has a sure and easy gait, both at the walk and trot; used for heavy draft and farm work.

sowar A trooper in an Indian cavalry regiment.

sow mouth *see* UNDERSHOT JAW

soybean A protein rich leguminous plant, *Glycine max*, used for forage (q.v.), and its seeds used as a source of oil, flour, and other foods.

soybean meal A high energy, high protein supplement produced from the residue of the soybean (q.v.) following oil extraction; contains the highest level of protein of all grains, varying from 41 to 50 percent, a fat content of 1.5 to 5 percent, is a good source of calcium, provides moderate amounts of riboflavin and thiamin, contains all ten essential amino acids, is highly digestible, low in fiber, and commonly fed to horses.

spa *see* TRIPLE BAR

spade (1) A bit with leverage like a curb (q.v.), having a high spoon (q.v.) instead of a port (q.v.); connected to the cheekpieces by copper braces. (2) *see* SPOON

spade bit *see* SPADE no. 1

span A pair of horses harnessed in a team to pull a vehicle.

Spanish Anglo-Arab *see* HISPANO

Spanish Arab *see* HISPANO

Spanish hackamore A bitless bridle consisting of a bosal (q.v.), headstall, and mecate (q.v.); control is achieved when the bosal is pulled against the bridge of the horse's nose by the reins, thereby restricting his wind.

Spanish Horse *see* ANDALUSIAN

Spanish jumping bit *see* KIMBLEWICK

Spanish Riding School *see* IMPERIAL SPANISH RIDING SCHOOL OF VIENNA

Spanish Riding School of Vienna *see* IMPERIAL SPANISH RIDING SCHOOL OF VIENNA

Spanish School *see* IMPERIAL SPANISH RIDING SCHOOL OF VIENNA

Spanish snaffle *see* KIMBLEWICK

Spanish walk An artificial air; an exaggerated, elevated walk, whereby the horse extends his straightened forelegs up and forward to about chest height; the forelegs show much greater activity and extension than the hind legs.

spare (1) A racing term; any horse in partial training who is not working with the main string. (2) A coaching term; an extra horse kept at a change (q.v.) on the coach route who was changed with a tired or lame horse in the team pulling the coach.

spasms of the gastrointestinal tract *see* COLIC

spavin Any of certain diseases or conditions of the horse affecting the hock including bog spavin (q.v.), bone spavin (q.v.), blood spavin (q.v.), and occult spavin (q.v.).

spavined Said of a horse suffering from a occult spavin (q.v.), bone spavin (q.v.), blood spavin (q.v.), or bog spavin (q.v.).

spavin shoe A horseshoe (q.v.) in which the toe of the shoe is rolled to prevent the hoof toe from hitting the ground and the heels are sloped and left high, approximately 1 inch (2.5 cm), to relieve stress on the joint; used on spavined (q.v.) horses.

spavin test A flexion test used as an aid in diagnosing and/or localizing lameness; to move the horse at a trot after holding the hock in a flexed position for a period of one to two minutes.

spay To perform any procedure on a mare or filly, such as surgically removing the ovaries, that renders her incapable of conception.

spayed mare A mare who has had a procedure to render her incapable of conception.

speak Also known as cry; a hunting term; said of a hound (q.v.) when he barks.

speck in the eye *see* FEATHER IN THE EYE

speckled Refers to a coat color pattern; an advanced version, not a separate pattern, of the snowflake (q.v.) pattern in which the horse becomes very light, appearing almost white, with small colored spots throughout the coat; often confused with flea-bitten grays.

specialized shoe Any horseshoe (q.v.) adapted for a specific breed or type of horse.

specialized shoeing A horseshoeing procedure for a specific breed or type of horse.

spectacles *see* IRISH MARTINGALE

speed figure A racing term; a handicapping tool used to assign a numerical value to a horse's performance.

speedy cut (1) A wound or injury to the knee or upper part of the cannon bone caused when the horseshoe of one foot, usually a hind, strikes the inside of the opposite front leg. (2) High scalping (q.v.) common to trotters.

speedy cutting Any limb interference occurring at a fast gait.

speedy-cutting shoe *see* FEATHER-EDGED SHOE

spelt A type of wheat (q.v.); grain of the genus *Triticum spelta*, grown as a livestock feed in western Asia and southern Europe; has a large fibrous hull, high fiber content, and a digestible energy slightly lower than that of oats (q.v.).

spent grains *see* BREWERS DRIED GRAINS

sperm Also known as seed, spermatozoa, or spermatozoon of which it is a contraction; the microscopic male fertilizing cell contained in the white, opaque seminal fluid of the male horse which is produced in the testicles; contains the genetic material of the stallion; consists of three fractions: watery containing little or no sperm, thin and watery containing the sperm, and gel from the vesicular gland.

spermatozoa *see* SPERM

spermatozoon *see* SPERM

spey *see* SPAY

spider *see* SPIDER WEB BANDAGE

spider bandage *see* SPIDER WEB BANDAGE

Spider Phaeton A light, four-wheeled, horse-drawn vehicle of the phaeton (q.v.) type popular in the 1860s; had a spindle-backed driving seat, a rumble seat for a groom, a skeletal structure mounted on arched irons for improved cut-under, and was hung on sideways-elliptical springs, front and rear; drawn either by a single horse in shafts or a pair in pole gear (q.v.).

spider web bandage Also known as a spider web bandage or spider; cloth or gauze used to apply pressure to the knee joint area; consists of a sufficient length of muslin to span 6 to 8 inches (15–20 cm) above and below the knee that is about 16 inches (41 cm) wide; the material is folded in half and strips are cut into the material which are 1 inch (19–25 mm) wide and approximately 5 inches (12.5 cm) long; the unstripped portion of the muslin rests on the inside and front of the leg while the strips are braided down the outside of the leg; the top left and right strips are tied and knotted and all subsequent strips are braided down the leg; may be applied over standing bandages (q.v.), dressings, ice packs, etc.

spiffing An antiquated practice; to blow snuff into the nostril of an unpredictable or cantankerous horse to control it.

spike (1) *see* UNICORN. (2) A hoof shape pattern in which the hoof is generally square, with straight quarters and sharply turned in heels with the widest part of the hoof located midway between the toe and heels.

spike team *see* UNICORN

spin A western term; a pivot or a 360 degree turn; similar to the canter pirouette; the forelegs swing 360 degrees, in bounding movements, around the hind legs, while the hind feet remain, more or less, in one place; the radius of the turn is equal to the length of the horse; lightness of the forehand is essential.

spinal column *see* VERTEBRAL COLUMN

spinal cord The cord of nervous tissue extending through the spinal canal, and enclosed within the spinal column (q.v.).

spine *see* VERTEBRAL COLUMN

spinny A hunting term; a small covert (q.v.).

spiral fracture A crack or break in a bone that turns or spirals around the bone circumference; caused by a sudden torque or twist of the bone; may or may not be comminuted (q.v.) or displaced (q.v.).

spirit level A glass tube nearly filled with alcohol, for determining a line or plane parallel to the horizon by the central position of an air bubble on its upper side.

spit box A racing term; a barn where horses are brought for post-race drug testing.

Spiti A pony breed indigenous to the Himalayan mountain region of Northern India; named for the Spiti tract in the central Himalayas; principally bred by the Kanyat, a high-caste Hindu tribe, who use it for trade; is tough, sturdy, sure-footed, vigorous, and ill-suited to the warm and humid conditions of the lowlands, being best suited for mountain use; stands approximately 12 hands, has a rather heavy neck, sharp ears, a strong, short back, short legs, round feet, and a full mane and tail; the coat is usually gray or steel gray; tends to temperamental; used for packing; is smaller, but similar in type and conformation to the Bhutia (q.v.).

spit out the bit Also known as spit the bit; a racing term; said of an exhausted horse who sucks back, releasing pressure on the bit.

spit the bit *see* SPIT OUT THE BIT

spiv Also known as a spivvey; an antiquated term; a groom (q.v.) lacking full-time employment who is capable and willing to perform odd jobs.

spivvey *see* SPIV

splashboard Also known as fender; a panel on a horse-drawn vehicle which protects the passengers from splashes of water, mud, etc., kicked up from the road.

splashed white Refers to a coat color pattern; an asymmetrical pattern of white consisting of large, distinctly marked patches, white legs, a predominantly white head, and a mostly white belly; the eyes are commonly blue.

splatter A cutting term; the action of a horse when it drops down in front of a cow.

splay footed *see* TOE-OUT

splenic fever *see* ANTHRAX

splint Also known as popping a splint; enlargement of the splint bones (q.v.) resulting from a proliferation of fibrous tissue and osteoperostitis; usually occurs in the forelegs of young horses in the early months or years of training on the medial aspect of the forelimbs between the second and third metacarpal bones; associated with hard training, poor conformation, improper hoof care, or malnutrition; characterized by swelling, heat, and lameness which is only observed during splint formation; splint size is usually dependent on the degree of inflammation and the surface area involved; usually assumes an elongated form lying parallel to the small metacarpal bone; of four types: interosseous splints (q.v.), edge splints (q.v.), creeping splints (q.v.), and knee splints (q.v.).

splint bone Also known as the small metacarpal, small metacarpal bones (foreleg), and metatarsus bone (hind leg); either of two small bones which lie along the posterior parts of the cannon bone (q.v.) in the fore or hind legs of the horse; braces the knee to prevent the knee from collapsing backward by anchoring tissues to the accessory carpal bone at the joint's rear.

splint boots *see* BRUSHING BOOTS

splinter bar *see* SWINGLE TREE

split A hunting term; said for the hound pack which separates into two different packs to follow the scents of two different foxes traveling in different directions.

split up behind Also known as split up quarters; a conformation fault; said of a horse with weak gaskins; when viewed from behind, the thighs divide too high, just below the dock (q.v.).

split up quarters *see* SPLIT UP BEHIND

SPAOPD The acronym for summer pasture-associated obstructive pulmonary disease (q.v.).

spoiled mouth Said of the mouth of the horse which is no longer sensitive to minimal bit and rein action to achieve the desired response.

spoke A western roping term; the length of rope between the honda (q.v.) and the roper's hand.

spoke brush A long, narrow brush with thick, hard bristles used to clean carriage wheels on a horse-drawn vehicle.

spokes Metal or wooden bars, radiating from the nave (q.v.) of the wheel of a horse-drawn vehicle on the inside and to the fellowe (q.v.) on the other, which support the rim.

sponge (1) A racing term; to insert a piece of sponge or other foreign material into the nostrils of a horse to impede its ability to breath, thus impacting his performance. (2) The skeleton or framework of any aquatic animal belonging to the phylum *Porifera*, composed of horny elastic fibers, easily compressible, readily imbibing fluids, and as readily giving them out again upon compression; used for bathing and general cleaning. (3) To cleanse or wipe with a sponge.

spook To cause to stampede; to frighten.

spooky Said a nervous or jumpy horse, who reacts to sounds, movement and changes of light and color.

spoon (1) Also known as a spade; a projection from the center of a spade bit (q.v.) usually from 3 to 4 inches (7.5–10 cm) long and approximately 1-1/2 inches (38 mm) wide near the top; commonly has a center opening to accommodate a cricket (q.v.); prevents the horse from getting his tongue up over the bit. (2) *see* LAME HAND

sport of kings *see* HORSE RACING

spot (1) A face marking (q.v.); any white mark on the horse's forehead less than 1 inch (25 mm) in diameter, except where the number of white hairs are very few. (2) A jumping term; the most suitable place from which a horse should leave the ground to clear an obstacle with ease and minimum effort; located in front of the obstacle at a distance determined by obstacle height and type as well as the jumping ability of the horse.

spot play A racing term; a wager in which the bettor (q.v.) only bets on races and horses he feels are worthwhile risks.

spotted blanket One of six symmetrical coat color patterns of the Appaloosa (q.v.) recognized by the Appaloosa Horse Club (q.v.); consists of a solid colored body with white over the hips and having colored spots on the white.

spotted horse (1) Any horse having a spotted coat pattern; known by a variety of names throughout history in Europe and Asia, notably the Danish Knabstruper (q.v.), French Tigre, British Blagdon, Chubbarie (q.v.), or Appaloosa (q.v.). (2) *see* APPALOOSA

spotters Employees of an auctioneer who, acting as intermediaries between the auctioneer and bidders, acknowledge each bid made on a horse and notify the auctioneer of such bids.

spotty scent A hunting term; said of uneven, periodic scent.

sprained tendon *see* BOWED TENDON

sprain of the suspensory ligament *see* SUSPENSORY DESMITIS

spread (1) The width of a jumping obstacle. (2) *see* SPREAD FENCE. (3) Also known as spreading a plate; a horseshoe (q.v.) that has shifted out of position or becomes loose on the hoof. (4) The distance between the heels of a horseshoe (q.v.).

spread fence Any show or cross country jumping obstacle which is both wide and high and has no more than one pole on the back upright; include, but are not limited to, parallel bars (q.v.), hog backs, triple bars (q.v.), oxers (q.v.), walls with rails behind, water ditches, and open water jumps (q.v.).

spreading a plate *see* SPREAD no. 2

spring bar *see* STIRRUP BAR

springing An old coaching term; to gallop.

spring tree A saddle tree (q.v.) with a strip of metal at the waist which gives the tree increased flexibility.

Spring Wagon A horse-drawn American passenger wagon with at least two rows of crosswise seating; mounted on shallow semi-elliptical or platform springs and drawn by a single horse in shafts (q.v.).

sprint (1) A racing term; a race seven furlongs or less in length. (2) To race, run, or move at a high speed especially at short intervals or over a short distance.

sprinter (1) A racing term; a horse who performs best over short distances, generally 1 mile (1.6 km) or less, and lacks the ability to compete over long distances. (2) Also known as wild cow; a cutting term; a cow who wants to run parallel to the herd. (3) One of three morphological types of Thoroughbred (q.v.); is tall, has a long back and loins, and is very fast.

spur (1) To encourage action of the horse with the spur (q.v.); from the modern German sporn, meaning to kick. (2) Also known as a gad; a metal instrument having a rowel (q.v.), or a blunt or sharp point, worn on the boot heel of the rider for decoration or to reinforce the rider's leg aids (q.v.); generally worn in pairs; attached to the boot by a spur strap.

spur box Also known as spur rest; a small, square piece of leather attached to and projecting from the heel of a boot upon which a spur rests.

spurred Said of the rider; wearing spurs (q.v.).

spur rest *see* SPUR BOX

spurrier One that makes spurs.

spur shield A square-shaped safe (q.v.) fitted beneath the top strap of the spur strap (q.v.) to prevent excessive buckle wear.

spur strap A leather or material strap by which the spur is attached to the boot of the rider.

square *see* STAND SQUARE

Square Landau *see* SHELBURNE LANDAU

square oxer Also known as parallel bars; a spread fence (q.v.) used in both show-jumping and cross-country courses consisting of two sets of standards (q.v.) and two sets of rails positioned one in front of the other at the same height which are jumped and scored as a single element.

square tail *see* BANG TAIL

square toe A square-toed horseshoe; the toe does not follow the natural curve of the toe of the hoof; and the toe of the hoof will extend over the front of the shoe; commonly used on the hind feet to speed breakover and/or to prevent injury to the foreleg should the horse be prone to overreaching.

square volte A dressage movement; a volte (q.v.) in which the horse describes a square, rather than a circle, cutting each corner with a short turn; the size of the square will depend on the ability of the horse and may be from 6 to 12 meters square.

squaw tail *see* RABICANO

squeeze into the cow A cutting term; said of the horse who, in response to leg pressure applied by the rider, drops down on and draws his haunches under his body; no forward movement of the front end actually occurs.

SSI The acronym for standard starts index (q.v.).

stabbing Said of a horse who strikes the ground with his hind hooves, toes first.

stable (1) A building in which one or more horses are kept. (2) Also known as livery, livery stable, and public stable; an establishment where privately owned horses belonging to one or more owner(s) are kept, exercised, and, in some cases trained, for a set fee. (3) A collection of horses owned by an individual or group or kept at one location. (4) To maintain a horse in a stable as opposed to keeping it at pasture. (5) *see* BOX STALL

stable bandage *see* STANDING BANDAGE

stable blanket *see* STABLE RUG

stable boots Also known as calking boots; round, disc-shaped, leather boots strapped onto the ground-side surface of the hoof to protect the other hooves from injury inflicted by the horseshoe heel.

stable colors The colors used to denote a trainer, stable, rider, farm, etc., as for awnings, blankets, show trunks.

stable connection Also known as connections; a racing term; those connected with a horse running in a race, e.g., the owner, trainer, stable staff, or groom.

stable fly Also known as *Stomoxys calcitrans*; a swarming daytime feeding fly (q.v.) slightly smaller and grayer than a housefly (q.v.) with needle-sharp mouthparts which inflict painful bites; adults are blood suckers which feed only once or twice daily on all warm-blooded animals, usually on the legs; particularly bloodthirsty just prior to weather changes; the primary cause of summer and fall foot stomping in horses; may contribute to the spread of anthrax (q.v.), swamp fever (q.v.), encephalomyelitis (q.v.), and trypanosomes.

stable fork *see* FORK no. 2

stable management The act of managing, treating, directing, or administrating the activities associated with stabled horses.

Stable Release A document, which is exchanged for the delivery order, which allows sale horses to be removed from the sale grounds.

stable return A racing term; a monthly summary of all race horse activity, e.g., transfers in and out of the track, death, etc.

stable rubber Also known as grooming stable rubber; a towel or cloth used to put the final polish on a horse following grooming.

stable rug Also known as a night rug, jute rug, or stable blanket; any protective covering used on the horse to protect it from the cold, particularly when clipped (q.v.); may be made from a variety of materials including jute, canvas, quilted nylon, etc. and is generally lined with wool or synthetic blanketing; held in place by means of a roller (q.v.) or strapping.

stables (1) An antiquated term; the first and last work or exercise of the day performed by a horse as in, morning stable. (2) The plural of stable (q.v.).

stable sheet *see* SUMMER SHEET

stable vice Any specific unpleasant or atypical habit, practice, and/or condition a horse may develop as a result of boredom, improper handling, or from mimicking other horses, e.g., cribbing (q.v.), wind sucking (q.v.), and weaving (q.v.).

stag (1) A male horse castrated after reaching maturity, the time at which the secondary sex characteristics develop. (2) An antiquated term; a gelding (q.v.) more than one year of age. (3) An English and European term; a male deer more than four years of age.

Stage *see* STAGE COACH

Stage Coach Also known as slow heavy, old heavy, or American stage coach; a four-wheeled, public transportation coach pulled by a team of two, four, or six horses operating between designated stopping places; heavier and slower than the mail coach (q.v.); always enclosed, with interior and roof-top passenger seating, with luggage was carried on the roof or in the boot (q.v.); driven from an elevated box seat, its footboard supported by brackets; a guard was positioned in the rear; at first unsprung or dead axle, but later hung on braces, elbow, and finally telegraph springs (q.v.).

stag face *see* DISH FACE

staggart An obsolete term; a four-year-old male deer.

staggers Also known historically as megrim; a disease of horses and cattle attended with sudden, short-term reeling and/or dizziness; may be caused by worm infestation, impaired circulation, poor digestion, etc.

stag hound One of a breed of hounds (q.v.) formerly used to hunt stag (q.v.).

stag hunting The sport of following, chasing, or searching, whether mounted or on foot, for stag (q.v.) behind a pack of hounds (q.v.).

stain *see* FOILED

stained *see* FOILED

stained line *see* FOILED LINE

staircase A series of obstacles in a cross country event.

stake A racing term; a commission paid to a winning jockey, trainer, or groom.

stake and bind *see* STAKE AND BOUND

stake and bound Also known as stake and bind; a jumping obstacle; a fence or hedge consisting of thin, vertical stakes interlaced horizontally with supple saplings, or wire, and bound between strong upright poles.

stake money *see* POOL

stakes *see* SWEEPSTAKES

stakes engagements A racing term; the stakes races (q.v.) to which a horse has been nominated.

stakes-placed A racing term; a second or third placing horse competed in a stakes race (q.v.).

stakes-producer A racing term; said of a mare who has produced at least one foal who finished first, second, or third in a stakes race (q.v.).

stakes race *see* SWEEPSTAKES

stale (1) *see* SOUR. (2) To discharge urine, as horses and cattle.

stale cattle *see* SOUR CATTLE

stale line Also known as cold line, cold scent, or pad scent; a hunting term; the scent (q.v.) of a fox (q.v.) or other hunted prey which is old, difficult to follow, and generally does not lead to a quarry (q.v.); is not necessarily a function of scent freshness.

stalking horse A horse behind which a hunter hides while pursuing game (q.v.).

stall (1) Also known as a box, box stall, stall, or loose box; a three- and frequently four-sided compartment in a stable (q.v.) for the accommodation of one horse or a mare and foal; opens on one side and may vary significantly in size, although 6 to 10 feet x 12 to 14 feet (1.8–3 m x 3.6–4.2 m) is common; normally occur in multiples sharing two common walls; include such types as standing stall (q.v.), pipe stall (q.v.), tie stall (q.v.), and box stall (q.v.). (2) To put or keep in a stall or stalls, as animals.

stalled An antiquated term; a horse who does not eat all his food, but appears to perform without problem.

stall gate A racing term; a starting gate in which each horse has its own compartment.

stalljack A miniature anvil (q.v.) attached to a stand on which farriers shape light horseshoes.

stallion Also known as entire, stud, stud horse, full, full horse, stone horse, or bull in Australia; an ungelded male horse of four years or older capable of reproducing the species; in Thoroughbreds, a horse five years or older; the term originated in Italy sometime in the 14th century, literally meaning one kept in a stall.

stallion breeding report A form listing the stallion's name, registration number, owner, the names of all mares bred during the calendar year, the dates they were bred, their breed and registration numbers, and the name of the mare's owner at the time of service.

stallion cage Also known as a stallion support; a truss used to support a strong, athletic, or big stallion during breeding.

stallion donkey *see* JACK

stallion groom One whose responsibility it is to care for stallions.

stallion hound A hunting term; a male hound used for breeding purposes.

stallion ring *see* STUD RING

stallion roll A padded stick placed between the stallion and the mare to prevent over penetration during breeding.

stallion season The period of time during the year when a stallion stands at stud (q.v.).

stallion share A lifetime breeding right to a specific stallion, with one breeding allowed per season per share.

stall-side diagnostic test Also known as a quick-response test or on-site evaluation test; any of a number of new biotechnologies developed to provide one- to ten-minute turn around time on tests conducted on site; currently tests exist to detect reproductive concerns (time of a mare's ovulation, pregnancy, prediction of an impending birth, and testing the status of a foal's passive immunity system), a variety of ailments, including influenza (q.v.) and equine infectious anemia (q.v.), and to monitor various body systems such as liver, kidney, muscle, and digestive function; stall-side diagnostic tools include test strips (q.v.) and ELISA (q.v.).

stallion support *see* STALLION CAGE

stall walker A horse who paces in his stall, consuming energy.

stampede A sudden rush or headlong flight of animals in fright such as horses.

stand (1) *see* STAND AT STUD. (2) A vaulting term; a compulsory exercise performed in vaulting competitions; the vaulter (q.v.), from the basic seat (q.v.) facing forward, swings both legs up and behind his body, bending at the hips, to land softly on both knees on the back of the horse; he then jumps into a crouched position and slowly straightens to stand with both arms outstretched to the side at eye level; in the Kür (q.v.) may be performed facing any direction. (3) A racing term; said of a non-cancelable wage, as in "the bet stands".

Standard One of three types of the Basque (q.v.) pony, a semi-wild, exceptionally hardy pony indigenous to the Basque region of France standing 11 to 13 hands.

standard (1) Also called jump stand, jump standard, or upright; a metal, wooden, or plastic stand used in jumping events to support horizontal rails (q.v.) over which horses jump; has calibrated holes on the inside portion, into which the cups that support the rail are inserted; the height of the cups, and therefore the jump, is adjustable; each standard sits upon a base for stability; two standards are required to support each rail(s). (2) In western events, any barrel, log, or pole used to mark a pattern or course to be completed by the horse and rider in competition. (3) The uprights at the end of the bolsters that hold the wagon bed in position on a horse-drawn wagon.

Standardbred Also known as an American Trotter or American Standardbred; an American-bred warmblood descended from the English Thoroughbred (q.v.) stallion, Messenger, a Darley Arabian descendant, imported to the United States in 1788; the foundation sireais Messenger's inbred descendant Hambletonian 10, foaled in 1849; more than 90 percent of the modern breed trace to four Hambletonian sons: George Wilkes, Dictator, Happy Medium, and Electioneer; early in breed selection, crossed with Morgan (q.v.) and Clay blood; stands 14.1 to 16 hands and generally has a bay, brown, black, or chestnut coat; the body shape varies from horse to horse as it is bred for speed not conformation; a muscular Thoroughbred type with a long back, short legs, and powerful shoulders; has tremendous speed and stamina, displaying great aptitude for harness racing, trotting, and pacing (q.v.); the breed name was first used in 1879, and refers to the speed standard for the mile distance required for entry into the American Trotter Register; the breed comprises both trotters and pacers, the average speed of which is 30 mph (48 kmph).

Standardbred racing *see* HARNESS RACING

standard donkey A donkey (q.v.) standing 36 to 48 inches (91–122 cm) tall.

standard event A rodeo term; any of five competitive events recognized by the Rodeo Cowboys Association including bareback (q.v.) riding, bull riding, calf-roping (q.v.), saddle bronc riding, and steer wrestling (q.v.).

standard hunting iron *see* HUNTING IRON

standards The plural of standard (q.v.).

standard starts index Also known by the acronym SSI; a racing term; a statistic by which the racing class of horses are compared based on earnings, with inflation factored out; the average earnings of each crop of foals at the start of the year is calculated and divided into male and female categories; any horse earning the average for his or her sex has a SSI of 1.00, while a horse with a SSI of 2.00 would have earned twice the average.

stand at stud Also known as stand or at stud; said of a stallion available to breed mares for a fee.

stand back A jumping term; said of a horse

who initiates his jump to clear an obstacle too far from the obstacle.

standing Said of a horse standing at stud (q.v.).

standing bandage Also known as a stable bandage; a thick, square-shaped cotton leg wrap used to support, protect, prevent swelling, and/or injury to the horse's lower leg during shipping or while stabled.

standing halter *see* STANDING MARTINGALE

standing martingale Also known as standing halter, fast martingale, tiedown martingale, or tiedown; an auxiliary, adjustable strap attached on one end between the forelegs to the girth (q.v.) and on the other to the underside of the cavesson noseband; the strap may be split and attach directly to the other side of the bit; may be fitted with a neck strap to keep it in place; used to prevent the horse from throwing up his head.

standing over *see* STANDING OVER IN FRONT

standing over in front Also known as standing over; a conformation defect in which the entire forelimb from the elbow down is placed in back of the perpendicular and too far under the body when the horse is viewed from the side; may also be caused by disease.

standing rein A vaulting term; a short, 3 foot (91 cm) rein (q.v.) sometimes attached to the center of the vaulting roller (q.v.) and always to a trick riding saddle used by the vaulter (q.v.) or trick rider (q.v.) when performing standing moves.

standing stall An 8 to 10 foot (2.4-3 m) long by approximately 5 to 6 feet (1.5-1.8 m) wide enclosure in a barn where a horse is kept at night or when not in use; enables the horse to stand, but not lie down or turn around.

stands near the ground Said of a deep-bodied horse with short legs.

stand square Said of a horse who stands straight with his weight evenly distributed over all four legs; fore and hind legs are abreast of each other.

standing under behind Also known as under behind; when viewed from the side, the entire horse's limb is placed too far forward under the body.

Stanhope *see* STANHOPE GIG

Stanhope Gig Also known as Stanhope; a horse-drawn vehicle of the gig (q.v.) type designed by the Hon. Fitzroy Stanhope in England around 1814; was open, had a stick-back driving seat balanced on two crosswise members above the passenger luggage compartment which was large enough for two seated side-by-side, double side or telegraph springs, iron-reinforced shafts attached to the axles by independent brackets, and 56 inch (1.4 m) wheels.

Stanhope Phaeton A light-weight, horse-drawn gentleman's driving phaeton (q.v.) popular in the early 19th century; noted for its detachable shafts attached to the axles by span irons; seated four forward-facing passengers, was hooded, had a railed-up rearward seat for a liveried groom, was hung on sideways-elliptical or telegraph springs, and driven to a small horse or pony or a pair.

star (1) A face marking (q.v.); any white mark on the forehead, except where the number of white hairs are very few, that varies from a small white spot to a large irregular area; the position, size, and shape of the star should be specified when describing the horse. (2) A racing term; credit extended to a horse by the racing secretary if it is excluded from an over-filled race, giving it priority placement in future races.

star and stripe A facing marking (q.v.); any white marking on the forehead with a stripe (q.v.) to the nasal peak; the stripe does not have to be an extension of the star.

star gazer A horse who holds his head too high.

staring coat Dull and generally unhealthy coat hair in which the hairs are dull and do not lay flat; may be an indication of malnutrition, parasite infestation, illness, etc.

starling An antiquated term; refers to coat color; a brown or blackish-gray coat intermixed with white.

star, stripe, and snip A face marking (q.v.); a white marking on the forehead which extends to between or below the nostrils.

start (1) To commence a course or race. (2) To move suddenly and spasmodically; to make a sudden and involuntary motion of the body caused by surprise, pain, or any sudden feeling. (3) *see* START A HORSE

start a horse Also known as start; to begin training of a young or previously untrained horse.

starter (1) A racing term; one responsible for ensuring the fair start of a horse race, includes loading the horses into and opening the starting gate (q.v.). (2) A racing term; any horse in the starting gate at the beginning of the race; may or may not run. (3) An animal who starts as a competitor.

starter race A racing term; any handicap race (q.v.) restricted to horses which have previously started for a specific claiming price or less at some time during their careers or during a fixed period of time.

starter's list A racing term; a list of horses entered to run in a specific horse race; maintained by the starter (q.v.) at the gate.

starter's orders A racing term; a determination by the official starter that all horses entered to compete in a specific race have been loaded into the starting gate (q.v.) and are ready to race.

starting gate Also known as gate or barrier; a racing term; a partitioned mechanical device consisting of stalls with front and back doors used to insure a fair and equal start to a horse race; starters (q.v.) enter by the rear door and are confined until the front doors are opened thus beginning the race; first used in London, England in 1900.

starting order *see* JUMPING ORDER

starting price A racing term; the betting odds on any horse at the beginning of a horse race in which the horse is competing.

starting price bookmaker A professional bettor who accepts wagers, cash or credit, placed by others on horses competing in a race or performance at prices posted at the start of the race or event and who does not vary the odds.

state-bred Said of a horse bred in a particular state in the United States; eligible to compete in races restricted to state-bred horses.

state coach Also known as coronation coach; an elegant, enclosed horse-drawn vehicle built for formal use by nobility on occasions of state; hung on cee-springs from a perch undercarriage, seated four, had elegantly appointed interiors, glass windows, painted panels, and a rear platform for standing servants; usually drawn by a team of four horses driven from the box and two leaders driven by a postillion (q.v.).

static exercises A vaulting term; any figure a vaulter holds for three canter strides in a freestyle competition or four in a compulsory test; include the basic seat (q.v.), flare (q.v.), and stand (q.v.).

station wagon *see* DEPOT WAGON

stay apparatus The anatomical structure of the horse which enables it to stand with little muscular effort.

stayer (1) A racing term; a horse who performs best over long distances, generally more than a mile, but who lacks the quick early speed required for shorter distances. (2) One of three morphological types of Thoroughbred (q.v.); is smaller and more gathered with good stamina over distances.

stay hooked A cutting term; said of a cutter (q.v.) who continues to work the same cow rather than quitting it and cutting a different cow from the herd.

St. Croix rim shoe A traction horseshoe (q.v.) developed in the United States during the 1980s; a steel shoe with a flat hoof-side and a rounded ground-side surface into which a hollow groove is cut along the circumference; the groove fills with dirt when the horse is used, the dirt becoming the traction device.

steadied A racing term; said of a horse taken in hand by his rider; generally necessary when a horse is in confined or tight quarters.

steady A hunting term; said of a hound (q.v.) who is not prone to riot (q.v.), chase farm livestock, or shy at the flurry of activity in a hunt (q.v.).

steed A horse, especially a spirited one.

steeplechase Also known as chase or steeplechase race; a cross-country jumping race over natural terrain; originated in 1752, at which time races were run from church to church, the steeples serving as markers; conducted over a long distance with approximately six different obstacles such as open ditches, water, and banks per mile; differ from hurdle races in that the obstacles are higher and include water hazards.

steeplechase jockey One who rides in steeplechases (q.v.); frequently weighs more than a jockey who races on the flat.

steeplechase meeting The location at which a steeplechase (q.v.) is held.

steeplechaser (1) A horse used in cross-country racing with jumps. (2) One who participates in a steeplechase.

steeplechase race *see* STEEPLECHASE

steeplechasers (1) A tall riding boot worn by a steeplechaser (q.v.); has a sturdy leg and generally fitted tops or cuffs. (2) More than one steeplechaser (q.v.).

steer A young castrated bovine, especially one raised for beef.

steer roping A standard rodeo event in which two mounted riders pursue a steer; one rider ropes the steer's head while the other ropes the heels; when successfully performed the steer is held taut between the two riders.

steer wrestler Also known as a bulldogger or wrestler; one who competes in steer wrestling (q.v.) events.

steer wrestling Also known as bulldogging or wrestling; a timed rodeo event in which a mounted rider gallops up along the side of a moving steer, drops from the back of the moving horse onto the horns of the steer, and attempts to throw it to the ground using the head and horns for leverage; the bulldogger (q.v.) locks the right horn into his right elbow and the left horn into the left, and after slowing the forward motion of the steer, twists the cow's head to bring it to the ground; a hazer (q.v.) rides on the far side of the steer wrestler (q.v.) to keep the steer moving in a straight direction; the contestant completing the event in the shortest time is the winner; steers used in this event may weigh in excess of 800 pounds (363 kg) and travel upwards of 35 mph (56 kmph).

step into the cow, to A cutting term; said of a horse who drops onto his haunches and moves toward the cow at the encouragement of the cutter (q.v.).

Steppe Bashkir Also known as Steppe Bashkir Curly; one of two distinct types of Bashkir (q.v.), a centuries-old pony breed originating in Bashkiria, around the southern foothills of the Ural Mountains in Russia; due to the introduction of Ardennais (q.v.) and Trotter blood, is heavier than the Mountain Bashkir (q.v.); is generally used for pulling troikas (q.v.), although it is also used for packing, riding, and to provide meat, milk and clothing – in a seven- to eight-month lactation period a mare can yield as much as 350 gallons (1,590 liters) of milk; stands 13.1 to 14 hands, has a distinctive thick, curly long winter coat which is spun into cloth, thick mane, tail, and forelock, a bay, chestnut or palomino coat, a short, long neck, low withers, elongated and sometimes hollow back, a wide and deep chest, short and strong legs, and a small foot for its size; the breed standard quotes a bone measurement of 8 inches (20 cm) below the knee and a girth measurement for stallions of 71 inches (1.8 m); is kept outdoors where it can withstand severe winter temperatures; is docile, strong, quiet, and hardy; due to the exceptionally hard hoof, is generally left unshod.

Steppe Bashkir Curly *see* STEPPE BASHKIR

stepper A horse who has a high or showy gait.

stepping pace *see* SLOW GAIT

step up A racing term; said of a horse who moves into a higher class to compete against faster competition.

sterile (1) Incapable of or not producing offspring. (2) Free from living germs or microorganisms.

sterility The quality or state of being sterile (q.v.).

sterilize (1) To inhibit or destroy by surgery the reproductive capabilities of the sex organs. (2) To render sterile, especially to free from living organisms.

stern The hind end of a hound (q.v.).

sternum *see* BREAST BONE

Steward Also known as stipendiary steward; a racing term; one of three appointed arbiters of racing law who judge the conduct of horses and personnel at each race meeting (q.v.).

steward's list A racing term; a list of horses ruled out of action by the official starter due to chronic misbehavior at the gate or for which ownership is an issue; such horses will be barred from racing or entry into future competitions until the bad habits or other matters are corrected and verified by the starter; maintained by the track stewards.

stick (1) To prod with a spur. (2) A riding crop; a jockey's whip. (3) *see* POLO MALLET. (4) A racing term; to whip a horse.

stick and ball A polo term; an exercise performed by a mounted rider to work hand to eye coordination; to practice polo strokes and movement of the ball down the field using a mallet.

stick and ball race A polo term; a mounted game in which each contestant, assigned a number or color, takes his place at the edge of the polo field opposite the polo ball with the same number or color, and when signaled, races to get his ball to the finish line; the first contestant to place his ball across the finish wins; contestants may utilize acceptable polo moves including the ride off (q.v.), backing (q.v.), and hooking (q.v.) to improve position.

stick basket Also known as an umbrella basket; a 2 to 3 foot (61-91 cm) deep and 10 inch (25 cm) wide basket with flat sides attached to the rear body of a horse-drawn coach (q.v.) in which the coach horn (q.v.), umbrellas, and sticks are carried.

sticker A light, sharp heel calk (q.v.) frequently used on the lateral side of hind horseshoes on race horses.

stick horse A racing term; a horse who runs better when the whip is applied.

sticky (1) A cutting term; cattle who bunch closely together and are difficult to separate. (2) Said of a horse uncertain when jumping fences; will generally slow down, half refuse to jump, then jump from a standstill or a slowed trot.

stiff (1) Said of the horse moving around a circle or corner without bend or even flexion. (2) A racing term; to prevent a horse from winning a race by deliberately riding him poorly, drugging him, or inappropriately training him. (3) A racing term; an unfit or outclassed horse.

stifle Also known as the genu or true knee; the equivalent of the patella (knee cap) in man; the joint in the hind leg where the tibia meets the femur above the hock.

stifled Said of a horse who has a permanent injury to the hind leg which affects his normal action.

stifle shoe Also known originally as a pattern shoe; a horseshoe that prevents the horse from bearing full weight on the shod foot.

stile A jumping obstacle consisting of a fence or wall elongated by wings on either side.

still birth (1) The birth of any fetus or offspring which is dead. (2) A fetus or offspring that is dead at birth.

still born Dead at birth.

stimulant Any substance or medication that produces a quickly diffused and transient increase of vital energy, activity, and strength in an organism or some part of it such as the circulatory, respiratory, and/or central nervous systems.

stint (1) *see* GAIT no. 2. (2) The right to pasture one or more horses on common or publicly owned land. (3) An antiquated term; said of a mare when serviced by a stallion.

stinted An antiquated term; mated, as in a mare.

stipe An antiquated racing term; slang; the office of the Stipendiary Steward (q.v.).

Stipendiary Steward *see* STEWARD

stirrup (1) Also known as pedal, stirrup iron, or iron; a loop, ring, or D-shaped metal, plastic, leather, or other material fitting connected to the saddle by stirrup leathers (q.v.) into which the rider places his foot; used to facilitate mounting, enhance the rider's seat, promote proper body alignment, and facilitate the smooth and moderate delivery of hand, leg, and seat aids; from the English stige-rap where stigan meant to mount and rap meant rope. (2) *see* VAULTING ROLLER

stirrup bar Also known as saddle bar or spring bar; one of two metal bars built into the front of the English saddle (q.v.) on either side of the seat beneath the skirt to which the stirrup leathers are attached; lie parallel to the seat and the vertical portion opens as a safety release.

stirrup cup Also known as jumping powder; the cup of wine or other refreshment offered to the traveler, who having mounted his horse, was in the stirrups and ready to proceed on his journey; one for the road.

stirrup iron *see* STIRRUP

stirrup leather *see* LEATHERS

stirrup lights Small, battery-powered, night-safety lights that attach to the English stirrups (q.v.) and emit a red light to the rear.

stirrup pad Also known as pad; a rubber, plastic, or brush insert fitted into the portion of the stirrup upon which the foot rests; provide improved grip for the foot in the iron.

stirrup strap *see* LEATHERS

stock (1) A restraining chute used on many breeding farms to allow palpation, culturing, insemination, suturing, etc. of mares. (2) Previously known as a hunt tie; part of the riding habit traditionally worn by participants in the hunt; a long, white neck cloth detachable from the shirt, so that in the event of an accident, could be used as a clean bandage or sling; now worn when hunting, competing, and for formal occasions. (3) The handle of a whip (q.v.). (4) A line of descent; a family or body of descendants from a common ancestor. (5) *see* BARSTOCK. (6) A large framework used to immobilize a horse and hold the hoof in position for shoeing; commonly used for heavy breed horses or unmanageable smaller ones.

stock class An equestrian show class for stock or ranch horses and ponies.

stocked (1) A mare served (q.v.) by a stallion. (2) A field or area when pastured with horses or other stock are pastured.

stocked up Said of a horse whose limbs are swollen, as following strenuous exercise.

stocker An animal, as a young steer, to be kept until matured or fattened before killing.

stock horse (1) Any horse trained to work and herd stock. (2) A stallion used at stud.

stocking A leg marking (q.v.); white extending from the coronet (q.v.) to the top of the cannon bone, but excluding the knee.

stockman One owning or having charge of stock (q.v.), as on a large ranch, as in a cattleman.

stock saddle Also known as western saddle or working saddle; a saddle design based on that used by conquistadors and popularized in the American west; has a large, deep seat bound on the front by two pommels (q.v.) between which projects a saddle horn (q.v.) and on the rear, by a cantle (q.v.); the stirrups are supported by wide fenders under which is a full leather, felt- or wool-lined skirt (q.v.).

Stock-Type Pinto One of four Pinto (q.v.) conformation types; a western horse of predominantly Quarter Horse (q.v.) breeding and conformation; may range from the small, heavy-muscled to the large, well-developed (modern) type; should display characteristics necessary for all standard western working events and include well-developed jaws, relatively heavy-muscled shoulders, withers the same height as the croup, deep chest, well-muscled forearm, and broad, well-muscled quarters.

stock up Also known as Monday morning leg, Monday morning complaint, Monday morning evil, filled leg, big leg, humour, humor, or historically as weed; a condition of the horse characterized by a generalized swelling of or the entire leg, or a portion of, caused by the accumulation of excess fluid in the soft tissues; commonly caused by stabling a horse without exercise following a period of strenuous exercise, especially if the ration is not adjusted during the period of inactivity; also triggered by strain, excessive standing, localized and systemic infection, and a decrease in the protein (q.v.) level in the blood plasma; in most cases, swelling will usually disappear following exercise in which case the flow of the lymph is increased by the massaging action of the muscles and tendons.

stock whip A short-handled whip (q.v.) with a very long thong (q.v.) used by mounted stockmen when driving cattle.

stockyard A yard, especially an enclosure with pens or sheds, connected with a slaughterhouse or market for the temporary keeping of cattle, horses, etc.

stökk The gallop (q.v.) of the Icelandic Horse (q.v.); a gallop.

stomach The pouchlike enlargement of the alimentary canal (q.v.) being the principal organ of digestion where food is acted upon to yield nutrients to the body; connects the gullet to the small intestine.

stomach staggers *see* COLIC

stomach worms Generally refers to parasitic worms of the species *Habronema* (*Habronema muscae*, *Habronema microstoma*, and *Draschia megastoma*) found in the large stomach; in some cases may also refer to *Trichostrongylus axei* found in the small stomach; vary in size from 6 to 25 mm; the eggs are ingested by larvae of house or stable flies, which serve as the intermediate hosts; horses are infected by ingesting infected flies or free larvae that emerge from flies as they feed around the mouth of the horse; *Draschia megastoma* occurs in tumor-like swellings in the stomach wall as large as 4 inches (10 cm) in diameter, while the other species are free in the stomach mucosa.

stomp divots *see* DIVOT STOMPING

stone *see* ENTEROLITH

stone bruise Also known as strawberry; an injury to the sole of the hoof with discoloration resulting from impact with a hard or sharp object as a rock, hard mud ball, ice, etc.

stone cold A racing term; a horse who has exhausted himself physically and cannot run any faster or in some cases further.

stone horse *see* STALLION

stone wall A solid jumping obstacle consisting of faux stone blocks; a wall (q.v.).

stoop *see* STOOP TO THE LINE

stooper An American racing term; one who collects discarded mutuel tickets at race tracks and cashes those thrown away by other bettors by mistake.

stoop to the line Also known as stoop; a hunting term; said of a hound (q.v.) who hunts with its nose close to the ground.

stop hound A hunting term; a hound who ceases to pursue the line of a fox (q.v.) and sits on his haunches and speaks (q.v.).

stop hounds A hunting term; to call the hounds off the line of the fox (q.v.) when they run into impassable or forbidden ground; stopped by the huntsman using his voice, a thong, and the aid of the whippers-in (q.v.).

stopper Any substance or medication which produces a quickly diffused and transient decrease in vital energy, activity, or strength in an organism or some part of it such as the circulatory, respiratory, and/or central nervous systems.

stopping earth *see* EARTH STOPPING

stopping the feet To moisturize the hoof.

stopped out A hunting term; said of the fox den (q.v.) when closed the night before a hunt.

stopping out A hunting term; the process of closing a fox den (q.v.) the night before a hunt.

stops (1) Metal projections on the shafts of a horse-drawn vehicle which keep the harness of a single horse at the proper place on the shafts; support much of the vehicle weight when descending a hill. (2) Round or rectangular pieces of rubber or leather through which the rein is threaded perpendicularly to prevent the rings of the martingale (q.v.) from sliding forward and catching on the bit rings or shafts. (3) Narrow strips of leather sewn incrementally across the width of English reins from the buckle approximately three quarters of the distance to the bit rings; improves the rider's grip on the reins.

straddle jump A vaulting term; a move in which the vaulter (q.v.), from a standing position on the horse, leaps into the air with arms and legs straight and stretched away from the sides of his upright body; post jump, the vaulter returns to a standing position on the back of the horse.

straight as a string A racing term; said of a horse competing in a race who gives his all.

straightaway Also known as stretch; a racing term; the straight part of the race course.

straight behind Said of the horse who, when viewed from the side, shows very little angle between the tibia and femur; the hock joint and pasterns are correspondingly straight; predisposes a horse to bog spavin (q.v.).

straight bucking *see* JACK-KNIFING

straight neck *see* STRAIGHT NECK FOX

straight neck fox A hunting term; a fox (q.v.) who runs in a straight line.

straightness Said of a horse; the extent to which a horse moves in a straight line, the hind feet following the track of the fore.

straight shoulder A conformation defect; said of the horse's shoulder which lacks sufficient angulation due to a scapula being either too short or too straight; when the line from the point of the shoulder (q.v.) to the withers is straight rather than rearward sloping.

strained tendon *see* BOWED TENDON

straight triactor *see* STRAIGHT TRIFECTA

straight trifecta Also known as a straight triple or straight triator in Canada; a betting option in which the bettor (q.v.) selects the first, second, and third place horses in that order in a specific race.

straight triple *see* STRAIGHT TRIFECTA

strangles Also known as distemper; an acute, infectious, transmissible disease of the lymph glands of the upper respiratory track or throat caused by bacterium *Streptococcus equi*, especially common in young horses; takes a number of days following initial infection to develop; symptoms include nasal discharge, elevated temperature, and swelling of the lymph glands; so called because if swelling in the lymph glands becomes too severe, breathing may become labored or strangled.

strap *see* GROOM no. 1

straps *see* LEATHERS

strappings (1) Ceremonial harness including the saddle and bridle. (2) Also known as grips or patches; leather or synthetic patches sewn onto the inside legs of riding breeches (q.v.) and jodhpurs (q.v.) which extend below and to slightly above the knee; lengthen the life of the breeches and provide additional grip.

stratum germinativum The horn-producing layer of cells that produces the horny sole (q.v.).

straw The stalk or stem of certain species of grain collectively when cut, and after being thrashed; used for bedding (q.v.) horse stalls, trailers, etc.; has a nice appearance, relatively wide availability, and is soft, affordable, and pleasantly scented, but lacks absorbency and can be quite moldy and dusty potentially aggravating or causing respiratory ailments.

strawberry *see* STONE BRUISE

strawberry corn *see* CORN no. 3

strawberry roan Also known as sorrel roan; refers to coat color; of the color group roan (q.v.); a clear light red coat uniformly mixed with white hairs, a colored head, and colored, nonblack points.

strawyard An outdoor area deeply bedded with straw (q.v.) in which horses on rest or recovery are turned out.

streak *see* STRIPE

street car *see* HORSE CAR

streptothricosis *see* RAIN SCALD

Strelets A horse breed indigenous to Russia; descended from native mares put to Anglo-Arab (q.v.), Turkish, Persian, and purebred Arab (q.v.) stallions; basically a large Arab; used for riding.

stress fracture A bone fracture (q.v.) resulting from repeated concussion; generally occurs in the front of the cannon bone (q.v.) and tibia where it causes a hard-to-diagnose hind limb lameness.

stretch (1) *see* STRAIGHTAWAY. (2) A harness racing term; the last 1/8 mile (201 m) portion of the race track before the finish line.

stretch call A racing term; a point, at the eighth pole (q.v.), usually one furlong (q.v.) from the finish on the straightaway (q.v.), where a call is made for charting purposes.

stretch runner A racing term; a horse who runs fastest near the finish of the race.

stretch the topline To encourage the horse to extend his head and neck out and downward to a loose rein.

stretch turn A racing term; the final turn on the racetrack before the homestretch (q.v.).

stride A single step measured from where one hoof leaves the ground to the spot where the same foot again touches the ground; an ideal horse will have four equal strides at the trot, e.g., Grayhound had a stride of more than 27 feet (8.2 m).

strike (1) To scrape or knock one leg with the other. (2) A vice; said of a horse who reaches out quickly with a foreleg to hit a handler or other horses. (3) *see* STRIKE A FOX. (4) Said of a tent pegger (q.v.) when he hits the tent peg in the mounted sport of tent pegging (q.v.), but does not successfully lift it from the ground.

strike a fox Also known as strike; a hunting term; said of a hound who finds a fox.

strike dog A hunting term; a hound who is adept at locating fox (q.v.).

strike off The first step of the canter (q.v.).

strike off early A dressage term; said of the horse when he takes the first step of the canter (q.v.) before the appropriate arena marker.

strike off late A dressage term; said of the horse when he takes the first step of the canter when taken after the appropriate arena marker.

striking Said of a horse who strikes (q.v.) because it is mean; a vice.

string (1) The horses owned by one stable or handled by one trainer or packer (q.v.). (2) A racing term; two or more racehorses exercised together.

stringhalt Also formerly known as snatch; a condition characterized by the sudden, abnormal, and excessive flexion of one hind leg upward, in some cases as high as the belly; usually seen at the walk or when the horse is turning, backing, or rising from lying down or rolling; diminishes as the horse is exercised; thought to be caused by strain or trauma to the hock resulting in scar tissue which restricts the movement of the extensor tendons (q.v.) and results in the jerky movement; is usually harmless and nondegenerative; may be surgically treated.

string the foot A roping term; said of the roper; to place the loop of the pigging string (q.v.) around one of the front feet of a calf in preparation for the tie (q.v.).

strip (1) A face marking (q.v.); a narrow white mark, no wider than the width of the flat nasal bones which does not extend onto the forehead and is more narrow than a stripe (q.v.). (2) *see* TRACK

stripe (1) Also known as streak, strip, or flash; a face marking; any long, narrow white marking on the face of the horse which runs in a relatively straight line from the forehead, at eye level, to, or almost to, an imaginary line which connects the top of the nostrils to the muzzle and which is no wider than the width of the nasal bone. (2) *see* DORSAL STRIPE

stripe and snip A face marking (q.v.); a narrow white marking extending vertically, from just below the eyes to just below or between the nostrils.

striped hoof A hoof having vertical stripes of alternating layers of pink and black; it is believed that the pink hoof is soft and the black hoof hard, almost brittle, and that the striped hoof perfectly combines the strong layers between softer pink layers; common in the Appaloosa (q.v.).

striped muscle A voluntary muscle (q.v.); any nonstriated muscle, as those controlled by will and which operate in such voluntary movements as kicking and walking, which attach to the bones by tendons and contract on stimulation to produce bodily motion.

strongyle Also spelled strongyl; any of certain nematode worms constituting the family *Strongylidae*, parasitic in the organs and tissues of the horse and often giving rise to serious pathological conditions; of two common types: large strongyle (q.v.) and small strongyle (q.v.).

strongyloide A parasitic roundworm of the species *Strongyloides westeri* found in the small intestine of foals during the first eight weeks of life; larvae are passed to the foal in the mare's milk.

strongylosis Any disease caused by strongyles (q.v.).

Strongylus edentatus A species of large strongyle measuring up to 45 mm in length; found in various parts of the horse's body including the liver, peri-renal tissues, flanks, and pancreas.

Strongylus equinusis A species of large strongyle (q.v.) measuring up to 50 mm in length; found in various parts of the body including the liver, peri-renal tissues, flanks, and pancreas.

Strongylus vulgaris A species of large strongyle (q.v.) measuring up to 25 mm in length; migrate extensively in the cranial mesenteric artery and its branches where they may cause parasitic thrombosis and arteritis.

stub-bred Also known as stub; a hunting term; a fox cub raised above the ground rather than in an earth (q.v.).

stub (1) *see* STUB-BRED. (2) An antiquated term; a wound on the sole of the hoof.

stubby A hoof shape pattern in which the hoof is generally round, but wider than it is long with the widest part of the hoof located midway between the toe and heels.

stud (1) *see* STALLION. (2) The singular of studs (q.v.). (3) Also known as stallion station or stud farm; a farm or place where horses are kept for breeding purposes. (4) Any large establishment of racehorses, hunters, and so on which belongs to one owner.

stud billet *see* STUD FASTENING

Stud Book Any permanent book or registry of breeding records for any established horse breed, the requirements for inclusion which vary by breed

Stud Book Also known as the General Stud Book, The Book, or Weatherby's; a permanent

book or registry of breeding records for the English Thoroughbred (q.v.); includes all purebred mares and their progeny, the pedigrees of these accepted purebred mares, and the sires of their offspring; any horse registered must be traceable to the Darley Arabian (q.v.), the Godolphin Arabian (q.v.), or the Byerley Turk (q.v.) on the male side and to the Royal Mares on the female side; founded in 1793 by the Weatherby family, it is still published by them under control of The Jockey Club (q.v.); all Thoroughbred Stud Books throughout the world are affiliated with this parent stud book.

stud-bred Any horse of a breed which maintains its own stud book (q.v.).

stud farm *see* STUD no. 3

stud fastening Also known as a French clip, stud billet, billet, and hook fastening; an L-shaped metal stud projecting approximately 4 inches (10 cm) from the end of a leather strip such as reins, which fits through a small slit, cut length-wise approximately 1/2 inch (13 mm) from the end of the same strip and which is pulled down against the end of the cut to lock it and create a closed loop.

stud fee Money paid to the stallion owner for breeding services whether by natural cover (q.v.) or artificial insemination (q.v.).

stud groom A senior groom, especially at a stud (q.v.).

stud horse *see* STALLION

stud mule An uncastrated male mule (q.v.); usually sterile.

stud ring Also known as a stallion ring; a metal, non-corrosive metal, or plastic ring slipped over the head of a horse's penis behind the glands to prevent masturbation, erection, and to discourage ejaculation when not being bred.

studs Also known as pegs; metal heads screwed into the bottom of a conventional horseshoe (q.v.) to increase traction on slippery or deep surfaces such as grass, snow, or asphalt; depending on the purpose, may be set into all four shoes as for snow or asphalt surfaces or the front or back only for grass or dirt; a maximum of three screws may be set in each shoe, one on each heel and, more rarely, one on the toe; the farrier drills a tap hole in the shoe and fills it with an Allen screw; when traction is required, the horse owner removes the Allen screw and screws in the appropriate stud; available in a variety of shapes and sizes including pointed, thick, flat, and oblong and may be made of a variety of materials including steel, borium, and tungsten.

stumble To trip when walking.

stumour Slang; a horse who does not exert himself.

stump sucking *see* CRIB

subacute laminitis A broad classification of laminitis (q.v.); inflammation of the laminae (q.v.) characterized by a rapid onset and a brief duration; often there will only be a mild change in the stance of the horse who may demonstrate an increased sensitivity on the soles of the affected feet; may lead to chronic laminitis (q.v.) if left untreated.

subluxation An incomplete dislocation in which the normal joint relationship is disturbed, but the articular surfaces are still in contact as in two vertebrae in a motor unit (q.v.).

submission Said of the horse; obedience to the rider or handler

subscription A racing term; the fees paid by the owner of a horse(s) to nominate or maintain eligibility for the horse in a stakes race (q.v).

substance The physical quality of a horse's body as due to bone width and depth, muscularity, etc.; the build of the horse.

sucked up *see* TUCKED UP

sucker *see* SUCKLING

sucking lice The plural of sucking louse (q.v.).

sucking louse Also known as *Haematopinas asini*; a lice (q.v.); an external, biting and sucking parasite which feasts on the blood of the horse; although less than 1/10 inch (2 mm) long, is visible to the naked eye as a small, light-gray object; may be detected by inspecting the mane, root of the tail, inside the thighs, or on the underside of the saddle blanket following exercise; are not transmitted to people.

suckling Also known as a sucker; a foal of either sex, up to weaning (q.v.) or, if unweaned, until it is ranked as a yearling (q.v.).

sudadero *see* FENDER

Sudan grass A grass sorghum, *Sorghum vulgare sudanensis*, introduced into the United States from the Sudan and grown for hay.

Sudan grass hay A cut and dried grass hay (q.v.) made from Sudan grass (q.v.) which is grown throughout the United States in most soil types; best cut at the pre- or early-bloom stage to ensure palatability and nutritional quality; if cut prematurely, may contain large amounts of prussic acid; in newer varieties the threat of prussic acid poisoning is reduced but still an issue; it is therefore advisable to test the prussic acid content prior to feeding; contains a digestible protein content of approximately 5 percent and 35 percent fiber.

sudden death A polo term; an overtime period played until one team scores in the event a match is tied at the end of the sixth chukker (q.v.).

Suffolk *see* SUFFOLK PUNCH

Suffolk Punch Also known as a Suffolk; the smallest and oldest of the British heavy-draft breeds native to Suffolk, Great Britain; descended from the Great Horse (q.v.) crossed with Norfolk Trotter (q.v.), Norfolk Cob, and English Thoroughbred (q.v.) around 1506; all modern Suffolks can be traced to one stallion, Blakes Farmer foaled in 1760, who handed his chestnut coat color to all his descendants; a pure breed, is frugal, early maturing, long-lived, possessed of exceptional pulling power, quiet and gentle; stands 15.3 to 16.2 hands, weighs 1,980 to 2,200 pounds (898–998 kg), has a compact, yet large body set on short, powerful, clean legs with little feather (q.v.); the coat color is exclusively chestnut which may be one of seven shades ranging from nearly brown to a pale, mealy shade; no white markings are permitted; historically used to draw omnibuses (q.v.) and brewer's drays and for farming and heavy draft while the modern horse is used for heavy draft.

Suffolk Horse Society An organization formed in Great Britain in 1878 to maintain the purity of, generate interest, and maintain the breed registry for the Suffolk Punch (q.v.).

sugar-beet pulp Also known as beet pulp; a by-product of the sugar production process, made by drying the residual beet chips after the sugar extraction; a highly digestible and palatable fiber with a high energy and fiber content; the digestible energy (q.v.) is slightly lower than that of oats (q.v.); a good source of calcium, but is low in phosphorus, selenium, and vitamins A and D; used for supplementing an inadequate hay supply and as a dust-free roughage substitute; available in cubed and shredded forms both of which must be rehydrated before feeding.

Suicide gig *see* COCKING CART

sulfur Also spelled sulphur or sulpur; a metallic element present in the amino acids methionine and cystine as well as in chondroitin sulfate; a constituent of cartilage; as no dietary requirements have been established for the horse, deficiency is not of practical concern, yet over-supplementation can result in death.

sulk A racing term; said of a horse who refuses to run or respond to urging of the jockey.

sulkette A horse-drawn exercising sulky (q.v.) similar in construction to a racing sulky (q.v.), but made of heavier construction.

sulky Also known as a bike or gig; a modern, very light, two-wheeled, one-horse, single-seated cart for one with a skeleton body used in harness racing; weighs 29 to 37 pounds (13–17 kg), uses bicycle-type wheels and is generally constructed with hardwood shafts, although aluminum and steel may be used; equipped with adjustable foot rests.

sulky stirrup An adjustable foot rest fitted on a sulky (q.v.).

Sullivan, Con A horse whisperer (q.v.) who practiced in the 19th century.

sulphonamides Antibacterial compounds used both topically and internally for the prevention and treatment of nonspecific infections by controlling multiplication of some bacteria; a common ingredient of wound powders and dressings.

sulphur *see* SULFUR

sulpur *see* SULFUR

Sumba A pony breed originating on the island of Sumba, Indonesia; similar in appearance to the Chinese and Mongolian ponies (q.v.) which suggests they may have common origins; is almost identical to the Sumbawa (q.v.); is very tough, willing, intelligent, and docile, and has good endurance; the coat may be any color although dun (q.v.) with an eel stripe (q.v.) and dark tail, mane, and points is most common; the mane is frequently shaggy and upright; has a slightly heavy head, almond-shaped eyes, a short, broad neck, long back, and short, strong legs; used for lance-throwing, dancing competitions (q.v.), riding, and packing.

Sumbawa A pony breed originating on the island of Sumbawa, Indonesia; similar in appearance to the Chinese and Mongolian ponies (q.v.) which suggests they may have common origins; almost identical to the Sumba (q.v.); is very tough, willing, intelligent, and docile, and has good endurance; the coat may be any color although dun (q.v.) with an eel stripe (q.v.) and dark tail, mane, and points is most common; the mane is frequently shaggy and upright; has a slightly heavy head, almond-shaped eyes, a short, broad neck, long back, and short, strong legs; used for lance-throwing, dancing competitions (q.v.), riding, and packing.

summering The turning out to pasture of horses during the summer months.

summer pasture-associated obstructive pulmonary disease Also known by the acronym SPAOPD; a chronic allergic airway disease due to developing hypersensitivity to soil- or grass-borne fungus; allergens cause constriction of the muscles in the walls of the small airways, swelling of the airways' lining, and excess mucus production, all of which contribute to narrowing of the airways and increased effort required to breath; symptoms include difficulty exhaling, flared nostrils, elevated heart and respiratory rates, abnormal respiratory sounds such as crackles and wheezes, and coughing not associated with exercise; affects pastured horses from June through September.

summer sheet Also known as stable sheet or paddock sheet; a light-weight, rectangular blanket used to keep a horse clean rather than warm.

summer sores *see* CUTANEOUS HABRONEMIASIS

sumpter *see* PACK HORSE

sunburn Inflammation of the skin caused by prolonged exposure to the sun's rays; usually appears on the white facial markings where hair is sparse; the skin may appear red and irritated or blisters may develop.

sun circle *see* SUNFLASH

sunfishing The action of a buckjumper (q.v.) when he twists his body into a crescent while off the ground.

sunflash Also known as sun circle; one of four primary historic patterns of horse brasses (q.v.) used on horse harnesses to ward off the Evil Eye; the pattern of the sun, one of the images of the pagan gods, was struck into brass or other metal and placed on the forehead of the horse; so called because it flashes gold in the sun as the horse or ox moves.

sunflower meal A high energy, high protein supplement produced from the residue of the sunflower seed following oil extraction; is a good supplement for horses, but lacks some essential amino acids and is low in lysine.

sunstroke *see* HEAT STROKE

superfecta A racing term; a betting option where the bettor (q.v.) selects perfectas (q.v.) in two nominated races; may be played straight or boxed (q.v.).

superficial crack Also known as a surface crack; any crack in the exterior hoof wall that does not expose sensitive tissues or result in lameness.

superficial digital flexor tendon Also known as superficial flexor tendon; a tendon (q.v.) that runs down the back of the foreleg between the knee and foot, and between the hock and foot in the hind leg (q.v.), splitting below the fetlock, and attaching to PI (q.v.) and PII (q.v.); functions to extend the hock (q.v.) and the foot in the hind leg and to flex the pastern and knee and extend the elbow in the foreleg; injuries most commonly occur in the front legs.

superficial flexor tendon *see* SUPERFICIAL DIGITAL FLEXOR TENDON

superficial laceration An injury penetrating only the upper layers of the skin; typically the edges of the wound will remain close together; generally result in more bleeding than an abrasion (q.v.).

superficial wound Any injury to the body of the horse which only damages the upper layers of skin such as abrasions (q.v.) and lacerations (q.v.).

superior check ligament A ligament (q.v.) originating above the knee and attaching to the superficial flexor tendon (q.v.) which it supports.

supple (1) Said of a horse who is pliant, flexible, smooth, and limber in movement; having the ability to shift its balance easily and quickly forward, backward, and/or sideways; may also be said of leather. (2) To make a horse supple through stretching, exercises, etc.

supporting hand Refers to the rider's hand; the hand that holds the rein which applies pressure to the neck of the horse in neck reining (q.v.); on the opposite side of the acting hand (q.v.).

supporting rein The rein that aids the direct rein (q.v.) during any movement off a straight line, as in a circle.

supporting limb lameness Lameness (q.v.) in the leg(s), other than that injured; evidenced when a horse is supporting weight on the foot, or when he lands on it.

surcingle Also known as overgirth; a 2-1/2 to 4 inch (6–7.5 cm) wide band of leather or webbing that encircles the horse just behind the forelegs which is used to hold a blanket or pad in place or as a secondary girth to hold a saddle on the back of a horse and prevent it from slipping.

surface crack *see* SUPERFICIAL CRACK

surfeit To stuff or gorge as with food.

surgical leg brace Also known as a leg brace; a device that holds or supports surgical or trauma damaged sites on the leg while they heal; many are made with hinged or bolt-on portions using a horseshoe as a base; vary according to the location and extent of the limb injury.

surgical shoe *see* THERAPEUTIC SHOE

surpanakh A game of mounted basketball.

Surrey A light, four-wheeled, horse-drawn passenger vehicle or family carriage drawn either by a single horse or pair of ponies in pole gear (q.v.) developed in Surrey, England from which the name derived; originally seated four on double, forward-facing cross-seats and later up to six; had a rearward folding half-hood, and later, an umbrella, canopy, or extension top; known as a jerky (q.v.) when not fitted with a hood (q.v.).

suspend (1) To debar or cause to withdraw temporarily from privilege, office, or function. (2) Also known as rule off; a racing term; to bar a horse, jockey, horseman, or stablehand from participation in a race, access to a race track, etc.; usually ordered by the race steward (q.v.).

suspension The act of suspending or the state or period of being suspended, interrupted, or abrogated, as to declare a jockey, horseman, or stablehand ineligible for participation in an event.

suspension time A jumping term; the period following take off during which the horse is in the air over the fence.

suspensory desmitis Also known as sprain of the suspensory ligament or pulled suspensory; a sprain of the suspensory ligament (q.v.) anywhere along its length; symptoms may include localized heat and/or enlargement of the medial palmar vein on the inside of the limb, slight lameness following fast work or long periods of exercise; the most common location of the injury is at the point where the suspensory ligament divides into two branches; if one of the branches of the suspensory ligaments is damaged, injury to the sesamoid bone to which it is attached may also occur; most common in race horses.

suspensory ligament Also known as interosseous tendon or superior sesamoidian ligament; a broad band of elasticized fibrous tissue attached to and behind the cannon bone over the fetlock joint to the pastern bones; supports the fetlock joint preventing it from sinking to the ground; may be strained or torn.

suspensory ligament strain Injury to the suspensory ligament (q.v.) due to excessive tension, work on rough ground, conformation, or incorrect shoeing; generally occurs on or near the lower end of the ligament in the region of the sesamoid bones; symptoms include swelling, pain, and lameness.

suture (1) The uniting of the lips or edges of a wound or incision by stitching. (2) The material by which a wound or incision is united by stitching.

suturing (1) *see* CASLICK'S OPERATION. (2) *see* SUTURE

swag block *see* SWEDGE BLOCK

swaged-side stirrup iron *see* HUNTING IRON

swallows his head Said of a bucking (q.v.) horse when he places his head well between his forelegs.

swallow-tail pad A cotton dressage saddle pad (q.v.) or numnah (q.v.); is square cut in the front, providing plenty of protection for the saddle flap (q.v.), but swoops up in a curved line carried a little beyond the "true square" of the pad, terminating in a long point or "swallow tail" just behind the flap, which keeps it out of the way of the whip; used to protect the back of the horse, provide padding, and absorb sweat.

swamp fever *see* EQUINE INFECTIOUS ANEMIA

swan neck (1) Also known as cock throttled; a conformation fault in which the upper neck of the horse is long and narrow through the throat and concave or lacking muscle development at the base where it joins the forequarters; the head joins the neck in a near vertical line and the gullet appears to stand out in a convex shape as in the throat of a cock. (2) *see* POLL HOOK

swap horses in the middle of the stream It is best not to switch political sides in the middle of the Civil War; a phrase coined by President Lincoln when renominated for the Presidency.

sway back Also known as hollow back, saddle back, or bobby back; said of the horse's back when concave between the withers and loin as caused by old age, faulty conformation, mineral imbalance, or in brood mares, by the weight of foals carried during pregnancy; the opposite of roach back (q.v.).

sway backed Also known as hollow backed, saddle backed, or bobby-backed; said of a horse with a sway back (q.v.).

sweat (1) Also known as perspire; to excrete fluid from the pores of the skin. (2) A treatment used to promote interosmotic passage of fluid from edematous tissue to reduce swelling; consists of the topical application of either an oil- or water-based mixture of which the most consistent ingredients include menthol and/or thymol and in some mixtures, capsicum due to its pain reducing capability, as to the legs; the treated area is normally covered with a wrapping such as plastic to promote heat.

sweat flaps The leather under portion of a saddle which lies against the body of the horse and/or the saddle pad, and protects the rider and finer leather of the saddle from the effects of the horse's sweat.

sweating The act or function of producing sweat (q.v.).

sweat scraper *see* SCRAPER

sweat the brass A racing term; to overwork a horse.

swedge block Also known as a swag block; a molding tool strapped onto an anvil (q.v.) and used to shape barstock (q.v.) which can then be forged into rim shoes, polo plates, and other specialized horseshoes with cross-sections.

swedged shoe Any horseshoe in which the ground-side surface is molded into a traction modifying pattern; will generally have a deep groove running the circumference of the shoe.

Swedish Ardennes A heavy-draft coldblood developed in 19th-century Sweden by crossing Belgian and French Ardennais (q.v.) horses with the Swedish Horse (q.v.); stands 15 to 16 hands and weighs upwards of 1,500 pounds (680 kg); similar in appearance to the Belgian Ardennes (q.v.); may have a black, bay, chestnut, or brown coat, has a heavy head, short, crested neck, short back, rounded and muscular (often double) croup and short, sturdy legs with light feathering; is docile and quiet but energetic in nature; used for heavy draft and farm work.

Swedish Gotland *see* GOTLAND

Swedish Halfbred *see* SWEDISH WARMBLOOD

Swedish Warmblood Also known as the Swedish Halfbred; a warmblood developed in 16th-century Sweden by crossing native mares with high-quality imported Arab (q.v.), Andalusian (q.v.), Friesian (q.v.), Hanoverian (q.v.), Trakehner (q.v.), and Thoroughbred (q.v.) stallions; once used for military purposes, it is a strong, sound riding horse of good temperament; popular as a dressage mount, but is equally suited to jumping, eventing, and driving; stands 16.2 to 17 hands, and may have a coat color of any solid color including bay, brown, chestnut, and gray; has had an open stud book maintained since 1812; foals are eligible for registration if sired by an approved Swedish Warmblood stallion and out of a mare approved by one of the recognized European registries (Hanoverian, Dutch Warmblood [q.v.], Holsteiner [q.v.], etc.) or out of a Thoroughbred registered by The Jockey Club (q.v.).

Swedish Warmblood Association An organization founded in Flyinge, Sweden to preserve the characteristics of the Swedish Warmblood (q.v.) and to maintain the stud book.

sweeney Also known as shoulder atrophy, slipped shoulder, or shoulder paralysis; atrophy of the muscles of the shoulder resulting from disuse following lesion of the leg or foot that leads to prolonged diminished use of the limb or damage to the suprascapular nerve; polo ponies (q.v.) are commonly affected because of competitive collisions; lameness may be difficult to detect until atrophy; if atrophy persists, may result in a noticeable hollowing on either side of the spine or scapula and a looseness in the shoulder.

swelled heel The heel of the horseshoe when folded up onto the hoof-side surface and leveled; raises the heels of the hoof without creating as much traction as blocked heels (q.v.) or heel calks (q.v.).

sweep A cutting term; the action of a horse when he sits back on his haunches and swings his forequarters left to right, with his legs spread, to track a cow.

sweeps *see* SWEEPSTAKES

sweepstakes Also known as sweeps; a racing term; a horse race in which the entry, nominating, eligibility, starting, or other fees or contributions of three or more owners, are divided amongst the first four place getters in previously agreed percentages of the total; entry fees are not required for any other races; all stakes can qualify a horse for black type (q.v.) in a sale catalogue; a higher class of race than allowance races (q.v.), overnight handicaps, and claiming races (q.v.).

sweet feed Any feed, single grain or mixed, to which molasses has been added to improve flavor.

sweet feed bumps *see* HIVES

sweet itch Also known as Culicoides hypersensitivity, Queensland itch, or Kasen; an annually recurring, widely occurring seasonal skin condition caused by an allergic reaction to the blood-sucking insect Culicoides or to midges, sandflies, punkies, and no-see-ums; the insects swarm only in the warmer months of the year before and at dusk feeding on the mane, tail, and belly of the horse, causing intense irritation and producing patches of thick, scaley, and sometimes ulcerated skin; immature horses are rarely affected.

swell (1) To grow bulkier; to increase in size or bulk; to protuberate. (2) Also known as a fork, swell fork, or western saddle fork; that portion of the western saddle (q.v.) in front of the pommel and below the horn in the front; available in a variety of shapes and widths as determined by purpose.

swell body cutter *see* CUTTER

swell fork *see* SWELL no. 1

swine chopped *see* PIG-MOUTHED

swing bars *see* SWINGLETREE

swingers *see* FLY TERRETS

swing horse The middle horse in a randem (q.v.).

swinging limb lameness Lameness (q.v.) evident when the limb is in motion.

swingle bar *see* SWINGLE TREE

swingle tree Also known as a bar, whippletree, whipple tree, splinter bar, badikins, single tree, swingle bar, or swing bar; the pivoted, horizontal swinging bar located at the front of a horse-drawn vehicle to which the harness traces or chains are fastened and by which a vehicle or implement is drawn.

swings *see* SWING TEAM

swing team Also known as swings; the middle pair in a six-horse hitch or the team in front of the wheelers (q.v.) in an eight-horse hitch.

swing up *see* INDIAN STYLE

swipe (1) A racing term; slang; a groom, stable hand, or exercise boy. (2) *see* GROOM no. 1

swirl A hair marking on the head of a horse in the shape of a twist or curl; may be used for identification purposes.

swishing tail The continuous movement of the horse's tail; a form of resistance.

Swiss Anglo-Norman *see* EINSIEDLER

Swiss Warmblood A horse breed developed in the 1960s in Switzerland by putting Thoroughbred (q.v.), Swedish and German horses to the Einsiedler (q.v.); stands 15 to 16.3 hands, has a straight back, slightly sloping croup, prominent withers, a slightly convex or straight head, strong, well-jointed legs, and a coat of any solid color with chestnut and bay occurring most commonly; used for riding and driving.

switch tail A tail pulled to about half its length with the terminal hairs either pulled or allowed to grow to a natural point.

swooping ends Said of a bucking horse when the hind end and head come together as a result of a very tight lateral bend in the body.

swung round A dressage term; said of the horse having performed a walk or canter pirouette (q.v.) too fast and without control; in the case of the canter pirouette, the strides of the canter may be lost and the horse may swing or pivot on one or both hind feet.

syce *see* SAIS

sympathetic nervous system That section of the autonomic nervous system (q.v.) originating in the thoracic and lumbar regions which stimulates the heart beat, dilates the pupils, contracts the blood vessels, and, in general, functions in opposition to the parasympathetic nervous system (q.v.).

synchronous diaphragmatic flutter Also known as thumps or by the acronym SDF; an abnormal heartbeat caused by the involuntary contraction of the diaphragm in rhythm with the beat of the heart resulting from electrolyte losses occurring during physical exertion, hypocalcemic tetany, or blister beetle toxosis; symptoms include a noticeable twitch or spasm in the flank area which may cause an audible sound, dehydration, decreased plasma volume, lack of gut motility, an increase in blood pH, and lowered levels of chloride (q.v.), calcium (q.v.), sodium (q.v.), and magnesium; most commonly seen in electrolyte-depleted/exhausted horses.

Syndicat des Eleveurs de Cheval Breton The French breed association established in 1909 which maintains the stud book for both the Heavy Draught Breton (q.v.) and Postier Breton (q.v.) and only admits horses born in the four departments of Brittany, France, and in the Loire-Latalnatique; registered foals are branded on the left side of the neck with two distinctive marks.

syndicate A partnership arrangement formed for the purpose of buying a horse for race, show, or breeding purposes; investors put up the money and share in the profits and tax benefits.

synovia *see* SYNOVIAL FLUID

synovial fluid Also known as synovia, joint fluid, tendon oil or joint oil; the sticky, transparent lubricating fluid in the joint cavities and tendon sheaths secreted by the synovial membrane (q.v.) which prevents friction and allows smooth joint and tendon action.

synovial joint A moveable joint consisting of articulating bone ends held together with a joint capsule and ligaments and which contains synovial fluid (q.v.).

synovial membrane The lining of the tendon sheaths and joint capsules which secretes synovial fluid necessary for smooth joint action.

synovial sheath The inner lining of a tendon sheath which produces synovial fluid (q.v.).

synovitis Inflammation of a synovial structure, usually the synovial sheath (q.v.).

Syrian An ancient pony breed originating in Syria; has similar origins to the Arab (q.v.) from which it is believed to have descended; stands 14.2 to 15.2 hands and has a gray or chestnut coat, is slightly larger than the Arab and has more angular conformation, yet is equally elegant; is long-lived, fast, frugal, energetic, and possessed of good endurance and strength; used for riding.

systemic lupus erythematosus Also known by the acronym SLE; an auto-immune disease rare in horses; symptoms can be quite diverse depending on the organ systems involved and may include swollen eyelids, facial pain and swelling, visual impairment, photosensitivity, whitening of the hair in patches, and scabbing.

T

tabanid Also known as tabained fly; any of a number of large, dipterous, bloodsucking insects belonging to the family *Tabanidae*, including horseflies (q.v.) and gadflies.

tabanid fly *see* TABANID

tables The polished surface of the front incisor teeth formed by contact with teeth of the lower jaw; table shape is an indicator of age.

Tables 1, 2, and 4 American Horse Show Association (q.v.) rules by which classes for jumpers (q.v.) are judged.

table bank A jumping obstacle consisting of a constructed mound of dirt with, generally, a three-stride platform or flat top and vertical takeoff and landing sides.

tack (1) Saddlery. (2) An abbreviation for harness tackle (q.v.). (3) A racing term; the weight of a jockey including his gear, e.g., The jockey tacks 110 pounds.

tack room Any room in which tack, saddlery, and/or accessories are kept.

tact The rhythmic beat of the horse's footfalls in all gaits.

tag (1) A racing term; the claiming price paid for a horse. (2) The tip of the fox's tail. (3) A farrier term; a hoof shape pattern in which the hoof is somewhat pointed at the toe, straight through the quarters, and turns sharply in at the heels with the widest part located across the rear one third of the hoof.

tail (1) Also known as a horse tail; that part of the horse which starts at the dock (q.v.) and includes the tail, bones, and tail hair; a direct extension of the spinal column consisting of coccygeal bones numbered 15 to 21. (2) The sire line or top line in a pedigree. (3) *see* TAIL SHOT.

tail bandage Also known as a tail wrap; a bandage (q.v.) approximately 2-1/2 to 3 inches (6–7.5 cm) wide made of stockinet or synthetic material wrapped around the tail from the dock to the end of the tail bone to protect it from injury or rubbing while traveling, to improve the appearance of the tail, and to keep the hairs of a pulled tail in place.

tail carriage The manner in which the horse carries his tail.

tail coat *see* SHADBELLY

tailer A roping term; one whose responsibility it is to rope the hind legs of a calf; works with a header (q.v.).

tail going round Said of a horse who swishes its tail in a circular motion; believed to be a sign of irritability or exhaustion.

tail guard A soft leather, cloth, or synthetic covering for the top 10 to 12 inches (25–30 cm) of the tail; used to protect the tail hair from being rubbed during trailering or while stabled.

tail hound A hunting term; a hound who follows at some distance behind the pack (q.v.), rather than leading, when running a fox (q.v.).

tailor seat A vaulting term; a static exercise (q.v.) in which the vaulter (q.v.) sits on the back of the horse with both legs crossed in front of him.

tail notch A cut or hollow cut into the tail hair of the horse to facilitate identification when turned out on public land.

tail rubbing Said of a horse; persistent rubbing of the dock (q.v.) of the tail against any object such as a stall wall as due to boredom, pinworm infestation, external parasite infestation, or any other localized skin irritation.

tail set (1) A rigid, crupper-like contraption used on a nicked (q.v.) tail to lift it sufficiently high to be doubled and tied down; maintaining the horse's tail in an unnatural, high-set position while the horse is stabled and to give it an arch and extremely high carriage when driven or ridden. (2) The set position or carriage of the horse's tail.

tail shot A polo term; a stroke on the ball in which the polo player strikes the ball from behind and across the rump of his horse.

tail string *see* TAIL FILLET

tail to the wall *see* RENVERS

tail wrap *see* TAIL BANDAGE

take Also known as take out; a racing term; money deducted from each mutuel pool (q.v.) to cover track revenue and state and local taxes.

take a fall (1) Said of a rider, to fall from a horse. (2) A hunting term; a fall of both the horse and rider.

take back *see* TAKE UP

take down A racing term; to disqualify a horse for an infraction after he has finished in the money (q.v.), at which point his number is removed from the list of early finishers.

take hold Said of the horse who bites down on the bit and pulls against the rider's or driver's hands through the reins.

taken up A racing term; said of a horse pulled up (q.v.) by the jockey to conserve the horse's energy or to avoid trouble on the track.

take off (1) A vaulting term; the moment when the vaulter (q.v.) leaves the ground in preparation to mount the horse. (2) A jumping term; the moment at which a horse leaves the ground in preparation to clear a jump; preceded by the approach (q.v.) and followed by flight (q.v.).

take off rail *see* GROUND POLE

take-off side The side of any jumping obstacle from which the rider begins his jump; the opposite of the landing side (q.v.).

take off too late A jumping term; said of the horse who begins to jump an obstacle too close to the jump to allow a full jumping stride; the horse will generally hit the jump with his forelegs.

take off too soon A jumping term; said of the horse who begins his jump of an obstacle too far away from the take off point appropriate for his stride; the horse will therefore descend from his jump before fully clearing the obstacle and thus may contact the jump with his body or hind legs.

takeout *see* TAKE

take the bump *see* POST

take up Also known as take back; a racing term; said of a jockey who sharply pulls up his horse to avoid a collision or other trouble on the track or to rate (q.v.) it.

take with the hand Said of the rider; to tighten the grip of the fingers on the reins to apply bit pressure on the bars of the horse's mouth.

taking down the purse An antiquated racing term; to award the purse to the winner of a horse race; originally, prize money was contained in a purse hung on a wire which crossed the finish line.

Tally-ho (1) Also known as tally o; a hunting term; the huntsman's cry to urge on his hounds; indicates a fox has been sighted. (2) *see* TALLY-HO BREAK

Tally-ho break Also known as a tally-ho; a horse-drawn, light, sporting break popular in the late 19th century with fox-hunting and horse-racing groups; supported by high wheels and hung on elliptical and/or semi-elliptical springs; drawn by a single horse in shafts or a pair in pole gear (q.v.).

tally-ho over *see* TALLY OVER

tally o *see* TALLY-HO

tally over Also known as tally-ho over; a hunting term; a cry to the field indicating that a fox has crossed a ride (q.v.) in a wood.

tampering *see* BISHOPING

tandem Two horses, one hitched in front of the other, who pull a vehicle; the wheeler (q.v.) is placed between the shafts of the vehicle and the leader is out in front.

tandem cart A two-wheeled, horse-drawn dogcart (q.v.) generally used for show purposes driven to a tandem (q.v.); had dummy slatted sides, as dogs were not carried, and a rear groom's seat situated at a slightly lower level than the driving seat.

tandem sporting A two-wheeled, tandem-drawn dogcart (q.v.) or gig (q.v.) used to transport a saddled, bridled, and harnessed

Hunter to a hunt; the Hunter was driven in the lead at the canter, while the wheeler (q.v.), a harness horse, was driven at the trot; with destination reached, the hunter was unharnessed from the lead and mounted; the vehicle was then drawn back to the stable by the wheeler, driven by a groom.

tandem whip *see* COACHING CROP

Tanghan A subgroup of the Bhotia (q.v.) pony breed which originated in the Himalayan mountains of northern India; stands 13.2 hands, has a gray coat, short neck, shaggy mane, straight shoulder, and short, strong legs; is frugal and has good endurance; used for riding.

tapadero The hooded leather covering of the front of a western stirrup (q.v.).

tape (1) *see* ADHESIVE TAPE. (2) To tie or secure with tape. (3) *see* BARRIER

tap root The direct female line of descent traced back to the origin.

tap root mare *see* FOUNDATION MARE

tapeworm Also known as a flat worm; a gastrointestinal parasite; of three species in the horse: *Anoplocephala manga* (q.v.), *Anoplocephala perforliata* (q.v.), and *Paranoplocephala mamillana*; vary in length from 8 to 25 cm; found in the cecum, small intestine, and occasionally the stomach where they feed on nutrients consumed by the horse; in light infestations, no signs of disease are present, while in heavy infestations, digestive disturbances, unthriftiness, and anemia (q.v.) may occur.

Tarai A horse breed indigenous to Nepal standing about 11.2 hands.

Tarbenian A horse breed from Tarbes located at the foot of the Pyrenees mountains between France and Spain; descended from the Iberian (q.v.) horse improved with Arab (q.v.) stallions imported by Napoleon Bonaparte at the beginning of the 19th century; later English Thoroughbred (q.v.) stallions were put to Tarbenian mares to increase breed height and create the Bigourdan Horse (q.v.); is light boned, stands about 15 hands, is fast, courageous, intelligent, and generally has good conformation.

tare Any of several species of vetch, especially *Vicia sativa*, or any seed of a vetch; a weed pest of grain fields.

target a cow A cutting term; said of a cutter (q.v.) who identifies a cow in the herd he wants to work and slowly and deliberately separates it from the herd; the opposite of cut for shape (q.v.).

Tarpan Also known by the scientific name *Equus ferus ferus*; until the end of the 18th century, was one of two subspecies of ancient wild horse found in eastern Europe and Asia; was about the size of a mule (q.v.) with a tan, Isabella (q.v.), or mouse coat with a whitish surcoat, an arched forehead with the ears set far back, thin neck, narrow, high, and pointed hooves, hock-length tail which was sometimes scant and at others bushy, and a high croup; the fronts of the fore and hind legs were black from the knees to the hoof; although the original breed is now extinct, two attempts have been made to breed it back; the Turkoman word for wild horse.

tarsus *see* HOCK

tarsus valgus *see* MEDIAL DEVIATION OF THE HOCK JOINTS

tat A native Indian pony.

Tattenham Corner A notorious, steep left-hand bend following the highest point of the 1-1/2 mile (2.4 km) Epsom Derby (q.v.) course; the turn located 1,154 yards (1,055 m) from the start of the course, drops 40 feet (12 m) in approximately 700 yards (640 m).

tattersall bit Also known as a yearling bit, ring bit, or colt bit; a circular bit that attaches to the headstall; the upper half of the circle is placed in the horse's mouth while the lower half fits under the horse's chin; may or may not have players (q.v.).

tattoo (1) The act or practice of marking the skin with indelible patterns, legends, or numbers by making punctures in it and inserting pigments. (2) A mark or marks in the skin of the horse made with a sharp instrument and injected indelible dye used to identify and/or register the horse; frequently a series of numbers or a code placed on the horse's inside upper or lower lip; a horse cannot be tattooed until it is at least two years of age as the immature immune system will recognize the dye as a foreign substance and sweep it to the lymph nodes; required by some stud books for registration purposes, and in the United States for race eligibility; will fade and stretch over time and may be temporarily altered or masked for a period of up to 48 hours by injection of condensed milk into the dyed areas.

tattooer One trained, certified, or registered to tattoo (q.v.) horses.

tattooing *see* TATTOO no. 1

Tattu A subgroup of the Bhotia (q.v.) pony breed originating in the Himalayan mountains of northern India; stands 11.2 hands, has a gray coat, short neck, shaggy mane, straight shoulder, and short, strong legs; is frugal and has good endurance; used for mountain packing.

TB *see* THOROUGHBRED

TBFV loop The acronym for tidal-breathing flow-volume loop (q.v.).

T-Cart *see* T-CART PHAETON

T-Cart Phaeton A light, horse-drawn, four-wheel vehicle of the phaeton (q.v.) type driven to a small horse or large pony; popular in military circles throughout the second half of the 19th century; had a forward driving seat much wider than the groom's rearward seat, which when viewed from above appeared T-shaped.

Tchenarani A half-breed indigenous to northern Iran; produced since 1700 by crossing Persian Arab (q.v.) stallions with Turkmene (q.v.) mares; stands 14.1 to 15.1 hands, has an athletic, wiry build, sloping croup, and powerful hindquarters, and usually has a bay, chestnut, or gray coat; is spirited and gentle; although historically used as a cavalry mount, now used for riding.

TDN *see* TOTAL DIGESTIBLE NUTRIENT SYSTEM

tea A racing term; any illegal chemical administered to a horse to hamper or improve his performance.

team (1) Two or more horses harnessed together to draw a wagon or other vehicle. (2) The draft horse(s) together with the harness and the drawn vehicle. (3) A number of riders associated by country, riding style, breed, etc. participating in a joint activity or action as in

sides of a competition.

team handicap A polo term; the sum of the goal ratings (q.v.) of each of four players on a team; used to equalize playing ability; the side with the lowest goal-rating total receives the difference between the two team totals as a score at the beginning of the match.

team penning Also known as penning; a relatively young mounted team competition fostered under the auspices of various cattlemen's associations and rooted in traditional ranch work; consists of three skills: cutting (q.v.), reining (q.v.), and sprinting; a trio of three horses and riders ride into one end of an arena toward a herd of 30 cattle clustered at the opposite end; each cow is identified by a number from zero to nine on its shoulder, and when the first horse and rider reach the start/foul line, a judge calls out a number and the clock begins; the team then attempts to isolate the three cows bearing the specified numbers, cut them from the herd, and drive them down the arena and into an enclosed pen within the allotted two minutes; when the last cow is confined, one or all the riders raises a hand, stopping the clock and ending the competition; generally conducted in three rounds; scored in one of two ways: (a) the team with the lowest cumulative time for all three rounds wins or (b) teams with the lowest times advance to second and third rounds, the one with the lowest third-time round wins; because it is governed by more than one association, the rules may vary among competitions.

team rope To participate in team roping (q.v.).

team roper A mounted horseman, either a header (q.v.) or healer (q.v.); who participates in team roping (q.v.).

team roping A timed horseback competition originating on American cattle ranches as a utilitarian event; in the fall of each season, cattle are rounded up and moved to winter ground at which time calves are pulled from the herd for branding (q.v.), inoculating, and marking; two mounted horsemen, consisting of a header (q.v.) and healer (q.v.) rope the head and hind legs of the calf, respectively, and hold it tight between them so that the ground team can perform branding, etc.; evolved into a timed event.

team sorting A relatively new sport originating in central California around 1990 as a ranch competition similar to team penning (q.v.); a timed event in which each participating team (consisting of three mounted contestants) attempts to herd 10 calves, numbered 0–9, to one end of a standard arena; the end quarter of the arena is marked with painted posts or flags on either side between which an imaginary line known as a foul line is drawn; this line serves as a starting line for the timer, a boundary line for the cattle, and should be located 50 to 75 feet (15–23 m) from the corners, depending on the width of the arena; one team at a time rides to the foul line and waits for the announcer to draw and call out a number from 0–9; the riders attempt to cut each of the 10 calves in numerical order (starting with the number called by the announcer) away from the herd and drive them across the foul line; the calves must be sorted in proper numerical order and cross the line in that order; "no-time" is called if any calf crosses the foul line out of order or passes across the line and then retreats to the original side; each team has two minutes (90 seconds in Southern California, USA) to cut 10 cattle; if more than one team sorts 10 cattle, the team with the fastest time wins; if no team sorts the entire herd in the allotted time, teams are scored by the number of calves correctly herded across the line within 90 seconds; the next team does not cut until the 10 calves are settled (q.v.).

tease To sexually stimulate the mare with a teaser (q.v.) to determine if she is ready to be mated and to encourage her to come into heat (q.v.); generally, a mare will be brought to a fence or padded partition such as a trying board (q.v.) on the other side of which is a stallion, ridgeling, or gelding; the partition prevents full contact between the horses; if the mare is ready she will adopt the mating posture (q.v.), holding her tail up and to the side.

teaser Also known as teaser stallion; a horse, usually a stallion or a ridgeling (q.v.), used to test the response of a mare prior to breeding, or to determine if a mare is in heat (q.v.) and ready to breed at which time the mare will be mated to a selected stallion, generally other than the teaser; use of a teaser prolongs stallion fertility and libido.

teaser stallion *see* TEASER

technical delegate One responsible for insuring that an international horse show or

three-day event competition is run according to international FEI (q.v.) rules and that the course is correct; usually from a country other than the host nation.

teeth The plural of tooth (q.v.).

telega A crudely made, four-wheeled, horse-drawn Russian passenger or stage coach; frequently unsprung or dead axle.

telegraph springs An elastic contrivance or body, as a wire of steel coiled spirally, which when compressed, bent, or otherwise forced from its natural shape, has the power of recovering this by virtue of its elasticity; specifically, a combination of four double-elbow springs, two lying sideways and two crossways used on such horse-drawn vehicles as the mail coach (q.v.), mail phaeton (q.v.), Stanhope gig (q.v.), etc.; so called because the first ones were used on the English telegraph coach.

teletheater A racing term; a movie theater in which horse races are simulcast.

teletimer A racing term; an electronic timer that flashes the fractional and final race times of horses running in races on the tote board (q.v.).

Tellington-Jones Equine Awareness Method Also known as TTEAM or TTEAM training; a system of integrated training, therapeutic and holistic healing, and overcoming common resistances or tension in the horse's body using a technique of functional integration and body work; developed by Linda Tellington-Jones (q.v.); consists of three sections: the Tellington TTouch (q.v.), ground exercises, and riding with awareness, including tools and exercises to improve equine and rider balance and coordination.

Tellington-Jones, Linda An accomplished horsewoman, educator, trainer, and healer most noted for her technique of holistic body work, ground exercises, and riding with awareness to train, heal, and overcome common resistances in the horse known as the Tellington-Jones Equine Awareness Method (q.v.).

Tellington TTouch Also known as TTouch; a method of training, healing, and overcoming common resistances in the horse developed by American Linda Tellington-Jones (q.v.) in the

1970s; based on the Feldenkrais method of functional integration and body work; a component of TTEAM (q.v.) training.

Tell that to the Horse Marines An antiquated phrase of derision said to one guilty of gross exaggeration.

temperature Body heat; the normal rectal temperature for a horse at rest is approximately 99.1 to 100.5° F (37.5 to 38° C); the temperature of a horse at work may rise by as much as five degrees.

tempi changes A dressage term; lead changes performed by the cantering horse at every stride or at intervals such as every second, third, or fourth stride.

tempo The measure of speed within the movements of the horse's various gaits, that is the number of feet or meters covered per minute; may be lengthened or shortened.

temporary teeth *see* DECIDUOUS TEETH

tendinous windgall *see* TENDINOUS WIND-PUFF

tendinous windpuffs A soft, fluid-filled enlargement of the digital flexor tendon sheath usually confined to above the fetlock and does not cause lameness; swelling occurs between the suspensory ligament and flexor tendon and should be distinguished from distension of the fetlock joint capsule (articular windpuff [q.v.]); may be caused by intense training followed by a period of rest, excessive exercise on hard surfaces, or the cumulative effects of imbalances produced by poor conformation or improperly trimmed hooves; must be regarded with suspicion in the presence of lameness.

tendon Also known as sinew; tough, fibrous, slightly elastic, white cords connecting muscle to bone and giving support to the joints; transmit the energy generated by muscular contraction to the bones.

tendon Achilles *see* ACHILLES TENDON

tendon boots Also known as run-down boots; a protective leg covering worn around the cannon bones of the forelegs of the horse to support the tendons in the back of the leg and to protect them from injury; may have a closed or open front.

tendon oil *see* SYNOVIAL FLUID

tendon bowed *see* BOWED TENDON

tendon contracted *see* CONTRACTED TENDON

tendon extensor *see* EXTENSOR TENDON

tendon flexor *see* FLEXOR TENDON

tendonitis Inflammation of the tendon (q.v.) caused by irritation from use or injury.

tenectomy The surgical removal of a portion of a tendon.

ten-minute halt An eventing (q.v.) term; a compulsory ten-minute stop required of the horse and rider at the end of Phase C of the Speed and Endurance Phase, during which time the second compulsory veterinary inspection occurs and the horse is cooled down and refreshed.

Tennessee Walker *see* TENNESSEE WALKING HORSE

Tennessee Walking Horse Also known as a Plantation Walking Horse, Southern Plantation Walking Horse, Tennessee Walker, Tennessee Walking Horse, Walking Horse, Walker, Turn-Row (because of its ability to travel between the rows of crops without damaging them), or Turn-Row Horse; a breed developed in 19th-century Tennessee, USA as a practical horse that could carry its owner in comfort for hours while inspecting plantation crops; descended from a mix of Standardbred (q.v.), Thoroughbred (q.v.), Morgan (q.v.), and the American Saddlebred (q.v.); the foundation sire, a black Standardbred stallion named Allan, came from a line of trotters out of a Morgan mare; noted for its three natural gaits: the running walk (q.v.), the flat-foot walk (q.v.), and the canter (rocking-chair canter [q.v.]); exhibits an overstriding action which serves as a shock absorber, whereby the hind foot is placed ahead of the track left by the forefoot by as few as 12 and as many as 50 inches (30–127 cm); is large-boned, deep and short-coupled, with a square appearance to the barrel, stands 15 to 17 hands, has a steady and reliable temperament, and most commonly a bay, black, or chestnut coat; recognized as a breed in 1950; included in the American Saddlebred Registry until the late 1950s as more than 25 percent of the foundation sires were registered American Saddlebreds.

Tennessee Walking Horse Breeders' and Exhibitors Association Also known by the acronym TWHBEA; an organization founded in 1935 in Lewisberg, Tennessee, USA, to collect, record, and preserve the pedigrees of the Tennessee Walking Horse (q.v.), maintain a registry, develop rules and regulations governing all aspects of the breed, and to sponsor promotional programs; the stud book opened in 1947; to qualify for the registry both parents must be registered Tennessee Walkers.

tenosynovitis *see* BOWED TENDON

tense Also known as worked up; the mental and physical state of the horse when not relaxed, obedient, and/or responsive to the aids of the rider.

tent pegger One who participates in the mounted sport of tent pegging (q.v.).

tent pegging A mounted sport originating in India for military purposes in which a mounted rider carrying a 10 to 12 foot (3–3.6 m) lance, would charge on a galloping horse at the tent of the enemy, place the tip of his lance through an eye in a tent peg and lift it from the ground, thus dropping the tent on those inside; now a competitive sport; the size of the peg varies depending on the expertise of the competitors with larger pegs used by beginners and progressively smaller pegs with more advanced riders.

Terek *see* TERSKY

termino The natural action of the forelegs of a Peruvian Paso (q.v.) when performing the paso (q.v.) gait in which the forelegs arc, or dish, to the outside in the forward strides.

terms race *see* CONDITION RACE

terra-à-terra Also known as terra terra and spelled terre à terre; an air (q.v.) which served as the foundation for the high airs (q.v.), although it is no longer performed in dressage (q.v.) today; a very cadenced, elevated canter (q.v.) performed in two time on two tracks (q.v.) in which the forelegs are raised together, then put down together, followed by the deeply engaged hindquarters in the same motion; a rocking movement of small, controlled, and low to the ground advancing prances forward and bearing sideways; often performed against the wall or between pillars (q.v.).

terra terra *see* TERRA-A-TERRA

terre-à-terre *see* TERRA-A-TERRA

terret One of the round loops or rings on the hames (q.v.), pad, or saddle through which the driving reins pass.

terrier man Also known as a fencing man; a hunting term; one responsible for repairing hunt jumps and fences damaged during the day's hunting, attending to the hunt terrier, and earth stomping.

Tersk *see* TERSKY

Terskij *see* TERSKY

Tersky Also known as a Tersk, Terskij, or Terek; a Russian-bred warmblood developed at the Tersk and Stavropol Studs in Northern Caucasus between 1921 and 1950; descended from the old Tersky breed which was founded on the Strelets Arabian selectively crossed with pure and part-bred Arabians (q.v.) which it closely resembles; stands 14.3 to 15.1 hands and always has a gray coat; is good-natured, active, and possessed of good stamina; used for riding, racing, and in the circus; officially recognized as a breed in 1948.

test barn A racing term; an area where blood and urine samples are taken immediately following each horse race to screen for the presence of illegal drugs.

testes Also known as nuts or testicles; the plural of testis; two reproductive glands in the male which produce spermatozoa and the male sex hormone testosterone.

testicle *see* TESTES

testis Also known as gonad; a single reproductive gland in the male which produces sperm and testosterone.

tetanus (1) Also known as lockjaw; an acute infectious disease characterized by tonic spasm of voluntary muscles especially of the jaw and caused by the bacillus toxin, *Costridium tetani*, which is usually introduced through a wound as in a puncture wound; found in spores in the soil; estimated to be fatal in at least 25 to 50 percent of all cases as horses are the most sensitive of all species of mammals; the incidence is generally higher in the warmer parts of the continents; the incubation period varies from one to several weeks, but usually averages 10 to 14 days following introduction of the bacteria into an anaerobic (q.v.) wound environment; symptoms include localized stiffness in the area of the wound, followed by generalized stiffness, increased intensity of the reflexes, excitement of the horse into spasms by sudden movements or noises, an inability to chew (hence the common designation lockjaw), protrusion of the third eyelid, erect ears, stiff tail, stiff walking, difficulty backing and turning, sweating, and due to leg muscle stiffness, a sawhorse stance (q.v.); the temperature usually remains slightly above normal, but may rise to 108-110° F (42–43° C) toward the end of a fatal attack; may be prevented by active immunization with tetanus toxoid (q.v.), including boosters at annual intervals; if a horse has not been immunized prior to the occurrence of the wound or puncture, tetanus antitoxin (q.v.) administered up to two days following the injury will still provide temporary protection. (2) The specific bacterium that causes tetanus.

tetanus antitoxin The antibody formed in a host inoculated with tetanus (q.v.) bacteria are injected into a horse to provide temporary protection against tetanus.

tetanus toxoid A tetanus toxin whose toxic property has been eliminated, usually by a chemical agent, but which retains its antigenic qualities that produce immunity on injection into the body by stimulating production of immune antibodies in the blood; provides prolonged protection against tetanus (q.v.).

tether (1) A rope or chain by which a horse is fastened to restrict range to a set radius of the object to which it is tethered. (2) To fasten or restrain by or as with a tether.

Tevis Cup Ride Also known as the 100-mile Western States Ride; a 100-mile (160 km) endurance race run in the United States from Tahoe City, Nevada to Auburn, California, over the steep Sierra Nevada mountain range; riders climb 9,500 feet (2,896 m) to Squaw Pass and drop into El Dorado Canyon where temperatures can reach 100° F (37.7° C); generally covered by the winners in 11 to 12 hours; first held in 1955.

Texas ditch The most grueling of 31 jumping obstacles in the Grand Pardubice (q.v.), a steeplechase (q.v.) held annually in Czechoslovakia every second Sunday in October since

1874; is 16 feet 5 inches (5 m) wide and fronted by a natural fence 5 feet (1.5 m) high and 5 feet (1.5 m) wide.

Texas fever *see* EQUINE PIROPLASMOSIS

Texas Racing Commission An eight-member board which governs all horse and Grayhound racing activities in Texas, United States.

The American Donkey and Mule Society *see* AMERICAN DONKEY & MULE SOCIETY

The American Stud Book *see* AMERICAN STUD BOOK, THE

The Blazers *see* BLAZERS, THE

The Book *see* STUD BOOK

the box *see* BOX no. 1

the brace *see* BRACE no. 5

The British Racehorse *see* BRITISH RACEHORSE, THE

The British Riding Club *see* BRITISH RIDING CLUB, THE

The British Percheron Horse Society *see* BRITISH PERCHERON HORSE SOCIETY, THE

the cart horse of the north *see* ARDENNAIS

The Connemara Pony Breeder's Society *see* CONNEMARA PONY BREEDER'S SOCIETY, THE

the cross Also known as a cross; a primitive marking (q.v.); a dorsal stripe (q.v.) of darker hair starting at the top of the head and running to the end of the tail which is crossed at the withers with another darker line of hair thus forming a cross; may be seen on any coat color, commonly found on donkeys; a dominant trait.

The Dales Pony Improvement Society *see* DALES PONY SOCIETY, THE

The Darby *see* EPSOM DERBY

the daughter of the horseleech An antiquated term originating in the 16th century; any rapacious insatiable person, or bloodsucker who clings to another robbing him of ideas, money, or other resources; the daughters of such people would, presumably, be more grasping.

The Derby Stakes *see* DERBY STAKES, THE

The Distance A racing term; the 240-yards (220 m) straightaway on a racecourse before the finish (q.v.).

The Downs *see* DOWNS

The English Connemara Pony Society *see* ENGLISH CONNEMARA SOCIETY

The English Jockey Club *see* ENGLISH JOCKEY CLUB, THE

The Epsom Derby *see* EPSOM DERBY

The Father of Classical Equitation *see* DE LA GUERINIERE, FRANCOIS ROBICHON

The Father of Foxhunting *see* WARDE, JOHN

The Fell Pony Society *see* FELL PONY SOCIETY, THE

The Foxhound Kennel Stud Book *see* FOXHOUND KENNEL STUD BOOK, THE

The Garden *see* NATIONAL HORSE SHOW

The Golden Horse Society *see* GOLDEN HORSE SOCIETY, THE

The Grand Liverpool Steeplechase *see* GRAND NATIONAL STEEPLECHASE

The Grand National *see* GRAND NATIONAL, THE

The Great Horse *see* GREAT HORSE, THE

The Hackney Horse Society *see* HACKNEY HORSE SOCIETY, THE

The Heythrop *see* HEYTHROP HOUNDS, THE

The Heythrop Hounds *see* HEYTHROP HOUNDS, THE

The Highland Pony Society *see* HIGHLAND PONY SOCIETY, THE

The Holyhead Mail *see* HOLYHEAD MAIL, THE

The International Federation of Pony Breeders *see* INTERNATIONAL FEDERATION OF PONY BREEDERS, THE

The Jockey Club *see* JOCKEY CLUB, THE

The Kadir Cup *see* KADIR CUP, THE

The Liverpool Steeplechase *see* GRAND NATIONAL STEEPLECHASE

The Loriners Company *see* LORINERS COMPANY, THE

The Maneige Royal *see* DE PLUVINEL, ANTOINE

The Master *see* MASTER

The Master of the Game *see* DE FOIX, GASTON

The Mounties *see* CANADIAN MOUNTED POLICE, THE ROYAL

The National (1) *see* GRAND NATIONAL STEEPLECHASE. (2) *see* NATIONAL HORSE SHOW

The Northern Dales Pony Society *see* DALES PONY SOCIETY, THE NORTHERN

Théodore Géricault *see* GERICAULT, THEODORE

the off *see* OFF no. 1

the office A British jumping term; said of the rider, the act of communicating the aids to the horse preparatory to the take off in jumping.

The Polo Association *see* UNITED STATES POLO ASSOCIATION

The Pony Club *see* PONY CLUB, THE

the prop Also known as number 1; a vaulting term; the first vaulter (q.v.) in the saddle when performing exercises in pairs and threes; is positioned closest to the vaulting roller (q.v.) and assists other vaulters mount and/or dismount the horse; dismounts first, at which time the second vaulter becomes the prop.

therapeutic riding Riding as used in physiotherapy or psychotherapy circumstances.

therapeutic shoe Also known as pathological shoe, surgical shoe, or corrective shoe; a horseshoe (q.v.) used in conjunction with veterinary medical treatment to treat or correct conformation defect, disease, or injury of the foot or leg such as founder (q.v.) or bruised heels.

therapeutic ultrasound The use of high frequency sound waves, above the range of the human ear, to break down unwanted tissues and promote healing by stimulating circulation.

The Ride and Tie Association *see* RIDE AND TIE ASSOCIATION, THE

The Ring *see* RING, THE

thermography A lameness diagnostic technique in which a visual image is produced from infrared radiation emitted from the skin surface; the infrared radiation is detected by a proton detector, converted to electrical impulses, and displayed in colors on a television monitor, the different colors corresponding to variances in body temperature with areas of trauma or injury registering an elevated temperature.

thermoregulation The control and/or regulation of the body temperature.

The Royal Canadian Mounted Police *see* CANADIAN MOUNTED POLICE, THE ROYAL

the scale *see* SCALE OF WEIGHTS

The School of Mounted Troop Instruction *see* FRENCH CAVALRY SCHOOL AT SAUMUR

The Shires *see* SHIRES, THE

the simpler's art *see* HERBALISM

Thessalian An ancient pony breed indigenous to Greece; now extinct.

the taller the port, the tighter the curb A rule of thumb used to estimate the tightness of a curb chain whereby the higher the port (q.v.) sits above the bit (q.v.), the tighter the curb chain should be adjusted.

the tie Also referred to as tie; a roping term; to place three of the calf's legs together, wrap a pigging string (q.v.) around them and secure the string with a half hitch.

the V A roping term; the V shape created by bringing and holding together the calf's fore

and hind legs in the middle of his body in preparation for the tie (q.v.).

The Worshipful Company of Farriers *see* WORSHIPFUL COMPANY OF FARRIERS OF LONDON

thiamin Originally known as vitamin B_1 and spelled thiamine; a white crystalline compound found in the outer coating of ceral grains, greens, brewer's yeast, peas, beans, liver, etc. and also prepared synthetically; essential for normal metabolism and nerve function; lacking in most horse rations, particularly low-quality hay and is destroyed by heat and cooking; deficiency is detected by blood analysis, the symptoms of which include loss of appetite, nervousness, reduced fertility, and a lack of coordination.

thick wind An American term; said of the horse; to have difficulty breathing.

thief A racing term; a horse who runs worst when his chances appear to be best.

thigh bone *see* FEMUR

thill *see* SHAFT HORSE

thiller *see* SHAFT HORSE

thill horse *see* SHAFT HORSE

third incisors *see* CORNER INCISORS

third man Also known as referee; a polo term; a referee (q.v.) who sits on the sidelines during a polo match and who arbitrates in the event the two field umpires disagree on a call.

third pastern Also known as os pedis, third phalanx, coffin bone, distal phalanx, distal phalange, pedal bone, or PIII; the largest bone in the horse's foot and the most distal bone in the leg; a hoof- or crescent-shaped bone which lies with the navicular and lower portion of the coronet bone to form the pedal or foot joint; one of three primary bones which make up the lower part of the horse's leg and hoof.

third phalanx *see* THIRD PASTERN

third sire The paternal great-grandfather of a horse.

this grass An antiquated term; this coming

spring, as in "the horse will be four years old this grass".

thong The long, plaited-leather portion of a whip attached to the crop (q.v.) on one end and to the lash (q.v.) on the other, the length of which varies from 1 to 2 yards (91-180 cm); generally found on lunge (q.v.) and hunting whips.

thoracic Pertaining to the thorax (q.v.).

thoracic cavity *see* CHEST

thoracic inlet The bony, oval opening in the front of the horse's chest through which the windpipe (q.v.), esophagus (q.v.), and major vessels to and from the head pass.

thorax *see* CHEST

thoropin *see* THOROUGHPIN

thorn bit A very severe bit (q.v.) with a spiked mouthpiece still used in some parts of the Orient.

thoroughbrace A strong leather strap(s) on which the body of a horse-drawn vehicle was sometimes suspended in lieu of shocks or springs.

Thoroughbred Also known as English Thoroughbred, British Thoroughbred, TB, blood-stock, blood horse, blood 'un (obs), Thro-bred, or bred horse (obs); a horse breed whose origins date back to the early 18th century and the importation of three Arab stallions into England: the Byerley Turk (q.v.), the Godolphin Arabian (q.v.), and the Darley Arabian (q.v.); these three stallions, and mares of varietal stock, are the foundation from which all Thoroughbreds can trace their descent on the male side; the General Stud Book (q.v.) dates back to 1791 and is kept by The Jockey Club (q.v.); does not present uniform physical characteristics, it can be categorized into three physical types: the stayer (q.v.), the sprinter (q.v.), and the middle-distancer (q.v.); stands 14.3 to 17 hands, has fine skin, a bay, dark bay, black, chestnut, or gray coat and white face and leg markings; roan and red roan are rarely found; used for riding, racing, and improving other breeds.

Thoroughbred Breeders Association An organization founded in 1917 in Great Britain to encourage and ensure the cooperation and unity of Thoroughbred (q.v.) breeders in improvement of the Thoroughbred.

Thoroughbred Racing Association Also known by the acronym TRA; a trade association of North American racetrack owners and managers founded in 1942 to maintain the integrity of racing, a data base of racing statistics, and to provide racetrack management support.

Thoroughbred Racing Protective Bureau An intelligence network operating in the United States responsible for fighting corruption within the racing association.

thoroughpin Also spelled thoropin; a distention of the tarsal sheath of the deep digital flexor tendon just above the hock (q.v.) characterized by a fluid-filled swelling visible above the point of the hock on either side; caused by trauma or strain to the tendon and is most common in draft and jumping horses although any sudden stop can cause the condition; considered a blemish which rarely affects the horse's performance.

Thracian An ancient pony breed indigenous to Greece; now extinct.

train off A British term; to overtrain a horse to the point that his performance deteriorates.

thread worm *see* STRONGYLOIDE

Three-Day Event Also known as Concours Complete, Concours Complete d'Equitation, or complete test; a three-phase competition conducted over a period of three days and consisting of dressage, show/stadium jumping, and speed and endurance phases, the later including steeplechase (Phase B), roads and tracks (Phases A and C), and cross country (Phase D); the three phases are performed by the same rider/horse team; three compulsory veterinary inspections take place, the first prior to when competition begins, the second following Phase C of the speed and endurance phase, and the third occurring on the third day before beginning the jumping phase; differs from horse trials (q.v.) in that it includes an endurance phase.

three-eighths pole A racing term; a distance marking pole located on the inside rail three furlongs (q.v.) from the finish line.

three feet of tin *see* COACH HORN

three-gaited Said of any horse who performs the three natural gaits of walk, trot, and canter.

three-gaited saddler One of three types of horse show classes for the American Saddlebred (q.v.) in which demonstration of the walk, trot, and canter is required.

three-quarter pole A racing term; a distance marking pole located on the inside rail (q.v.) exactly six furlongs (q.v.) from the finish.

three-quarters brothers A relationship between male horses having the same dam (q.v.) and whose sires (q.v.) had identical sires but different dams.

three-quarters in blood Said of male or female horses having the same dam and whose sires had identical sires but different dams.

three-quarters sisters A relationship between female horses having the same dam (q.v.) and whose sires (q.v.) had identical sires but different dams.

three to one Also known as 3 to 1; one of three methods of holding the reins of a double bridle; three reins are held in the left hand (the two curb reins divided by the ring finger and the left snaffle rein around the little finger) with the right snaffle rein and the whip held in the right hand; the method is only effective if the horse has been properly trained and worked through on the snaffle; the only method accepted at the Spanish Riding School (q.v.).

thrifty A horse who is healthy, alert, and active.

throat (1) The passage that leads from the nose and mouth to the lungs and stomach and includes the esophagus and pharynx; the front part of the neck. (2) The bottom of the inside of a collar (q.v.).

throat lash *see* THROAT LATCH

throat latch Also known as throat lash; the narrow strap of the bridle which encircles the head from the crown piece of the bridle under the throat (q.v.) where it buckles; prevents the bridle from slipping over the horse's head.

throat latching A coaching term; a method of restraining a horse inclined to pull; to pass the coupling rein of the puller through his partner's throat latch (q.v.) before buckling it to the puller's bit.

Thro-bred *see* THOROUGHBRED

thrombosis A coagulation of blood in a blood vessel or in the heart during life.

thrombus A fibrous clot of blood which forms in and obstructs a blood vessel.

throw (1) To toss or fling through the air, as a cow to the ground in preparation for branding, the tie (q.v.), etc. (2) *see* THROW A RACE

throw a race Also known as throw or pull; a racing term; said of the jockey, to intentionally restrain a horse or use other means to prevent the horse from winning a race.

throw a shoe Said of a horse who loses a horseshoe by any means other than intentional removal.

throw his tongue *see* GIVE TONGUE

throw-in Also known as bowling; a polo term; the action of the umpire tossing the polo ball into play between the two teams from midfield.

throwing hobbles A set of leather straps attached to the pasterns and used to throw a horse to the ground.

throwing their tongues A hunting term; said of the hounds when they give tongue (q.v.).

thrown (1) Said of a rider bucked or tossed off the back of the horse; an unintentional dismount. (2) Said of the horse when intentionally cast to the ground by its handlers as for medical treatment, etc. (3) Said of a horseshoe which, for any reason other than intentional removal, becomes detached from the hoof.

thrown out A hunting term; said of a member of the field who becomes lost or falls behind when hunting.

throw off A hunting term; said of the huntsman (q.v.) when he takes the hounds (q.v.) from the meet to search for a fox (q.v.)

throw tongue *see* GIVE TONGUE

thrush Also known as frush (obs); a yeast infection of the frog resulting in degeneration of frog tissue; caused by standing in wet, dirty conditions for prolonged periods of time and failure to clean the hooves; most common in the hind feet; symptoms include a softening of the hoof horn and a black, thick, foul smelling discharge; if left untreated may result in lameness.

thrust A hunting term; said of a member of the field when he/she rides hard to the hounds (q.v.).

thruster A hunting term; a member of the field who rides too aggressively and close to the hounds (q.v.) and/or hunting staff (q.v.).

thumb a horse To make a horse buck by digging one's thumb deep into the horse's neck and running it along the neck muscles.

thumb of the Prophet *see* PROPHET'S THUMB

thumps *see* SYNCHRONOUS DIAPHRAGMATIC FLUTTER

thymus Also known as the thymus gland; a ductless gland located in the upper thoracic cavity near the throat.

thymus gland *see* THYMUS

thyroid Also known as the thyroid gland; the two-lobed endocrine gland located in the neck on either side of the larynx that controls the rate at which basic body functions proceed and release of the hormone thyroxin (q.v.).

thyroid gland *see* THYROID

thyroid stimulating hormone Also known by the acronym TSH, a hormone secreted by the pituitary gland; stimulates the thyroid gland to increase production of thyroxin (q.v.).

thyroxin Also spelled thyroxine; the hormone produced by the thyroid gland (q.v.) which regulates the metabolic rate of all cells.

thyroxine *see* THYROXIN

Tibetan A pony breed originating in the mountains of Tibet thought to have descended from Mongolian and Chinese ponies; related to the Bhutia (q.v.) and Spiti (q.v.) which it closely resembles; stands approximately 12 hands, may have a coat of any color although yellow dun (q.v.) is most common, has a straight profile, broad forehead, full forelock, mane and tail, small ears and eyes, a short, muscular neck, short back, and short, sturdy legs; used for riding, packing, and farm work.

tibia The inner and usually larger of the two bones of the hind limb between the knee and ankle.

tick (1) A jumping term; said of a horse who barely touches, but does not dislodge any portion of the jump. (2) An external, bloodsucking parasite belonging to the order *Acarina* and family *Ixodidae;* each species may have one or more favored feeding sites on the host, although in severe infestations other areas of the host body may be utilized; feed chiefly on the head, neck (including the mane), shoulders, ears, and tail; infestation can cause anemia, unthriftiness, and can result in the transmission of a large variety of diseases including equine encephalomyelitis, swamp fever (q.v.), and billary fever (q.v.).

ticket (1) A racing term; a bet (q.v.) placed on a horse, e.g., a combination pari-mutuel ticket. (2) Also known as betting ticket, slip, or card; a slip, usually of paper or cardboard, serving as evidence or token of the holder's title by reason of payment.

tick fever *see* EQUINE PIROPLASMOSIS

tick-tack A British racing term; hand signals by which tick-tack men (q.v.) communicate betting odds to the bookmakers.

tick-tack men A British racing term; those employed by the bookmakers who communicate betting odds, bets laid, and prices quoted by means of hand signals.

tidal-breathing flow-volume loop Also known by the acronym TBFV loop; a breath-by-breath measurement of the changing airflow, volumes, pressures, and frequencies occurring throughout the breath cycle, from inhale to exhale, breath after breath; is usually dumbbell shaped showing one airflow peak as the horse inhales and another as he exhales; in horses with heaves (q.v.) there is a peak in airflow, but only when the horse exhales.

tie *see* THE TIE

tie-back surgery *see* LARYNGOPLASTY

tied in at the knee Also known as tied-in knees; a conformation defect in which the flexor tendons appear to be too close to the cannon bone at a point just below the knee; inhibits free movement.

tied in below the knee Also known as short of bone; said of legs that are much narrower just below the knee than near the fetlock (q.v.); a conformation fault that indicates a horse is light of bone (q.v.).

tied-in knees *see* TIED IN AT THE KNEE

tied on A racing term; knotted and crossed reins; give the jockey a stronger hold.

tiedown *see* STANDING MARTINGALE

tiedown martingale *see* STANDING MARTIN-GALE

tie man One who regularly ties his lariat (q.v.) to the saddle horn.

tie off A roping term; to tie and secure the feet of a roped calf or steer with a piggin' string (q.v.).

tierce *see* TOTALIZATOR

tie stall A partitioned space about 6 x 12 feet (1.8–3.6 m), normally occurring in multiples, in which a horse is tied, in some cases using a log headcollar (q.v.), when not being used; allows limited movement, although fighting between the horses sharing a common wall may occur.

tie up (1) To restrain a horse with a halter and rope to a rail or post so he cannot move away. (2) *see* TYING-UP

tiger An antiquated British term; a tiny groom who rode behind a cabriolet (q.v.) standing on the platform; always immaculately dressed in a yellow and black horizontally striped waistcoat (denoting a member of the outside staff); it was from the tiger-colored waistcoat that the name derived.

tiger stripes *see* ZEBRA STRIPES

tight A racing term; said of a horse ready to race.

tightener (1) A racing term; a race intended to bring a horse to his peak physical fitness level, a level not attainable in morning workouts alone. (2) A leg brace.

tight on a cow A cutting term; said of a horse who controls a cow in tight confrontation.

Tilbury Also known as seven spring gig or Tilbury gig; a light, two-person, two-wheeled horse-drawn vehicle of the gig (q.v.) type developed by Hon. Fitzroy Stanhope in early 19th-century Britain, and built by the Mr. Tilbury for whom it was named; much heavier than the Stanhope gig (q.v.); hung on seven springs and two braces which made it cumbersome, but comfortable for travel over rough roads; had a spindle-backed driving seat, generally no luggage space, and was entered by means of bucket-shaped shaft steps.

Tilbury gig *see* TILBURY

Tilbury tug Also known as a French Tilbury tug; a stout, oval-shaped, metal reinforced leather loop buckled to each side of the short harness backband used to support and stabilize the shafts; principally used on four-wheeled horse-drawn vehicles.

tilt (1) A mounted knightly sport and military exercise practiced between 476 and 1450 AD and an exhibition commonly performed at 17th-century weddings; a mounted participant would strike, by means of a lance, a revolving figure, tree trunk, post, pile, or shield against which he would break his lance; if not struck properly, when used, the object struck could swing around and strike the tilter (q.v.). (2) The cloth covering of a cart or wagon.

tilter One who tilts (q.v.).

tilt the quintaine Said of a knight or sportsman who successfully broke his lance against a revolving figure, tree trunk, pile, shield, or post in quintaine (q.v.) exercises; performed from the 476 AD through the 17th century.

tilting head *see* TIPPING HEAD

tilting the head *see* TIPPING HEAD

timber (1) A racing term; a hurdle or other obstacle constructed of wood which is jumped. (2) Growing trees.

timber rider A racing term; a steeplechase jockey.

timber splitter A horse skilled in maneuvering his way through an area of burned timber.

timber topper A racing term; a horse who runs in jump races; most accurately, a horse who jumps over timber fences.

time allowed The period of time in which a competitor must complete a course (q.v.) or event to avoid time faults (q.v.).

time fault Also known as time penalty; a point handicap assessed for exceeding the time allowed (q.v.) to complete an event or course.

time keeper One who monitors the official game or event clock used to regulate the period of play or competition.

time limit: The period of time in which a competitor must complete a course (q.v.) or event to avoid elimination from the competition.

time line A line which marks the location of a timing beam projected by an electronic timer (q.v.) which starts and stops the time clock.

time out A polo term; a temporary cessation of action in a polo match (q.v.) called by an umpire (q.v.) when a foul is committed, an accident occurs, or at his own discretion or by a player due to broken tack or injury to himself or his horse; may not be called to replace a broken mallet or change horses.

time penalty *see* TIME FAULT.

Timor A pony breed indigenous to the island of Timor, Indonesia; the smallest of the Indonesian breeds standing 9 to 11 hands, usually has a black, bay, or brown coat, a relatively large and heavy head, short ears, flared nostrils, short neck, short back, and strong quarters; has good endurance, is surefooted, agile, strong, docile, and willing; used for riding, farm work, and light draft; has been exported to Australia where it contributed to the development of the Australian Pony (q.v.).

Timothy *see* TIMOTHY GRASS

Timothy grass Also known as Timothy; a perineal European coarse grass, *Phleum*

pratense, with dense cylindrical spikes or bristly spikelets widely grown for hay.

timothy hay A cut and dried coarse grass, *Phleum pratense*, with cylindrical spikes valuable as fodder; of average nutritional quality; preferred as a feed hay because it is generally free of dust and mold; highest in nutritional content, palatability, and quality in the pre-bloom stage; second and third cuttings tend to have the highest nutritional value with a digestible protein content of approximately 6.6 percent; the fiber content of all cuttings is just above 30 percent; frequently grown in a mixture with legumes such as alfalfa (q.v.) and clover (q.v.).

tipping head Also known as tilting head, tilting the head, or tipping the head; a dressage term; said of a horse whose head is held in a position to the left or right of the vertical.

tipping the head *see* TIPPING HEAD

tip (1) To give private or secret information. (2) Private or secret information, as in the anticipated success of a horse in a race or event. (3) *see* TIP SHOE. (4) To strike lightly and sharply; to tap. (5) To give a small present of money for some service. (6) The pointed, tapering, or rounded end or top of something long and slim, as a whip.

tip shoe Also known as tip or slipper; a horseshoe (q.v.) that only covers the bearing surface of the hoof from just in front of the quarters to the toe, or approximately 25 percent of the hoof circumference; provides no protection to the quarters or heels of the foot.

tipster A racing term; one who makes a business of providing betting information or tips about horses competing in races to bettors (q.v.).

tits (1) A 19th-century term; a pair of horses. (2) Slang; light and/or little horses.

tittup An antiquated term; said of a horse who moves with a jittery action, as if on his toes; to jig (q.v.).

toad eyes A British term; said of the eyes of a horse when prominent with mealy upper and lower lids; typical of the Exmoor Pony (q.v.).

tobiano Refers to a coat color pattern; a white base coat with large, asymmetrical patterns of colored, vertically arranged patches typically originating from the head, chest, flank, buttocks, and often including the tail; the color will cover one or both flanks; there is a sharp definition between the white and colored areas and the spots will be regular and distinct as ovals or round patterns that extend down over the neck giving an appearance of a shield; all four legs are generally white, at least below the hocks and knees; the head is usually conservatively patterned with patterns like those of a solid-colored horse – solid or with a blaze (q.v.), star (q.v.), or snip (q.v.); the pattern may range from little spotting to a predominantly white body and colored head; the eyes are generally not blue; results from a dominant gene and requires at least one tobiano parent; the most common Pinto Horse (q.v.) coloring in the United States.

tocopherol *see* VITAMIN E

toe angle *see* HOOF ANGLE

toe calk A calk (q.v.) affixed to the toe of the horseshoe.

toe clip A V-shaped extension of the horseshoe (q.v.) at the toe pressed into the hoof wall to hold the shoe onto the hoof in those situations or on those hoofs where nails are insufficient.

toe crack A crack in the hoof wall at the toe, starting at the bearing surface and extending to a variable distance up the hoof wall, or cracks originating at the coronary band (q.v.), and extending downward; may occur in either the front or hind feet.

toed in *see* PIGEON TOED

toe-flipping *see* FALSE EXTENSION

toe grab Also known as cleat; a toe calk that follows the contour of the toe of the horseshoe and is usually sharper than conventional calks; used on race horses to prevent slipping.

toe-in *see* PIGEON TOED

toeing knife A mallet-driven blade used to trim the hoof wall; now largely replaced by hoof nippers (q.v.).

toe-out Also known as splay-footed; when viewed from the front, the toes of the hoof point away from each other; generally a con-

genital condition; may cause the forelegs to swing in during movement as in winging (q.v.) and results in stress on the outside and inside of the fetlock and pastern joints respectively.

toe plate A horseshoe used on race horses having a cleat in front and is used to prevent slipping.

toe tapper A discouraged and outdated method of the rider tumbling a horse headfirst to perform a stunt as in the movie industry; so called because the toes of the horse's forefeet are tapped with screws between the horseshoe and hoof and to which are connected cables that run to a ring on a surcingle where the cables merge into a single cable attached to a wooden handle held by the rider; on the upstride of the horse, and on cue, the rider will pull the wooden handle vertically towards the sky thus pulling the horse's feet out from under him.

toe weight A metal weight attached by clips to the front feet of trotters and harness horses to improve stride by changing the balance in motion.

to fence *see* FENCE no. 3

to flog a dead horse *see* FLOG A DEAD HORSE

to have whip A harness racing term; a horse possessed of geat speed.

to lock the stable door after the horse is stolen *see* LOCK THE STABLE DOOR AFTER THE HORSE IS STOLEN

tølt The natural rack (q.v.) of the Icelandic horse (q.v.); a fast, four-beat, running walk (q.v.) in which the horse can escalate his speed from a stop to upwards of 35 mph (56 kmph).

Tonga An Indian two-wheeled, hooded vehicle originally pulled by two horses and subsequently by one.

tongue (1) The freely moving organ within the horse's mouth with the power to shape itself for different purposes including grazing and drinking. (2) *see* CRY no. 2

tongue-bar shoe A therapeutic horseshoe (q.v.); a combination of a heart bar (q.v.) and egg bar (q.v.) shoes; the egg bar, which connects the two heels of the shoe, is squared to give lateral support and the heels are bent down to raise heel angle without putting pressure on the heel wall or rear of the frog; the tongue is welded to the center of the bar to distribute weight over the front third of the frog; used in conjunction with a strong toe clip.

tongue loller A horse who evades bit action by putting his tongue over the top of the mouthpiece (q.v.).

tongue out Said of a horse who evades bit action by putting his tongue out the side of his mouth.

tongue over the bit Said of the horse who evades bit action and control by putting his tongue over the top of the bit rather than underneath.

tongue strap Also known as tongue tie; a leather or cloth band laid over the top of the tongue and connected under the chin by means of a buckle; prevents a race horse from swallowing his tongue during a race or other workout, or to prevent the tongue from sliding up over the bit.

tongue swallowing *see* SOFT PALATE DISEASE

tongue tie *see* TONGUE STRAP

tool A coaching term; to drive a horse-drawn vehicle.

tool budget A leather box attached to the fore-carriage of a horse-drawn vehicle in which tools are stored.

too low *see* ON THE FOREHAND

tooth One of the hard bodies or processes attached in a row to each jaw, serving for the prehension and mastication of food and as a weapon of defense and attack; composed chiefly of dentin surrounding a sensitive pulp and covered on the crown with enamel; of two types: deciduous teeth (q.v.) and permanent teeth (q.v.); tooth wear patterns may be used to determine, with some degreee of accuracy, horse age; tooth infections will generally drain through the nose; specific teeth include the caninine teeth (q.v.), incisors (q.v.), molars (q.v.), temporary teeth (q.v.), premolars (q.v.), and wolf teeth (q.v.).

tooth decay *see* CARIES

tooth rasp A long-handled file having separate, point-like teeth used to smooth off the rough edges on the molar teeth (q.v.) of the horse.

tooth rasping *see* FLOAT

tooth star *see* DENTAL STAR

top *see* CARRIAGE HOOD

top boot A tall, riding boot with a cuff of a different color than the leg; traditionally and, still formally, worn by members of a Hunt (q.v.); women's boots have a black patent leather cuff and a black leg, while men's have a brown or cordovan (q.v.) cuff and black boot leg; tops are earned and are a symbol of status in each Hunt with the conditions upon which tops are awarded varying from Hunt to Hunt.

top horse A racing term; the first horse listed in a race program.

top line (1) Also known as back line; the visual line created by the horse's back and croup. (2) On a pedigree (q.v.) chart, the breeding on the sire's side.

top of the ground A hunting term; said of the footing over which the hunters travel when it so firm that the horses' feet do not sink into it.

top pommel *see* HUNTING HEAD

top rein The cord bearing rein used on Hackneys (q.v.) in show; released from the hook on the pad when the horse comes to a standstill in the race lineup and which is refastened when the horse moves off.

top rider An accomplished rider; an "A" rider whether professional or amateur.

top weight *see* HIGH WEIGHT

Toric Also known as the Estonian Klepper, Double Klepper, or Torisky; an Estonian-bred warmblood of fairly recent origin; developed in the 19th century by crossing Arab (q.v.), Ardennais (q.v.), Hackney (q.v.), East Friesian (q.v.), Hanoverian (q.v.), Orlov (q.v.), Thoroughbred (q.v.) and the Trakehner (q.v.) with the Klepper (q.v.); a fast moving, active, light draft horse with a good temperament; stands 15 to 15.2 hands and may have a bay or chestnut coat; has quite a long neck, a short back, deep and wide chest, and a notably tough hoof; the name derived from the Toric Stud where breeding first began; well suited to draft and farm work.

Torisky *see* TORIC

torsion When one end of a body part is twisted in one direction, while the other end remains motionless, or twisted in the opposite direction; common in the intestine.

torsion colic Also known as twisted gut or twisted bowel; colic (q.v.) resulting when the digestive tract twists on itself, blocking passage of feed through the intestines; may be caused by falls, heavy feed following hard work, etc.; causes intense abdominal cramping.

torso *see* BODY no. 1

tostado Refers to point color; a Spanish term; brown points; sometimes used in conjunction with other color distinctions for greater color specificity, e.g., chestnut tostado.

total digestible nutrient system Also known by the acronym TDN; a method of measuring the energy value of feed by rating the different nutrient components of the feed according to digestibility; the evaluated feed is given a numerical value which indicates the percentage of the nutrients in the feed which are used by the horse; the sum of the contents of the digestible protein, digestible crude fiber, digestible nitrogen-free extract, and digestible ether extract (crude fat) times 2.25; the preferred method of determining energy value is now calories.

totalisator *see* TOTALIZATOR

totalizator Also known as a tote or tierce and spelled totalisator; a mechanical apparatus that automatically registers and totals each betting ticket as it is issued on a per race basis in pari-mutuel wagering (q.v.), keeps a running total of all money bet on each horse in the win, place (q.v.), and show (q.v.) pools, and calculates the betting odds on each horse; the betting odds and number of bets placed on each horse are openly displayed to the public on the totalizator board (q.v.).

totalizator board Also known as board, odd board, or tote board; an electronic board located in the infield upon which the up-to-the-minute betting odds for each horse, as

calculated by the totalizator (q.v.) on a per race basis, are displayed; may also show the amounts wagered in each mutuel pool and changes in equipment and jockeys.

total plasma protein Also known by the acronym TPP; a blood test performed to determine dehydration in the horse; levels of plasma protein increase with dehydration.

tote *see* TOTALIZATOR

tote board *see* TOTALIZATOR BOARD

touched in the wind Said of a horse slightly unsound in the wind (q.v.).

touched up fox *see* DOPED FOX

touch the horn A hunting term; to blow the hunt horn (q.v.).

tournament A series of games or athletic events in which teams, individuals, or horses compete against one another.

tout A racing term; one who obtains information on horses for betting purposes and peddles such information or tips and betting systems to the racegoer in advance of a race.

tovero Refers to a coat color pattern; a horse showing both overo (q.v.) and tobiano (q.v.) coat patterns.

towel An old coaching term; to flog a coach horse.

Town coach A heavy, elegantly appointed, horse-drawn vehicle driven from a box-seat covered with a fringed hammer cloth; seated four passengers vis-à-vis, and had a rear platform for two footmen; originally hung on cee springs, but later on elliptical and semi-elliptical side springs; drawn by a pair of matching coach horses, usually bays with black tails; is less formal than the state coach (q.v.).

toxaemia *see* TOXEMIA

toxemia Also spelled toxaemia; the presence of a toxin in the bloodstream; generally results from absorption of bacterial products formed at a localized source of infection.

toxicosis An abnormal or diseased condition produced by the action of a toxin or poison.

toxin An unstable organic poison produced in living or dead organisms or their products, e.g., venom.

to you A hunting term; a verbal warning from a rider to other members of the field to indicate the presence of a ditch on the near side of an upcoming fence.

TPP An acronym for total plasma protein (q.v.).

TRA The acronym for the Thoroughbred Racing Association (q.v.).

trace (1) A path or trail made by the passage of animals or people. (2) Either of two straps, chains, or lines of a harness by which the horse is attached to a vehicle to be drawn.

trace bearer *see* BEARING STRAP

trace carrier *see* BEARING STRAP

trace clip To remove the coat hair from a horse in a broad line from the shoulder, belly, haunches (historically, the area where the traces would go), and occasionally from under the neck leaving the legs, back, neck, and head unclipped; a common clip for harness horses.

trace element *see* TRACE MINERAL

trace heel The end of the trace (q.v.) closest to the horse-drawn vehicle.

trace horse The leader of a tandem (q.v.); any horse added to the existing equipage to assist in pulling a vehicle up an incline.

trace mineral Also known as trace element; a chemical element essential to the physiology of a horse in minute quantities.

trachea Also known as windpipe; the tube extending from the larynx to the bronchi which serves as the passage for conveying air to and from the lungs.

trachectomy *see* TRACHEOTOMY

tracheotomy Also known as trachectomy or tubing; to surgically incise the trachea (q.v.) and insert a breathing tube to enable a horse to breath in emergency situations where the trachea is obstructed or swollen.

track (1) Also known as racetrack – race-track, race track, racecourse, course, racing strip, or strip; a racing term; any specific area where horses run during training or racing; is generally grass or dirt footed, fenced, and maintained. (2) The beaten path or trail left by repeated passage of persons, animals, or vehicles. (3) A series of footprints or other marks left by a horse, fox, etc. (4) To leave tracks or footprints, as a fox.

track bandage *see* EXERCISE BANDAGE

track bet Also known as on course bet or on track bet; a racing term; any wager placed at the racetrack (q.v.).

track bias A racing term; a racing surface that favors a particular running style or position.

track condition A racing term; the nature of a racing surface, as in fast tract (q.v.), muddy track (q.v.), good track (q.v.), sloppy track (q.v.), frozen track (q.v.), hard track (q.v.), firm track (q.v.), soft track (q.v.), or heavy track (q.v.).

tracking A cutting term; said of a horse who follows the movements of a cow from behind.

tracking up A dressage term; said of a horse whose body is straight and the hind feet overlap the impressions of the forefeet in all gaits except the collected ones.

track master A racing term; one responsible for maintaining the condition of the racing strip (q.v.).

track sour Said of a horse having temporary vitamin B complex deficiency; commonly diagnosed in racehorses; symptoms include reduced performance, nervousness, weight loss, and shuffling of the feet.

traditional acupuncture *see* ACUPUNCTURE

Traekehner *see* TRAKEHNER

traffic jam *see* JAM

trail (1) To drag or let drag behind one, especially on the ground. (2) To make a mark (path, track, etc.,) as by treading down; the usual, repeated passage of men or animals.

trailer (1) To haul one or more horses. (2) Also known as box; any vehicle attached to, and drawn by, a car, truck, tractor, or van used to haul one or more horses; does not have an engine. (3) An extended outside heel (1/4 inch (6 mm) or more beyond the heel of the horse's foot) of a hind-hoof horseshoe commonly turned 45 degrees away from the center line of the hoof and the line of travel; used only on the hind legs.

trailing A cutting term; said of a horse in a working position who lags behind the movements of the cow.

trailing leg Also known as nonleading leg; the horse's foreleg which does not lead in the canter.

trail horse A horse trained, bred, or used for cross country riding either on or off trail.

trail ride To ride a horse outside of the manège or stable on a groomed or blazed path or track through the country.

trail up A racing term; said of a physically fit horse who loses its competitive edge.

trainer (1) Also known as a horse breaker, horse tamer, or horse trainer; one who teaches horses to move or perform in a predetermined manner. (2) One responsible for teaching another the art of horsemanship (q.v.).

training barn (1) Also known as barn; refers to a training operation located within a larger facility where all boarders and their horses are trained by a professional horse trainer (q.v.). (2) A boarding facility if one of the horses must be in training to board there.

training cavesson *see* LUNGEING CAVESSON

training gallop A racing term; to gallop (q.v.) a horse on stretches of turf or other track surfaces in preparation for running on the race course; the stretches may be of varying lengths.

training plate A very lightweight horseshoe, commonly made of steel, used on racehorses between races and on some young riding and show horses.

training roller Also known as a breaking roller; a girth (q.v.) or surcingle of leather or webbing with two pads separated by a space attached to the underside that fit on either side of the withers; the pads prevent pressure and rubbing on the withers; is adjustable on both sides and is fitted with rings to which a crupper (q.v.), side reins (q.v.), and bearing reins may be attached; used in the ground training of a horse.

training track A racing term; a racetrack used for exercising, rather than competing horses; may be located on the track grounds or offsite.

training yoke *see* RUNNING MARTINGALE

Trait du Nord Also known as the Ardennais du Nord; a horse breed originating in the northeastern France around the turn of the 20th century; descended from a cross of Ardennais (q.v.), Belgian Draft (q.v.) and Boulonnais (q.v.) blood; is heavily built, incredibly strong for its size, hardy, calm, stands 15.3 to 16.1 hands, and weighs 1,320 to 1,760 pounds (599–798 kg); the coat may be bay, roan, or red roan; has a large head set on a thick neck and a short-coupled, muscular body set on short legs; used for heavy draft and farm work; breed population is on the decline; the stud book was established in 1919.

Trakehner Also known as East Prussian horse and spelled Traekehner; a warmblood indigenous to that part of Prussia which is now Poland; developed at the stud of Trakehnen which was founded in Lithuania in 1732 by Frederick William I of Prussia to breed horses for military purposes and from which the name derived; breed development was particularly influenced in the 16th century by the native Schweiken infused with Oriental blood, followed by Arab blood in the early 19th century, and thereafter, Thoroughbred (q.v.) blood; made an excellent cavalry remount due to its tremendous stamina and was capable of light farm work; in 1945, when the Germans retreated from Poland, approximately 1,000 of the horses registered in the stud book were taken on a three-month trek to West Germany where the stud farms were reconstructed; Trakehners who remained in East Prussia became known as Masuren (q.v.), which was amalgamated with the Poznan to create the Wielkopolski (q.v.); stands 16 to 16.2 hands, may have a chestnut, bay, brown, or black or rarely gray coat, has pronounced withers, a well-proportioned head, long neck, slightly sloping croup, and deep chest; is intelligent, lively, and kind; used for riding and competition.

trandem Also known as a Manchester team; three horses driven abreast.

transfer dray *see* DRAY

transition Said of a horse; any change of pace or speed as from one gait or movement to another.

transition not defined A change from one pace to another in which there is no distinct difference between the speed or pace, e.g., medium to collected canter; said of a horse who drifts from one gait to another.

transition rough A change from one gait to another which is other than smooth, straight, and balanced as resulting from resistance to the hand.

transom A wood or iron transverse member used to secure the wheel plate or fifth wheel to the body of a four-wheeled, horse-drawn vehicle.

transom plate An iron reinforcement plate placed above and below the axle-tree bed on a four-wheeled, horse-drawn vehicle.

transtracheal aspirate Also known by the acronym TTA; a procedure to remove fluid from the lungs by inserting a needle into the windpipe through the skin, about halfway down the underside of the neck; moderately flexible, fine-gauge tubing is threaded through the needle and into the airway down towards the lungs, and the needle removed; finally a syringe is used to flush the airway with sterile saline solution, which dilutes and liquefies lung exudate for sampling.

trap Any two-wheeled, horse-drawn cart designed for country driving.

trapper Slang; a trotting harness horse.

trappings Ceremonial harness including the saddle, bridle, and all ornamental coverings.

trappy (1) Short and rapid action of the horse; a condition predisposed in horses with upright pasterns and straight shoulders. (2) Also known as trappy country; any rough country which has a number of blind or semi-blind jumps or where the jumps have difficult approaches and/or landings.

trappy country *see* TRAPPY no. 2

trauma A wound or bodily injury produced by violence or some kind of shock.

travel in straw Said of stablehands who travel in the vans with the horses during transport.

traveling boots *see* SHIPPING BOOTS

travers Also known as haunches in, quarters in, or head to the wall; a dressage movement performed on two tracks (q.v.); the horse's head, neck, and shoulders follow a straight track along the wall, while the loins and quarters are bent around the rider's inside leg and follow a track approximately 1 yard (91 cm) off of the wall at an angle of around 30 degrees; the horse's head is flexed in the direction of the movement.

traverse Also known as sidestep; a lateral, two-track movement of the horse without forward or backward motion.

travois Also spelled travoise or travoy; an A-shaped carrying frame consisting of two trailing poles serving as shafts bridged by woven twigs, small planks, or thongs for supporting a load; the apex rested on the back or hind quarters of a dog or horse; widely used by the North American Indians for conveying people and belongings.

travoise *see* TRAVOIS

travoy (1) *see* TRAVOIS. (2) A military stretcher used during World War I; attached on one end to a horse, mule, or pony, while the rear end was supported and steered by a medical orderly on foot.

tread Any wound to the coronet (q.v.) of a coach horse as caused by another horse.

treadmill A machine consisting of a wide belt which rotates around two moving cylinders upon which the horse is forced to walk, trot, and/or canter; the speed is adjustable up to 37 mph (60 kmph) and the incline adjustable up to 6 degrees; used by practitioners to conduct orthopedic, cardiovascular, and pulmonary workups on horses.

treats Also referred to as nibbles; any food item given to the horse that is not normally part of his regular ration such as apples, carrots, molasses, and sugar; are generally more flavorful than nutritional; may be used as a training aid.

treble *see* TRIPLE COMBINATION

tree *see* SADDLE TREE

trencher A square or circular flat piece of wood on which food, traditionally bread, was formerly served or cut; from the French trenchier meaning to cut.

trencher-fed A hunting term; said of hounds who live with and are fed by individual farmers and other Hunt supporters rather than kept in a hunt kennel (q.v.); from the French trenchier meaning to cut.

triactor *see* TRIFECTA

trial A racing term; a preparatory race or workout in which the horse is asked for speed; generally held near the time to of a more important race, e.g., the Derby Trial.

Tribus A three-passenger horse-drawn cab introduced in 1840; passengers entered from a door on the nearside rear of the vehicle and driven from a seat on the offside of the roof.

tri-color hound Refers to hound coat color; any hound with a mixed black, tan, and white coat.

trifecta Also known as triple or as triactor in Canada; a betting option in which the bettor (q.v.) selects the first, second, and third place horses in any order in a specific race; of two types: straight trifecta (q.v.) and boxed trifecta (q.v.).

trifecta box A betting option; a trifecta (q.v.) wager in which all possible combinations for a specific number of horses are used; the total number of combinations is calculated using the formula $x^3 - 3x^2 + 2x = y$ multiplied by the amount wagered on each combination (where x equals the total number of horses in the box).

Triga A Grecian chariot pulled by three horses harnessed abreast.

trim To free of extraneous or extra matter by or as if by cutting; the process of cleaning up a horse including, but not limited to, pulling the mane and tail and clipping the whiskers, feathers, bridle path, and ears.

trimmer One responsible for upholstering the interior of carriages and other horse-drawn vehicles with materials such as silk and lace.

trip (1) Said of a horse who stumbles in one or more strides. (2) A racing term; the course taken by a horse from the start to finish.

triple *see* TRIFECTA

triple bar Also known as spa; any single-element jumping obstacle consisting of three or more rails (q.v.) set up as a ramped slant with the highest pole at the backside of the jump and lowest in the front.

triple buckboard A horse-drawn vehicle of the buckboard (q.v.) type having three seats in a row.

triple combination Also known as a treble; any show or cross country jumping obstacle consisting of three consecutive elements (q.v.), with one or two strides between each element, numbered and judged as one; may include any type of fence or any combination of non-jumping strides between the elements.

triple crown A series of three important races.

Triple Crown Also known as the American Triple Crown; a program of three classic races for three-year-olds run in the United States since 1867; consists of the 1-1/4 mile (2 km) Kentucky Derby (q.v.), the 1 mile, 1-1/2 furlong (1.9 km) Preakness Stakes (q.v.), and the 1-1/2 mile (2.4 km) Belmont Stakes (q.v.); equivalent programs are run in England (the 2,000 Guineas, Epsom Derby, and St. Leger Stakes) and also in Canada (the Queen's Plate, Prince of Wales Stakes, and Breeders' Stakes); always written capitalized in written reference.

triple oxer A jumping obstacle; a triple combination (q.v.) consisting of three oxers (q.v.) in a line, each separated by one to two strides.

tripler (1) A horse able to perform the Dutch triple (q.v.). (2) A Gaucho term; a horse with a fast rolling gait between a trot and canter.

Tri-Super A racing term; a betting option in which the bettor (q.v.) selects the top three finishing horses in a race; if the wager wins, the bettor is paid a price from the wagering pool and is allowed to make a second trifecta (q.v.)

bet, free, on the race that comprises the second half of the bet; in the second half, the bettor must select the top four finishers.

tristeza *see* EQUINE PIROPLASMOSIS

triticale A grain; a cross between wheat (q.v.) and rye (q.v.) developed in 1969 to combine the quality and uniformity of wheat with the hardiness and disease resistance of rye; the name derived from a contraction of triticum (wheat) and secale (rye); has a high yield and rich protein content; uncommonly fed to horses.

trocha The diagonal trot of the Paso Fino horse (q.v.); an unacceptable gait which most young horses grow out of; the Paso Fino should always travel with a lateral gait.

Troika Also known as Russian style; a method of harnessing three, specially trained horses abreast in which the two outside horses are bent to the outside by tight side reins and canter or gallop, while the center horse, held in an arched douga (q.v.), works at a fast trot; a Russian word meaning two or three.

Troika Curricle A large vehicle of the curricle (q.v.) type drawn by three horses abreast in the Russian style (q.v.); the center horse was put to, between shafts, under a douga (q.v.) while the outside horses were harnessed to outriggers, with swingle trees, and put to outside shafts.

Trojan Horse In classical mythology, a large, hollow horse made of wood used by the Greeks to win the Trojan War; in a plan devised by Odysseus, the Greeks hid soldiers inside the horse, left it outside the gates of Troy, and set sail, apparently for Greece; instead, they anchored their ships just beyond sight of Troy; a man they left behind was instructed to say to the Trojans that the goddess Athena would be pleased if they would bring the horse inside the city and honor it, which they did; that night, the Greek army returned to Troy and were let inside the gates of the walled city by the men who emerged from within the horse; as a result, the Greeks won the war.

tropilla A South American term; six to 12 horses owned by a gaucho (q.v.); only the male horses are ridden and a usually piebald (q.v.) bell mare (q.v.) is used to hold the herd together.

trot Also known as pure trot or in Western terms, jog; a natural two-beat gait in which the diagonal legs, such as the left fore and right hind, leave the ground simultaneously followed by a moment of suspension where the feet do not touch the ground and then the simultaneous strike of right fore and left hind; this sequence remains unchanged in the collected trot (q.v.), working trot (q.v.), ordinary, and extended trot (q.v.) tempos and only the length of stride and duration of suspension change; the speed of the ordinary trot is approximately 220 yards (201 m) per minute, although the gait will vary considerably from breed to breed.

trot level Said of a sound (q.v.) horse who moves at the trot without defect.

trotter (1) Any horse bred and gaited to trot (q.v.), especially in harness racing (q.v.). (2) *see* PUFFER

trotting light *see* POST

trotting vanner *see* VANNER

trouble line An American racing term; the words included in the eastern edition of the Daily Racing Form which appraise a horse's past-performance efforts or excuse his loss.

TRTA The acronym for The Ride and Tie Association (q.v.).

truck (1) A two- or four-wheeled, horse-drawn, heavy freight vehicle popular in the 18th century; headed by a length of canvas stretched over hoops and drawn by teams of two or more; from the Latin *trochus* meaning hoop; (2) A class of mechanized vehicle of various sizes and designs used to transport goods or livestock; may have a separate trailer unit attached.

true canter Also known as galop juste; said of a cantering horse who leads with his foreleg on the side to which he is turning.

true gallop *see* GALLOP

true Kimblewick *see* KIMBLEWICK

true knee *see* STIFLE

true lethal Any disease or condition genetically transmitted to the foal which results in death of the foal shortly before or after birth.

trueness of gait The lack of medial or lateral deviation from the line of travel as seen in the horse's limbs.

true splint A sprain or tear of the interosseous ligament generally in the forelegs of young horses resulting in an enlargement of the splint bones; the enlargement is most frequently seen 2 1/3–2 3/4 inches (6–7 cm) below the carpus (q.v.) on the medial side.

true skin *see* CORIUM

true to type Said of a horse who shows characteristics typical of his breed, e.g., conformation, size, temperament, aptitude, and coloring.

trunk (1) *see* BOOT no. 4. (2) The body apart from the head and limbs.

trying board Any fence or padded partition used to separate a mare from the teaser (q.v.) or stallion (q.v.) to determine if she is ready to be mated or to encourage her to come into heat (q.v.).

Tschenburti A Russian equestrian sport similar to polo (q.v.) in which two teams of six riders attempt to score by placing the ball into the opponents' goal using sticks similar to long tennis raquets.

Tschiffely, Aimé Felix (1895–1954) The naturalized Argentinean who rode his Criollo (q.v.) horses Mancha (q.v.) and Gato (q.v.) approximately 10,000 miles (16,000 km) from Buenos Aires, Argentina to Washington DC, USA in a period of 2 1/2 years.

TTA The acronym for transtracheal aspirate (q.v.).

TTouch *see* TELLINGTON TOUCH

TTEAM The acronym for Tellington-Jones Equine Awareness Method (q.v.).

TTEAM training *see* TELLINGTON-JONES EQUINE AWARENESS METHOD.

Tubal Cain A farrier; the first shoeing professional of whom written record exists as noted in Genesis, chapter 4, verse 22.

Tub Car *see* GOVERNESS CART

Tub Cart *see* GOVERNESS CART

tubed horse A horse having had a tracheotomy (q.v.) and in whose trachea (q.v.) a breathing tube still exists.

tucked up Also known as sucked up or ganted up; said of a horse whose loins are drawn up tightly behind the ribs as due to illness, overwork, lack of water or bulk in the diet, and/or underfeeding rather than conformation.

tuck jump A vaulting term; a leap performed by a vaulter (q.v.) on the back of a horse; the vaulter, from a standing position on the horse's back, jumps into the air, bends his knees and brings them into his chest while his body remains upright and the arms straight with the fingers pointing towards the ground; he returns to a standing position on the horse's back.

tufted whorl A whorl (q.v.); a change in direction of the flow of the hair in which hairs converge from different directions and pile into a tuft.

tufter A stag hunting term; an old hound (q.v.) selected by the Harbourer (q.v.) and brought to a hunt to start the chase of the stag (q.v.).

tug A stout, oval-shaped, leather loop connected to the harness (q.v.) backband through which the shafts pass when a horse is hitched to a vehicle; prevents the shafts from moving up and down when the vehicle is moving; types include the Tilbury tug (q.v.) and open tug (q.v.).

tumbleweed *see* HORSE DEVIL

Tumbrel (1) Also known as Tumbril; a traditional farm cart used throughout Western Europe. (2) Also known as Tumbril; a low-slung ammunition cart used by many European armies throughout the 18th century; drawn by a single horse in shafts.

Tumbril *see* TUMBREL

tune *see* TUNE-UP

tune-up Also known as tune; to polish the performance of the horse by conducting gymnastics or exercises prior to a competition.

turf (1) A racing term; the sport or business of horse racing. (2) A racing term; the upper stratus of soil bound by grass and plant roots into a thick mat. (3) see TURF COURSE

turf course Also known as turf; a racing term; a grass track or course used for horse racing.

turfman One interested in or devoted to the sport of horse racing.

turgid Swollen, distended beyond its natural state.

Turinsky A lesser-known native horse breed indigenous to the former Soviet Union.

Turk Also known as a Turkish Horse; a horse breed indigenous to Turkey; a characteristic oriental type, having predominantly Persian and Arab (q.v.) blood.

turkey bit see MAMELUKE BIT

turkey curb see MAMELUKE BIT

Turkmen see TURKOMAN

Turkmene see TURKOMAN

Turkoman (1) Also known as Turkmen or Turkmene; an Iranian-bred warmblood indigenous to the region of Turkmenistan where it was bred for centuries; survived by the Akhal-Teké (q.v.) and the Iomud (q.v.); horses bred in the Turkmenistan region which have exceptional speed and endurance and used for flat racing. (2) Any horse bred in the Turkmenistan region of Iran.

turn To change direction.

turnback help see TURNBACK RIDER

turnback rider Also known as turnback help or turnback; a cutting term; a mounted rider in a cutting horse competition positioned between the performing cutter, time line, and judge(s) responsible for turning the cow being worked back toward the cutter; work in pairs; considered herd help (q.v.).

turnback see TURNBACK RIDER

turn down(s) A horseshoe (q.v.) used on race horses; the heels of the rear shoes are turned down 3/4 to 1 inch (19-25 mm) to provide better traction on an off-track; illegal in many jurisdictions.

turn on center Also known as turn on the center, pirouette on the center, or pirouette sur le centre; a dressage term; a pirouette (q.v.) in which the horse fails to keep his hindquarters on the spot, swinging them against the outside leg instead of keeping them still.

turn on the center see TURN ON CENTER

turn on the forehand A movement in which the horse pivots around his inside foreleg, cutting an outer concentric circle with the other legs; the pivot leg marks time in the rhythm of the pace.

turn on the haunches Also known as turn on the quarters; a movement in which the horse turns around his inner hind leg, which remains on the spot or describes a small circle, cutting a larger outer concentric circle with the other legs.

turn on the quarters see TURN ON THE HAUNCHES

turn-out (1) To turn a horse out in a paddock (q.v.) to exercise. (2) The general appearance of either a horse or rider.

turned Also known as turned to the horse; said of a mare whose last mating will not produce a foal.

turned out Said of a horse kept at pasture (q.v.).

turned to the horse see TURNED

Turn-Row see TENNESSEE WALKING HORSE

Turn-Row Horse see TENNESSEE WALKING HORSE

turn tail A cutting term; a horse who quit a working cow; results in a 5-point penalty action in competition.

turtle boot Also known as turtle back boot; the fore-boot (q.v.) located beneath the box seat of some horse-drawn coaches and carriages; detached from the main body work.

tush see CANINE TEETH

TWHBEA The acronym for the Tennessee Walking Horse Breeders' Association of America (q.v.).

twin One of two young brought forth at birth usually resulting from the fertilization of two eggs; the young will not be identical.

twinning The conception of twins (q.v.).

Twin Trifecta A racing term; a betting option in which the bettor (q.v.) places a trifecta (q.v.) wager on one race; if that wager wins, the bettor is paid a winning price from the pool (q.v.) and is allowed to make a second trifecta bet, free, on a second race.

twist a horse To break (q.v.) a horse.

twisted bowel *see* TORSION COLIC

twisted gut *see* TORSION COLIC

twisted snaffle A variably sized snaffle bit (q.v.) in which the mouthpiece has corrugations along the entire length; the tightness of the twist may vary – the thinner the mouthpiece and the greater the number of twists, the more the severe the bit.

twitch A device used to distract the attention of, or restrain, a horse for a specific purpose such as clipping, covering, shoeing, performing minor operations, or administering medication; of many varieties, the most common of which consists of a loop of rope or other material, fastened to a wooden, plastic, or metal handle, which is then passed over the upper lip or the base of the ear of the horse, the latter of which is illegal in Britain; the handle is turned until the rope is sufficiently tight around the lip or ear to restrain the horse; releases endorphins and concentrates the horse's attention on the discomfort, causing it to submit and stand still.

two-day event A three-phase eventing (q.v.) competition consisting of dressage, show jumping, and speed and endurance phases, the later including steeplechase, roads and tracks, and cross country conducted by the same rider and horse over a period of two days; dressage and show jumping phases are generally conducted on the first day while the speed and endurance phase takes place on the second.

two hole position Also known as a win hole; a harness racing term; the position immediately behind the leading horse.

two sweats *see* BOTH SIDES OF THE ROAD

Two Thousand Guineas A 1 mile (1.6 km) horse race for three-year old fillies run annually since 1809 in Great Britain.

two time Any pace marked by two hoof beats per stride.

two track Also known as a pass, sidestep, two track movement, or in French as appuyer; any movement where the horse's hind legs travel on a track parallel to, but different than that of the forelegs; in dressage, such movements include shoulder in (q.v.), shoulder out (q.v.), half pass (q.v.), renvers (q.v.), travers (q.v.), pirouettes (q.v.), and haunches out (q.v.).

two tracking Said of a horse performing any two track (q.v.) movement.

two track movement *see* TWO TRACK

two/two A method of holding the reins of a double bridle (q.v.) in which two reins are held in each hand, the curb rein around the little finger and the snaffle through the ring finger.

two-wheeler (1) *see* HANSOM CAB. (2) Any two-wheeled horse-drawn vehicle.

two-year old Also known by the acronym T-Y-O or two-year-old horse; a horse having reached the second, but not the third anniversary of its birth.

two-year-old horse *see* TWO YEAR- OLD

tying up *see* TYING-UP SYNDROME

tying-up disease *see* TYING-UP SYNDROME

tying-up syndrome Also known as tying up, tying-up disease, cording up, set fast, or incorrectly as exertion myopathy (q.v.); a mild form of azoturia (q.v.) with some similar signs, but not to the same degree; a disease affecting the skeletal muscles following prolonged, exhaustive physical activity, appearing to occur primarily as a result of muscle energy depletion; the urine may be dark-colored varying from a red wine to a dark coffee color because of the myoglobin released by the breakdown of affected muscle tissue; symptoms include profuse sweating, rapid pulse, a stiff, stilted gait, particularly of the hind quarters, muscle trembling, cramping, spasms of varying degrees, and a disinclination to move; survivors sometimes suffer from lameness and prolonged, or occasionally permanent, muscle atrophy; symptoms are similar to those seen in exercise related myopathy (q.v.), although the metabolic changes responsible may be quite different; more common in mares than geldings.

T-Y-O The acronym for a two-year-old horse (q.v.).

type (1) *see* BREED TYPE. (2) A horse who serves a particular purpose, but who does not belong to a specific breed, e.g., hunter, cart horse, cob, hack.

U

Ukrainian Riding Horse A horse breed developed in the former Soviet Union in the late 1940s by crossing Trakehner (q.v.), Hanoverian (q.v.), and Thoroughbred (q.v.) stallions with local mares or with Nonius (q.v.), Furioso (q.v.) and Gidran Arabian (q.v.) mares imported from Hungary; breed selection continued using only Thoroughbred and Hanoverian stallions; stands approximately 15.1 to 16.1 hands, usually has a chestnut, bay, or black coat, has a long neck, slightly-hollowed back, deep chest, and long croup; colts are broken at 18 months at which time they undergo aptitude testing consisting of flat racing, cross-country, show jumping, or dressage, with top colts in each category going on to serve as breeding stock in state-owned studs; used for competition, light draft, and farm work.

ulcerative lymphangitis Also known as equine ulcerative lymphangitis; a slightly contagious skin condition which develops in the lower pectoral and ventral abdominal regions characterized by diffuse or local swelling, pitting edema, and lameness of the adjacent limb; abscesses have a thick, fibrous capsule and may enlarge up to 8 inches (20 cm) before rupturing; the incidence is highest in warm climates.

ultrasound Also known as sonogram or ultrasonography; a technique in which high frequency sound waves, above the range of the human ear, produced by the conversion of high-frequency electrical energy waves to sound waves by a piezoelectric crystal in the head of a machine are directed into the tissue to break down unwanted tissues, promote healing by stimulating circulation (therapeutic ultrasound [q.v.]), and as a diagnostic aid (diagnostic ultrasound [q.v.]).

ultrasonography *see* ULTRASOUND

umbilical hernia The protrusion of the intestine through the incompletly closed umbilical opening shortly after birth; reasonably common in foals and is easily correctable; if the condition appears in horses older than 12 months of age, complications may set in.

umbrella basket *see* STICK BASKET

umpire One of two mounted officials who enforces the rules of play in polo (q.v.), polocrosse (q.v.), or other mounted sports; there is one positioned on either end of the field during the game with a referee on the sidelines; may consult with each other and impose penalties.

unbacked A racing term; a horse competing in a horse race upon whom no bets have been placed.

unbalanced Said of the horse when his weight and the weight of the rider are not distributed equally over the foot of each leg; the rider's seat, posture, and/or leg position may prevent the horse from performing his natural gaits freely and correctly.

uncertain fencer A horse who jumps a fence tentatively; one who balks (q.v.), half refuses a jump and then jumps from a standstill or slow trot.

under behind *see* STANDING UNDER BEHIND

under-carriage *see* CARRIAGE no. 1

underlay A racing term; a horse running at odds shorter than seem warranted by his past performances.

under pad A saddle pad (q.v.) positioned between the back pad and the vaulting roller (q.v.); is slightly wider than the roller and long enough to go completely around the circumference of the horse; used to distribute the weight of the roller and vaulter (q.v.) evenly on either side of the spine and prevents the formation of girth galls (q.v.).

underpinning The legs and feet of a horse.

under reach A gait defect; said of the horse when the toe of the front horseshoe strikes the toe of the hind shoe at the trot.

underrun heels Also known as run-under heels or underslung heels; said of heels of the hoof when the angle is greater than that of the toe; largely due to poor trimming.

under saddle Said of a horse in tack including the saddle, bridle, martingale, etc.

undershot Said of the horse's jaw when the lower jaw protrudes beyond the upper.

under-shot jaw Also known as bull-dog bite, hog mouth, sow mouth, or prognathism; a congenital malformation of the mouth in which the lower jaw protrudes beyond the upper; as a result, the incisors do not meet properly and are therefore not worn down by use and impair the ability of the horse to graze or eat; frequent floating of the incisors is necessary to prevent the intruding teeth from lacerating the soft tissue of the mouth.

underslung heels *see* UNDERRUN HEELS

under starter's orders A racing term; said of the jockeys and their mounts when loaded in the starting gate and ready to race.

under wraps A racing term; said of a horse running under restraint to prevent him from pulling away from the competition by too wide a margin.

unentered A hunting term; a hound who has not completed his first cub hunting (q.v.) season.

unharness To remove harness (q.v.) from a horse.

unhooked A cutting term; said of a cutting horse who loses the attention of the cow being worked.

unhorsed *see* UNSEATED

unhulled peanut meal One of two types of peanut meal (q.v.) in which the peanut shells are left on the nuts during processing; contains about 60 percent less protein and energy than hulled peanut meal (q.v.).

unicorn Also known as a spike team or spike and incorrectly as a pick-axe team (q.v.); a hitch of three horses consisting of two wheelers (q.v.) and one leader; evolved to enable a team to continue its journey when one of the horses was unable to continue travel or to hitch a fresh horse to the front of a tired pair for additional pulling power; commonly used by breweries and other trade operations.

unilateral Pertaining to or affecting only one side.

united Said of the action of the horse, gener-

ally the canter, when properly coordinated and executed.

United States Combined Training Association Also known by the acronym USCTA; an organization founded in the United States in 1959 to educate horse owners and riders in those principles and practices of horsemanship embodied in the term combined training (q.v.), and founded on the essential relationship between classical dressage and cross-country riding; sponsors and/or facilitates organization of horse trials, combined tests, two-day events, and three-day events.

United States Equestrian Team Also known by the acronym USET; an organization founded in the United States to support teams representing the United States in international show jumping, eventing, dressage, and driving competitions.

United States Polo Association Originally known as The Polo Association; an organization founded in New York in 1890 to coordinate polo matches, standardize rules, and establish handicaps for the game in the United States; at the time of its founding, seven clubs were accepted into the association.

United States Team Penning Association Also known by the acronym USTPA; one of three organizations in the United States devoted to the sport of team penning (q.v.); publishes Team Penning USA.

unkennel Also known as find; a hunting term; to dislodge a fox from his covert and to get it moving.

unlevel A dressage term; said of a horse who takes uneven strides by placing more weight on one fore foot than the other, one leg coming further forward than the other, and/or one hock lifting higher than the other; gives the appearance of slight lameness; may be due to the horse being bridle lame (q.v.), having uneven physical development, or unbalanced training from side to side.

Unmol A rare pony bred indigenous to Northern Punjab, India; is strong, elegant, and shapely having a compact body and long mane.

unnerve *see* NERVE no. 2

un pas un saut A movement performed in

three stages: a short gallop, courbette (q.v.), and a capriole (q.v.).

unpatterned leopard Refers to a coat color pattern; a distinct type of leopard spotting in which the spots on the coat tend to be more round and do not appear to flow from the flank as on a patterned leopard (q.v.).

unraced A racing term; a horse who has not yet competed in his first race.

unsaddle (1) To remove the saddle from a horse. (2) To be unseated from the saddle, as in the rider.

unsaddled *see* UNSEATED

unseated Also known as unsaddled or unhorsed; said of a rider who has been, for any reason, dislodged from the saddle, but not necessarily from the horse.

unsettled *see* FRESH no. 2

unshod *see* BAREFOOT

unskid A coaching term; to remove the skid (q.v.) from the wheel of a horse-drawn vehicle.

unsound Said of a horse who is not free from illness, disease, physical or conformation defect, injury, or blemish that affects his future performance or ability to work.

unsoundness A condition of the horse affecting his ability to perform; may result from injury, accident, disease, conformation defect, unnatural stress caused by use for which he is not trained, and/or poor feed.

unsteady halt Said of a horse who comes to a halt, but does not remain motionless; the horse may fidget or shift his legs or head, or move off the line.

unsteady head Said of a horse lacking steadiness of the head and/or head carriage; may result from loss of balance of either the horse or rider or failure of the horse to accept the bit (q.v.).

untried (1) A racing term; a horse not previously raced or tested for speed. (2) A stallion who has not been previously bred.

unwind (1) A racing term; to gradually withdraw a horse from intense training. (2) Said of

a horse who starts to buck. (3) To make relaxed or less tense.

upper aids Both hands of the rider when employed to communicate pace, speed, and direction to the horse by acting, resisting, or yielding on the bit through the reins.

upper Benjamin *see* BENJAMIN

upper-cheek snaffle A half-cheek snaffle bit (q.v.); consists of a straight or jointed mouthpiece fitted at either end with fixed rings to which straight- or spoon-shaped (wider and slightly curved toward the horse's jaw at the top) arms attached above the mouthpiece; the arms prevent the bit from running through the mouth of a horse if he runs sideways or refuses to turn; the straight-arm upper-cheek snaffle bit acts on the sides of the mouth, the lips, and the corners of the mouth, while the spoon-cheek provides a small amount of leverage and places more pressure on the jaw; is accepted in the dressage ring.

upright (1) *see* STANDARD. (2) *see* VERTICAL

upright shoulder *see* STRAIGHT SHOULDER

upset price The minimum acceptable price which opens bidding on a horse offered for sale at an auction.

up to their bits A coaching term; said of the horses pulling a horse-drawn vehicle when they move freely forward.

up-wind In the direction from which the wind is blowing.

urea A colorless, soluble basic nitrogenous compound $CO(NH_2)_2$, the chief solid component of urine and an end product of protein composition produced in the liver; synthesized from carbon and ammonia and is used in animal rations and fertilizer; excess urea or nitrogen containing compounds in the blood may result in azotemia (q.v.).

urethra A tubular canal through which urine is discharged from the bladder; in males also serves as the sperm duct.

urine The liquid, deep yellow to brown color secretion from the kidneys, conducted to the bladder by the ureters, and discharged through the urethra (q.v.); a full-grown horse will average 5.5 quarts (6.2 liters) of urine per day.

urine test Chemical analysis of a horse's urine to detect if illegal substances were administered to alter his performance or mask an injury.

Urocyon cineroargenteus *see* GRAY FOX

used up Said of an exhausted horse.

USCTA The acronym for the United States Combined Training Association (q.v.).

USPA The acronym for the United States Polo Association (q.v.).

USTPA The acronym for the United States Team Penning Association (q.v.).

uterine body That portion of the uterus (q.v.) which lies between the uterine horns and the cervix.

uterine horn That portion of the uterus (q.v.) which lies between the Fallopian tube (q.v.) and the uterine body (q.v.).

uterine prolapse Inversion of the uterus (q.v.) resulting in partial or complete expulsion from the vulva.

uterus The hollow, muscular organ in the female of a species consisting of the cervix, uterine body (q.v.), and uterine horns (q.v.), serving as a protective place for the ovum (q.v.) while it develops into an embryo (q.v.) or fetus.

uticaria A rash triggered by a histamine (q.v.).

utility cart A two-wheeled, horse-drawn, skeleton cart used for breaking young horses; usually low-slung with the seat positioned near road level; is difficult to overturn.

utility saddle *see* ALL PURPOSE SADDLE

Uxeter kimblewick One of five types of kimblewick (q.v.) bit; a pelham (q.v.) bit requiring one instead of two reins (q.v.), having a straight, low-ported mouthpiece (q.v.), and short cheeks (q.v.) with flat, double-slotted D rings running the full length, and a square eye on the upper end of the cheeks; the reins may be attached at the mouthpiece or lower down on the cheeks; when the rider's hands are held in a standard position, the bit acts as a snaffle (q.v.), but when the hands are lowered, or when used in conjunction with a martingale (q.v.), the resulting action is similar to that of a curb (q.v.).

V

vaccine A preparation of matter from a killed micro-organism, living attenuated organisms administered to produce or artificially increase immunity to a particular disease.

valet A racing term; one responsible for a jockey's clothing and tack, to carry the saddle and equipment to the paddock (q.v.), help the trainer saddle the horse, and meet the rider after the race to carry the saddle and equipment back to the jockeys' room (q.v.).

valeting room A hunting term; a room used by the whippers-in for the cleaning and drying of hunting clothes and boots following a hunt.

van (1) To transport a horse in a van. (2) A high-sided, two- or four-wheeled, generally headed, horse-drawn vehicle used by tradesmen and business men for the delivery and collection of goods; drawn by a single horse in shafts or, less frequently, by a pair in pole gear (q.v.); frequently pulled by a vanner (q.v.).

vanity brand *see* RANCH BRAND

vanner Also known as a parcel carter or trotting vanner; any horse used to pull a tradesman's van (q.v.); generally a cross between a light horse such as a Thoroughbred (q.v.) and a draft horse.

vaquero *see* BUCKAROO

varmint Hunting slang; a fox.

varnish marks Refers to coat color pattern; a concentration of dark hairs occurring on the bony prominences; common to the Appaloosa (q.v.), specifically the roan Appaloosa.

varnish roan Also known as marble; one of six symmetrical coat color patterns of the Appaloosa (q.v.) recognized by the Appaloosa Horse Club (q.v.); a pattern of white that may vary from a roan (red or blue) blanket to white hairs scattered over the entire body of the horse including the head with colored hairs concentrated over the bony prominences; a progressive pattern (q.v.), with horses being born sorrel.

vasculogenic shock: Circulatory collapse characterized by a progressively diminishing circulating blood volume relative to the capacity of the vascular system, leading to acute failure of vital organs; blood volume is normal, but blood is pooled in dilated peripheral vessels; may be caused by endotoxins or trauma.

vault *see* VAULTING

vaulter One who vaults (q.v.).

vaulting Also known in French as voltige; an ancient competitive equine sport consisting of gymnastics performed on the back of a horse circling at a trot or canter on the end of a 25 to 30 foot (7.6–9 m) lunge line (q.v.); first included as an Olympic sport at the 1920 Games where individual teams were formed from cavalry regiments, was brought to the United States in the 1960s, and was recognized by the FEI (q.v.) as an international equestrian sport in 1985.

vaulting barrel Also known as barrel or metal horse; 1-1/2, 55-gallon (250 liter) drums welded together to which four legs and handles are attached, which stands 4 feet (1.2 m) high and is covered with padding; used by vaulters (q.v.) to develop a sense of balance, learn movements, and practice; spares the horse from overuse and wear and tear.

vaulting pad *see* UNDER PAD

vaulting roller Also known as a vaulting surcingle; a wide leather band which fits around the girth of the horse behind the shoulder and buckles on both sides; has two leather padded handles built onto rigid steel plates on either side of the withers and two, optional, Cossack hung straps (stirrups); the position of the handles may vary both in size and angle to the roller.

vaulting surcingle *see* VAULTING ROLLER

vault on A compulsory exercise in a vaulting (q.v.) competition; the vaulter (q.v.), from a position facing the horse's haunches places his left hand on the vaulting roller (q.v.), swings his right leg high above the horse, rotates his hips to a position parallel to the horse's back at a height above the level of the horse's head, and lowers himself onto the back of the horse behind the vaulting roller (q.v.) facing forward.

veal Also known as vealer; the flesh of the calf as used for food.

vealer *see* VEAL

vealers Any English riding boot made with veal hide, the leather of which is extremely fine and soft.

VEE The acronym for Venezuelan Equine Encephalomyelitis (q.v.).

vehicle skid *see* DRAG SHOE

velvet The skin-like sheath covering the developing bone of the antler of species including members of the deer family consisting of the dermis (q.v.) and the hair-covered epidermis; velvet covered antlers develop beginning in April; as the bone of the antler hardens, and preparatory to the mating season (sometime around July or August), the animal rubs the velvet off the antlers onto trees; this rubbing polishes and stains the bone; while the velvet is visible on the antlers, the stag is said to be in velvet (q.v.).

venery The act or practice of hunting from horseback using hounds; became common to the English language in the early 14th century; an important aspect of social life for the European feudal elite; derived from venari meaning to hunt.

Venezuelan Equine Encephalomyelitis Also known as sleeping sickness or by the acronym VEE; a mosquito-borne viral disease affecting horses, mules, donkeys, zebras, and in some cases humans; causes inflammation of the white matter of the brain and spinal cord; infected horses may exhibit high fever, aggression, excitability, and stiffness, which is followed by head pressing, incoordination, inability to swallow, convulsions, coma, and death; manifests itself within two to five days of contact; fatal in about 90 percent of cases; surviving victims generally have irreversible brain damage; a vaccine is available.

venous bleeding The loss of blood from veins varying from minimal to profuse, depending on the size of the blood vessels involved; the blood is less red than from an artery.

ventral Toward the belly.

ventral hernia Protrusion of the intestine through the weakened abdominal wall; may be caused by kicks from other horses, falls, or, in mares, because of the weight of having carried many foals, etc.

ventricle stripping *see* LARYNGEAL VENTRICULOTOMY

venule Any of the small vessels that collect blood from the capillaries to join and form veins.

verminous aneurysm Thickening of the arteries or veins of the horse caused by irritation of some types of immature strongyles (q.v.) which are able to migrate within the arteries of the horse and within the walls of the arteries and intestines; thickening may reduce blood flow through the arteries and veins and cannot be removed once it occurs; most commonly affects the blood supply to the intestines, resulting in colic; reduced blood supply to the hind legs may result in thrombosis (q.v.), while restricted blood flow from the heart will result in death.

vertebra Any of the bones or segments composing the spinal column; typically of a more or less cylindrical body and an arch with various processes, forming a foramen through which the spinal column passes.

vertebrae More than one vertebra (q.v.).

vertebral Of or pertaining to the vertebra (q.v.).

vertebral column Also known as the spine, backbone, or spinal column; the series of small bones or vertebrae (q.v.) forming the axis of the skeleton and protecting the spinal cord.

vertical (1) Also known as upright or vertical jump; jumping term; any show or cross country jumping obstacle consisting of a fence built vertical to the ground, with all parts placed one above the other, the width of which may vary; has no spead; include, but are not limited to, gates, planks, stiles, walls, straight posts, and rails; requires the horse to make a steep arc in his effort to jump. (2) Said of the horse's head; perpendicular to the plane of the horizon; upright; a horse may be in front of the vertical (q.v.) or behind the vertical (q.v.).

vertical jump *see* VERTICAL no. 1

vesicant *see* BLISTER no. 2

vesicle A small blister (q.v.).

vesicular stomatitis A contagious viral disease resulting in an inflammation, usually in the form of blisters, of the mouth, tongue, teats, coronary band (q.v.), and occasionally, other parts of the body; occurs epidemically in temperate and warmer regions between late spring and early fall; thought to be spread by insect vectors and the movement of animals; the route of infection is unknown, but may be through the skin or respiratory system; affected horses may stop drinking and develop mild lameness; in severe cases may lead to laminitis (q.v.); recovery is usually complete within about two weeks.

vestigial lower canines *see* CANINE TEETH

vet *see* VETERINARIAN

vet clean Said of a horse who, when inspected by a veterinarian, is found to be sound (q.v.) and free from contagious disease, structural degeneration, injury or other disorder or condition.

vetch Any of the various, usually climbing, leguminous plants of the genus *Vicia*, allied to the bean, some of which are cultivated for fodder for cattle and rarely horses.

vet check *see* VETERINARY INSPECTION

veterinarian Also known as horse doctor, vet, veterinary surgeon, or veterinary medical doctor; one who practices the prevention, diagnosis, medical and surgical treatment, and general study of animals; a practitioner of veterinary medicine (q.v.).

veterinarianitis Slang; excessive use of a hoof knife (q.v.) by a veterinarian.

veterinary Of or pertaining to the medical or surgical treatment of cattle, horses, and other animals.

veterinary certificate A certificate of soundness which documents the veterinarian's evaluation of a horse's physical condition.

veterinary examination *see* VETERINARY INSPECTION

veterinary inspection Also known as a vet check, soundness examination, or veterinary examination; to evaluate the physical condition and/or soundness of a horse identifying illness, disease, physical or conformation defect, injury, or blemish that may affect the horse's present or future performance or ability to work; generally performed on a horse offered for sale or trade and compulsory in endurance riding and eventing.

veterinary medical doctor Also known by the acronym VMD; a veterinarian (q.v.).

veterinary medicine The branch or division of medical science concerned with the prevention, diagnosis, treatment, and general study of animal diseases.

veterinary surgeon *see* VETERINARIAN

vet's list A racing term; a list of ill or injured horses declared ineligible to run by the track veterinarian.

Vettura A usually four-wheeled, horse-drawn, Italian cab or hired carriage; was headed and drawn by a single horse in shafts.

Viatka A pony breed indigenous to the former Soviet Union where it is bred primarily in the Viatka and Obva river basins; descended from the Klepper (q.v.) and Konik (q.v.); stands 13 to 14 hands, may have a bay, gray, roan, mouse dun, palomino, or dun coat (ponies with dun and palomino coats will also have an eel strip [q.v.]), zebra markings (q.v.) on the legs, and a full, black mane, forelock and tail; has pronounced jaws, flared nostrils, a rather snub profile, a muscular, long neck, long back, wide and deep chest, and solid legs; is sturdy, lively, energetic and quiet; the action of the trot is more vertical and forward and is particularly well suited to travel on snow-covered terrain; a good all-around pony used to draw troikas (q.v.) and perform light farm work; is an easy keeper; breeding is government controlled.

vice Any specific unpleasant or atypical habit, practice, and/or condition a horse develops and exhibits, as from boredom, mimicry, or improper handling; include biting (q.v.), balking (q.v.), bolting (q.v.), bucking (q.v.), cribbing (q.v.), halter pulling (q.v.), wood chewing (q.v.), kicking (q.v.), striking (q.v.), weaving (q.v.), rearing (q.v.), savaging (q.v.), and napping (q.v.).

Viceroy A horse-drawn vehicle; a very light-weight, cut-under, elegant, four-wheeled, air-tired, single-horse vehicle of the spider phaeton (q.v.) type designed and built by Mills & Sons; used for some heavy harness classes, and especially for showing Hackney (q.v.), Shetlands (q.v.), and harness show ponies.

Victoria A low, semi-open, horse-drawn carriage with a rearward half hood seating two forward-facing passengers side-by-side; hung on four elliptical side springs, but often having double suspension with rearward cee springs; the English version of a Victorian pleasure carriage; popular in the late 19th century and named for Queen Victoria in 1869; frequently used for semi-formal or park driving; driven from a box-seat (q.v.) to a single horse in shafts or, less often, to a pair in pole gear (q.v.).

video endoscope A diagnostic instrument consisting of a flexible tube containing light-conducting fiber bundles which reflect an image into an eyepiece and a small camera at the tip of the instrument, inserted through a body passage; enables a veterinarian (q.v.) to view and film the interior of a body cavity.

view A hunting term; to see a fox.

viewed A hunting term; said of a fox when seen.

viewed away A hunting term; said of a fox seen leaving a covert (q.v.).

view halloa *see* VIEW HALLOO

view halloo Also known as halloo and spelled view halloa; a hunting term; an utterance by the huntsman (q.v.) when the fox is viewed.

viral abortion Expulsion of the fetus before fully developed as due to viral infection.

viral arteritis *see* EQUINE VIRAL ARTERITIS

vis-à-vis (1) Face-to-face; said of seating arrangements in some horse-drawn vehicles in which the occupants sat facing each other on opposite seats. (2) A narrow passenger or pleasure carriage popular in the late 18th century large enough for two passengers facing each other; eventually replaced by the town or state chariot (q.v.).

visiting fox A hunting term; a dog fox who has left his home territory in search of a vixen (q.v.).

vital force The dynamic energy of an organism which is stimulated by the homeopathic remedy (q.v.).

vitamin Also spelled vitamine; one of several organic compounds occurring in minute amounts in natural foods and necessary for the proper metabolism of the horse; of two groups: fat-soluble vitamins (q.v.) consisting of vitamin A (q.v.), vitamin D (q.v.), vitamin E (q.v.), and vitamin K (q.v.) and water-soluble vitamins (q.v.) consisting of thiamin (q.v.), riboflavin (q.v.), niacin (q.v.), pyridoxine (B_6), pantothenic acid (q.v.), biotin (q.v.), folic acid (q.v.), vitamin B_{12} (q.v.), and vitamin C (q.v.).

vitamin A A fat-soluble, aliphatic alcohol, $C_{20}H_{29}OH$, derived from carotene in carrots and other vegetables such as good quality hay required for healthy skin, hair, and hooves, proper eye function, reproduction and lactation; the exact daily requirement for the horse is undetermined, although it has been approximated at 12,500 IU per day for the mature horse weighing about 1,000 pounds (454 kg); supplementation is necessary for pregnant mares and horses in heavy training or under stress; deficiency can cause infertility, fragile bones, night blindness (q.v.), loss of appetite, reduced resistance to infection, respiratory illnesses, elevated spinal fluid pressure, convulsions, rough coat, poor hoof growth, and scaly hooves; overdose is uncommon, but may cause bone fragility; as much as a six-month's supply may be stored in the liver; first discovered in 1913.

vitamin B_1 *see* THIAMIN

vitamin B_2 *see* RIBOFLAVIN

vitamin B_6 *see* PYRIDOXINE

vitamin B_{12} Also known as cobalamin or cyanocobalamin; a complex, cobalt containing compound essential to normal blood formation, neural function, and growth; sufficient levels are produced in the cecum and large intestine to meet daily requirements; is not stored in the cells and all excess is excreted in the urine; deficiency can cause anemia, weight loss, reduced performance, and poor coat hair.

vitamin B complex A group of ten water-soluble vitamins consisting of thiamin (q.v.), niacin (q.v.), riboflavin (q.v.), pyridoxine (q.v.), folacin (q.v.), biotin (q.v.), choline (q.v.), inositol (q.v.), pantothenic acid (q.v.), and vitamin B_{12} (q.v.) which were previously thought to be members of the same group; are present as co-enzymes in virtually all metabolic processes occurring in the horse necessary for the utilization of proteins, carbohydrates, and fats; although daily dietary requirements have not been established, it appears sufficient amounts are synthesized in the intestines to prevent deficiency; supplementation is not harmful, and may be helpful in horses with poor appetites, slow growth patterns, in competition, or late gestation; temporary deficiency is known as track sour (q.v.); are sensitive to heat and strong light.

vitamin C Also known as ascorbic acid; a water-soluble vitamin (q.v.) required for production of certain essential amino acids and building of intracellular material; synthesized in the liver of the horse and other tissues from glucose in sufficient amounts to meet the dietary requirements; found in most growing plants; supplementation is thought to improve reproductive performance in both mares and stallions, to decrease the incidence of eptistaxis and respiratory diseases, and to calm stressed horses; excess destroyed in the digestive tract.

vitamin D A fat-soluble vitamin (q.v.) required for the formation of calcium-binding protein, which aids in the absorption, transportation, and metabolism of calcium and phosphorus; the exact daily dietary requirement of the mature horse is undetermined although requirements will generally be met by grazing or exercising the horse regularly in sunlight and feeding it sun-cured hay; hay may not supply sufficient amounts to horses for which exposure to sunlight is limited; excess is stored in the liver; toxicity may occur and is characterized by weakness, loss of body weight, calcification of the blood vessels, heart, lungs, and other soft tissues, and bone abnormalities such as enlargement of the head and jaw; deficiency can result in poorly mineralized bones (rickets), swollen joints, stiffness of gait, and reduced serum calcium and phosphorus levels.

vitamine *see* VITAMIN

vitamin E Also known as tocopherol; the tocopherols collectively; a fat-soluble vitamin (q.v.) associated with muscle development,

oxygen transportation in the blood stream, proper development of red blood cells, and fertility and works in conjunction with selenium (q.v.) to prevent nutritional muscular dystrophy; if the levels are sufficient, then vitamin A is used more efficiently and less of the latter is required; deficiency can cause white muscle disease, anemia, infertility, myositis, muscular dystrophy in foals, and may be a factor in azoturia; supplementation is shown to improve breeding performance and speed and stamina in performance horses, particularly race horses; is quickly oxidized by air and is therefore lost from feeds during storage.

vitamin H *see* BIOTIN

vitamin K A fat-soluble vitamin (q.v.) synthesized by the microorganisms of the cecum and colon in sufficient quantities to meet the minimum daily dietary requirement of the mature horse and occurring in certain green vegetables, etc. promotes blood clotting and is required for the formation of prothrombin by the liver; deficiency is rare in horses, but may cause internal hemorrhage.

vitiligo A skin disorder characterized by the loss of pigmentation of the hair or skin due to disease; results in white skin patches and, in some cases, if hair growth returns, white hair.

vixen A female fox.

Vladimir Heavy Draft A heavy draft breed developed in the second half of the 19th century in the former state of Vladimir, Soviet Union from which the name derived; descended from crossings of heavy draft breeds including the Ardennais (q.v.), Suffolk Punch (q.v.), Cleveland Bay (q.v.), Clydesdale (q.v.) and Shire (q.v.); in the 1930s a policy of no interbreeding was invoked and introduction of all non-breed blood was eliminated; registered as a breed in 1946 under its present name; selection of breed stock is strictly controlled by means of rigorous practical trials; stands 15.1 to 16.1 hands and may have a chestnut, bay, brown, or black coat; white markings are common; has an average head, but heavy jaw line, arched neck, high and long withers, short back, deep chest, and short, powerful, well-feathered legs; is energetic, vigorous and willing; used for heavy draft and farm work.

VMD The acronym for veterinary medical doctor (q.v.).

vocal folds Membranes in the larynx (q.v.) attached to the arytenoid cartilages (q.v.) which when vibrated, produce vocalization.

voice *see* CRY no. 2

voice box *see* LARYNX

void Also known as a void bet; a racing term; any bet declared off (q.v.) in which the money bet is returned to the bettors (q.v.).

volar *see* PALMAR

volte A High School (q.v.) movement in which the horse scribes a 6 meter circle on one or two tracks (q.v.) with complete bending from poll to dock; when performed correctly, the horse will circumscribe the circle vertically, rather than leaning in; of several varieties including half volte (q.v.), renversvolte (q.v.), half volte and change (q.v.), double volte (q.v.), and square volte (q.v.).

voltige *see* VAULTING

voluntary muscle Any nonstriated muscle, such as those controlled by will and which operate in such voluntary movements as kicking and walking; attached to the bones by tendons and contract on stimulation to produce bodily motion.

voluntary withdrawal Said of a rider who makes a unilateral decision not to continue participation in a competitive event and to leave the competition area; will usually nod the head or tip the hat in the direction of the judge(s) to indicate withdrawal as due to a problem with the horse, failure to remember, or negotiate the course, accumulation of too many faults, injury, etc.

vomit To eject the contents of the stomach through the mouth; almost impossible for a horse.

von Achenbach, Benno *see* BENNO VON ACHENBACH

von Osten, William A Russian psychologist who developed a theory of equine intelligence in 1990 using a group of stallions known collectively as the Elberfeld Horses (q.v.); he purported to have trained one of the horses, a Russian stallion named Kluge Hans (q.v.), to calculate by pawing the ground with his hoof, read, and differentiate colors, up to the general standard of knowledge of a 14-year-old-child; von Osten's studies gained enormous publicity, but in 1904, the German psychologist Oskar Pfungst demonstrated that the stallion answered to unconscious signs from von Osten.

Vulpes fulva *see* RED FOX

vulpecide To kill foxes (q.v.) by some means other than with hounds (q.v.).

W

wager *see* BET

waggon *see* WAGON no. 1

waggoner *see* WAGONER

waggonette *see* WAGONETTE

wagon (1) Also known in early English as wain and spelled waggon; a four-wheeled, medium-heavy, horse-drawn vehicle originally designed without brakes, suspension, or any type of driving seat; had semi-open or ladder sides and a pivoting fore-carriage connected to the hind-carriage by a reach pole or under-perch; later types had box-shaped bodies, hand brakes, and sprung driving seats; derived from the German or Dutch wagen, meaning wheeled vehicle. (2) Any lightly built, four-wheeled show vehicle.

wagoner Also spelled waggoner; one who drives a wagon.

wagonette Also spelled waggonette; a four-wheeled passenger vehicle drawn by a single horse in shafts or a pair in pole gear (q.v.) first constructed in the 1840s; usually open, entered through the rear via a small door and step iron, fitted with three interior, inward-facing seats, a lever brake which acted on both rear wheels, and a fairly low driving seat; widely used throughout Britain and North America throughout the second half of the 19th century; hung on sideways-elliptical springs in the front and sideways semi-elliptical springs in the rear.

Wagonette Break A large wagonette (q.v.), having a high box seat and, commonly, a canopy top on fixed standards; seated eight passengers and drawn by a pair of horses in pole gear (q.v.).

Wagonette Omnibus A wagonette (q.v.) with a raised coach- or carriage-type driving seat elevated well above the passenger level, generally drawn by a four-in-hand team (q.v.).

Wagonette Phaeton A small, light wagonette (q.v.) having a double driving seat.

Wagonette Trap A four-wheeled American phaeton (q.v.) drawn by a single horse in shafts and having a shifting rear seat.

wagon-lock *see* DRAG-SHOE

wagon train A group or train of wagons (q.v.) traveling together for a common purpose as for transporting people and supplies.

wain (1) *see* WAGON. (2) Any two-wheeled, horse-drawn farm dray or float used in harvesting; frequently spindle-sided and drawn by a single horse in shafts.

wainwright A wagon maker.

waist That narrowest point of the seat of a saddle.

wait on your horse A cutting term; said of a rider who waits for his horse to react to a cow.

Waler Also known as an Australian Waler; a type rather than a breed; predominantly Thoroughbred with some Arab (q.v.) and pony blood; the foundation stock for the Australian Stock Horse (q.v.); the name derived from its place of origin in New South Wales, when in the early days of settlement waler was a name given to all newly settled areas of Australia.

walk (1) Also known as ordinary walk or working walk; a natural, flat-footed, four-beat gait, executed in four-time in which each diagonal pair of feet is lifted alternately off the ground and in which each foot strikes the ground separately and independently in sequence – near fore, off hind, off fore, and near hind without a moment of suspension; the sequence of steps remains unchanged in the ordinary, walk (q.v.), extended walk (q.v.), and collected walk (q.v.); the average speed is approximately 4 mph (6.4 kmph). (2) Also known as at walk or out to walk; a hunting term; the time when hound puppies between the ages of two and seven months of age are sent, usually in couples, to boarding facilities and farms to learn their names and to be trained and socialized.

Walker *see* TENNESSEE WALKING HORSE

Walking Horse *see* TENNESSEE WALKING HORSE

Walking Horse bit A curb bit (q.v.) having shanks, usually S-shaped, approximately 7-9 inches (18-23 cm) long.

Walking Horse class Any of a number of competitions held for the Tennessee Walking Horse (q.v.) in the United States.

walking out A hunting term; said of hounds (q.v.) when exercised by a huntsman on foot.

walk on a free rein Said of the horse allowed to walk freely with the reins completely loose and unrestricted by the rider's hands.

walk on a loose rein Said of the horse allowed to walk with the reins long enough to allow slack and retain bit contact, which permits the horse to drop his head.

walkover A racing term; a race in which all horses but one have been scratched; the one remaining horse wins the race and collects the purse by walking or galloping, rather than running, the distance; a rare occurrence.

walk ring A racing term; an oval enclosure located near the racetrack (q.v.) where horses are walked and riders mount before the start of the post parade (q.v.).

walk the course To walk on foot the jumping or cross country course as set by the course designer, to evaluate the footing and obstacles, determine distance between the jumps, and plan the track between them prior to riding in the competition; neither the rider nor horse may practice on a course prior to actual competition.

walk-up start A racing term; a start of a horse race conducted without a starting gate (q.v.); the horses walk toward the starting line and begin running at the starter's command.

wall (1) An upright show jumping obstacle made of hollow wooden blocks painted and stacked to look like bricks or stone. (2) A cross country obstacle constructed of brick or stone. (3) see HOOF WALL

wall eye Also know as glass eye, smoky eye, watch eye, china eye, blue eye, fish eye, or crockery eye; the eye of the horse lacking iris pigmentation, either partial or complete; the eye has a white or blue- or pinkish-white color; is not indicative of blindness.

wall of the hoof see HOOF WALL

wallop (1) American slang; to strike hard. (2) A quick, rolling, movement; a gallop (q.v.).

wanderer see BARKER

wandering (1) Deviation of the horse from the straight line or circumference of a circle which he is supposed to be executing. (2) see WALK ABOUT DISEASE

wap-John An antiquated coachman's term of contempt; a gentleman's coach (q.v.).

warble (1) A small, hard tumor or swelling on a horse's back produced by galling (q.v.) from the saddle. (2) A tumor or small swelling found under the skin on an animal's back, caused by the larvae of a warble fly (q.v.).

warble fly Any of the various flies of the families *Oestridae* and *Hypodermatidae*, the larvae of which cause subdermal warbles (q.v.) in the horse and other animals; lays its eggs on the lower extremities of the horse, which when hatched, migrate beneath the skin towards the subdermal tissue of the back where they secrete an enzyme to make a breathing hole through the skin; within four to six weeks the larvae emerge through the holes and drop to the ground.

warbles The plural of warble (q.v.).

war bonnet paint Refers to a coat color pattern; the specific arrangement of colored areas on a predominantly white horse in which both ears and/or eyes, the poll, and most of the neck have color, while the body shows little color; some American Indian tribes thought horses so colored were imbued with supernatural powers; it was further believed that the rider of such a horse could not be injured in battle.

Warde, John (b.1752) Also known as The Father of Foxhunting; born in 1752 in Britain, he pioneered the modern style of fast foxhunting (q.v.) and invented the telegraph springs (q.v.).

'ware A hunting term; said by the huntsman to the field to advise or caution, e.g., 'ware hound, 'ware hole, 'ware wire.

war horse A horse used in war; a charger.

warmblood Also known as halfblood; in general terms, a cross between coldblood (q.v.) and hotblood (q.v.) breeds.

warmblooded said of a warmblood (q.v.)

warm out of it Also known as work out of it or work sound; said of a horse who does not move freely and/or soundly until his muscles have warmed up as with exercise.

warm up Any process of gradual activity performed to prepare the horse for strenuous activity or competition.

warrantable An English term; a deer five years or older.

war shield A coat color pattern; pigmented patches on the chest, flanks, and base of the tail on a white body.

wart A small, dry, hard, nonmalignant lesion of the skin.

washed out Said of a horse suffering from systemic and physical exhaustion resulting from heavy use or stress beyond his condition level; such a horse will be electrolyte and fluid deplete.

washy (1) A racing term; said of a horse who breaks into a heavy sweat prior to the race. (2) Said of a horse who is washed out.

waste energy The usable power or energy lost in the urine and other nitrogenous wastes, in the feces, the bacterial fermentation process in the intestines, and in body heat lost through energy used in consuming and digesting feed.

watch eye *see* WALL EYE

water (1) To take a horse to, or provide it with, water to drink. (2) *see* WATER JUMP. (3) The liquid which in a more or less impure state constitutes rain, oceans, lakes, and rivers, and which in a pure state is transparent, odorless, tasteless liquid; a compound of oxygen and hydrogen freezing at 32° F(0° C) and boiling at 212°F (100° C). (4) A hunting term; a ditch or stream having no fence, but containing water.

water bag *see* AMNIONIC SAC

water brush (1) A grooming tool made of bristles set into a handle used to wash the coat,

mane, and tail of the horse. (2) *see* WATER BUSH

water bush Also known as water brush; a small hedge or row of bushes positioned on the takeoff side of a water jump (q.v.) over which a horse jumps; the height does not exceed 2 feet 6 inches (76 cm); considered part of the jumping obstacle.

water founder A founder (q.v.) condition; inflammation of the sensitive laminae (q.v.) of the hoof caused by too-rapid an intake of copious amounts of water, particularly cold water, following strenuous exercise.

water jump Also known as water; any show or cross country jumping obstacle consisting of a shallow, water-filled ditch at least 6 to 12 inches (15-30 cm) deep and approximately 16 feet (5 m) wide by 14 feet (4.25 m) in spread; always preceded by a water bush (q.v.) and may or may not include a fence in front of, or over the water; used to test jumping ability and bravery.

water line The inner, unpigmented, white-colored hoof wall which is sometimes mistaken for the white line (q.v.).

water out A racing term; to water a horse while he cools down following exercise.

water scraper *see* SCRAPER

water soluble vitamin Any vitamin having the property of dissolving in water; is not stored in the body tissues and must be ingested or manufactured in the body to meet the minimum daily requirements; excess amounts are secreted in the urine.

wattle A hunting term; a hurdle or jumping obstacle.

wax The buildup of dried colostrum (q.v.) on the teats of a pregnant mare ready to foal.

waxing The slow leakage and drying of colostrum (q.v.) from the teats of a pregnant mare prior to foaling; occurs between 48 and two hours of foaling.

way of going The way in which a horse moves.

WBC The acronym for white blood cell (q.v.).

WCF The acronym for the Worshipful Company of Farriers (q.v.).

WCTPA The acronym for the World Champion Team Penning Association (q.v.).

wean To accustom a foal to do without the mare's milk as food; can occur at any time from a foal age of three to ten months.

weanling A foal separated from his dam and accustomed to do without her milk as food until his first birthday, regardless of when it was actually weaned.

weanling colt A male foal accustomed to taking nourishment otherwise than by nursing from the mare.

weanling filly A female foal accustomed to taking nourishment otherwise than by nursing from the mare.

wear itself well Also known as carry both ends; said of a horse who moves with his head and tail carried high.

Weatherby An English family who maintained and first published the Stud Book (q.v.) for the English Thoroughbred (q.v.) for the Jockey Club (q.v.).

Weatherby's *see* STUD BOOK

weaving A vice; the rhythmic swaying of the horse from side to side in which the horse shifts his weight from one foot to the other while nodding or swinging his head and neck back and forth; usually results from boredom, is most common in stall-bound horses, and is generally corrected when the horse is turned out to pasture.

weaver A horse who weaves.

web (1) The area between the left and right sides of a horseshoe (q.v.). (2) The width of the barstock (q.v.) from which a horseshoe is made.

webfoot *see* MUDDER

web martingale *see* BIB MARTINGALE

wedge A piece of horseshoe-shaped leather, plastic, or rubber thick at the heels and tapering to the toes placed between the horseshoe and ground-surface of the hoof to elevate the

heel of the hoof and thus change the hoof angle (q.v.).

wedge-heeled shoe *see* WEDGE SHOE

wedge pad A saddle pad, the thickness of which gradually increases towards the rear-portion of the pad; used to level the saddle on the back of the horse; available in a variety of thicknesses.

wedge shoe A horseshoe which graduates in thickness from a thin toe to a thicker heel; elevates the heel of the hoof and thus changes the hoof angle (q.v.).

wedging *see* BEANING

weed (1) *see* STOCK UP. (2) A small, underdeveloped horse generally lacking stamina and quality.

weedon lane *see* JUMPING CHUTE

weedy Said of a long-legged, unimpressive horse.

weigh in A racing term; to measure the weight of the rider, saddle, and associated gear prior to a race or competition; the starting weight of the rider and gear should be equal to ending weight; required to ensure that the horse has carried the correct weight during the performance.

weighing room A racing term; the place on a racecourse where the jockeys (q.v.) are weighed in (q.v.).

weigh out A racing term; to weigh the rider, saddle, and associated gear upon completion of a race or competition; the ending weight of the rider and gear should be equal to beginning weight; required to ensure that the horse has carried the correct weight during the performance.

weight (1) The amount of heaviness of the horse as measured on a scale or approximated from the heart girth (q.v.). (2) The extra poundage a horse carries; the average horse can carry loads or riders equal to 25 to 30 percent of his weight, with lateral-gaited horses such as the Tennessee Walking Horse (q.v.) often tolerating heavier loads because they keep at least two legs on the ground during each of their gaits and are able to more evenly support the weight. (3) *see* LEAD no. 3

weight aid The rider's body weight when employed to communicate pace, speed, and direction to the horse, as by shifting the position of the weight in the saddle.

weight allowance A racing term; a reduction in the amount of weight carried by an apprentice jockey (q.v.) or other jockey due to inexperience or lack of success in riding winners or carried by a mare or filly when racing against colts and geldings.

weight cloth *see* LEAD PAD

weight for age Also known by the acronym WFA; a racing term; a race condition in which the weight a horse carries depends on his age and is determined according to a scale developed by The Jockey Club (q.v.); the spread of weight carried by horses of different ages depends on the time of year and the distance run, with younger horses carrying less weight than older horses.

weight-for-age race A racing term; any race that is neither a handicap race (q.v.) nor a selling race in which participating horses carry scale weight (q.v.) or weight assigned arbitrarily according to age, distance, and month of the year.

well let down (1) Said of the hocks of the horse when long, low, and dropping straight to the ground. (2) Said of the body of the horse when cylindrical in shape from the ribs through the flanks; the opposite of tucked-up (q.v.).

well-ribbed up *see* RIBBED UP

well-sprung Also known as well-sprung ribs; said of the ribs of the horse when the front ribs are flat and the back ribs are long and well rounded/arched allowing ample room for expansion of the heart and lungs.

well-sprung ribs *see* WELL SPRUNG

well to the ground *see* KNEES AND HOCKS TO THE GROUND

Welsh *see* WELSH MOUNTAIN PONY

Welsh Cart Horse An ancient pony breed indigenous to Wales where it evolved around the 12th century; was moderately sized and powerful.

Welsh Cob Also known as a Section D pony or generically as a native pony (q.v.); an ancient pony breed native to Wales, developed in the early 11th century by crossing Welsh Mountain ponies (q.v.) with Spanish, Barb-type horses to produce the Powys Cob (q.v.) and the Welsh Cart Horse (q.v.), which in the 18th and 19th centuries were put to Norfolk Roadsters (q.v.) and Yorkshire Coach Horses to create the present breed; has splendid action, a dished face, strong shoulder, compact body, deep powerful back, and slight, silky feathering (q.v.); stands 14 to 15.2 hands and is the strongest and largest of the Welsh breeds; all coat colors are permitted except piebald (q.v.) and skewbald (q.v.); historically used as a carriage horse, but now also used for competitive driving and riding including, hunting, jumping, eventing, and trekking; famed for its trotting ability; previously shown with both a hogged mane (q.v.) and docked tail (q.v.), now only the hogged mane is legal.

Welsh Mountain *see* WELSH MOUNTAIN PONY

Welsh Mountain pony Also known as a Welsh, Welsh Mountain, Section A pony (q.v.) or generically as a native pony (q.v.); the smallest of the four purebred pony and cob breeds native to Wales; descended from Arab (q.v.), Andalusian (q.v.), and Thoroughbred (q.v.) stock crossed with native mares; originally used in the underground to haul coal, now used for both riding and harness; stands up to 12 hands generally has a gray coat, although brown, chestnut, and palominos do occur with piebald (q.v.) and skewbald (q.v.) not permitted; has a compact body with great girth depth, powerful loins and hind legs, a dished face, wide and alert eyes, strong hock joints engaged well under the body, and exceptionally hard hooves; is an easy keeper (q.v.), has an easy and elegant flowing action, and is sure-footed; is spirited, intelligent, and possesses good endurance.

Welsh pony Also known as Merlin due to the influence of a small Thoroughbred (q.v.) named Merlin, Section B pony (q.v.), or generically as a native pony (q.v.); one of four ponies and cobs native to Wales; derived from the Welsh Mountain pony (q.v.), upgraded with Hackney (q.v.), and small Thoroughbred blood; the coat may be of any solid color, but not piebald (q.v.) or skewbald (q.v.); the second smallest of the Welsh breeds standing 12 to 13.2 hands; characteristics are similar to those of the Welsh Mountain pony (q.v.), but the action is lower to the ground with less, yet notably straight, knee action; has good girth depth, a full mane and tail, long, well-proportioned limbs, and strong quarters and hocks; is hardy, quiet, and energetic; historically used for shepherding, now used primarily for riding and harness.

Welsh Pony and Cob Society An organization established in Great Britain in 1901 to encourage the breeding of and maintain registries for Welsh cobs and ponies; the stud book, established in 1902, has four sections: Section A – Welsh Mountain Pony (q.v.) standing under 12 hands, Section B – Welsh Pony standing 12 to 13.2 hands, Section C – Welsh Pony of Cob Type standing 13.2 to 14 hands, and Section D – Welsh Cob standing 14 to 15.1 hands.

Welsh Pony of Cob Type Also known as a Section C pony or farm pony; a pony breed indigenous to Wales descended from the Welsh Mountain (q.v.) mares put to smaller Norfolk Trotters (q.v.) and Hackneys (q.v.); a smaller version of the Welsh Cob (q.v.); neared extinction in 1949, although the numbers are now on the incline; the mane and tail are silky with a small amount of heel feather (q.v.); has good girth depth, powerful quarters, a laid-back shoulder, straight profile, long neck, slightly pronounced withers, short back, deep chest, and relatively short legs, originally used for shepherding and general farm work is now popular for light draft and riding, particularly as a children's or small adult hunter; the coat may be of any solid color.

welter weights A racing term; 28 pounds (13 kg) over the official scale of weights carried by horses competing in a race; used to test the weight-bearing ability of entrants.

western A novel, movie, or play of the western United States, especially relating to Indians, pioneers, and cowboys.

western bit A bit consisting of two metal cheek pieces and, typically, a ported mouthpiece which brings pressure to bear on the bars of the mouth using leverage instead of direct pressure; the reins are attached to shanks (q.v.); used in conjunction with a curb strap (q.v.) or curb chain (q.v.); has longer shanks and is bigger than a curb bit (q.v.).

western equine encephalomyelitis Also known by the acronym WEE; one of three primary strains of encephalomyelitis (q.v.).

western horse A type of horse rather than a breed suited to trail, cutting, roping, etc.

Western Isles Highland Pony One of two distinct morphological types of Highland Pony (q.v.) standing 12.2 to 13.2 hands.

western riding Also known as western style; a riding technique popularized by the American cowboy, in which a stock saddle (q.v.) and western-type bridle are used.

western saddle *see* STOCK SADDLE

western show classes Competitive events for western-type horses; of four main divisions: Western Riding Horse, Pleasure Horse, Trail Horse, and Parade Horse.

western stirrup Any stirrup (q.v.) attached to a western saddle by means of a fender; available in a variety of shapes and sizes.

western stirrup leather *see* FENDER no. 1

western style *see* WESTERN RIDING

Westfaliches Pferd *see* WESTPHALIAN

Westlands pony *see* FJORD PONY

Westphalian Also known as a Westfaliches Pferd; a Hanoverian (q.v.) bred in Westphalia, Germany; stands 16 to 17 hands, is quiet, powerful, and athletic, has a solid build and may have a coat of any solid color; used as a competition and riding horse.

wet mare A mare with a nursing foal.

wet work A cutting and reining term; to train, work, or show a horse using cattle.

Weymouth bit A curb bit (q.v.) with straight shanks about 6 inches (15 cm) long upon which the mouthpiece slides up and down within a -1/2 inch (13 mm) space.

Weymouth bridle *see* DOUBLE BRIDLE

WFA. The acronym for weight for age (q.v.).

whangtree A yellow riding cane having closely spaced rings or knots, made from the stem of Chinese or Japanese plants similar to bamboo.

wheal A welt or other raised surface of the skin.

wheat The grain of the widely distributed cereal grass of the genus *Triticum*; most commonly fed as milling by-products, specifically wheat bran (q.v.) or middlings.

wheat bran The outer coating of the wheat grain separated from the flour in milling; contains less digestible energy but more protein, fiber, and phosphorus than whole grain; is highly laxative, contains 1.3 percent phosphorus, 11 to 13 percent digestible protein, and 5 percent fat.

wheatgrass hay A cut and dried grass hay made from crested wheatgrass; contains high quality roughage with a fiber content of about 34 percent and a digestible protein content of approximately 4.4 percent at first cutting and 3.4 percent for second-cut; grows best in moist climates and is best cut before it blooms after which the nutritional value drops dramatically and the grass becomes tough and fibrous.

wheat middlings The coarser particles of ground wheat mingled with bran; although a good source of niacin and vitamins B_1 and B_2, tends to pack in the stomach and cause digestive disturbances such as colic (q.v.).

wheel (1) A racing term; said of a horse who turns sharply. (2) A racing term; said of a bettor who bets every type of combination (daily-double [q.v.], perfecta [q.v.], or quinella [q.v.]) for a specific horse(s).

wheel back A hunting term; said of a hound (q.v.) who has an upwardly curved spine over the loins; characteristic of Walker field trial hounds.

wheel bar *see* SWINGLE TREE

wheelers A pair of horses in a four or more horse team who are hitched directly to the vehicle.

wheel hub *see* HUB

wheeling *see* BASEBALL

whelp (1) A hunting term; an unweaned hound puppy. (2) A hunting term; said of a gyp (q.v.) when pregnant. (3) A hunting term; said of a gyp (q.v.) when she gives birth.

whicker *see* NICKER

whiffletree *see* SWINGLE TREE

whinny (1) Also known as neigh; the common calling or communication between horses. (2) To neigh in a low and gentle way.

whip (1) Also known as a fiddle, horsewhip, or absolute ensurer; a hand-held device used as an aid to control, drive, correct, or punish the horse; generally consists of a wood, fiberglass, bone, plastic, metal, or leather rod to which is attached a thong of leather or cord of varying lengths as determined by intended use. (2) *see* WHIPPERS-IN. (3) One who handles the whip expertly. (4) One who drives a carriage. (5) To lash or flagellate with or as with a horsewhip.

whip-across bars Also known as Canadian bars; a therapeutic horseshoe (q.v.) of the bar shoe (q.v.) type; the outside, trailing heel is turned to the outside of the opposite heel; used most frequently on harness horses to keep the shoes from spreading when they become worn.

whipcord (1) A hard, twisted cord from which whip lashes are made. (2) A hard, woven, diagonally ribbed fabric, often used for making riding habits or sportswear.

whip hand Historically, the coachman's hand used to hold the whip when driving; now, to the hand used to hold the whip in any equestrian event.

whip-in A hunting term; to keep the hounds in the pack from scattering by use of a whip.

whiplash *see* LASH

whip off A hunting term; to use the whip to redirect the hounds from one line to another.

whipper-in *see* WHIPPERS-IN

whippers-in Also known as whip, the whip, or whipper-in; a hunting term; the principal assistant to the huntsman (q.v.) from whom he takes his orders; traditionally there are two whippers-in: the first whippers-in (q.v.) and the second whippers-in (q.v.); of four levels of proficiency: (a) learning the name and appearance of every hound (q.v.) in the pack, (b) learning the characteristics of each hound, (c) learning the temperament of each hound, and

(d) learning the voice of each hound; proficiency in all four levels must be attained before hunting the pack, as when the huntsman is absent or unable to complete the hunt.

whipping To punish a horse with a whip; to flagellate.

whippletree *see* SWINGLE TREE

whipple tree *see* SWINGLE TREE

whirlicote *see* LONG WAGON

whisk *see* DANDY BRUSH

whiskey A light, one-horse chaise popular in the late 18th and early 19th centuries; hung on shallow, sideways platform springs, was seldom headed, frequently lacked a dashboard, and seated either one or two passengers; in some cases the bodywork was covered in canework those being known as caned whiskies (q.v.) while others had panel or half-panel sides; so named because it "whisked" over the ground at great speed

whiskey-curricle A large, horse-drawn vehicle of the whiskey (q.v.) type driven to a pair of horses in curricle gear (q.v.).

whisperers *see* HORSE WHISPERERS

whistling *see* LARYNGEAL HEMIPLEGIA

whistle on the play A polo term; to blow a whistle to indicate a foul has been committed; an indication to stop play.

white Refers to coat color; a symmetrical pattern of white in which the coat is solid white; will usually have brown eyes and a few spots of pigmented skin; if the white coat results from extremely marked overos (q.v.), sabinos (q.v.), and blanket patterns, the horse will have pink skin and blue eyes.

white blanket One of six symmetrical coat color patterns of the Appaloosa (q.v.) recognized by the Appaloosa Horse Club (q.v.); a solid colored body with white over the hips and an absence of colored spots.

white blood cell Also known as leukocyte, leucocyte, or by the acronym WBC; a colorless blood cell active in the defense against infection and bacteria, and occasionally found in the body tissues.

white brass *see* GERMAN SILVER

white castor Slang; a white coaching hat.

white face *see* BALD FACE

white flag A white piece of cloth of varying size, shape, design, and hue, usually attached at one edge to a staff or cord, and used to mark the left side of a jumping obstacle.

White Horse of the Sea *see* CAMARGUE

white lethal A inherited genetic condition of a foal with a lethal dominant white (q.v.) gene.

white line The 1/8 inch (3 mm) wide, pale yellow-colored juncture between the laminae (q.v.) of the wall and the tubules of the sole; is only as deep as the inner layer of the sole and is not a specially secreted structure.

white line disease Any physiological or mechanical damage of the white line (q.v.); may be brought about by bacteria, any mechanical disruption of the white line brought about by concussion, or poor or incorrect shoeing, e.g., trimming, pressure on the sole by the shoe.

white mark *see* WHITE SPOT

white muscle disease Also known as nutritional muscular dystrophy or by the acronym WMD; a disease occurring in foals up to seven months triggered by either vitamin E or selenium (q.v.) deficiency in the pregnant mare leading to muscle-cell death in the embryo; symptoms include lethargy and a stilted, stiff gait; when muscle damage is extensive, the foal will generally go down and die unless treatment is administered; so called, because of the white striations and patches that occur in the muscles, particularly those of the hind legs and neck.

white muzzle A face marking (q.v.); white hairs covering both lips and extending into the area of the nostrils.

white of the eye Said of a horse when some part of the white sclera shows between partially closed eye lids.

white pastern *see* PASTERN

white sclera The area encircling the dark or pigmented iris of the eye; may be used as a distinguishing characteristic of the Appaloosa (q.v.).

white spot (1) Also known as white mark; the smallest of the leg markings (q.v.) consisting of a concentration of white hairs on the foot anywhere but on the heel. (2) A mark on the eye of the horse; indicates a past eye injury that may or may not interfere with vision.

Whitmore kimblewick One of five types of kimblewick (q.v.); a pelham (q.v.) bit requiring one instead of two reins (q.v.), having a straight, low-ported mouthpiece (q.v.), and short cheeks (q.v.) with D rings running the full length, a square eye on the upper end of the cheeks, and a second curb ring directly below the D ring; when used with a single rein and the rider's hands are held in a standard position, the bit acts as a snaffle (q.v.), but when the hands are lowered, or when used in conjunction with a martingale (q.v.) or second rein, the resulting action is similar to that of a curb (q.v.).

whoa A verbal command to the horse to stop or stand still, or when repeated softly, to slow down or pay attention.

whole colored Refers to coat color; the coat of the horse, inclusive of the head, body, and limbs, when entirely composed of hairs of one color.

whorl A hair pattern; changes in direction of the flow of the hair; may take various forms, depending on the interface at which two or more flows of hair meet, e.g., simple whorl (q.v.), tufted whorl (q.v.), linear whorl (q.v.), crested whorl (q.v.), feathered whorl (q.v.), and sinuous whorl (q.v.); may be used for identification purposes.

wid An obsolete term; a horse unsound in the wind.

widner breaking cart An American version of the breaking cart (q.v.) with balloon-type cycle tires.

Wielkopolski Also known as Polish Warmblood; a recently developed, Polish-bred warmblood descended from the Ponzan and Masuren (q.v.) regional types having Arab (q.v.), Hanoverian (q.v.), Trakehner (q.v.), and Thoroughbred (q.v.) ancestry; matures early, has a free-flowing action, is sturdy, well-balanced, and hard-working; stands 15.1 to 16

hands, has a compact body, and a high, deep chest; any solid-color coat is acceptable; used for riding and driving.

wiggler *see* PACER

wild burro An American term; a feral ass (q.v.) running wild in the western part of the United States; is registered as standard donkey (q.v.) with the American Donkey and Mule Society with the origin and breeding identified as wild burro.

wild cow *see* SPRINTER no. 2

wild game *see* GAME

wild goose chase One of two types of drag hunting sport popular in late 16th and early 17th-century England; the predecessor of drag hunting (q.v.) in which the drag (q.v.) was laid and the hounds were put on the line (q.v.) to run it at a racing pace; the horse in the lead at the end of the drag was declared the winner.

wild horse (1) *see* MUSTANG. (2) Any horse living and breeding in a wild, undomesticated state.

Wild Horses of America Registry An organization established in the United States in 1974 to register and campaign for the protection of wild horses and burros in North America; dissolved as a corporation in 1992 and subsumed into the International Society for the Protection of Mustangs and Burros (q.v.).

Wild Huntsman A spectral huntsman who, in European, especially German, folklore, with a phantom host of followers, ran through the woods, fields, and villages during the night, accompanied by shouts of huntsmen and the baying of hounds.

William Cavendish Newcastle *see* NEW-CASTLE, WILLIAM CAVENDISH, DUKE OF

William von Osten *see* VON OSTEN, WILLIAM

Wilson snaffle A jointed driving snaffle (q.v.) with tapered arms and two rings on each side; one ring is attached to the mouthpiece while the other, to which the cheekpieces are attached, floats on the mouthpiece; the reins may be connected to the cheek rings for normal and mild action and to the floating rings for more severe action; available in many variations.

win (1) Also known as straight and win only; a racing term; a betting option in which the bettor (q.v.) places a wager on a horse to come in first place. (2) To gain victory through competition.

win and place A racing term; a betting option in which the bettor selects the winner and the second place horses.

win by a nose *see* NOSE no. 2

wind (1) A horse's capacity for breath. (2) *see* FLATULENCE. (3) *see* WIND A FOX

wind a fox Also known as wind; a hunting term; said of the hounds (q.v.) when they catch the scent (q.v.) of a fox (q.v.) before finding his line (q.v.).

wind broke *see* ROARING

windgall *see* WIND PUFF

winding *see* ROPE WALKING

windpipe *see* TRACHEA

windpuff Also known as windgall or road puff; a soft, painless, fluid-filled swelling commonly found near the fetlock joint and occasionally elsewhere on the lower portion of the fore- and hind legs, generally without associated lameness or heat; occur when excessive levels of synovial fluid fill a stretched fetlock joint capsule or associated tendon sheath; of two types which often occur together: articular windpuff (q.v.) and tendinous windpuff (q.v.); may be caused by intense training followed by a period of rest, excessive exercise on hard surfaces, and the cumulative effects of imbalances produced by poor conformation or improperly trimmed hooves; must be regarded with suspicion in the presence of lameness; bandaging overnight or massaging the area may temporarily reduce swelling, but reoccurrence is common when established, and treatment difficult.

wind sucker A horse who exhibits the habit of wind sucking (q.v.).

wind sucking Also known as cribbing or aerophagia; a vice; the aspiration and swallowing of air by the horse through the mouth; the horse arches his neck and inhales air; may be facilitated by the horse biting or setting his teeth against a firm object; an acquired habit; may be controlled by the use of a cribbing collar (q.v.).

windy *see* ROARING

wing One of a pair of standards (q.v.).

winging *see* DISHING

win hole *see* TWO HOLE POSITION

winkers *see* BLINKERS

win in a canter A racing term; said of a horse who passes the finish line at an easy pace, well ahead of the rest of the field (q.v.).

winner A person or horse who wins; a victor in a competition.

winner's circle Also known as winner's enclosure; a racing term; the location on the racecourse reserved for the first three placing horses where awards are given and photographs taken.

winner's enclosure *see* WINNER'S CIRCLE

winning post *see* FINISHING POST

win only *see* WIN

winter horse An Australian term; a horse kept at the home ranch for use during the winter, rather than being turned out on the range.

winter out To leave a horse out to pasture or on the range during the winter rather than stabling him.

wire (1) *see* FINISH LINE. (2) *see* BARBED WIRE

wire cutters A metal, hand-held device used to cut wire, as in barbed wire (q.v.).

wisp An egg-shaped, grooming brush without a handle made of horse hair, straw, rope, or hay coiled in the form of a figure eight to make a tight pad; used to massage the horse to stimulate circulation and tone the muscles.

with a strain Said of a well-bred horse who has some common blood (q.v.).

wither pad *see* POMMEL PAD

withers The ridge located at the junction of the base of the horse's neck, his back at the point of the first thoracic vertebra, and the top of the scapula between the shoulders; the highest part of the horse's back.

with foal at foot Said of a mare after birth of a live foal.

WMD The acronym for white muscle disease (q.v.).

wobbler A horse afflicted with ataxia (q.v.).

wobbler disease *see* ATAXIA

wobbler syndrome *see* ATAXIA

wobbles *see* ATAXIA

wolf teeth Also known as permanent premolars or first premolars; one of up to four shallow-rooted, rudimentary teeth occasionally present in front of the premolars (q.v.) which have no function in the intake or chewing process; appear in the top of the mouth in front of the first premolars (q.v.) at the age of about six months and occasionally appear in the bottom of the mouth; mythically thought their presence would impair the horse's vision, ultimately causing blindness if not removed; may interfere with bit placement, in which case they are extracted.

wolfing feed Said of a horse who eats extremely fast.

wood chewing *see* CRIB-BITING

wood shavings Thin slices of wood; used as bedding (q.v.) material in horse stalls, trailers, etc.; are absorbent, soft, unpalatable, fragrant, and carry less mold spores than straw (q.v.); can be dusty and may be treated with chemicals that irritate the horse's skin and are difficult to store; any type of wood shaving may be used except black walnut which has been linked to laminitis (q.v.); sometimes combined with sawdust (q.v.) to improve absorbency.

World Champion Team Penning Association Also known by the acronym WCTPA; an organization founded in the United States in 1978 to promote, organize, and regulate the sport of team penning (q.v.).

work To exercise a horse.

work a line *see* CARRY A LINE

worked up *see* TENSE

work for a dead horse *see* PAY FOR A DEAD HORSE

working advantage A cutting term; said of the horse when he is parallel to the cow, his head next to the cow's shoulder, a position from which he is able to influence the cow's actions.

working canter A rocking, three-beat gait between the collected and the medium canter (q.v.); the horse is more collected and has a slightly shorter stride than at the medium canter (q.v.), but not as much as at the collected; the horse is balanced, on the bit and moves forward with even and light strides.

working cow A cutting term; a cow who is trying to return to the herd from which it has been separated; enables the horse to work it.

working cow horse A reining (q.v.) event consisting of two dry work (q.v.) and wet work (q.v.) competitions.

working saddle *see* STOCK SADDLE

working trot A natural two-beat gait in which the pace is between the collected and the medium trots (q.v.); the horse displays a slightly shorter stride than at the medium, but not as short as at the collected trot (q.v.); the hind feet will be placed on the ground near the rear of the marks for the forefeet; the horse is balanced and moves with an even and elastic gait; ridden sitting or rising.

working walk *see* WALK

work in the hand To train the horse from the ground; the trainer, standing at the horse's shoulder, controls the frame and movement of the horse using the curb reins held in one hand and a dressage whip (q.v.) held in the other; care must be taken to produce even results on either rein, as unbalanced training may result in a lack of symmetry.

workman Coaching slang; a good coachman (q.v.).

work off Any tie-breaking competition.

work on the long reins To train a horse from the ground using two long reins (q.v.) attached to the snaffle bit (q.v.) rings or hackamore (q.v.) to influence the rhythm, activity, and lateral bend of the horse in all lateral movements as well as in forward movements.; the trainer holds one rein in each hand and a 4-1/2 foot (1.3 m) whip, pointing forwards, in the right; whether the trainer stands behind or to the inside of the horse, the reins will run from the bit along the sides of the horse to the trainer's hands.

work on two tracks *see* LATERAL WORK

work out *see* AIRING

work out of it *see* WARM OUT OF IT

work sound *see* WARM OUT OF IT

work tab A racing term; a list of morning race workouts identified according to distance and time.

World Elephant Polo Association Games An invitation-only polo tournament played on elephants; held every December (usually the 8–13) at the Tiger Tops Jungle Lodge in southern Nepal; conceived by Jim Edwards and James Manclark in 1982.

worm *see* LARVA

worry *see* KILL no. 1

Worshipful Company of Farriers, The *see* THE WORSHIPFUL COMPANY OF FARRIERS OF LONDON

Worshipful Company of Farriers of London Also known as The Worshipful Company of Farriers or by the acronym WCF; one of the oldest active guilds in the world being organized and having remained active in Great Britain since 1356 AD to train, conduct exams, and certify farrier members at three levels: Diploma of the Worshipful Company of Farriers (q.v.), Associate of Farriers Company of London (q.v.), and Fellow of the Worshipful Company of Farriers (q.v.).

wound (1) A cut or rupture in the skin or flesh of a person or animal caused by violence. (2) To inflict a wound on.

wrangle Also known as wrangling; the act of herding or rounding up horses or other livestock.

wrangler A cowboy or herdsman; one who looks after horses.

wrangling *see* WRANGLE

wrestler *see* STEER WRESTLER

wrestling *see* STEER WRESTLING

wring off the nails Said of the farrier when he twists off the nail points protruding from the hoof wall when attaching a horseshoe to the hoof; the nail point is positioned in the fork of the shoeing hammer and the hammer twisted.

wrong bend A dressage term; failure of the horse to achieve and maintain the correct degree of bend when executing corners, circles, etc.; may result in a loss of balance and rhythm in the movements.

wrong leg not corrected A dressage term; said of the rider who allows the horse to strike off in the canter on the wrong lead and who fails to correct it.

wrung withers Said of the withers (q.v.) of the horse when bruised, but not chafed, by an ill-fitting saddle.

wry nose A congenital abnormality of the horse in which the horse's nose is askew.

Württemburg A German warmblood developed in the late 16th century by putting native mares to Arab (q.v.) and Suffolk Punch (q.v.) stallions from the Marbach stud; East Prussian (q.v.) and Norman blood (q.v.) was later introduced, followed by infusions of Oldenburg (q.v.), Nonius (q.v.), Anglo-Norman (q.v.), and Trakehner (q.v.); originally used for farm work in the Württemburg area from which the breed name derived; the stud book was established in 1895; is strong and hardy, cob-like, stands about 16 hands, and may have a bay, brown, black, or chestnut coat; a good worker and economical feeder; used for riding and driving.

X

X A dressage term; the center point of a dressage arena located midway from each short and long side and through which many movements are performed.

xanthos The color of all ancient Greek chariot horses; probably chestnut or dun.

Xanthus One of two mythical horses who pulled the chariot of Achilles; was given the power of speech and foretold of Achilles' death.

Xenophon (427/8–354 BC) An Athenian cavalry officer, writer, historian, and horseman; achieved fame for his essays on horsemanship and hunting, most notably, *The Art of Horsemanship.*

xeroradiography (1) Radiography (q.v.) that produces an image using X-rays (q.v.).

(2) A process in which an electrostatically charged selenium-coated aluminum plate is exposed by an X-ray (q.v.) to image internal structures; provides greater resolution than X-rays.

xerosis Abnormally dry skin.

X-ray photograph A picture produced by an X-ray (q.v.).

X-ray High-frequency, short-wave electromagnetic rays generated by the impact of high-speed electrons on a metal target; capable of penetrating solid masses, destroying living tissue, and affecting a photographic plate; used in medical diagnosis.

X-ray therapy Treatment of certain diseases such as cancer, by the use of X-rays.

Y

yaboo *see* NAG

yabusame Classical Japanese equitation in which fully armed, mounted Samurai warriors shoot arrows at a target while galloping; now generally performed in Whinto ceremonies.

Yamoote An Arab-type breed; a Plateau Persian (q.v.).

yap Said of a hound; to bark or yelp.

yard of tin *see* COACH HORN

yearling A foal of either sex between one and two years of age.

yearling bit *see* TATTERSALL BIT

yearling colt A male foal between one and two years of age.

yearling filly A female foal between one and two years of age.

yeld *see* OPEN MARE

yellow body *see* CORPUS LUTEUM

Yellow Bounder *see* POST CHAISE

yellow dun Refers to coat color; yellow coat hair with nonblack points, specifically brown points; differences between the shades of yellow are difficult to discern; resemble buckskins (q.v.) and zebra duns except that the points are brown instead of black.

yelp To give a quick, short, shrill cry, as hounds or foxes, as from surprise, pain, or excitement.

yerk (1) Said of the horse; to lash or strike out with the heels. (2) To crack a whip.

yielding A racing term; said of a turf course with a high moisture content.

yoi A hunting term; a cheer to encourage the hounds, e.g. yoirouse 'im.

yoick *see* YOICKS

yoicks Also known as hoicks, yoick, or huick; an antiquated hunting term; a cry of excitement and encouragement to the hounds.

yoke (1) A wooden frame or bar with loops or bows at either end, fitted around the necks of a pair of oxen, etc., for harnessing them together. (2) A pair of animals harnessed together. (3) The pair used in double harnessing to connect the horse's collar (q.v.) to the tongue of the wagon or carriage. (4) To harness an animal to a plow, etc.

Yomud *see* IOMUD

Yorkshire boot A light-duty brushing boot (q.v.) used to protect the fetlock consisting of a triangular piece of felt, heavy, lined cloth, or other material with a long strip of tape stitched horizontally to the boot; the boot is placed on and above the fetlock joint where it is tied in place using the tape; the portion of the boot above the tape is then folded over the tape providing a double-layer of protection to the fetlock.

Yorkshire Coach Horse A horse breed indigenous to England where it evolved about 1790; similar in appearance to the Cleveland Bay (q.v.) from which the breed descended when crossed with Thoroughbred (q.v.), Arab (q.v.), Barb (q.v.), and, in the 19th century, Hackney (q.v.) blood; stands about 16.2 hands, has a long body and relatively short legs, deep girth, and a bay or brown coat.

Yorkshire Derby *see* KIPLINGCOTES RACE

Yorkshire Gallop A British term; a medium canter (q.v.).

Yorkshire Packhorse *see* CLEVELAND BAY

you can lead a horse to water, but you can't make him drink A proverb; you can show people the way to do things, but you cannot force them to act.

young entry A hunting term; a young hound (q.v.) until completing its first formal hunting season.

Y'sabella *see* PALOMINO

yucca Any of the genus Yucca of sometimes

arborescent plants of the lily family having long, often rigid fibrous, margined leaves on a woody base; native to North America; used by ancient cultures including the Roman Empire and several North American Indian tribes as a treatment for arthritis; *Yucca shidigera* is the source of most yucca-based supplements fed to horses.

Z

zebra An African mammal of the genus *Equus*, which is related to the horse and ass, and having a whitish body striped with numerous brownish-black or black bands.

zebra dun Refers to coat color; a dun (q.v.) with a yellow coat, black points, a head of a similar color as the body, and primitive marks; an ancestral color in the Norwegian Fjord Horse (q.v.) and the Highland Pony (q.v.).

zebra marks *see* ZEBRA STRIPES

zebra stripes Also known as zebra marks, tiger stripes, or leg barring; a primitive mark (q.v.); a color pattern of dark-colored stripes wrapping front to back at the level of the hocks and knees.

zebroid Offspring of a male zebra and a female ass; a hybrid; generally sterile.

Zeeland horse An ancient Dutch breed originating sometime before the 6th century; had a snub nose, broad and deep chest, muscular loins, wide-set flanks, and good bone and feet.

Zemaituka Also known as a Zhmud, Zmudzin, and spelled Semaituka; a pony breed indigenous to Lithuania; thought to have descended from the Asiatic wild horse (q.v.) with recent infusions of Arab (q.v.) blood; stands 13 to 13.1 hands, has a brown, bay, black, mouse dun, dun (q.v.), or palomino (q.v.) coat with an eel stripe (q.v.) and zebra marks common in the duns and palominos, a medium-sized, coarse head, broad forehead, medium neck, low withers, short back, and short, reasonably well-muscled legs; is exceptionally frugal, indifferent to fatigue and cold, and is capable of covering 40 miles (64 km) per day; used for riding, light draft, and farming.

Zhmud *see* ZEMAITUKA

zigzag (1) A jumping obstacle consisting of timbers placed at overlapping angles to each other with a V created in the center of the jump. (2) A dressage movement; a line or course of progression characterized by angled turns from one lead to the other.

zig-zag half pass *see* COUNTER HALF PASS

zinc A metallic element essential in the diet of the horse; although no exact levels have been established, a level of 12 parts per million in the diet is considered sufficient; required for several enzyme systems and occurs in epidermal tissues, bone, muscle, blood, and internal organs; deficiency is not common, but can cause depressed appetite, skin lesions, and stunted growth, particularly in foals; excess zinc can be toxic.

zoonosis A disease communicable from animals to man or vice versa under natural conditions.

zoophobia An abnormal fear of animals.